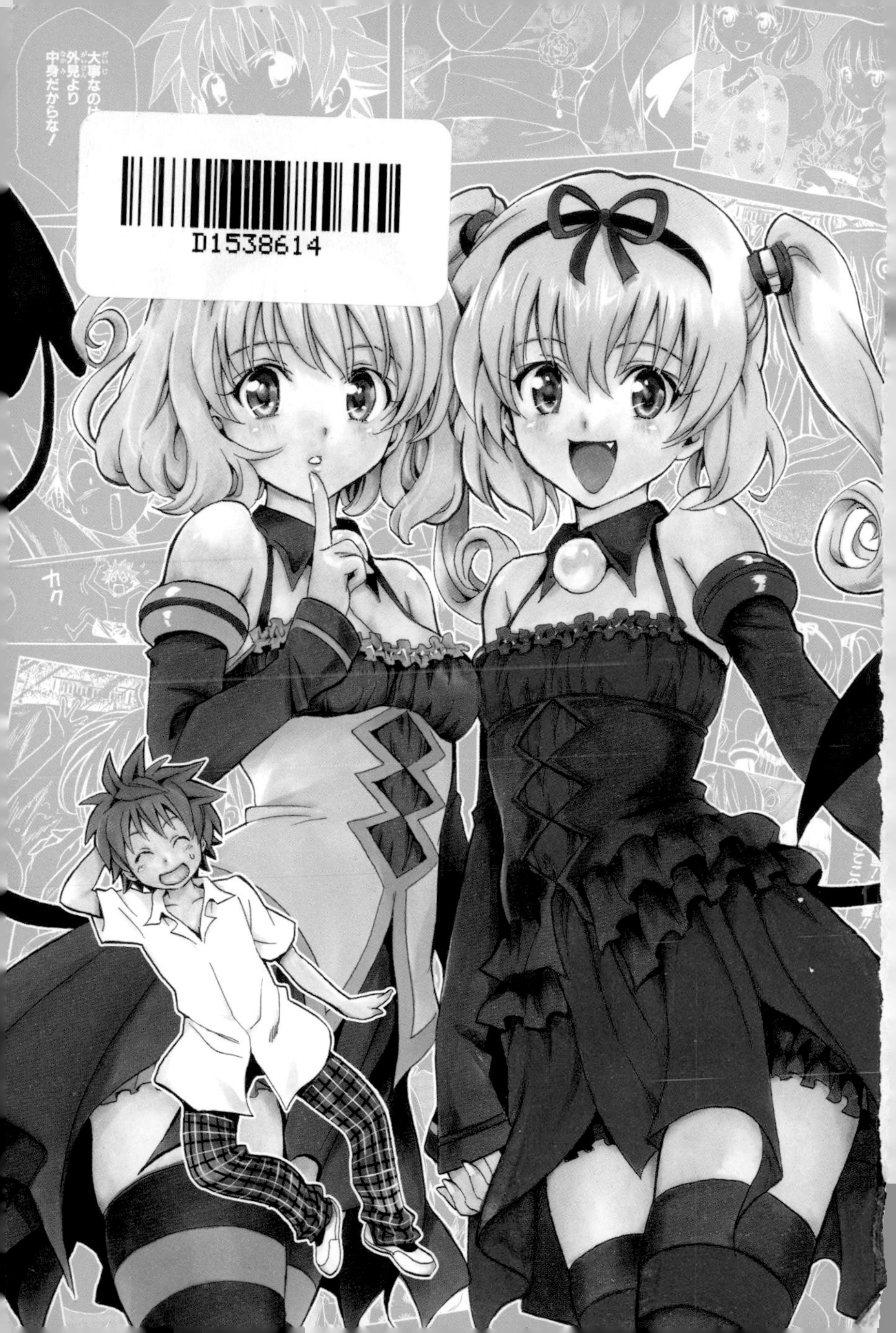
大事なのは
外見より
中身だからな！
カク

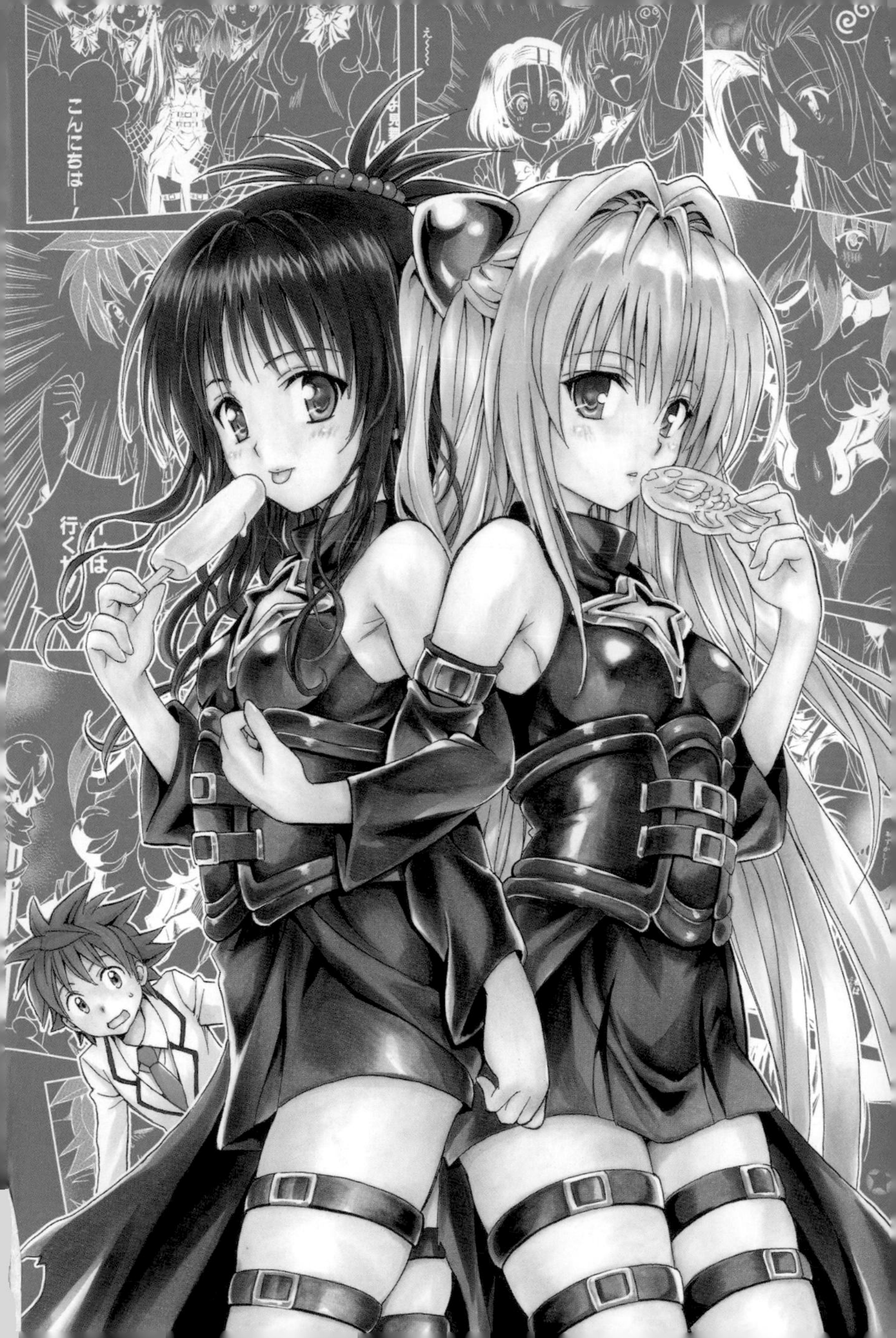
え～～
こんにちはー!

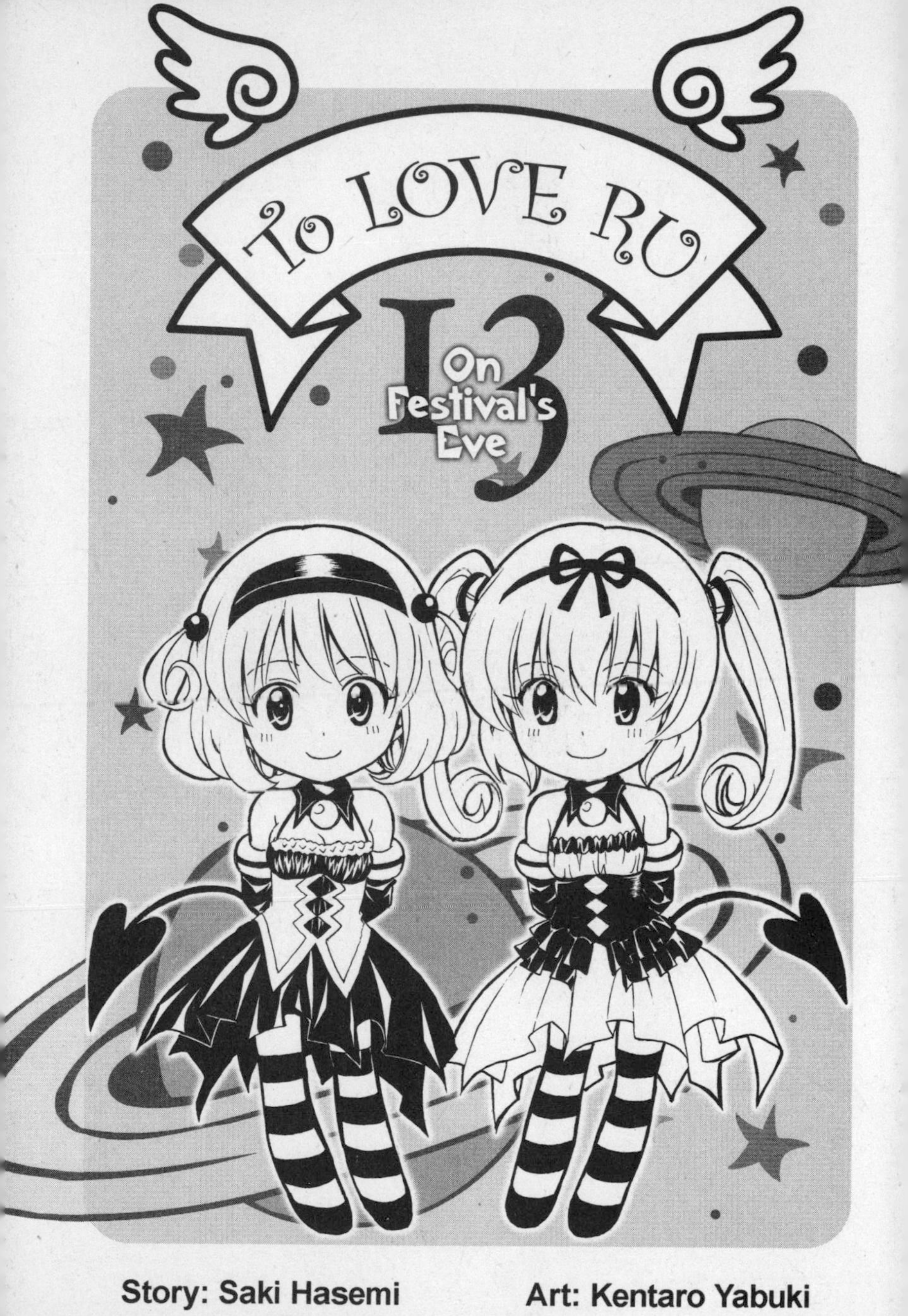
To LOVE RU
13
On Festival's Eve

Story: Saki Hasemi Art: Kentaro Yabuki

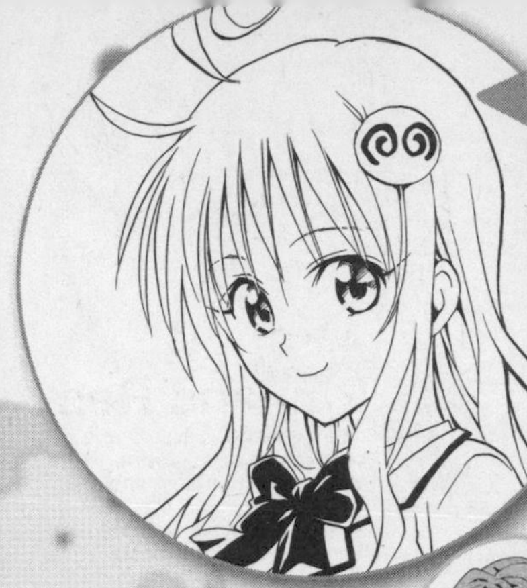

Lala Satalin Deviluke

The first princess of Planet Deviluke, seat of power for the entire Milky Way Galaxy.
She rejected the suitors her father has selected, and ran away from home to Earth. However, after truly falling for Rito, whom she met in a chance encounter, they started living together (?!).
Somehow, the fact that she's an alien was a secret, but (without her really being aware of it) a trivial occurrence let it slip out. Still, everybody pretty much took it in stride.

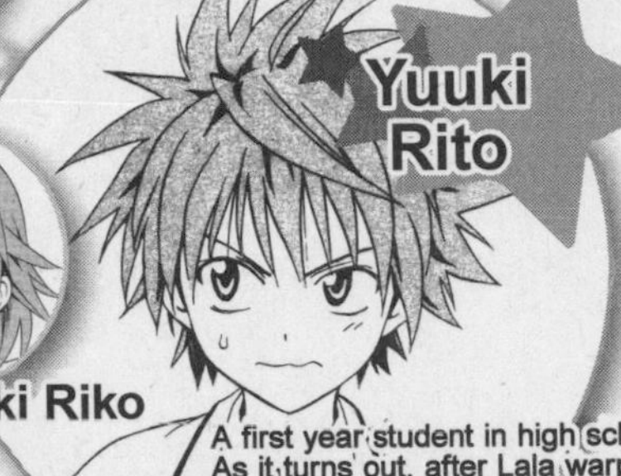

Yuuki Rito

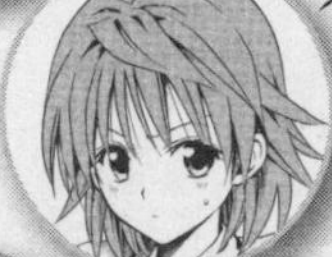

Yuusaki Riko

A first year student in high school. As it turns out, after Lala warped away from her ship, a sudden bath-time encounter led to them living together. He's a late-bloomer when it comes to romance. He was in the middle of trying to confess his feelings for Haruna--the girl he's crushed on since junior high--when, in the heat of the moment, he accidentally confessed to Lala, who appeared in between them. He ended up becoming her lone fiancé.

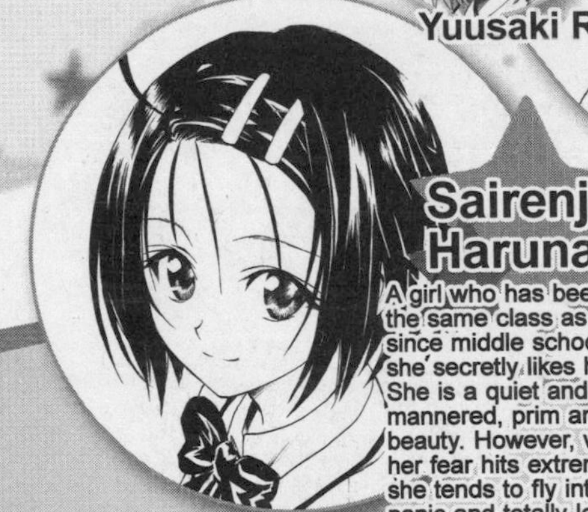

Sairenji Haruna

A girl who has been in the same class as Rito since middle school. And she secretly likes him?! She is a quiet and mild-mannered, prim and proper beauty. However, when her fear hits extreme levels, she tends to fly into a panic and totally lose it...

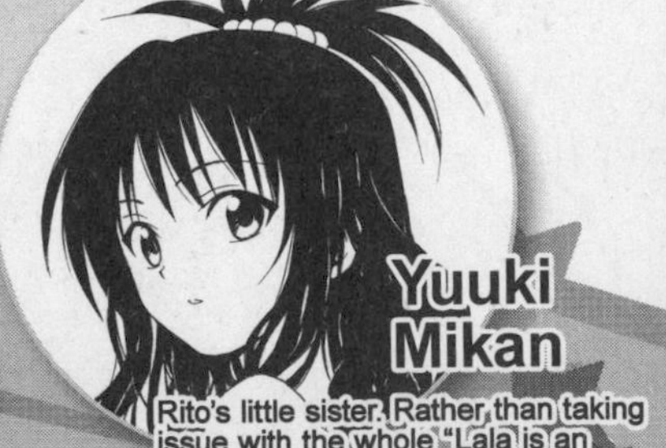

Yuuki Mikan

Rito's little sister. Rather than taking issue with the whole "Lala is an alien" thing, Mikan welcomes her into their home with open arms. She had to grow up fast and is quite a stable, level-headed person.

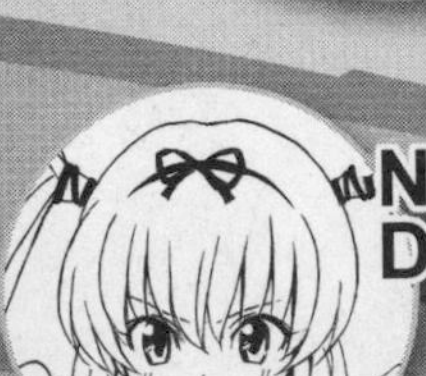

Nana Asta Deviluke

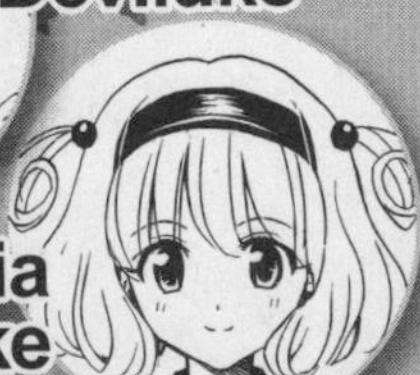

Momo Belia Deviluke

Lala's younger twin sisters. Nana is the second princess of Deviluke, and Momo is the third.

Characters & Story

Super-sweet, super-innocent Rito, and the girl whose beauty is the pride of the cosmos, Planet Deviluke's Princess Lala, along with Rito's classmate Haruna, are all woven together throughout this cute,♥ teensy-bit naughty, slapstick romantic comedy!!

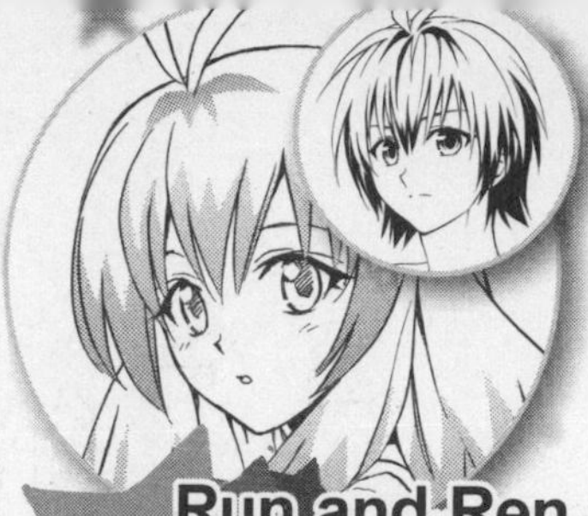

Run and Ren

Lala's childhood friend who switches between a boy and a girl when they sneeze. The girl's name is Run, and the boy's name is Ren. Run has made her debut as an idol star!

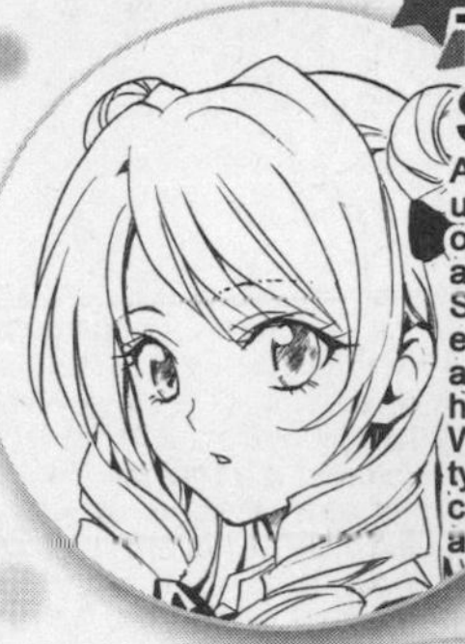

Tenjouin Saki

A super-rich and upper-crusty girl who is one year ahead of Rito and his pals in school. She holds herself in high esteem, and burns with a passion that makes her see Lala as a rival. Whenever the opportunity presents itself, you can bet she'll be picking a fight with Lala.

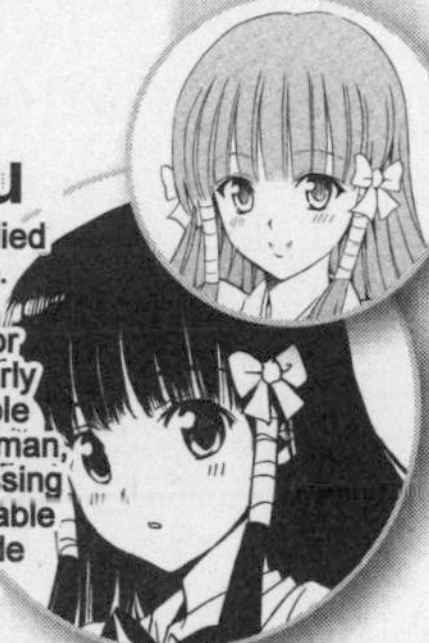

Oshizu

A ghost who died 400 years ago. Mikado built a bioroid body for her that is nearly indistinguishable from a real human, and by possessing it, she is now able to live alongside everyone else.

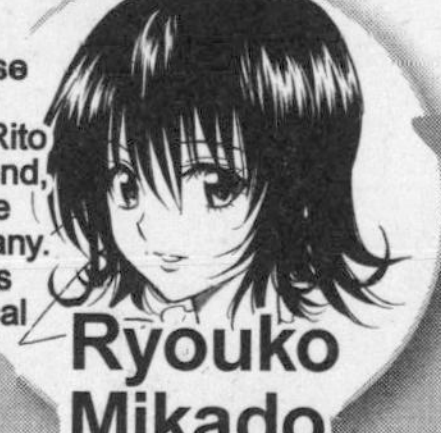

Ryouko Mikado

The school nurse at Sainan High School, which Rito and friends attend, and an alien like Lala and company. Her secret job is providing medical care for aliens living on Earth.

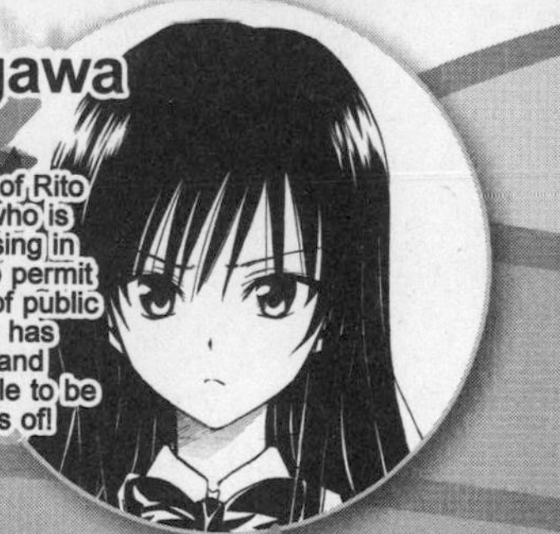

Kotegawa Yui

A classmate of Rito and friends who is uncompromising in her refusal to permit any flouting of public morality. She has marked Rito and Lala as people to be extra cautious of!

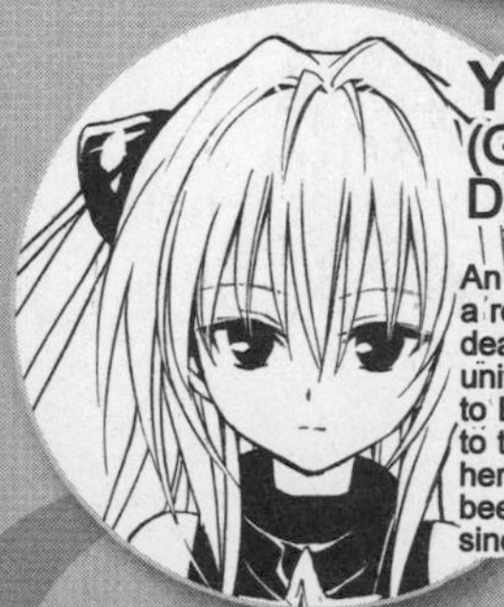

Yami (Golden Darkness)

An assassin with a reputation as the deadliest in all the universe. She came to Earth on a mission to take Rito out, but her attitude has slowly been changing ever since she first met Lala!

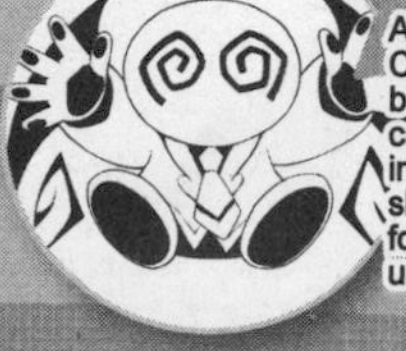

Peke

A Universal Costume Robot, built by Lala. He can transform into a variety of shapes, taking the form of a dress, a uniform, and more.

To LOVE Ru

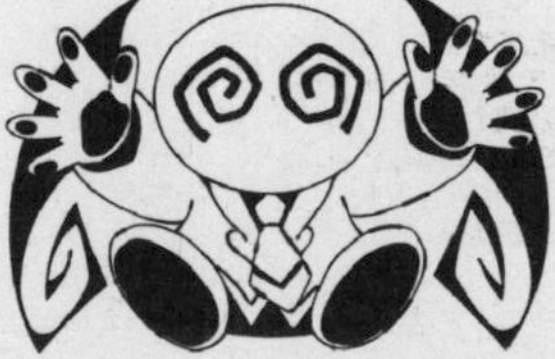

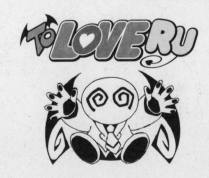

Trouble 107: The Curious Sound of Love♡

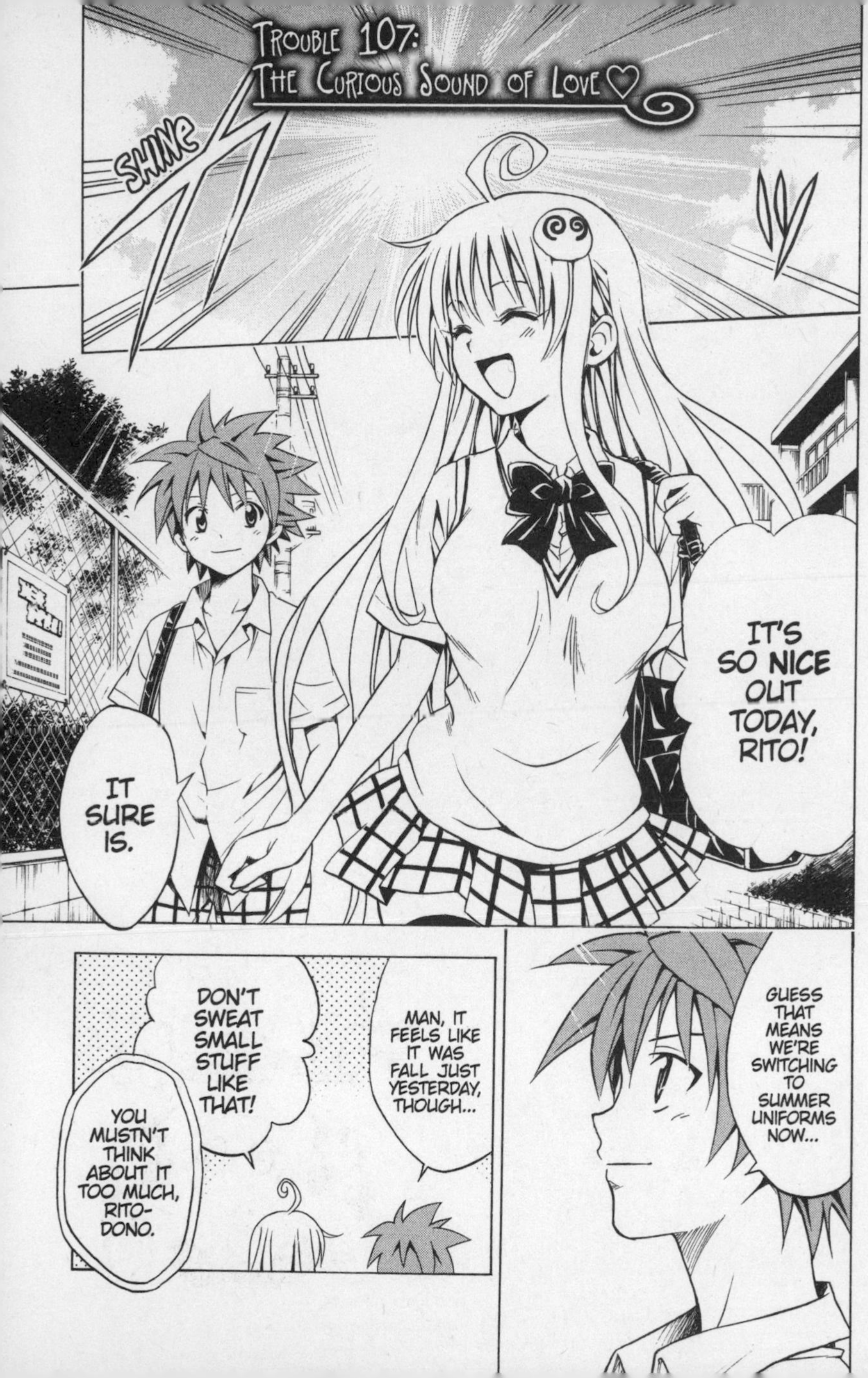
SHINE
IT'S SO NICE OUT TODAY, RITO!
IT SURE IS.
GUESS THAT MEANS WE'RE SWITCHING TO SUMMER UNIFORMS NOW...
MAN, IT FEELS LIKE IT WAS FALL JUST YESTERDAY, THOUGH...
DON'T SWEAT SMALL STUFF LIKE THAT!
YOU MUSTN'T THINK ABOUT IT TOO MUCH, RITO-DONO.

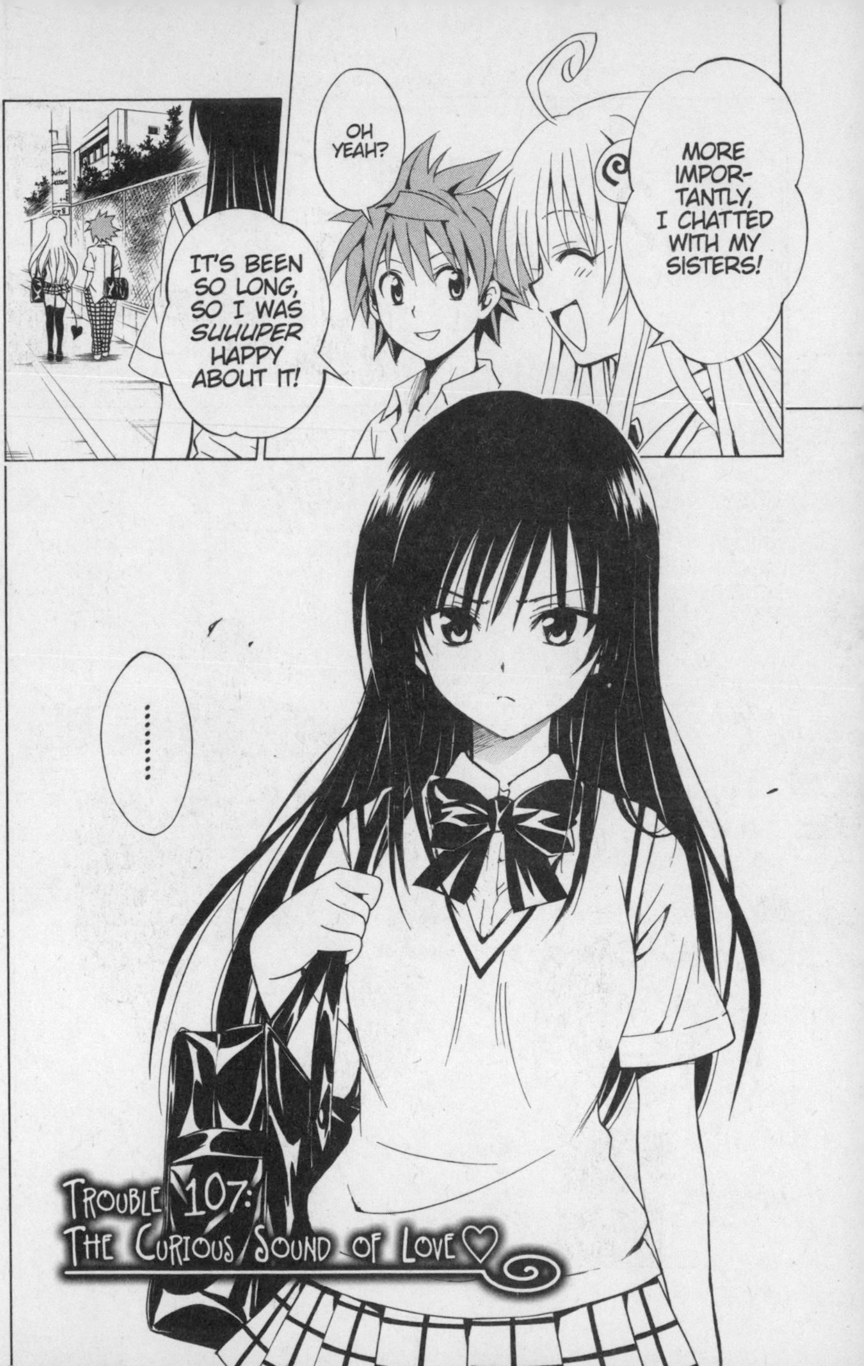
MORE IMPORTANTLY, I CHATTED WITH MY SISTERS!
OH YEAH?
IT'S BEEN SO LONG, SO I WAS SUUUPER HAPPY ABOUT IT!
……
TROUBLE 107: THE CURIOUS SOUND OF LOVE♡

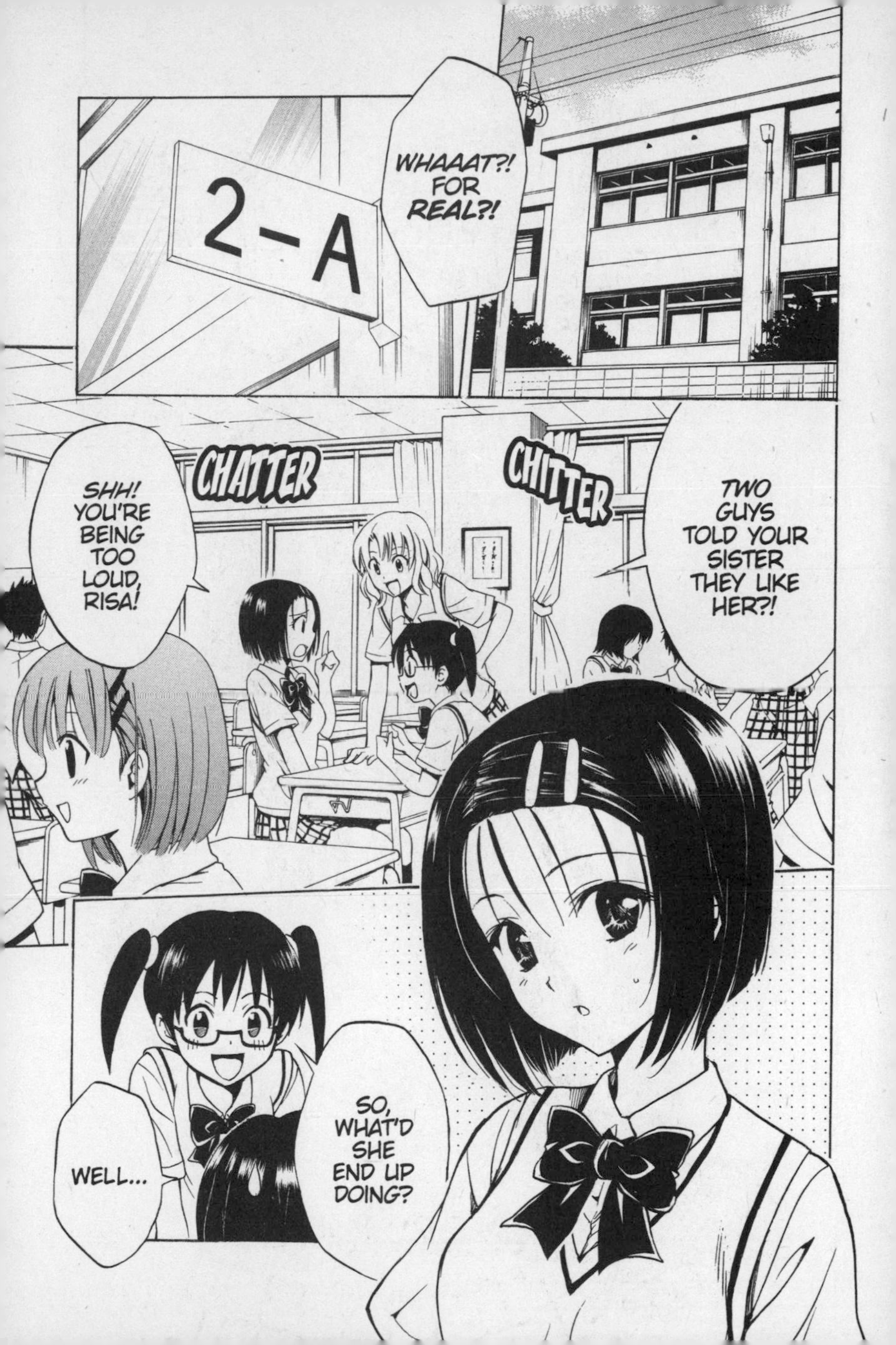
2-A
WHAAAT?! FOR REAL?!
TWO GUYS TOLD YOUR SISTER THEY LIKE HER?!
CHITTER
CHATTER
SHH! YOU'RE BEING TOO LOUD, RISA!
SO, WHAT'D SHE END UP DOING?
WELL...

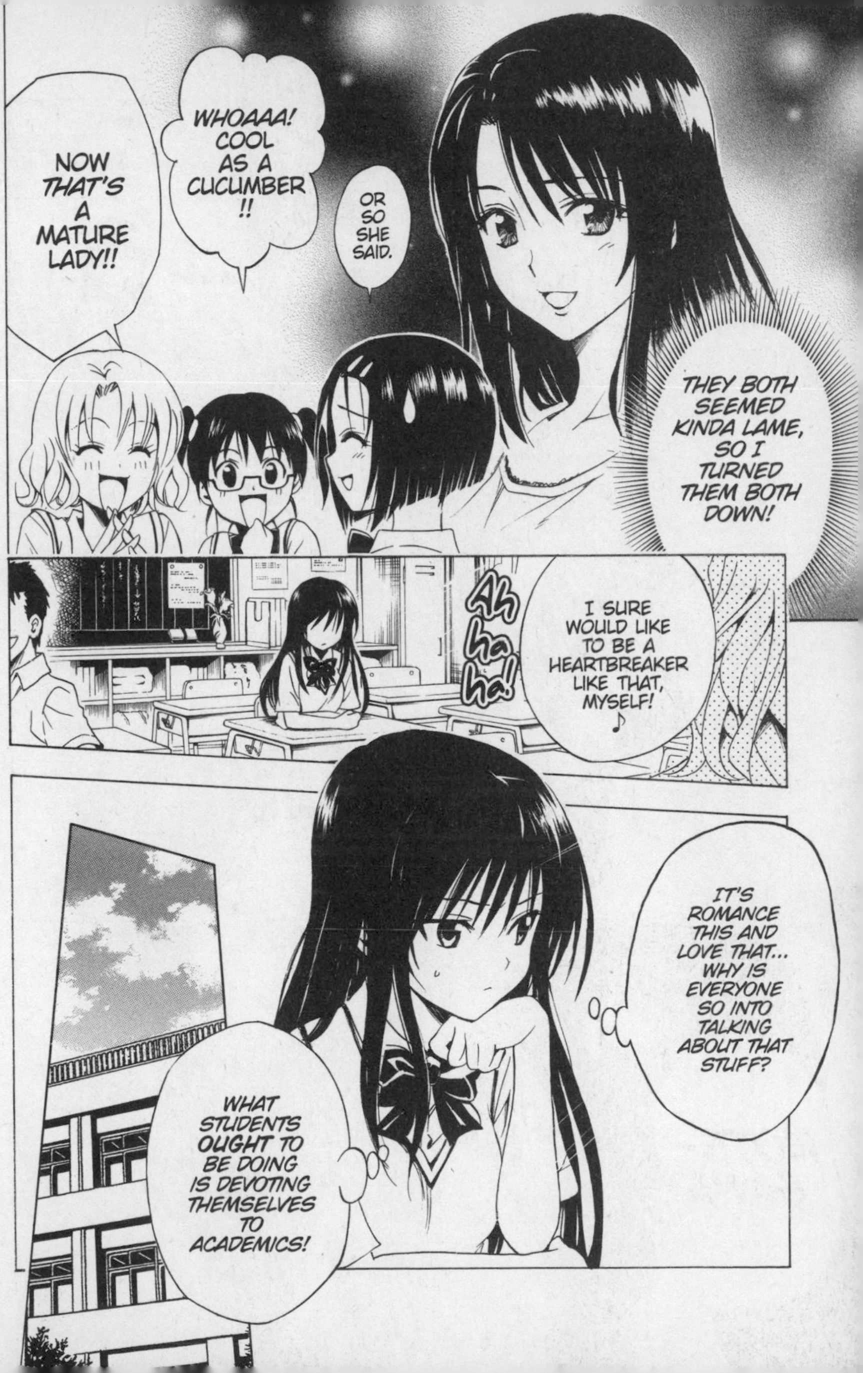
THEY BOTH SEEMED KINDA LAME, SO I TURNED THEM BOTH DOWN!
OR SO SHE SAID.
WHOAAA! COOL AS A CUCUMBER!!
NOW THAT'S A MATURE LADY!!
I SURE WOULD LIKE TO BE A HEARTBREAKER LIKE THAT, MYSELF! ♪
Ah ha ha!
IT'S ROMANCE THIS AND LOVE THAT... WHY IS EVERYONE SO INTO TALKING ABOUT THAT STUFF?
WHAT STUDENTS OUGHT TO BE DOING IS DEVOTING THEMSELVES TO ACADEMICS!

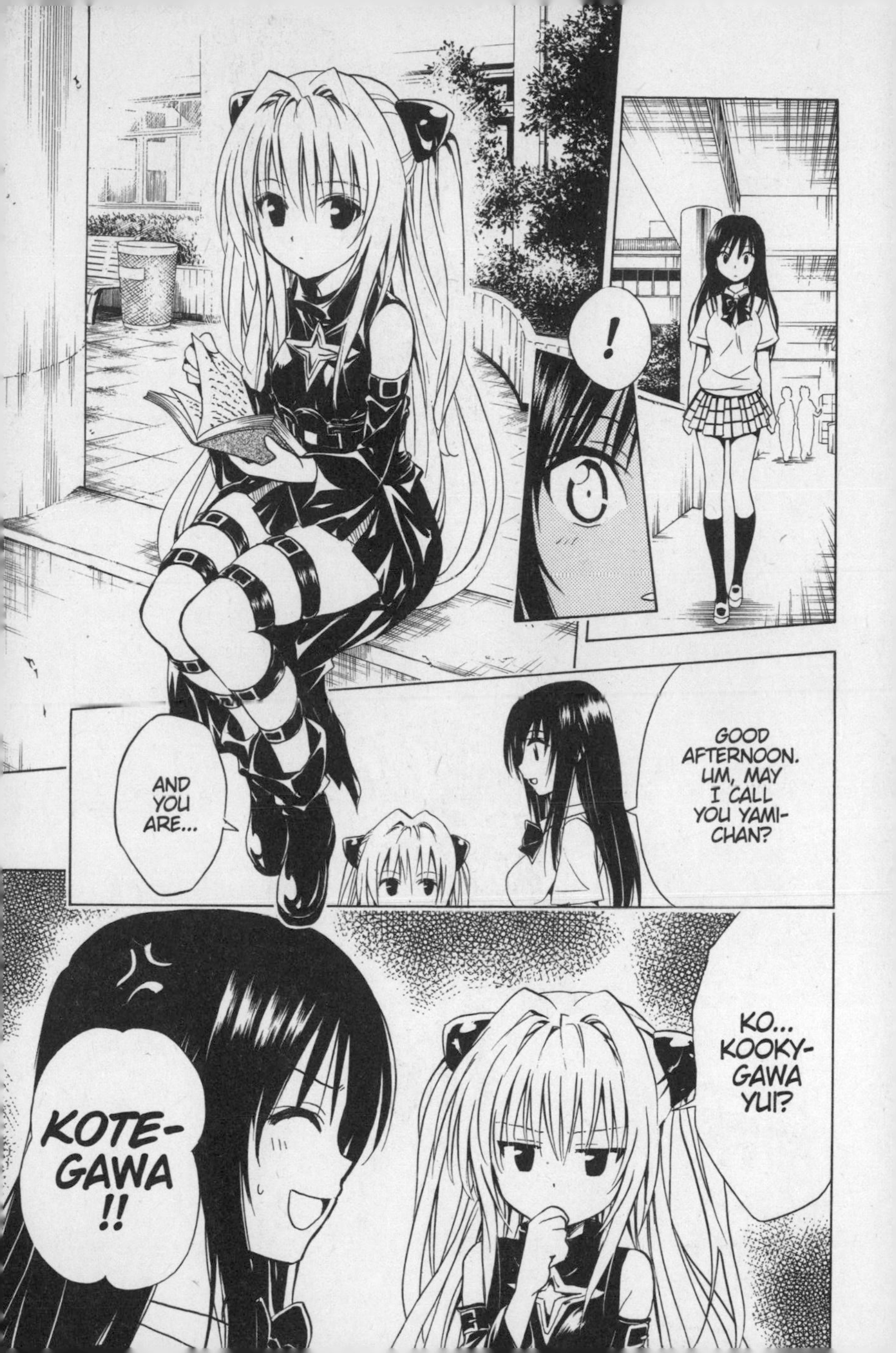
!
GOOD AFTERNOON. UM, MAY I CALL YOU YAMI-CHAN?
AND YOU ARE...
KO... KOOKY-GAWA YUI?
KOTE-GAWA!!

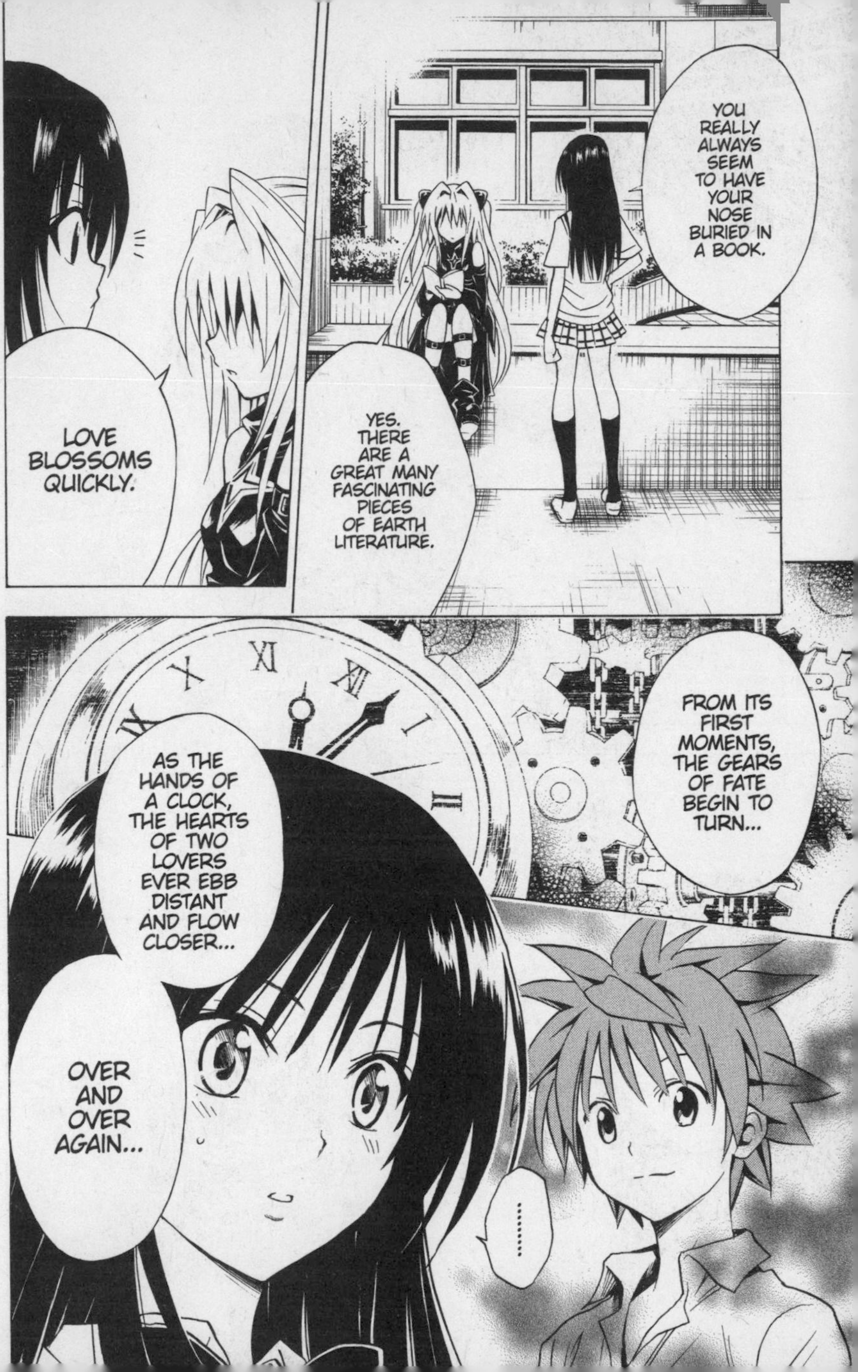
YOU REALLY ALWAYS SEEM TO HAVE YOUR NOSE BURIED IN A BOOK.
YES. THERE ARE A GREAT MANY FASCINATING PIECES OF EARTH LITERATURE.
LOVE BLOSSOMS QUICKLY.
FROM ITS FIRST MOMENTS, THE GEARS OF FATE BEGIN TO TURN...
AS THE HANDS OF A CLOCK, THE HEARTS OF TWO LOVERS EVER EBB DISTANT AND FLOW CLOSER...
OVER AND OVER AGAIN...
....

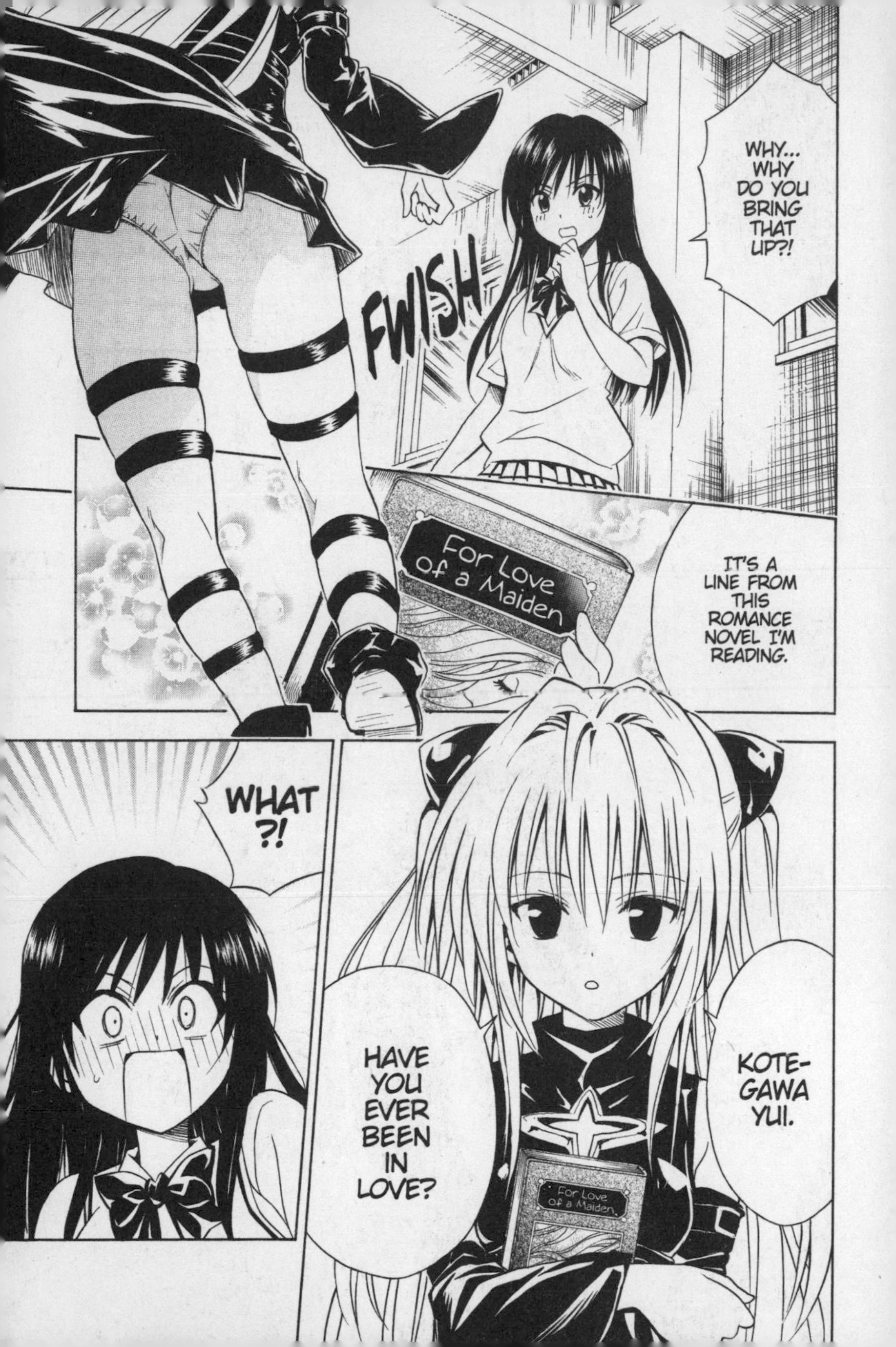
WHY... WHY DO YOU BRING THAT UP?!
FWISH
IT'S A LINE FROM THIS ROMANCE NOVEL I'M READING.
For Love of a Maiden
KOTE-GAWA YUI.
HAVE YOU EVER BEEN IN LOVE?
For Love of a Maiden
WHAT?!

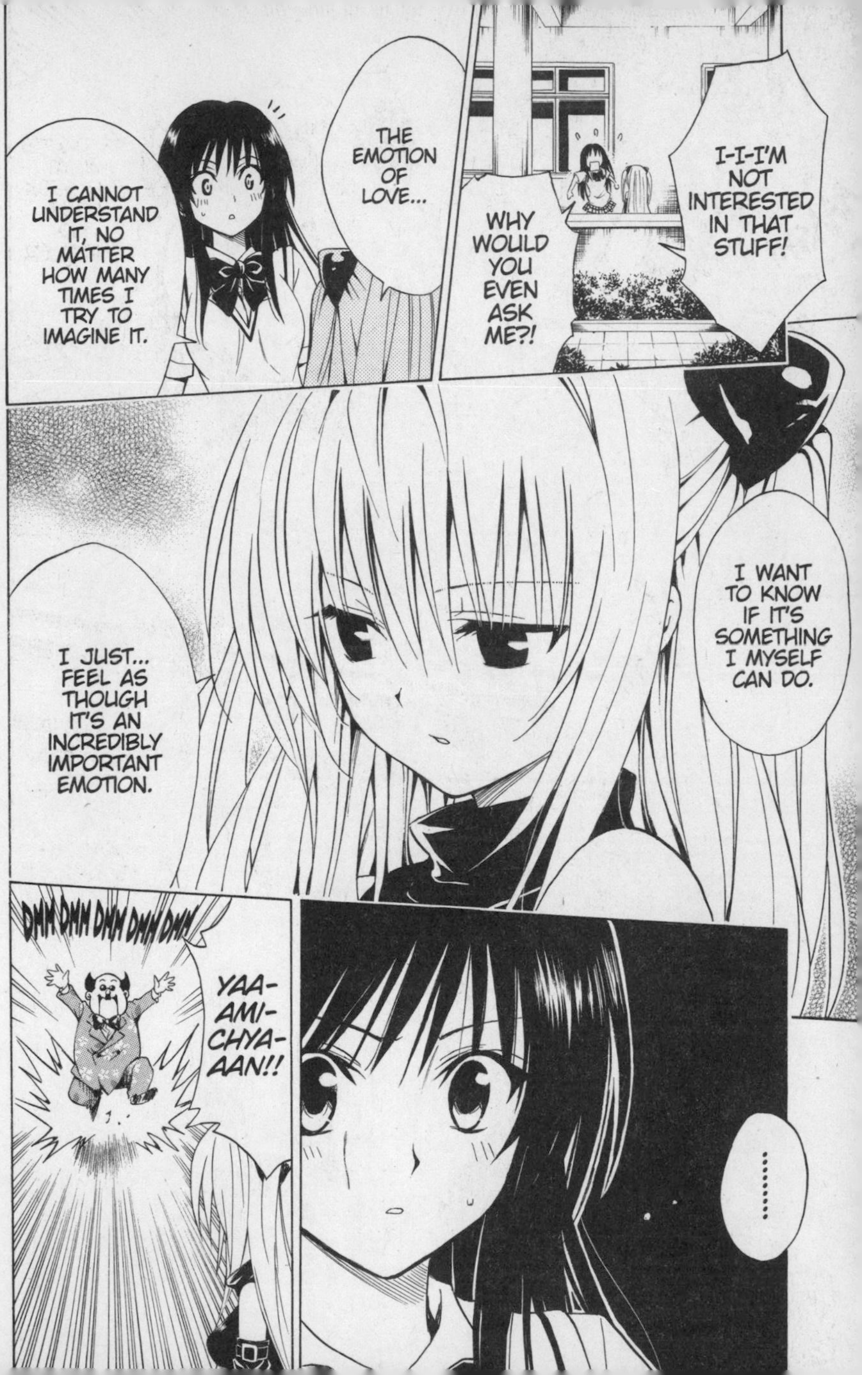
I-I-I'M NOT INTERESTED IN THAT STUFF!
WHY WOULD YOU EVEN ASK ME?!
THE EMOTION OF LOVE...
I CANNOT UNDERSTAND IT, NO MATTER HOW MANY TIMES I TRY TO IMAGINE IT.
I WANT TO KNOW IF IT'S SOMETHING I MYSELF CAN DO.
I JUST... FEEL AS THOUGH IT'S AN INCREDIBLY IMPORTANT EMOTION.
....
DMM DMM DMM DMM DMM
YAA-AMI-CHYA-AAN!!

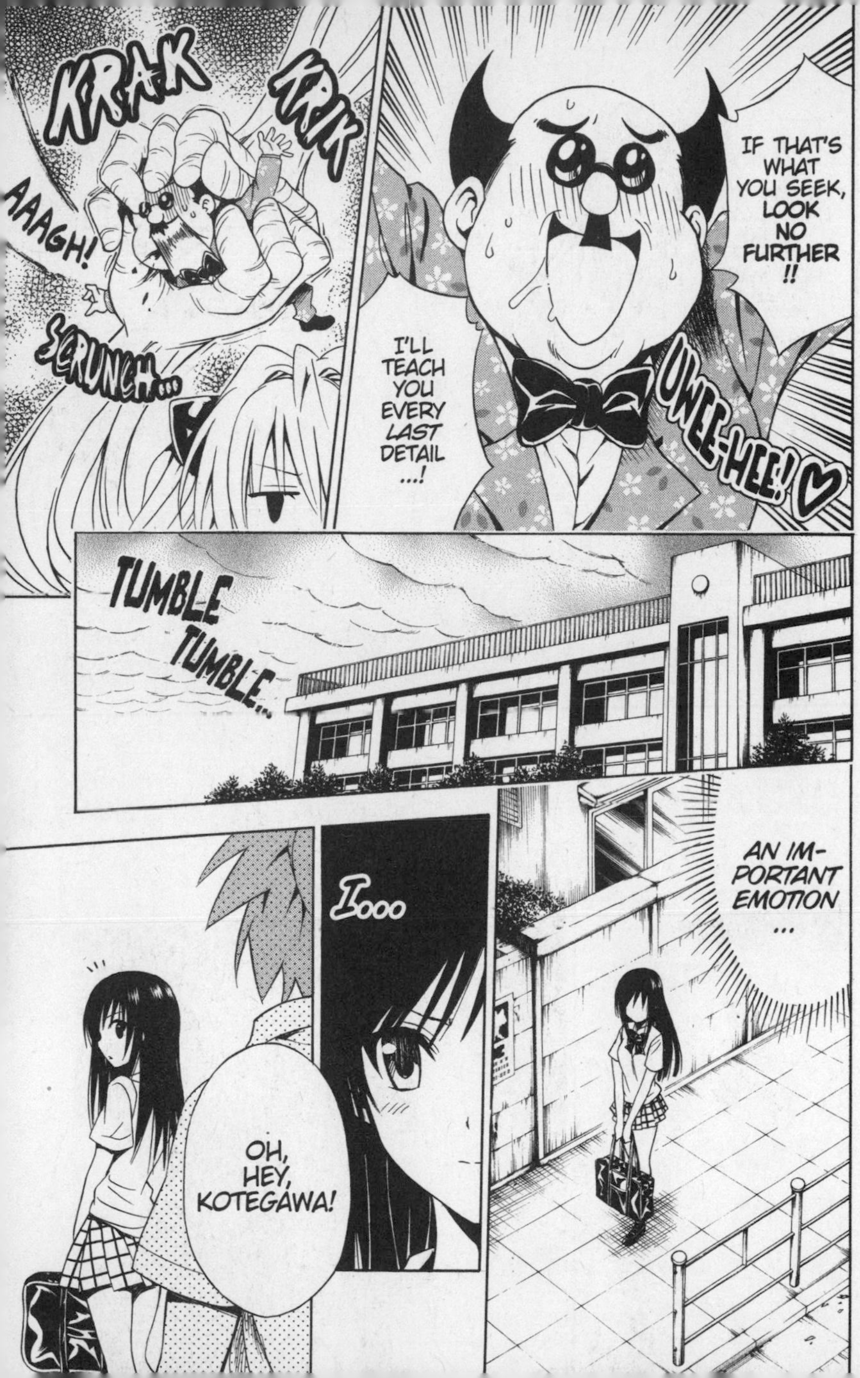

IF THAT'S WHAT YOU SEEK, LOOK NO FURTHER !!
I'LL TEACH YOU EVERY LAST DETAIL ...!
UWEE-HEE! ♥
KRAK
KRIK
AAAGH!
SCRUNCH...
TUMBLE TUMBLE...
AN IM-PORTANT EMOTION ...
Iooo
OH, HEY, KOTEGAWA!

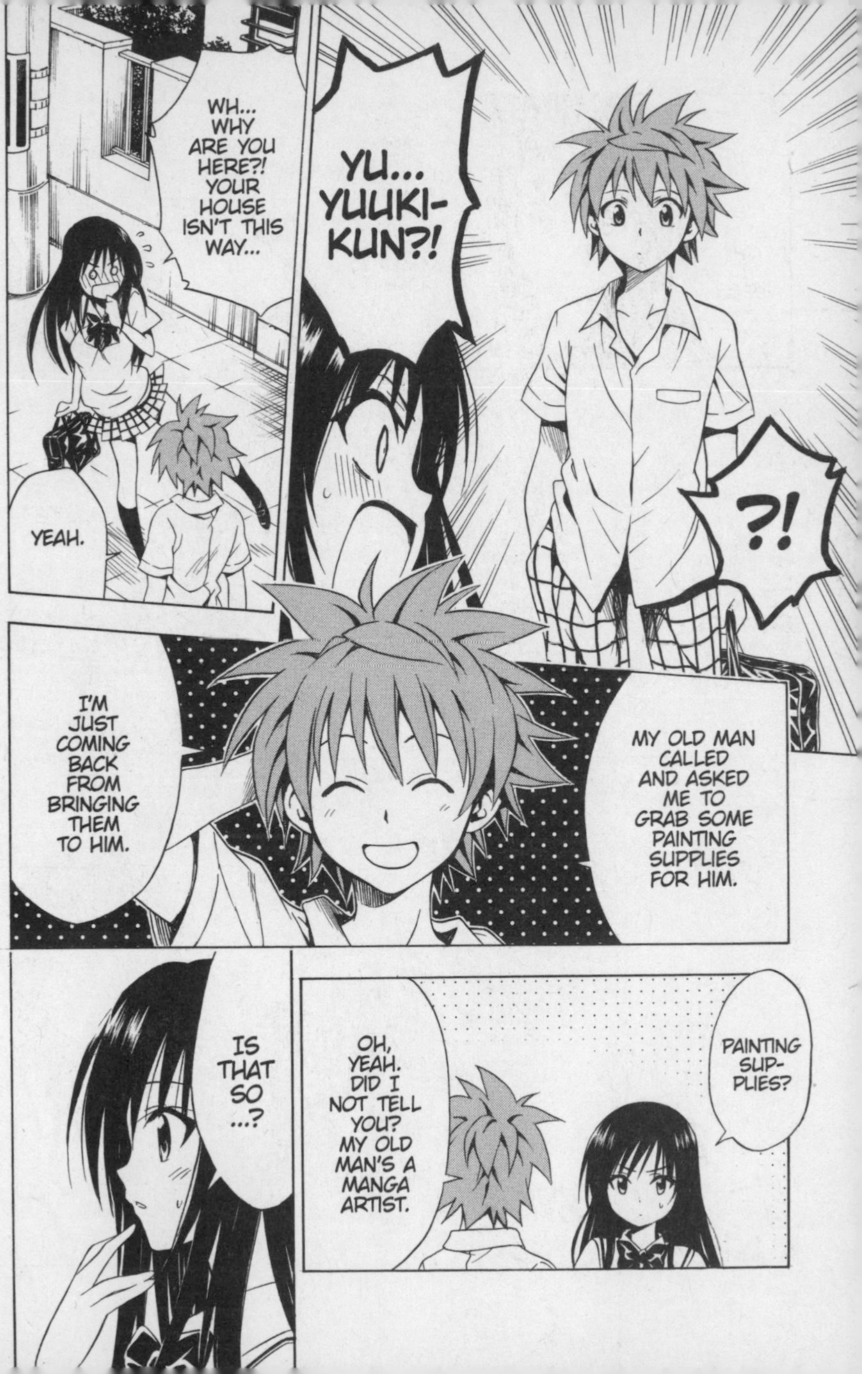
?!
YU... YUUKI-KUN?!
WH... WHY ARE YOU HERE?! YOUR HOUSE ISN'T THIS WAY...
YEAH.
MY OLD MAN CALLED AND ASKED ME TO GRAB SOME PAINTING SUPPLIES FOR HIM.
I'M JUST COMING BACK FROM BRINGING THEM TO HIM.
PAINTING SUP-PLIES?
OH, YEAH. DID I NOT TELL YOU? MY OLD MAN'S A MANGA ARTIST.
IS THAT SO ...?

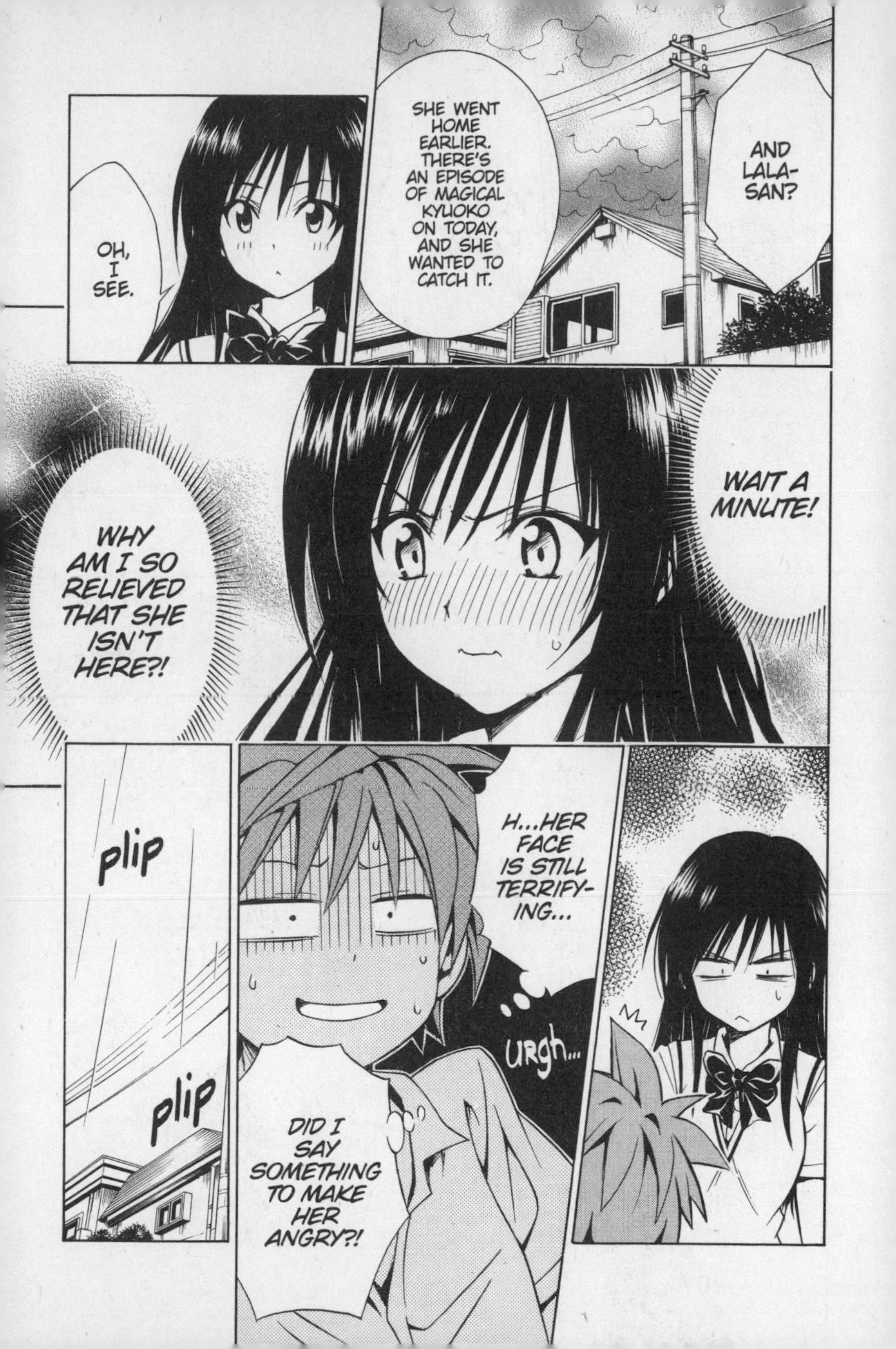
AND LALA-SAN?
SHE WENT HOME EARLIER. THERE'S AN EPISODE OF MAGICAL KYUOKO ON TODAY, AND SHE WANTED TO CATCH IT.
OH, I SEE.
WAIT A MINUTE!
WHY AM I SO RELIEVED THAT SHE ISN'T HERE?!
H...HER FACE IS STILL TERRIFY-ING...
urgh...
DID I SAY SOMETHING TO MAKE HER ANGRY?!
plip
plip

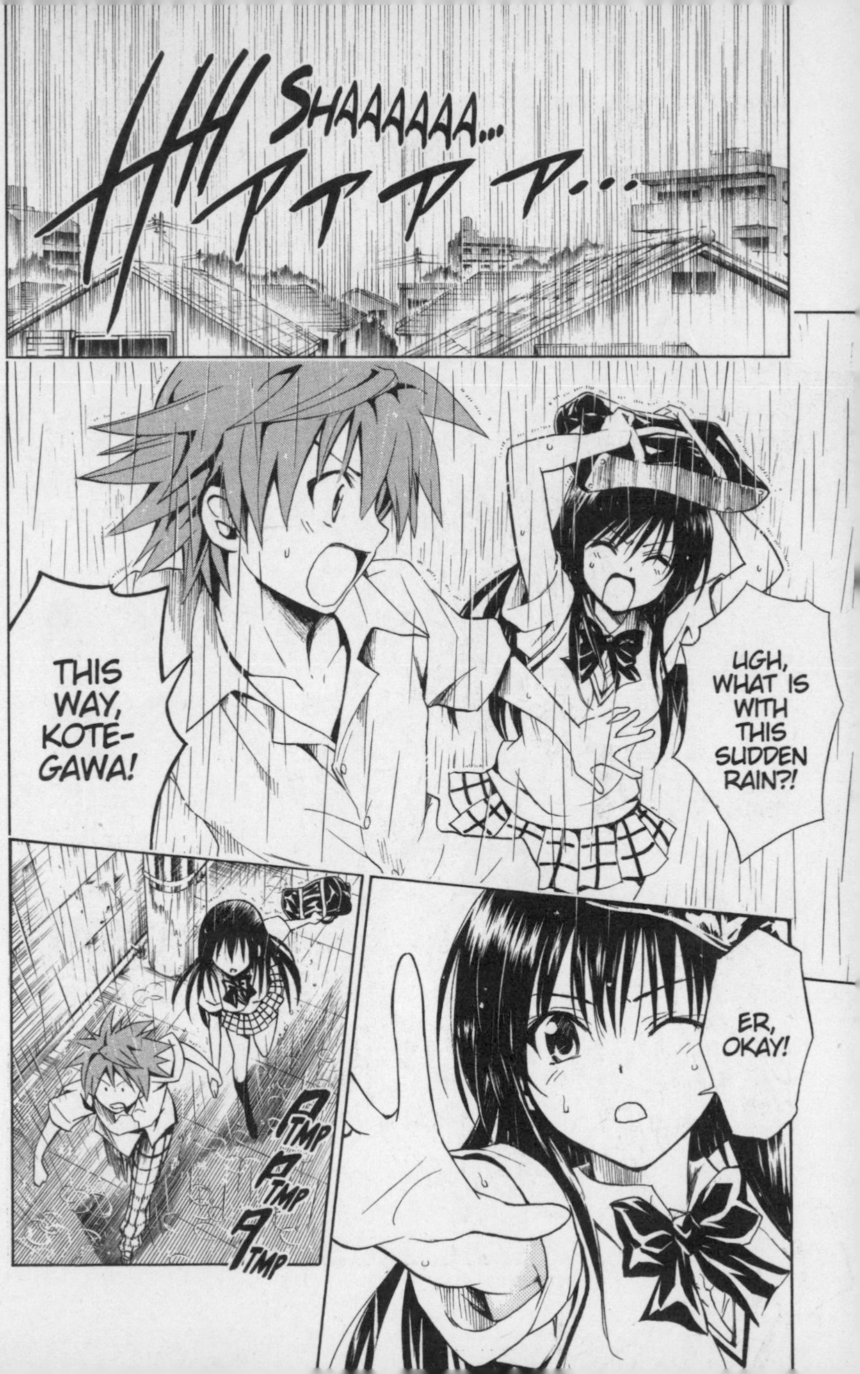
SHAAAAAA...
UGH, WHAT IS WITH THIS SUDDEN RAIN?!
THIS WAY, KOTE-GAWA!
ER, OKAY!
TMP
TMP
TMP

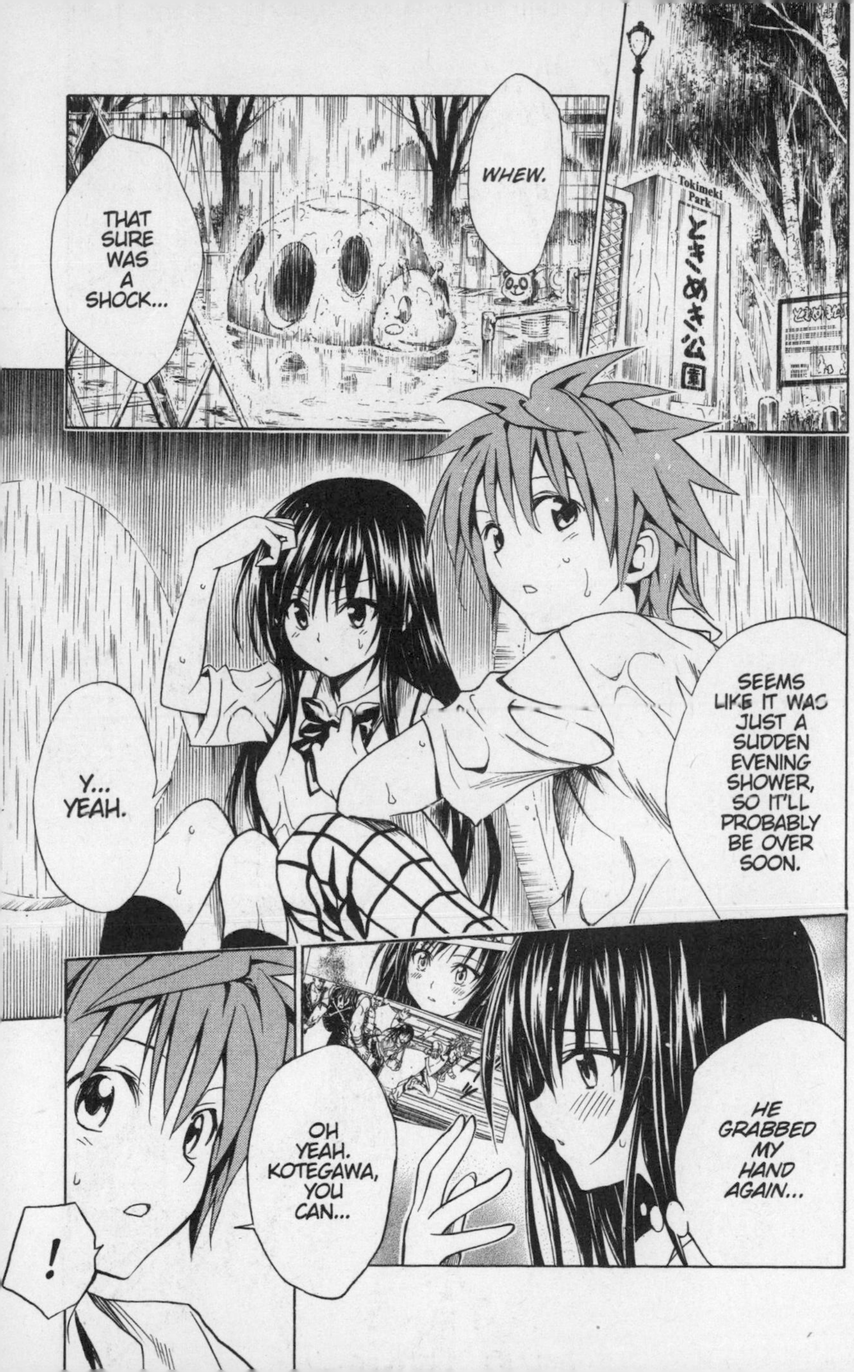
Tokimeki Park
ときめき公園
WHEW.
THAT SURE WAS A SHOCK...
SEEMS LIKE IT WAS JUST A SUDDEN EVENING SHOWER, SO IT'LL PROBABLY BE OVER SOON.
Y... YEAH.
HE GRABBED MY HAND AGAIN...
OH YEAH. KOTEGAWA, YOU CAN...
!

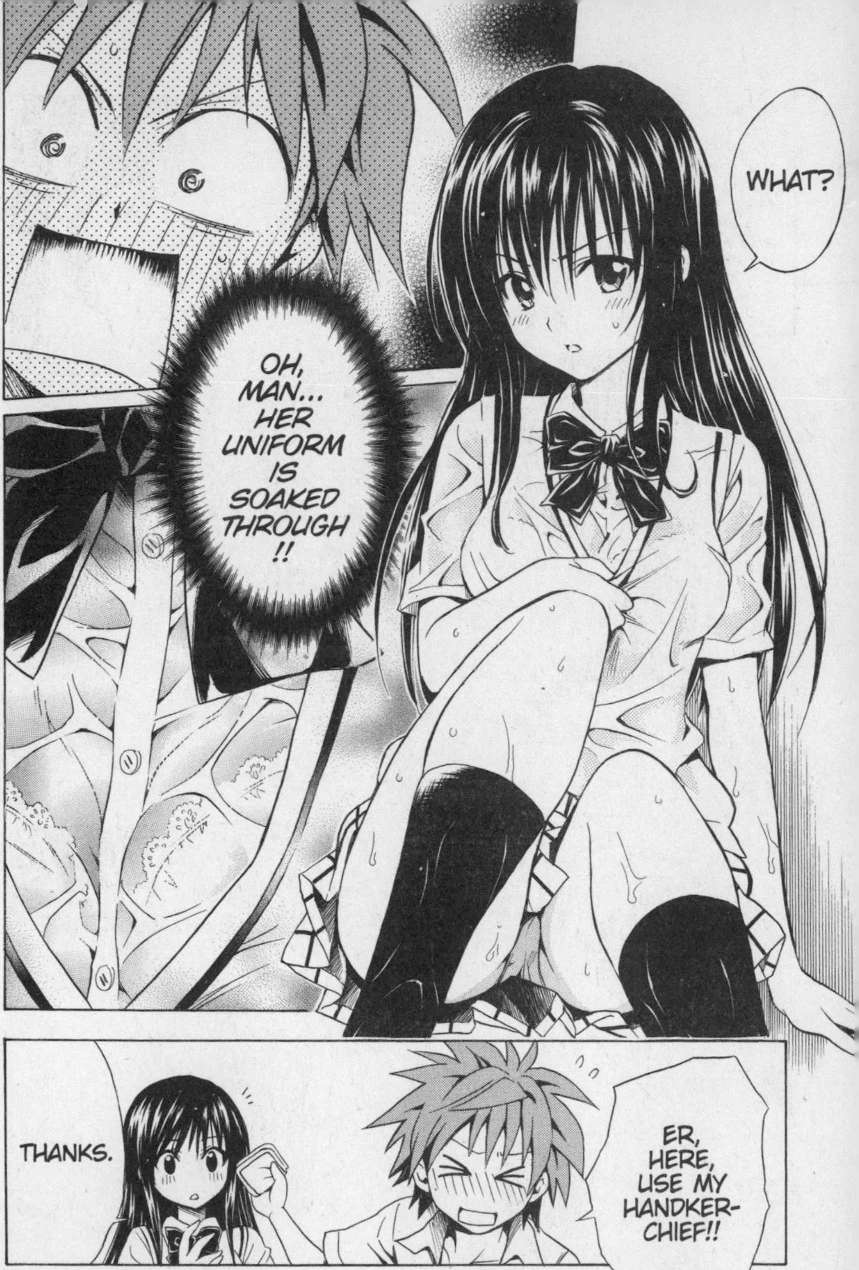
WHAT?
OH, MAN... HER UNIFORM IS SOAKED THROUGH!!
ER, HERE, USE MY HANDKER-CHIEF!!
THANKS.

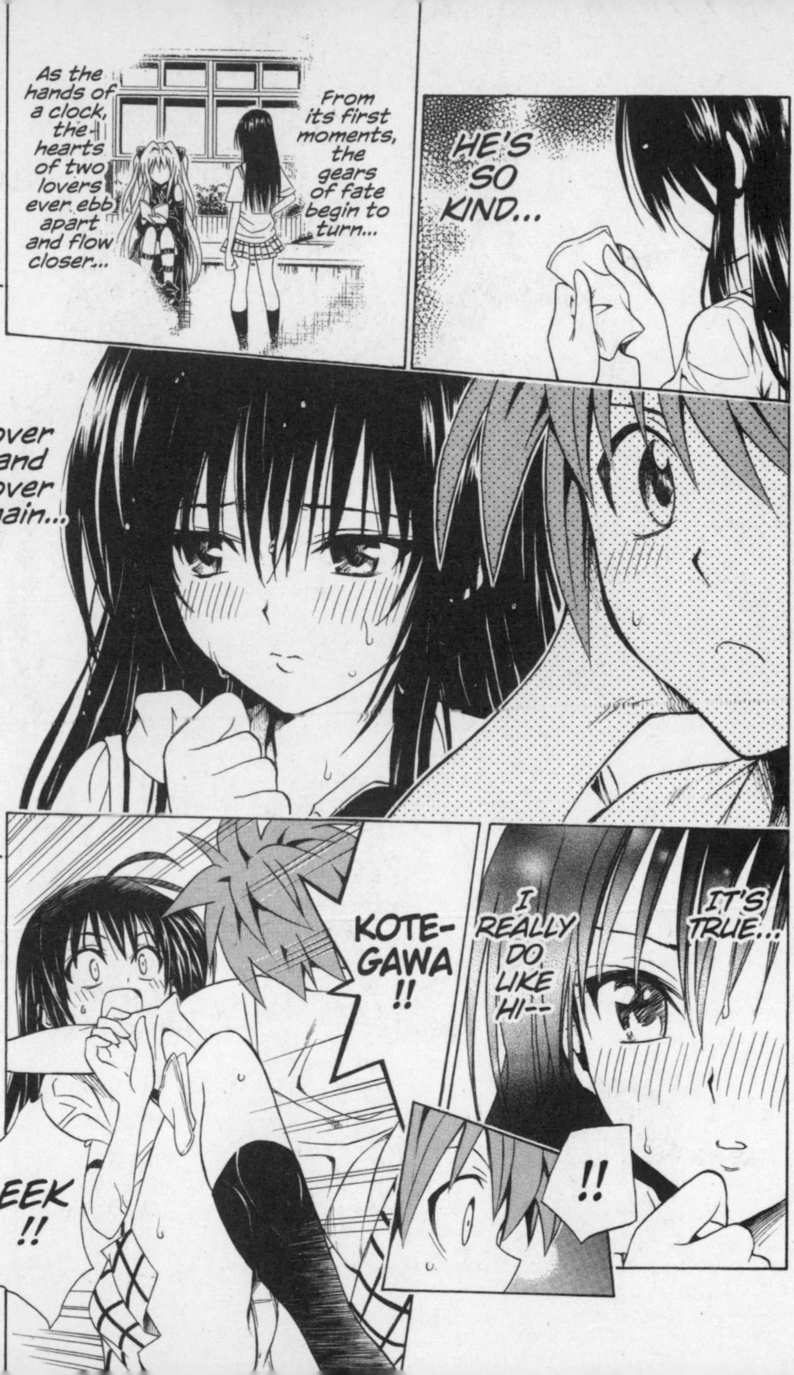
HE'S SO KIND...
From its first moments, the gears of fate begin to turn...
As the hands of a clock, the hearts of two lovers ever ebb apart and flow closer...
over and over again...
IT'S TRUE...
I REALLY DO LIKE HI--
!!
KOTE-GAWA!!
EEK!!

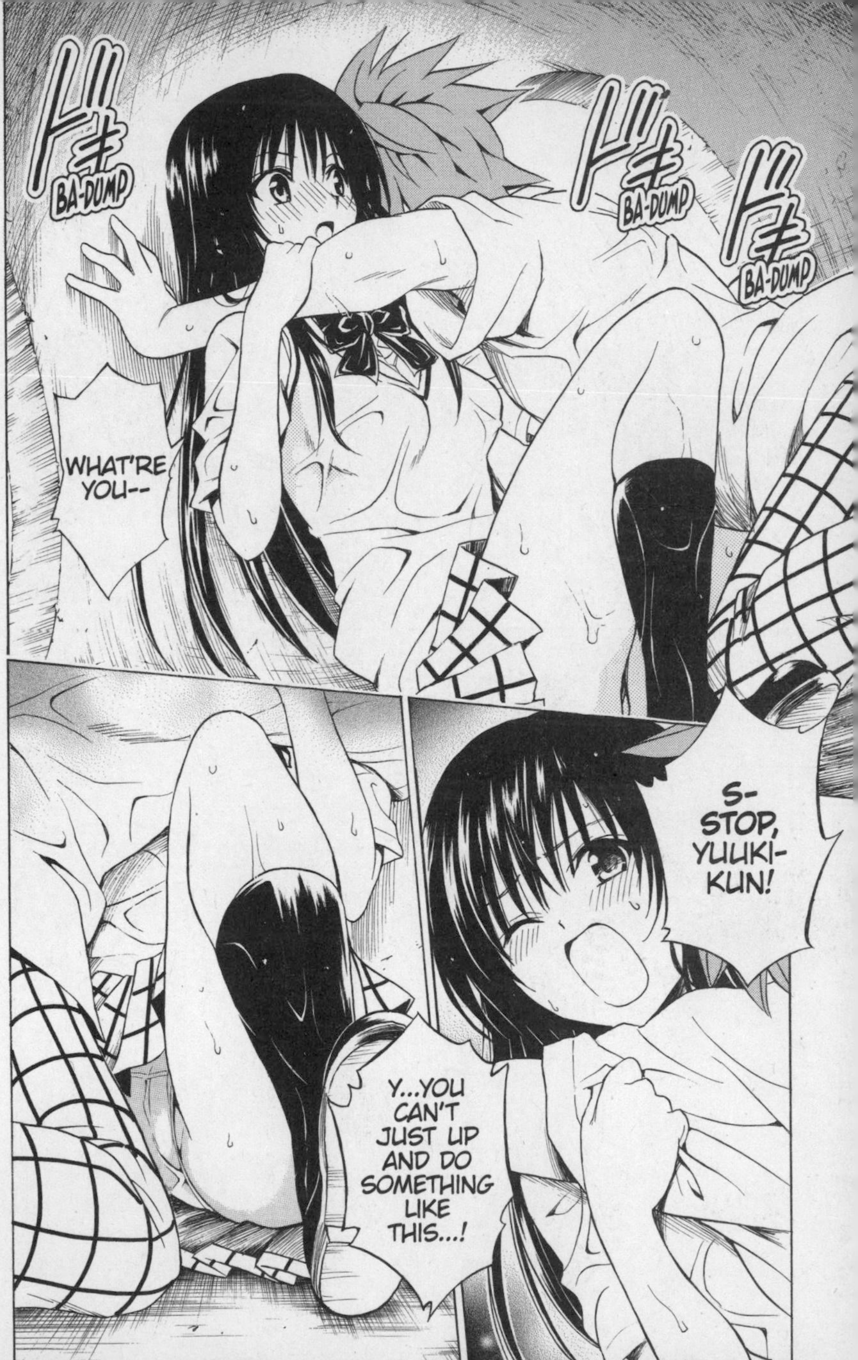
ドキ
BA-DUMP
ドキ
BA-DUMP
ドキ
BA-DUMP
WHAT'RE YOU--
S-STOP, YUUKI-KUN!
Y...YOU CAN'T JUST UP AND DO SOMETHING LIKE THIS...!

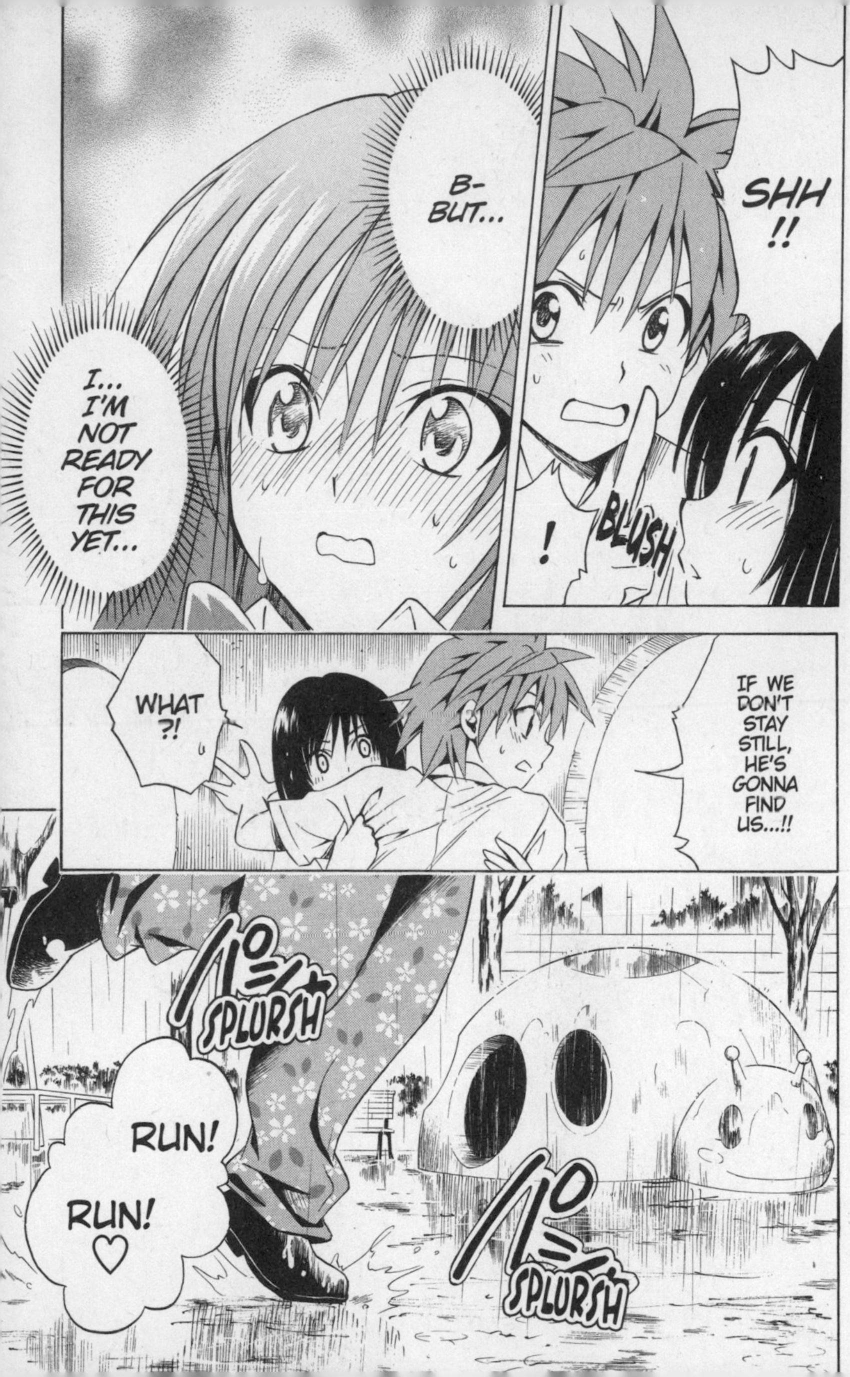
SHH!!
BLUSH
!
B-BUT...
I... I'M NOT READY FOR THIS YET...
IF WE DON'T STAY STILL, HE'S GONNA FIND US...!!
WHAT?!
SPLURSH
SPLURSH
RUN!
RUN! ♡

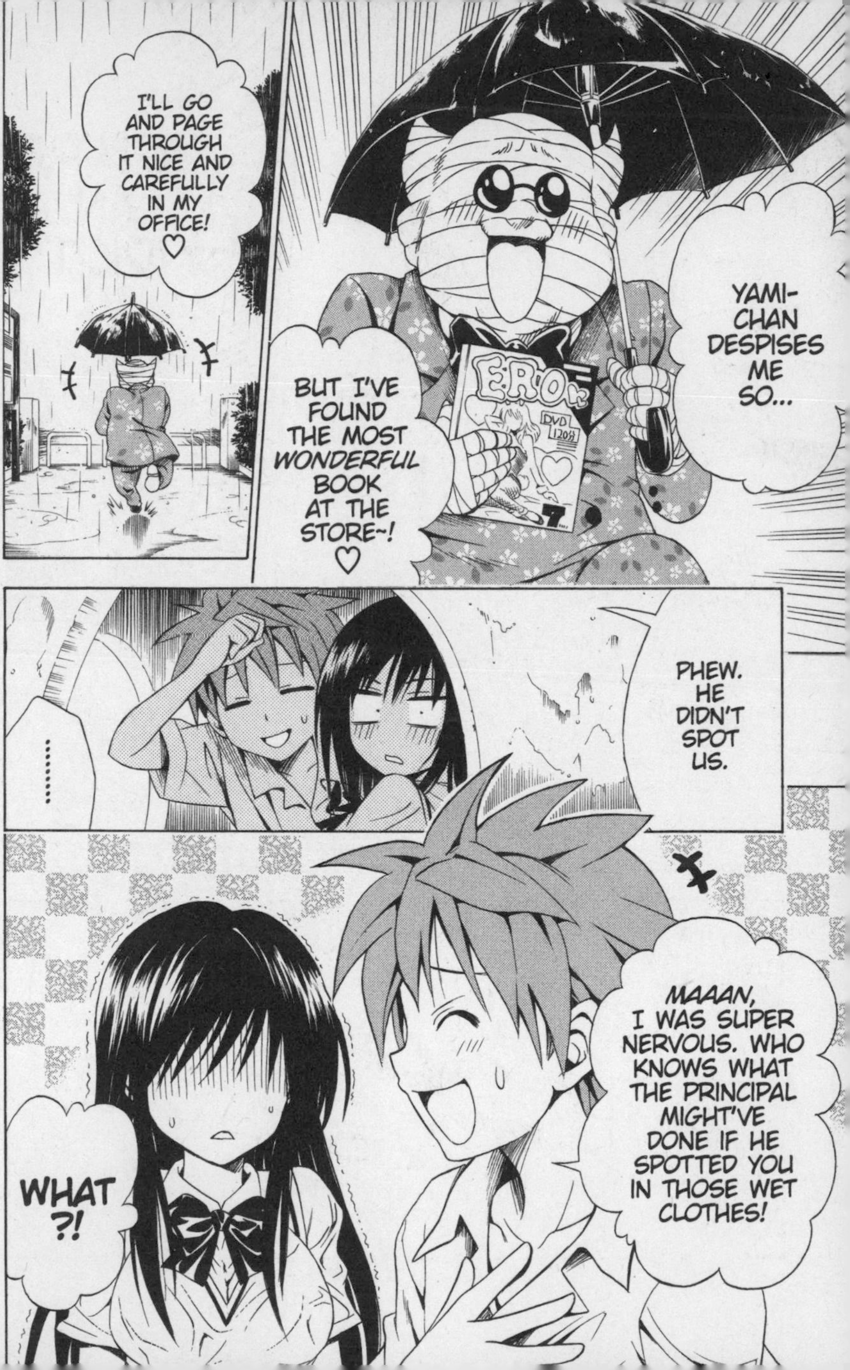
YAMI-CHAN DESPISES ME SO...
BUT I'VE FOUND THE MOST *WONDERFUL* BOOK AT THE STORE~! ♡
I'LL GO AND PAGE THROUGH IT NICE AND CAREFULLY IN MY OFFICE! ♡
PHEW. HE DIDN'T SPOT US.
....
MAAAN, I WAS SUPER NERVOUS. WHO KNOWS WHAT THE PRINCIPAL MIGHT'VE DONE IF HE SPOTTED YOU IN THOSE WET CLOTHES!
WHAT ?!

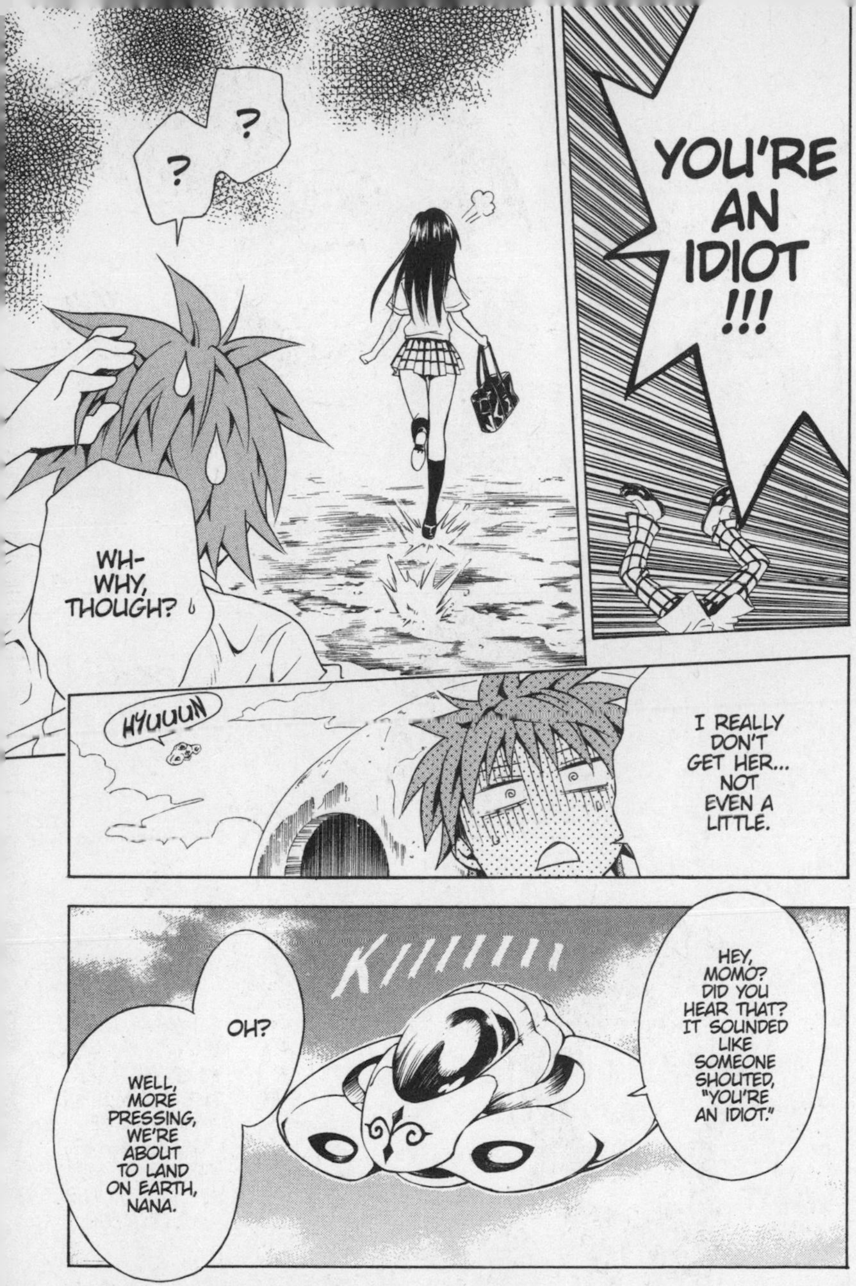
YOU'RE AN IDIOT !!!
? ?
WH- WHY, THOUGH?
I REALLY DON'T GET HER... NOT EVEN A LITTLE.
HYUUUN
HEY, MOMO? DID YOU HEAR THAT? IT SOUNDED LIKE SOMEONE SHOUTED, "YOU'RE AN IDIOT."
KIIIIII
OH?
WELL, MORE PRESSING, WE'RE ABOUT TO LAND ON EARTH, NANA.

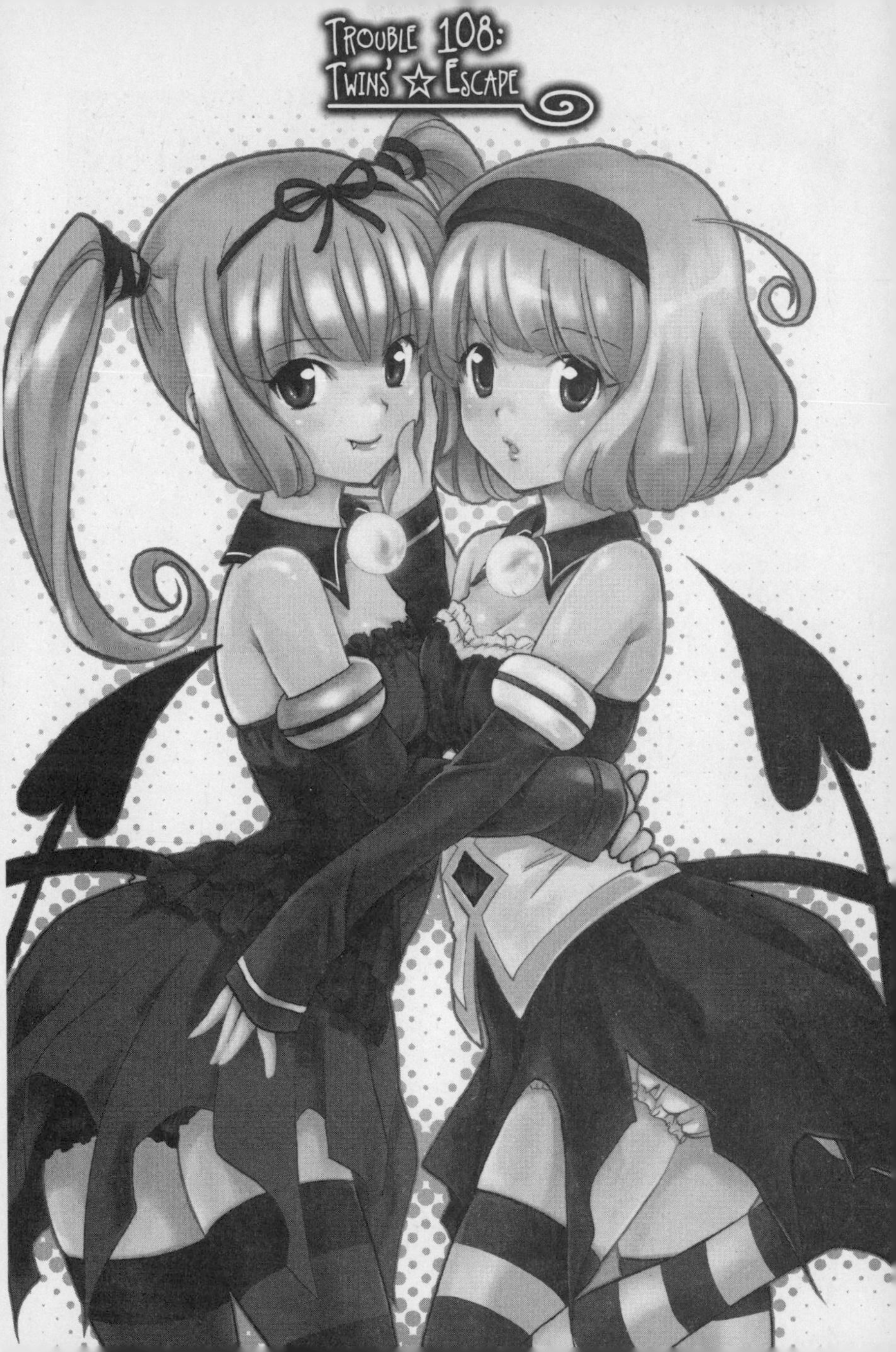
TROUBLE 108:
TWINS' ☆ ESCAPE

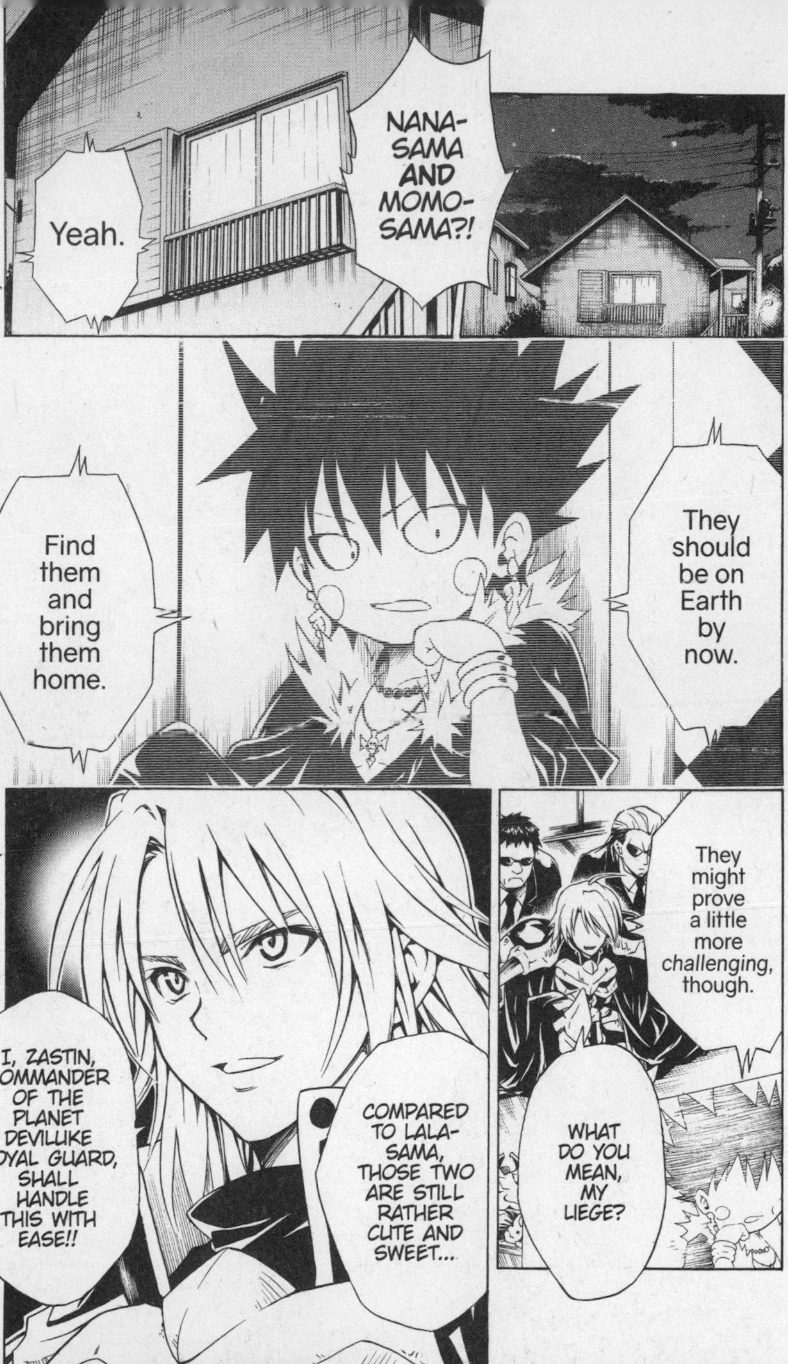
NANA-SAMA AND MOMO-SAMA?!
Yeah.
They should be on Earth by now.
Find them and bring them home.
They might prove a little more *challenging*, though.
WHAT DO YOU MEAN, MY LIEGE?
COMPARED TO LALA-SAMA, THOSE TWO ARE STILL RATHER CUTE AND SWEET...
I, ZASTIN, COMMANDER OF THE PLANET DEVILUKE ROYAL GUARD, SHALL HANDLE THIS WITH EASE!!

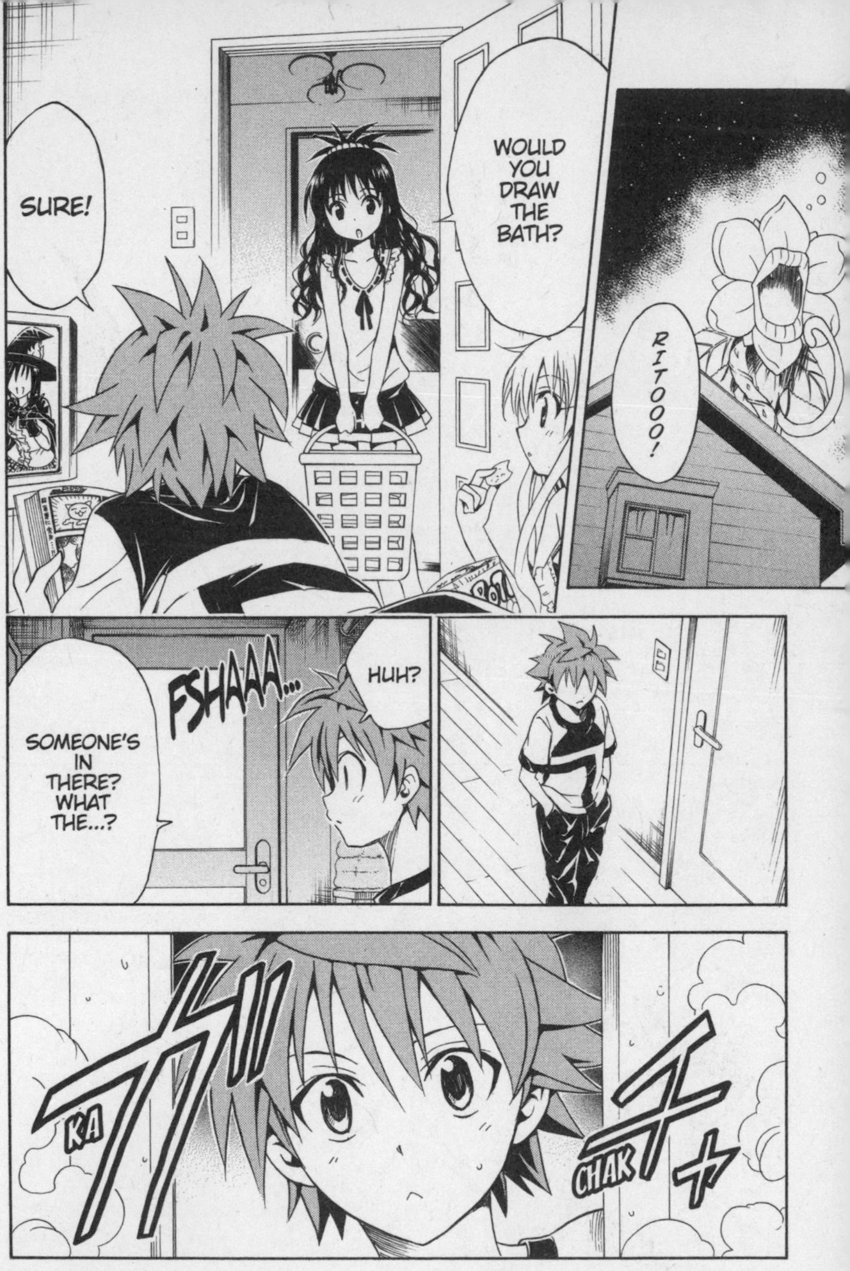
RITOOOO!
WOULD YOU DRAW THE BATH?
SURE!
HUH?
FSHAAA...
SOMEONE'S IN THERE? WHAT THE...?
KA
CHAK

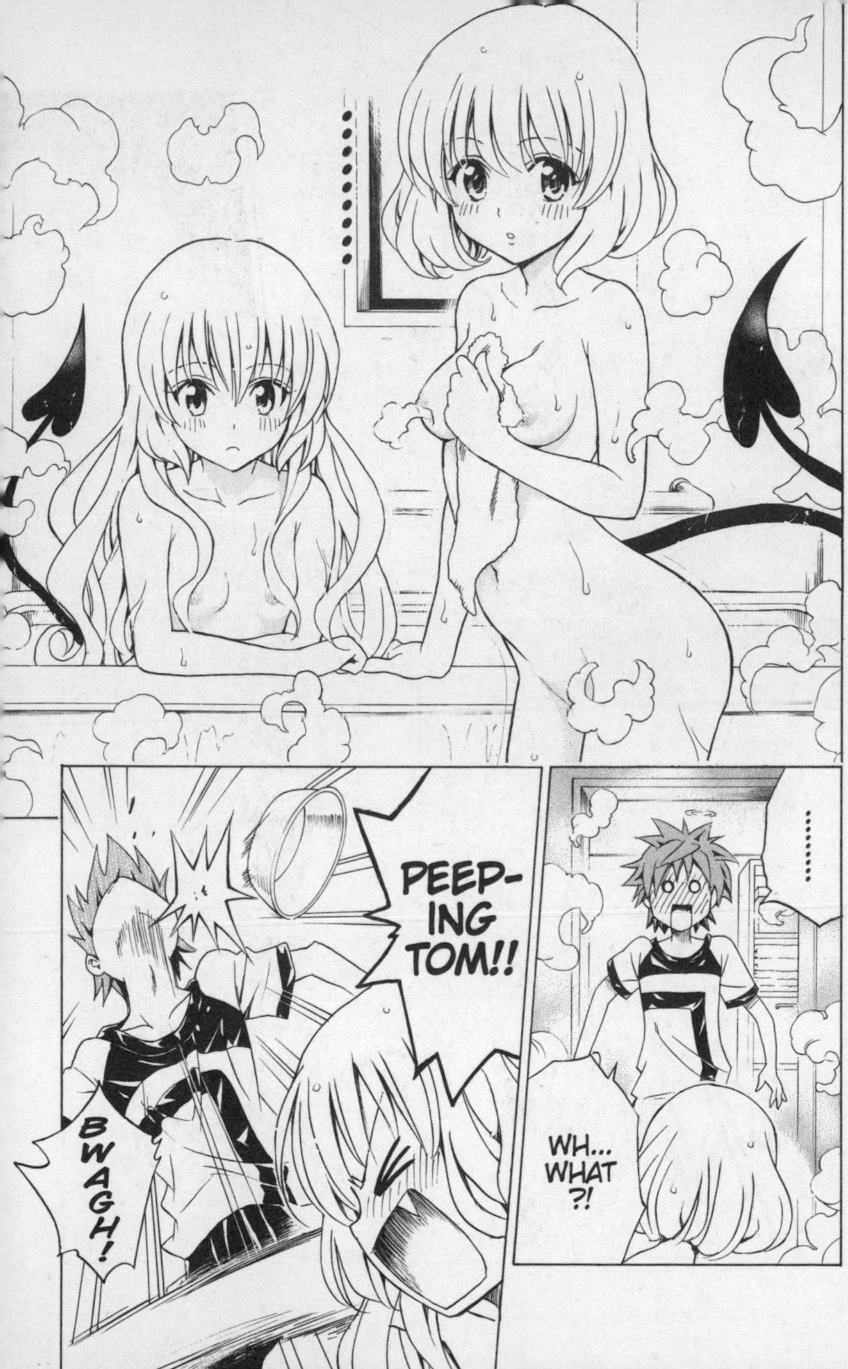
......
WH... WHAT?!
PEEP-ING TOM!!
BWAGH!

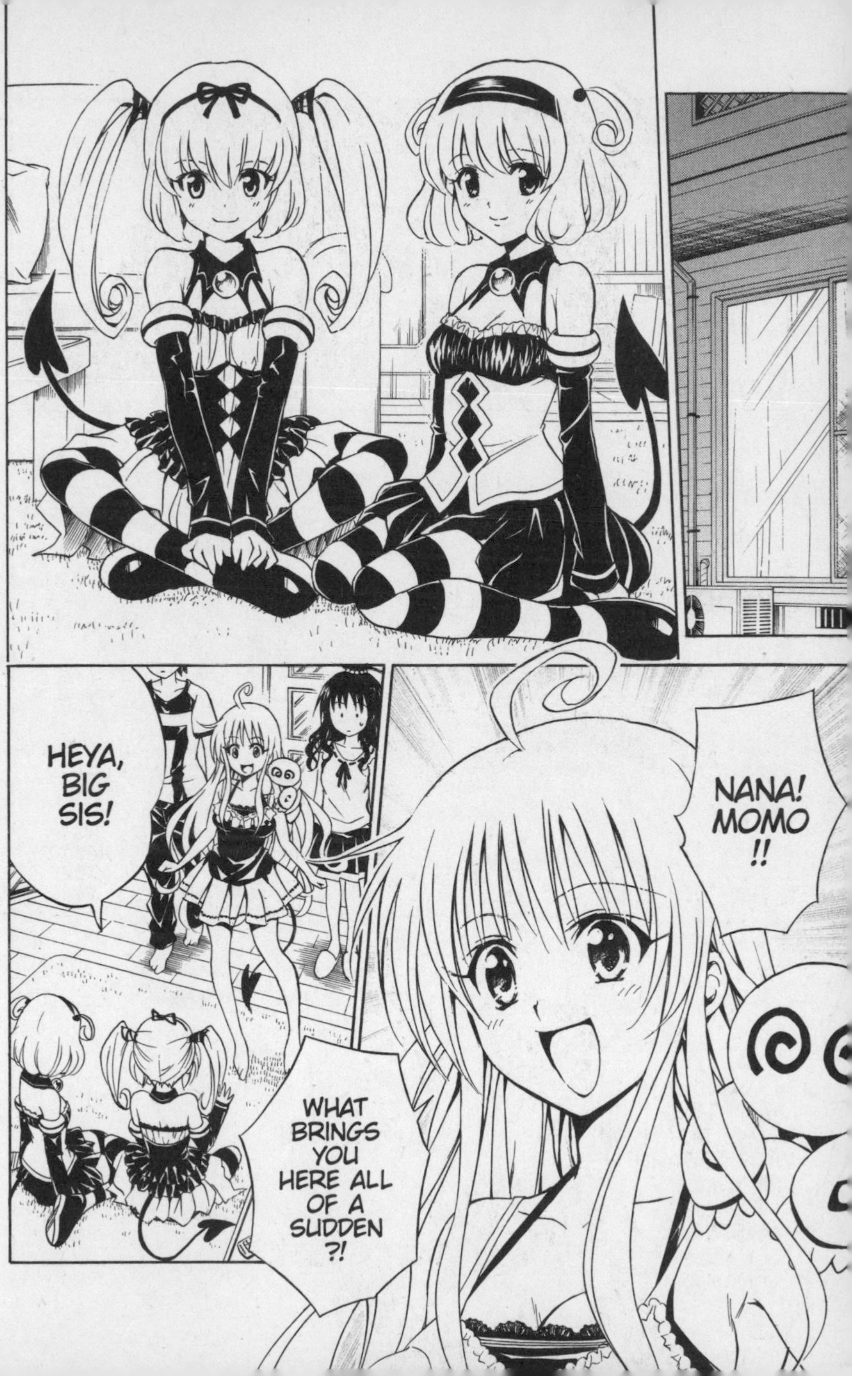
NANA! MOMO!!
WHAT BRINGS YOU HERE ALL OF A SUDDEN?!
HEYA, BIG SIS!

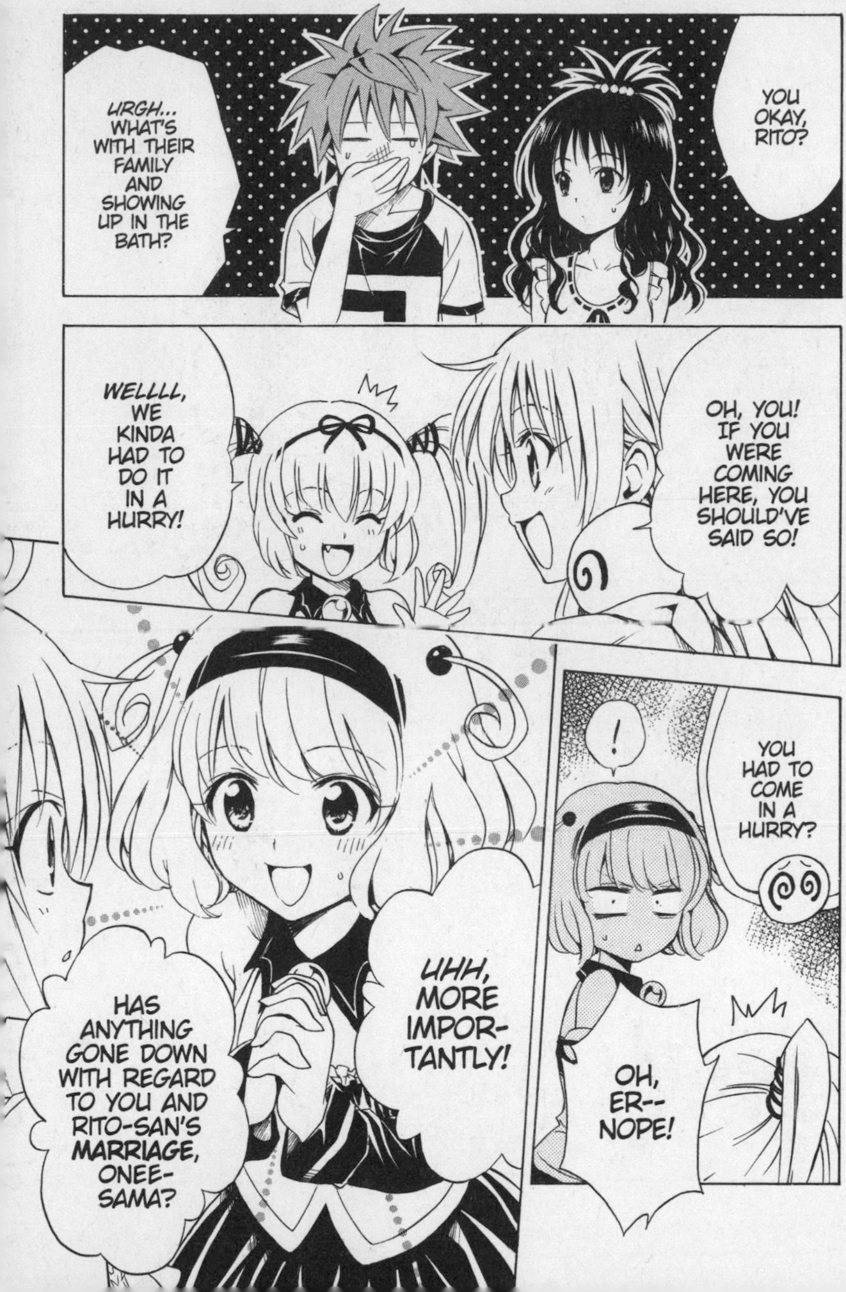
YOU OKAY, RITO?
URGH... WHAT'S WITH THEIR FAMILY AND SHOWING UP IN THE BATH?
OH, YOU! IF YOU WERE COMING HERE, YOU SHOULD'VE SAID SO!
WELLLL, WE KINDA HAD TO DO IT IN A HURRY!
YOU HAD TO COME IN A HURRY?
!
OH, ER-- NOPE!
UHH, MORE IMPOR-TANTLY!
HAS ANYTHING GONE DOWN WITH REGARD TO YOU AND RITO-SAN'S MARRIAGE, ONEE-SAMA?

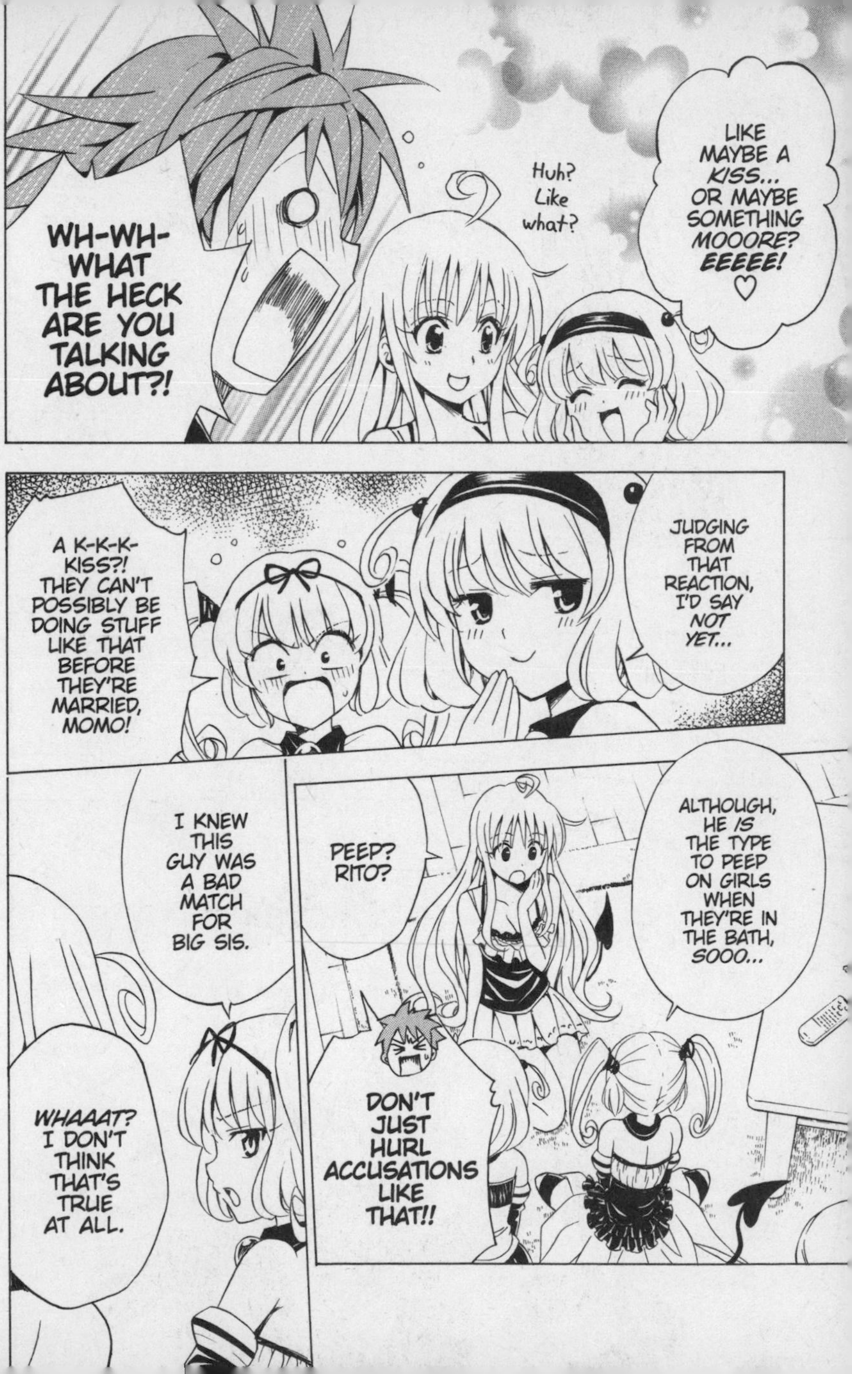
LIKE MAYBE A KISS... OR MAYBE SOMETHING MOOORE? EEEEE! ♡
Huh? Like what?
WH-WH-WHAT THE HECK ARE YOU TALKING ABOUT?!
JUDGING FROM THAT REACTION, I'D SAY NOT YET...
A K-K-K-KISS?! THEY CAN'T POSSIBLY BE DOING STUFF LIKE THAT BEFORE THEY'RE MARRIED, MOMO!
ALTHOUGH, HE IS THE TYPE TO PEEP ON GIRLS WHEN THEY'RE IN THE BATH, SOOO...
PEEP? RITO?
DON'T JUST HURL ACCUSATIONS LIKE THAT!!
I KNEW THIS GUY WAS A BAD MATCH FOR BIG SIS.
WHAAAT? I DON'T THINK THAT'S TRUE AT ALL.

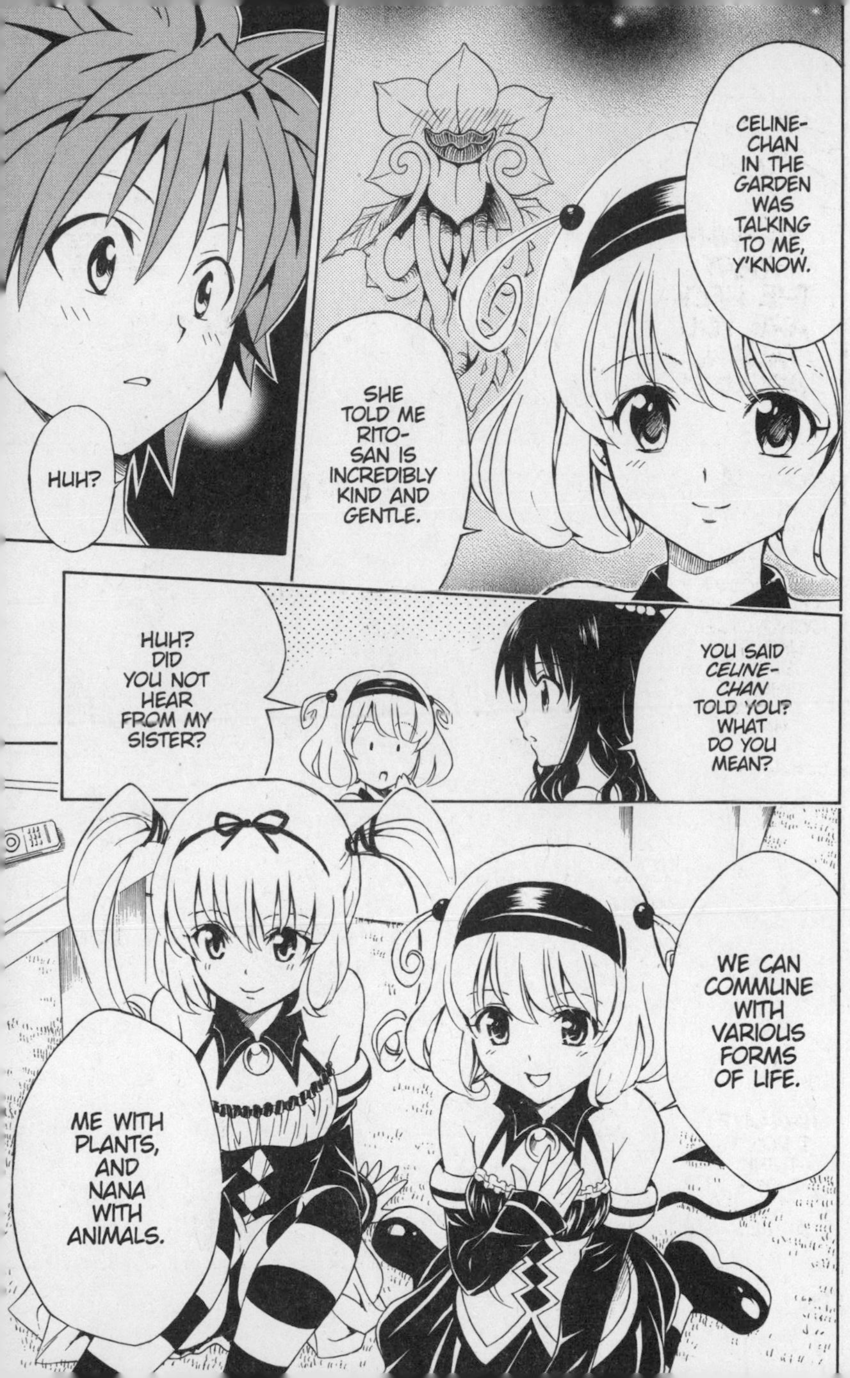
CELINE-CHAN IN THE GARDEN WAS TALKING TO ME, Y'KNOW.
SHE TOLD ME RITO-SAN IS INCREDIBLY KIND AND GENTLE.
HUH?
YOU SAID CELINE-CHAN TOLD YOU? WHAT DO YOU MEAN?
HUH? DID YOU NOT HEAR FROM MY SISTER?
WE CAN COMMUNE WITH VARIOUS FORMS OF LIFE.
ME WITH PLANTS, AND NANA WITH ANIMALS.

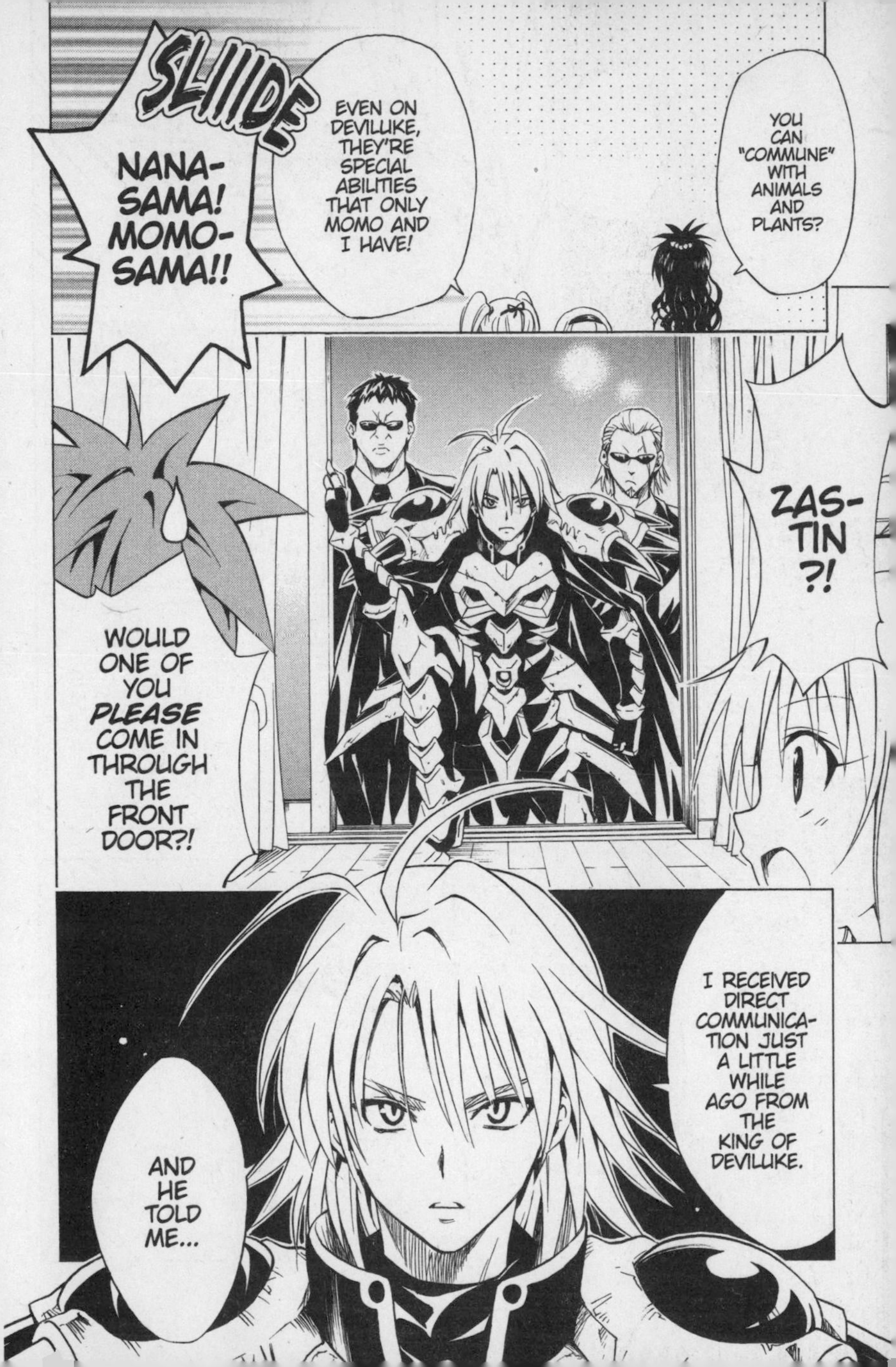
YOU CAN "COMMUNE" WITH ANIMALS AND PLANTS?
EVEN ON DEVILUKE, THEY'RE SPECIAL ABILITIES THAT ONLY MOMO AND I HAVE!
SLIIIDE
NANA-SAMA! MOMO-SAMA!!
ZAS-TIN?!
WOULD ONE OF YOU *PLEASE* COME IN THROUGH THE FRONT DOOR?!
I RECEIVED DIRECT COMMUNICATION JUST A LITTLE WHILE AGO FROM THE KING OF DEVILUKE.
AND HE TOLD ME...

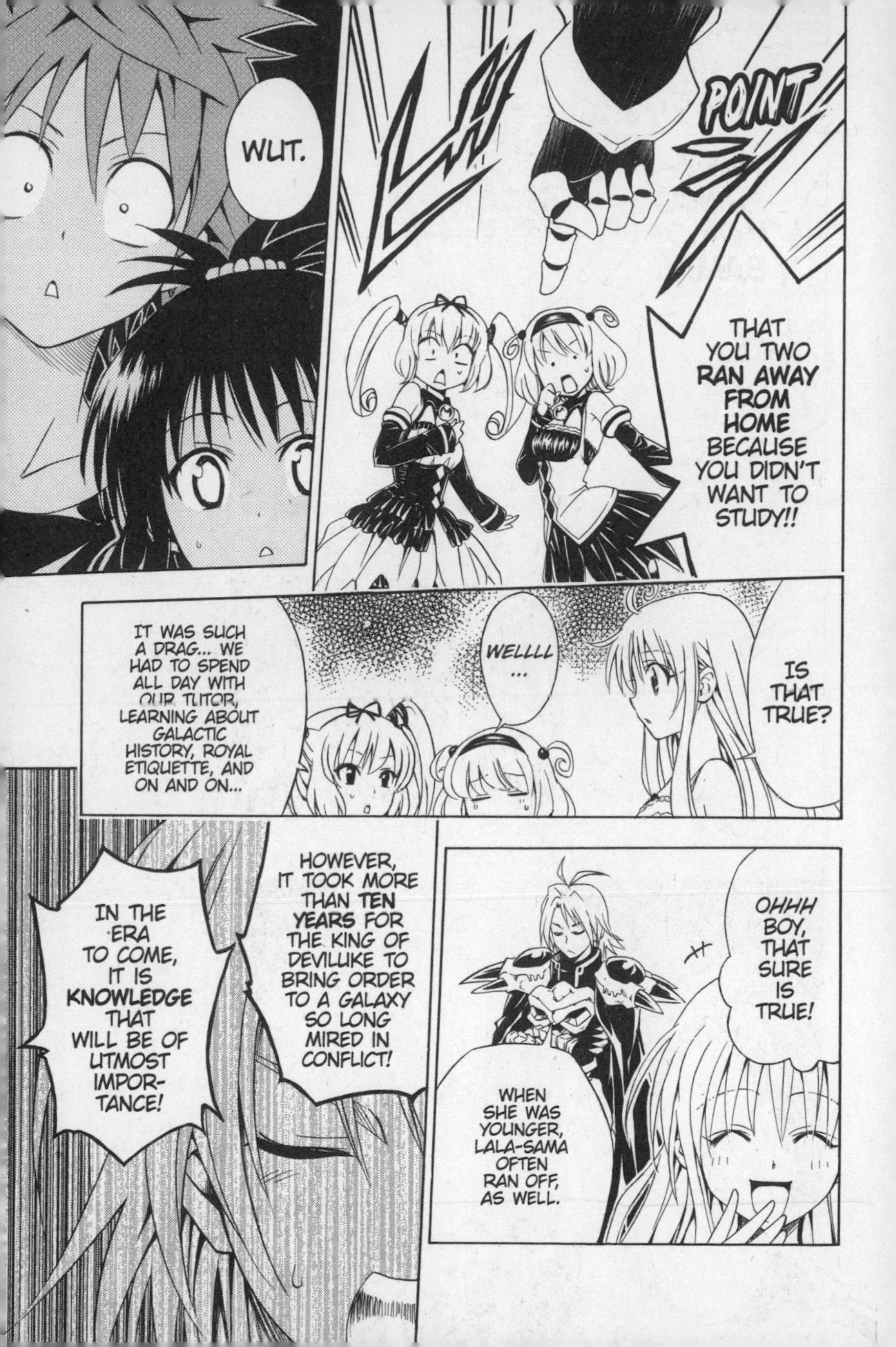
POINT
THAT YOU TWO RAN AWAY FROM HOME BECAUSE YOU DIDN'T WANT TO STUDY!!
WUT.
IS THAT TRUE?
WELLLL ...
IT WAS SUCH A DRAG... WE HAD TO SPEND ALL DAY WITH OUR TUTOR, LEARNING ABOUT GALACTIC HISTORY, ROYAL ETIQUETTE, AND ON AND ON...
OHHH BOY, THAT SURE IS TRUE!
WHEN SHE WAS YOUNGER, LALA-SAMA OFTEN RAN OFF, AS WELL.
HOWEVER, IT TOOK MORE THAN TEN YEARS FOR THE KING OF DEVILUKE TO BRING ORDER TO A GALAXY SO LONG MIRED IN CONFLICT!
IN THE ERA TO COME, IT IS KNOWLEDGE THAT WILL BE OF UTMOST IMPORTANCE!

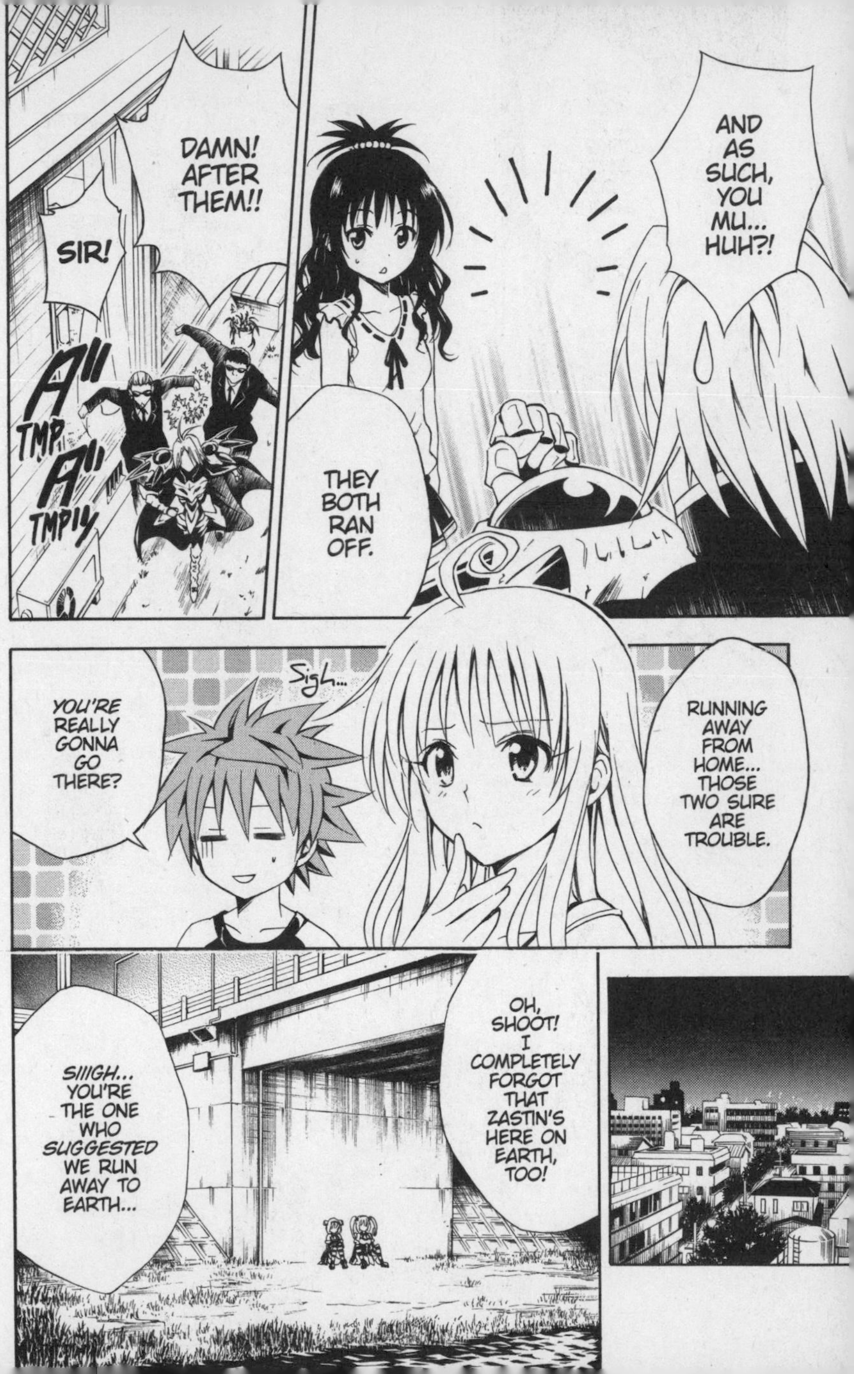
AND AS SUCH, YOU MU... HUH?!
THEY BOTH RAN OFF.
DAMN! AFTER THEM!!
SIR!
TMP
TMP
RUNNING AWAY FROM HOME... THOSE TWO SURE ARE TROUBLE.
Sigh...
YOU'RE REALLY GONNA GO THERE?
OH, SHOOT! I COMPLETELY FORGOT THAT ZASTIN'S HERE ON EARTH, TOO!
SIIIGH... YOU'RE THE ONE WHO SUGGESTED WE RUN AWAY TO EARTH...

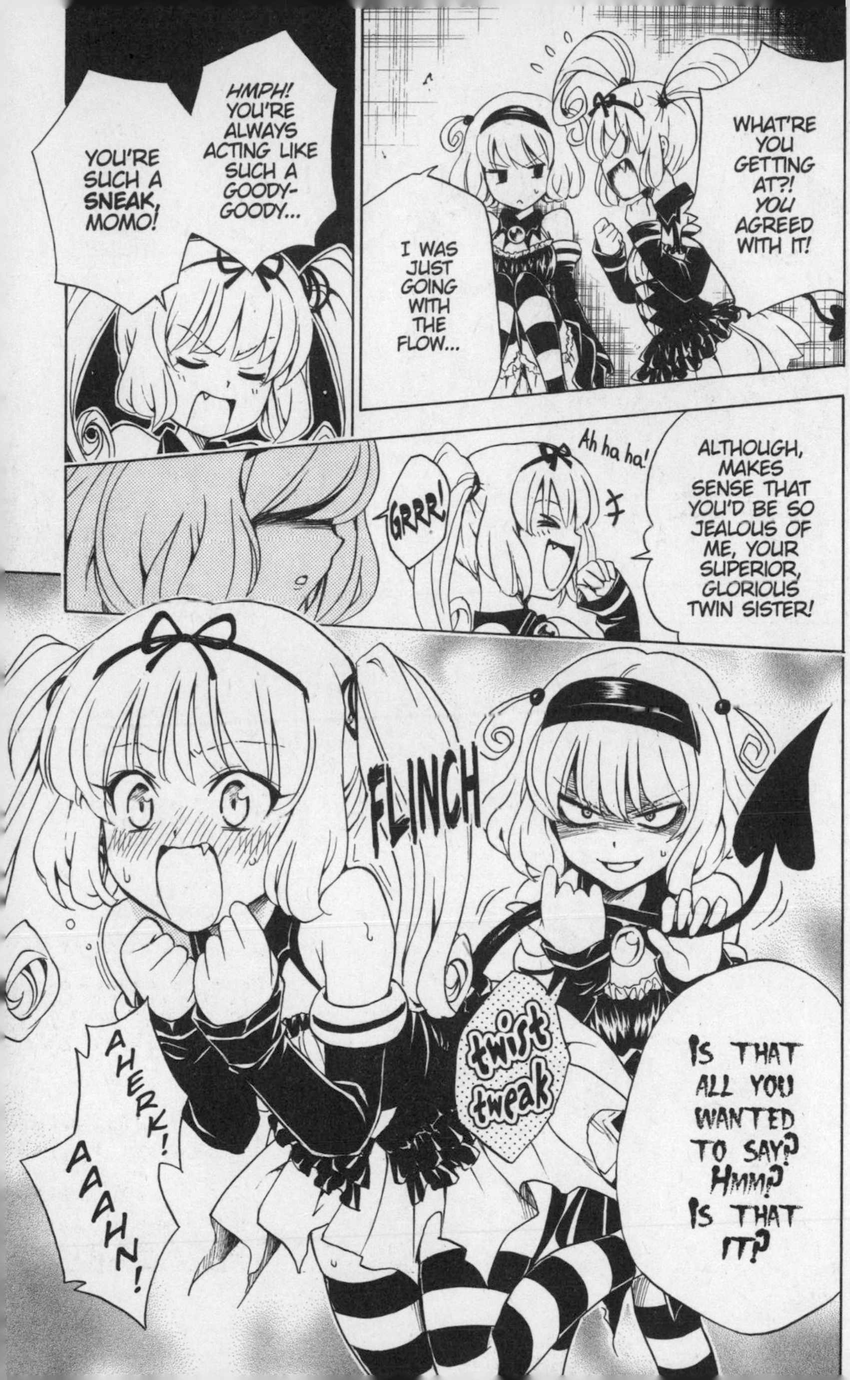
WHAT'RE YOU GETTING AT?! YOU AGREED WITH IT!
I WAS JUST GOING WITH THE FLOW...
HMPH! YOU'RE ALWAYS ACTING LIKE SUCH A GOODY-GOODY...
YOU'RE SUCH A SNEAK, MOMO!
ALTHOUGH, MAKES SENSE THAT YOU'D BE SO JEALOUS OF ME, YOUR SUPERIOR, GLORIOUS TWIN SISTER!
Ah ha ha!
GRRR!
IS THAT ALL YOU WANTED TO SAY? HMM? IS THAT IT?
twist tweak
FLINCH
AHERK!
AAAHN!

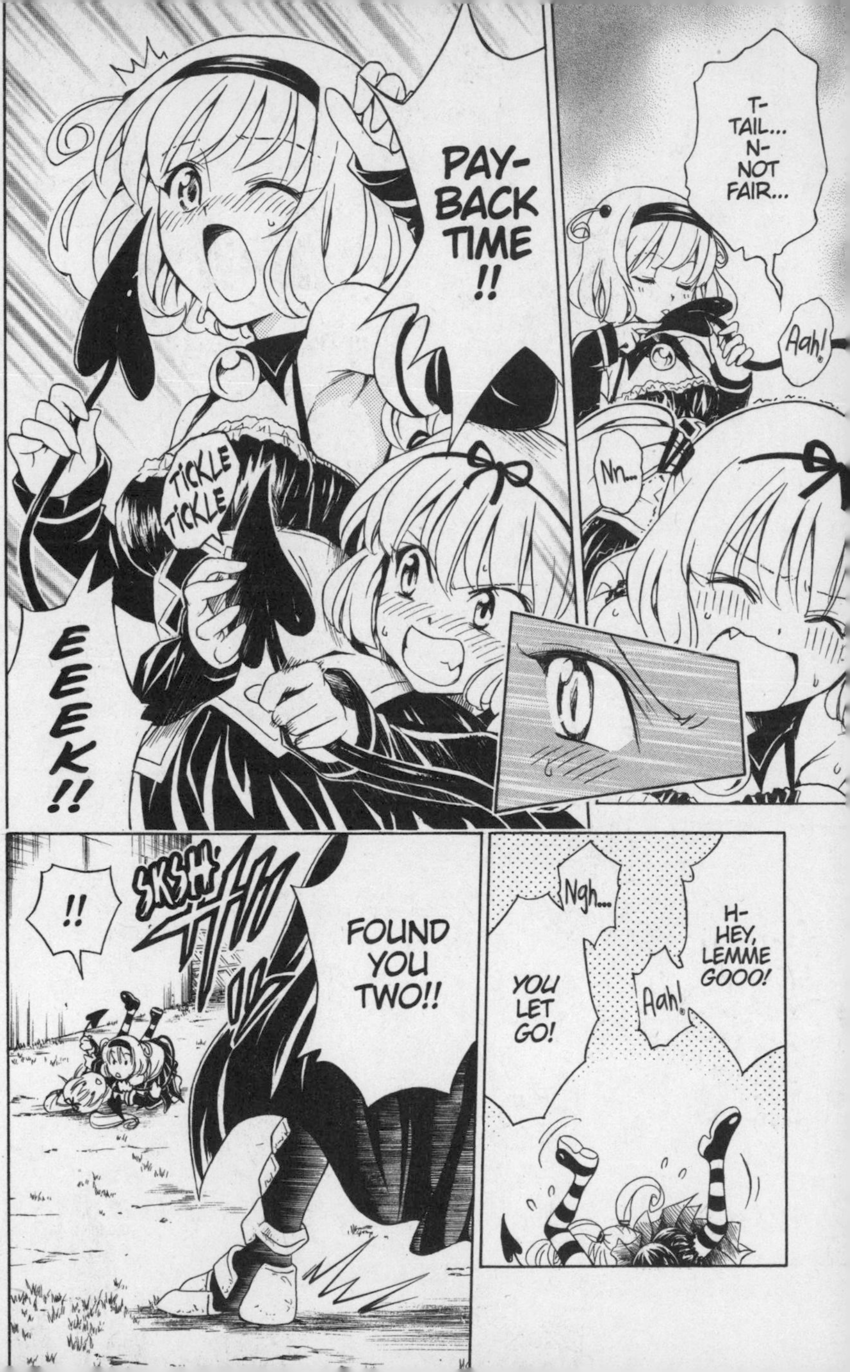
T-TAIL... N-NOT FAIR...
Aah!
Nn...
PAY-BACK TIME!!
TICKLE TICKLE
EEEEK!!
Ngh...
H-HEY, LEMME GOOO!
Aah!
YOU LET GO!
SKSH
FOUND YOU TWO!!
!!

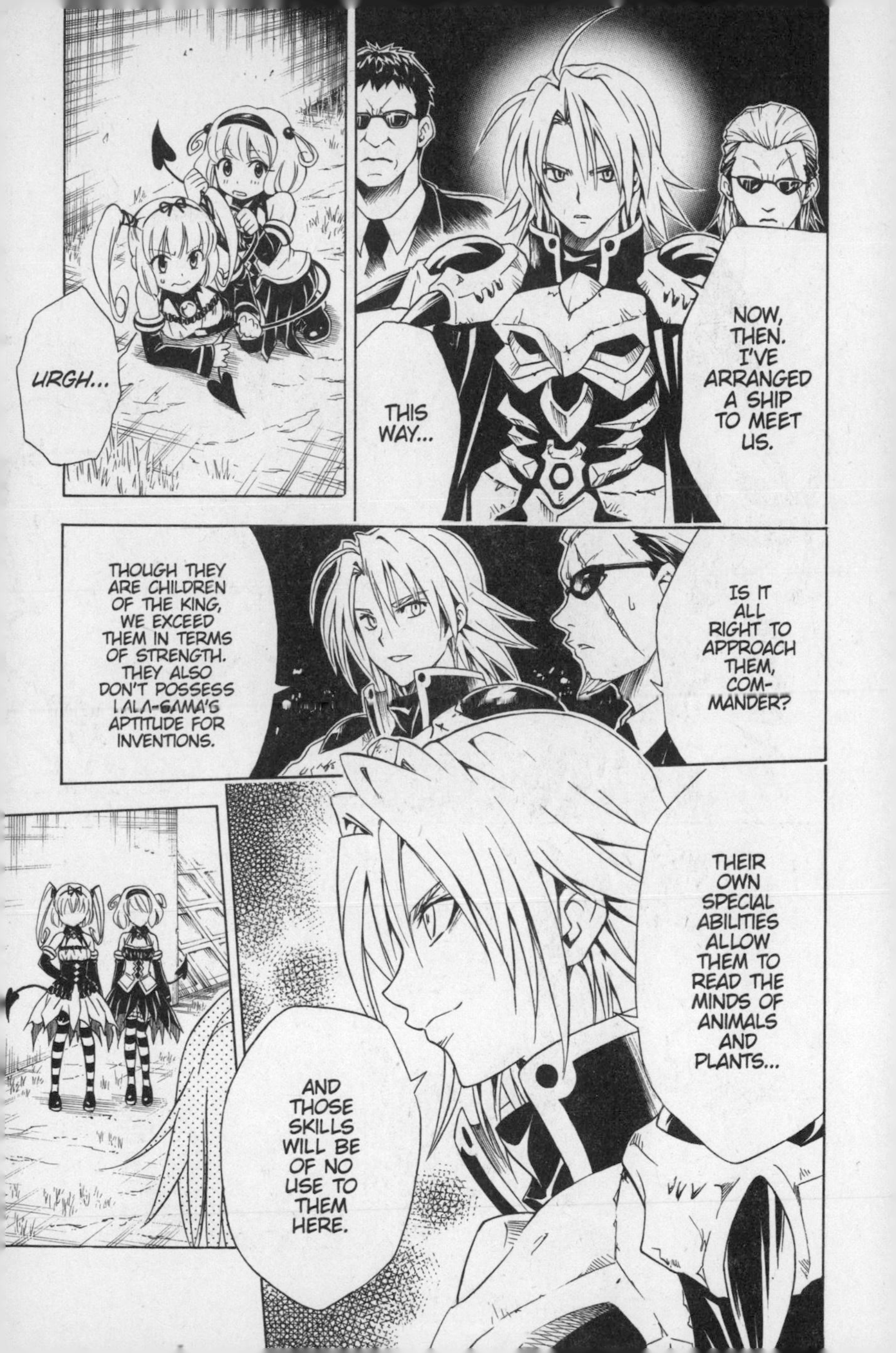

NOW, THEN. I'VE ARRANGED A SHIP TO MEET US.
THIS WAY...
URGH...
IS IT ALL RIGHT TO APPROACH THEM, COM-MANDER?
THOUGH THEY ARE CHILDREN OF THE KING, WE EXCEED THEM IN TERMS OF STRENGTH. THEY ALSO DON'T POSSESS LALA-SAMA'S APTITUDE FOR INVENTIONS.
THEIR OWN SPECIAL ABILITIES ALLOW THEM TO READ THE MINDS OF ANIMALS AND PLANTS...
AND THOSE SKILLS WILL BE OF NO USE TO THEM HERE.

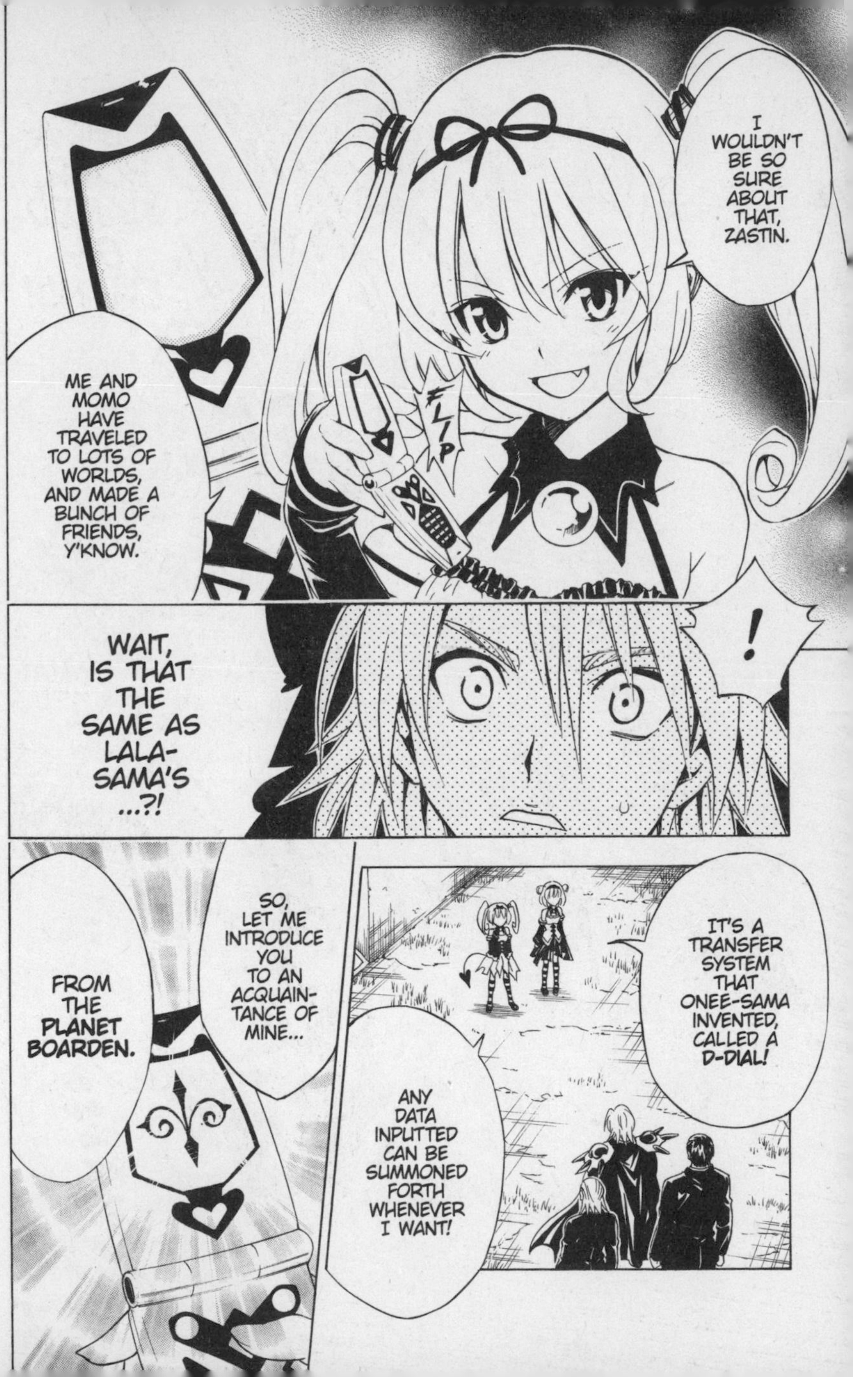
I WOULDN'T BE SO SURE ABOUT THAT, ZASTIN.
FLIP
ME AND MOMO HAVE TRAVELED TO LOTS OF WORLDS, AND MADE A BUNCH OF FRIENDS, Y'KNOW.
!
WAIT, IS THAT THE SAME AS LALA-SAMA'S ...?!
IT'S A TRANSFER SYSTEM THAT ONEE-SAMA INVENTED, CALLED A D-DIAL!
ANY DATA INPUTTED CAN BE SUMMONED FORTH WHENEVER I WANT!
SO, LET ME INTRODUCE YOU TO AN ACQUAIN-TANCE OF MINE...
FROM THE PLANET BOARDEN.

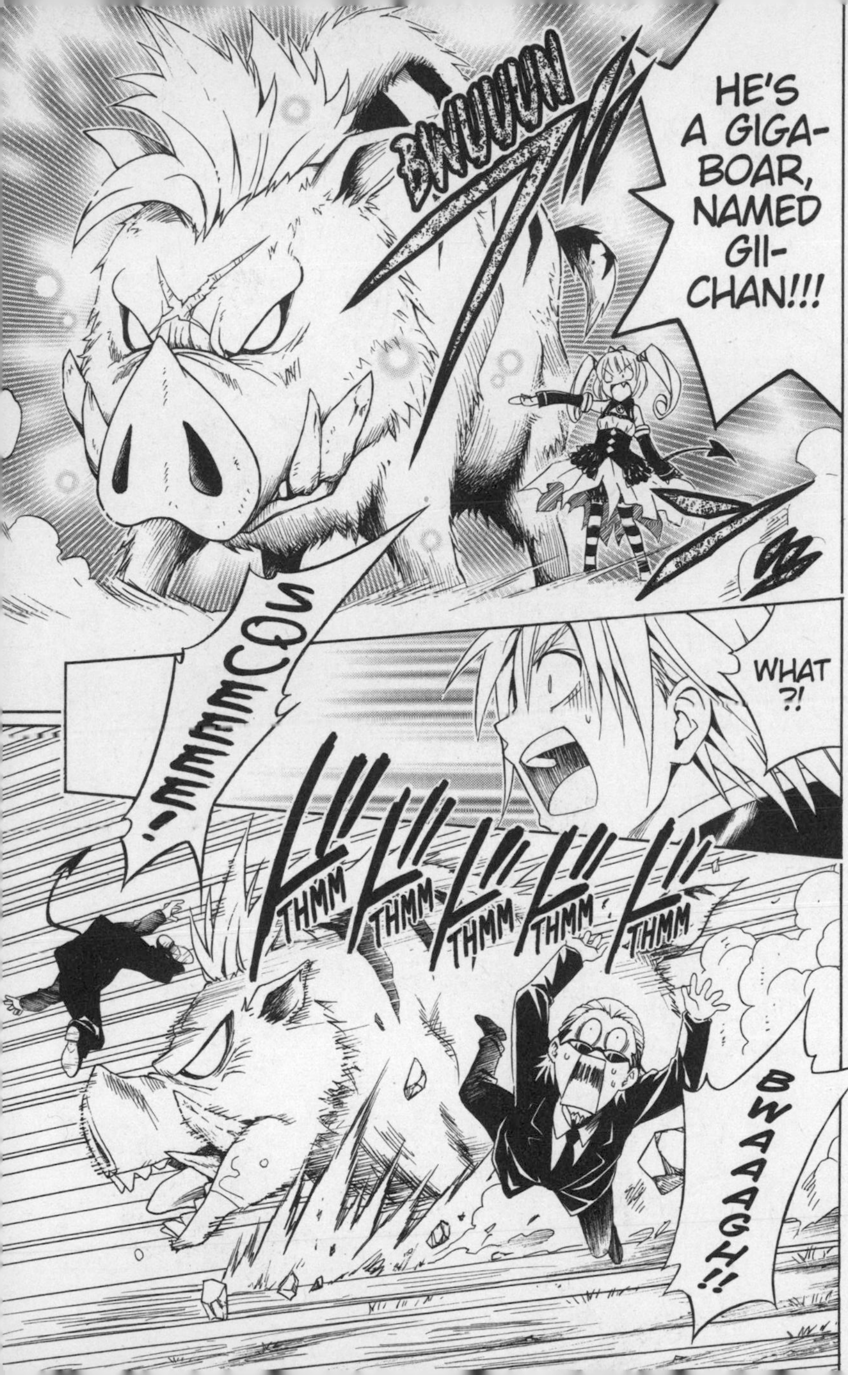
HE'S A GIGA-BOAR, NAMED GII-CHAN!!!
BWUUUN
SQUEEEEEE!
WHAT?!
THMM
THMM
THMM
THMM
THMM
BWAAAAGH!!

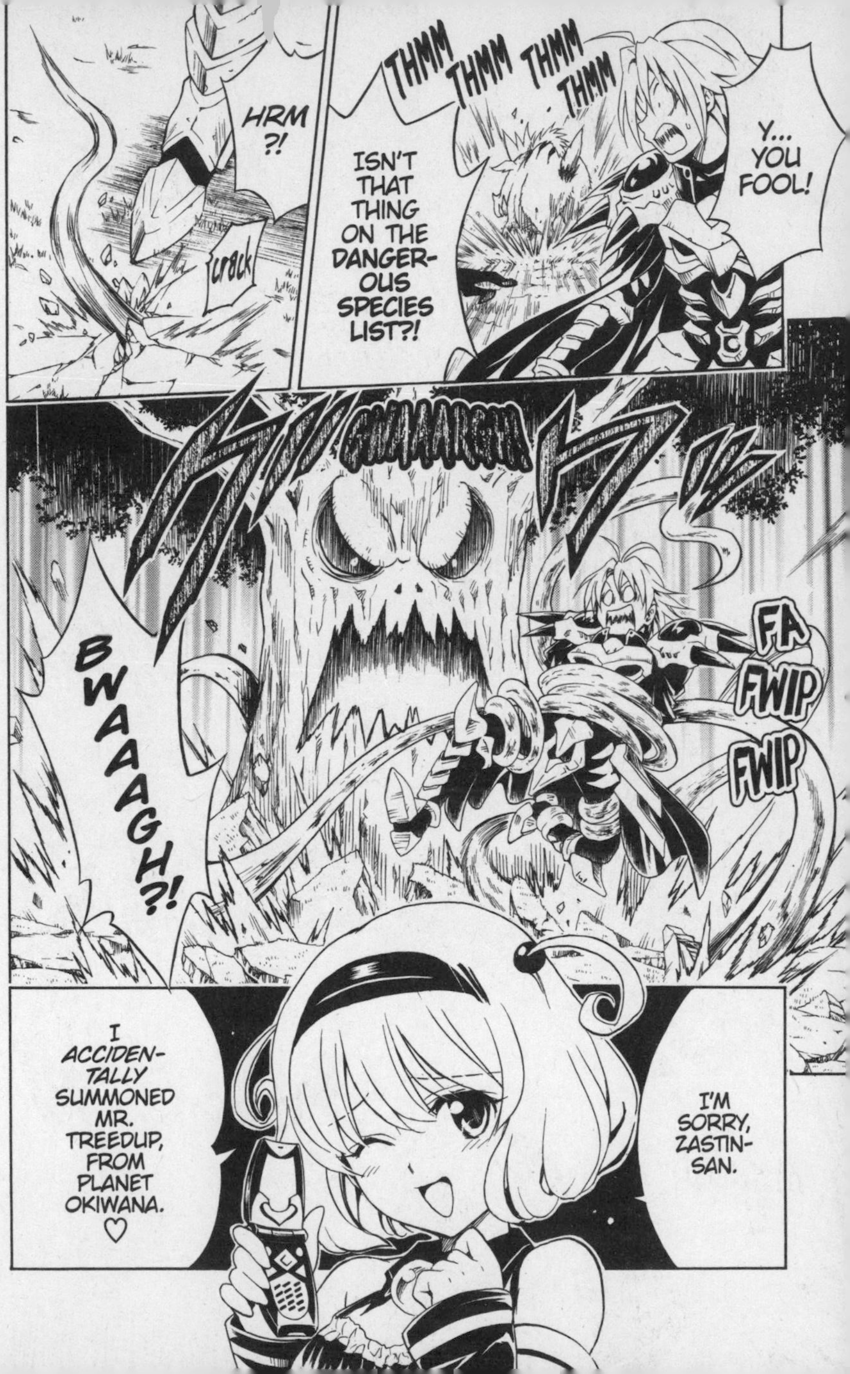
THMM THMM THMM THMM
Y... YOU FOOL!
ISN'T THAT THING ON THE DANGER-OUS SPECIES LIST?!
HRM ?!
crack
GWAAARGH
FA FWIP FWIP
BWAAAGH?!
I'M SORRY, ZASTIN-SAN.
I ACCIDEN-TALLY SUMMONED MR. TREEDUP, FROM PLANET OKIWANA. ♡

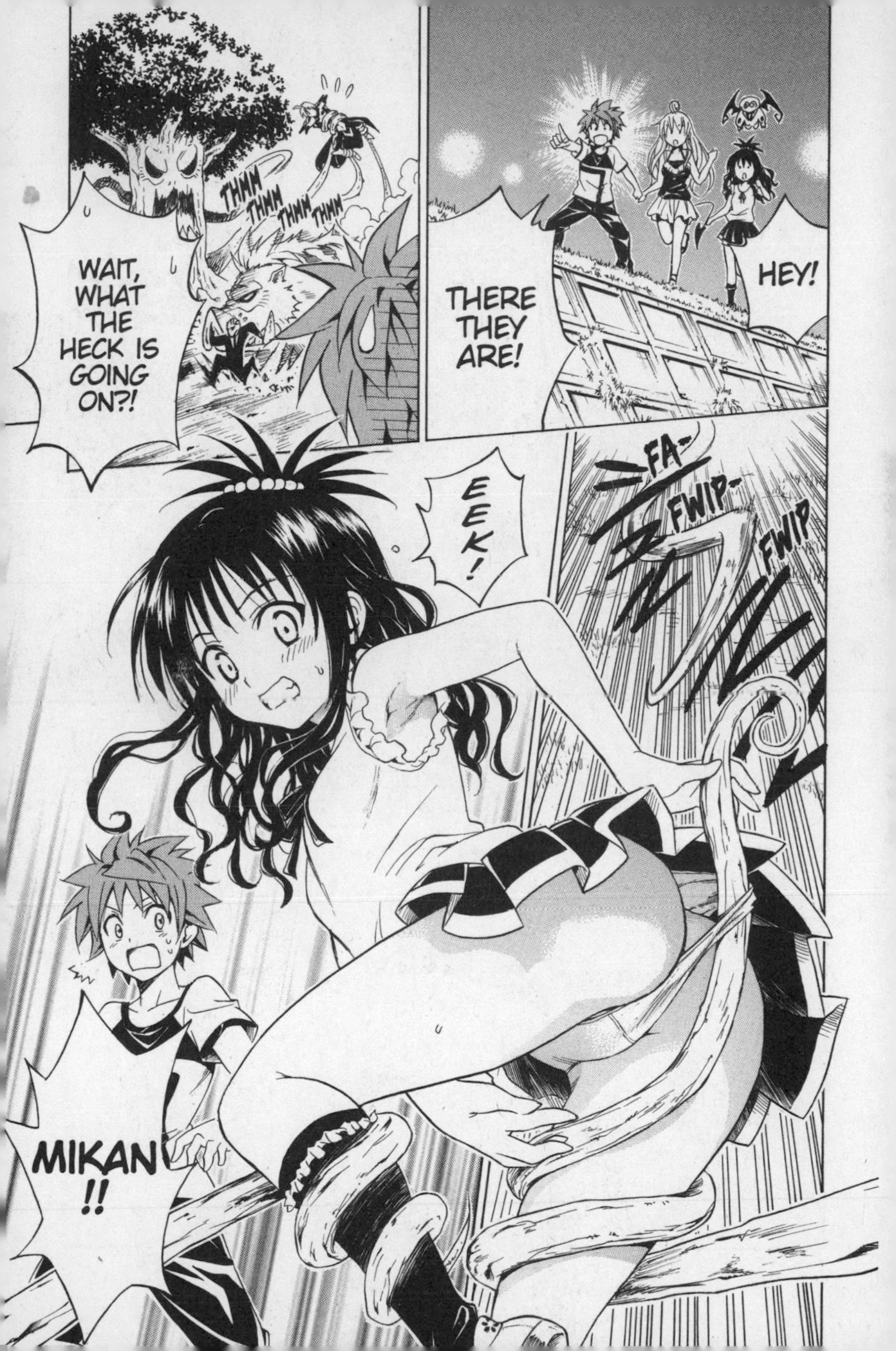
HEY!
THERE THEY ARE!
THMM THMM THMM THMM
WAIT, WHAT THE HECK IS GOING ON?!
FA- FWIP- FWIP
EEK!
MIKAN!!

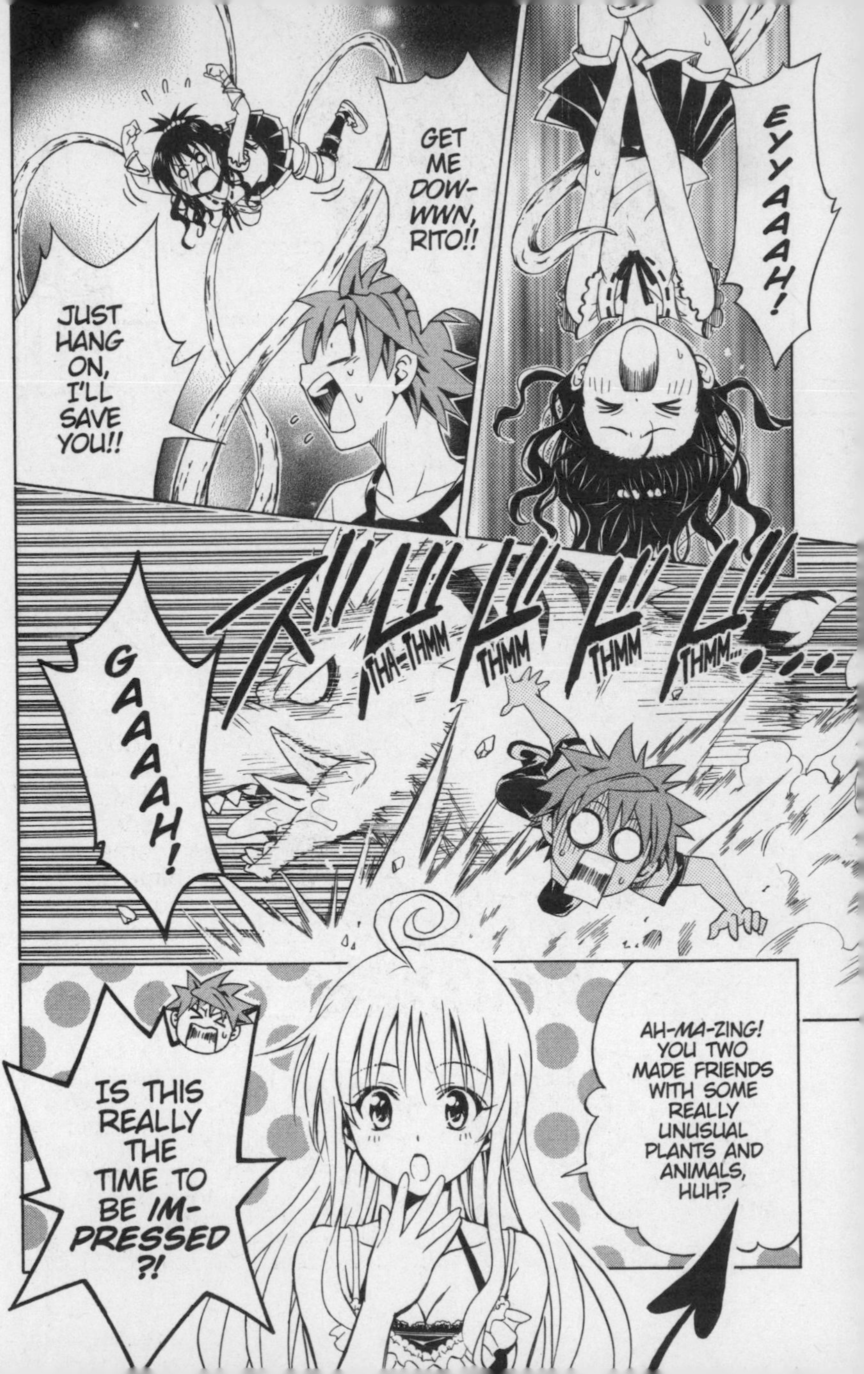
EYYAAAH!
GET ME DOWWWN, RITO!!
JUST HANG ON, I'LL SAVE YOU!!
THA-THMM THMM THMM THMM...
GAAAAH!
AH-MA-ZING! YOU TWO MADE FRIENDS WITH SOME REALLY UNUSUAL PLANTS AND ANIMALS, HUH?
IS THIS REALLY THE TIME TO BE *IMPRESSED*?!

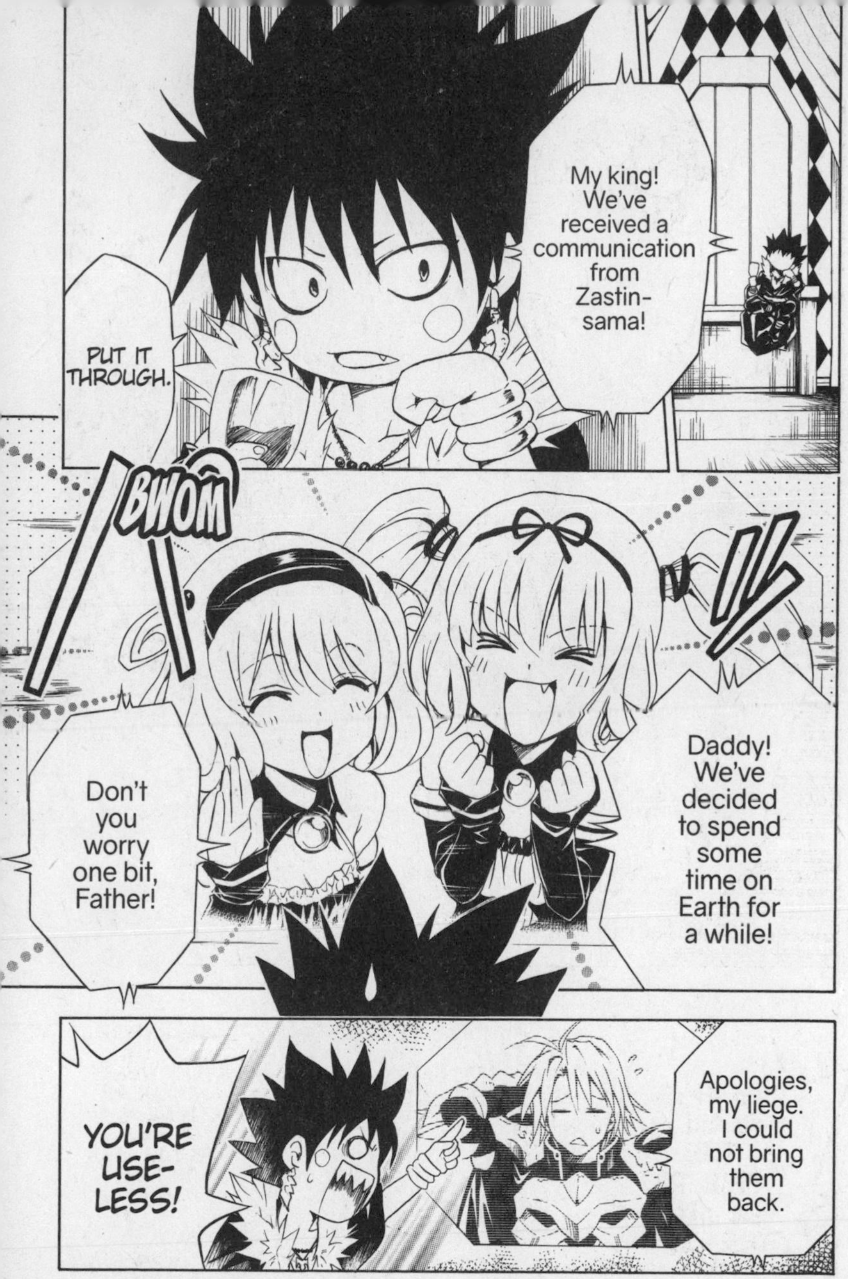
My king! We've received a communication from Zastin-sama!
PUT IT THROUGH.
BWOM
Daddy! We've decided to spend some time on Earth for a while!
Don't you worry one bit, Father!
Apologies, my liege. I could not bring them back.
YOU'RE USE-LESS!

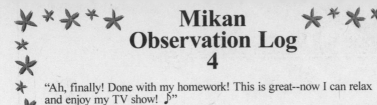

Mikan
Observation Log
4

"Ah, finally! Done with my homework! This is great--now I can relax and enjoy my TV show! ♪"

× × ×

Later that evening, Mikan sat clutching a mug with a round-eyed bear on it in one hand. A few discarded chocolate wrappers sat on the table, seemingly lined up in a row.

"Gahah, I'm sitting here munching on sweets while I watch TV... I'm kinda like an old grandma..."

× × ×

THUD! CREAAAK...

"Huh? Upstairs? That Rito, making some kind of fuss again..."

Mikan typically attributed any loud noises or trouble to Lala-san or her brother, but something had her more worried than usual this time.

× × ×

"Have your sisters come to play again, Lala-san? They said they'd be on Earth for a while, but where exactly are they living? On their space-ship?!"

"..."

"You couldn't possibly have told them to live here, right? Haha, no way..."

"..."

"It totally is possible..."

Mikan drank down the rest of her now-cooled herbal tea, and breathed a small sigh.

"Well, even if you did, the more people here, the more fun it is, so it's fine with me, but... Don't Nana-san and Momo-san have school to go to on Deviluke? Is there no homework? (Though it sure sounds like history and etiquette in the palace were rough...)"

Mikan thought to herself that it might be nice to have no homework for a little while.

Trouble 109: Through the Looking-Goggles

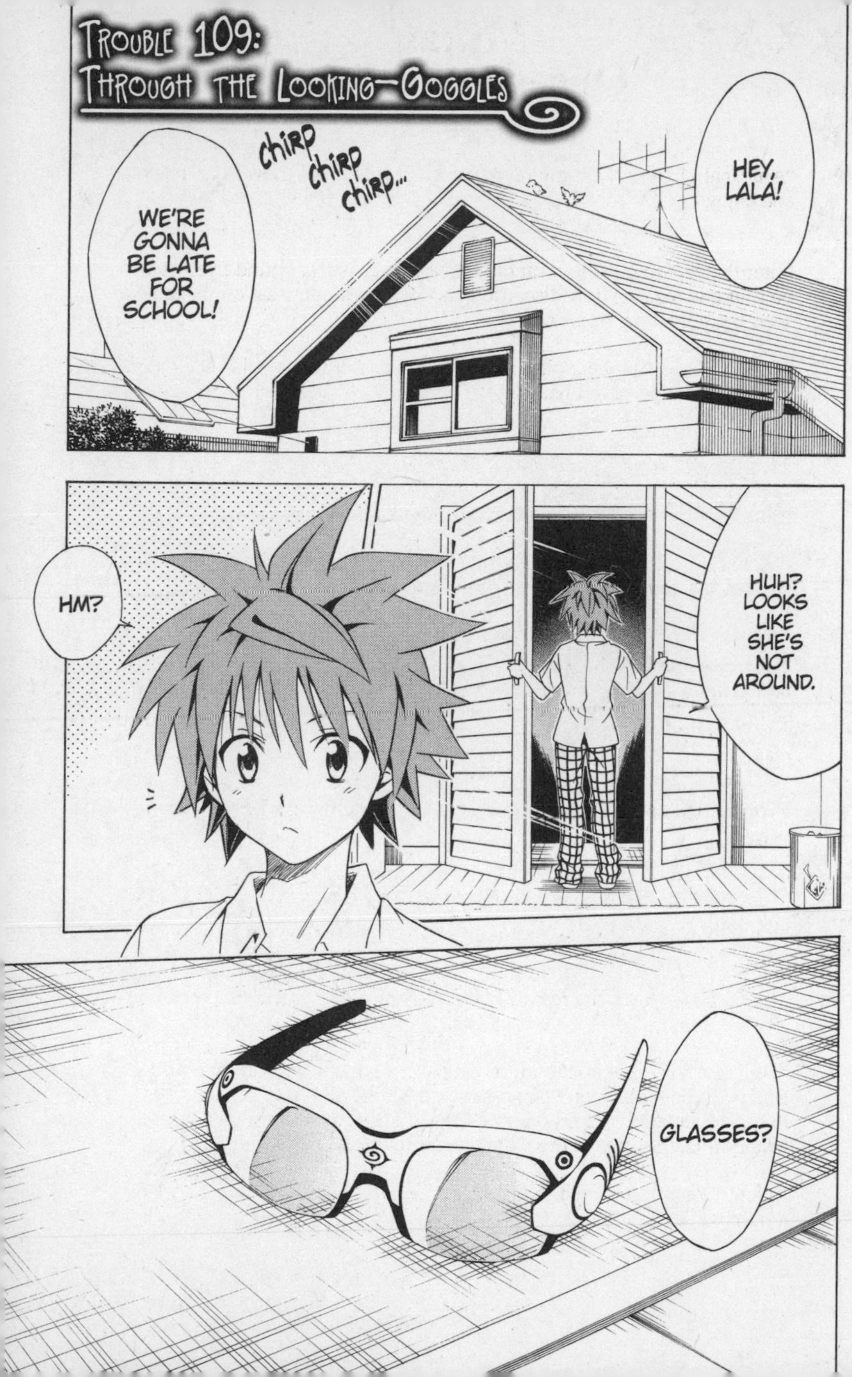
HEY, LALA!
chirp chirp chirp...
WE'RE GONNA BE LATE FOR SCHOOL!
HUH? LOOKS LIKE SHE'S NOT AROUND.
HM?
GLASSES?

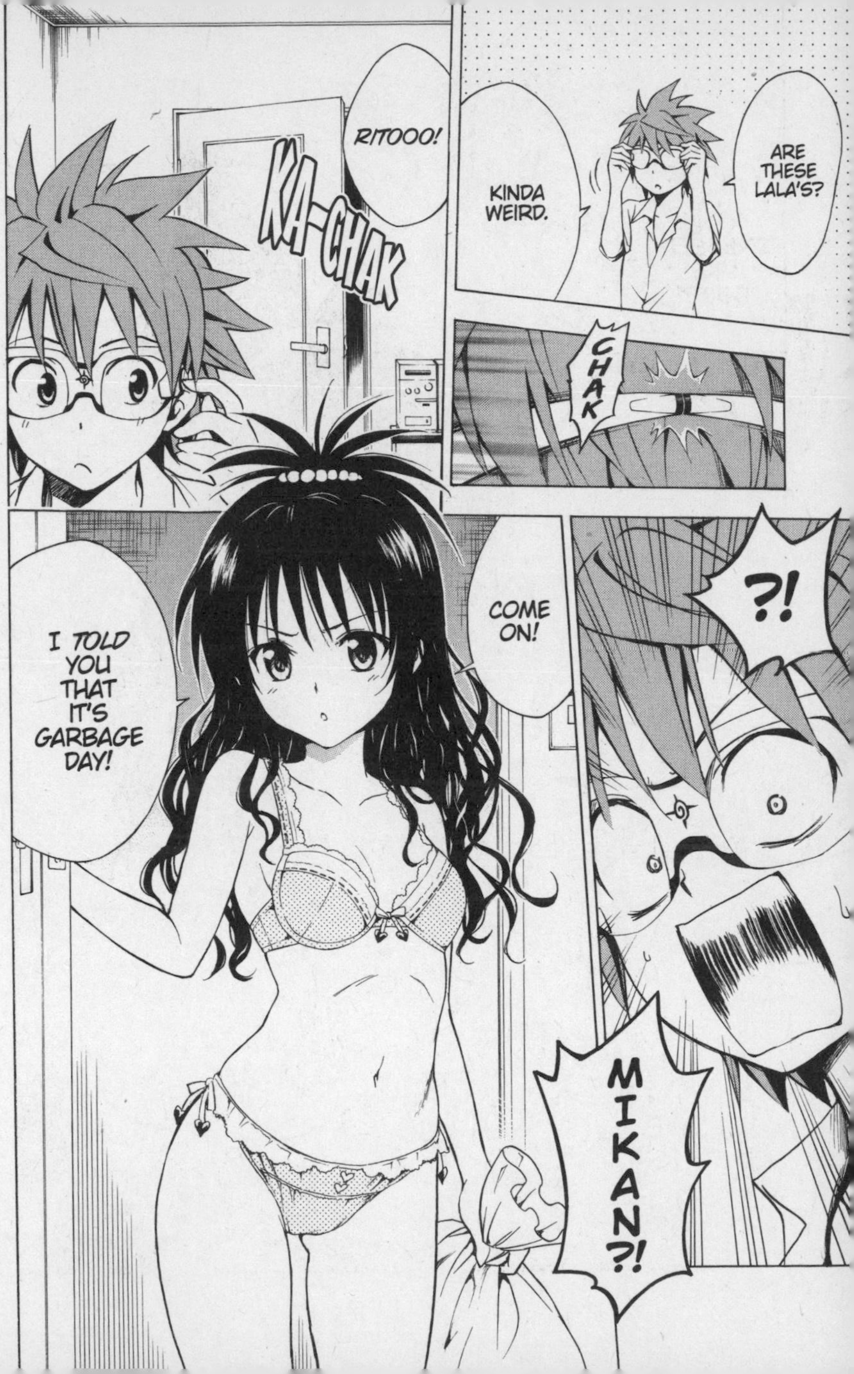
ARE THESE LALA'S?
KINDA WEIRD.
CHAK
CHAK
RITOOO!
KA-CHAK
?!
MIKAN?!
COME ON!
I TOLD YOU THAT IT'S GARBAGE DAY!

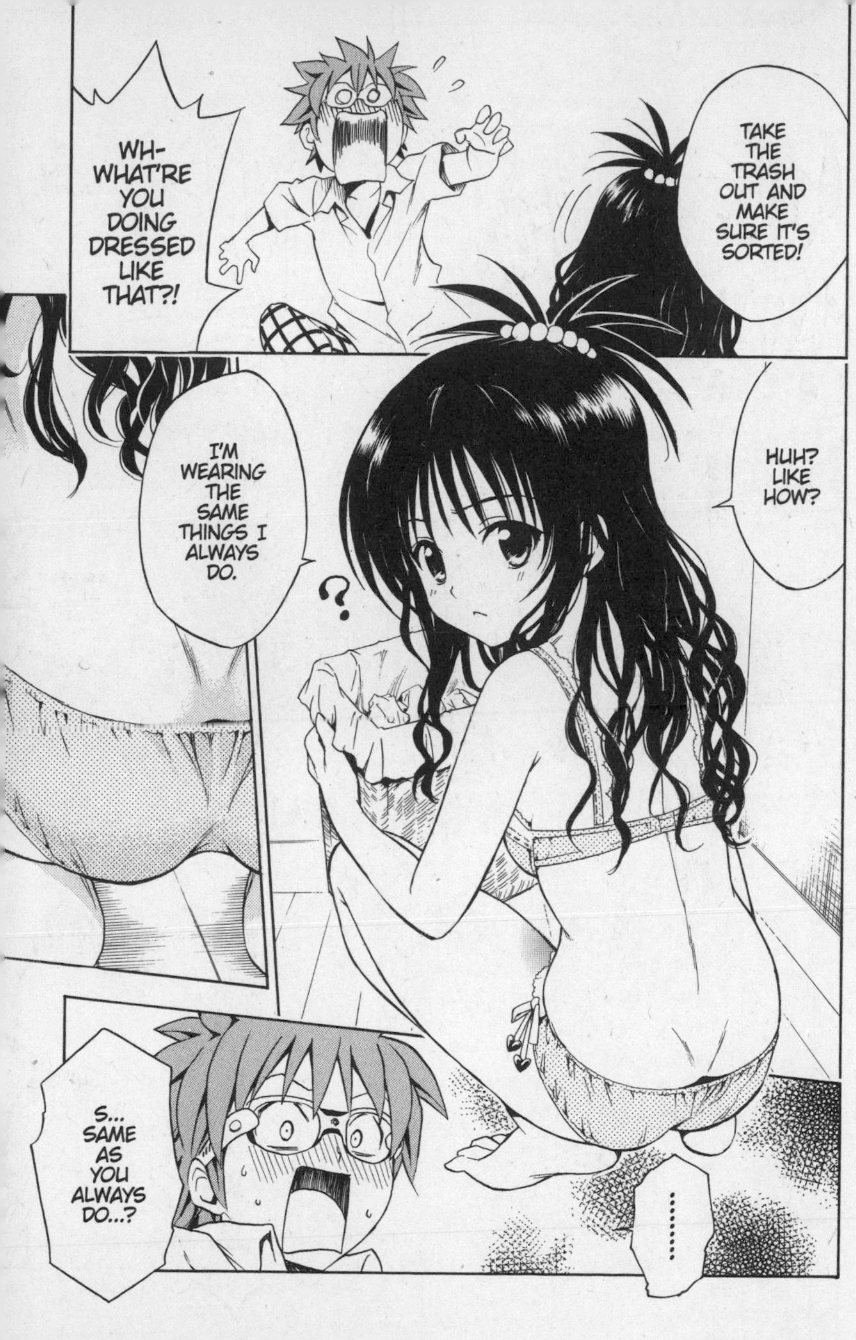
TAKE THE TRASH OUT AND MAKE SURE IT'S SORTED!
WH- WHAT'RE YOU DOING DRESSED LIKE THAT?!
HUH? LIKE HOW?
I'M WEARING THE SAME THINGS I ALWAYS DO.
S... SAME AS YOU ALWAYS DO...?
......

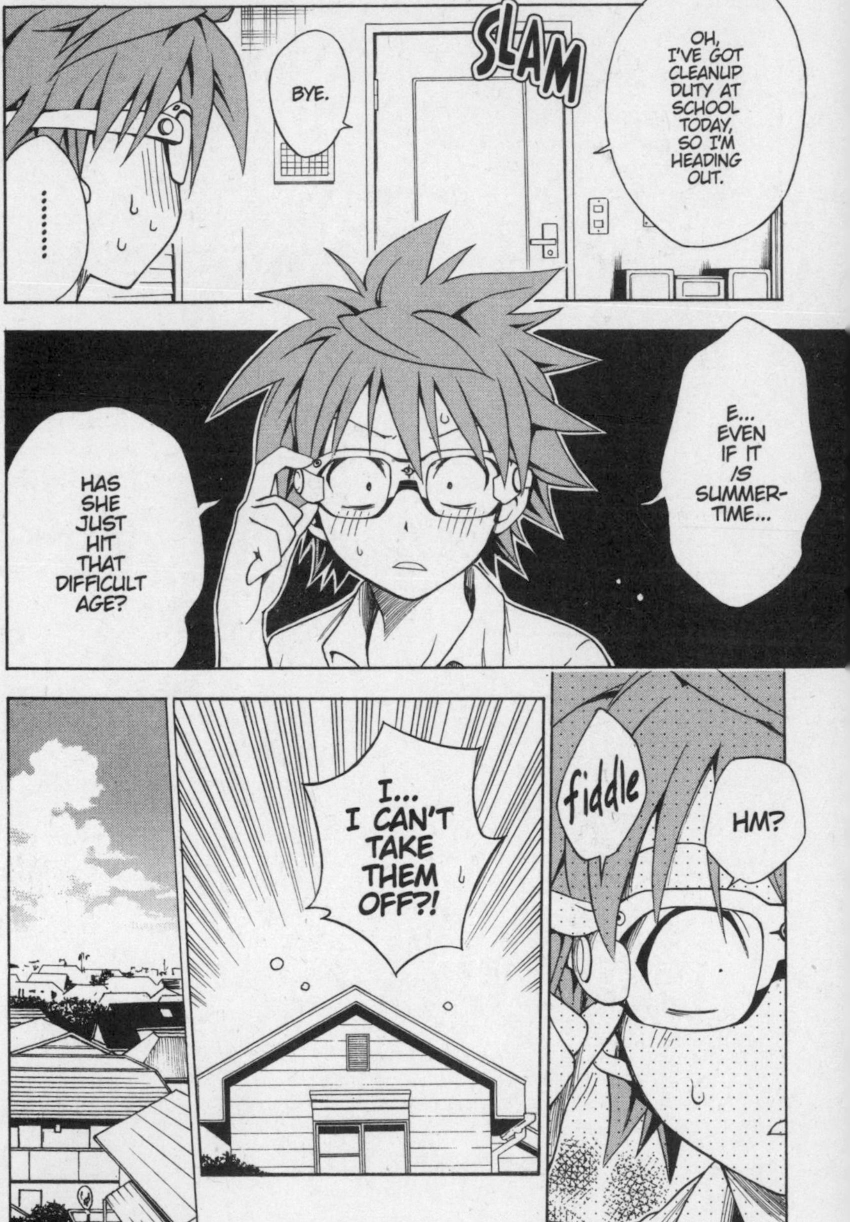
OH, I'VE GOT CLEANUP DUTY AT SCHOOL TODAY, SO I'M HEADING OUT.
SLAM
BYE.
......
E... EVEN IF IT IS SUMMER-TIME...
HAS SHE JUST HIT THAT DIFFICULT AGE?
HM?
fiddle
I... I CAN'T TAKE THEM OFF?!

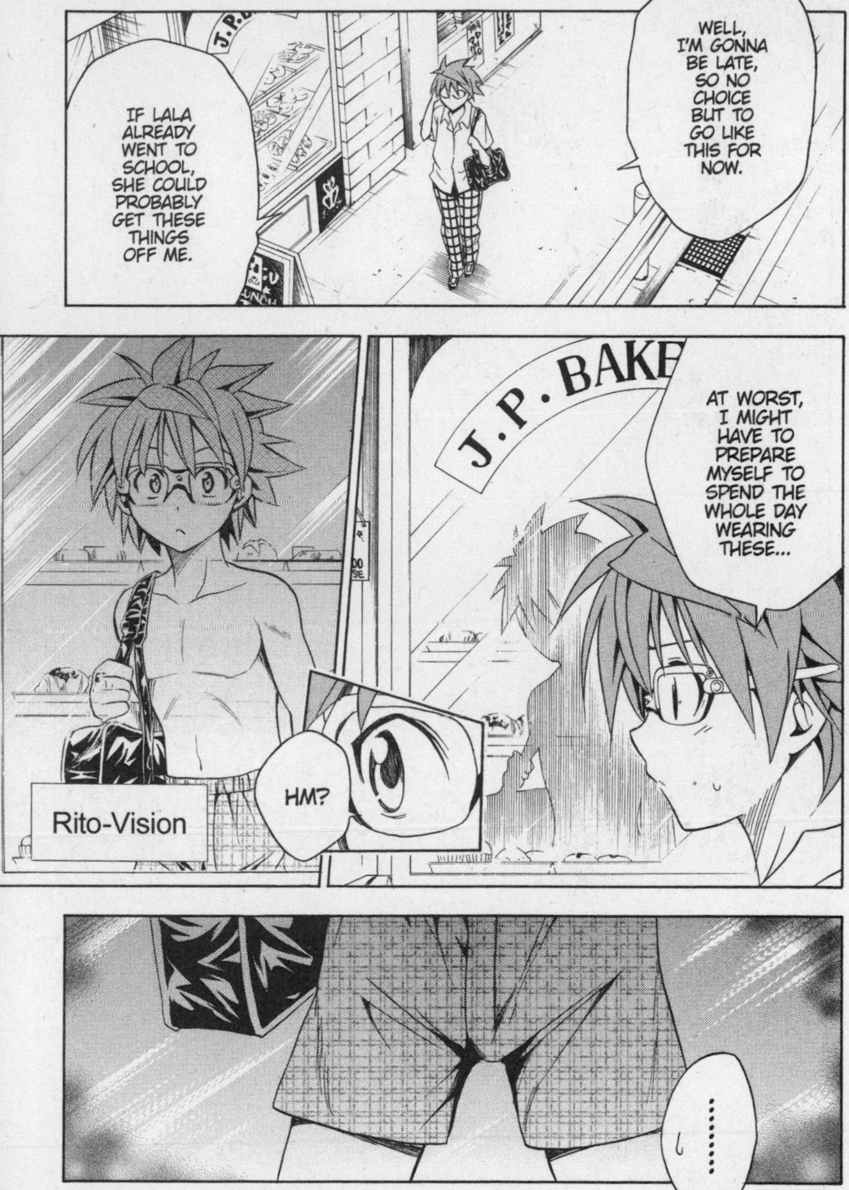
WELL, I'M GONNA BE LATE, SO NO CHOICE BUT TO GO LIKE THIS FOR NOW.
IF LALA ALREADY WENT TO SCHOOL, SHE COULD PROBABLY GET THESE THINGS OFF ME.
J.P. BAKE
AT WORST, I MIGHT HAVE TO PREPARE MYSELF TO SPEND THE WHOLE DAY WEARING THESE...
HM?
Rito-Vision
....

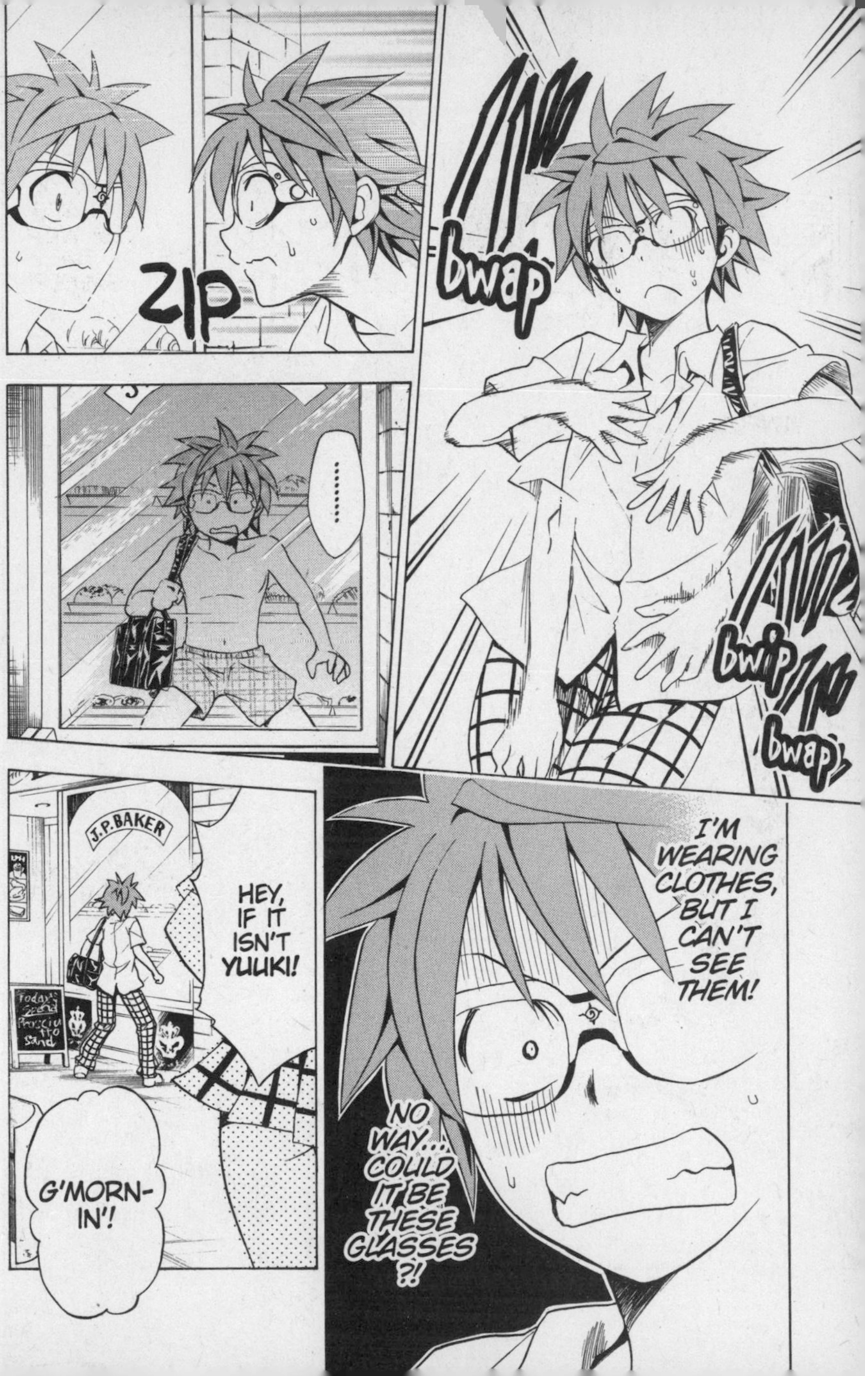
bwap
bwip
bwap
ZIP
......
I'M WEARING CLOTHES, BUT I CAN'T SEE THEM!
NO WAY... COULD IT BE THESE GLASSES?!
J.P.BAKER
HEY, IF IT ISN'T YUUKI!
G'MORN-IN'!

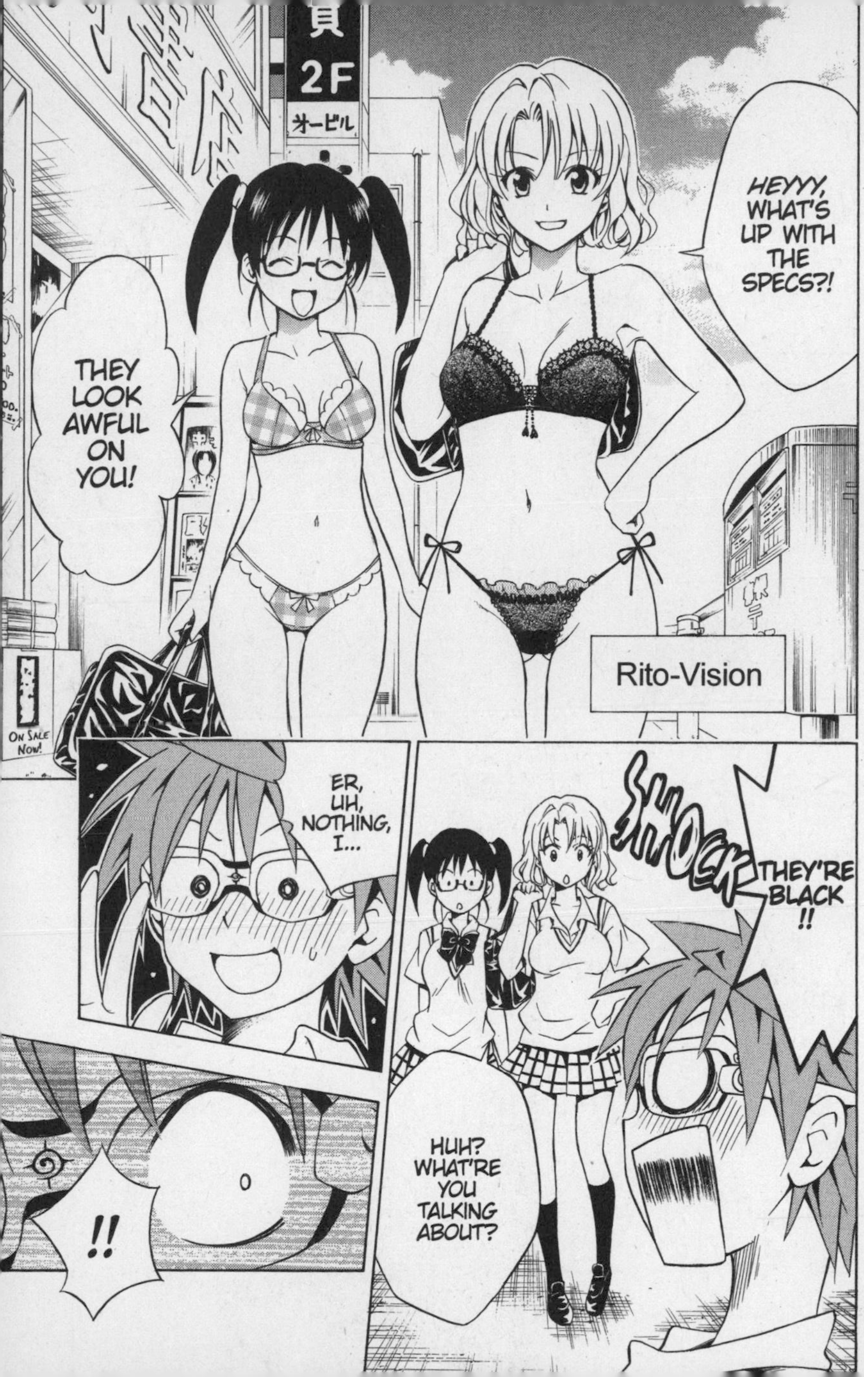
2F
オービル
HEYYY, WHAT'S UP WITH THE SPECS?!
THEY LOOK AWFUL ON YOU!
Rito-Vision
ON SALE NOW!
SHOCK
THEY'RE BLACK!!
HUH? WHAT'RE YOU TALKING ABOUT?
ER, UH, NOTHING, I...
!!

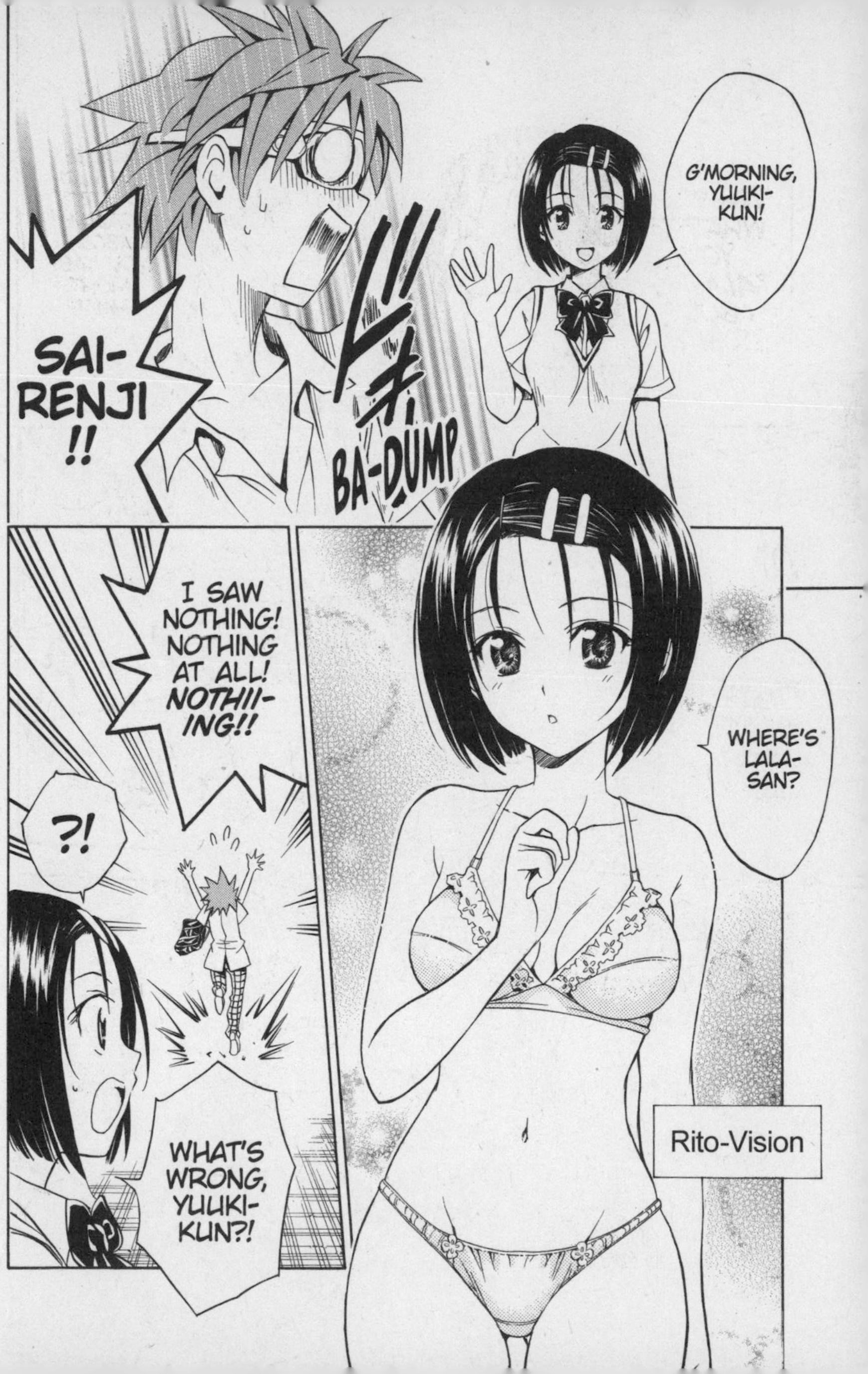
G'MORNING, YUUKI-KUN!
BA-DUMP
SAI-RENJI!!
WHERE'S LALA-SAN?
Rito-Vision
I SAW NOTHING! NOTHING AT ALL! NOTHIIING!!
?!
WHAT'S WRONG, YUUKI-KUN?!

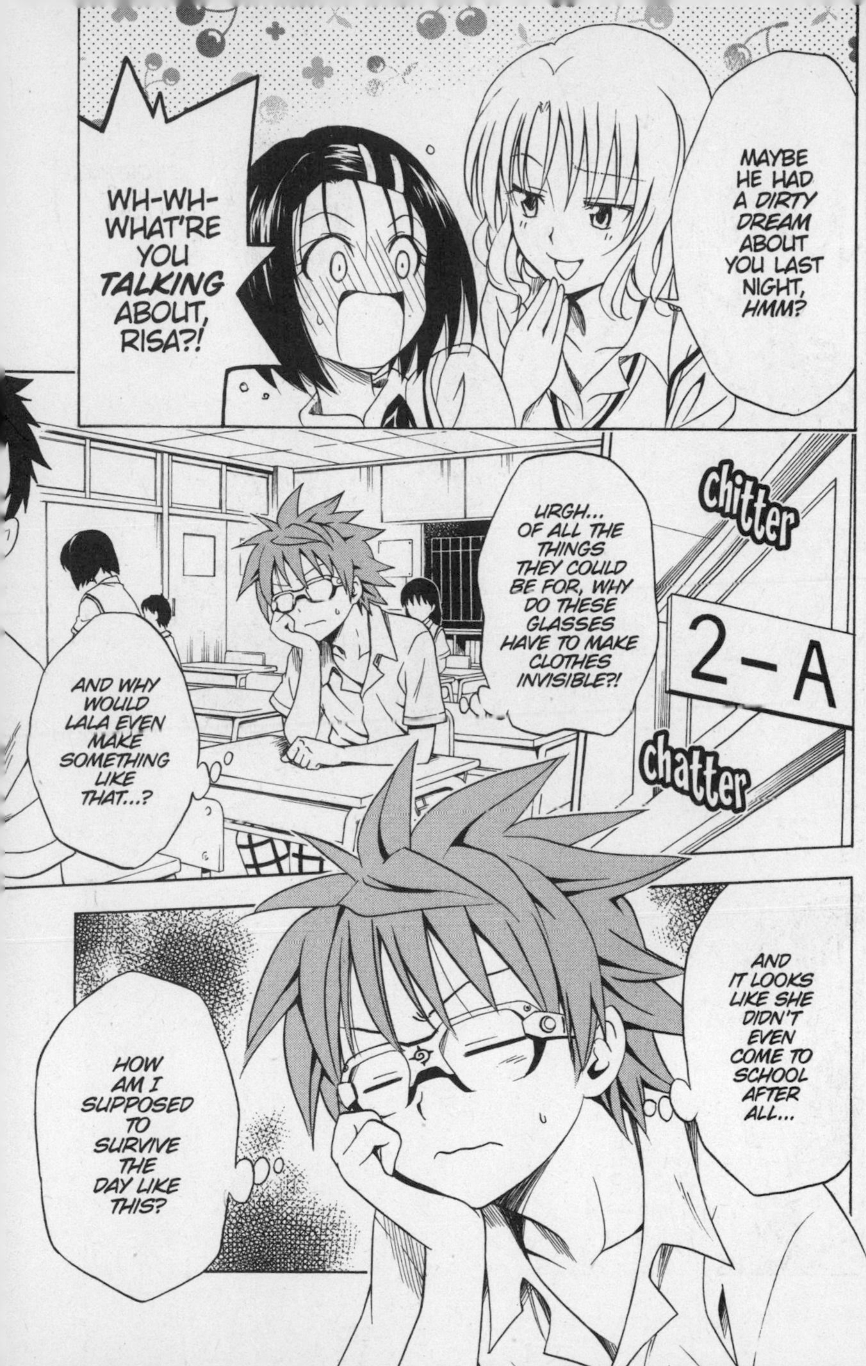
MAYBE HE HAD A DIRTY DREAM ABOUT YOU LAST NIGHT, HMM?
WH-WH-WHAT'RE YOU TALKING ABOUT, RISA?!
chitter
URGH... OF ALL THE THINGS THEY COULD BE FOR, WHY DO THESE GLASSES HAVE TO MAKE CLOTHES INVISIBLE?!
2-A
chatter
AND WHY WOULD LALA EVEN MAKE SOMETHING LIKE THAT...?
AND IT LOOKS LIKE SHE DIDN'T EVEN COME TO SCHOOL AFTER ALL...
HOW AM I SUPPOSED TO SURVIVE THE DAY LIKE THIS?

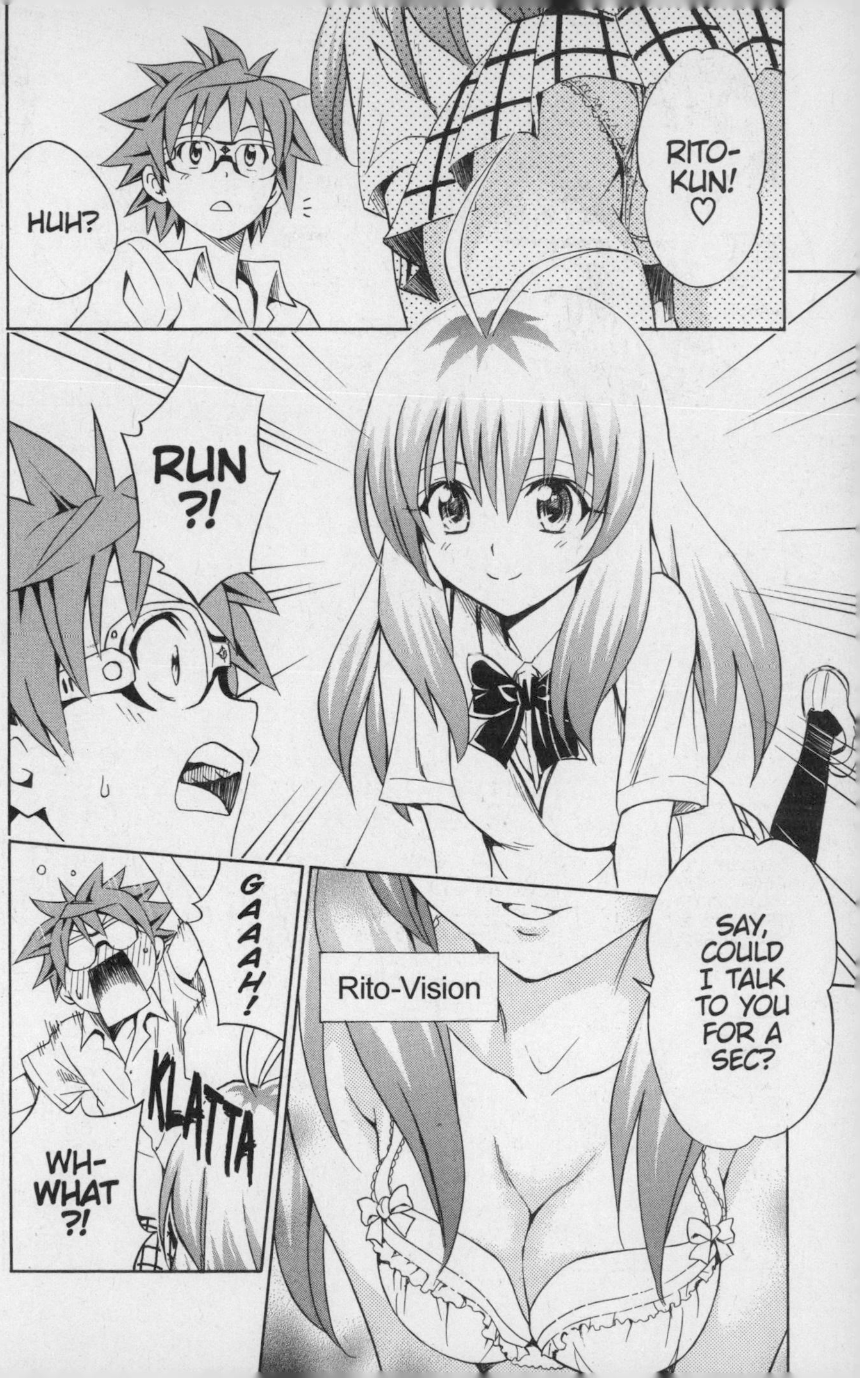
RITO-KUN! ♡
HUH?
RUN ?!
SAY, COULD I TALK TO YOU FOR A SEC?
Rito-Vision
GAAAH!
KLATTA
WH-WHAT ?!

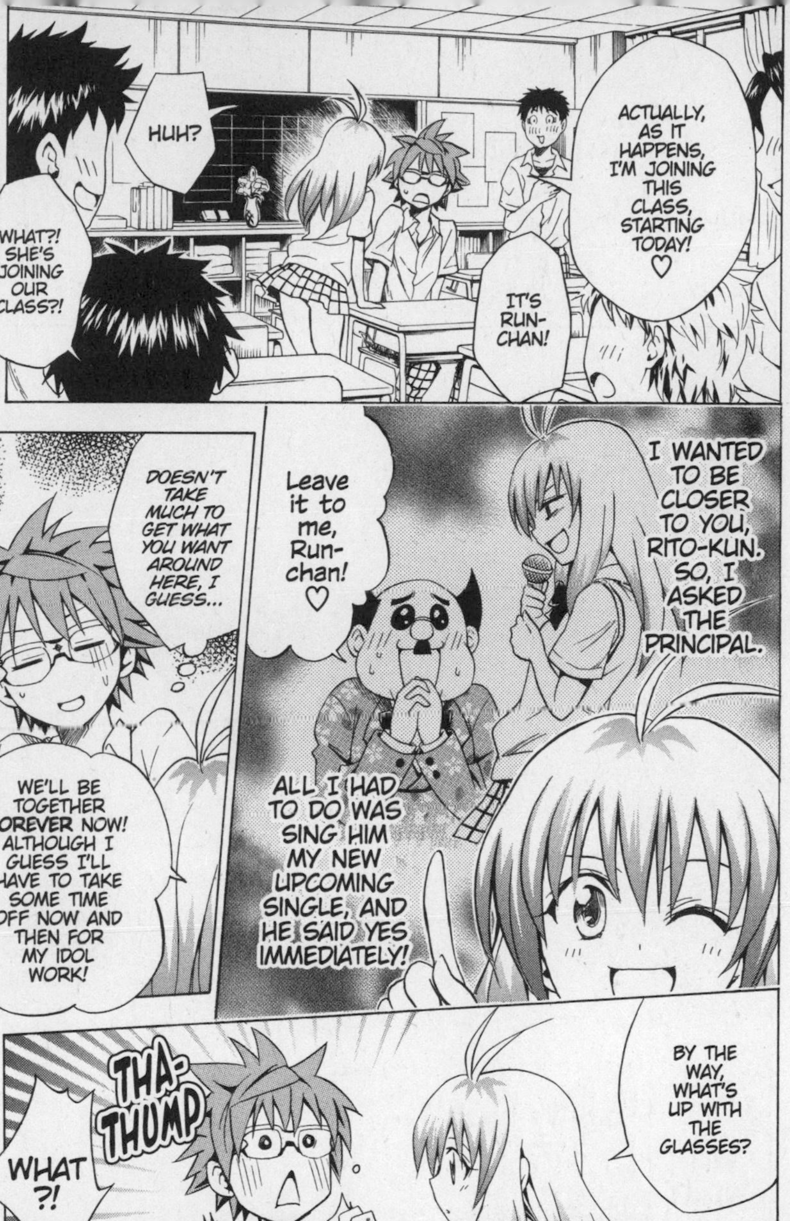
ACTUALLY, AS IT HAPPENS, I'M JOINING THIS CLASS, STARTING TODAY! ♡
IT'S RUN-CHAN!
HUH?
WHAT?! SHE'S JOINING OUR CLASS?!
I WANTED TO BE CLOSER TO YOU, RITO-KUN. SO, I ASKED THE PRINCIPAL.
Leave it to me, Run-chan! ♡
ALL I HAD TO DO WAS SING HIM MY NEW UPCOMING SINGLE, AND HE SAID YES IMMEDIATELY!
DOESN'T TAKE MUCH TO GET WHAT YOU WANT AROUND HERE, I GUESS...
WE'LL BE TOGETHER FOREVER NOW! ALTHOUGH I GUESS I'LL HAVE TO TAKE SOME TIME OFF NOW AND THEN FOR MY IDOL WORK!
BY THE WAY, WHAT'S UP WITH THE GLASSES?
THA-THUMP
WHAT ?!

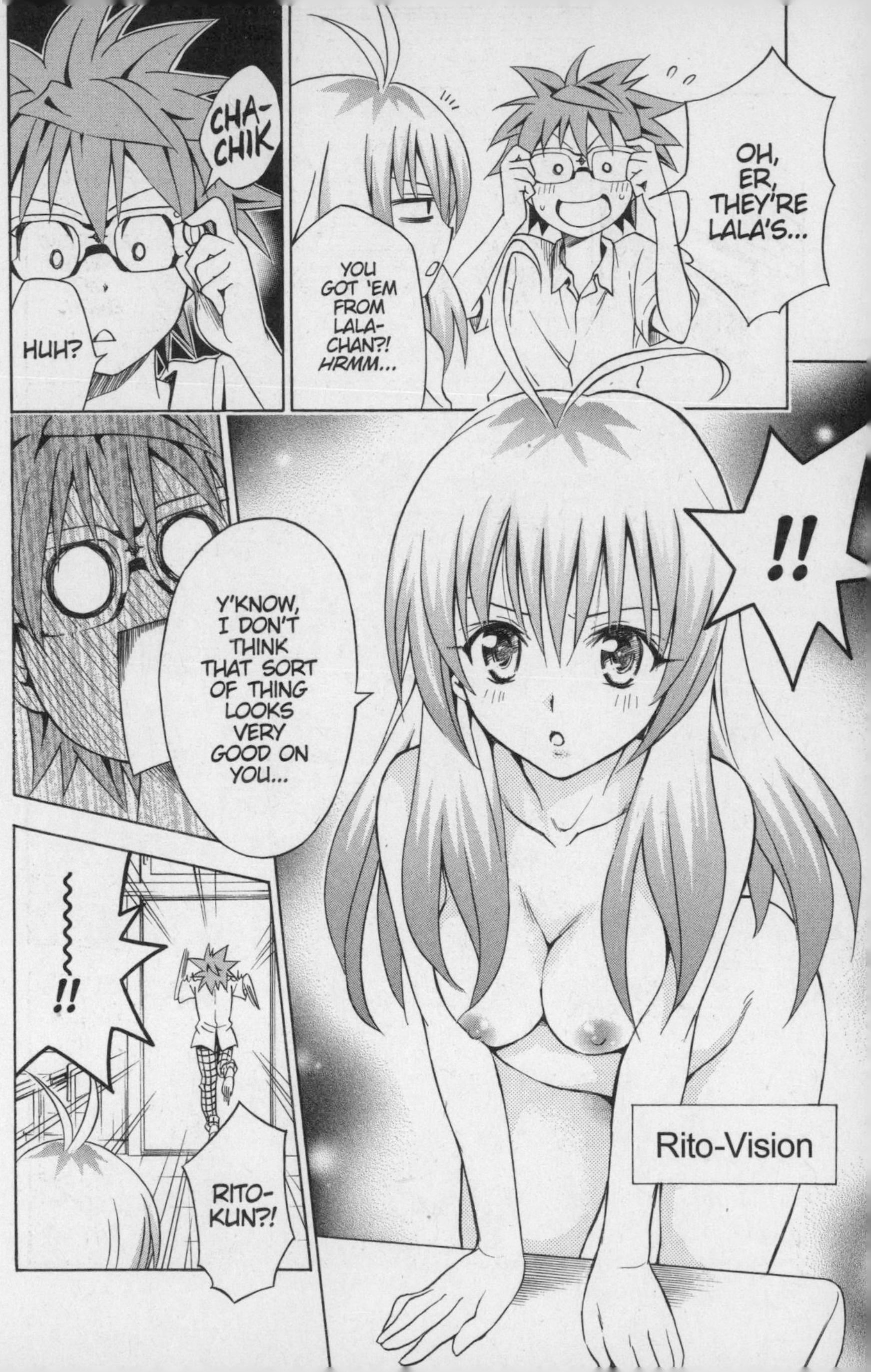
OH, ER, THEY'RE LALA'S...
YOU GOT 'EM FROM LALA-CHAN?! HRMM...
CHA-CHIK
HUH?
!!
Rito-Vision
Y'KNOW, I DON'T THINK THAT SORT OF THING LOOKS VERY GOOD ON YOU...
~~~~!!
RITO-KUN?!
~~~~

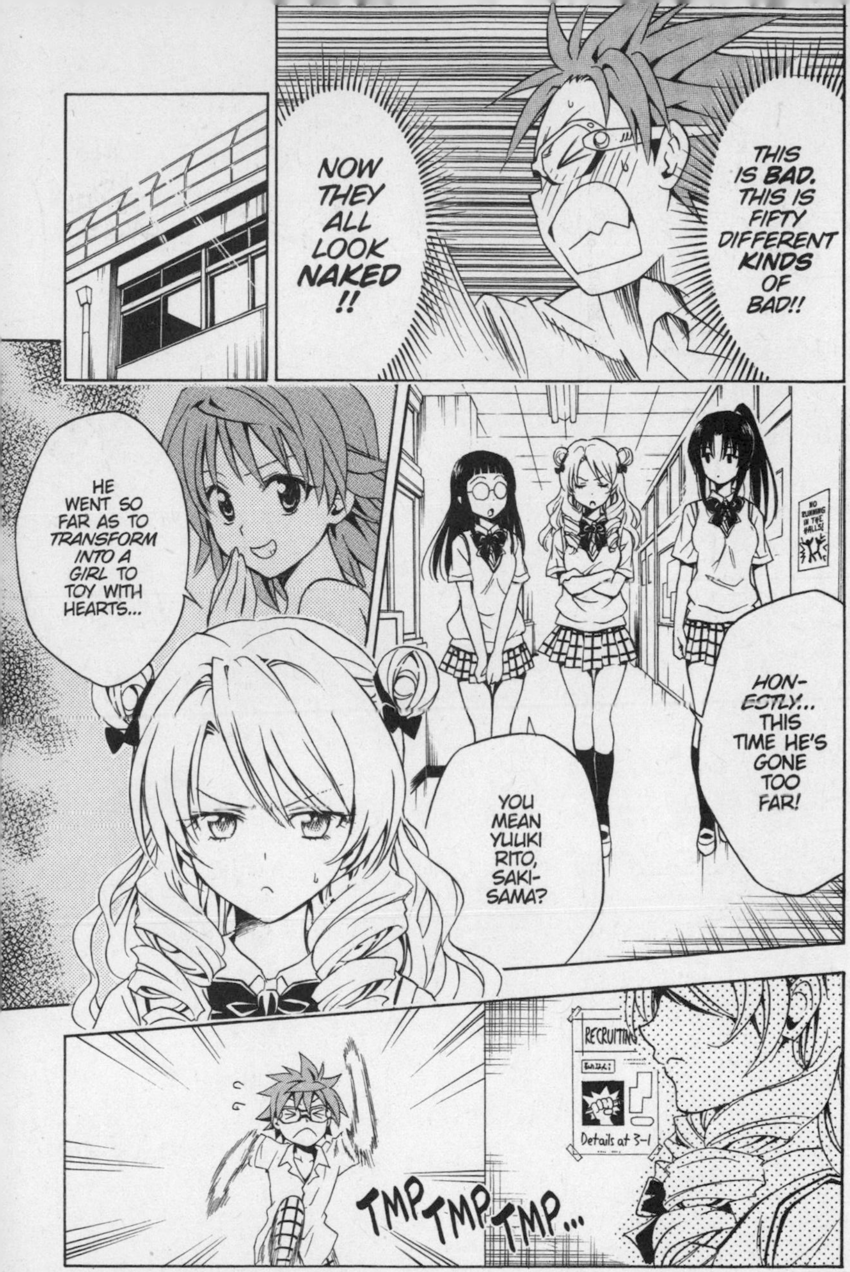
THIS IS BAD. THIS IS FIFTY DIFFERENT KINDS OF BAD!!
NOW THEY ALL LOOK NAKED!!
HON-ESTLY... THIS TIME HE'S GONE TOO FAR!
YOU MEAN YUUKI RITO, SAKI-SAMA?
NO RUNNING IN THE HALLS!
HE WENT SO FAR AS TO TRANSFORM INTO A GIRL TO TOY WITH HEARTS...
RECRUITING
Details at 3-1
TMP TMP TMP...

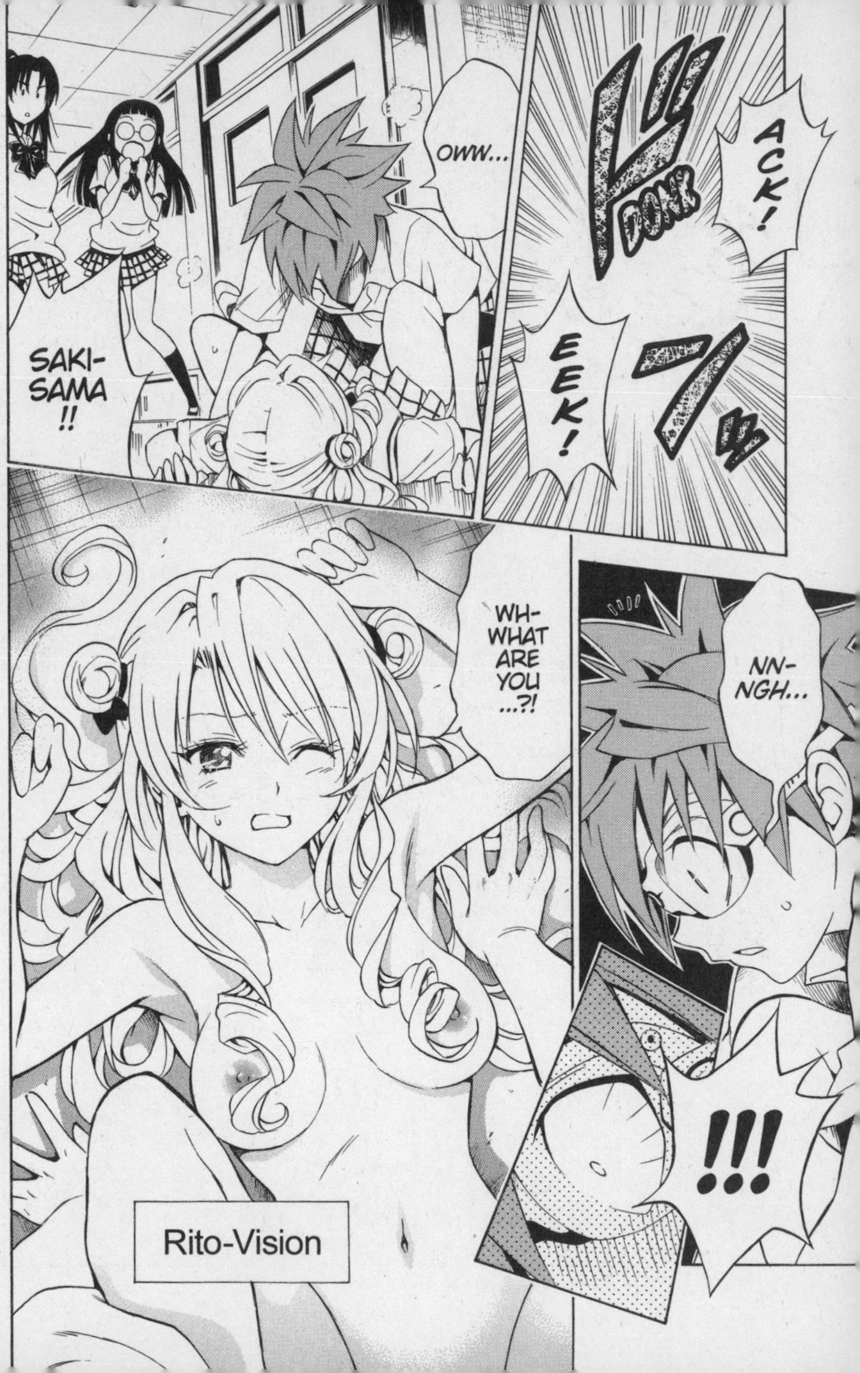
ACK!
DONK
EEK!
OWW...
SAKI-SAMA!!
NN-NGH...
!!!
WH-WHAT ARE YOU...?!
Rito-Vision

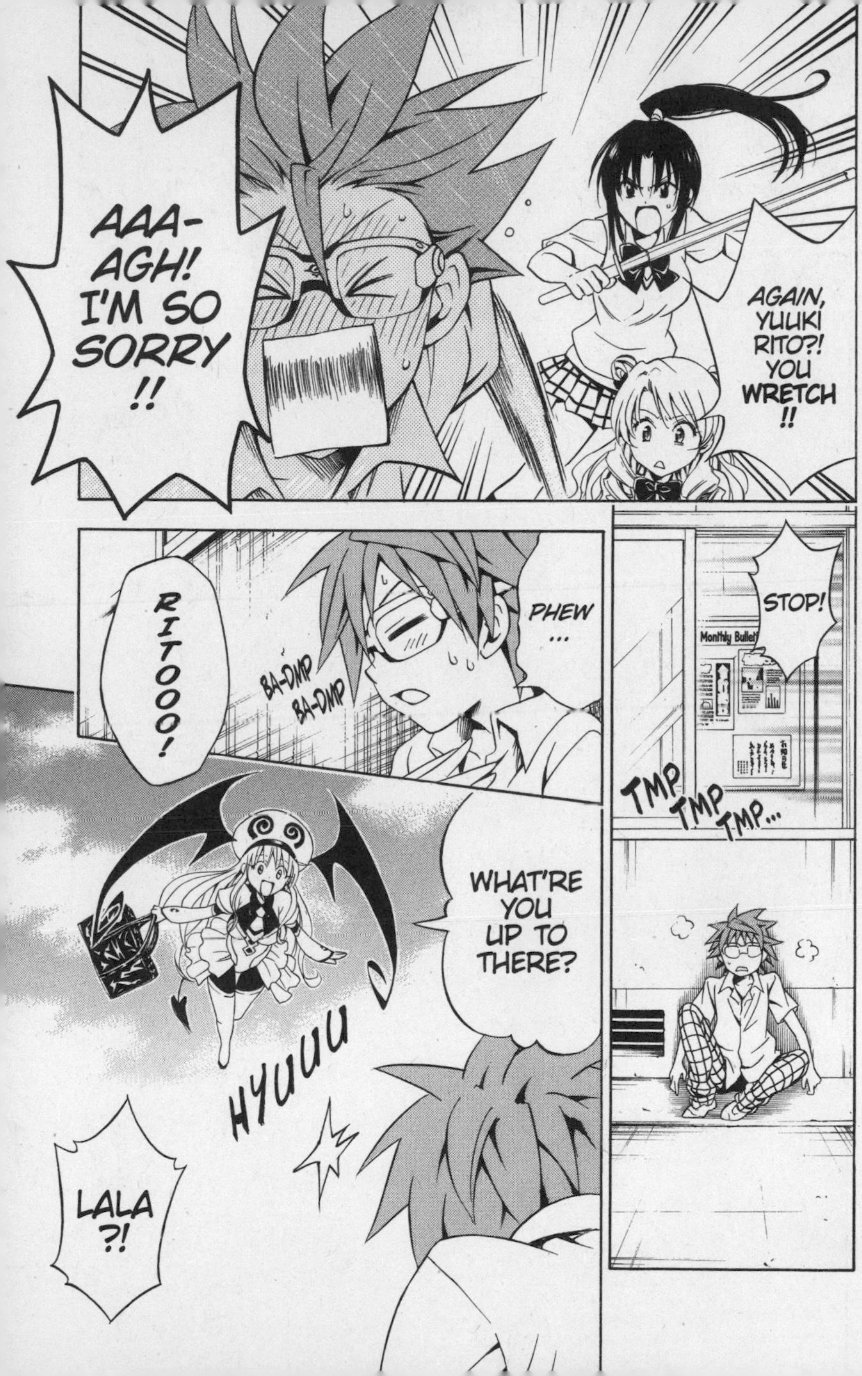
AGAIN, YUUKI RITO?! YOU WRETCH!!
AAA-AGH! I'M SO SORRY!!
STOP!
Monthly Bullet
TMP TMP TMP...
PHEW...
BA-DMP BA-DMP
RITOOOO!
WHAT'RE YOU UP TO THERE?
HYUUU
LALA?!

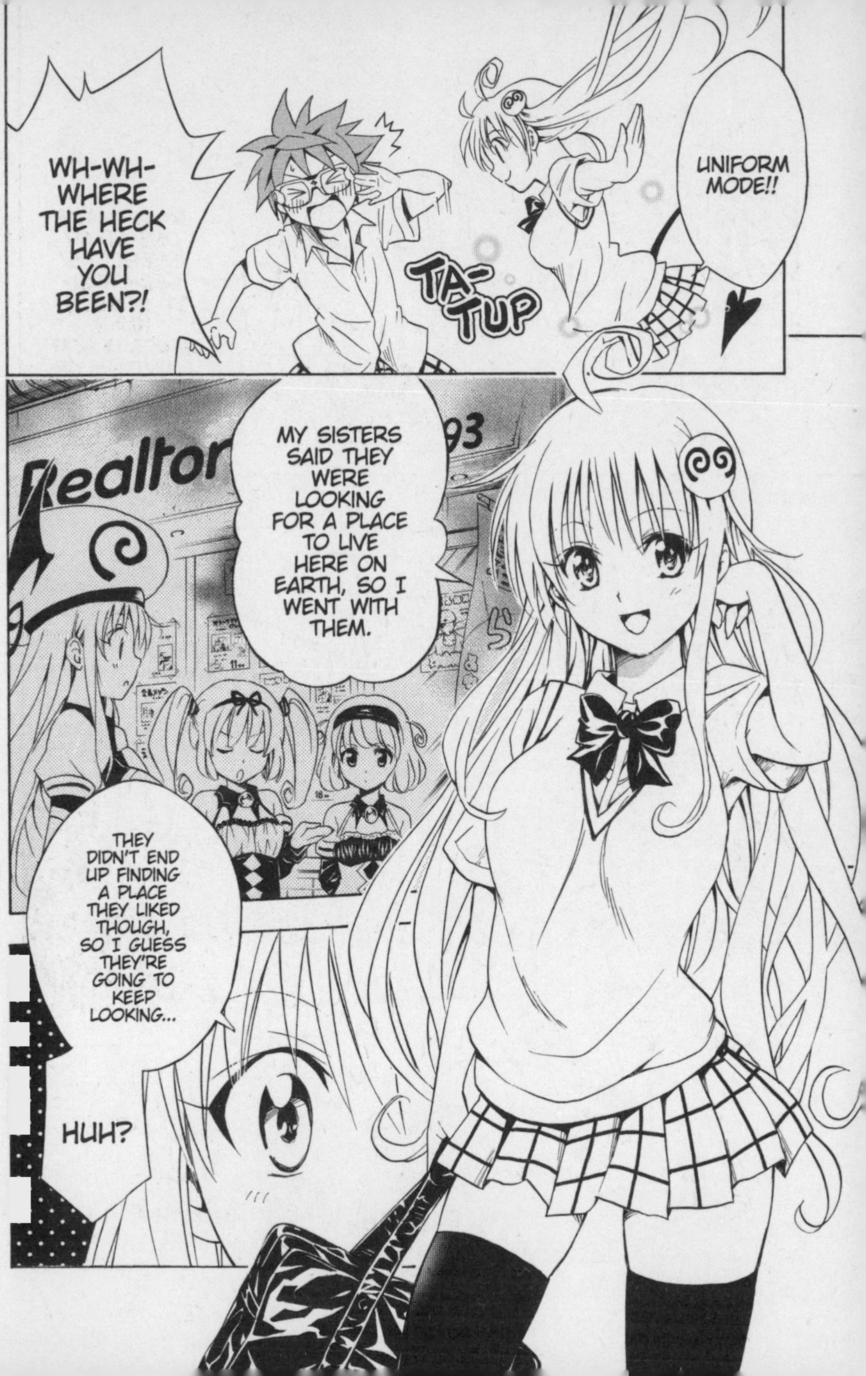
UNIFORM MODE!!
TA-TUP
WH-WH-WHERE THE HECK HAVE YOU BEEN?!
Realtor
93
MY SISTERS SAID THEY WERE LOOKING FOR A PLACE TO LIVE HERE ON EARTH, SO I WENT WITH THEM.
THEY DIDN'T END UP FINDING A PLACE THEY LIKED THOUGH, SO I GUESS THEY'RE GOING TO KEEP LOOKING...
HUH?

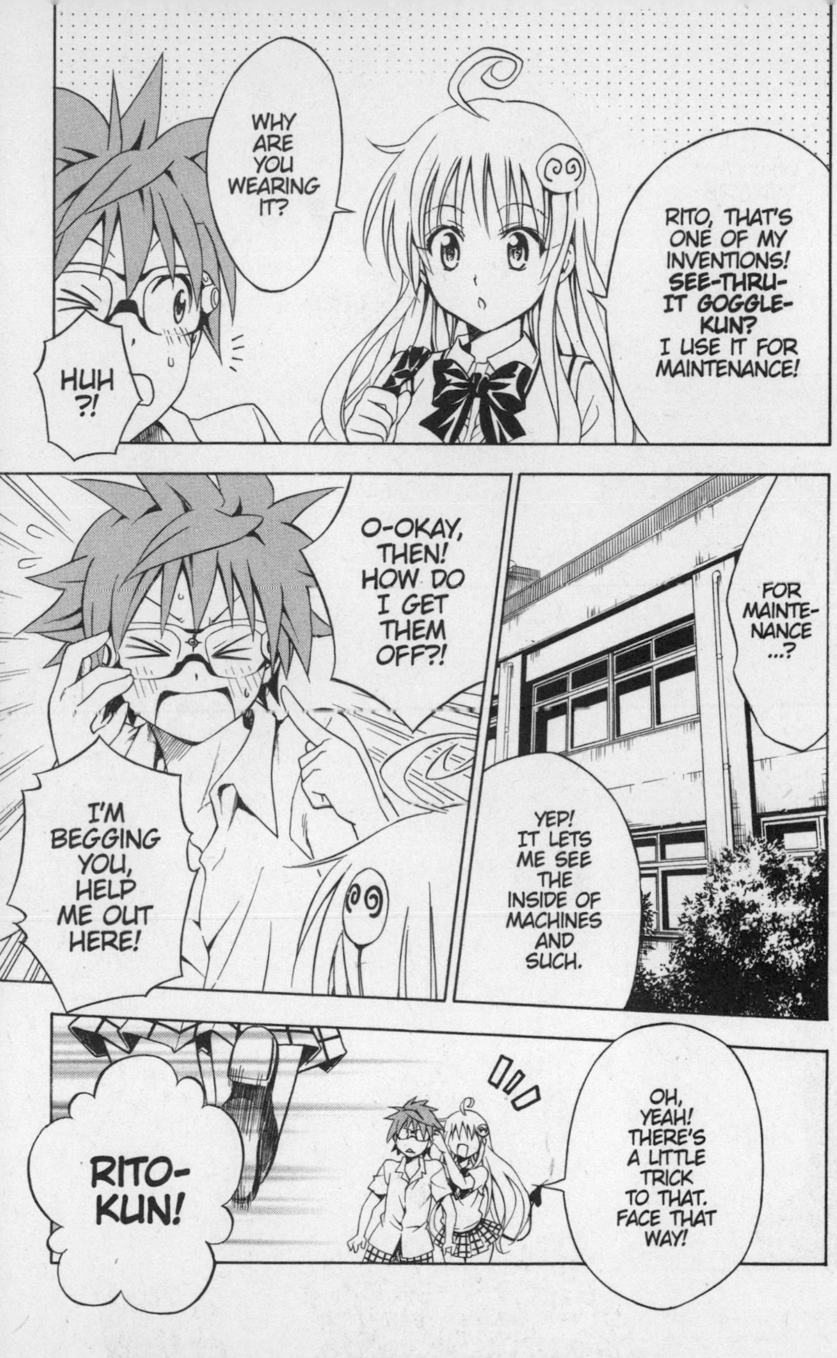
RITO, THAT'S ONE OF MY INVENTIONS! SEE-THRU-IT GOGGLE-KUN? I USE IT FOR MAINTENANCE!
WHY ARE YOU WEARING IT?
HUH?!
FOR MAINTENANCE...?
YEP! IT LETS ME SEE THE INSIDE OF MACHINES AND SUCH.
O-OKAY, THEN! HOW DO I GET THEM OFF?!
I'M BEGGING YOU, HELP ME OUT HERE!
OH, YEAH! THERE'S A LITTLE TRICK TO THAT. FACE THAT WAY!
RITO-KUN!

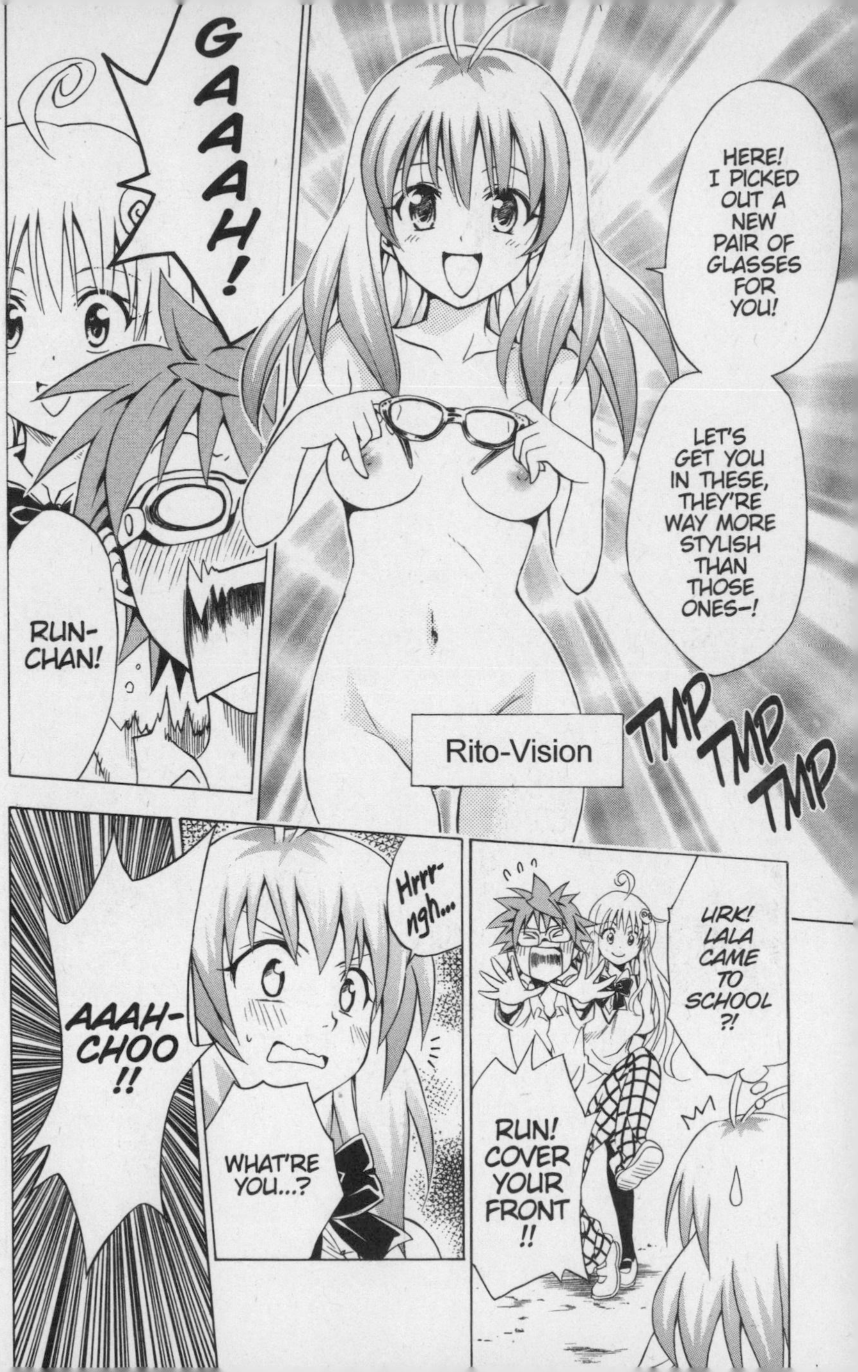
HERE! I PICKED OUT A NEW PAIR OF GLASSES FOR YOU!
LET'S GET YOU IN THESE, THEY'RE WAY MORE STYLISH THAN THOSE ONES–!
Rito-Vision
TMP TMP TMP
GAAAH!
RUN-CHAN!
URK! LALA CAME TO SCHOOL ?!
RUN! COVER YOUR FRONT !!
Hrrr-ngh...
WHAT'RE YOU...?
AAAH-CHOO !!

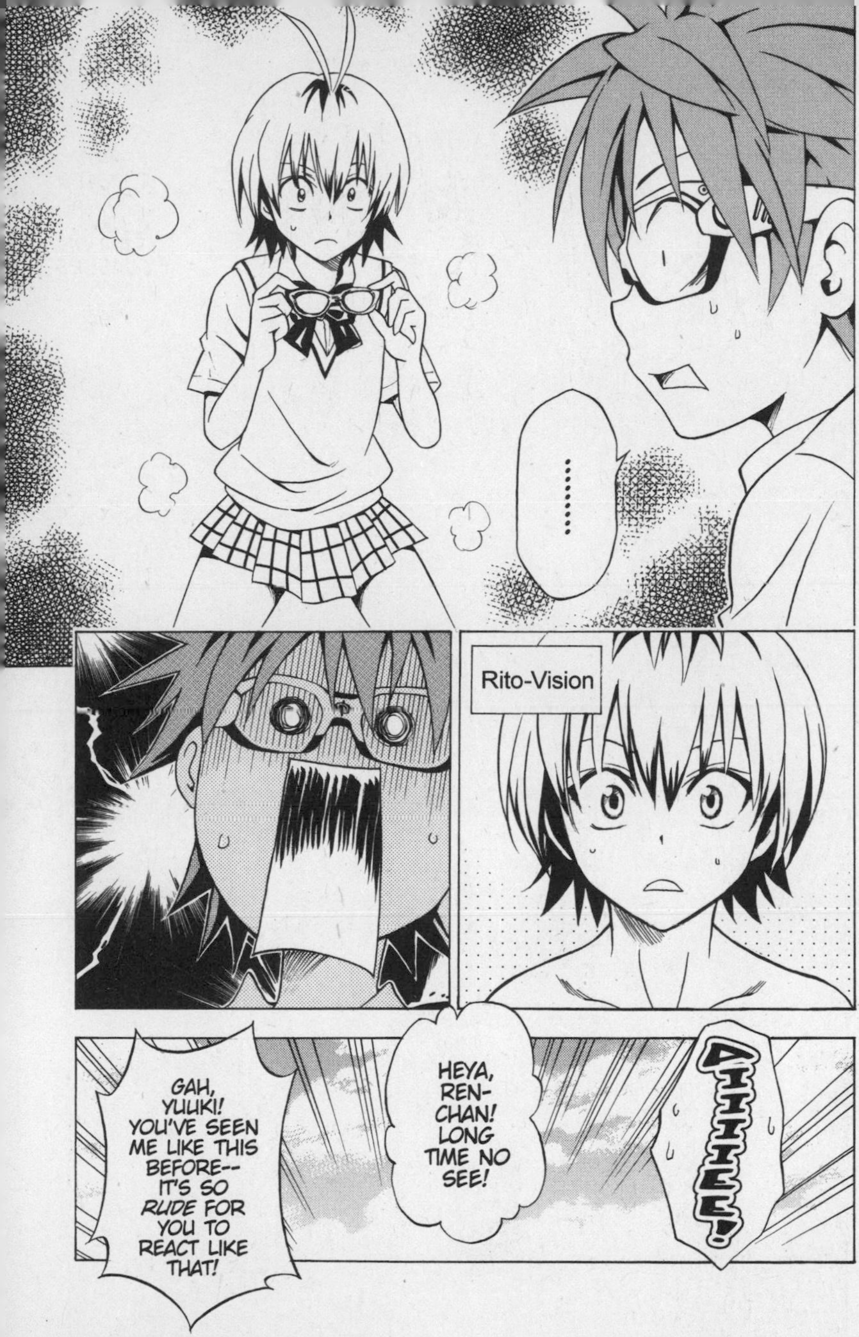
......
Rito-Vision
AIIIIEE!
HEYA, REN-CHAN! LONG TIME NO SEE!
GAH, YUUKI! YOU'VE SEEN ME LIKE THIS BEFORE-- IT'S SO *RUDE* FOR YOU TO REACT LIKE THAT!

To LOVE Ru

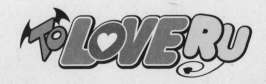

Trouble 110: On Festival's Eve

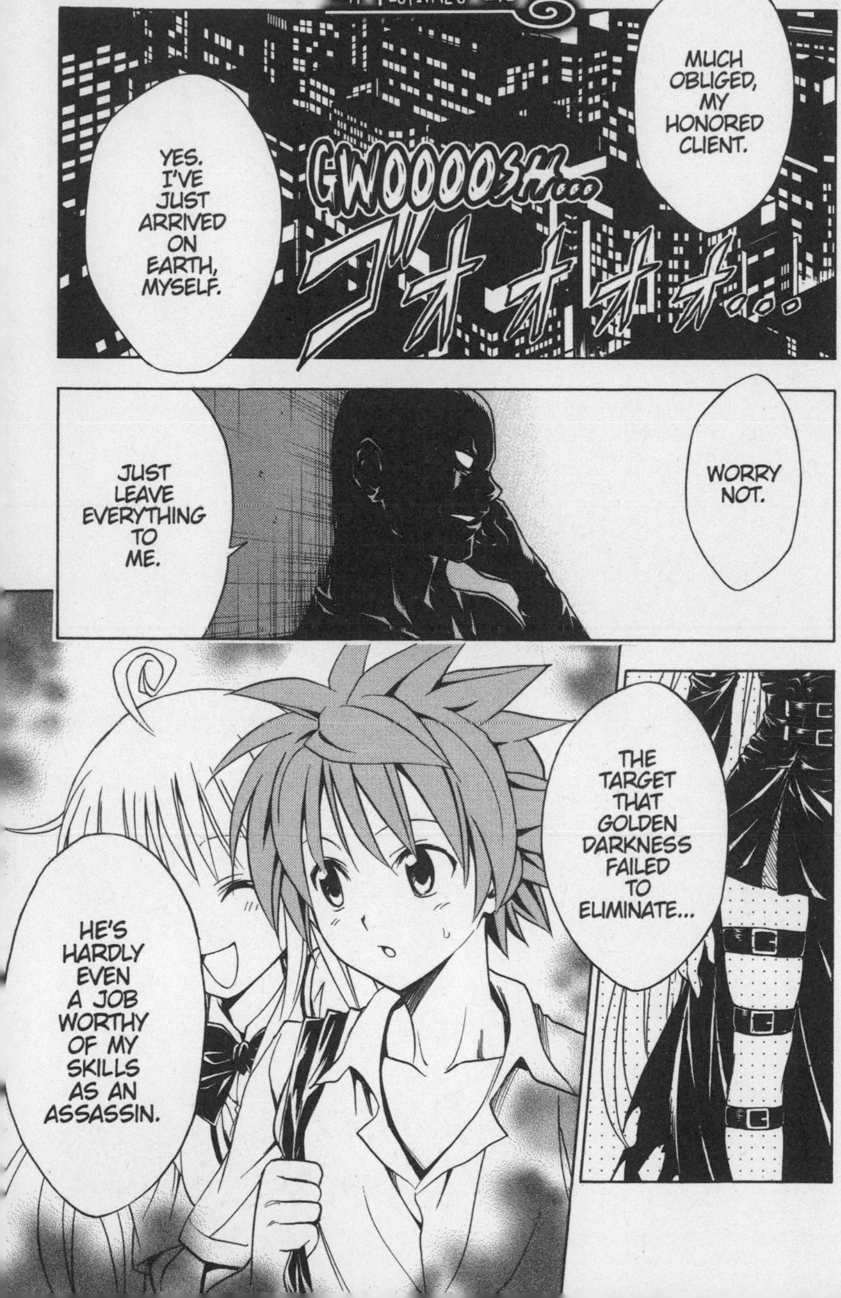
MUCH OBLIGED, MY HONORED CLIENT.
GWOOOOSH...
ゴオオオオ...!
YES. I'VE JUST ARRIVED ON EARTH, MYSELF.
WORRY NOT.
JUST LEAVE EVERYTHING TO ME.
THE TARGET THAT GOLDEN DARKNESS FAILED TO ELIMINATE...
HE'S HARDLY EVEN A JOB WORTHY OF MY SKILLS AS AN ASSASSIN.

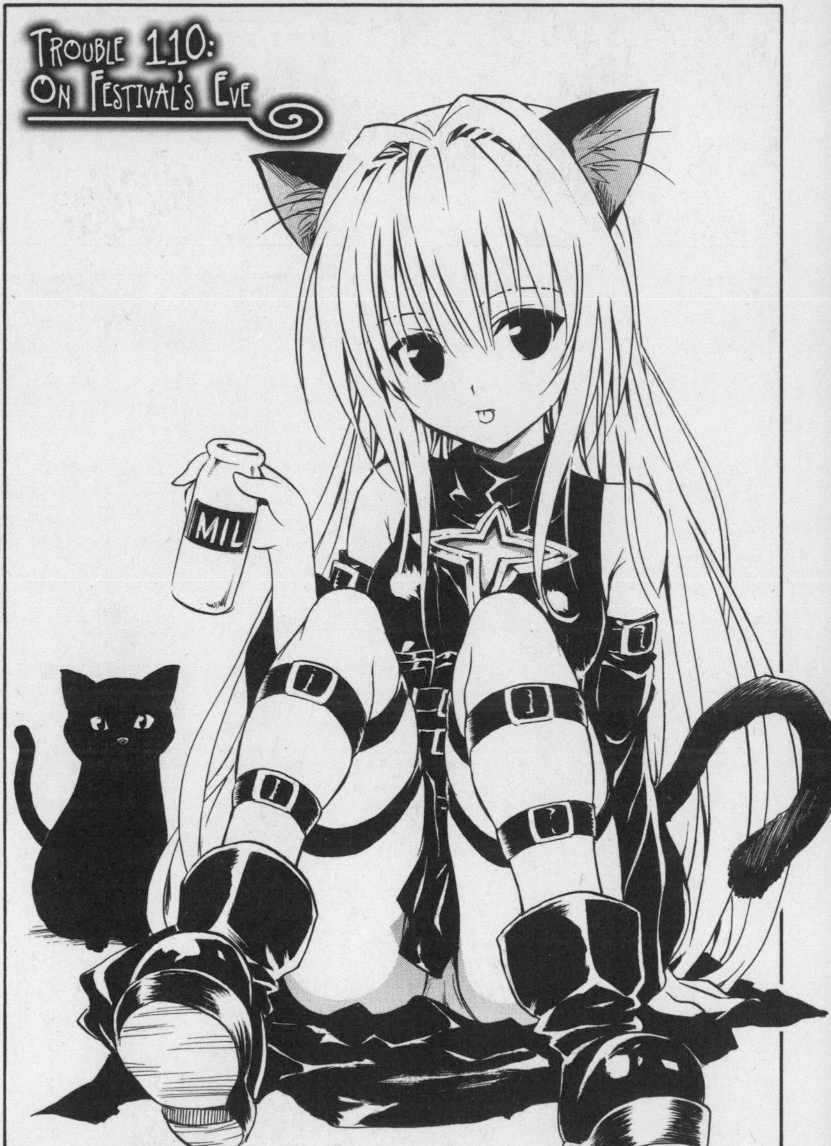
Trouble 110:
On Festival's Eve
MIL

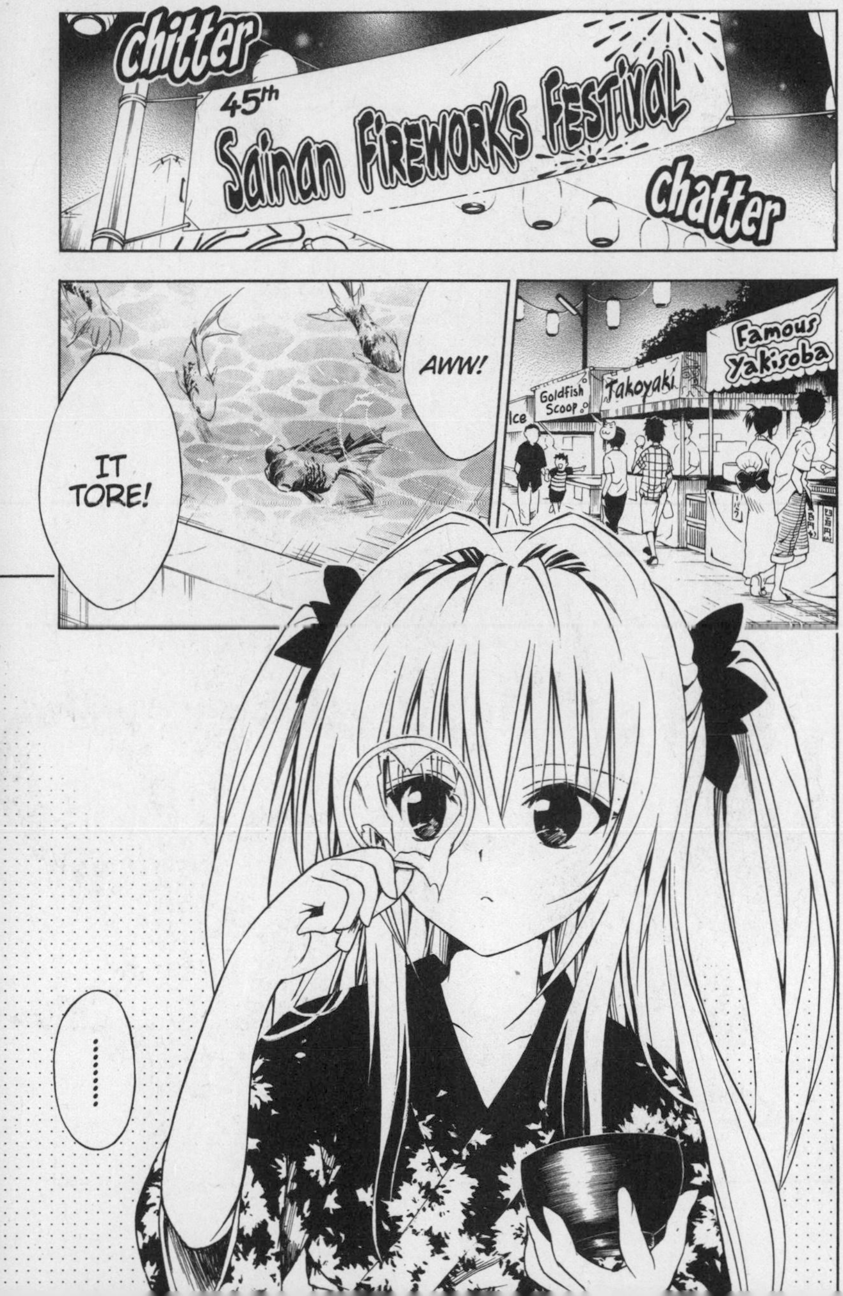
chitter
45th Sainan Fireworks Festival
chatter
Famous Yakisoba
Takoyaki
Goldfish Scoop
Ice
AWW!
IT TORE!
……

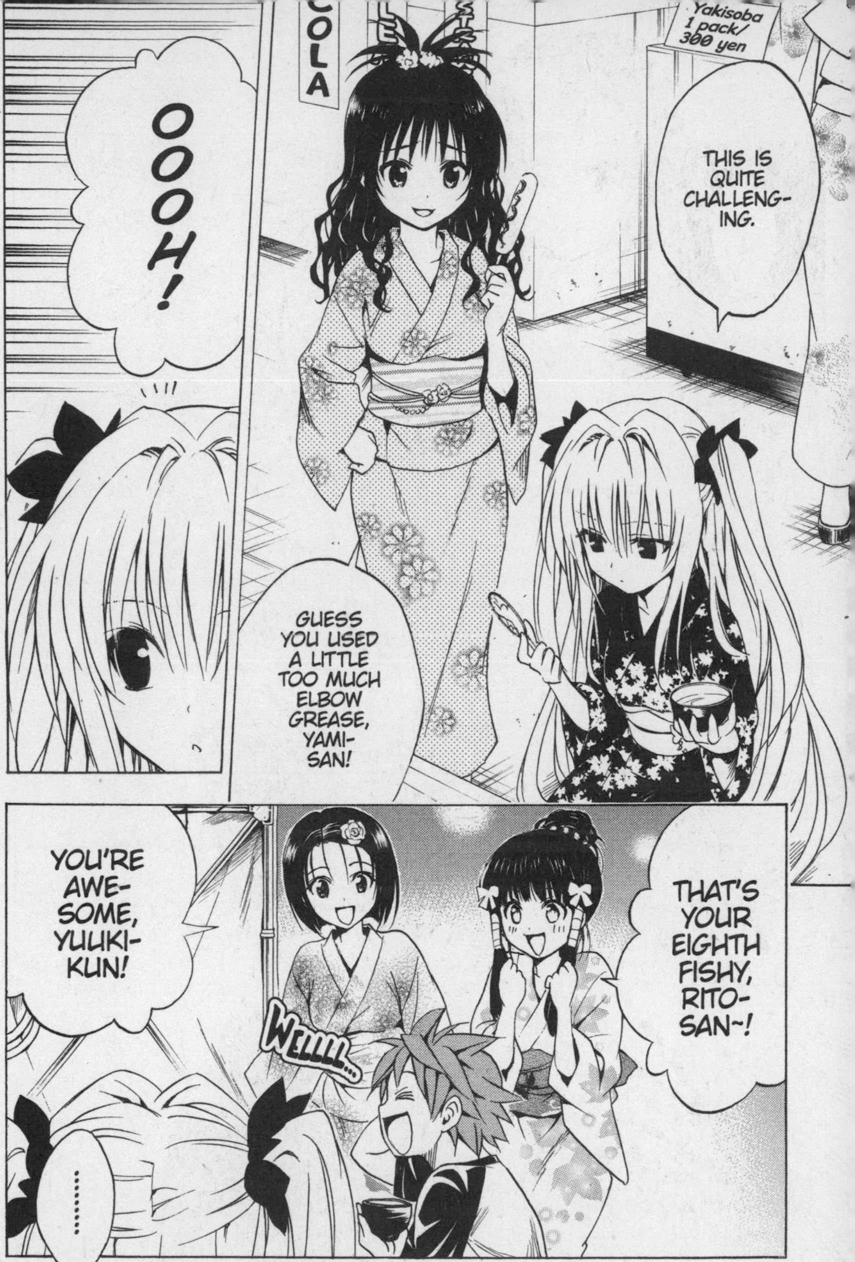
Yakisoba 1 pack/ 300 yen
THIS IS QUITE CHALLENG-ING.
COLA
GUESS YOU USED A LITTLE TOO MUCH ELBOW GREASE, YAMI-SAN!
OOOH!
THAT'S YOUR EIGHTH FISHY, RITO-SAN~!
YOU'RE AWE-SOME, YUUKI-KUN!
WELLLL...
....

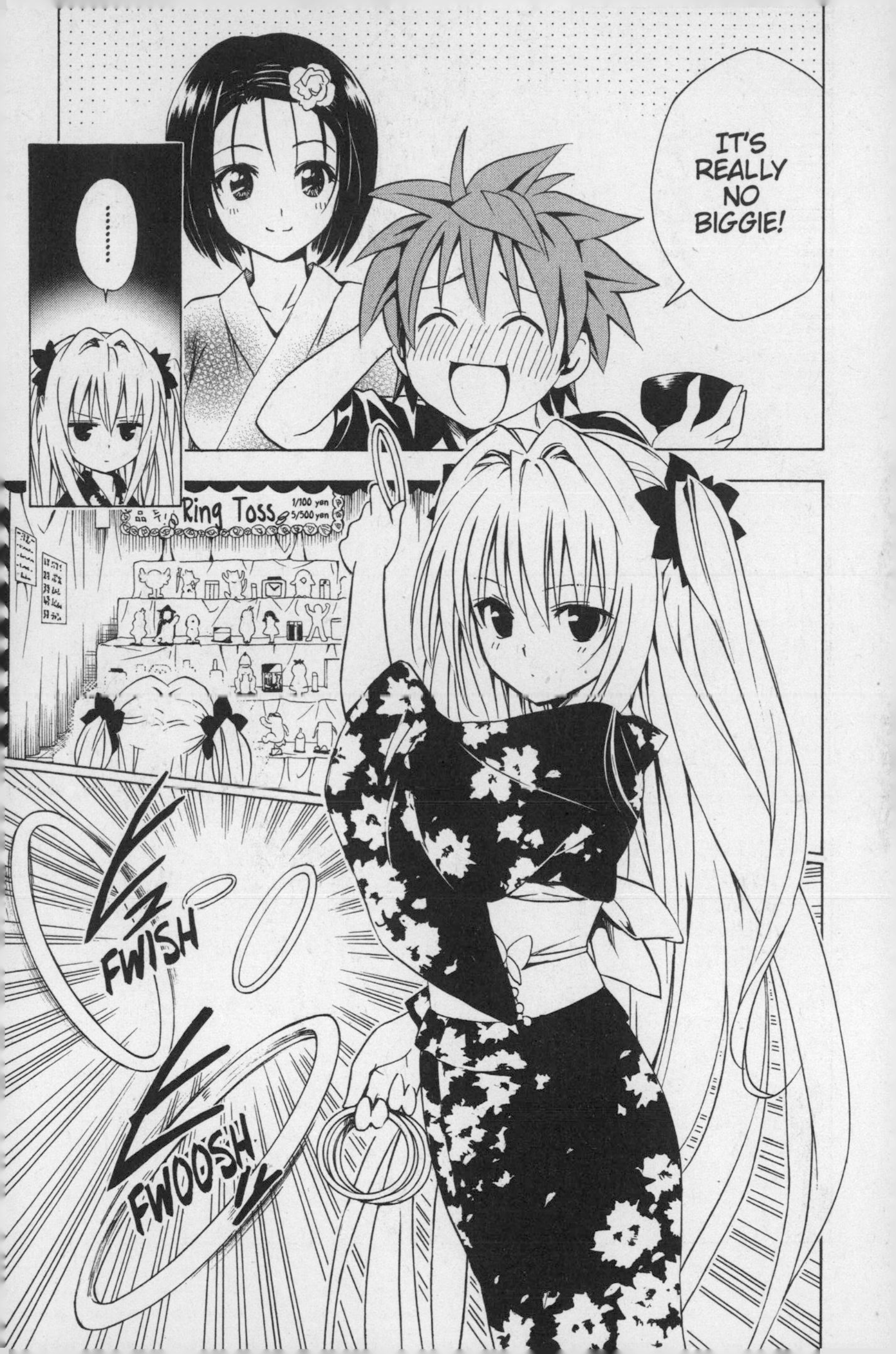
IT'S REALLY NO BIGGIE!
......
Ring Toss
1/100 yen
5/500 yen
FWISH
FWOOSH

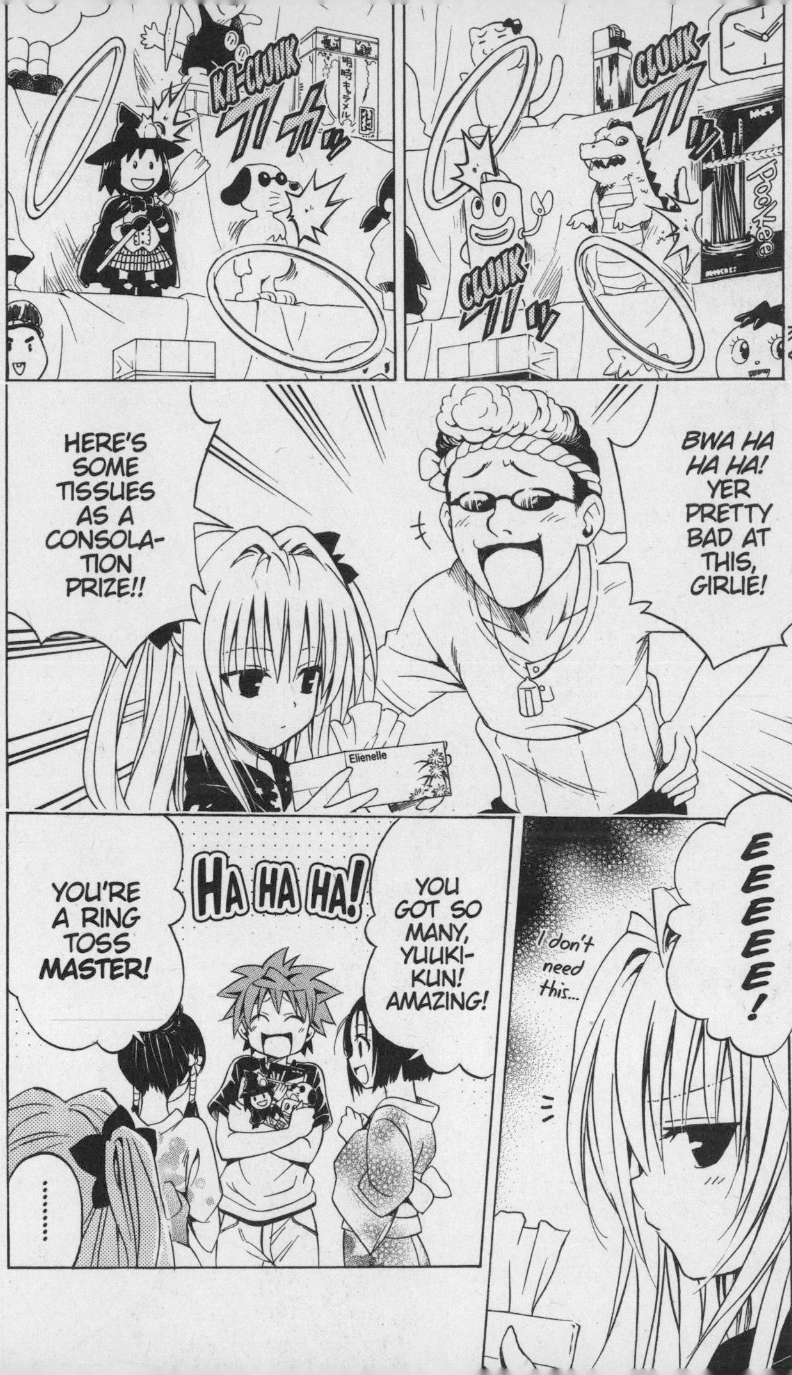
CLUNK
CLUNK
KA-CLUNK
BWA HA HA HA! YER PRETTY BAD AT THIS, GIRLIE!
HERE'S SOME TISSUES AS A CONSOLATION PRIZE!!
Elienelle
EEEEEE!
I don't need this...
YOU GOT SO MANY, YUUKI-KUN! AMAZING!
HA HA HA!
YOU'RE A RING TOSS MASTER!
......

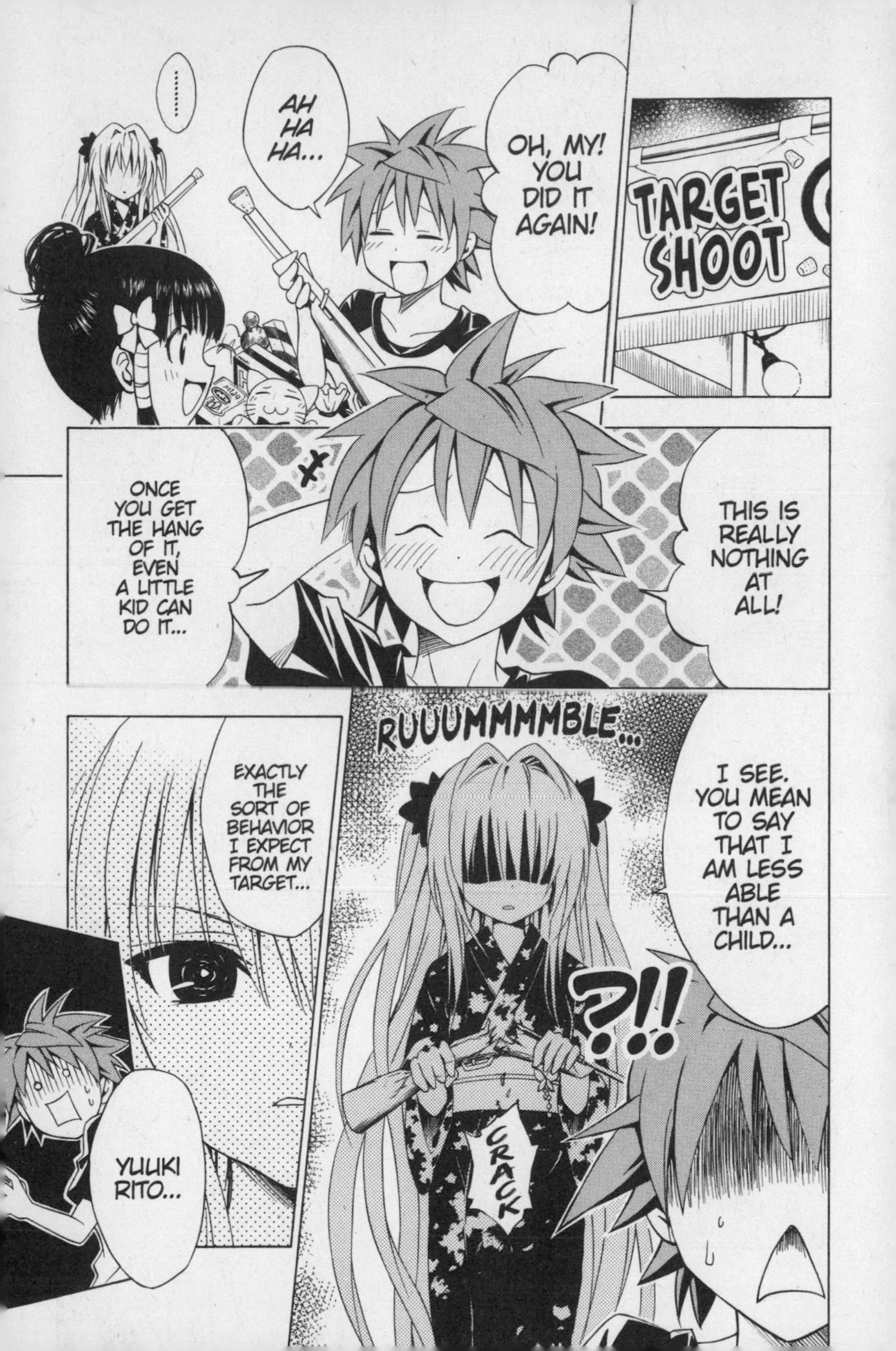
TARGET SHOOT
OH, MY! YOU DID IT AGAIN!
AH HA HA...
......
THIS IS REALLY NOTHING AT ALL!
ONCE YOU GET THE HANG OF IT, EVEN A LITTLE KID CAN DO IT...
RUUUMMMMBLE...
I SEE. YOU MEAN TO SAY THAT I AM LESS ABLE THAN A CHILD...
?!!
CRACK
EXACTLY THE SORT OF BEHAVIOR I EXPECT FROM MY TARGET...
YUUKI RITO...

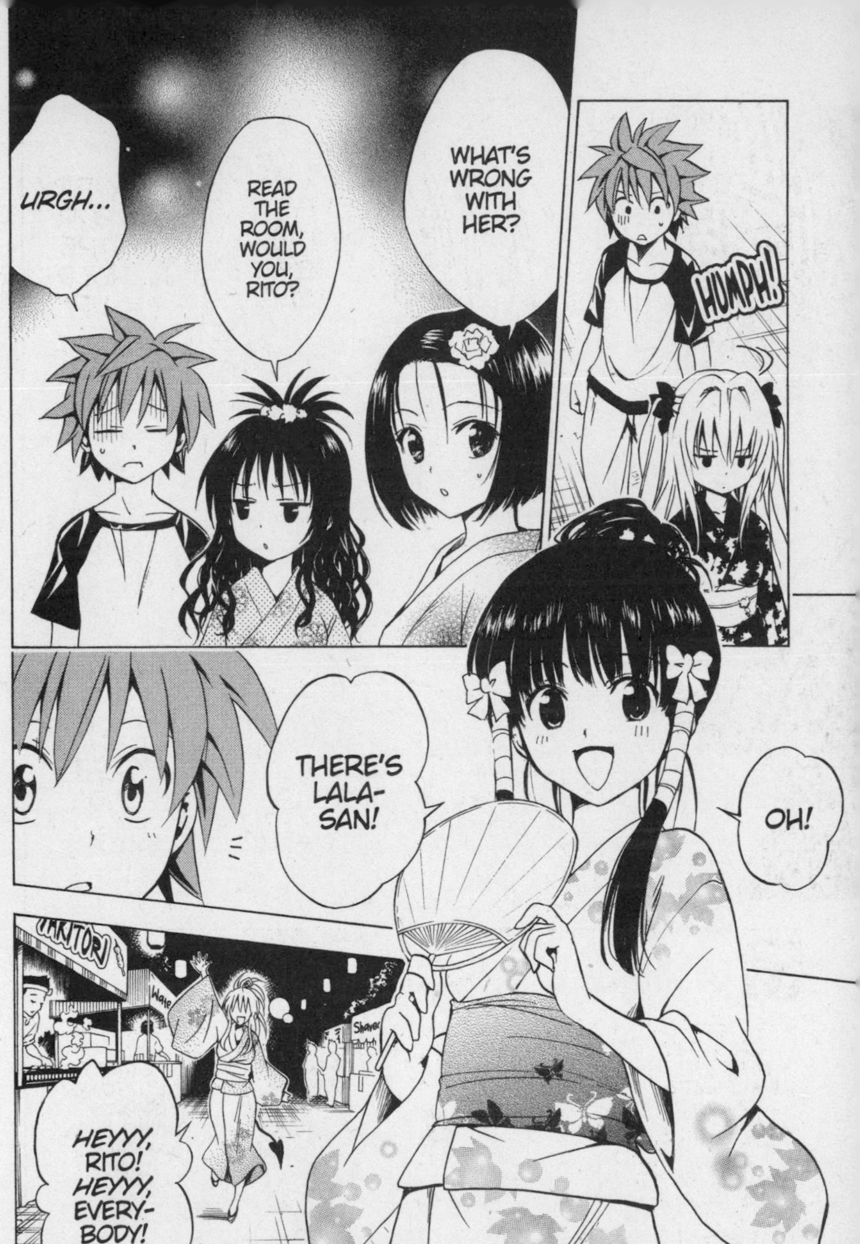
HUMPH!
WHAT'S WRONG WITH HER?
READ THE ROOM, WOULD YOU, RITO?
URGH...
OH!
THERE'S LALA-SAN!
HEYYY, RITO! HEYYY, EVERY-BODY!

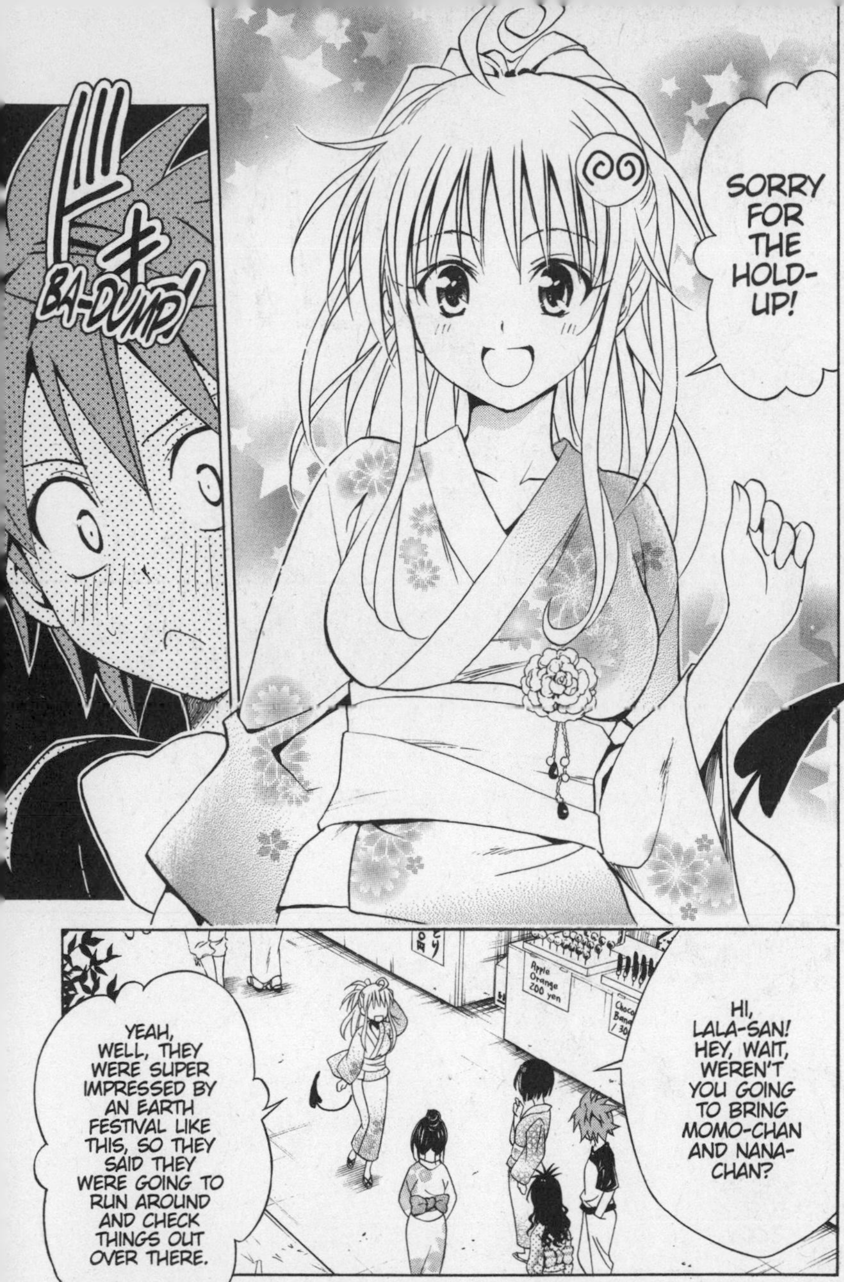
SORRY FOR THE HOLD-UP!
ドキ
BA-DUMP!
Apple Orange 200 yen
HI, LALA-SAN! HEY, WAIT, WEREN'T YOU GOING TO BRING MOMO-CHAN AND NANA-CHAN?
YEAH, WELL, THEY WERE SUPER IMPRESSED BY AN EARTH FESTIVAL LIKE THIS, SO THEY SAID THEY WERE GOING TO RUN AROUND AND CHECK THINGS OUT OVER THERE.

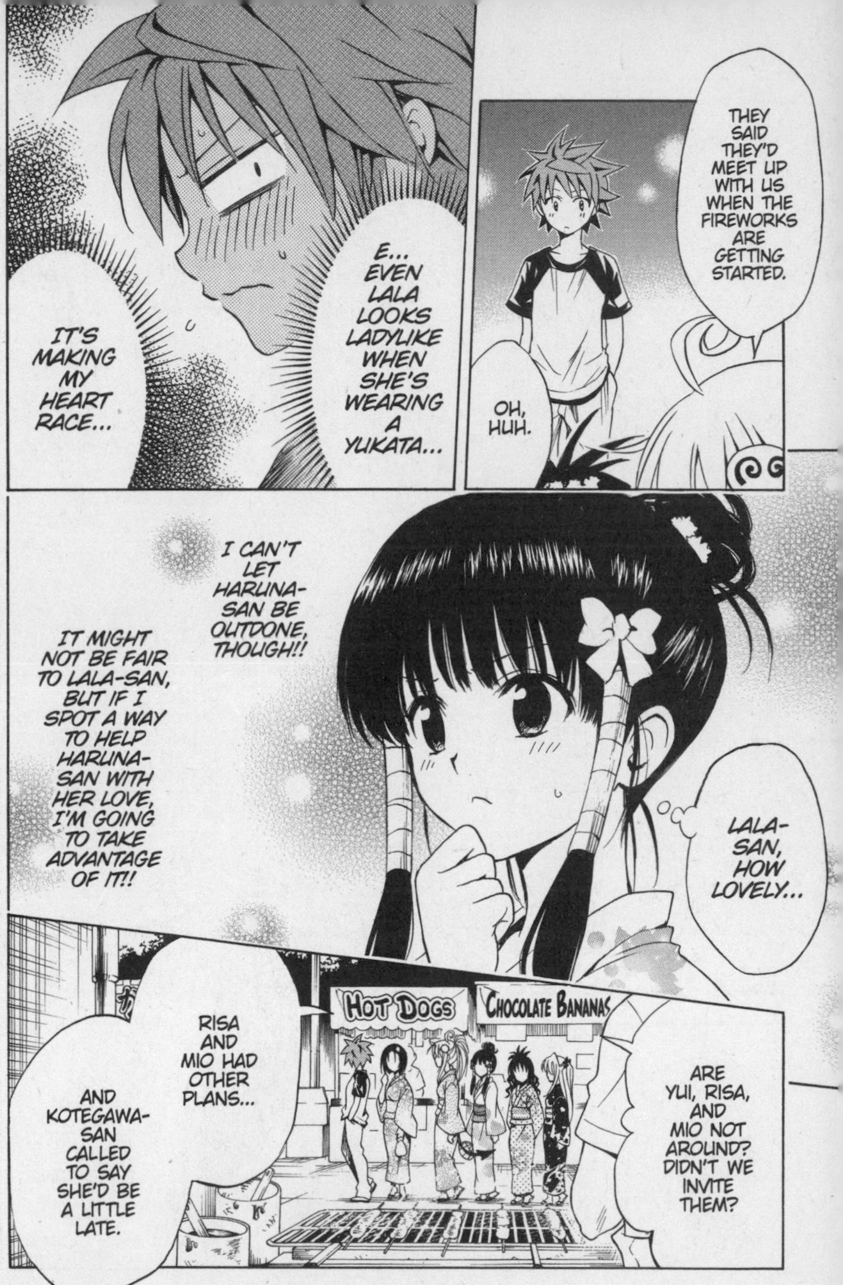
THEY SAID THEY'D MEET UP WITH US WHEN THE FIREWORKS ARE GETTING STARTED.
OH, HUH.
E... EVEN LALA LOOKS LADYLIKE WHEN SHE'S WEARING A YUKATA...
IT'S MAKING MY HEART RACE...
LALA-SAN, HOW LOVELY...
I CAN'T LET HARUNA-SAN BE OUTDONE, THOUGH!!
IT MIGHT NOT BE FAIR TO LALA-SAN, BUT IF I SPOT A WAY TO HELP HARUNA-SAN WITH HER LOVE, I'M GOING TO TAKE ADVANTAGE OF IT!!
CHOCOLATE BANANAS
HOT DOGS
ARE YUI, RISA, AND MIO NOT AROUND? DIDN'T WE INVITE THEM?
RISA AND MIO HAD OTHER PLANS...
AND KOTEGAWA-SAN CALLED TO SAY SHE'D BE A LITTLE LATE.

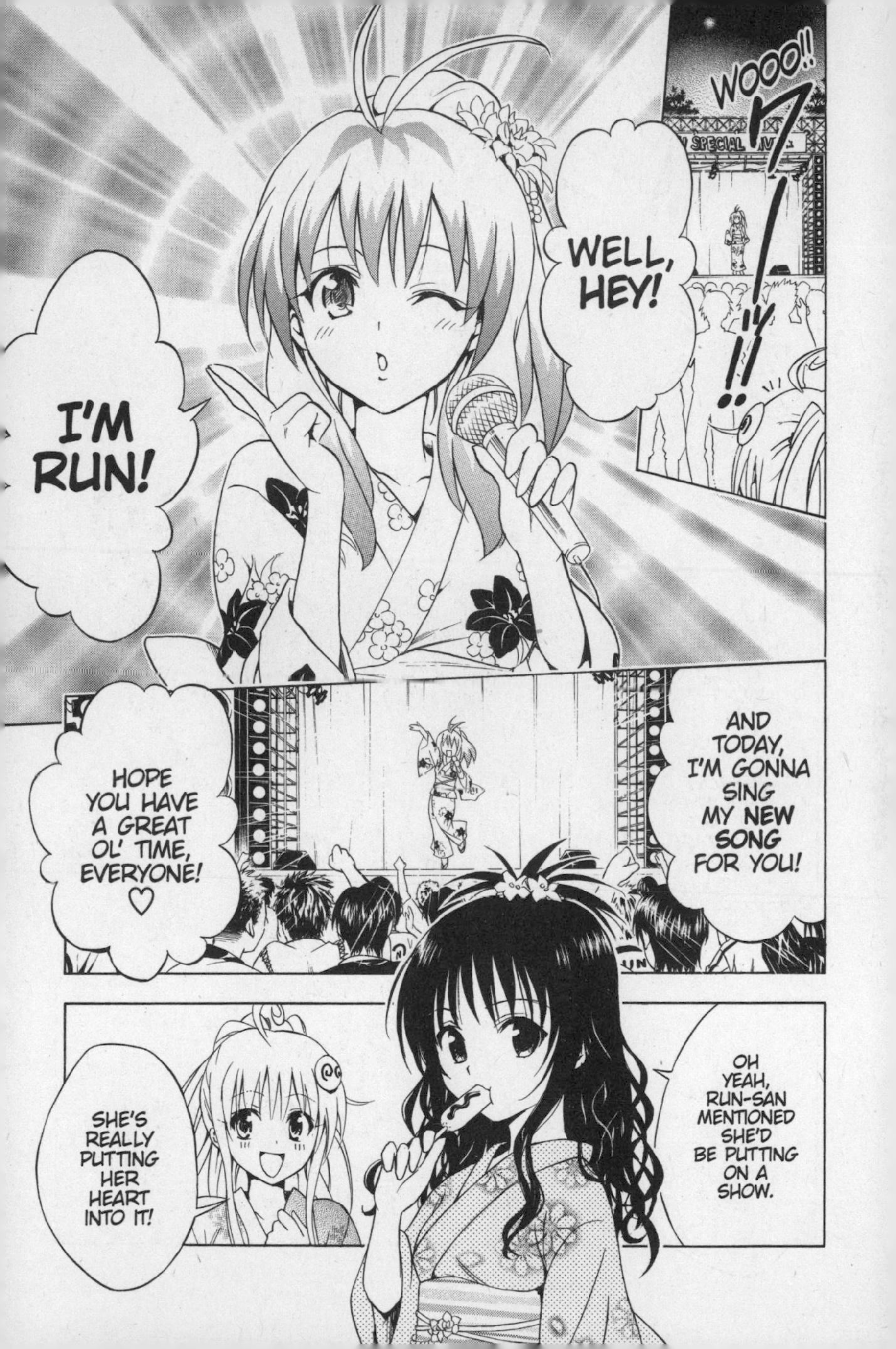
WOOO!!
WELL, HEY!
I'M RUN!
AND TODAY, I'M GONNA SING MY NEW SONG FOR YOU!
HOPE YOU HAVE A GREAT OL' TIME, EVERYONE! ♡
OH YEAH, RUN-SAN MENTIONED SHE'D BE PUTTING ON A SHOW.
SHE'S REALLY PUTTING HER HEART INTO IT!

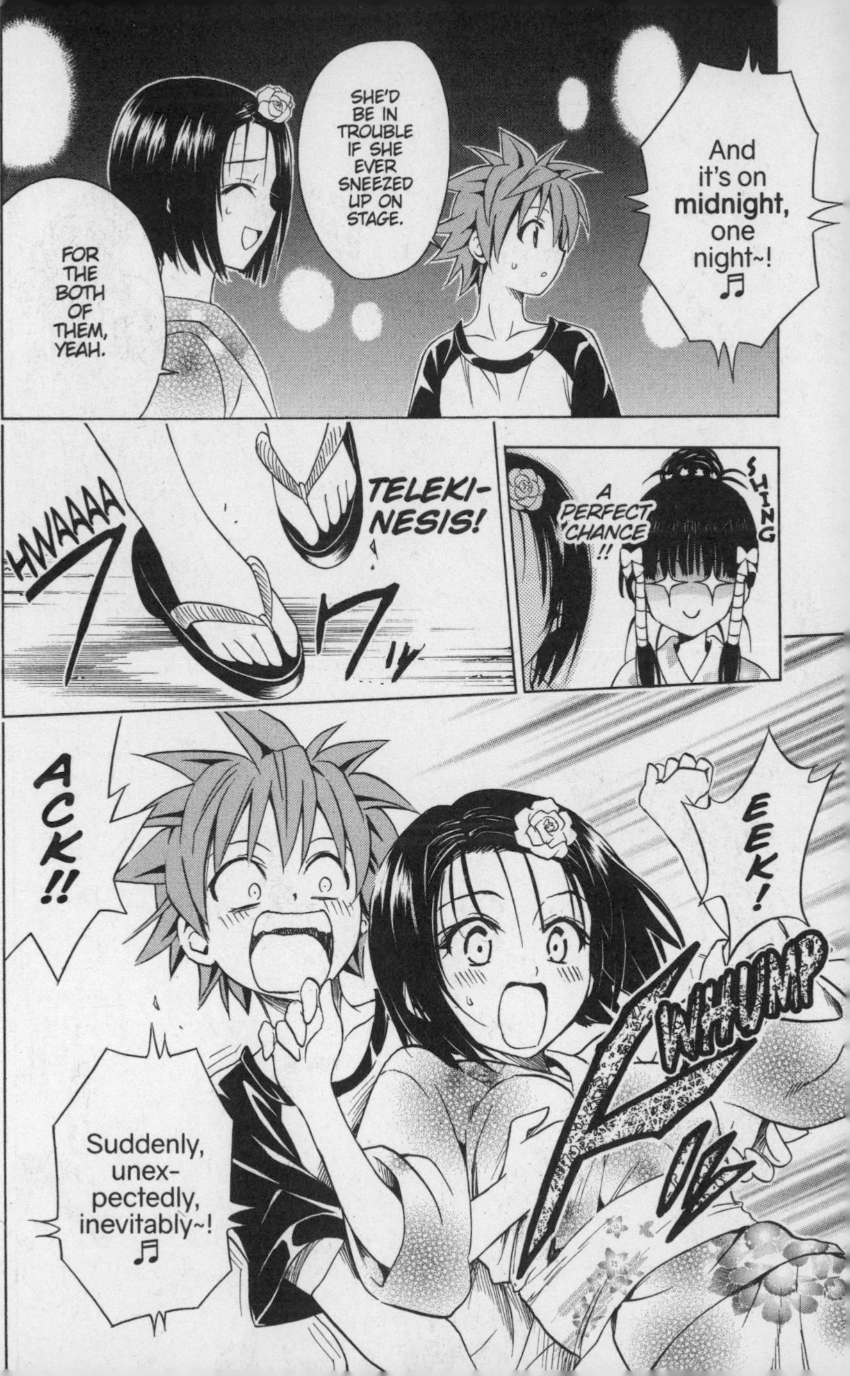
And it's on **midnight,** one night~! ♫
SHE'D BE IN TROUBLE IF SHE EVER SNEEZED UP ON STAGE.
FOR THE BOTH OF THEM, YEAH.
SHING
A PERFECT CHANCE!!
TELEKI-NESIS!
HWAAAA
EEK!
WHUMP
ACK!!
Suddenly, unex-pectedly, inevitably~! ♫

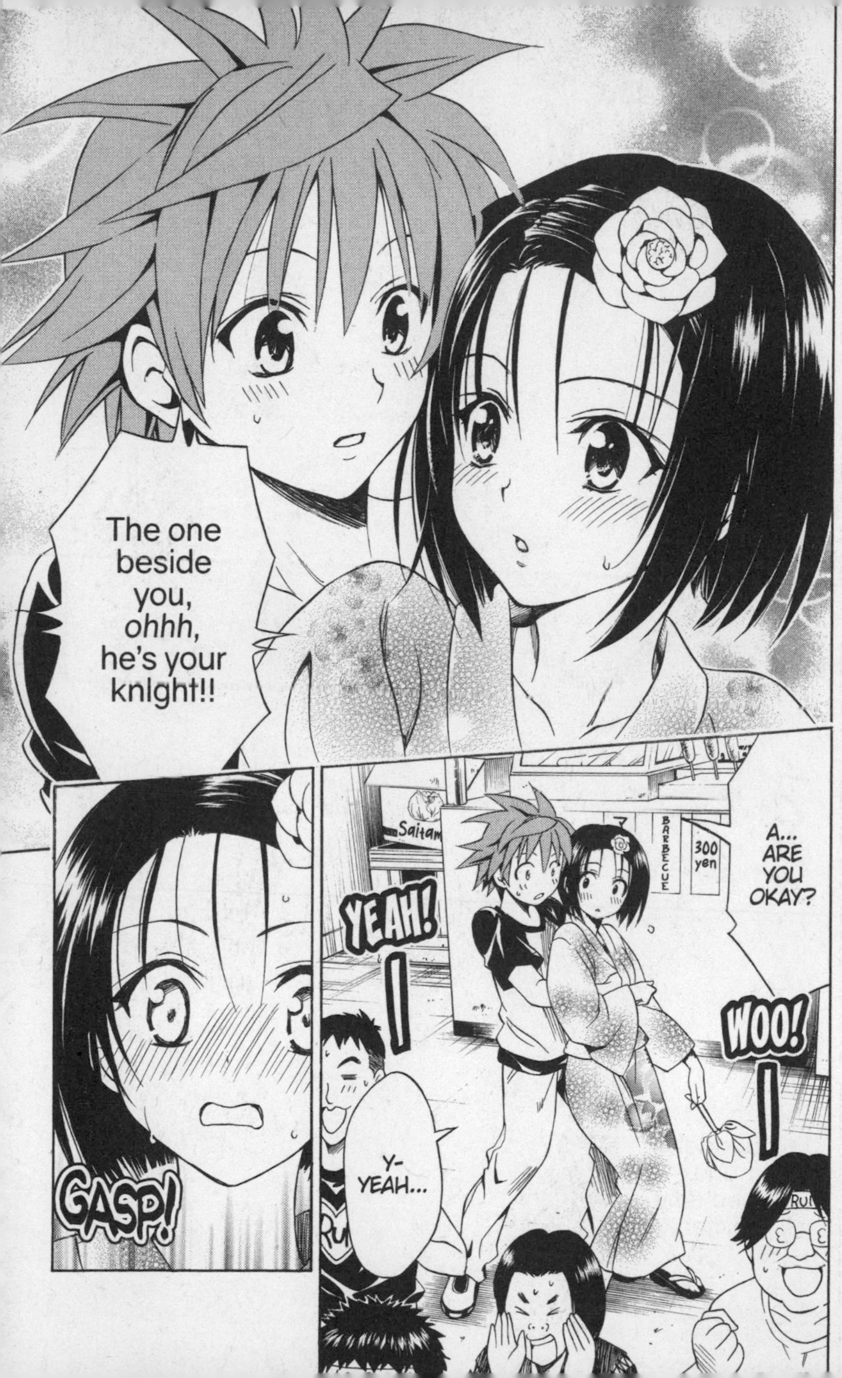
The one beside you, *ohhh*, he's your knight!!
A... ARE YOU OKAY?
300 yen
BARBECUE
WOO!
YEAH!
Saitam
Y-YEAH...
GASP!

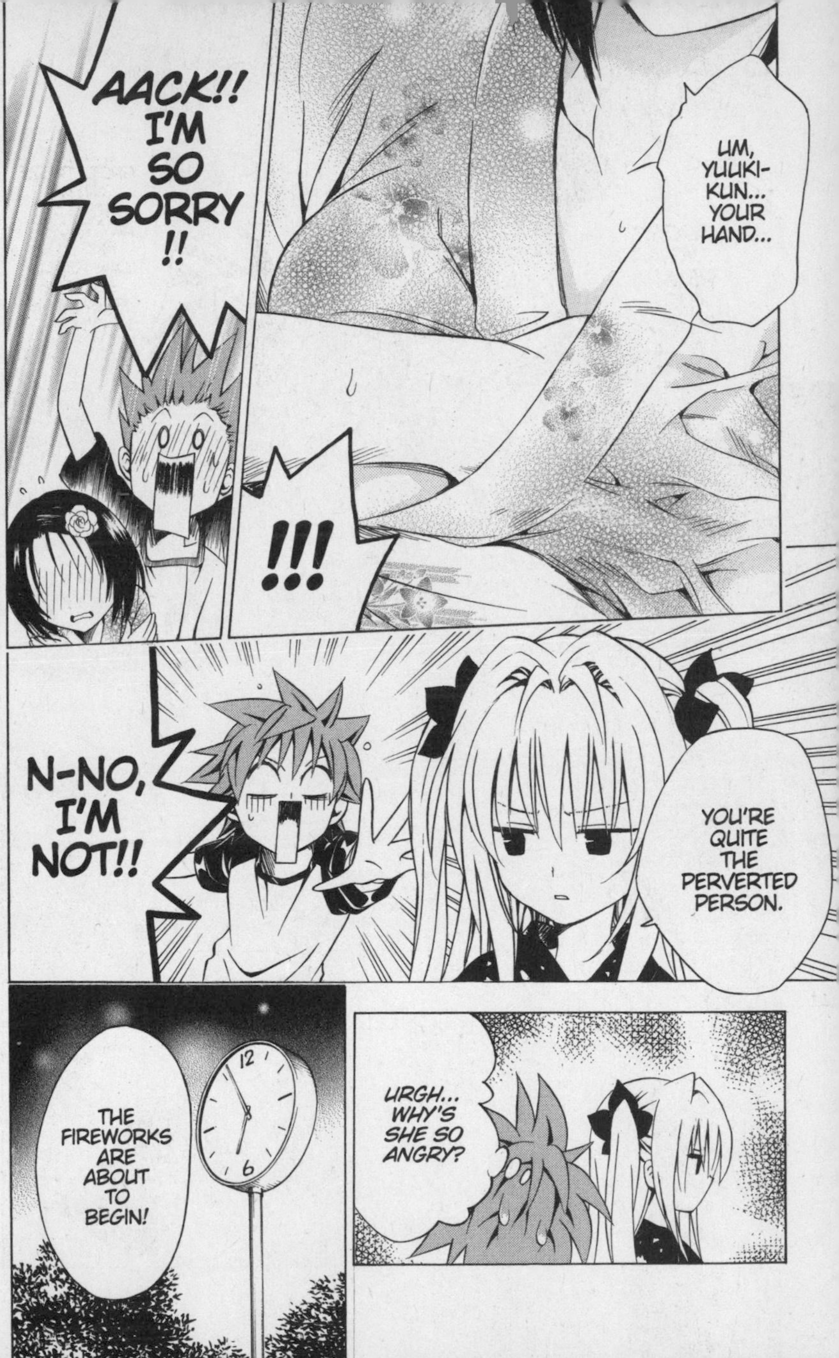

UM, YUUKI-KUN... YOUR HAND...
!!!
AACK!! I'M SO SORRY!!
YOU'RE QUITE THE PERVERTED PERSON.
N-NO, I'M NOT!!
URGH... WHY'S SHE SO ANGRY?
THE FIREWORKS ARE ABOUT TO BEGIN!

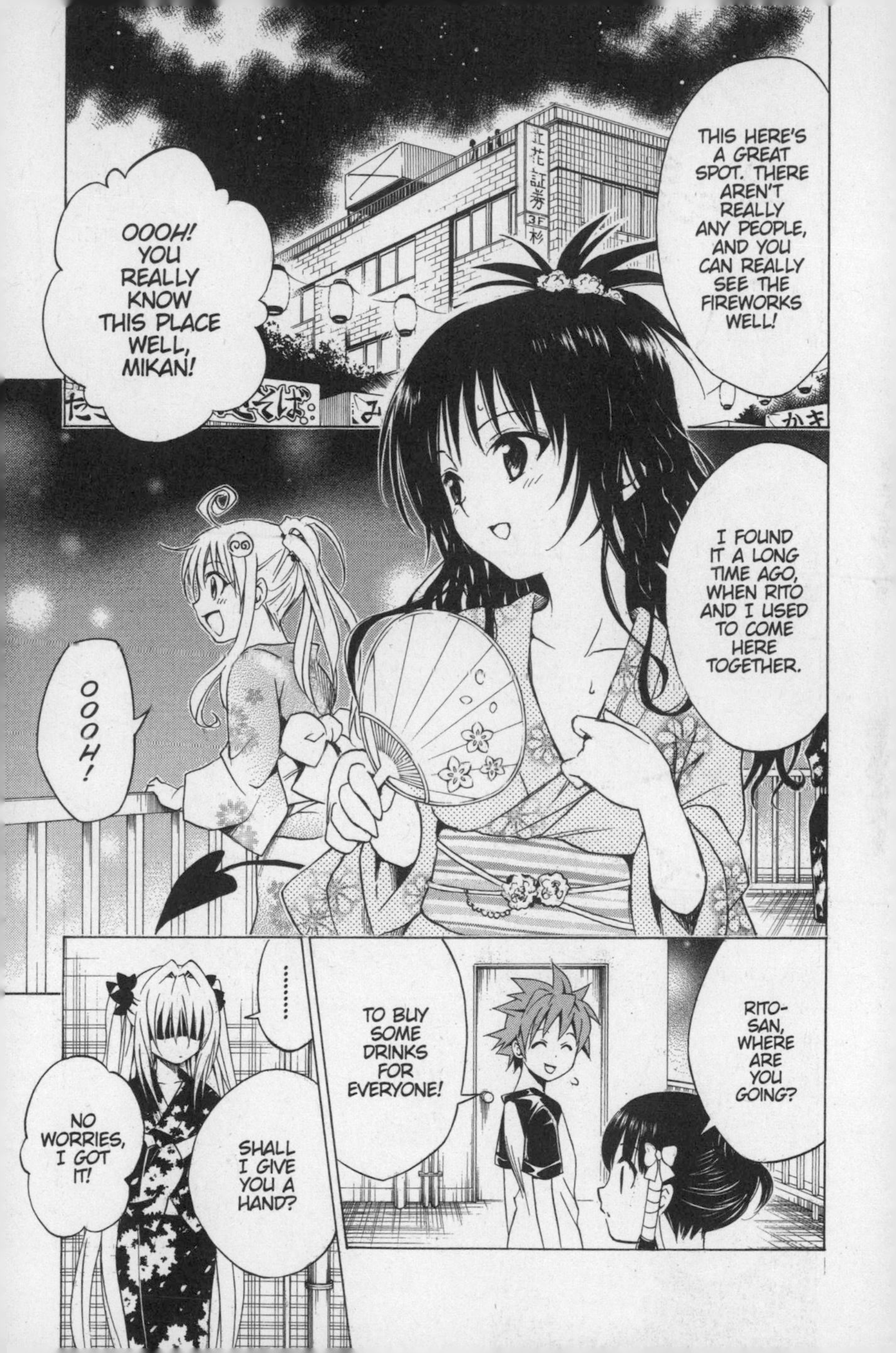

立花証券
3F 杉
THIS HERE'S A GREAT SPOT. THERE AREN'T REALLY ANY PEOPLE, AND YOU CAN REALLY SEE THE FIREWORKS WELL!
OOOH! YOU REALLY KNOW THIS PLACE WELL, MIKAN!
I FOUND IT A LONG TIME AGO, WHEN RITO AND I USED TO COME HERE TOGETHER.
OOOOH!
RITO-SAN, WHERE ARE YOU GOING?
TO BUY SOME DRINKS FOR EVERYONE!
......
SHALL I GIVE YOU A HAND?
NO WORRIES, I GOT IT!

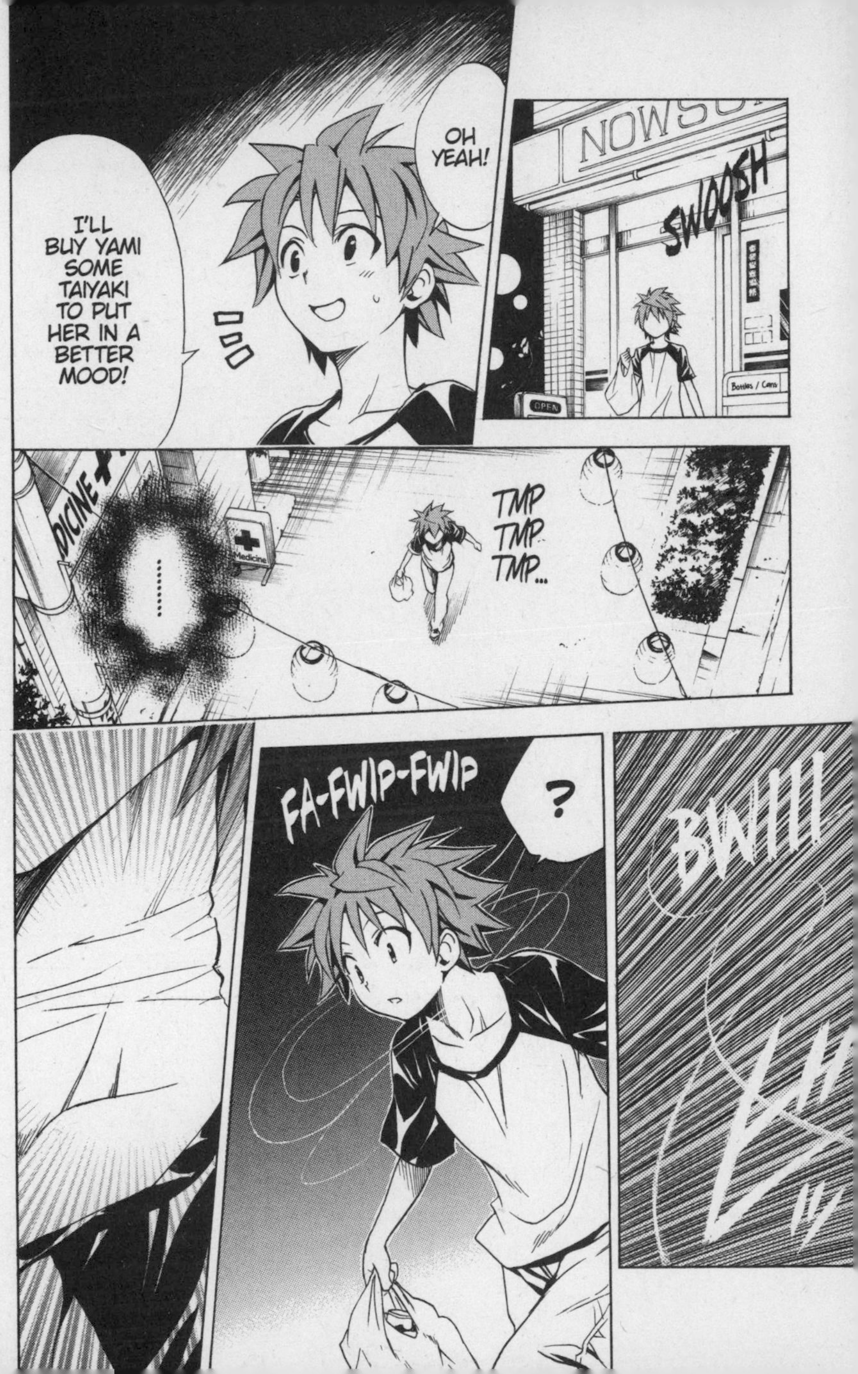
SWOOSH
Bottles / Cans
OPEN
OH YEAH!
I'LL BUY YAMI SOME TAIYAKI TO PUT HER IN A BETTER MOOD!
TMP TMP TMP...
Medicine
......
BWIII
FA-FWIP-FWIP
?

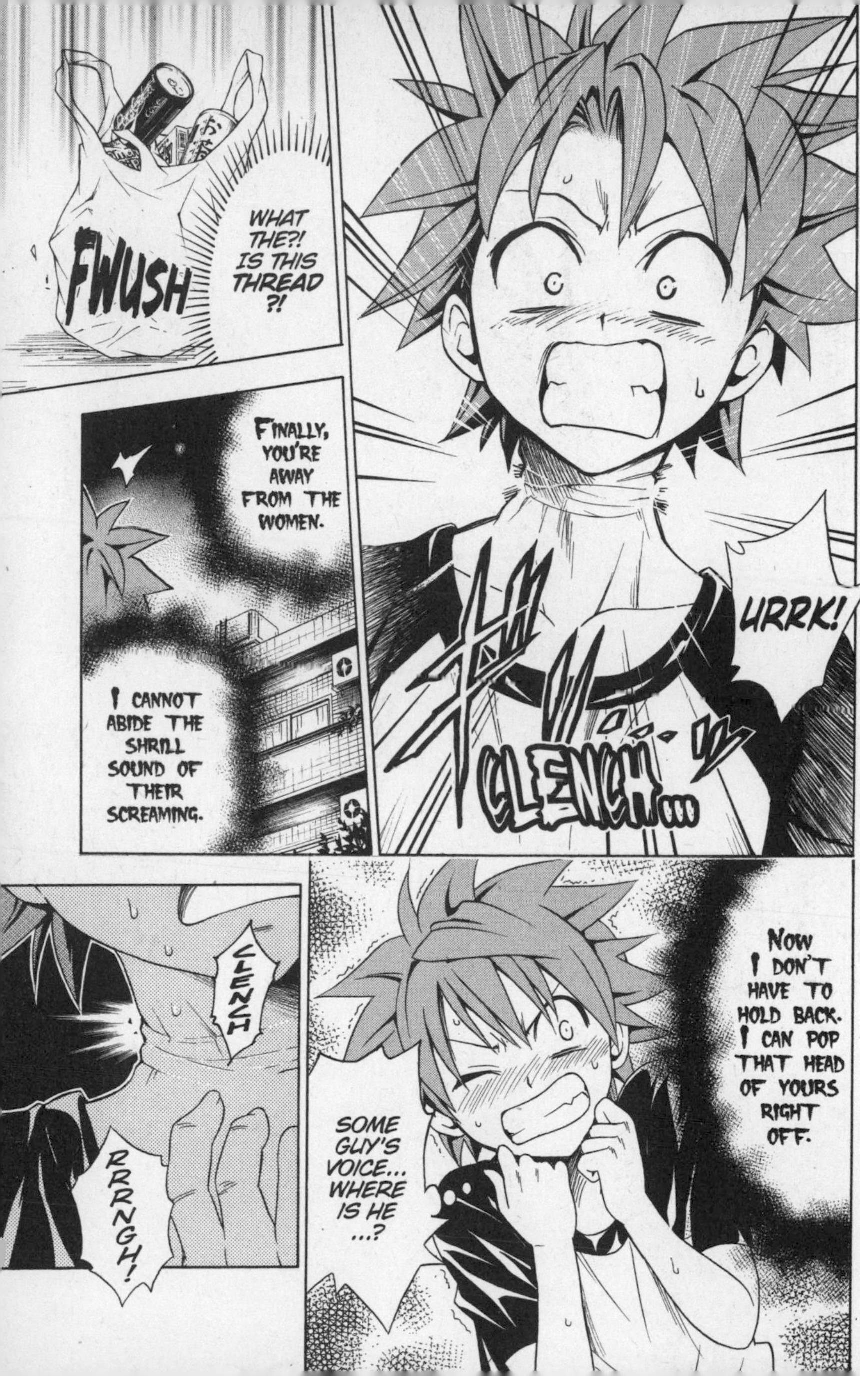
URRK!
CLENCH...
FWUSH
WHAT THE?! IS THIS THREAD ?!
FINALLY, YOU'RE AWAY FROM THE WOMEN.
I CANNOT ABIDE THE SHRILL SOUND OF THEIR SCREAMING.
NOW I DON'T HAVE TO HOLD BACK. I CAN POP THAT HEAD OF YOURS RIGHT OFF.
SOME GUY'S VOICE... WHERE IS HE ...?
CLENCH
RRRNGH!

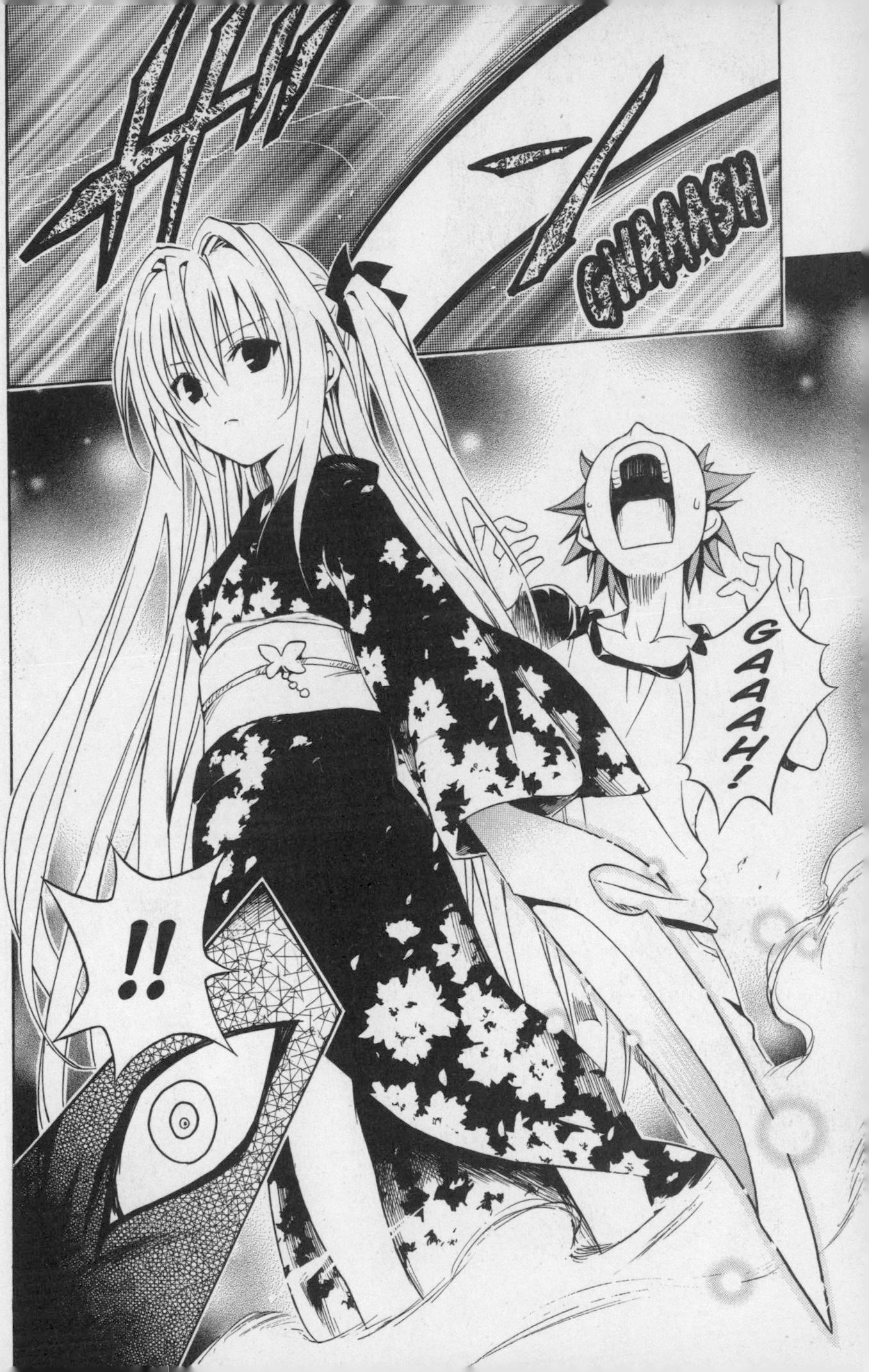
GWAASH
GAAAH!
!!

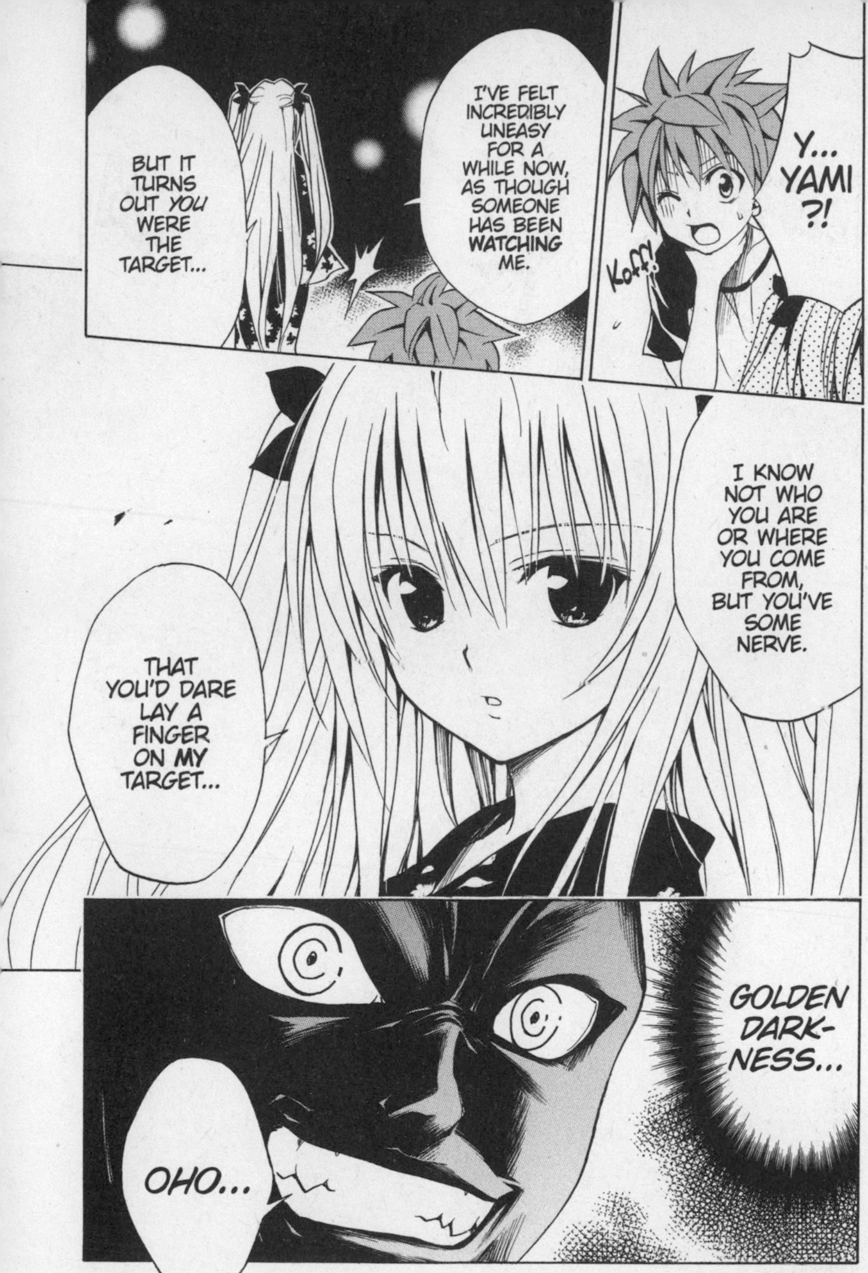
Y... YAMI ?!
Koff!
I'VE FELT INCREDIBLY UNEASY FOR A WHILE NOW, AS THOUGH SOMEONE HAS BEEN WATCHING ME.
BUT IT TURNS OUT YOU WERE THE TARGET...
I KNOW NOT WHO YOU ARE OR WHERE YOU COME FROM, BUT YOU'VE SOME NERVE.
THAT YOU'D DARE LAY A FINGER ON MY TARGET...
GOLDEN DARKNESS...
OHO...

To LOVE Ru

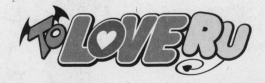

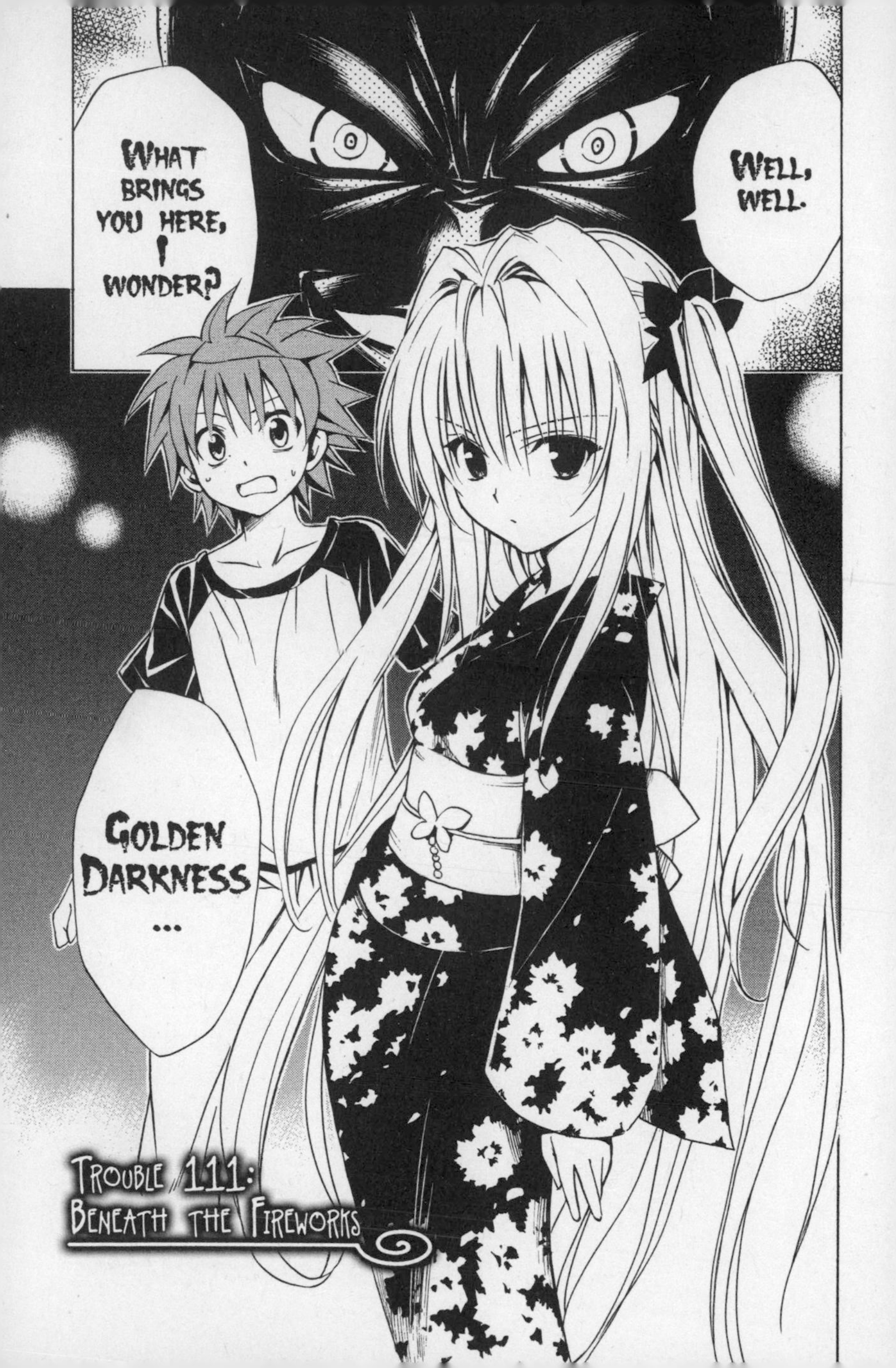
WELL, WELL.
WHAT BRINGS YOU HERE, I WONDER?
GOLDEN DARKNESS ...
TROUBLE 111: BENEATH THE FIREWORKS

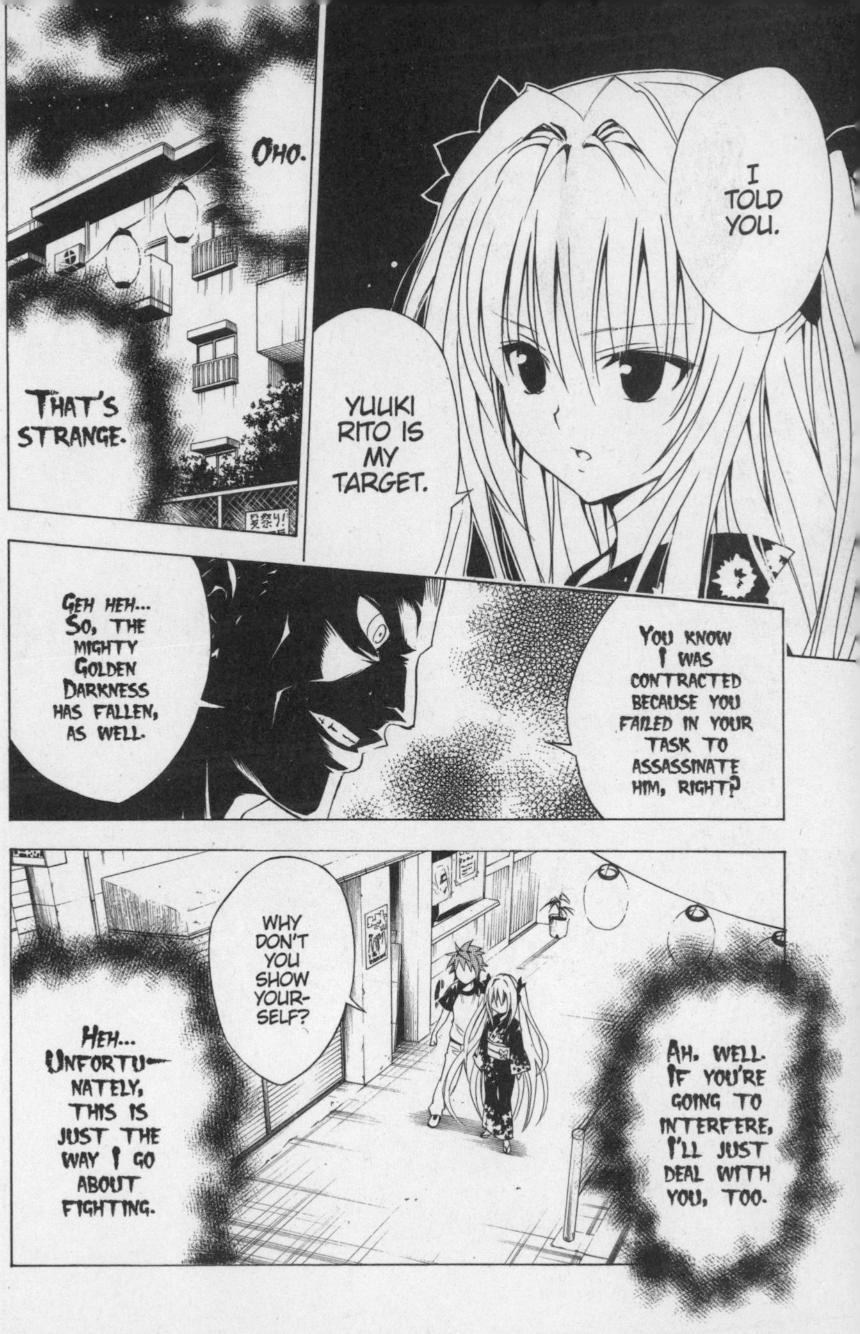
I TOLD YOU.
YUUKI RITO IS MY TARGET.
OHO.
THAT'S STRANGE.
夏祭り!
YOU KNOW I WAS CONTRACTED BECAUSE YOU FAILED IN YOUR TASK TO ASSASSINATE HIM, RIGHT?
GEH HEH... SO, THE MIGHTY GOLDEN DARKNESS HAS FALLEN, AS WELL.
AH. WELL. IF YOU'RE GOING TO INTERFERE, I'LL JUST DEAL WITH YOU, TOO.
WHY DON'T YOU SHOW YOURSELF?
HEH... UNFORTUNATELY, THIS IS JUST THE WAY I GO ABOUT FIGHTING.

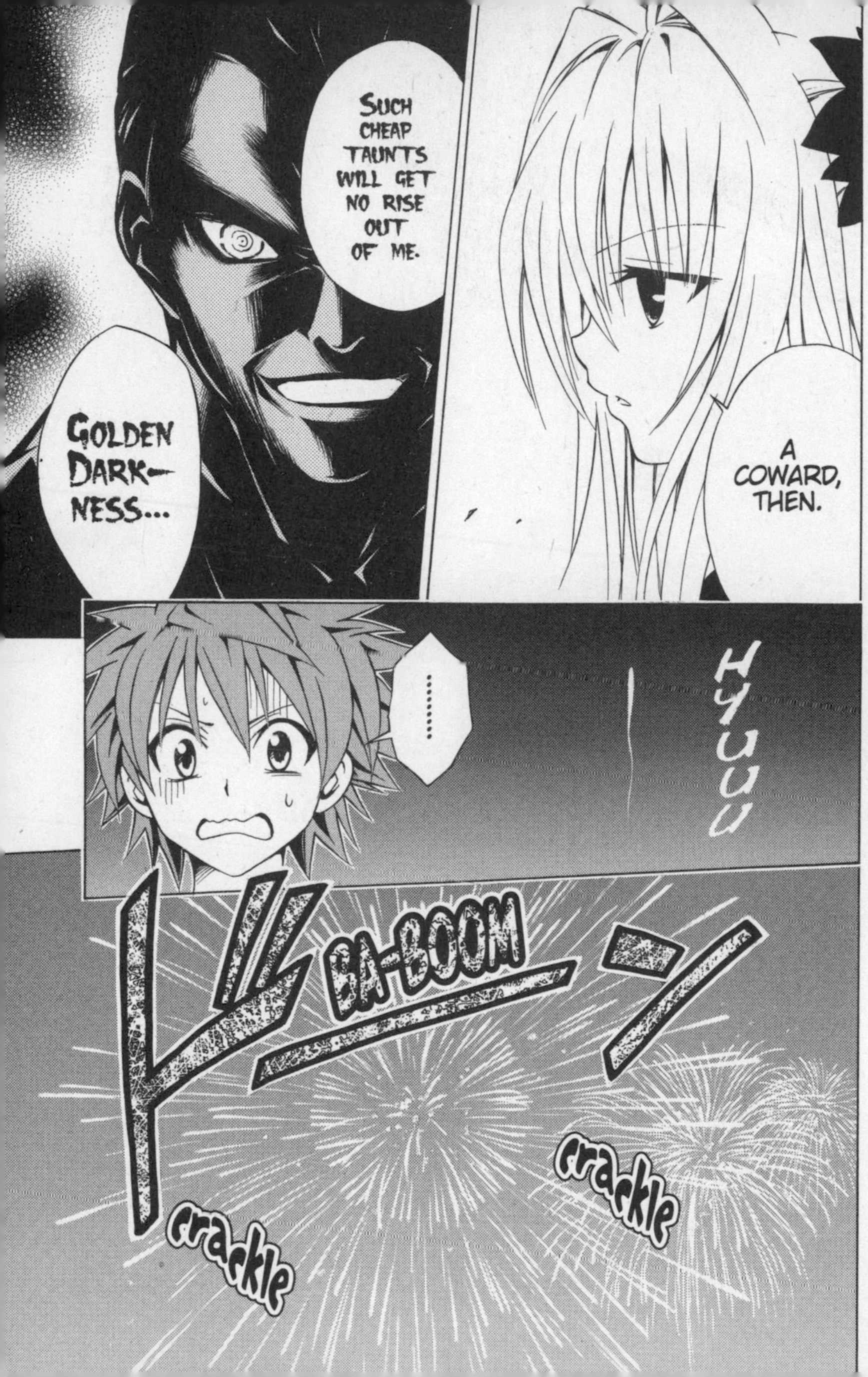
A COWARD, THEN.
SUCH CHEAP TAUNTS WILL GET NO RISE OUT OF ME.
GOLDEN DARK-NESS...
HYUUUU
......
BA-BOOM
crackle
crackle

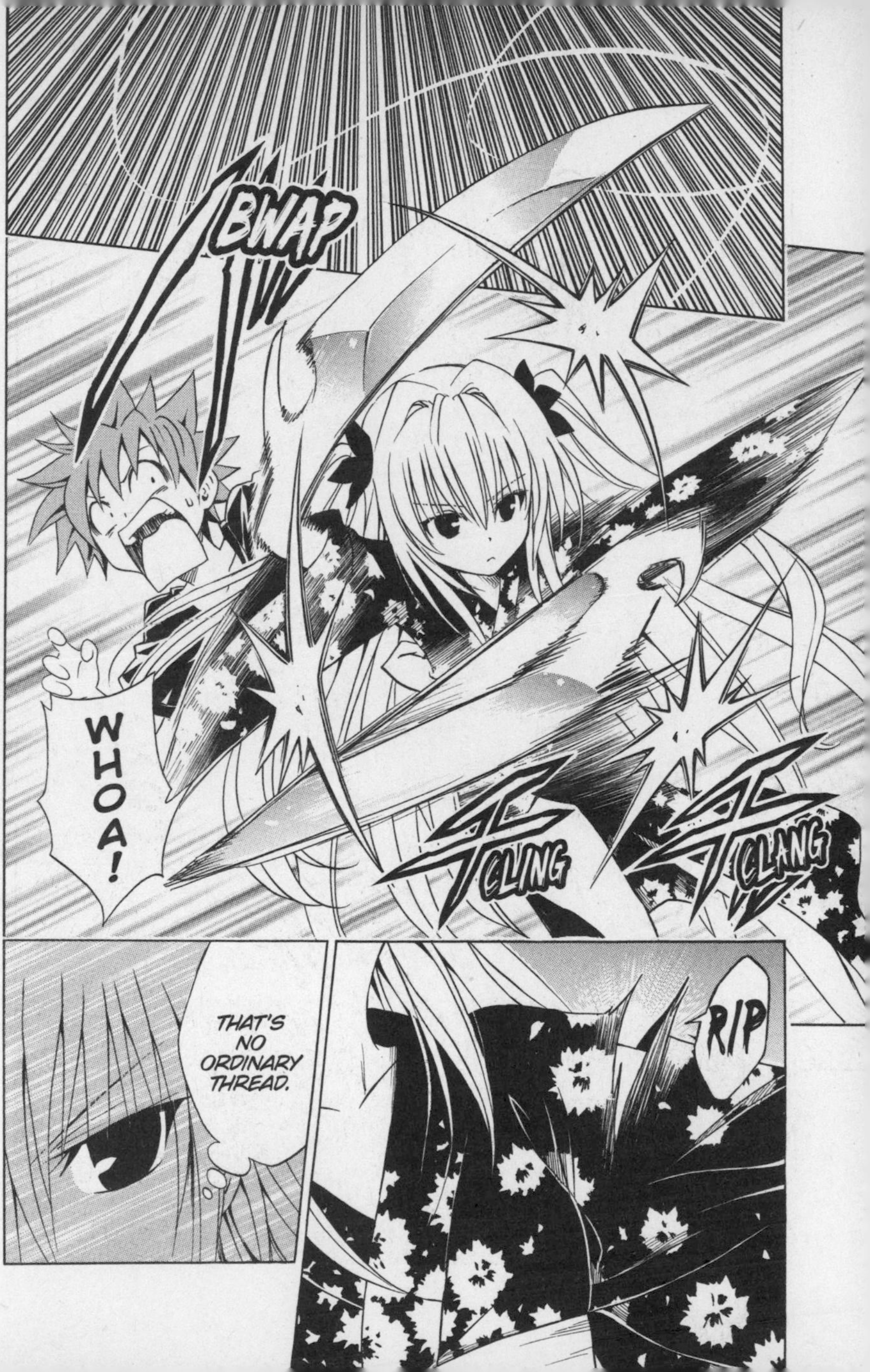
BWAP
CLANG
CLING
WHOA!
RIP
THAT'S NO ORDINARY THREAD.

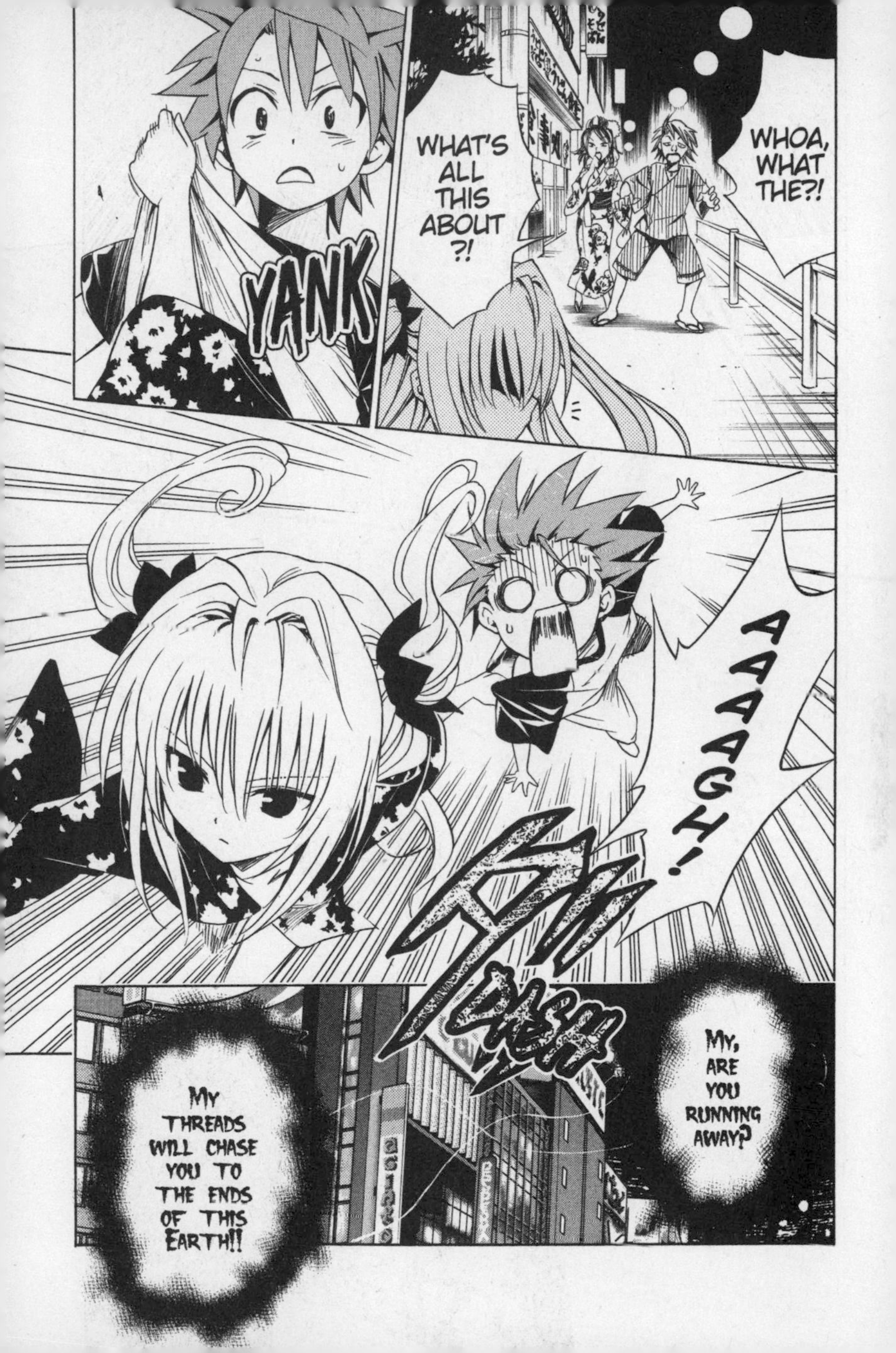
WHOA, WHAT THE?!
WHAT'S ALL THIS ABOUT?!
YANK
AAAAAGH!
MY, ARE YOU RUNNING AWAY?
MY THREADS WILL CHASE YOU TO THE ENDS OF THIS EARTH!!

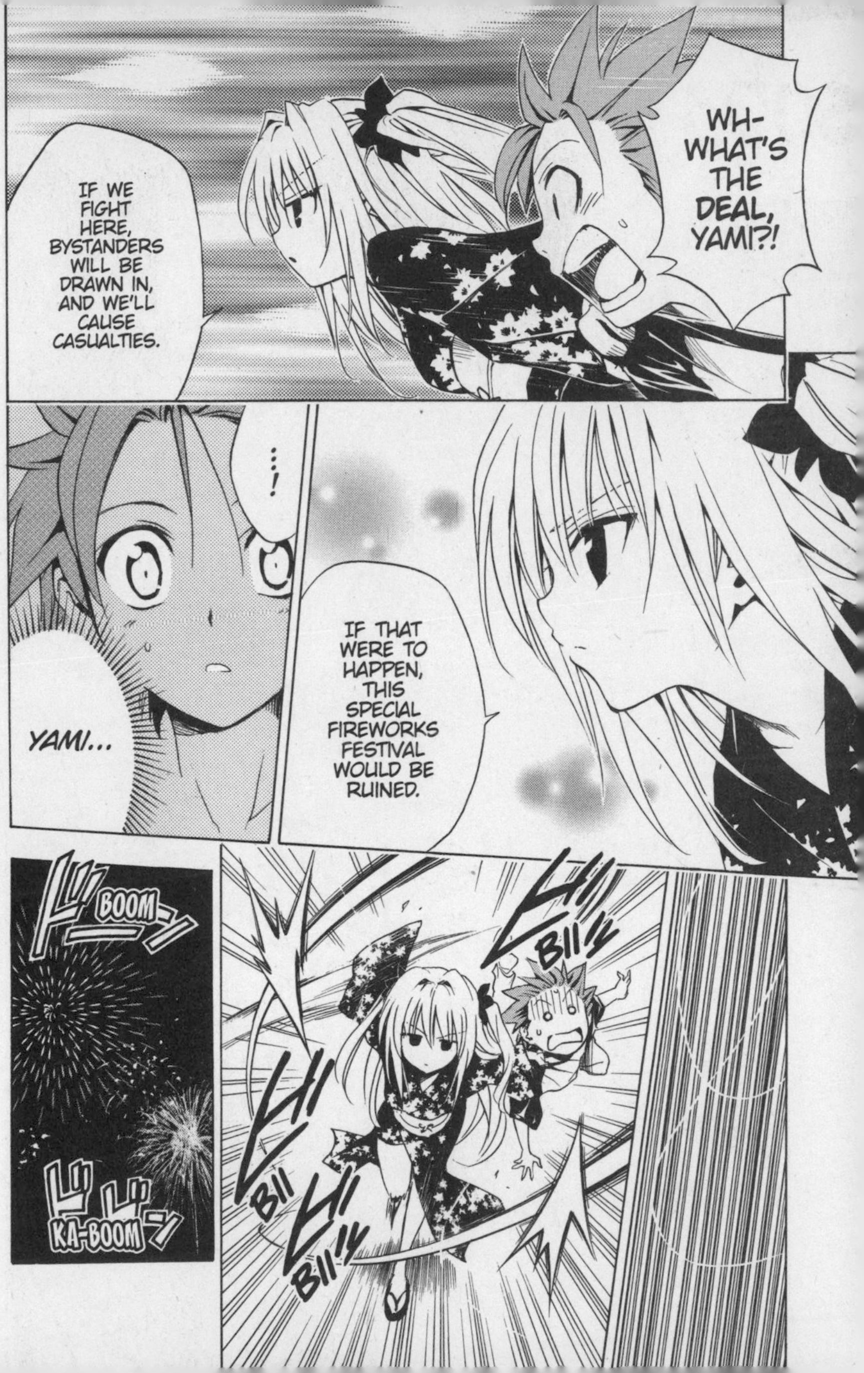
WH-WHAT'S THE DEAL, YAMI?!
IF WE FIGHT HERE, BYSTANDERS WILL BE DRAWN IN, AND WE'LL CAUSE CASUALTIES.
IF THAT WERE TO HAPPEN, THIS SPECIAL FIREWORKS FESTIVAL WOULD BE RUINED.
...!
YAMI...
BII
BII
BII
BOOM
KA-BOOM

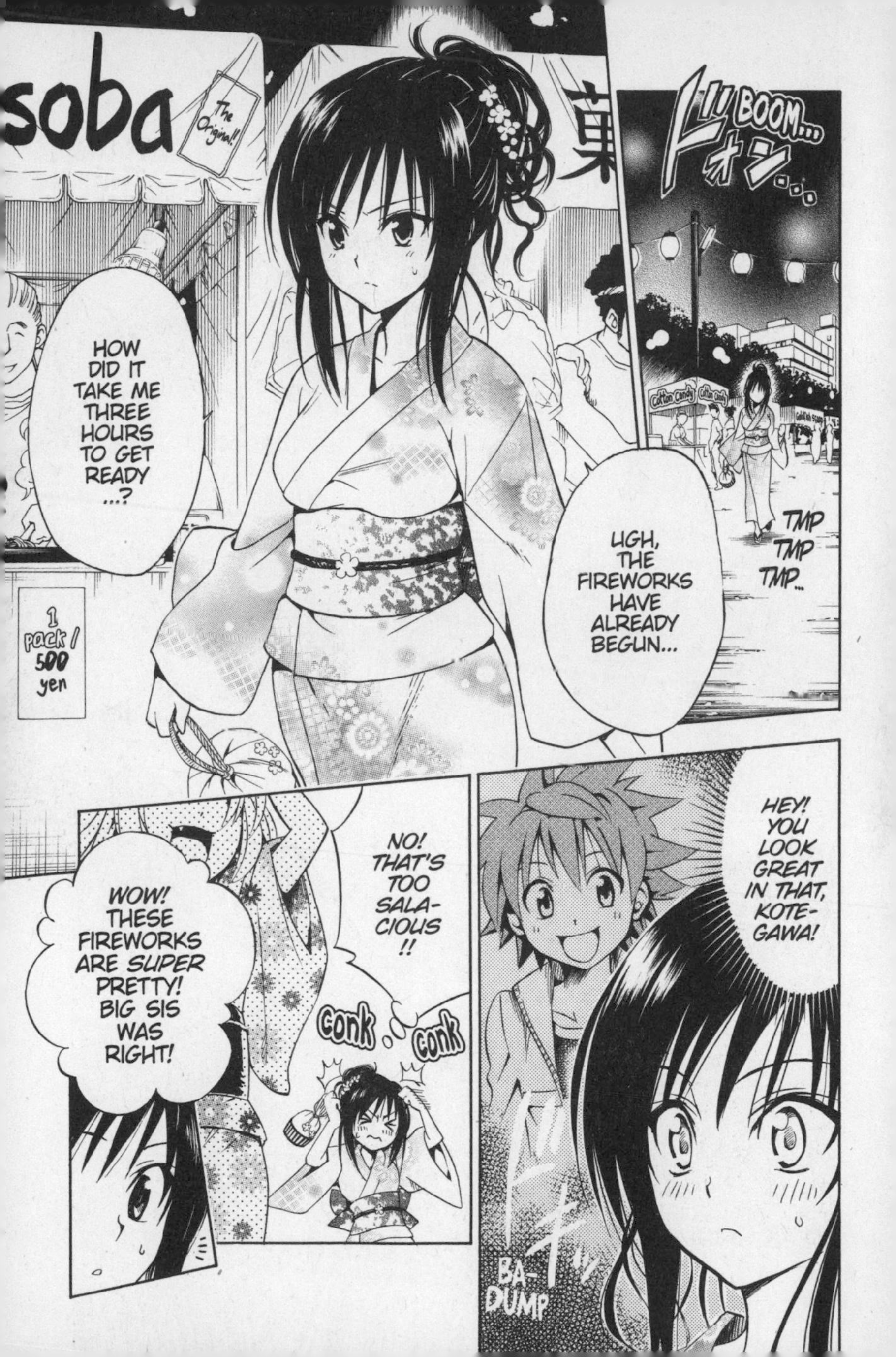
BOOM...
TMP TMP TMP...
Cotton Candy
UGH, THE FIREWORKS HAVE ALREADY BEGUN...
soba
The Original!!
HOW DID IT TAKE ME THREE HOURS TO GET READY ...?
1 pack / 500 yen
HEY! YOU LOOK GREAT IN THAT, KOTEGAWA!
BA-DUMP
NO! THAT'S TOO SALACIOUS !!
WOW! THESE FIREWORKS ARE SUPER PRETTY! BIG SIS WAS RIGHT!
conk conk

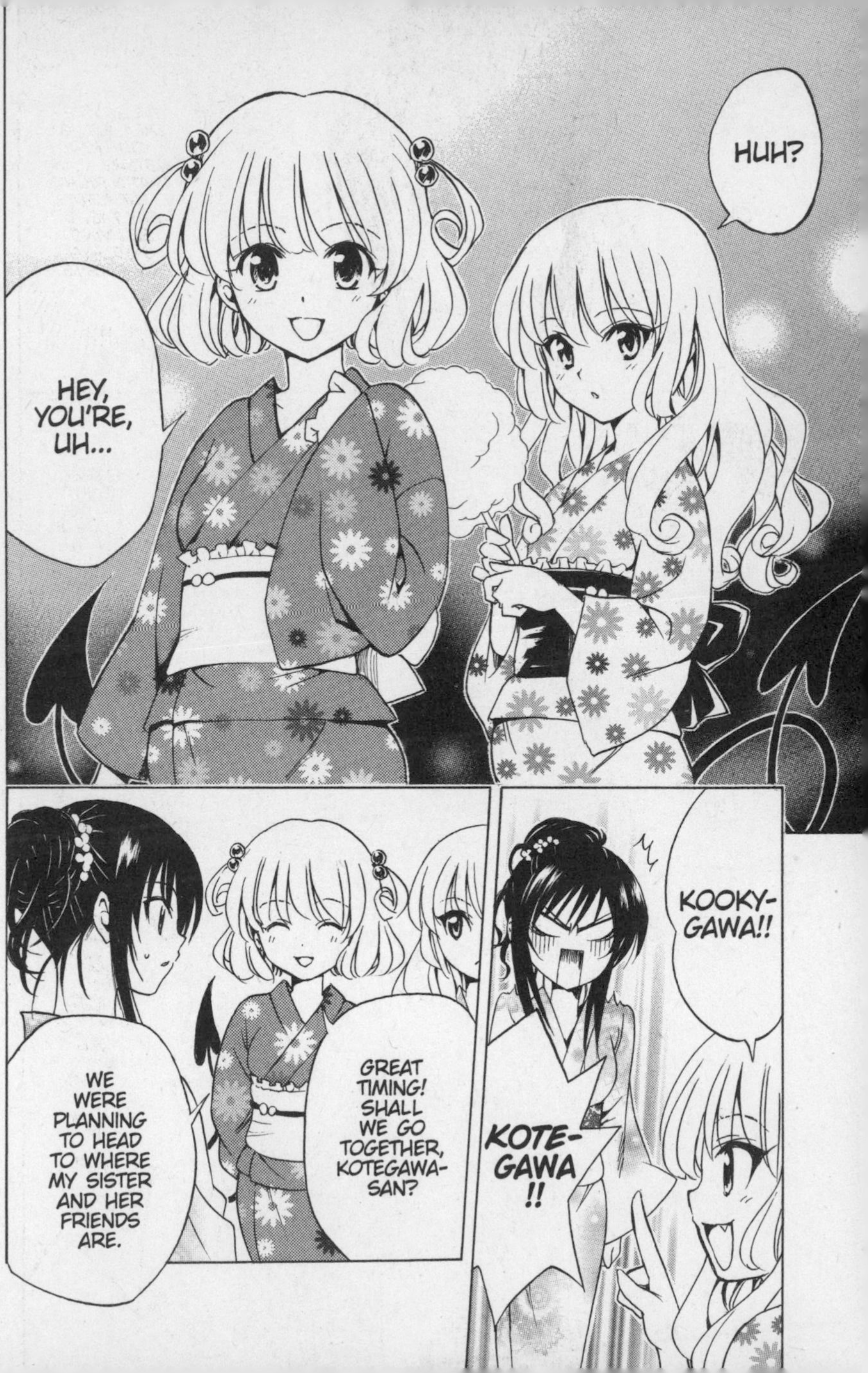
HUH?
HEY, YOU'RE, UH...
KOOKY-GAWA!!
KOTE-GAWA !!
WE WERE PLANNING TO HEAD TO WHERE MY SISTER AND HER FRIENDS ARE.
GREAT TIMING! SHALL WE GO TOGETHER, KOTEGAWA-SAN?

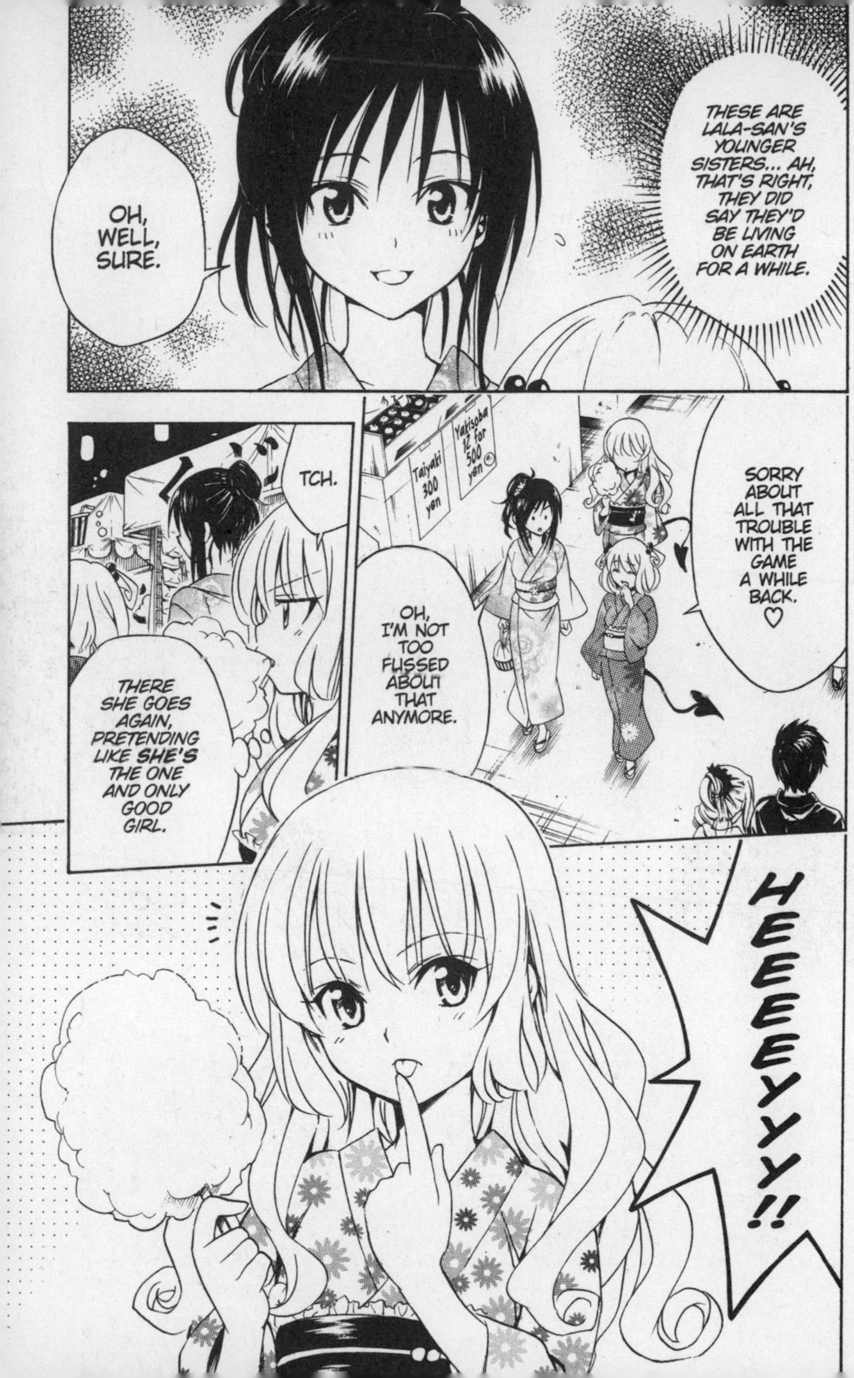
THESE ARE LALA-SAN'S YOUNGER SISTERS... AH, THAT'S RIGHT, THEY DID SAY THEY'D BE LIVING ON EARTH FOR A WHILE.
OH, WELL, SURE.
SORRY ABOUT ALL THAT TROUBLE WITH THE GAME A WHILE BACK. ♡
Yakisoba 12 for 500 yen
Taiyaki 300 yen
OH, I'M NOT TOO FUSSED ABOUT THAT ANYMORE.
TCH.
THERE SHE GOES AGAIN, PRETENDING LIKE SHE'S THE ONE AND ONLY GOOD GIRL.
HEEEEYYY!!

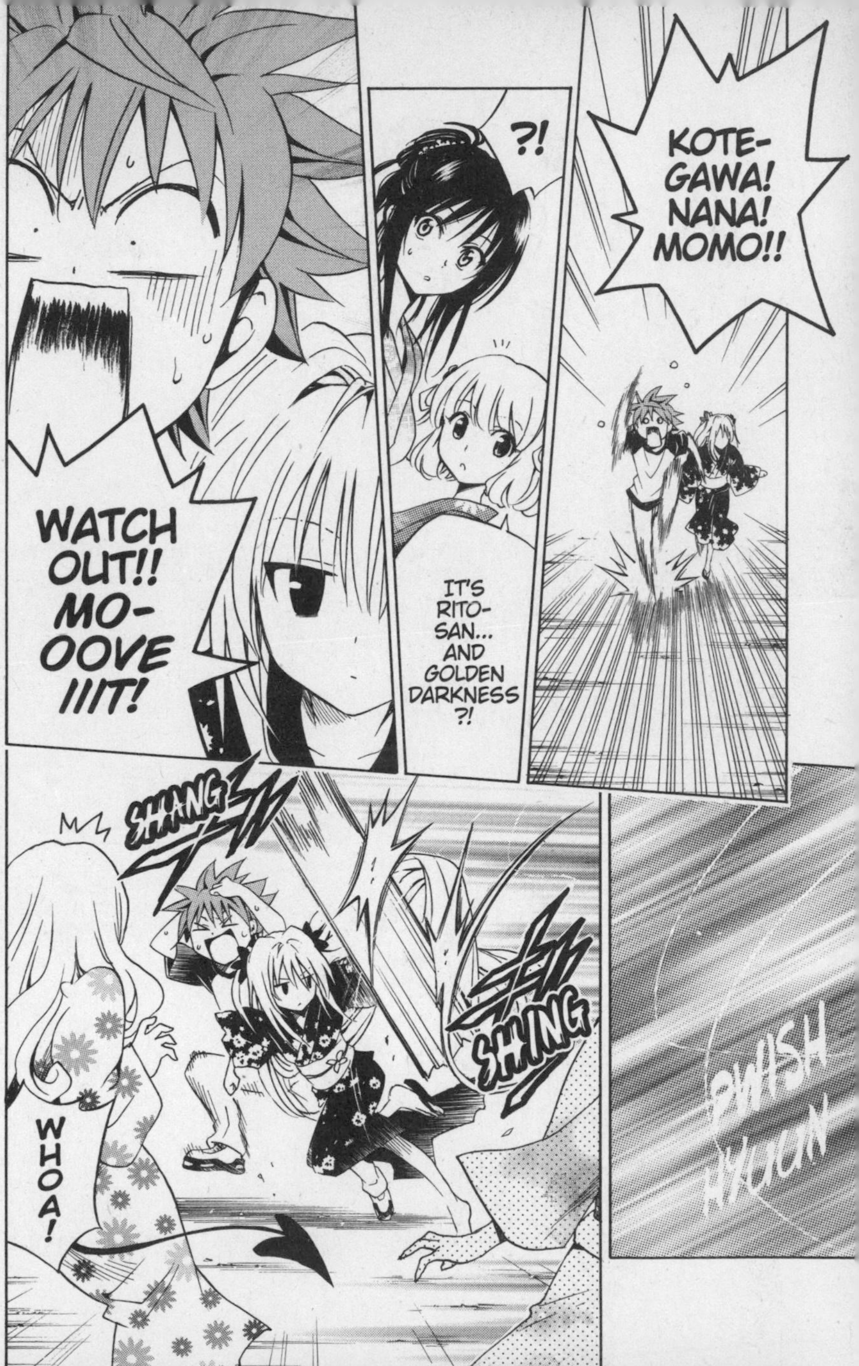
KOTE-GAWA! NANA! MOMO!!
?!
IT'S RITO-SAN... AND GOLDEN DARKNESS ?!
WATCH OUT!! MO-OOVE IIIT!
SHANG
SHING
WHOA!

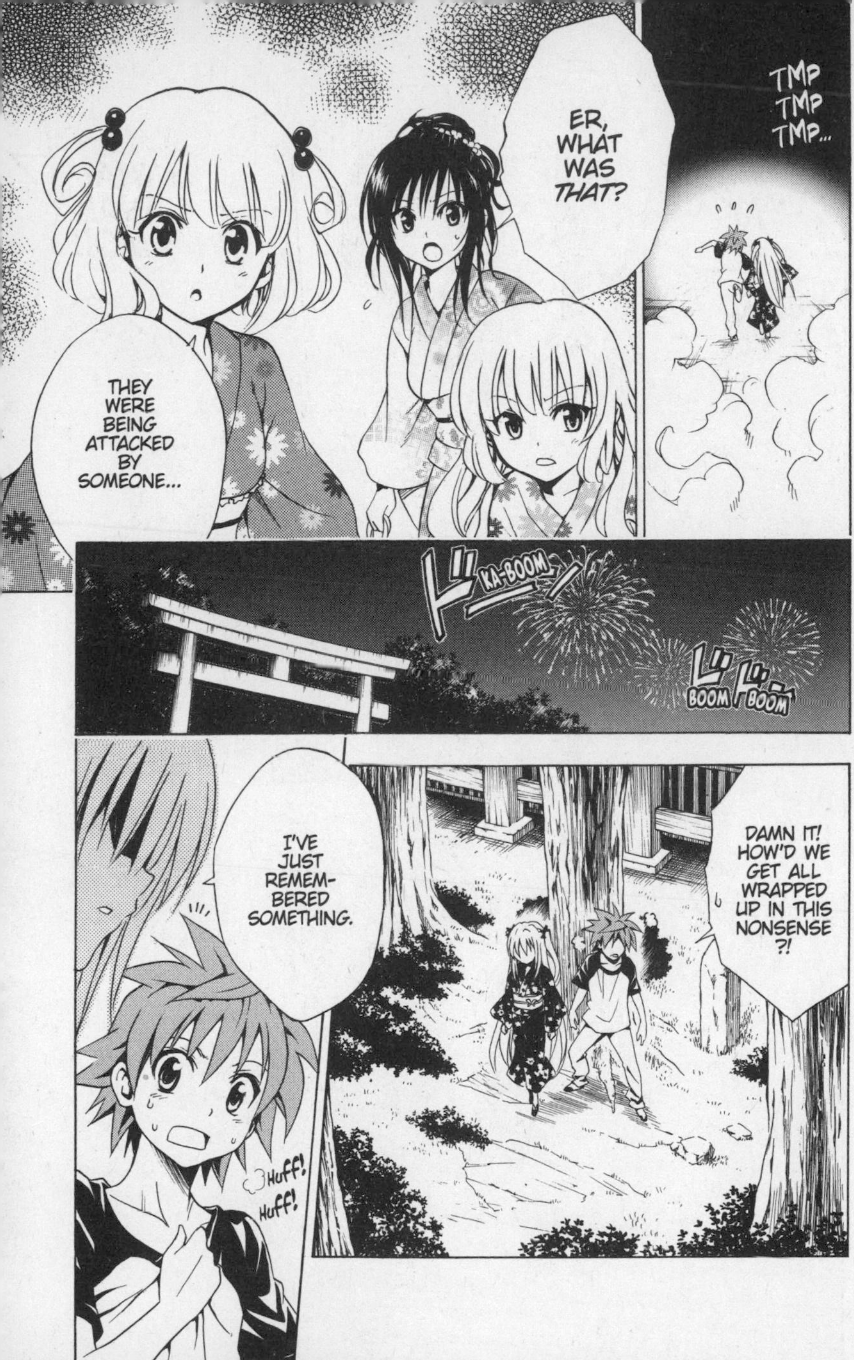
TMP TMP TMP...
ER, WHAT WAS THAT?
THEY WERE BEING ATTACKED BY SOMEONE...
KA-BOOM
BOOM BOOM
DAMN IT! HOW'D WE GET ALL WRAPPED UP IN THIS NONSENSE?!
I'VE JUST REMEM-BERED SOMETHING.
Huff! Huff!

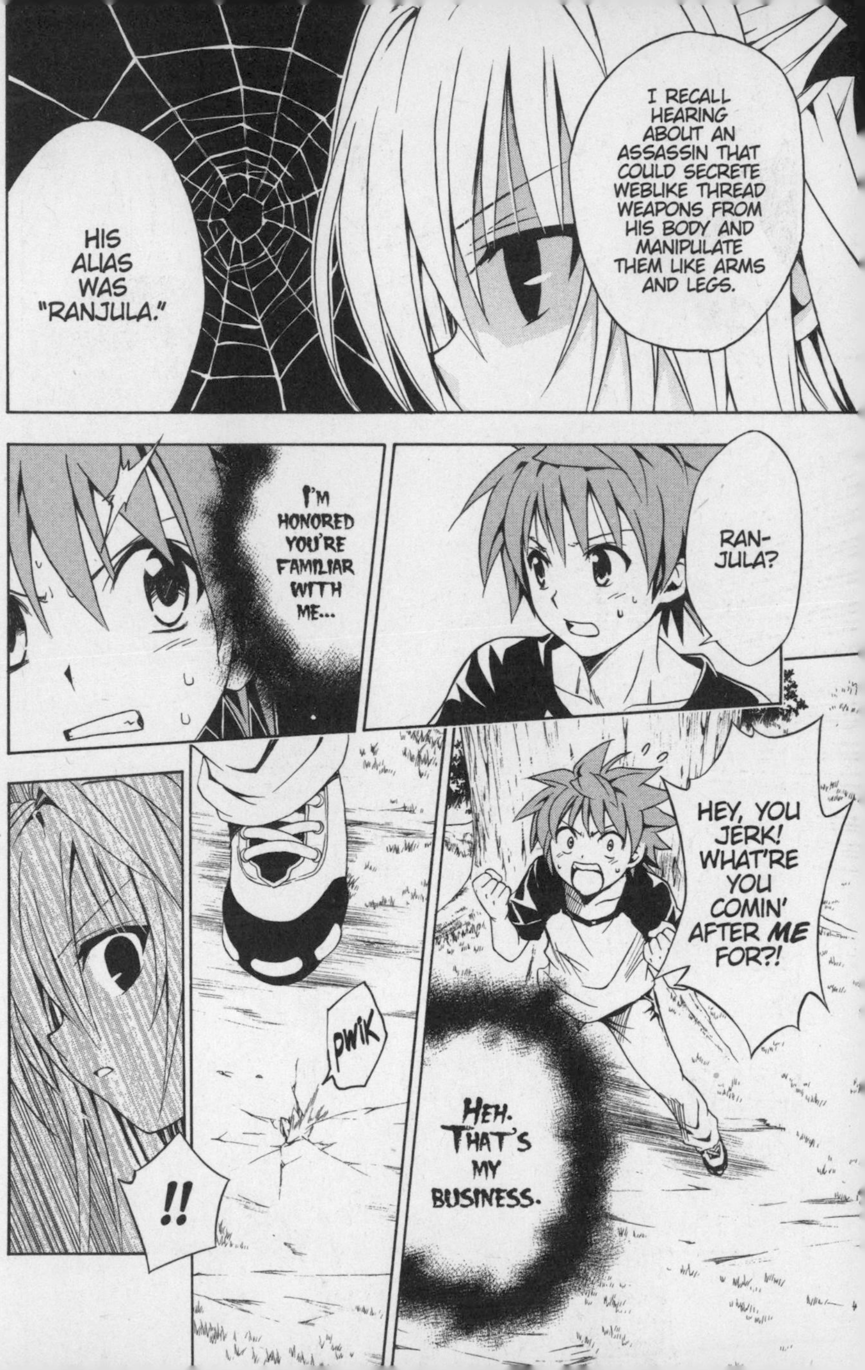
I RECALL HEARING ABOUT AN ASSASSIN THAT COULD SECRETE WEBLIKE THREAD WEAPONS FROM HIS BODY AND MANIPULATE THEM LIKE ARMS AND LEGS.
HIS ALIAS WAS "RANJULA."
RAN-JULA?
I'M HONORED YOU'RE FAMILIAR WITH ME...
HEY, YOU JERK! WHAT'RE YOU COMIN' AFTER *ME* FOR?!
HEH. THAT'S MY BUSINESS.
pwik
!!

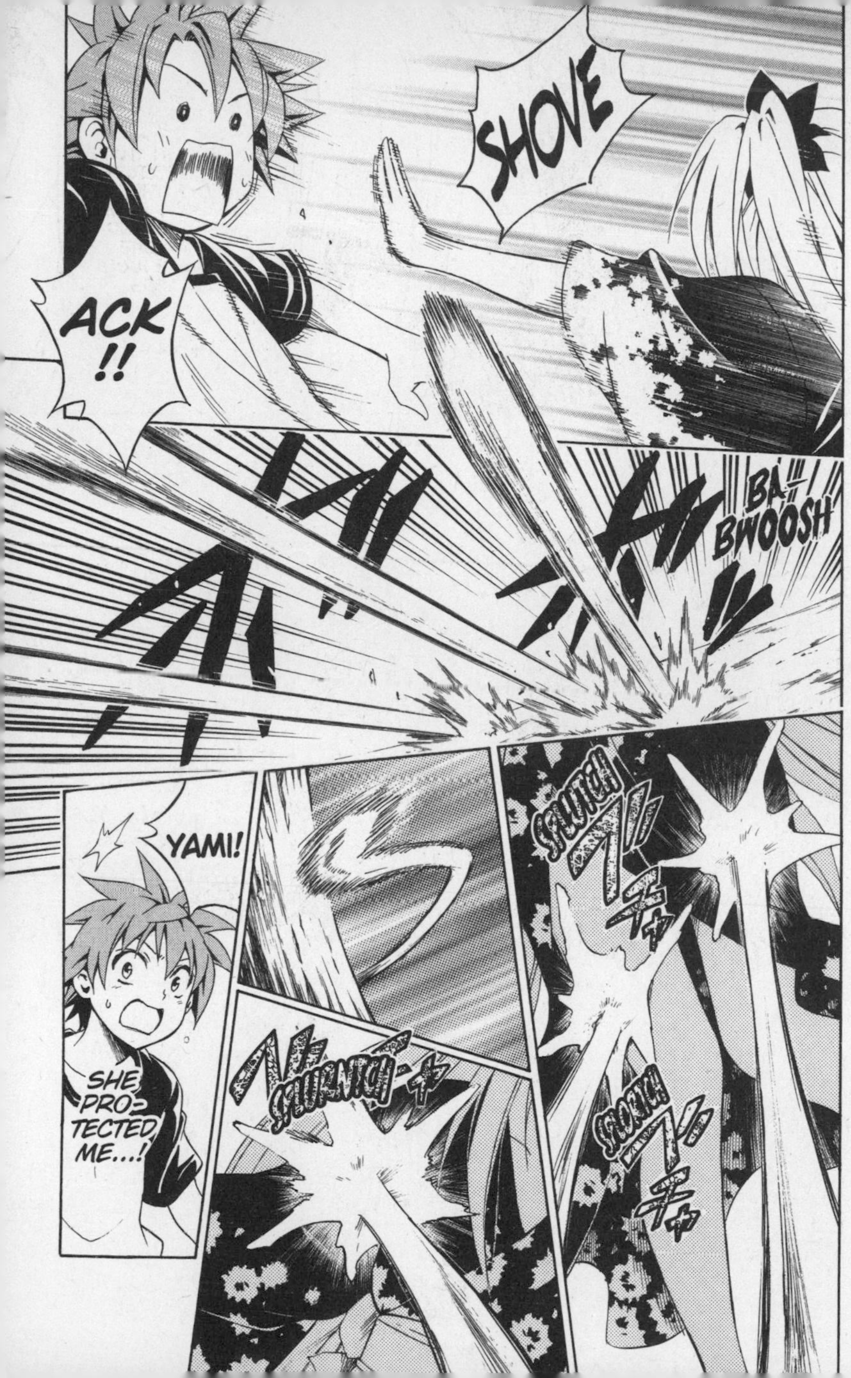
SHOVE
ACK!!
BA-BWOOSH
SPLUTCH
SPLORTCH
YAMI!
SHE PROTECTED ME...!

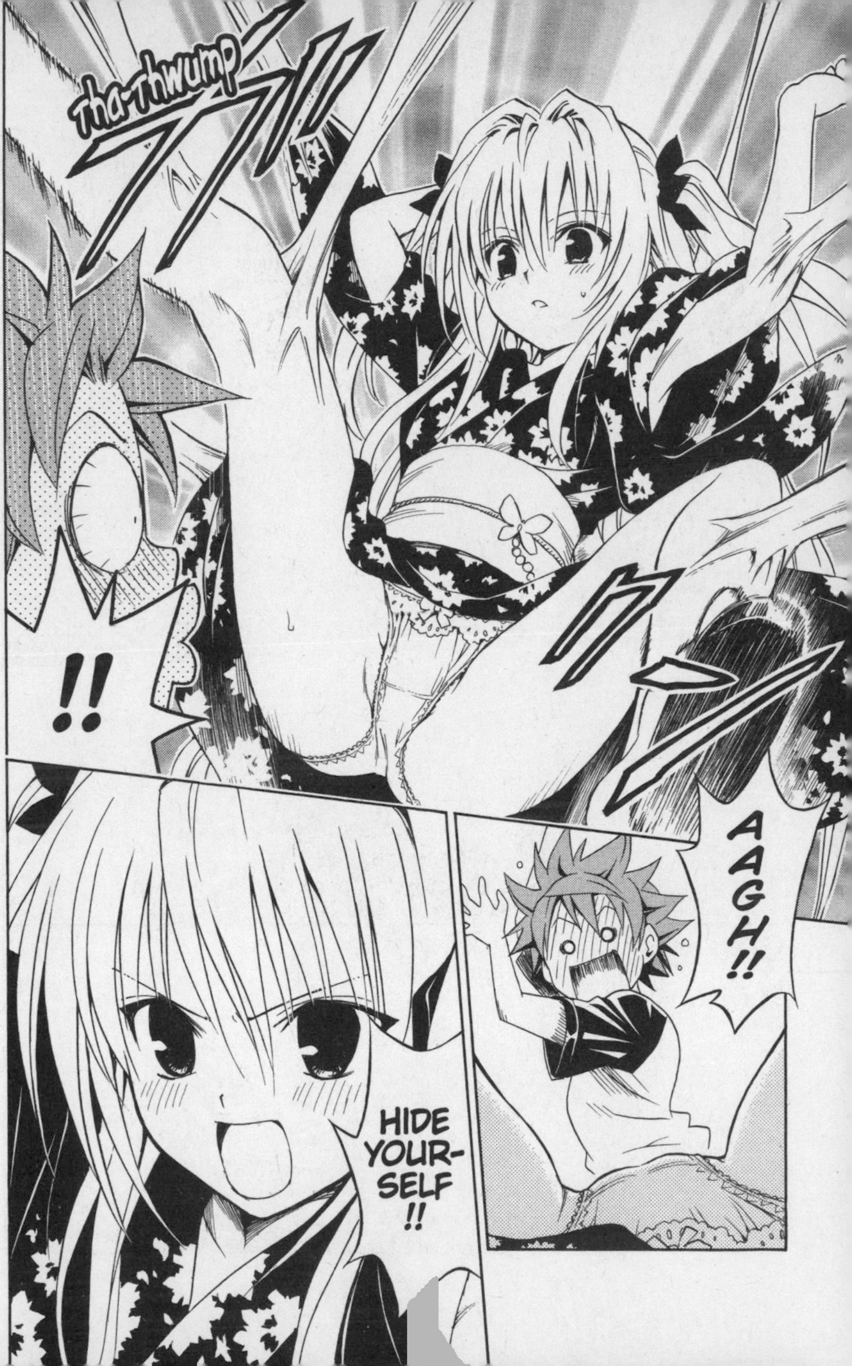
tha-thwump
!!
AAGH!!
HIDE YOURSELF!!

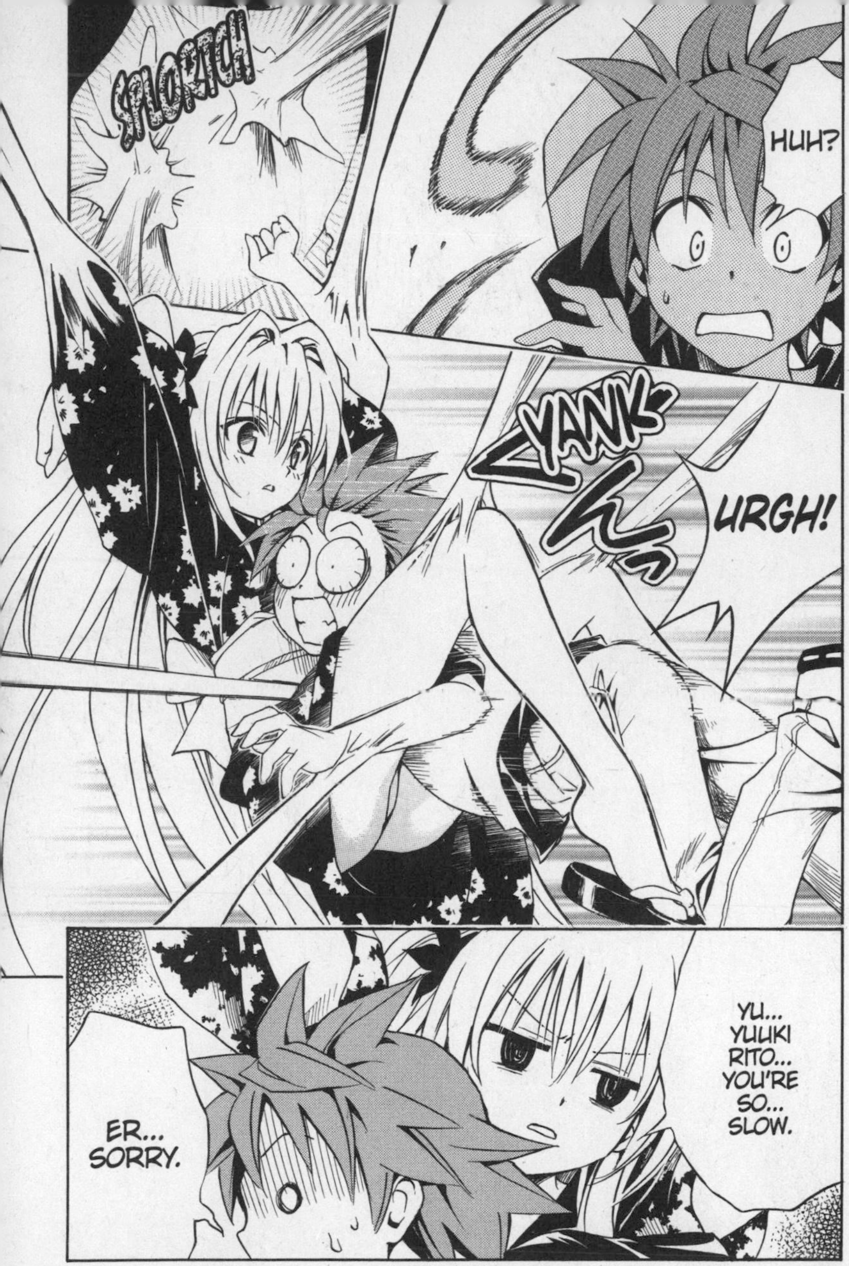
HUH?
SPLORTCH
YANK
URGH!
YU... YUUKI RITO... YOU'RE SO... SLOW.
ER... SORRY.

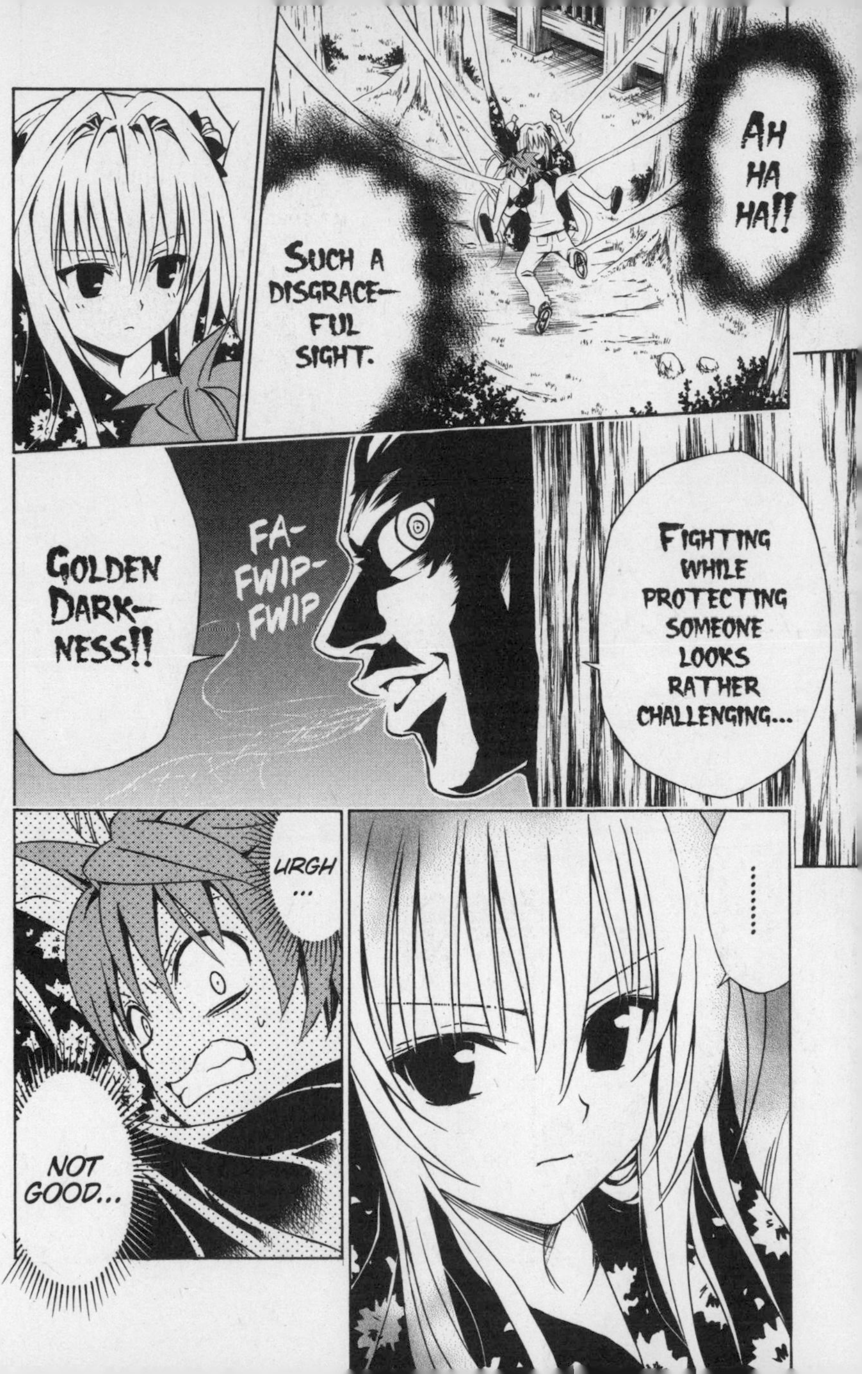
AH HA HA!!
SUCH A DISGRACEFUL SIGHT.
FIGHTING WHILE PROTECTING SOMEONE LOOKS RATHER CHALLENGING...
FA-FWIP-FWIP
GOLDEN DARKNESS!!
......
URGH ...
NOT GOOD...

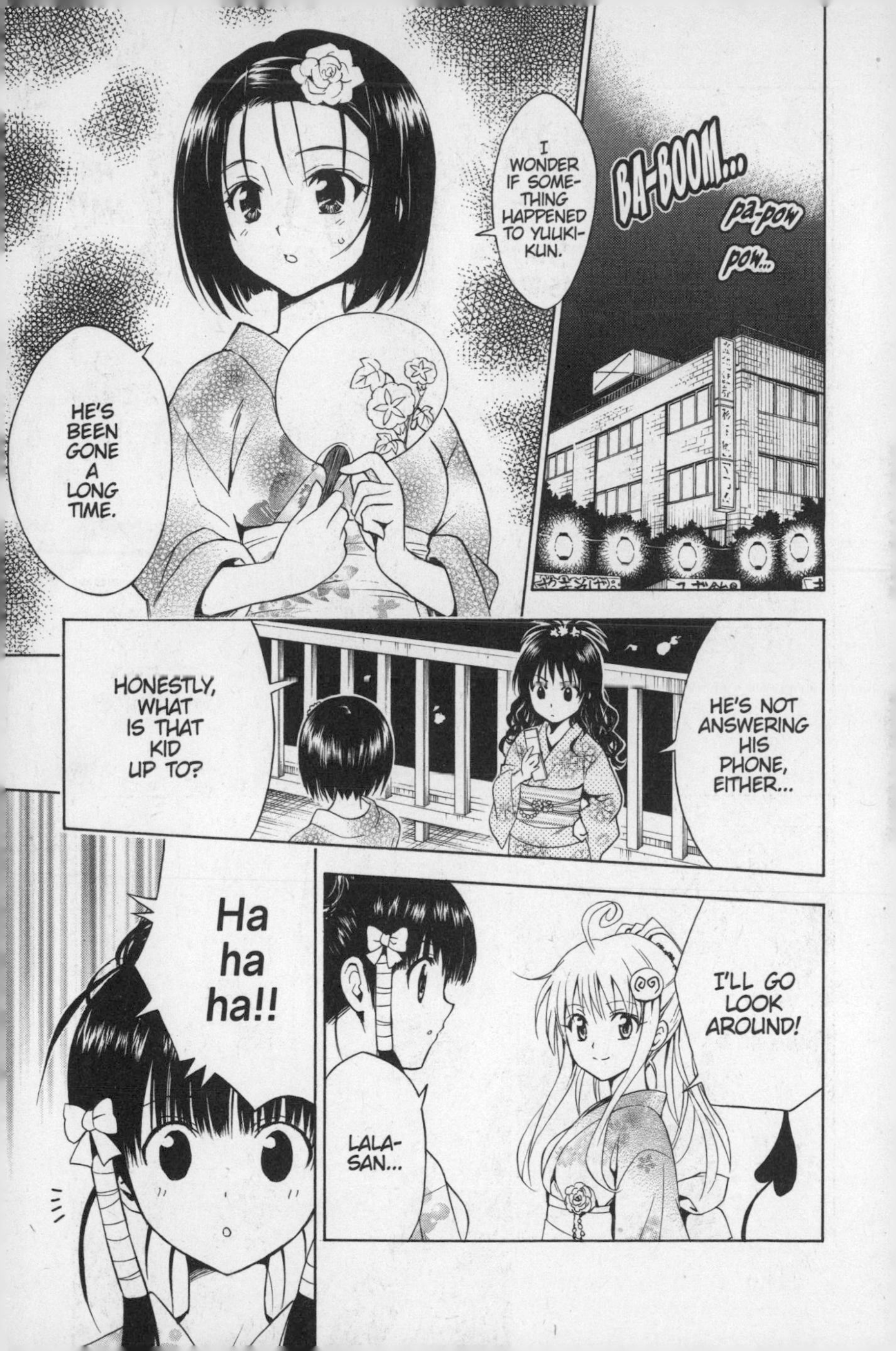
BA-BOOM...
pa-pow pow...
I WONDER IF SOME-THING HAPPENED TO YUUKI-KUN.
HE'S BEEN GONE A LONG TIME.
HE'S NOT ANSWERING HIS PHONE, EITHER...
HONESTLY, WHAT IS THAT KID UP TO?
I'LL GO LOOK AROUND!
LALA-SAN...
Ha ha ha!!

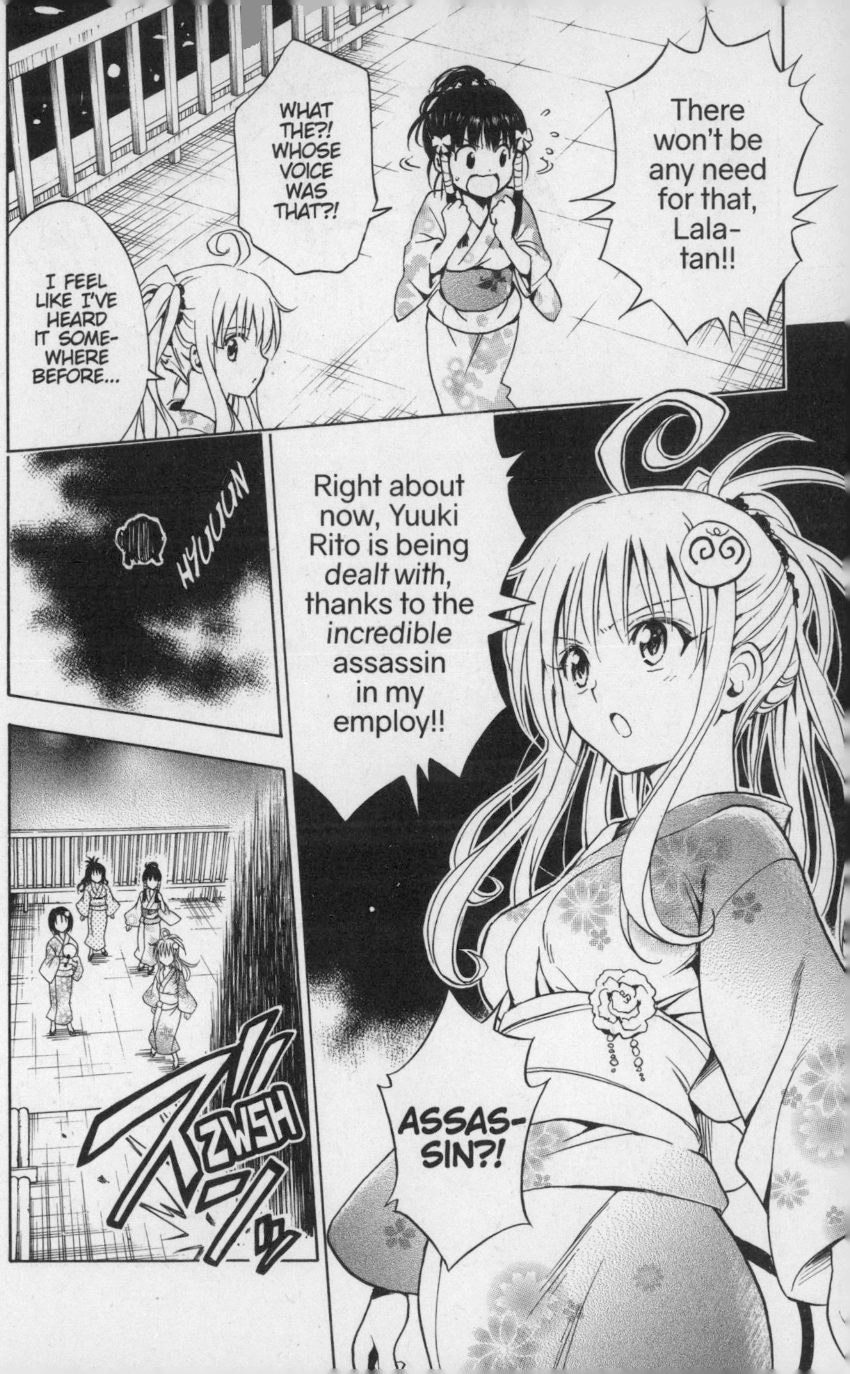

There won't be any need for that, Lala-tan!!
WHAT THE?! WHOSE VOICE WAS THAT?!
I FEEL LIKE I'VE HEARD IT SOME-WHERE BEFORE...
Right about now, Yuuki Rito is being *dealt with*, thanks to the *incredible* assassin in my employ!!
ASSAS-SIN?!
HYUUUN
ZWSH

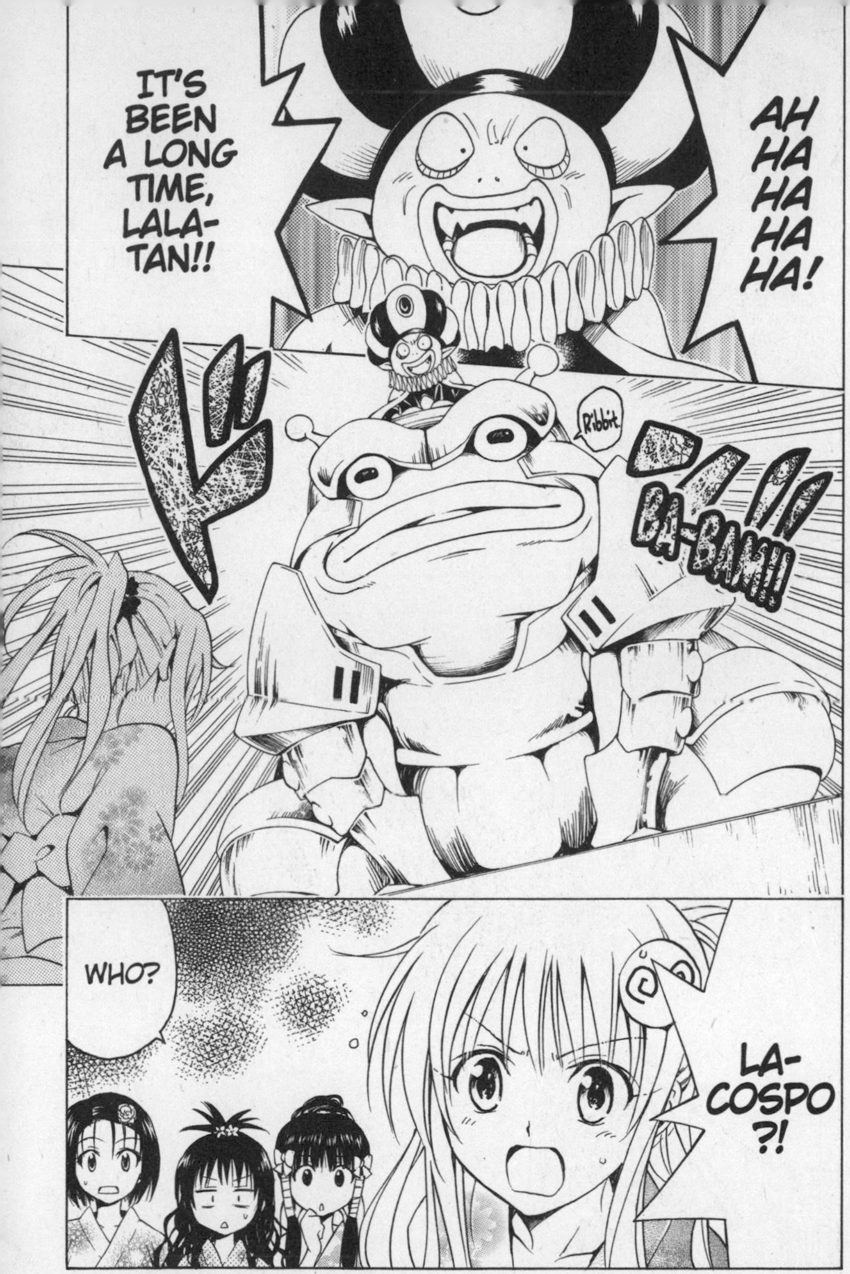
AH HA HA HA HA HA!
IT'S BEEN A LONG TIME, LALA-TAN!!
Ribbit
BA-BAM!!
LA-COSPO?!
WHO?

To LOVE Ru

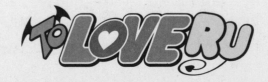

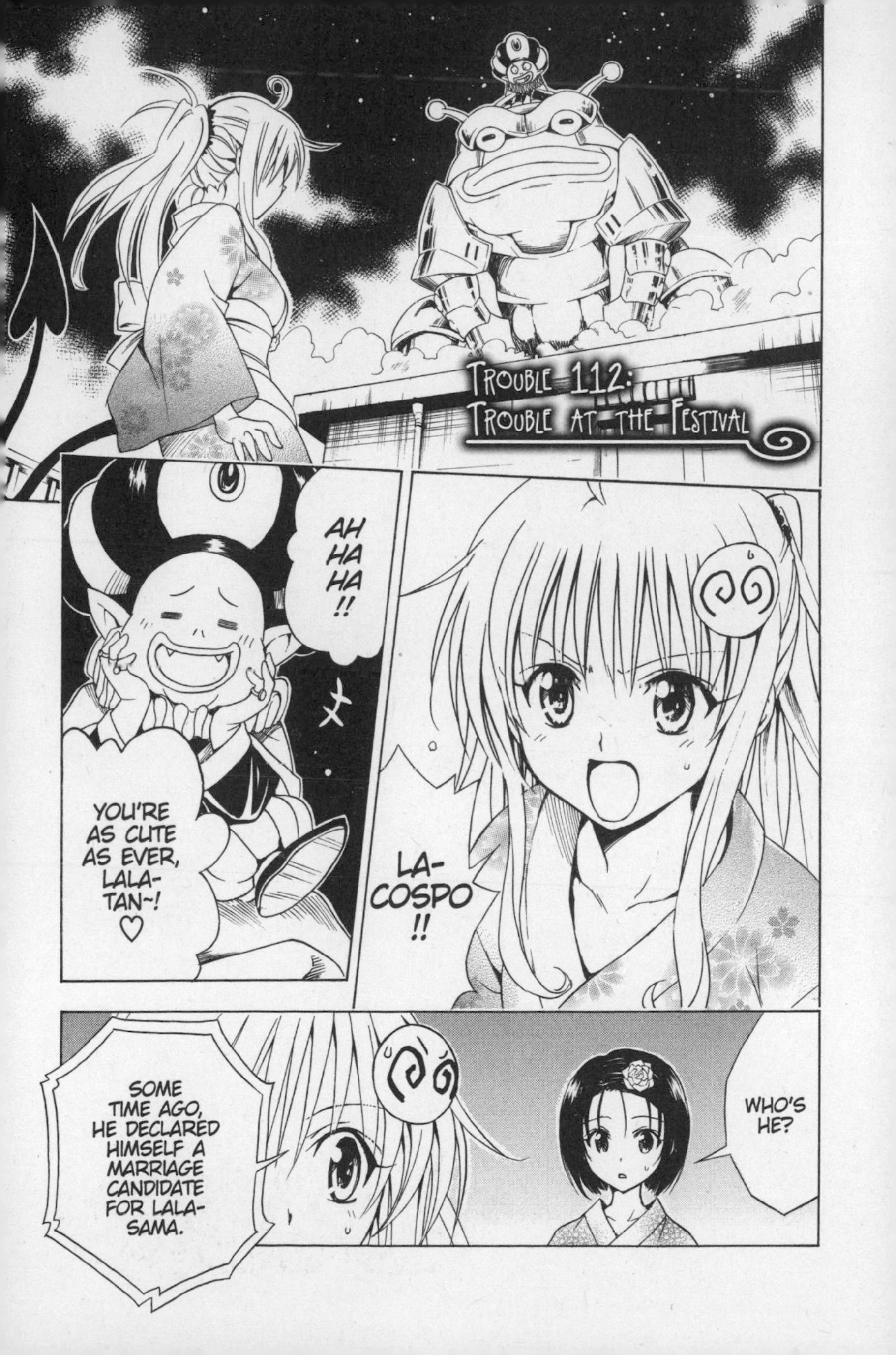
TROUBLE 112:
TROUBLE AT THE FESTIVAL
LA-COSPO!!
AH HA HA!!
YOU'RE AS CUTE AS EVER, LALA-TAN~! ♡
WHO'S HE?
SOME TIME AGO, HE DECLARED HIMSELF A MARRIAGE CANDIDATE FOR LALA-SAMA.

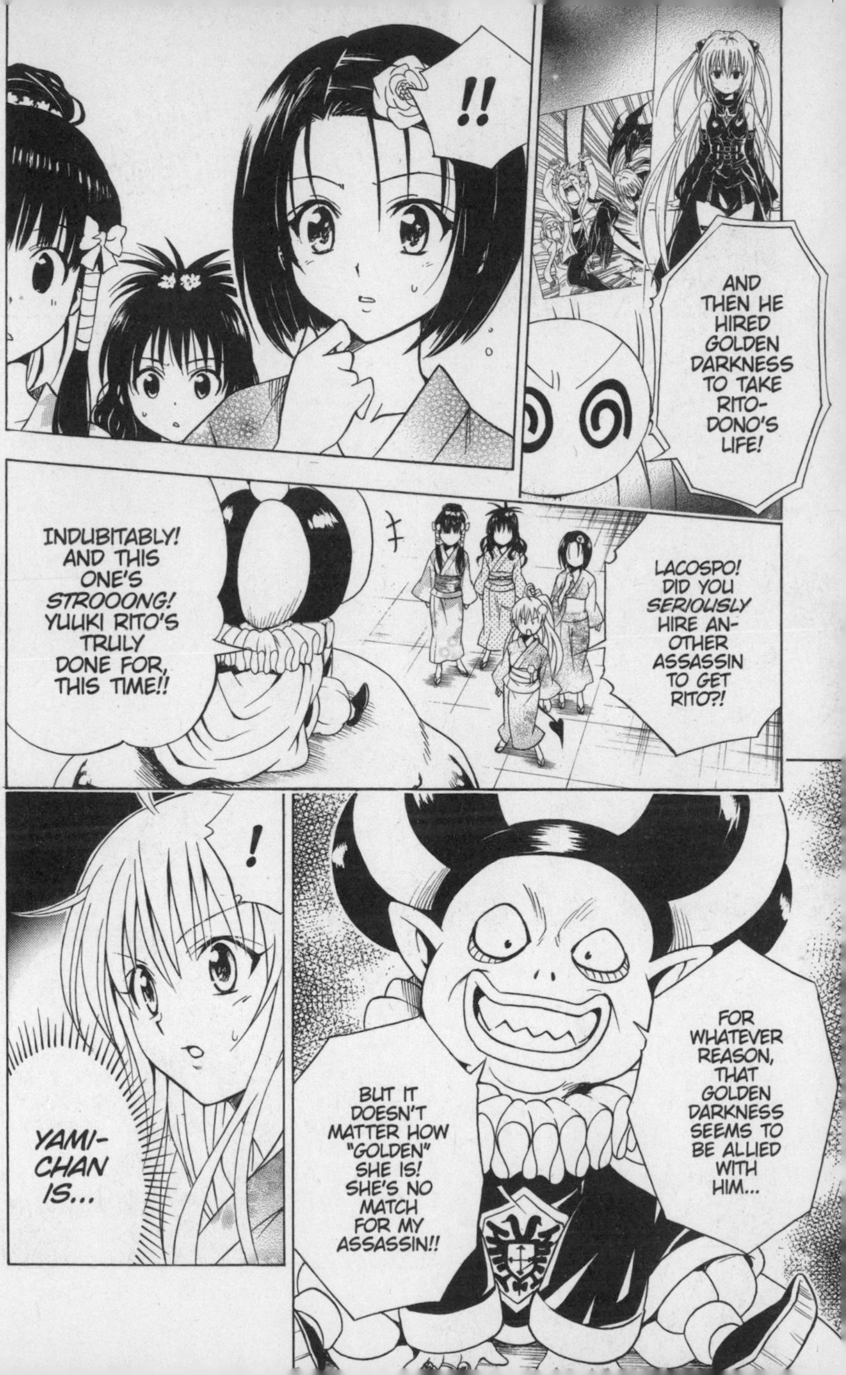
AND THEN HE HIRED GOLDEN DARKNESS TO TAKE RITO-DONO'S LIFE!
!!
LACOSPO! DID YOU *SERIOUSLY* HIRE AN-OTHER ASSASSIN TO GET RITO?!
INDUBITABLY! AND THIS ONE'S *STROOONG!* YUUKI RITO'S TRULY DONE FOR, THIS TIME!!
FOR WHATEVER REASON, THAT GOLDEN DARKNESS SEEMS TO BE ALLIED WITH HIM...
BUT IT DOESN'T MATTER HOW "GOLDEN" SHE IS! SHE'S NO MATCH FOR MY ASSASSIN!!
!
YAMI-CHAN IS...

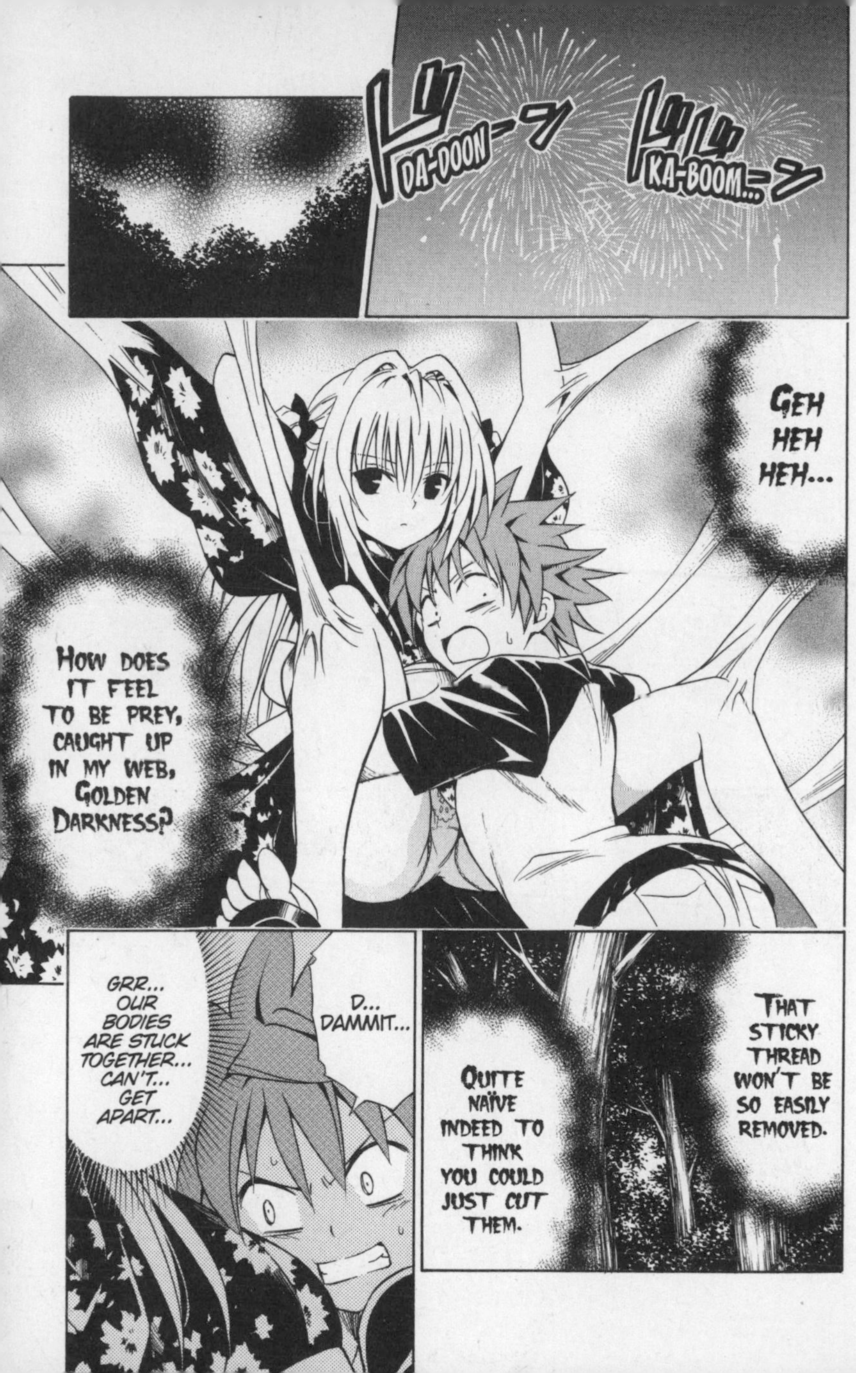
KA-BOOM...
DA-DOON
GEH HEH HEH...
HOW DOES IT FEEL TO BE PREY, CAUGHT UP IN MY WEB, GOLDEN DARKNESS?
THAT STICKY THREAD WON'T BE SO EASILY REMOVED.
QUITE NAÏVE INDEED TO THINK YOU COULD JUST CUT THEM.
D... DAMMIT...
GRR... OUR BODIES ARE STUCK TOGETHER... CAN'T... GET APART...

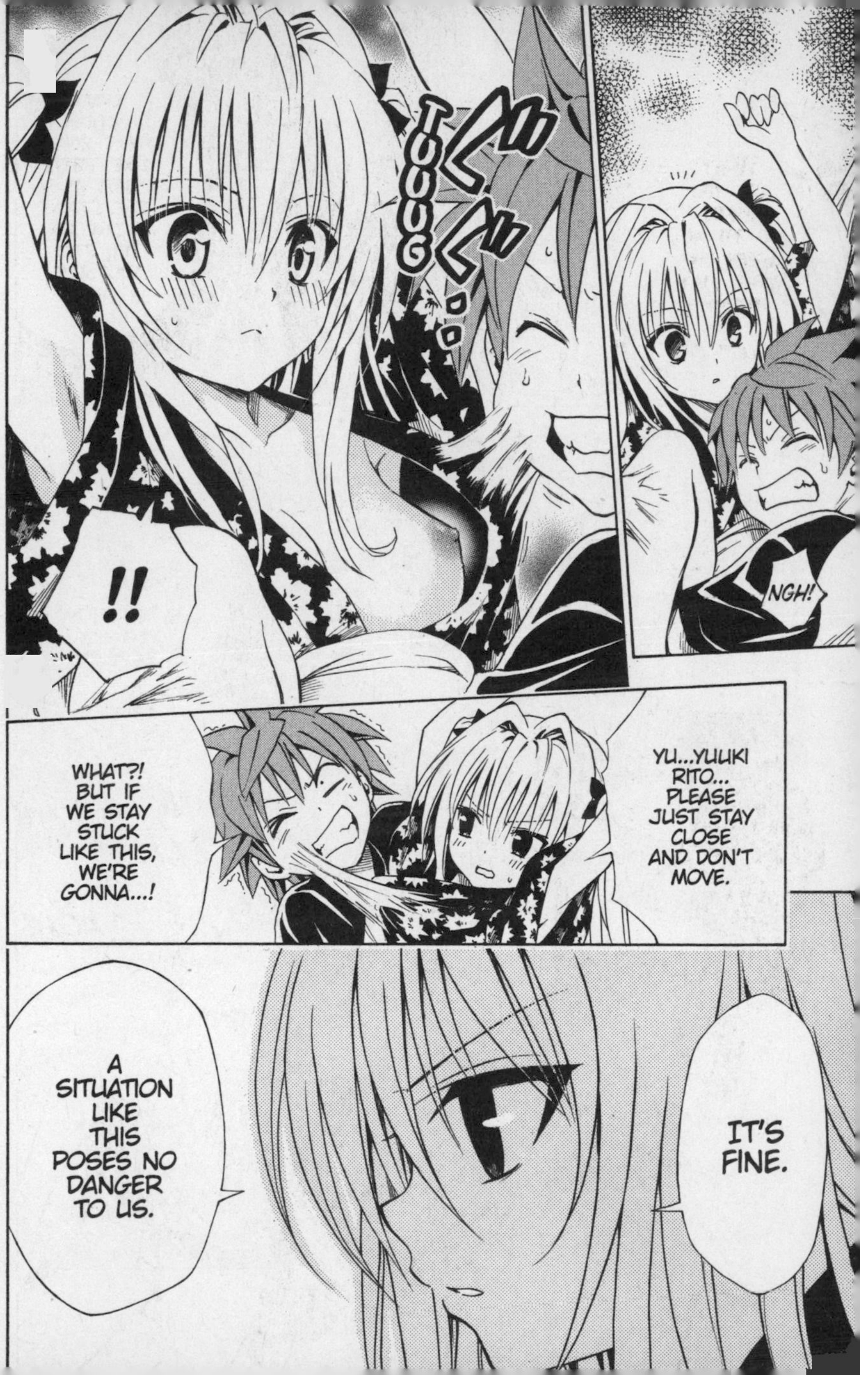
NGH!
TUUUG
!!
YU...YUUKI RITO... PLEASE JUST STAY CLOSE AND DON'T MOVE.
WHAT?! BUT IF WE STAY STUCK LIKE THIS, WE'RE GONNA...!
IT'S FINE.
A SITUATION LIKE THIS POSES NO DANGER TO US.

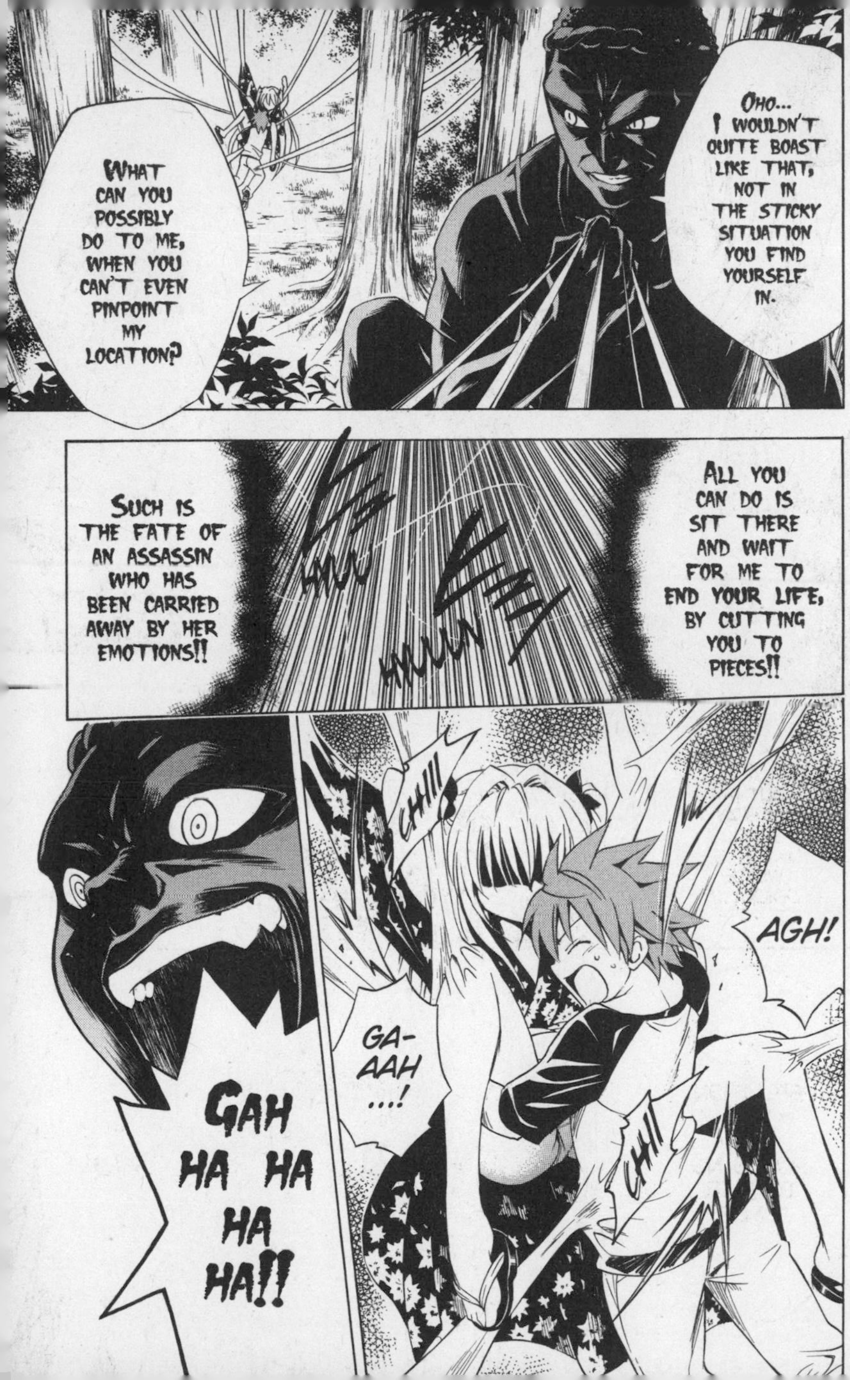
OHO... I WOULDN'T QUITE BOAST LIKE THAT, NOT IN THE STICKY SITUATION YOU FIND YOURSELF IN.
WHAT CAN YOU POSSIBLY DO TO ME, WHEN YOU CAN'T EVEN PINPOINT MY LOCATION?
ALL YOU CAN DO IS SIT THERE AND WAIT FOR ME TO END YOUR LIFE, BY CUTTING YOU TO PIECES!!
SUCH IS THE FATE OF AN ASSASSIN WHO HAS BEEN CARRIED AWAY BY HER EMOTIONS!!
KYUUU
KYUUUN
CHI!!
AGH!
GA-AAH ...!
CHI!!
GAH HA HA HA HA!!

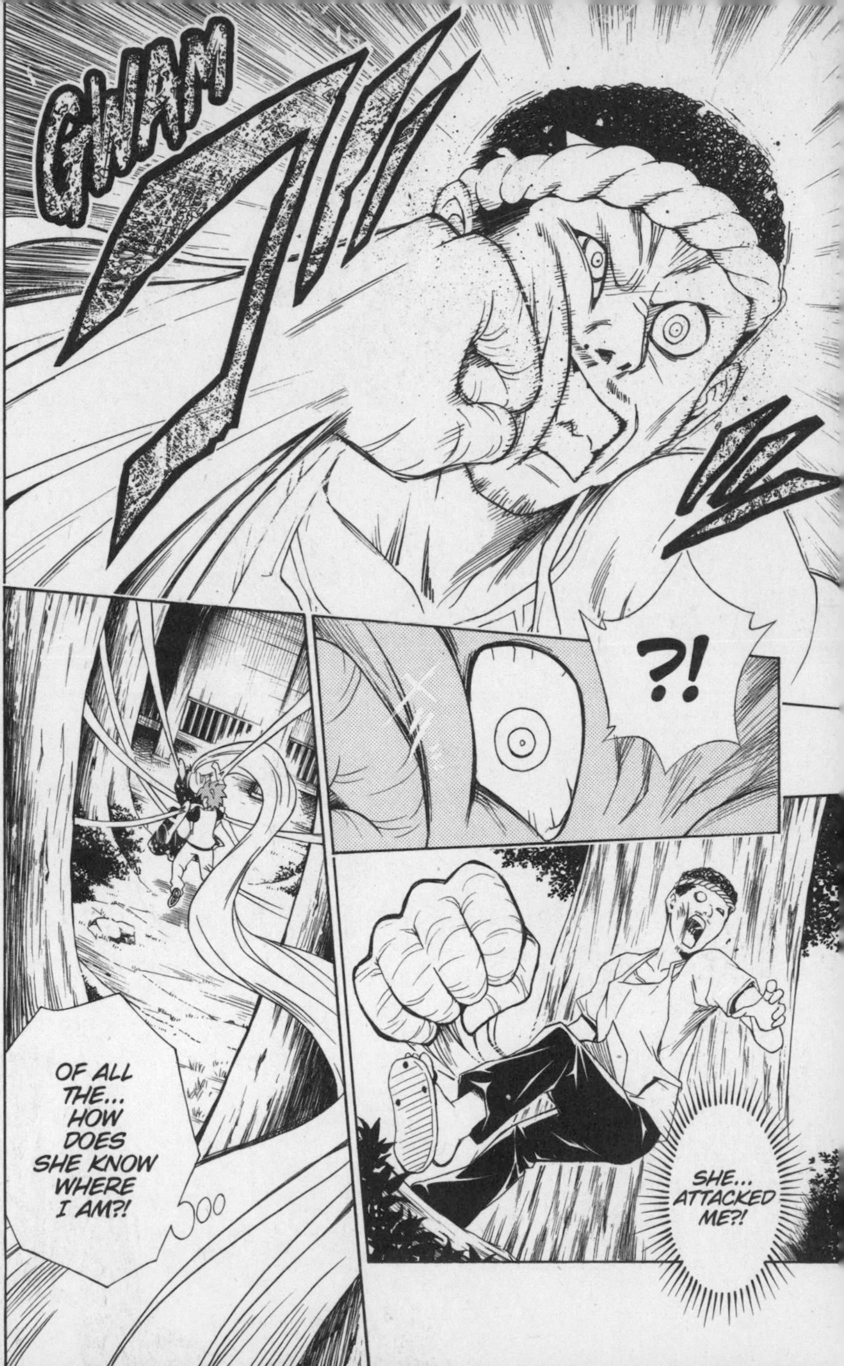
GWAM
?!
SHE... ATTACKED ME?!
OF ALL THE... HOW DOES SHE KNOW WHERE I AM?!

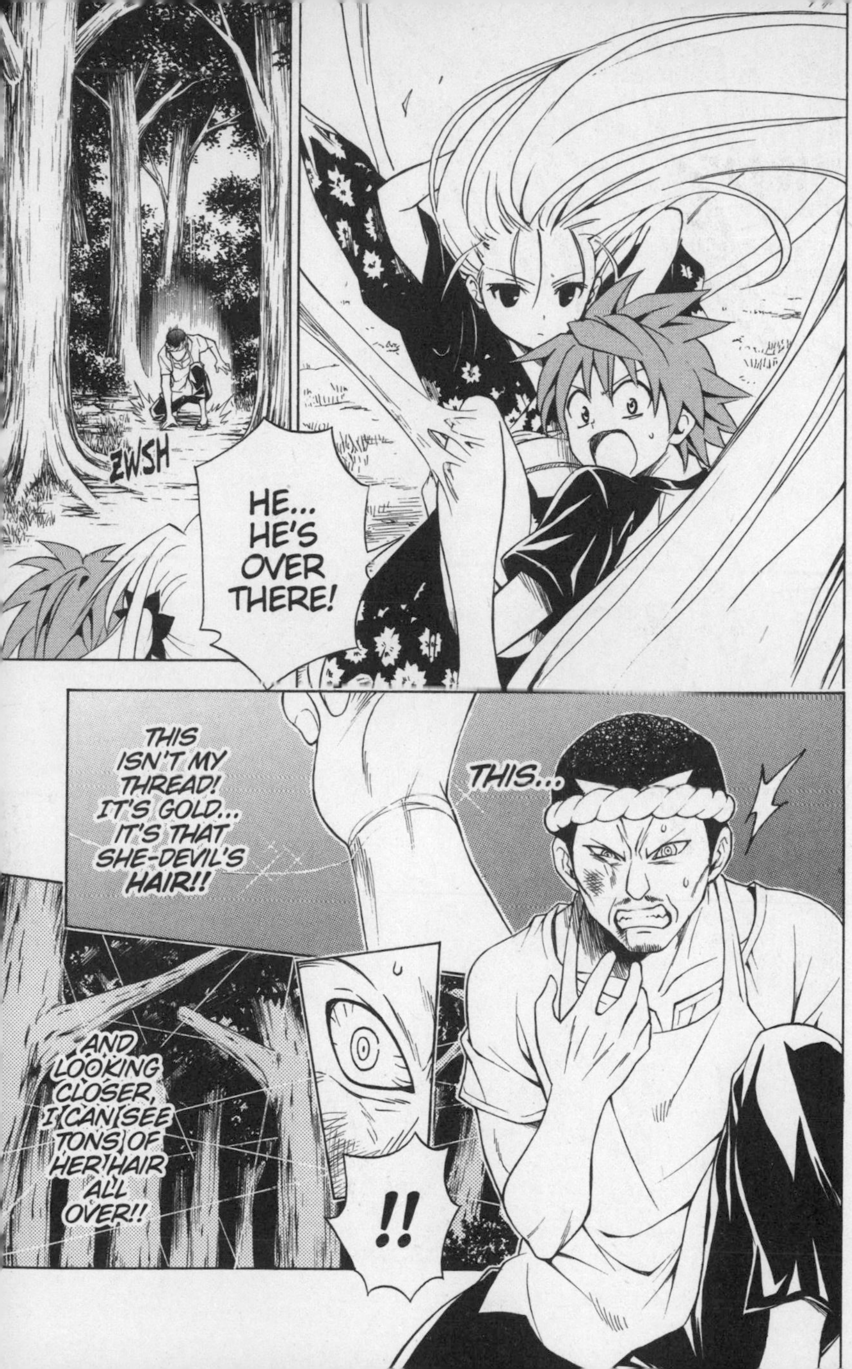
HE... HE'S OVER THERE!
ZWSH
THIS...
THIS ISN'T MY THREAD! IT'S GOLD... IT'S THAT SHE-DEVIL'S HAIR!!
!!
AND LOOKING CLOSER, I CAN SEE TONS OF HER HAIR ALL OVER!!

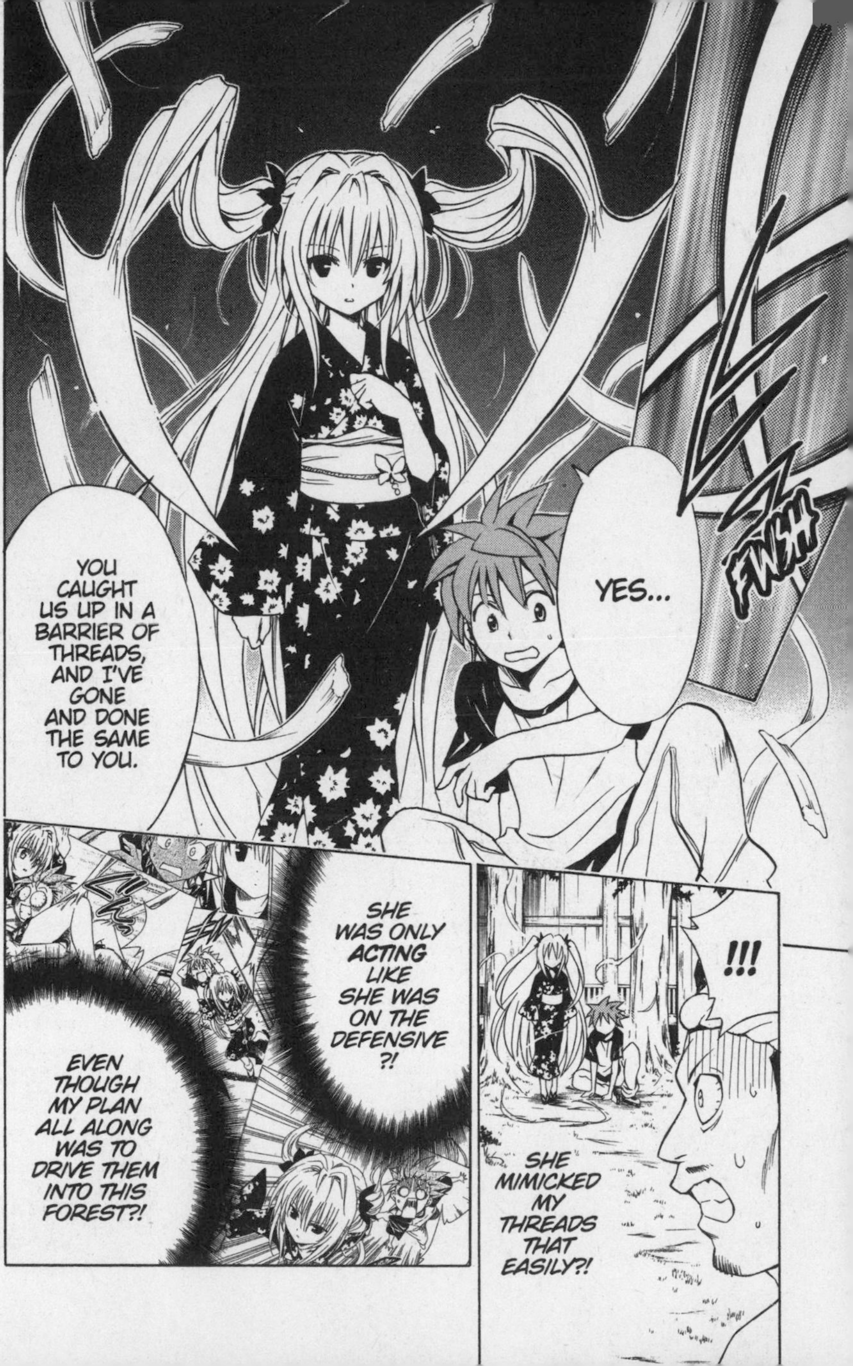
FWSH
YES...
YOU CAUGHT US UP IN A BARRIER OF THREADS, AND I'VE GONE AND DONE THE SAME TO YOU.
!!!
SHE MIMICKED MY THREADS THAT EASILY?!
SHE WAS ONLY ACTING LIKE SHE WAS ON THE DEFENSIVE?!
EVEN THOUGH MY PLAN ALL ALONG WAS TO DRIVE THEM INTO THIS FOREST?!

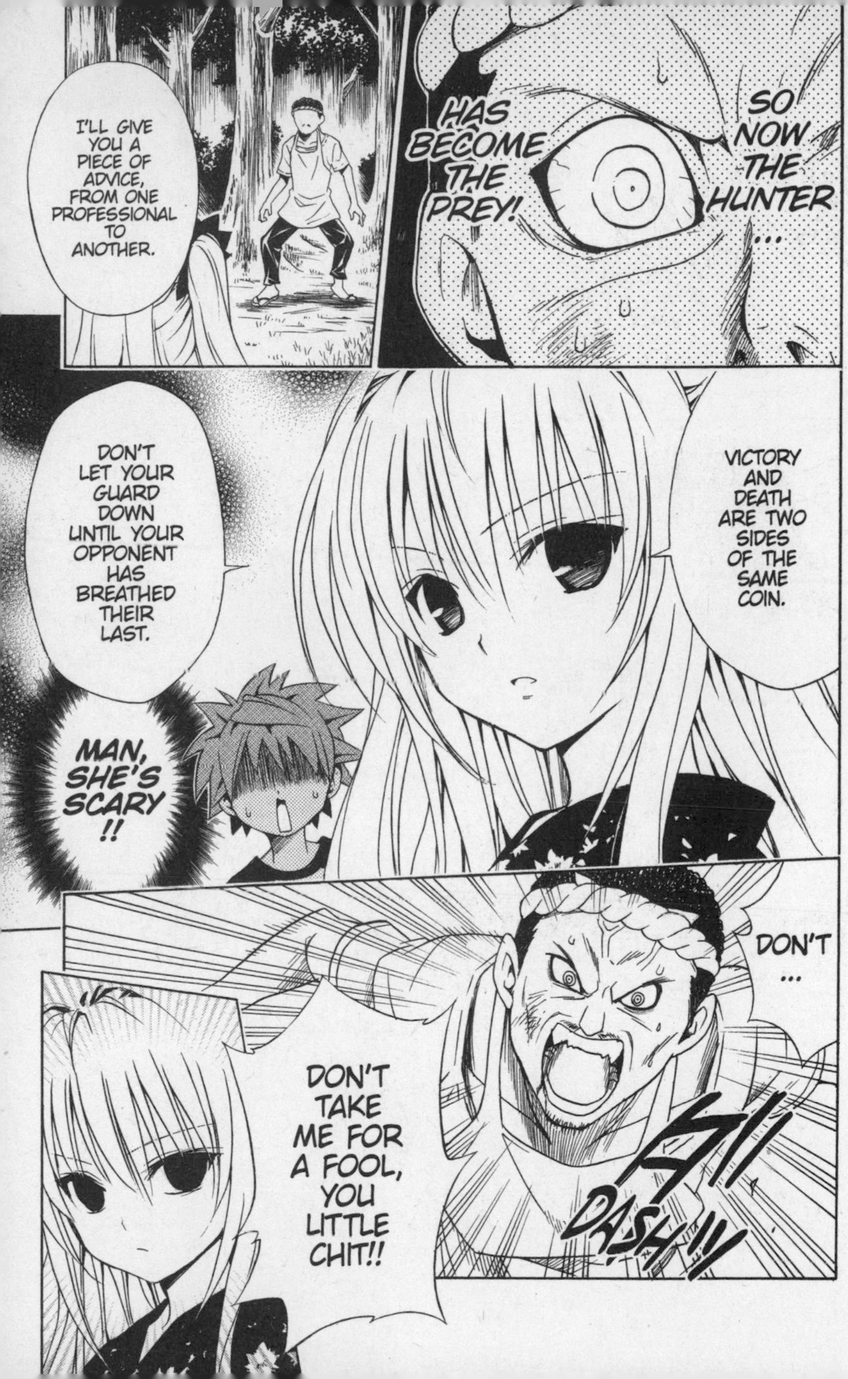
SO NOW THE HUNTER...
HAS BECOME THE PREY!
I'LL GIVE YOU A PIECE OF ADVICE, FROM ONE PROFESSIONAL TO ANOTHER.
VICTORY AND DEATH ARE TWO SIDES OF THE SAME COIN.
DON'T LET YOUR GUARD DOWN UNTIL YOUR OPPONENT HAS BREATHED THEIR LAST.
MAN, SHE'S SCARY!!
DON'T...
DON'T TAKE ME FOR A FOOL, YOU LITTLE CHIT!!
DASH!!!

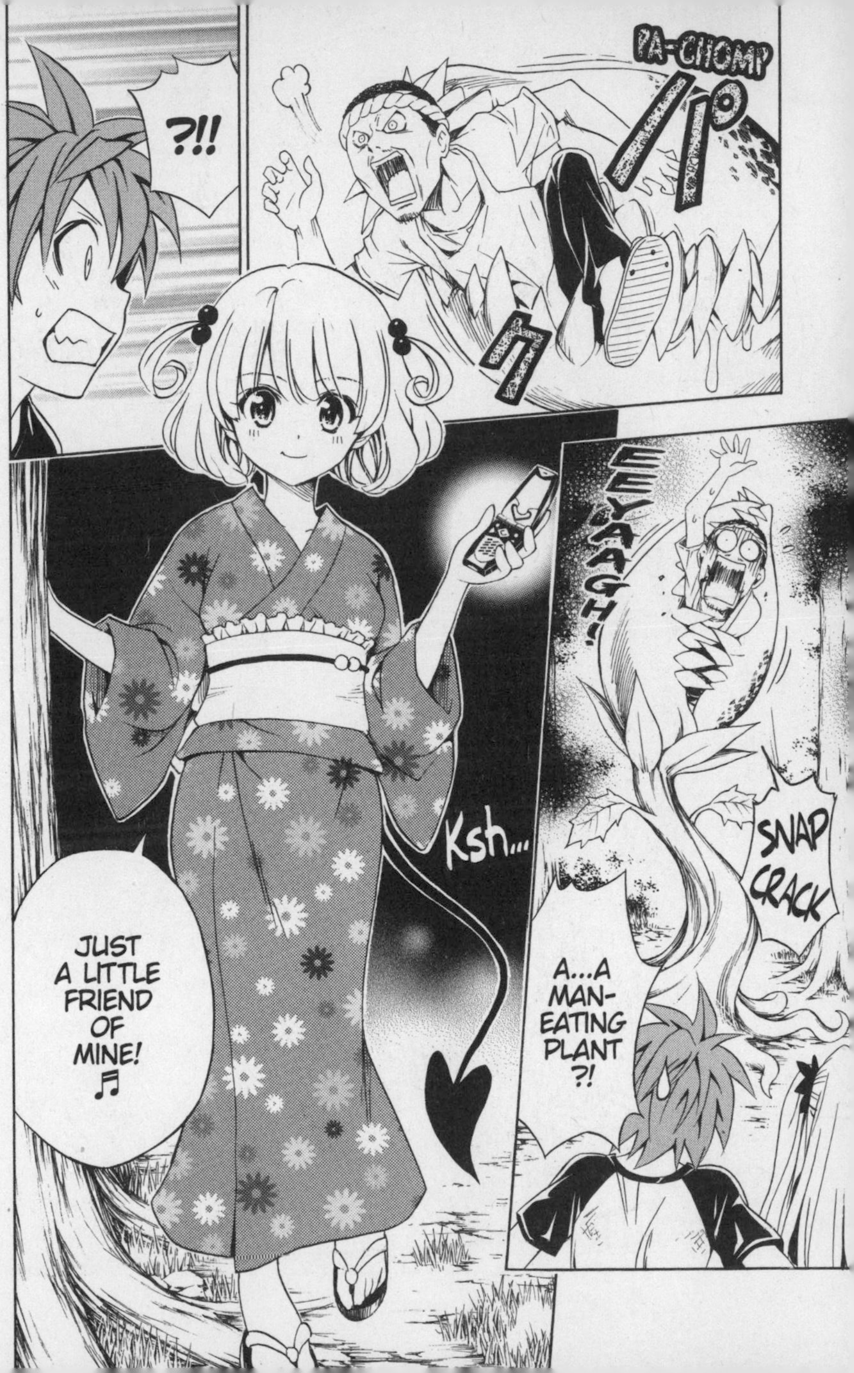
PA-CHOMP
?!!
EEYAAGH!
SNAP CRACK
A...A MAN-EATING PLANT?!
Ksh...
JUST A LITTLE FRIEND OF MINE! ♬

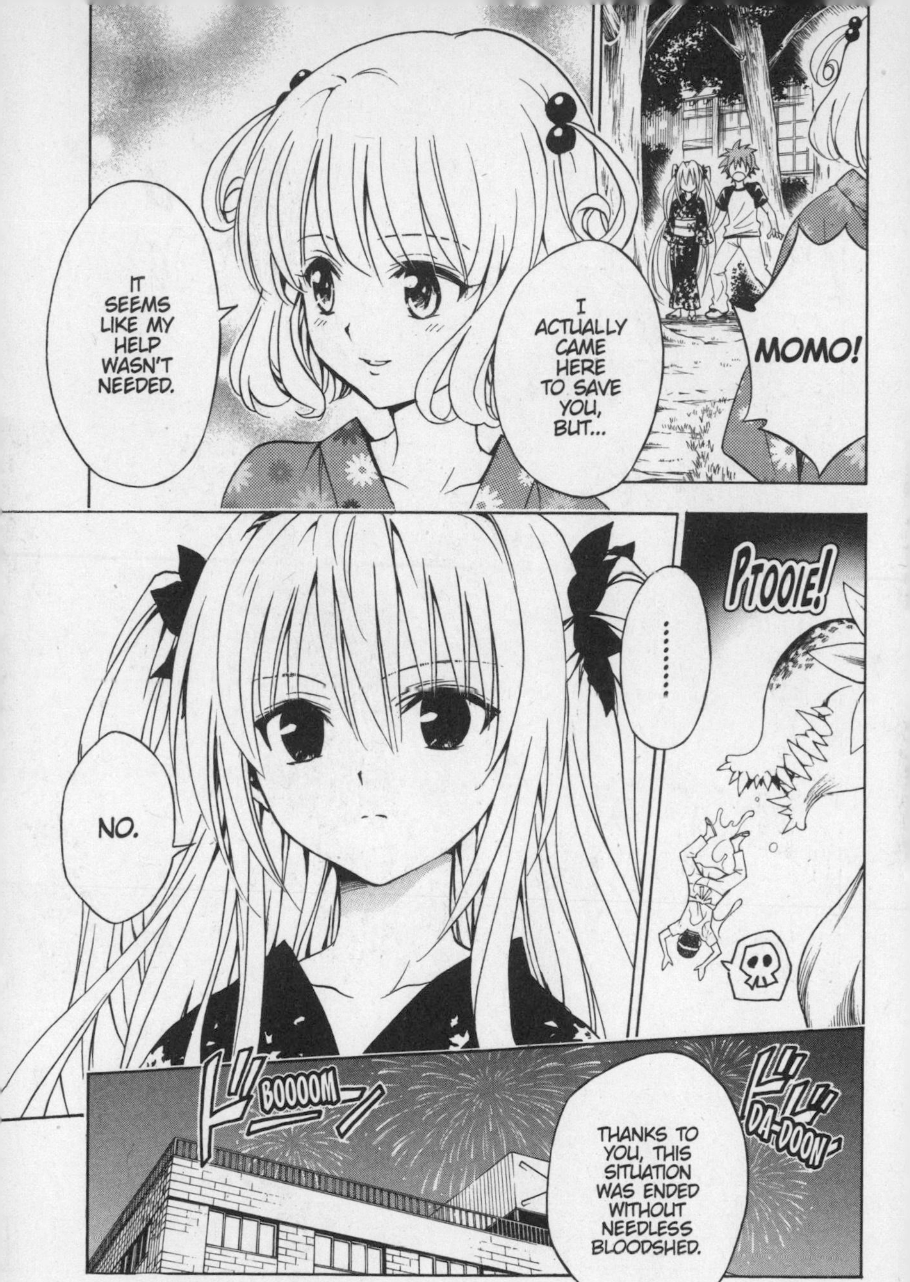
MOMO!
I ACTUALLY CAME HERE TO SAVE YOU, BUT...
IT SEEMS LIKE MY HELP WASN'T NEEDED.
PTOOIE!
......
NO.
DA-DOON
THANKS TO YOU, THIS SITUATION WAS ENDED WITHOUT NEEDLESS BLOODSHED.
BOOOM

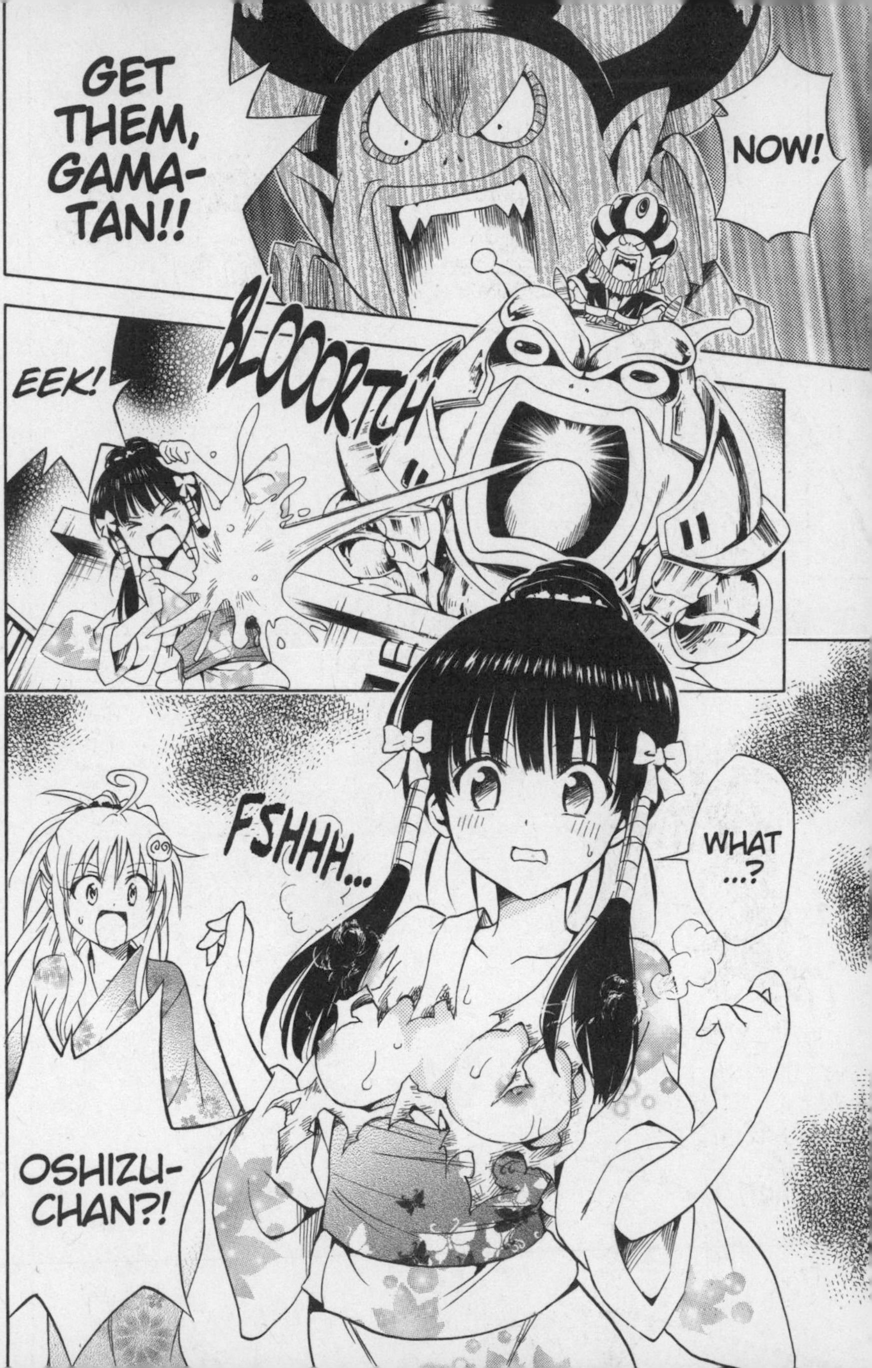
NOW!
GET THEM, GAMA-TAN!!
BLOOORTCH
EEK!
WHAT ...?
FSHHH...
OSHIZU-CHAN?!

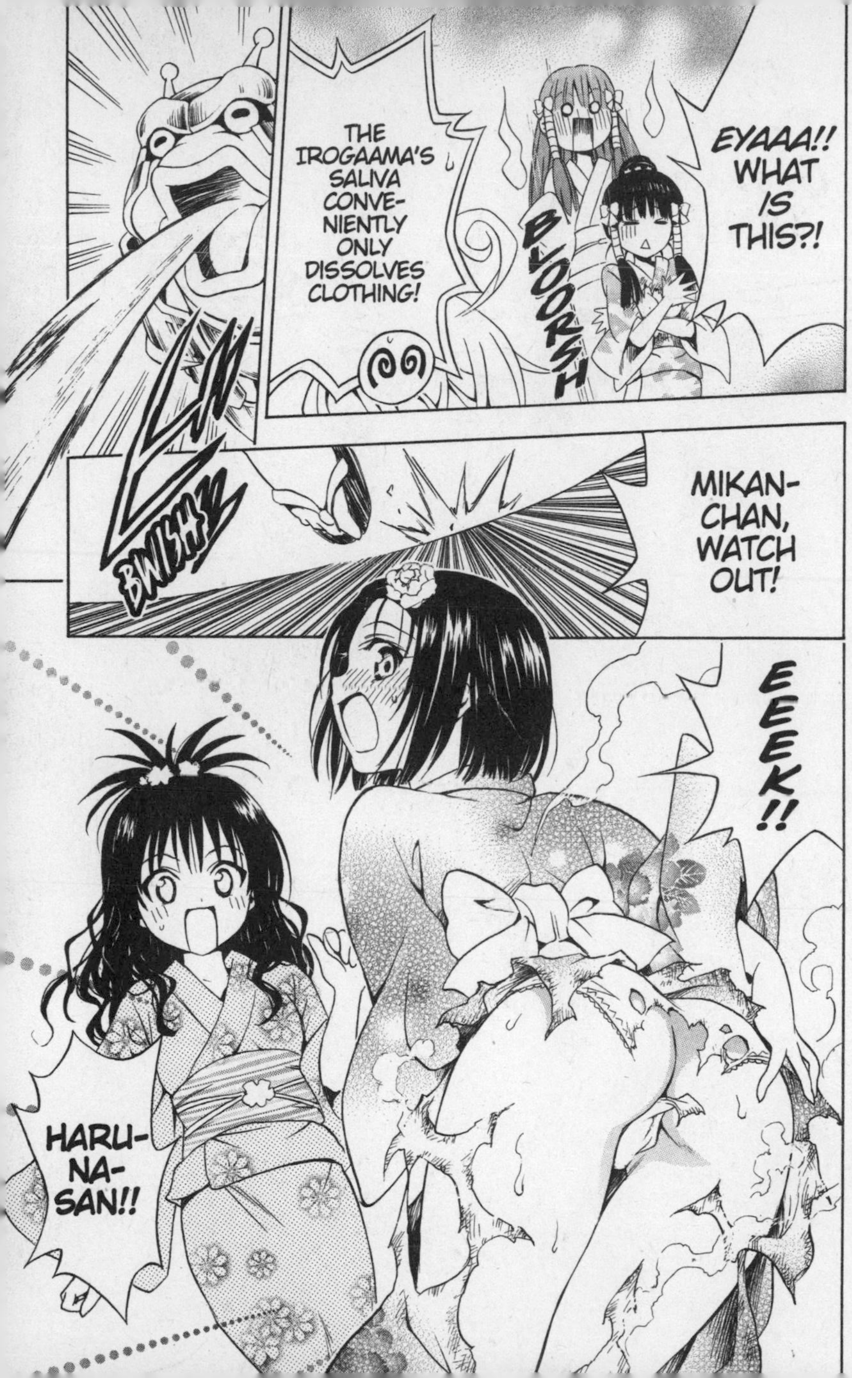
EYAAA!! WHAT IS THIS?!
THE IROGAAMA'S SALIVA CONVENIENTLY ONLY DISSOLVES CLOTHING!
BLOORSH
MIKAN-CHAN, WATCH OUT!
BWISH
EEEEK!!
HARU-NA-SAN!!

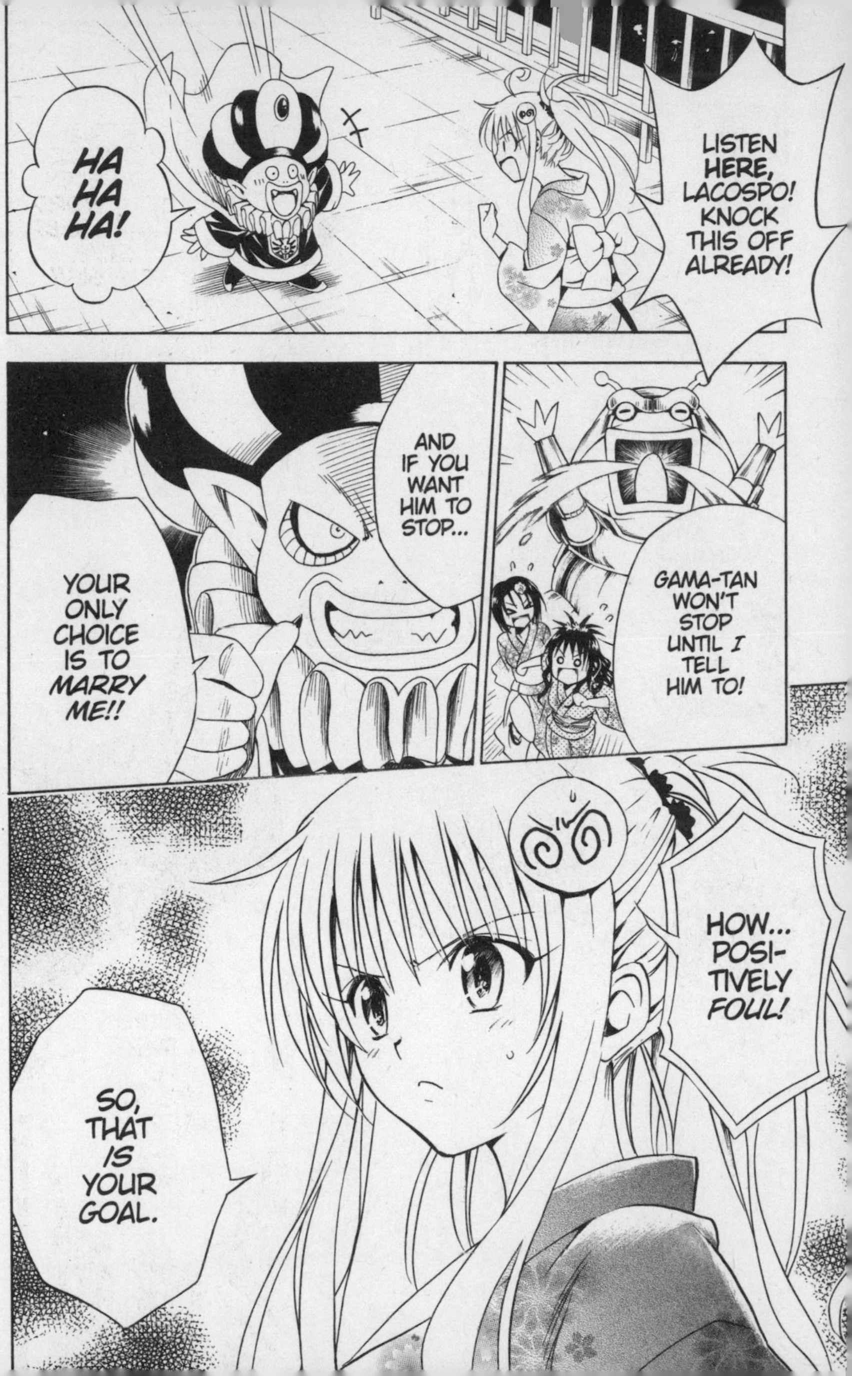
LISTEN HERE, LACOSPO! KNOCK THIS OFF ALREADY!
HA HA HA!
GAMA-TAN WON'T STOP UNTIL I TELL HIM TO!
AND IF YOU WANT HIM TO STOP...
YOUR ONLY CHOICE IS TO MARRY ME!!
HOW... POSI-TIVELY FOUL!
SO, THAT IS YOUR GOAL.

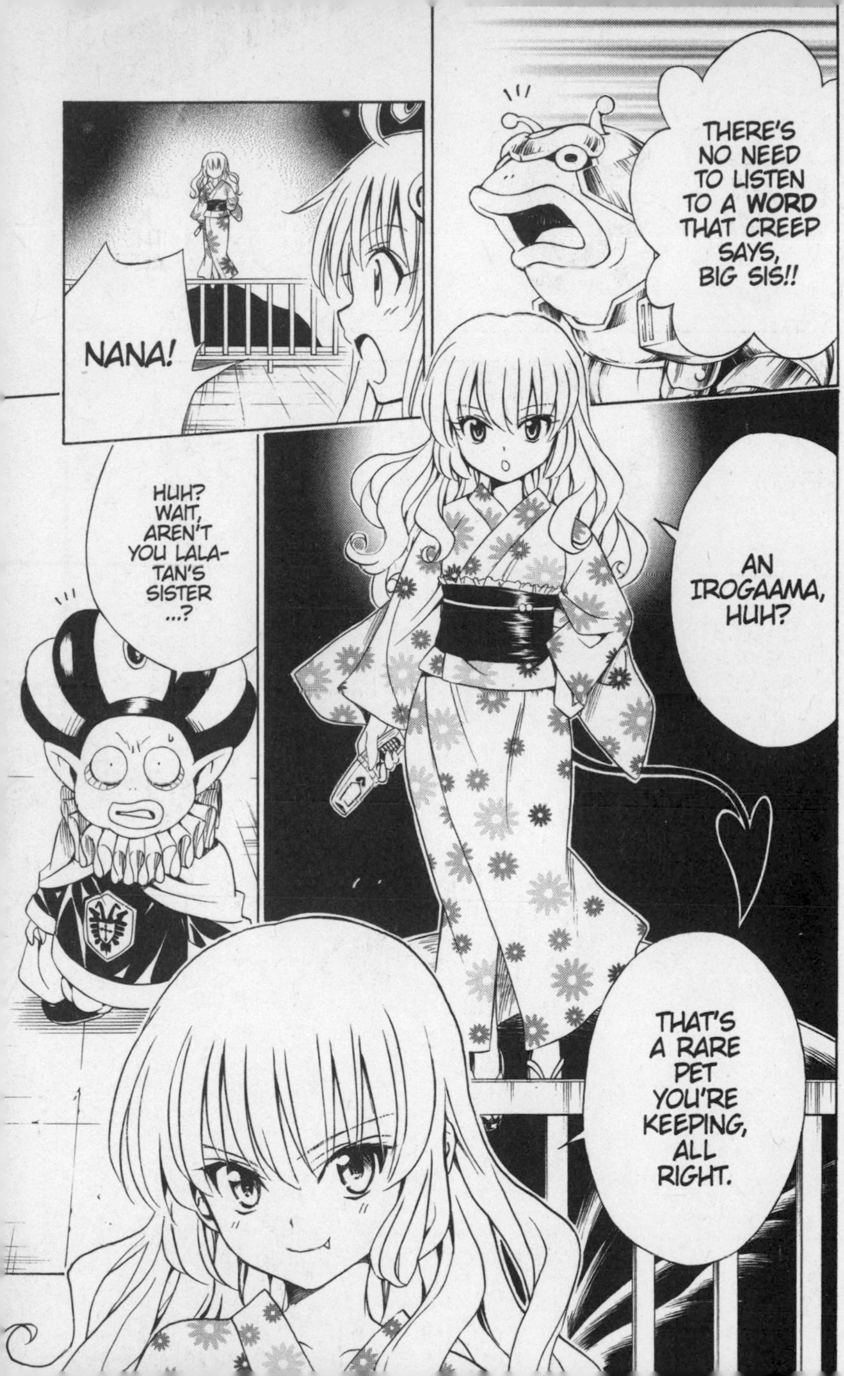
THERE'S NO NEED TO LISTEN TO A WORD THAT CREEP SAYS, BIG SIS!!
NANA!
AN IROGAAMA, HUH?
THAT'S A RARE PET YOU'RE KEEPING, ALL RIGHT.
HUH? WAIT, AREN'T YOU LALA-TAN'S SISTER ...?

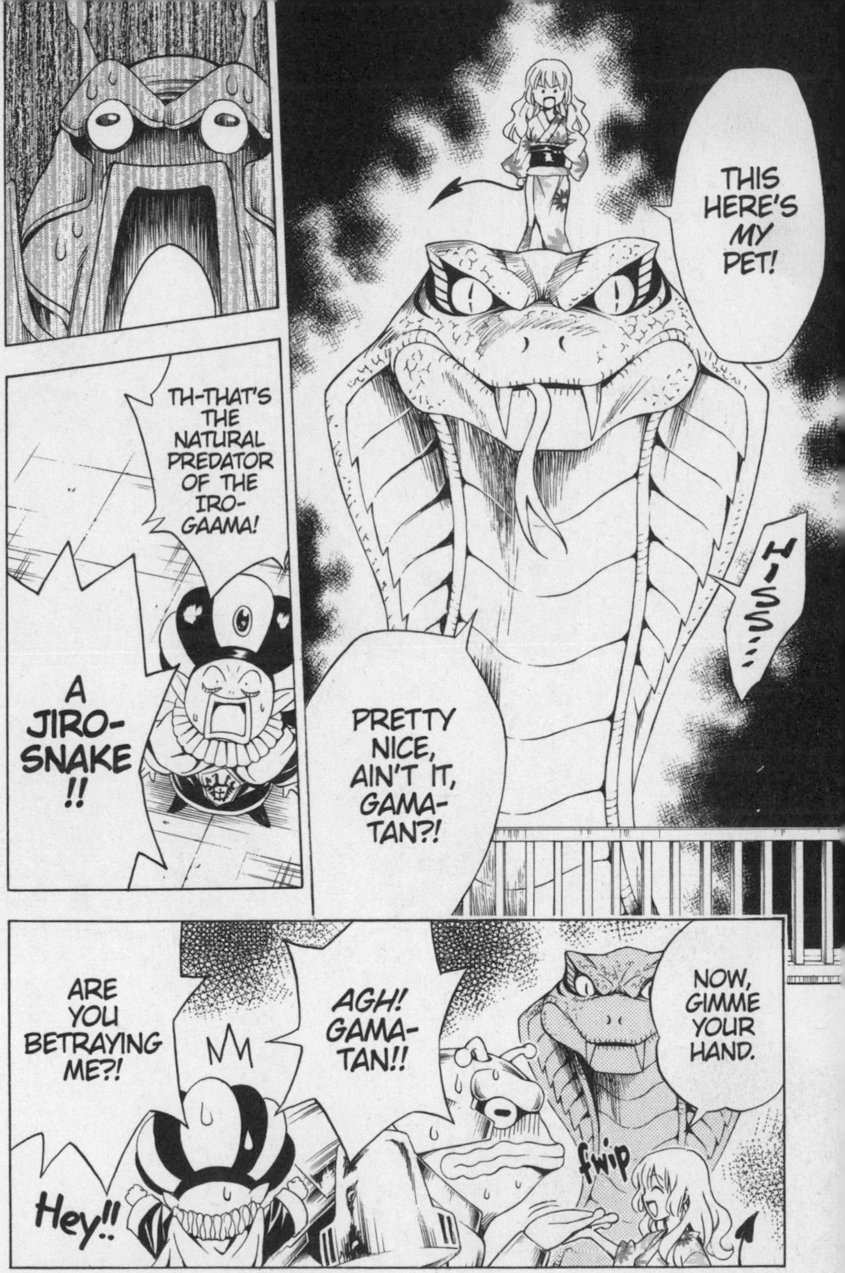
THIS HERE'S MY PET!
HISS...
PRETTY NICE, AIN'T IT, GAMA-TAN?!
TH-THAT'S THE NATURAL PREDATOR OF THE IRO-GAAMA!
A JIRO-SNAKE!!
NOW, GIMME YOUR HAND.
fwip
AGH! GAMA-TAN!!
ARE YOU BETRAYING ME?!
Hey!!

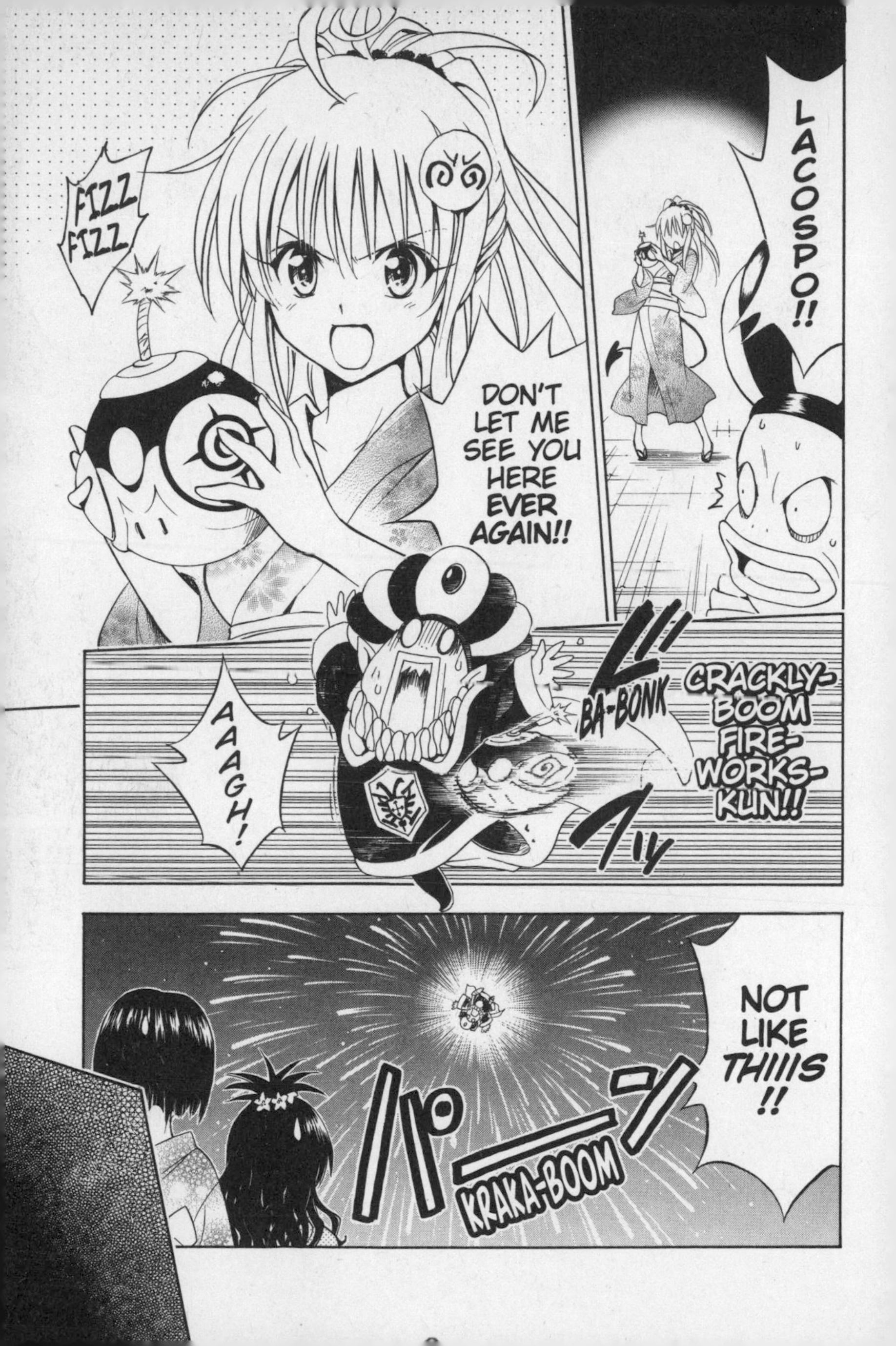
LACOSPO!!
DON'T LET ME SEE YOU HERE EVER AGAIN!!
FIZZ FIZZ
CRACKLY-BOOM FIRE-WORKS-KUN!!
BA-BONK
AAAGH!
NOT LIKE THIIIS!!
KRAKA-BOOM

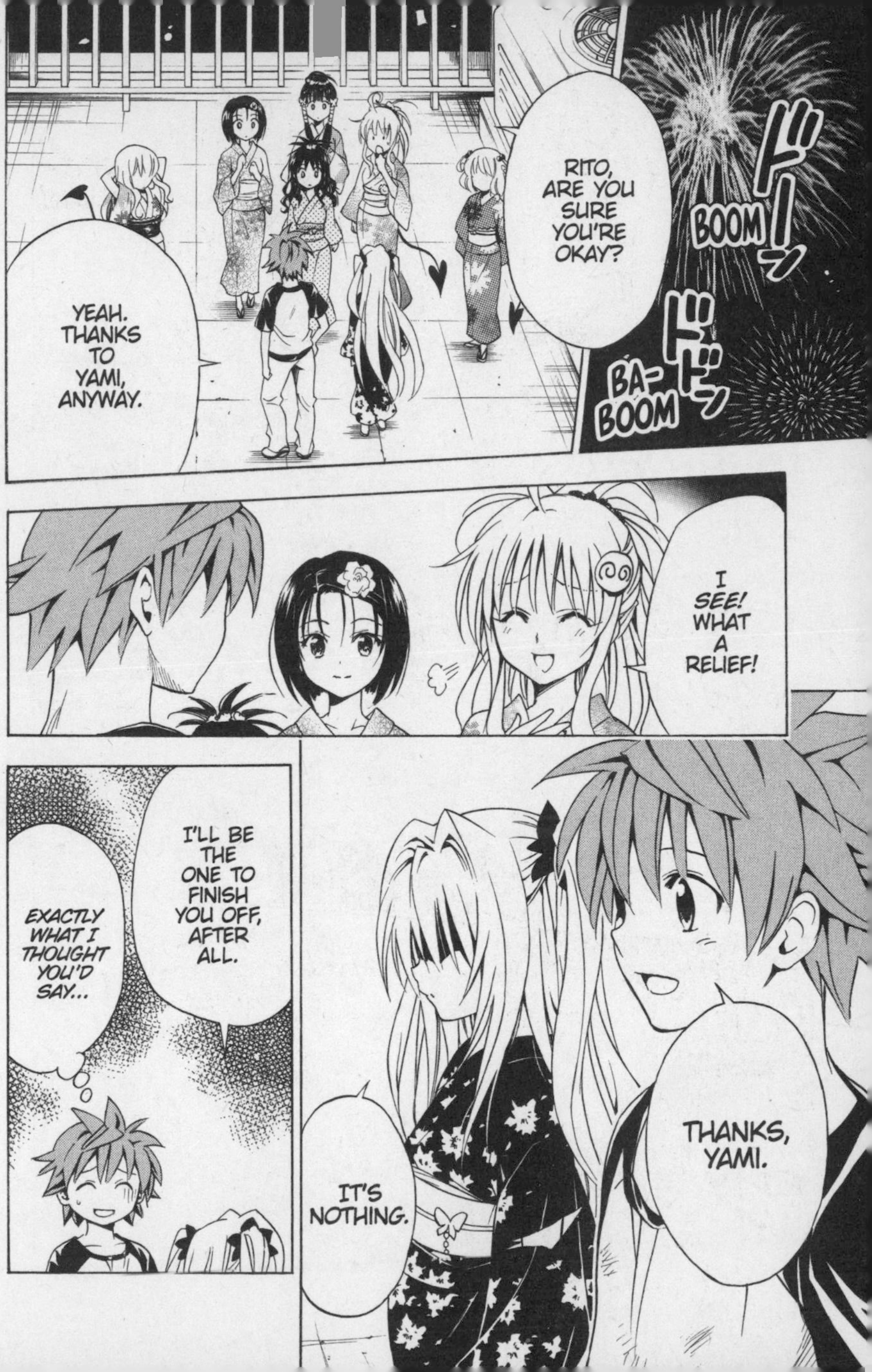
RITO, ARE YOU SURE YOU'RE OKAY?
BOOM
BA-BOOM
YEAH. THANKS TO YAMI, ANYWAY.
I SEE! WHAT A RELIEF!
THANKS, YAMI.
IT'S NOTHING.
I'LL BE THE ONE TO FINISH YOU OFF, AFTER ALL.
EXACTLY WHAT I THOUGHT YOU'D SAY...

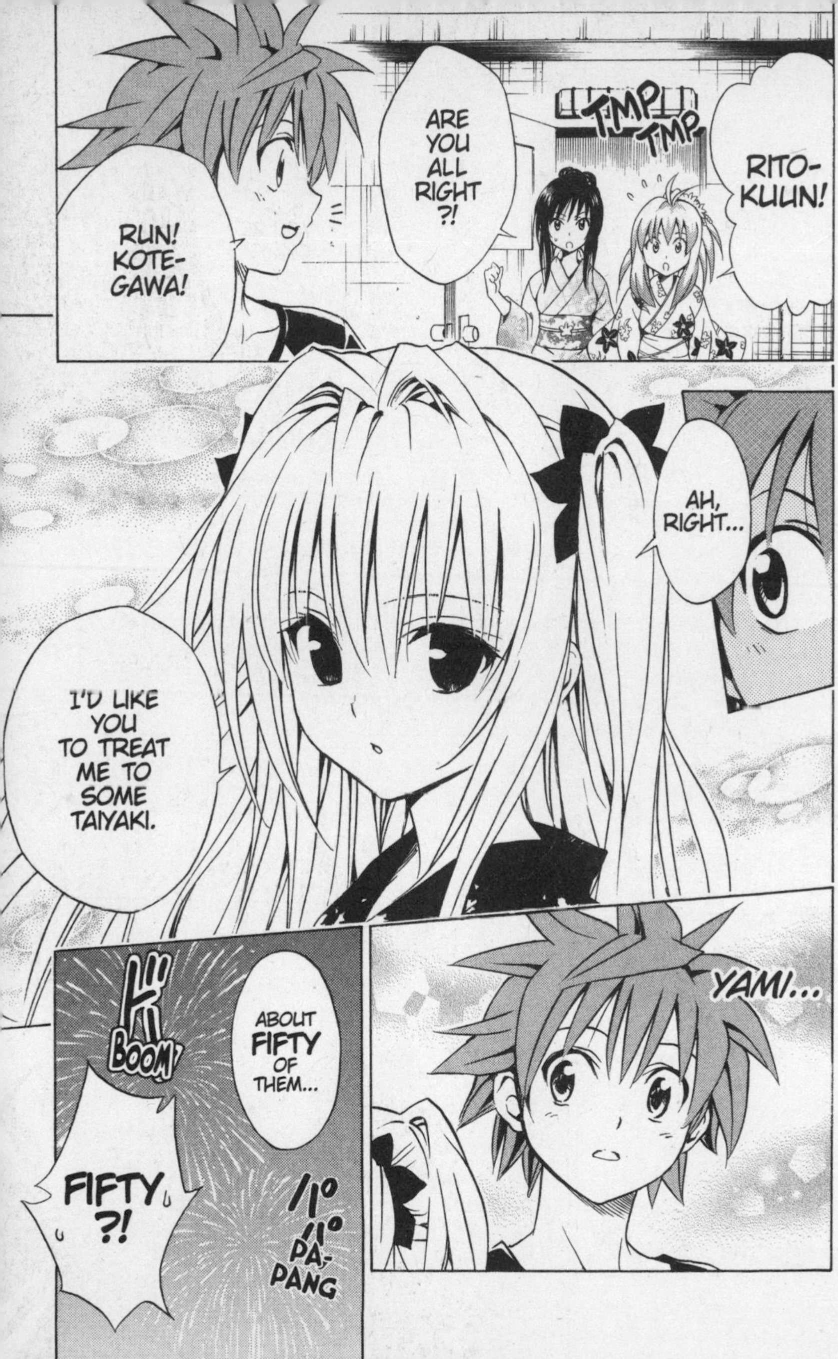
RITO-KUUN!
TMP TMP
ARE YOU ALL RIGHT?!
RUN! KOTE-GAWA!
AH, RIGHT...
I'D LIKE YOU TO TREAT ME TO SOME TAIYAKI.
YAMI...
ABOUT FIFTY OF THEM...
BOOM
PA-PANG
FIFTY?!

To Love Ru Gaiden
Galaxy Legend ☆ Zastin

PRESENTED BY SAKI HASEMI

Shueisha HQ. Right now, Zastin is in a second-floor meeting room, having a storyboarding discussion with supervisor Uchida.

Uchida: Phew...
Zastin: How is it?
Uchida: It was interesting.
Zastin: Really?!
Uchida: Yeah. It certainly was interesting, but we can't do it.
Zastin: Huh?
Uchida: Well, your story's just too bland. If I had to be specific, I'd say it's like something you'd find in a textbook. Or no, it's like a manga you'd find in an instruction manual.
Zastin: An instruction manual manga?
Uchida: A manga can't *just* be "that was interesting!" If the readers of *Jump* finished a volume and just said "that was interesting," it'd be finished!
Zastin: Um... I really don't have a clue what you're talking about.
Uchida: I'm not looking for "that was interesting." I'm looking for "this *is* interesting."
Zastin: !
Uchida: Your manga ends with the reader going, "That was interesting." But if you want to get picked up for serialization, it's essential that the story feels like it's ongoing! You gotta hook 'em with that "To be continued!" You need the reader to go "This is interesting," and not "That *was* interesting!" It has to beg the question, "What's gonna happen next?!" And so, unfortunately, yours doesn't have that.
Zastin: Meaning...
Uchida: Meaning your manga doesn't have that novel *spark* that grabs hold of a reader's imagination. And without it, never mind getting serialized, you'd be lucky to get it printed on the office copier.
Zastin: I-I see... Very well. I will take it back to the drawing board, then.

Zastin trudges his way out of the meeting room. However, he doesn't appear to be discouraged in the slightest. In the next moment, a lone man appears before Uchida in the meeting room.

Editor-in-Chief: Uchida...
Uchida: Sir, he ought to have what it takes to create a great work, but he just doesn't deliver...
Editor-in-Chief: Hey, come on, the girl in it is cute, so isn't that enough?
Uchida: I've *got* to do something about this guy...

This event occurred one week before meetings to choose the new lineup began.

Be aware that this story is purely fiction made to appear in the pages of this volume. It has no bearing or relation to any actual editorial department (named above) whatsoever.

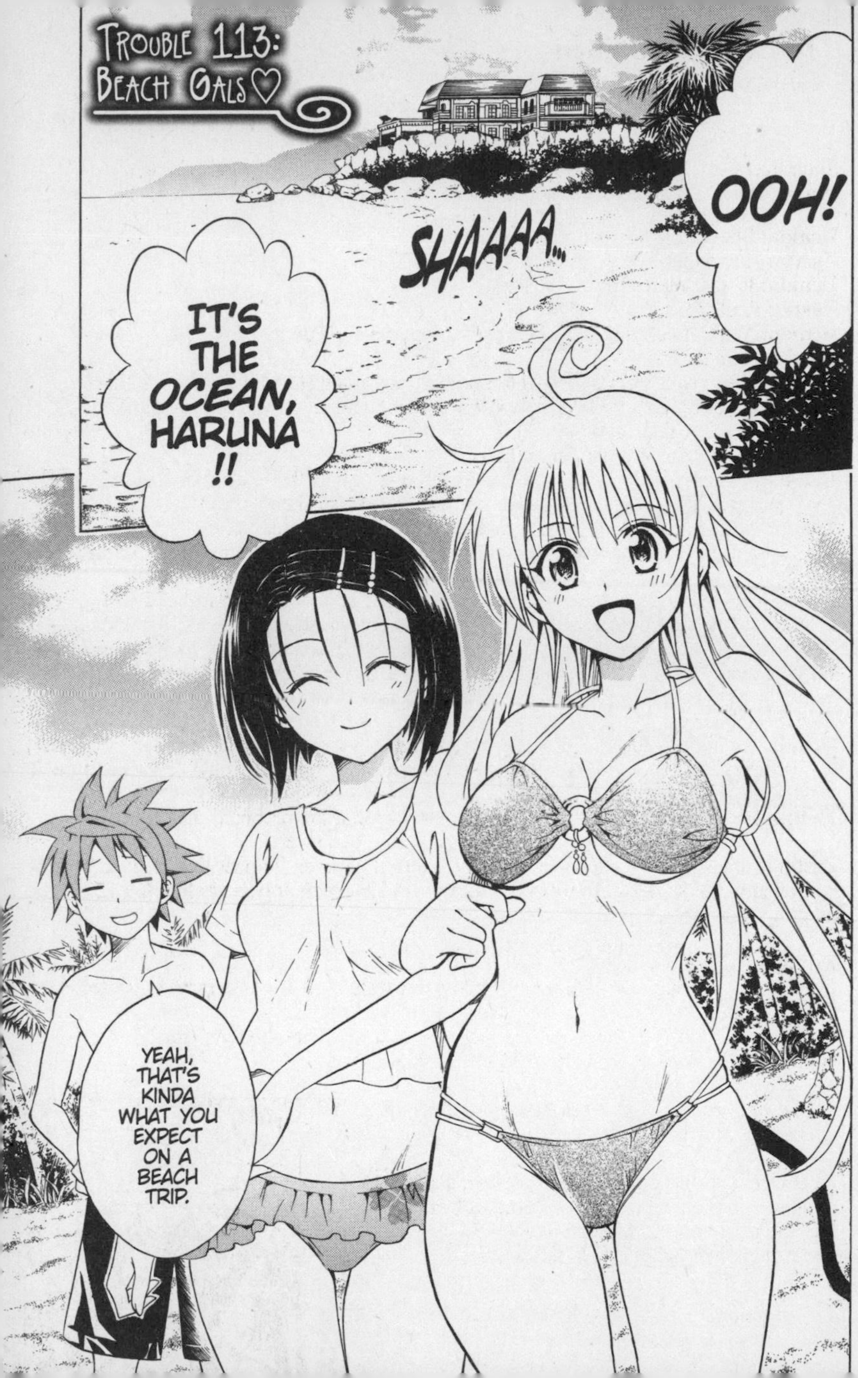
TROUBLE 113: BEACH GALS♡
OOH!
SHAAAA...
IT'S THE OCEAN, HARUNA!!
YEAH, THAT'S KINDA WHAT YOU EXPECT ON A BEACH TRIP.

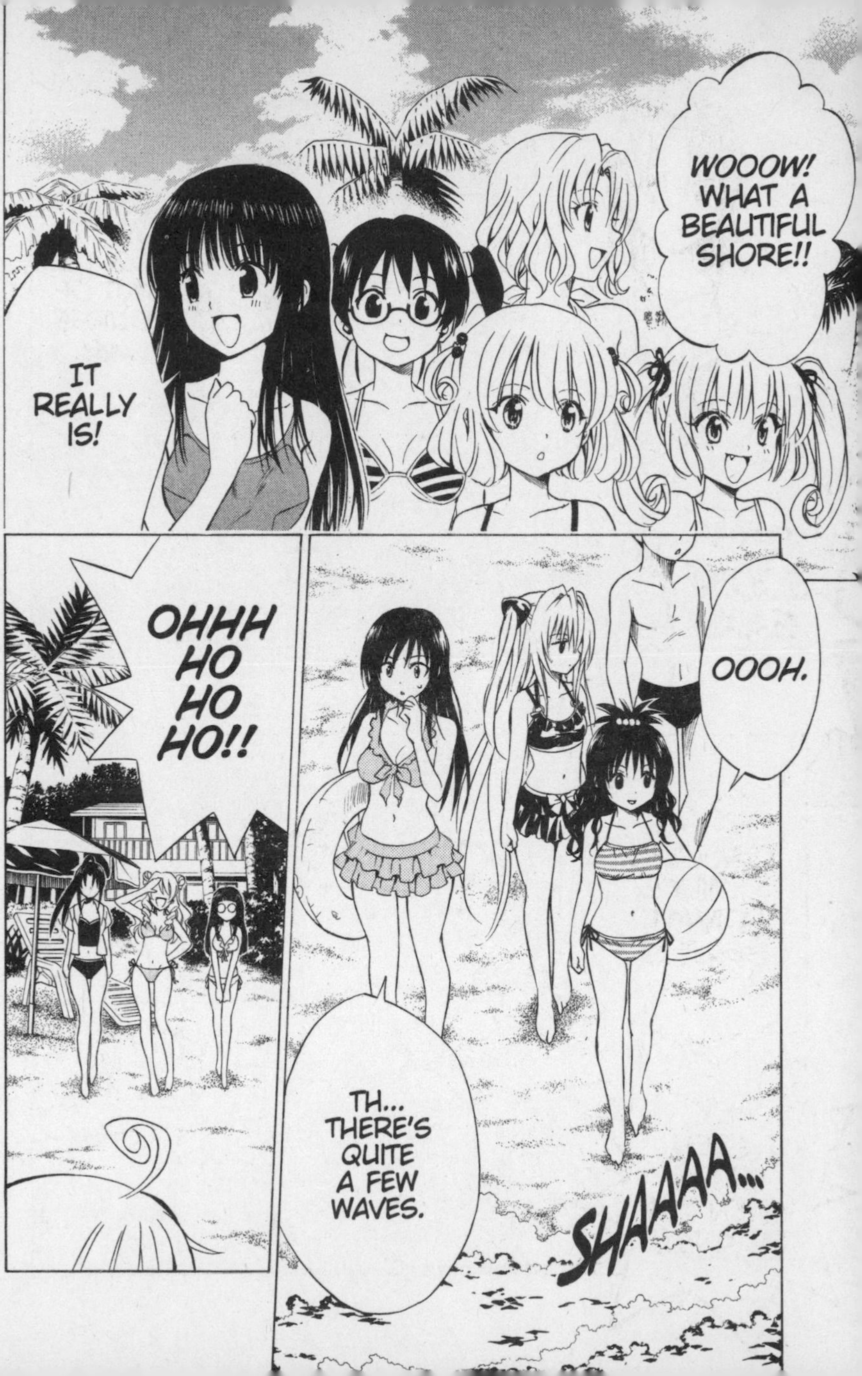
WOOOW! WHAT A BEAUTIFUL SHORE!!
IT REALLY IS!
OOOH.
TH... THERE'S QUITE A FEW WAVES.
SHAAAA...
OHHH HO HO HO!!

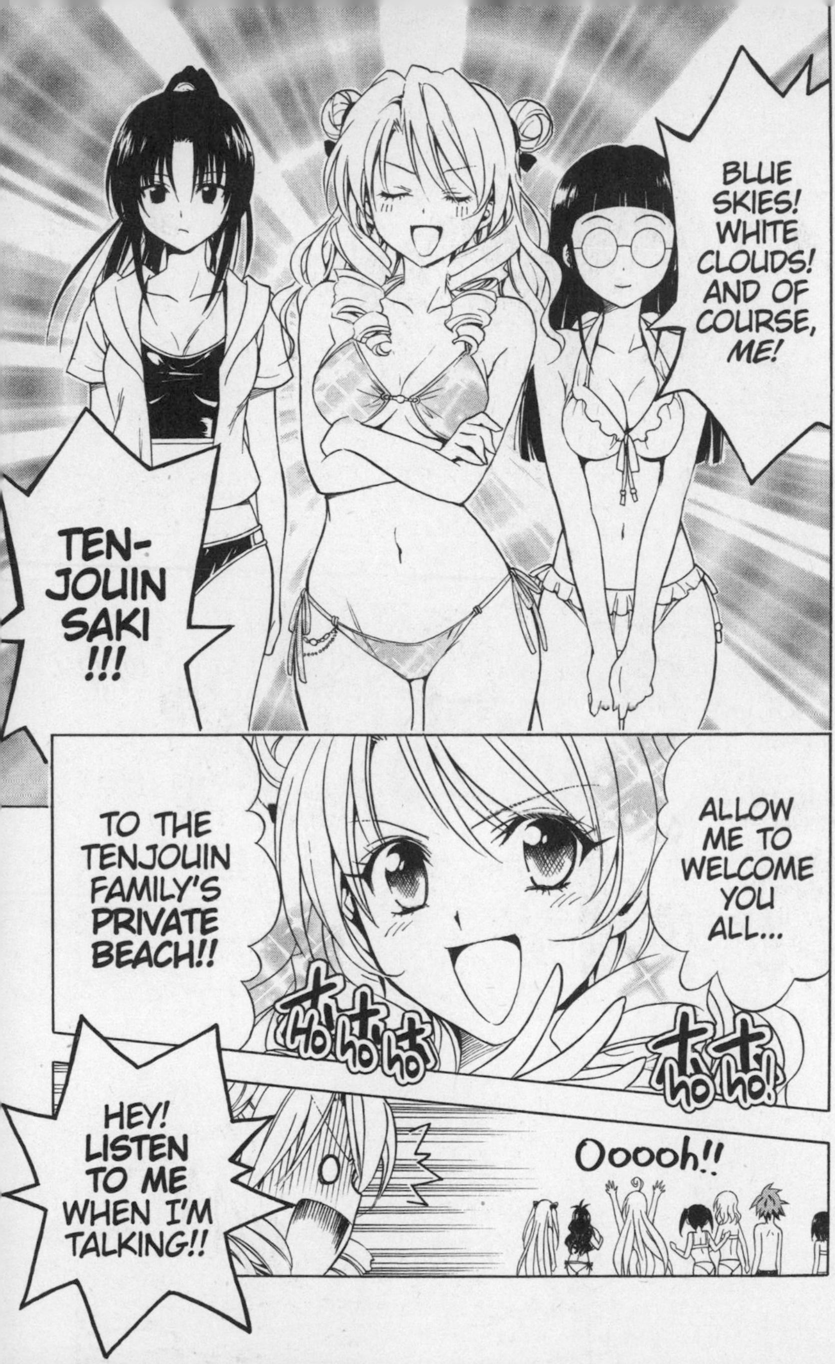
BLUE SKIES! WHITE CLOUDS! AND OF COURSE, ME!
TEN-JOUIN SAKI !!!
ALLOW ME TO WELCOME YOU ALL...
TO THE TENJOUIN FAMILY'S PRIVATE BEACH!!
Ho ho ho
ho ho!
Ooooh!!
HEY! LISTEN TO ME WHEN I'M TALKING!!

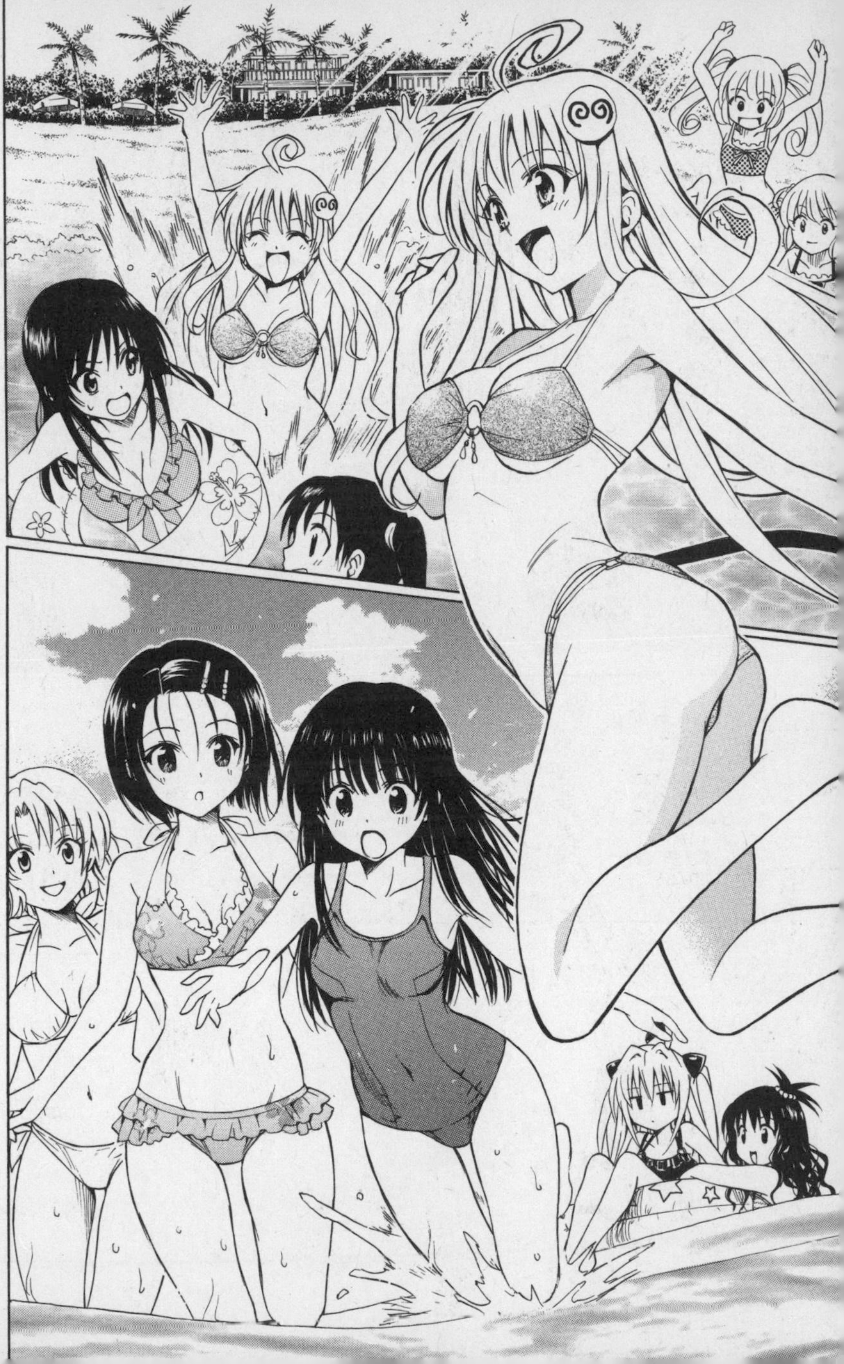

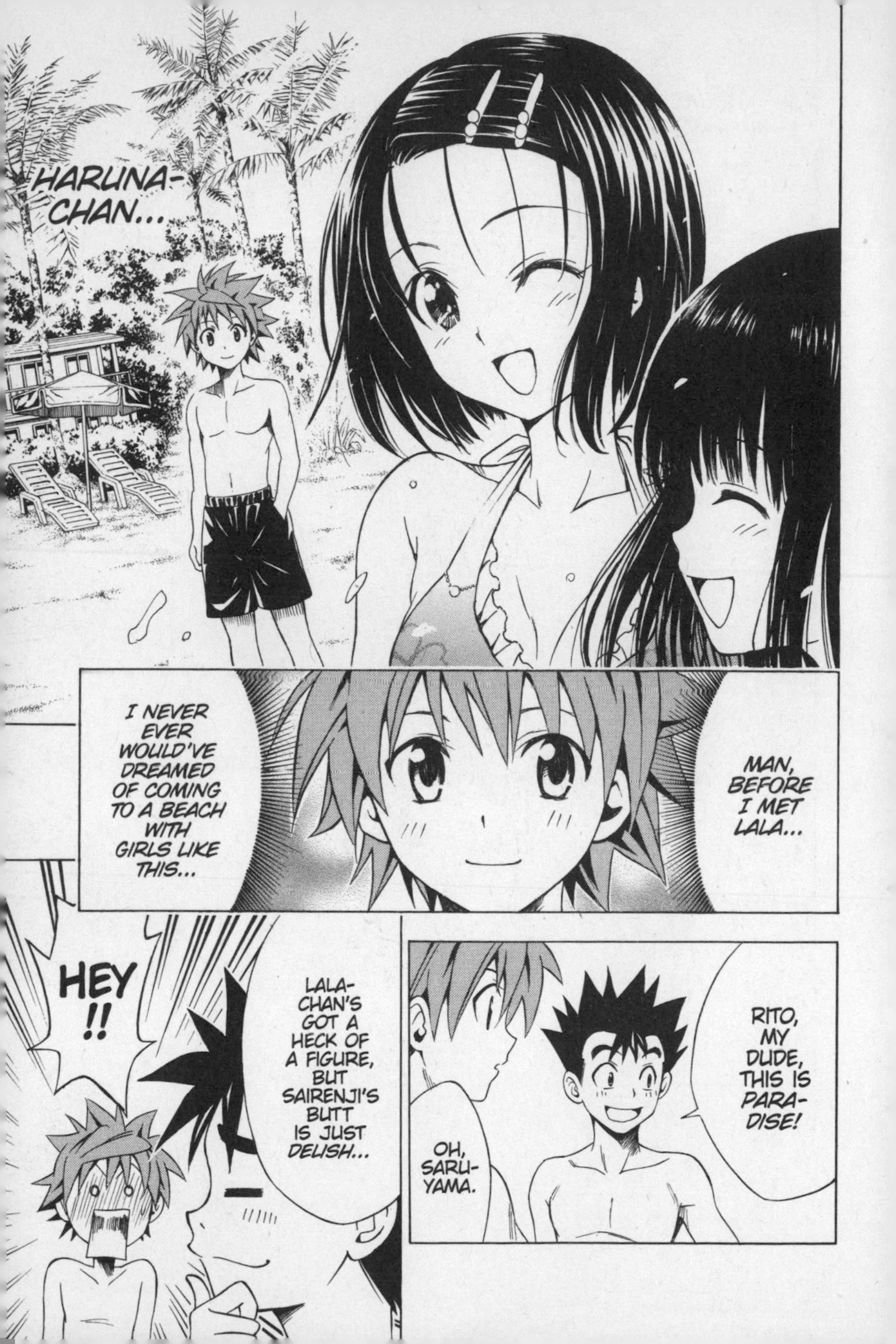
HARUNA-CHAN...
MAN, BEFORE I MET LALA...
I NEVER EVER WOULD'VE DREAMED OF COMING TO A BEACH WITH GIRLS LIKE THIS...
RITO, MY DUDE, THIS IS PARA-DISE!
OH, SARU-YAMA.
LALA-CHAN'S GOT A HECK OF A FIGURE, BUT SAIRENJI'S BUTT IS JUST DELISH...
HEY !!

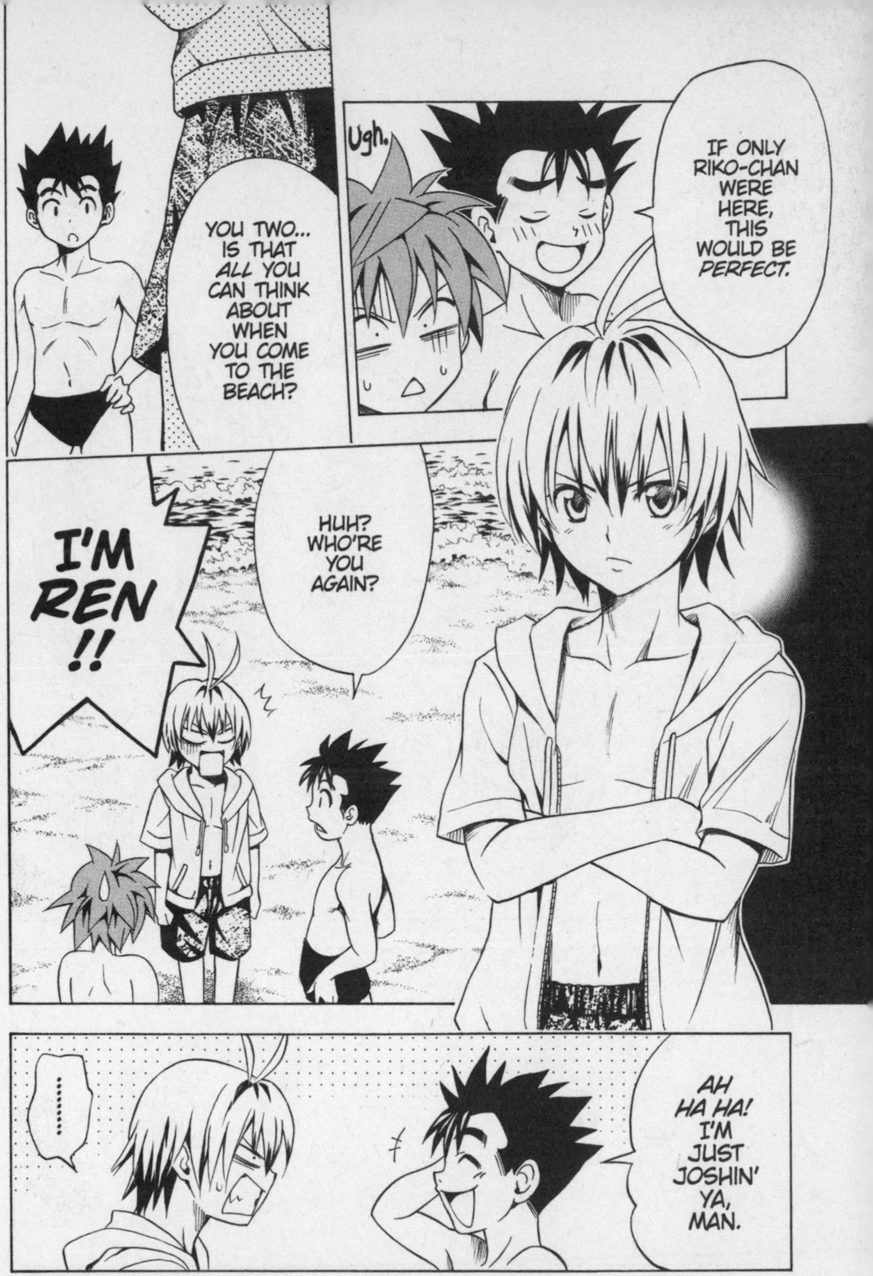
IF ONLY RIKO-CHAN WERE HERE, THIS WOULD BE PERFECT.
Ugh.
YOU TWO... IS THAT ALL YOU CAN THINK ABOUT WHEN YOU COME TO THE BEACH?
HUH? WHO'RE YOU AGAIN?
I'M REN!!
AH HA HA! I'M JUST JOSHIN' YA, MAN.
....

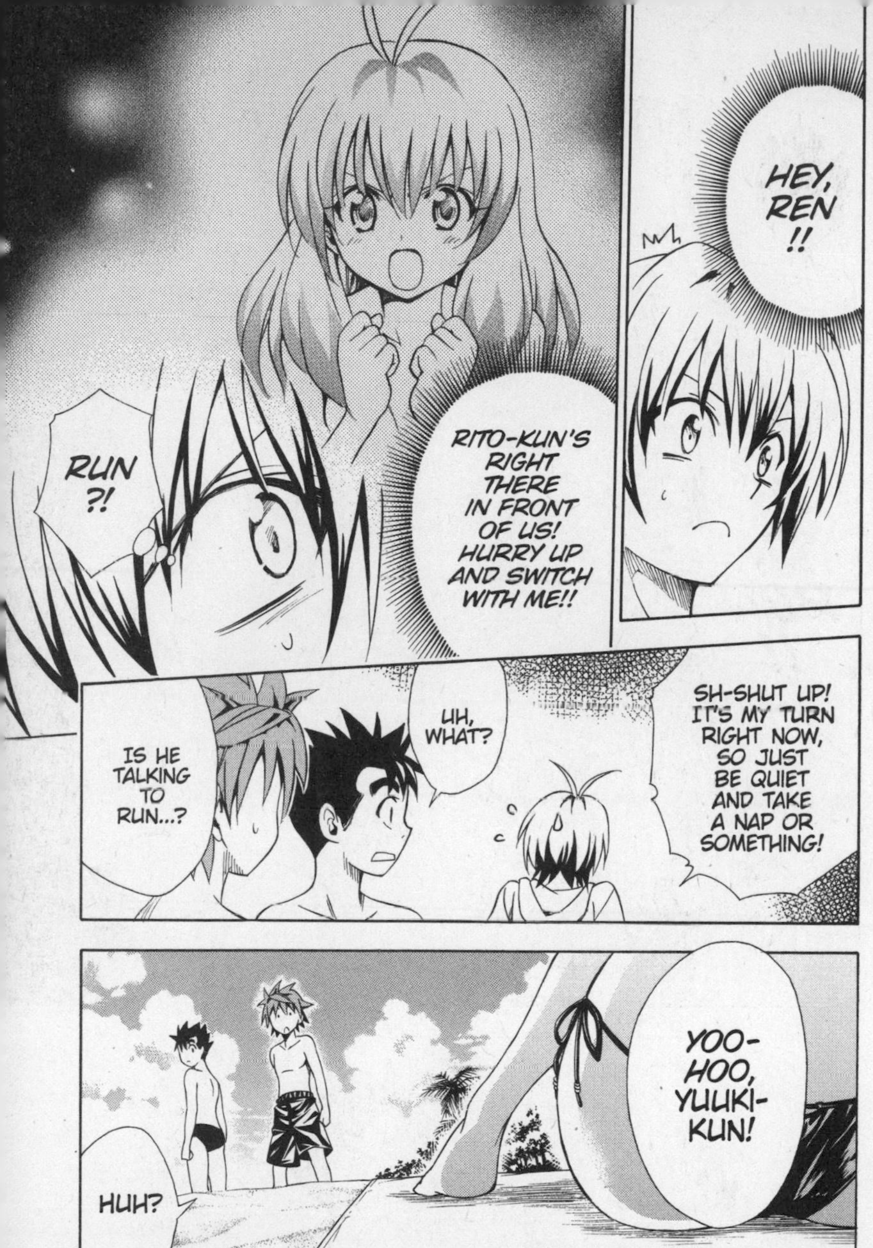
HEY, REN!!
RITO-KUN'S RIGHT THERE IN FRONT OF US! HURRY UP AND SWITCH WITH ME!!
RUN?!
SH-SHUT UP! IT'S MY TURN RIGHT NOW, SO JUST BE QUIET AND TAKE A NAP OR SOMETHING!
UH, WHAT?
IS HE TALKING TO RUN...?
YOO-HOO, YUUKI-KUN!
HUH?

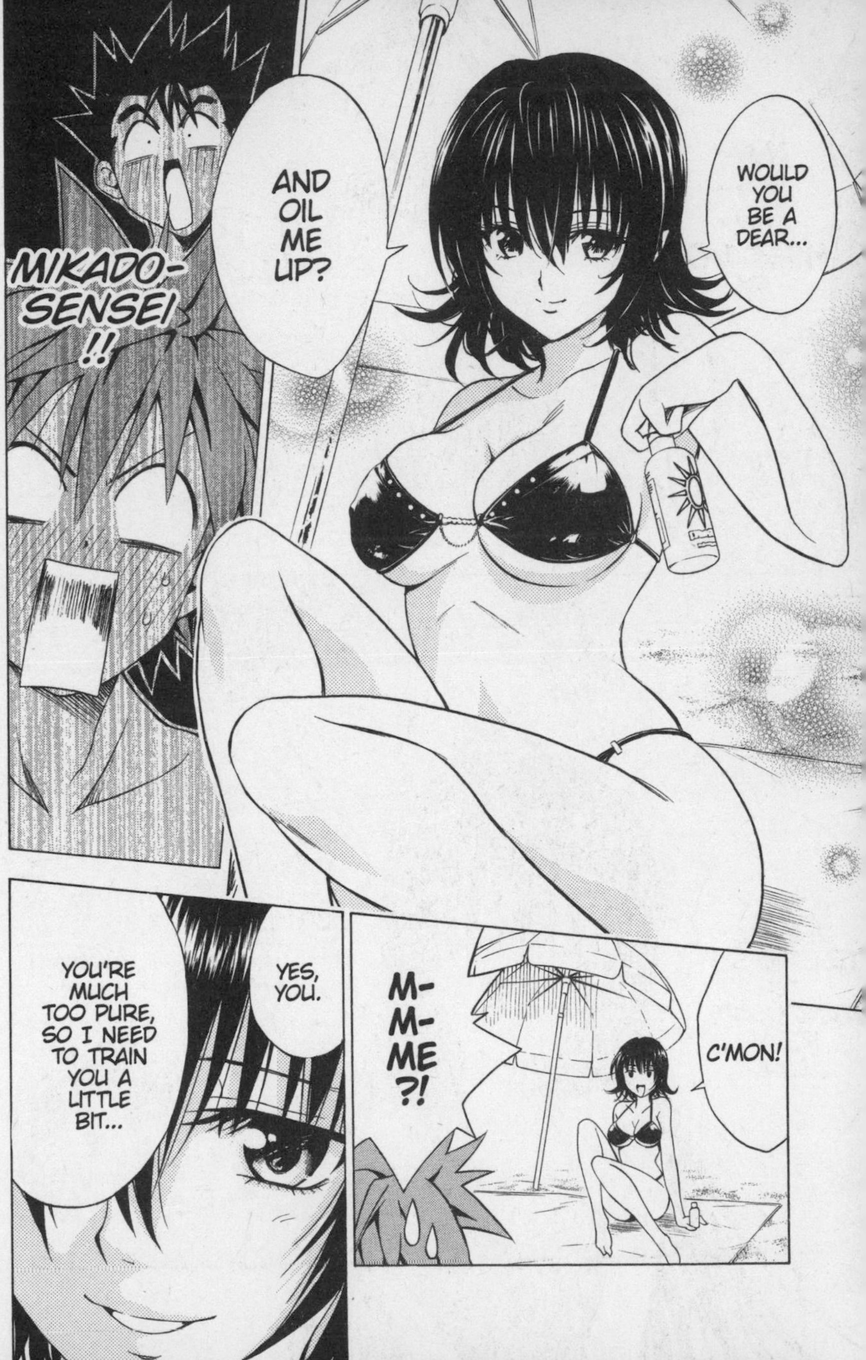
WOULD YOU BE A DEAR...
AND OIL ME UP?
MIKADO-SENSEI!!
C'MON!
M-M-ME?!
YES, YOU.
YOU'RE MUCH TOO PURE, SO I NEED TO TRAIN YOU A LITTLE BIT...

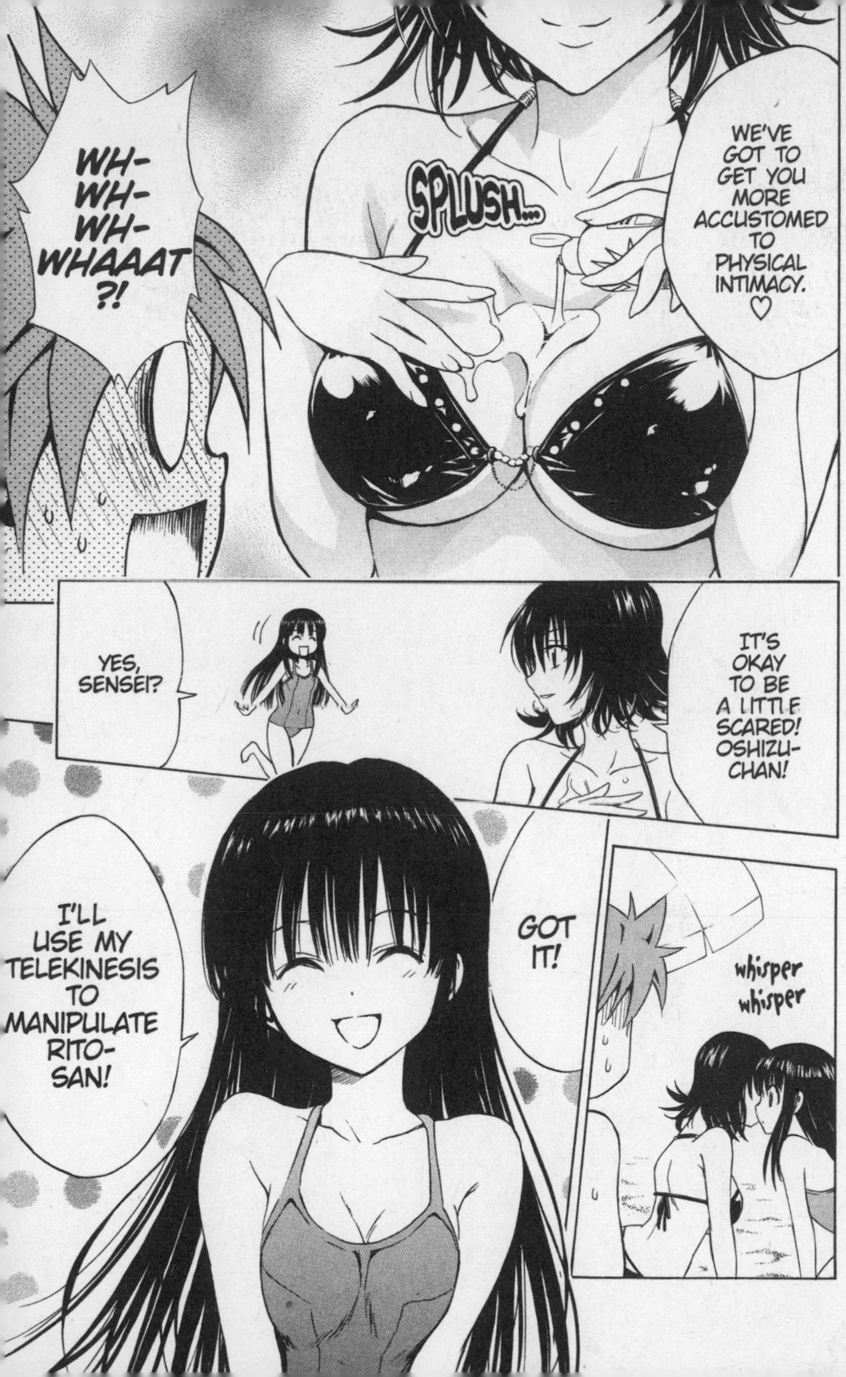
WE'VE GOT TO GET YOU MORE ACCUSTOMED TO PHYSICAL INTIMACY. ♡
SPLUSH...
WH-WH-WH-WHAAAT?!
IT'S OKAY TO BE A LITTLE SCARED! OSHIZU-CHAN!
YES, SENSEI?
whisper whisper
GOT IT!
I'LL USE MY TELEKINESIS TO MANIPULATE RITO-SAN!

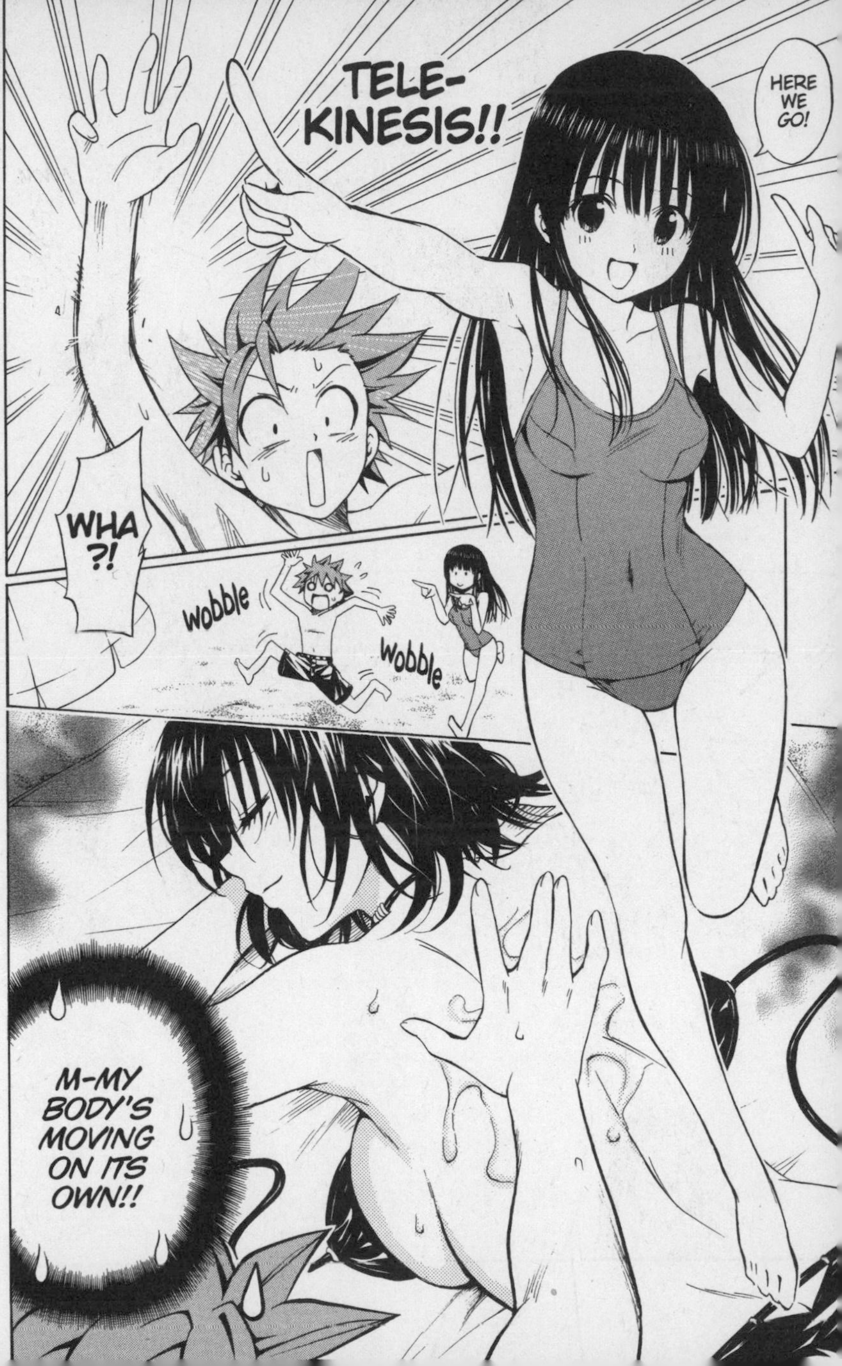
HERE WE GO!
TELE-KINESIS!!
WHA?!
wobble
wobble
M-MY BODY'S MOVING ON ITS OWN!!

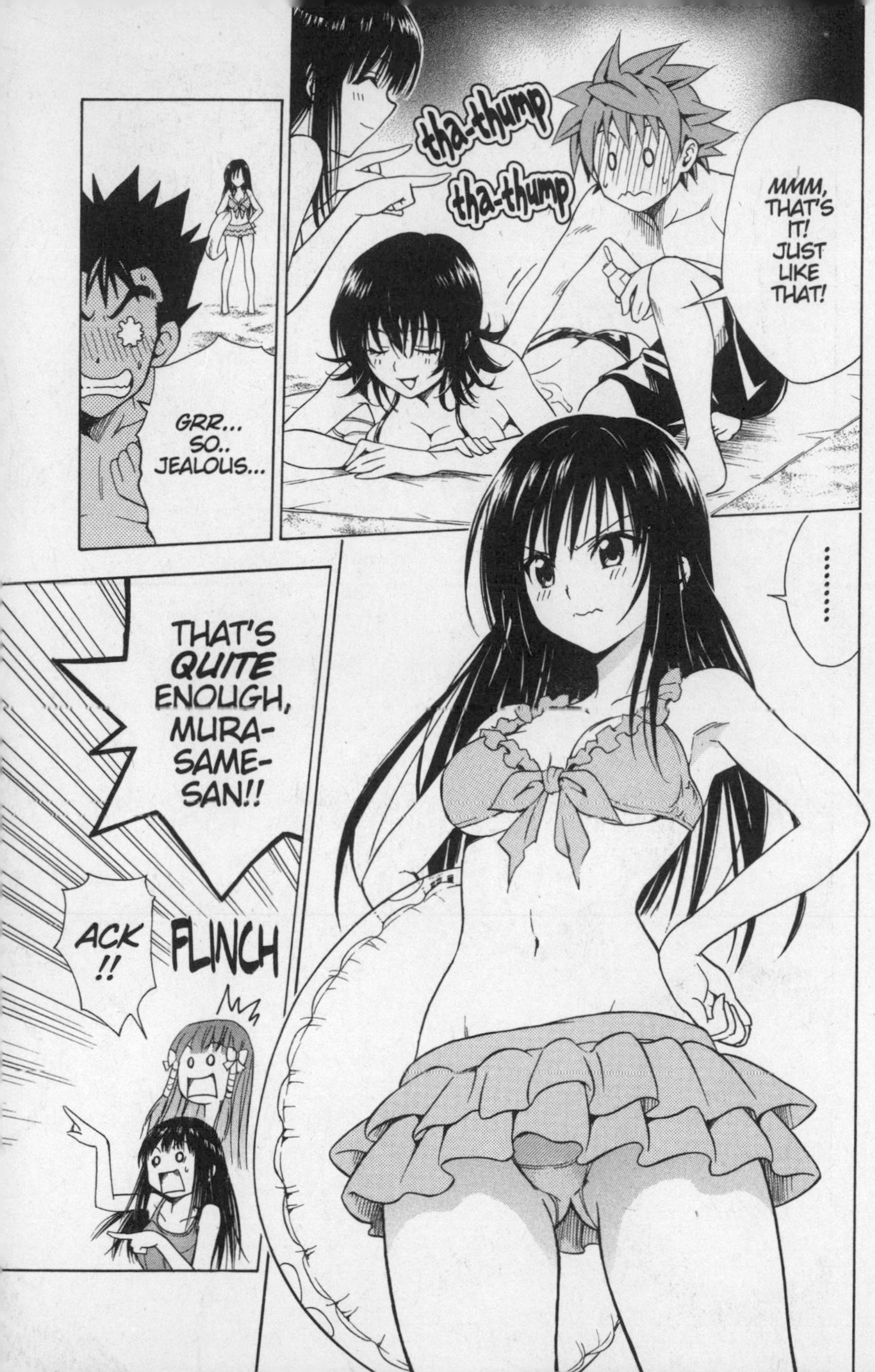
tha-thump
tha-thump
MMM, THAT'S IT! JUST LIKE THAT!
GRR... SO.. JEALOUS...
......
THAT'S QUITE ENOUGH, MURA-SAME-SAN!!
FLINCH
ACK!!

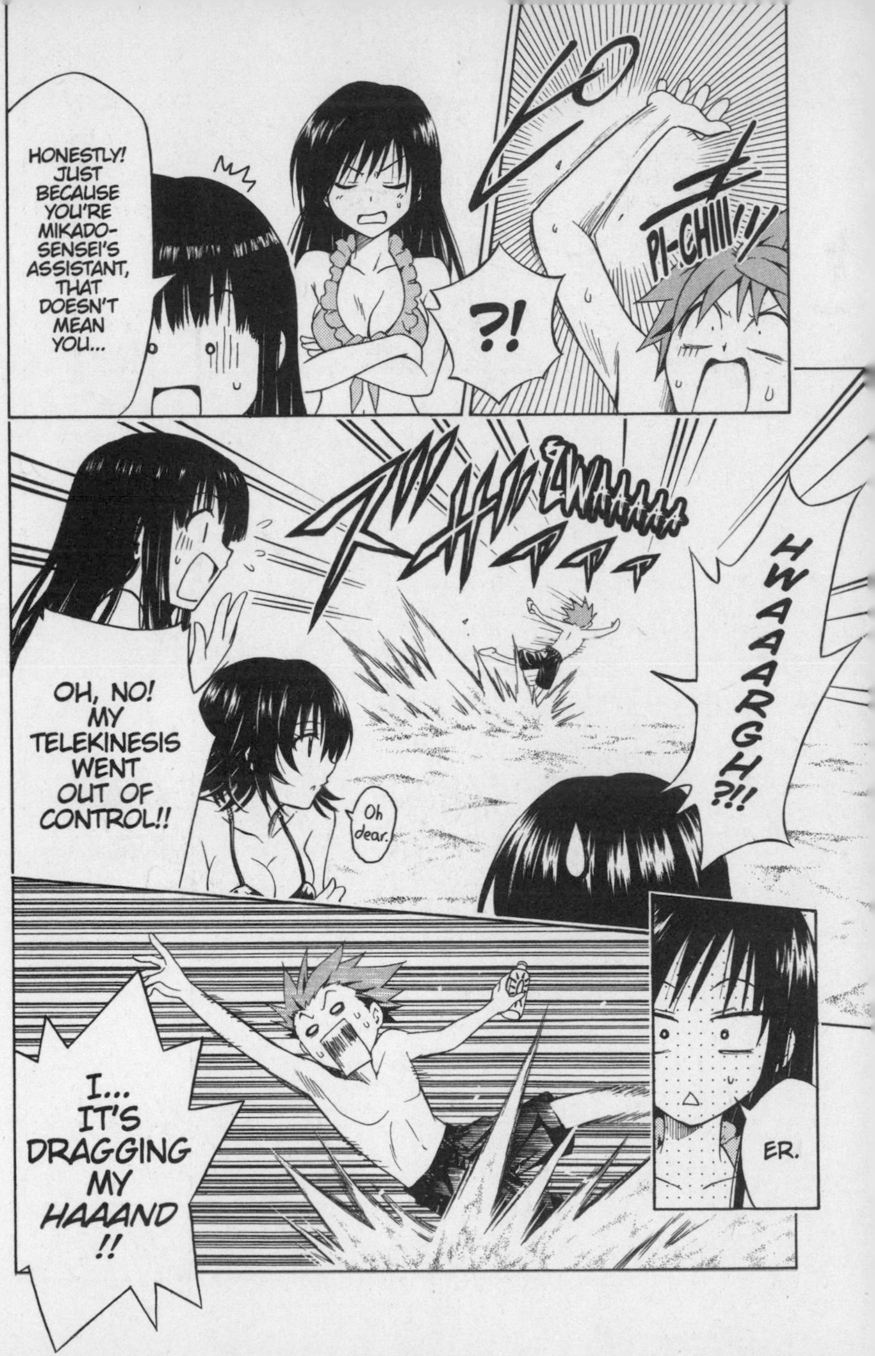
PI-CHIIII!!
?!
HONESTLY! JUST BECAUSE YOU'RE MIKADO-SENSEI'S ASSISTANT, THAT DOESN'T MEAN YOU...
HWAAAARGH?!!
OH, NO! MY TELEKINESIS WENT OUT OF CONTROL!!
Oh dear.
ER.
I... IT'S DRAGGING MY HAAAND!!

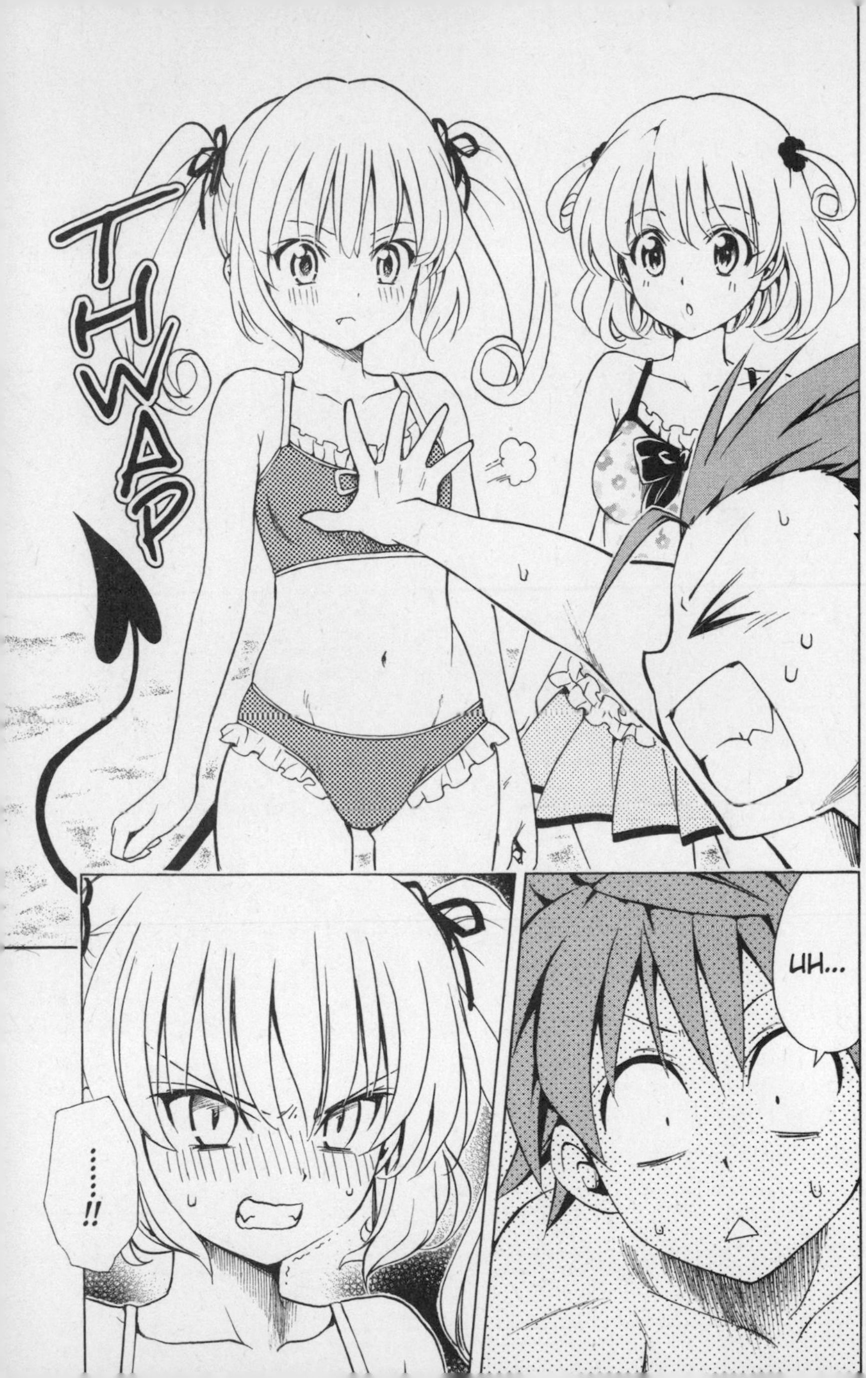
THWAP
UH...
......!!

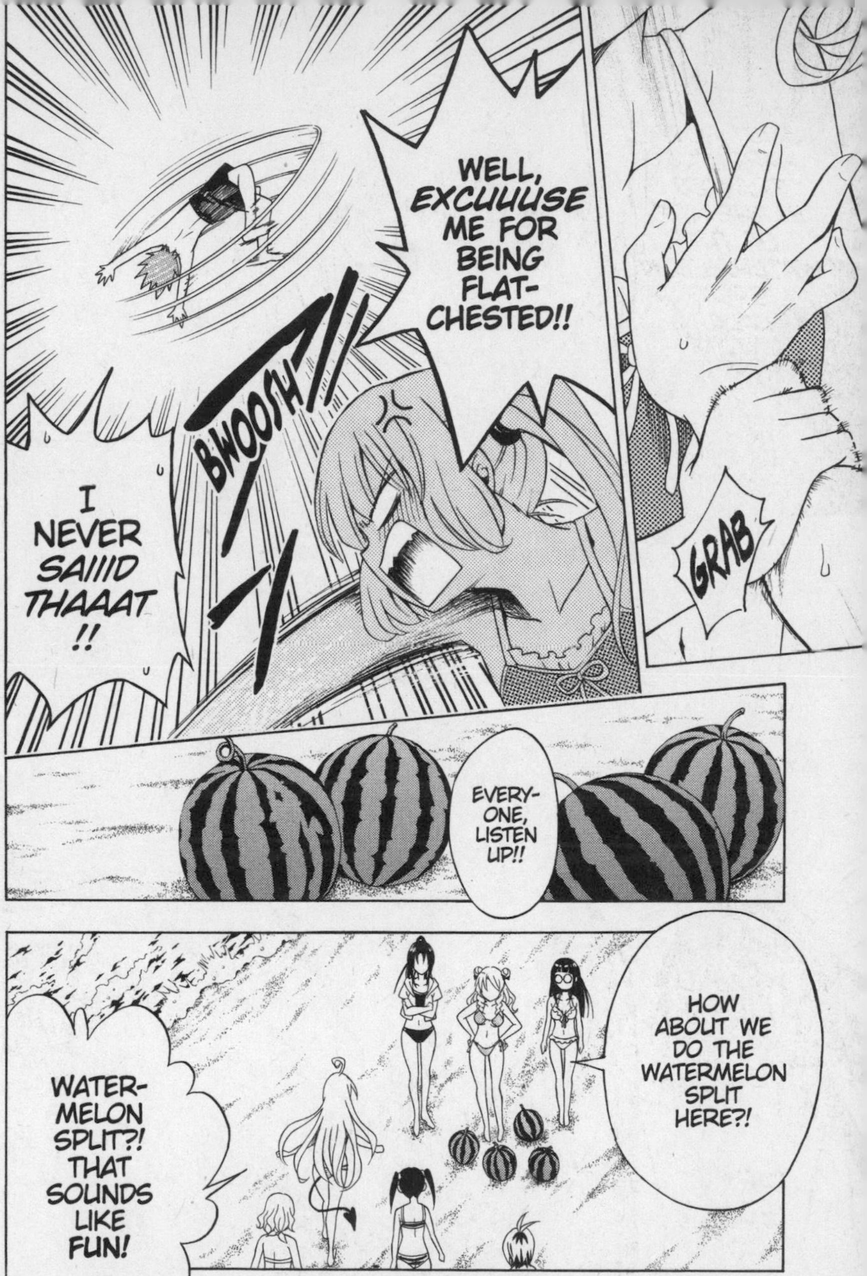
GRAB
WELL, EXCUUUSE ME FOR BEING FLAT-CHESTED!!
BWOOSH
I NEVER SAIIID THAAAT!!
EVERY-ONE, LISTEN UP!!
HOW ABOUT WE DO THE WATERMELON SPLIT HERE?!
WATER-MELON SPLIT?! THAT SOUNDS LIKE FUN!

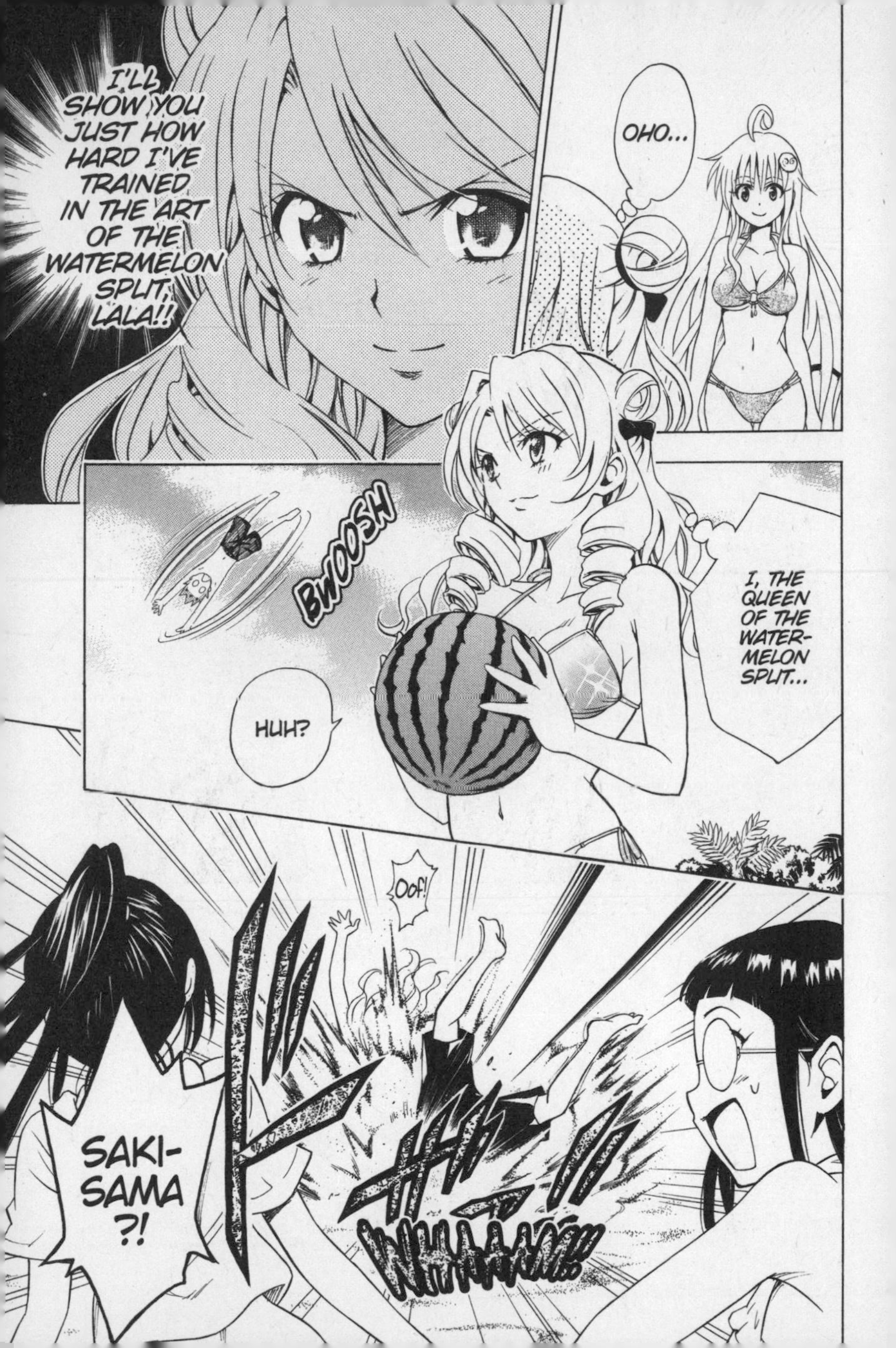
OHO...
I'LL SHOW YOU JUST HOW HARD I'VE TRAINED IN THE ART OF THE WATERMELON SPLIT, LALA!!
I, THE QUEEN OF THE WATER-MELON SPLIT...
BWOOSH
HUH?
Oof!
SAKI-SAMA ?!

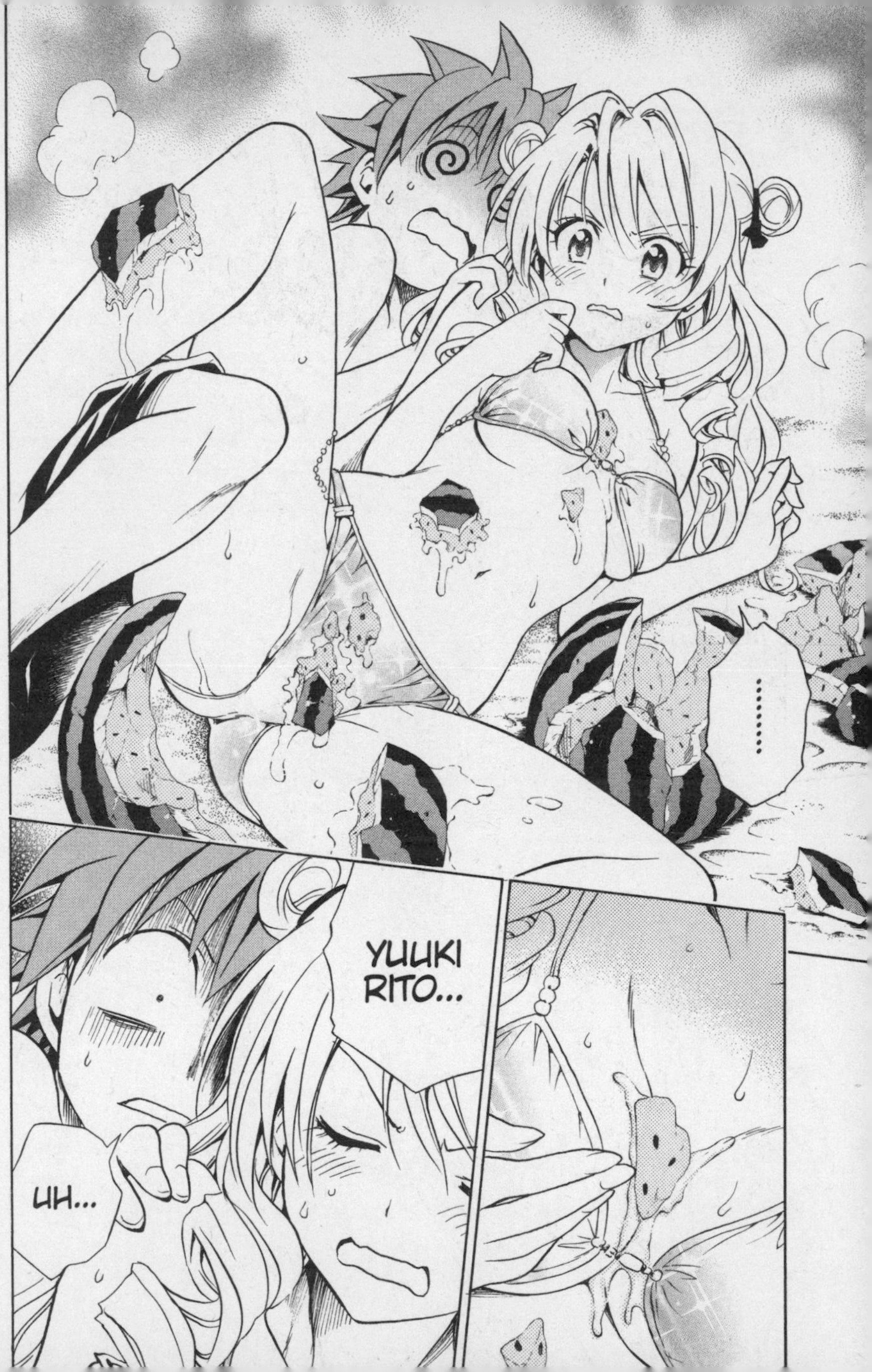
......
YUUKI RITO...
UH...

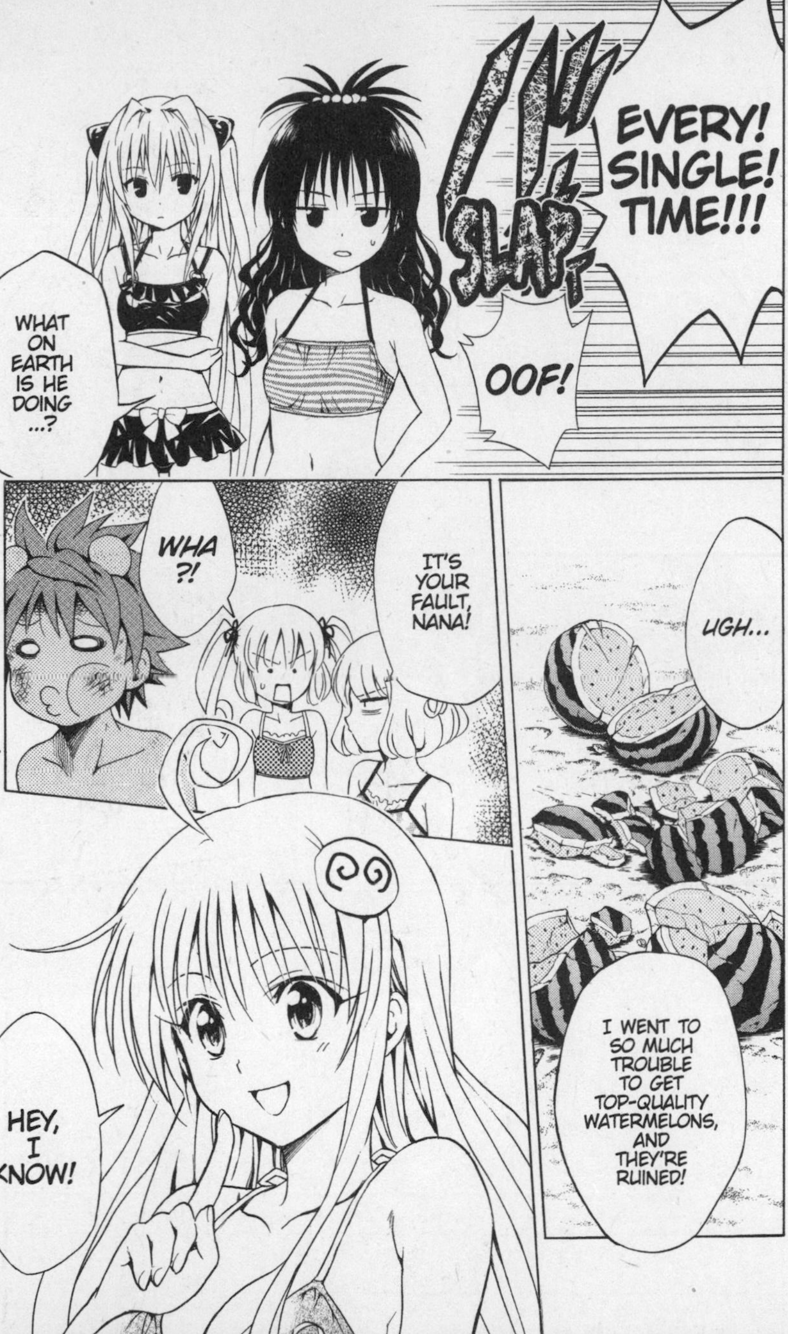
EVERY! SINGLE! TIME!!!
SLAP
OOF!
WHAT ON EARTH IS HE DOING ...?
UGH...
I WENT TO SO MUCH TROUBLE TO GET TOP-QUALITY WATERMELONS, AND THEY'RE RUINED!
IT'S YOUR FAULT, NANA!
WHA ?!
HEY, I KNOW!

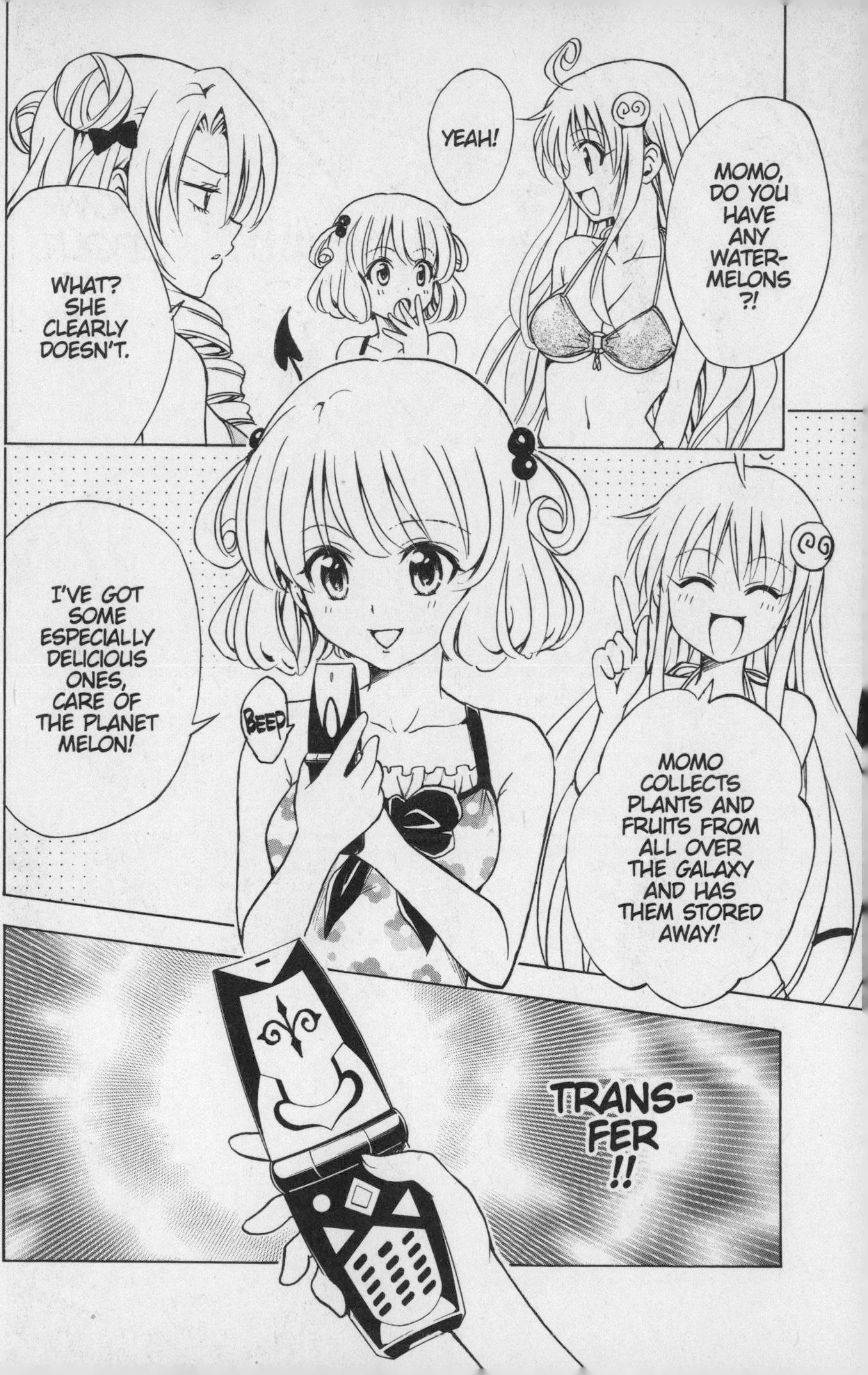
MOMO, DO YOU HAVE ANY WATER-MELONS?!
YEAH!
WHAT? SHE CLEARLY DOESN'T.
I'VE GOT SOME ESPECIALLY DELICIOUS ONES, CARE OF THE PLANET MELON!
BEEP
MOMO COLLECTS PLANTS AND FRUITS FROM ALL OVER THE GALAXY AND HAS THEM STORED AWAY!
TRANS-FER!!

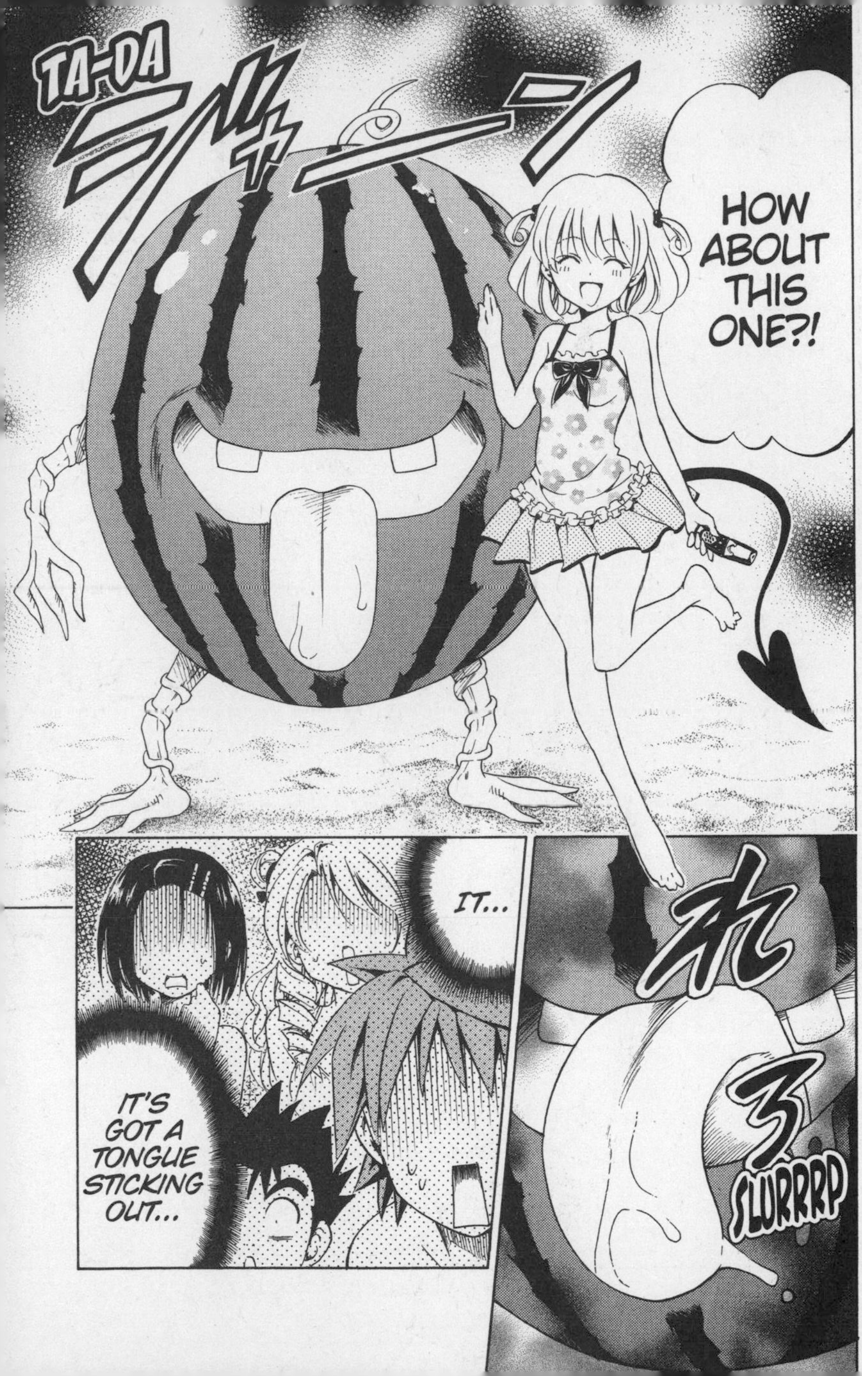
TA-DA
HOW ABOUT THIS ONE?!
れろ
SLURRRP
IT...
IT'S GOT A TONGUE STICKING OUT...

To LOVE Ru

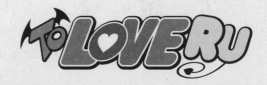

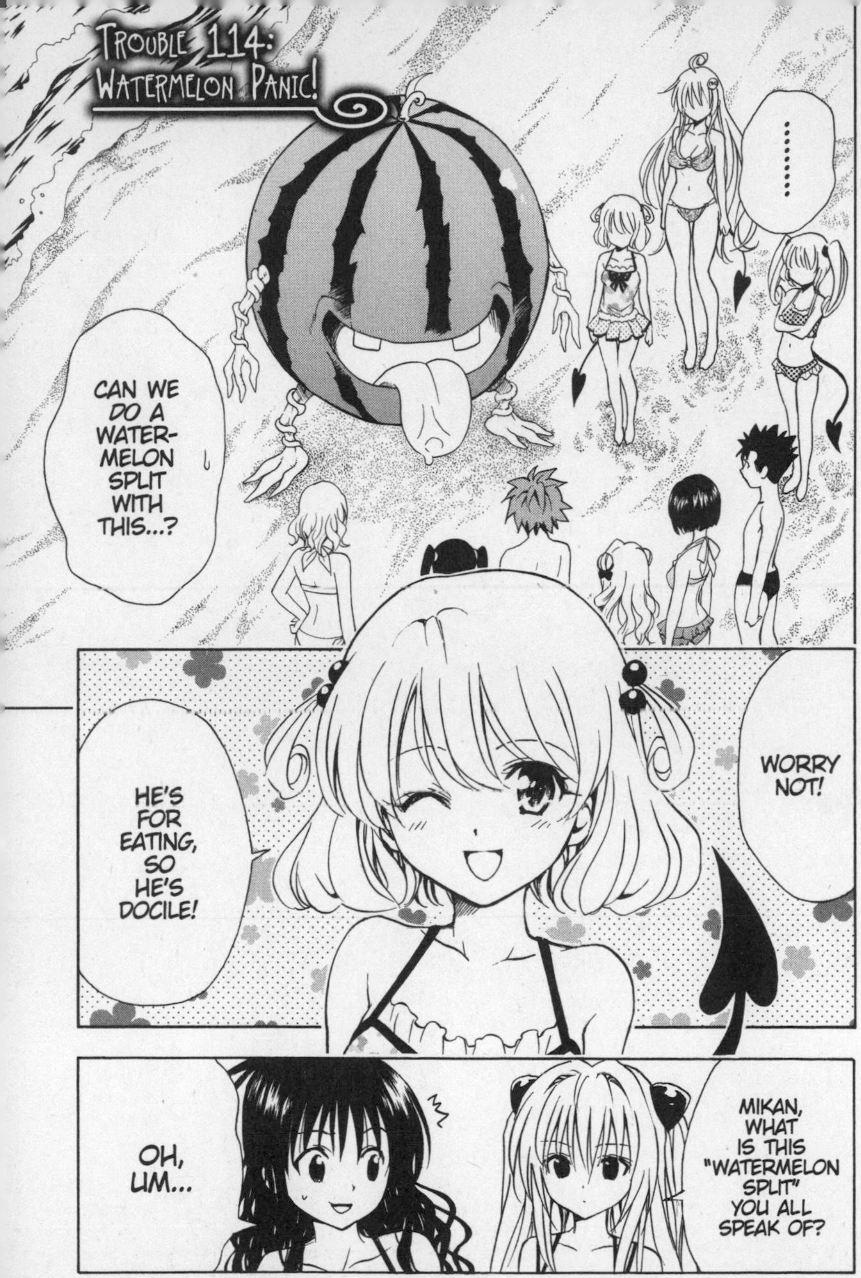
Trouble 114: Watermelon Panic!
......
Can we do a watermelon split with this...?
Worry not!
He's for eating, so he's docile!
Mikan, what is this "watermelon split" you all speak of?
Oh, um...

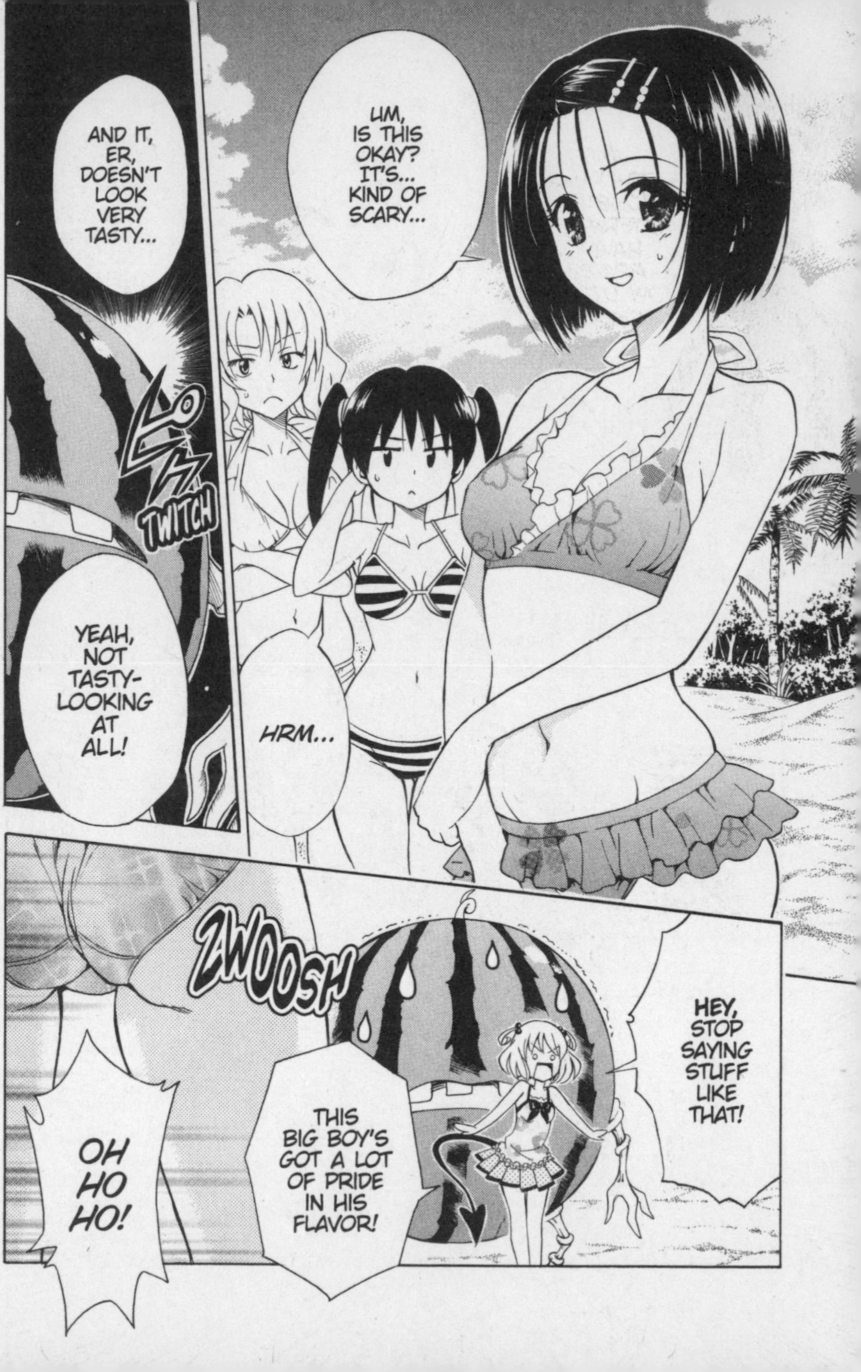
UM, IS THIS OKAY? IT'S... KIND OF SCARY...
HRM...
AND IT, ER, DOESN'T LOOK VERY TASTY...
TWITCH
YEAH, NOT TASTY-LOOKING AT ALL!
ZWOOSH
HEY, STOP SAYING STUFF LIKE THAT!
THIS BIG BOY'S GOT A LOT OF PRIDE IN HIS FLAVOR!
OH HO HO!

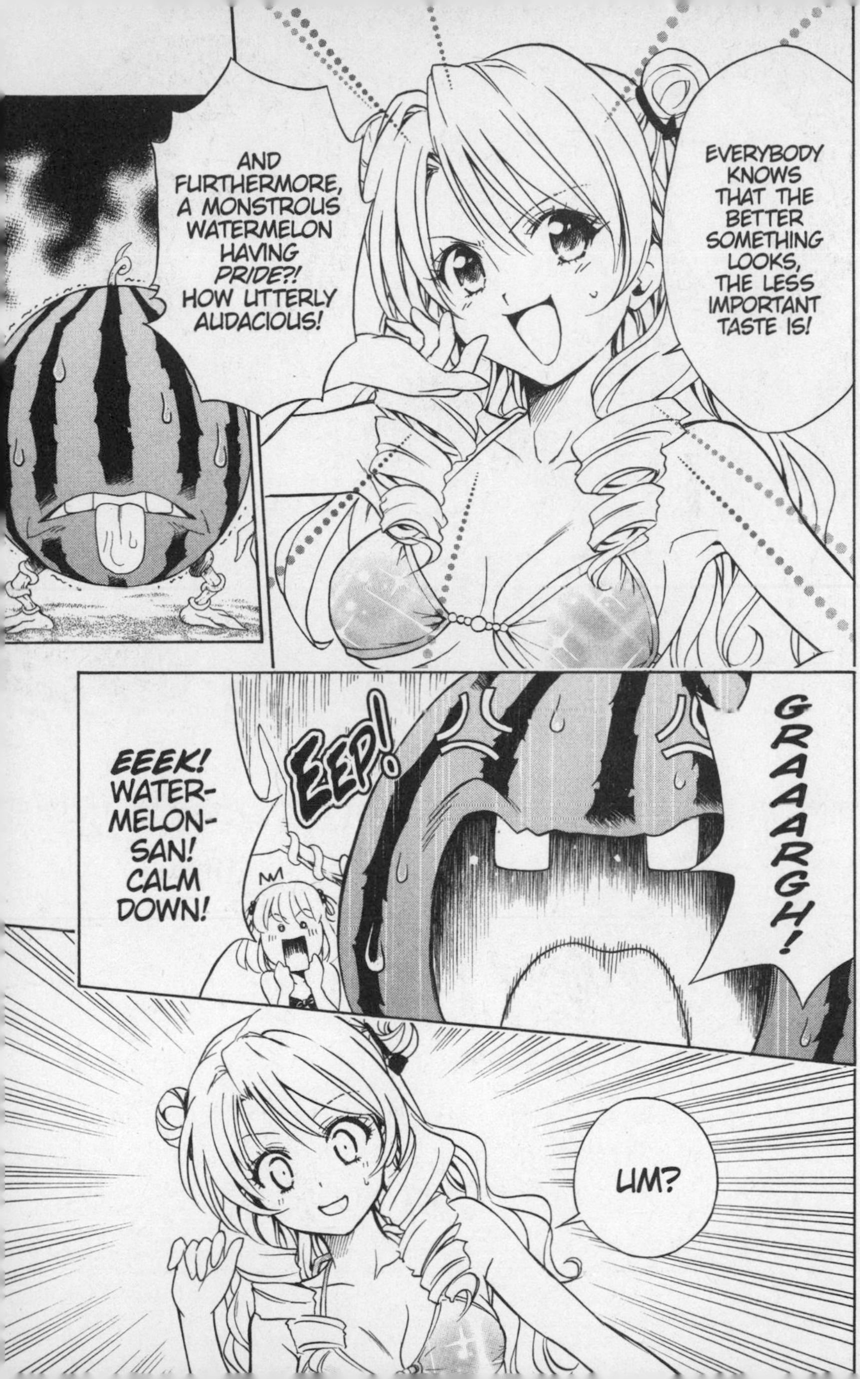
EVERYBODY KNOWS THAT THE BETTER SOMETHING LOOKS, THE LESS IMPORTANT TASTE IS!
AND FURTHERMORE, A MONSTROUS WATERMELON HAVING *PRIDE*?! HOW UTTERLY AUDACIOUS!
GRAAARGH!
EEP!
EEEK! WATER-MELON-SAN! CALM DOWN!
UM?

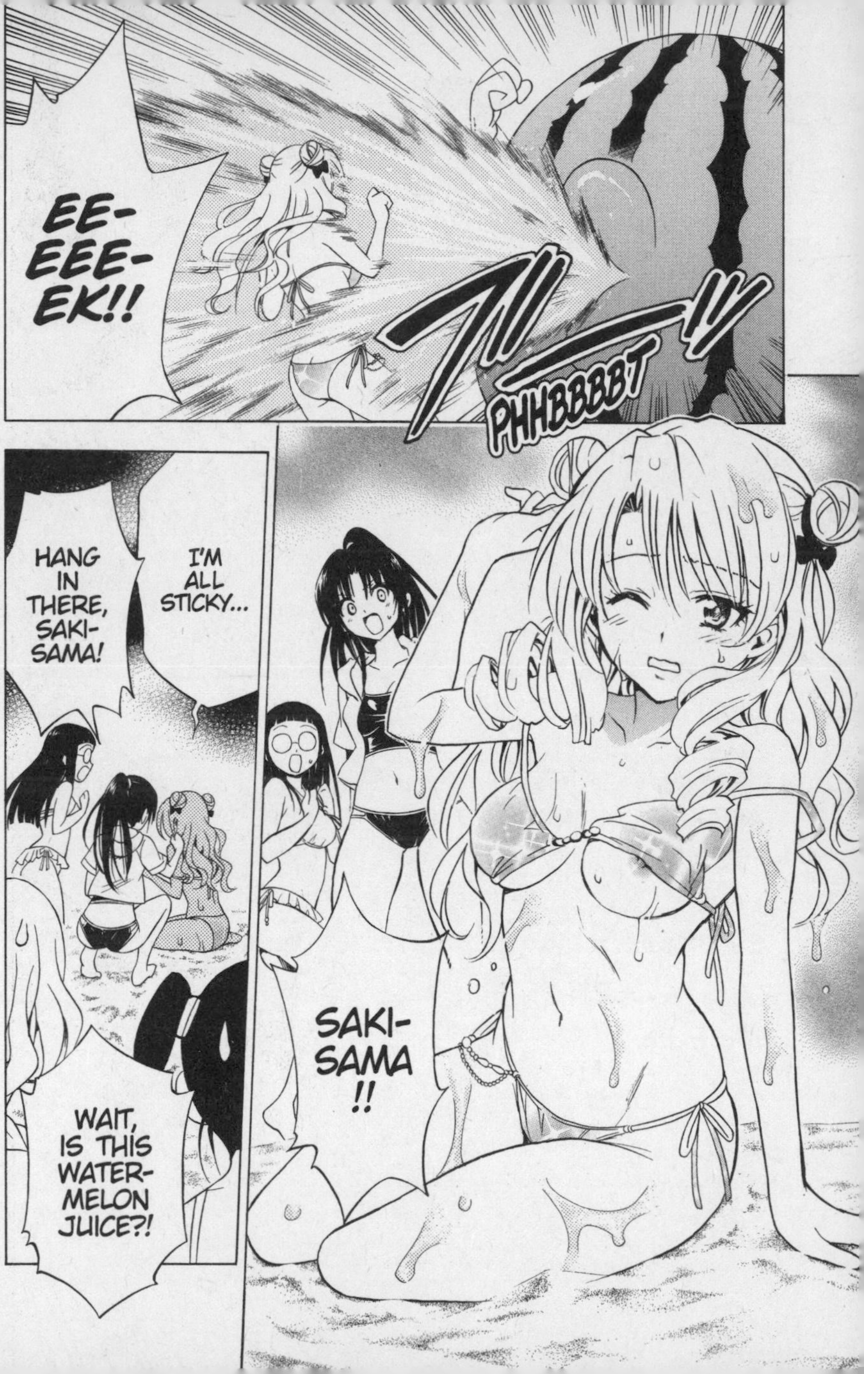
EE-EEE-EK!!
PHHBBBBT
SAKI-SAMA!!
I'M ALL STICKY...
HANG IN THERE, SAKI-SAMA!
WAIT, IS THIS WATERMELON JUICE?!

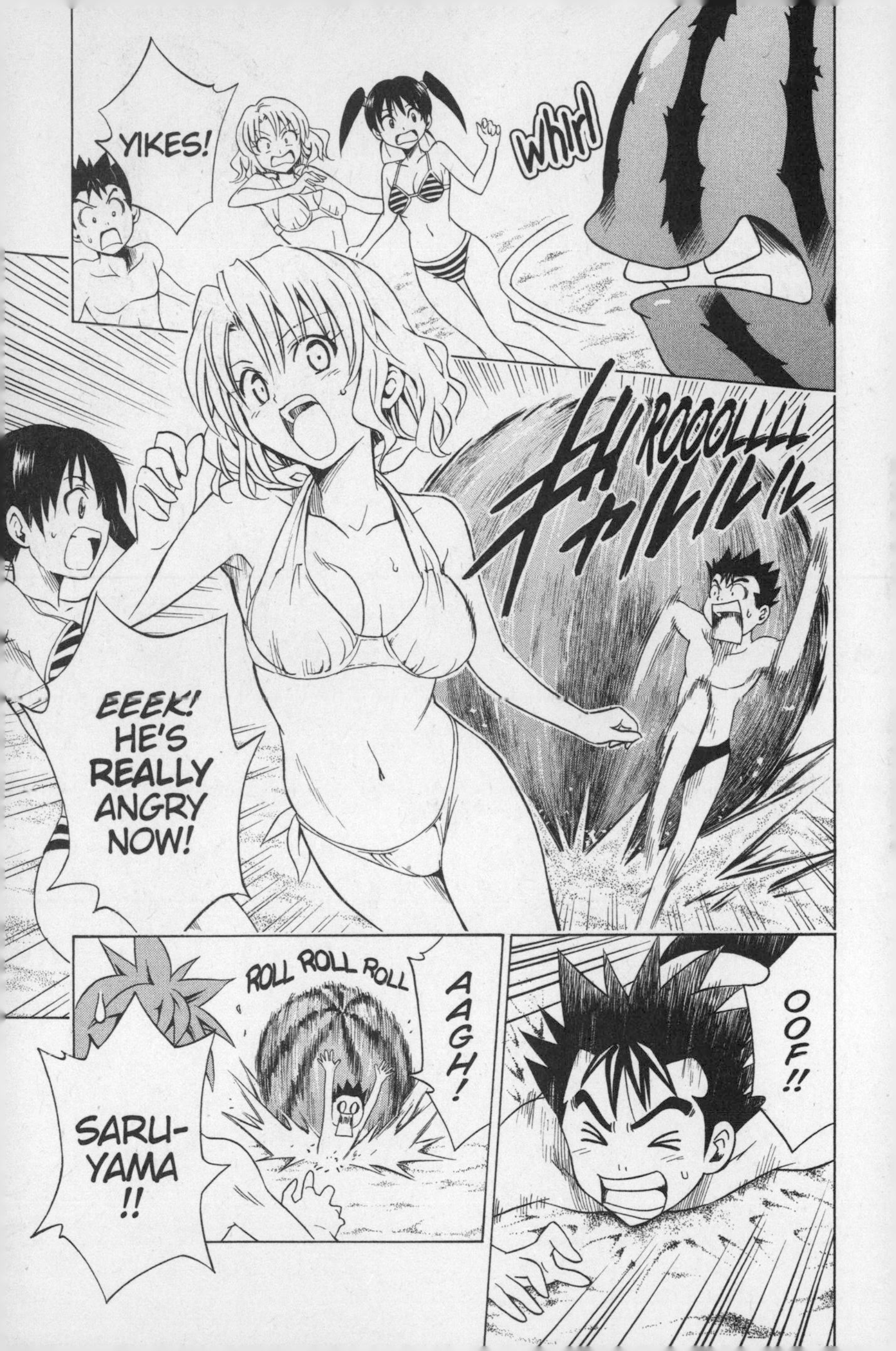
whirl
YIKES!
ROOOLLLL
EEEK! HE'S REALLY ANGRY NOW!
OOF!!
AAGH!
ROLL ROLL ROLL
SARU-YAMA!!

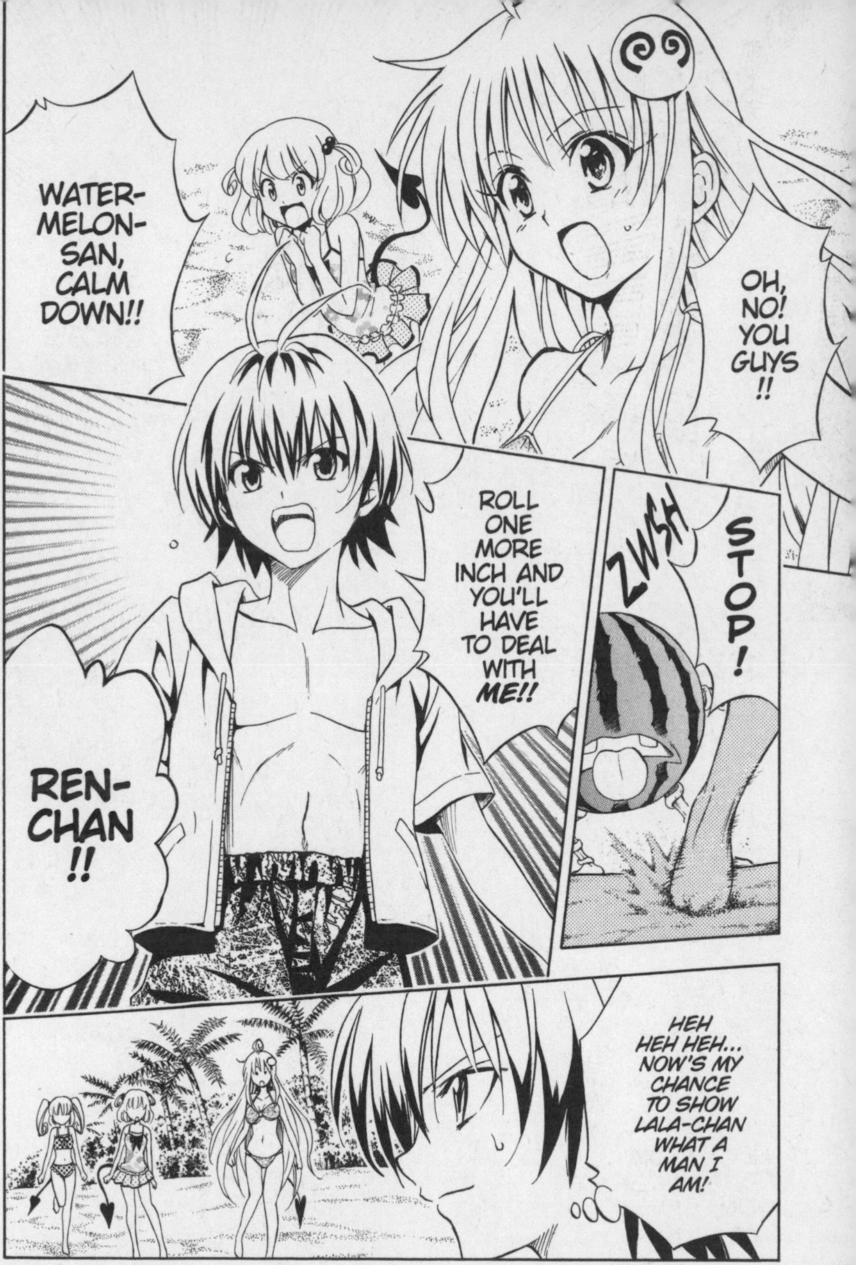
OH, NO! YOU GUYS!!
WATER-MELON-SAN, CALM DOWN!!
ZWSH
STOP!
ROLL ONE MORE INCH AND YOU'LL HAVE TO DEAL WITH *ME!!*
REN-CHAN!!
HEH HEH HEH... NOW'S MY CHANCE TO SHOW LALA-CHAN WHAT A MAN I AM!

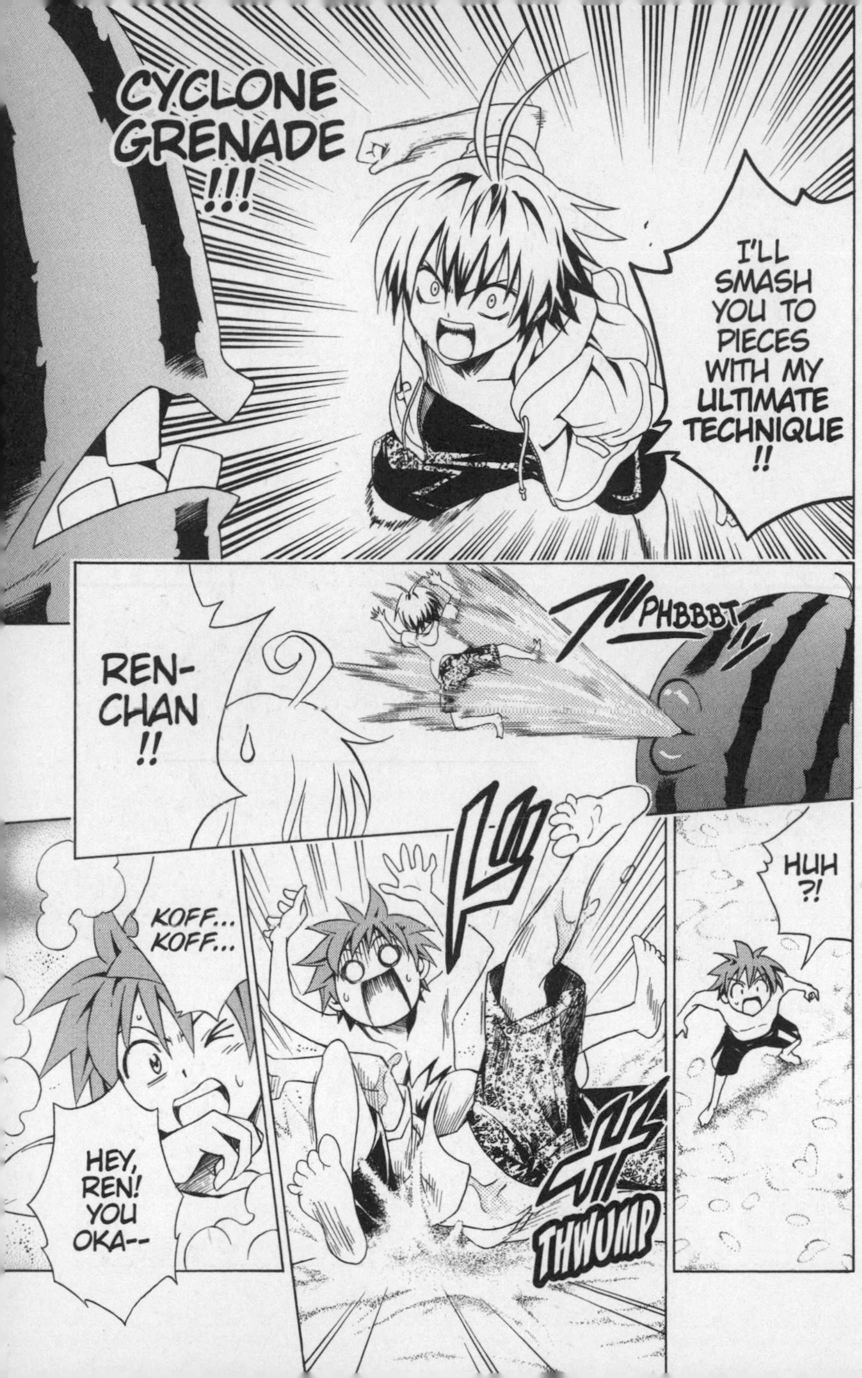
I'LL SMASH YOU TO PIECES WITH MY ULTIMATE TECHNIQUE!!
CYCLONE GRENADE!!!
PHBBBT
REN-CHAN!!
HUH?!
THWUMP
KOFF... KOFF...
HEY, REN! YOU OKA--

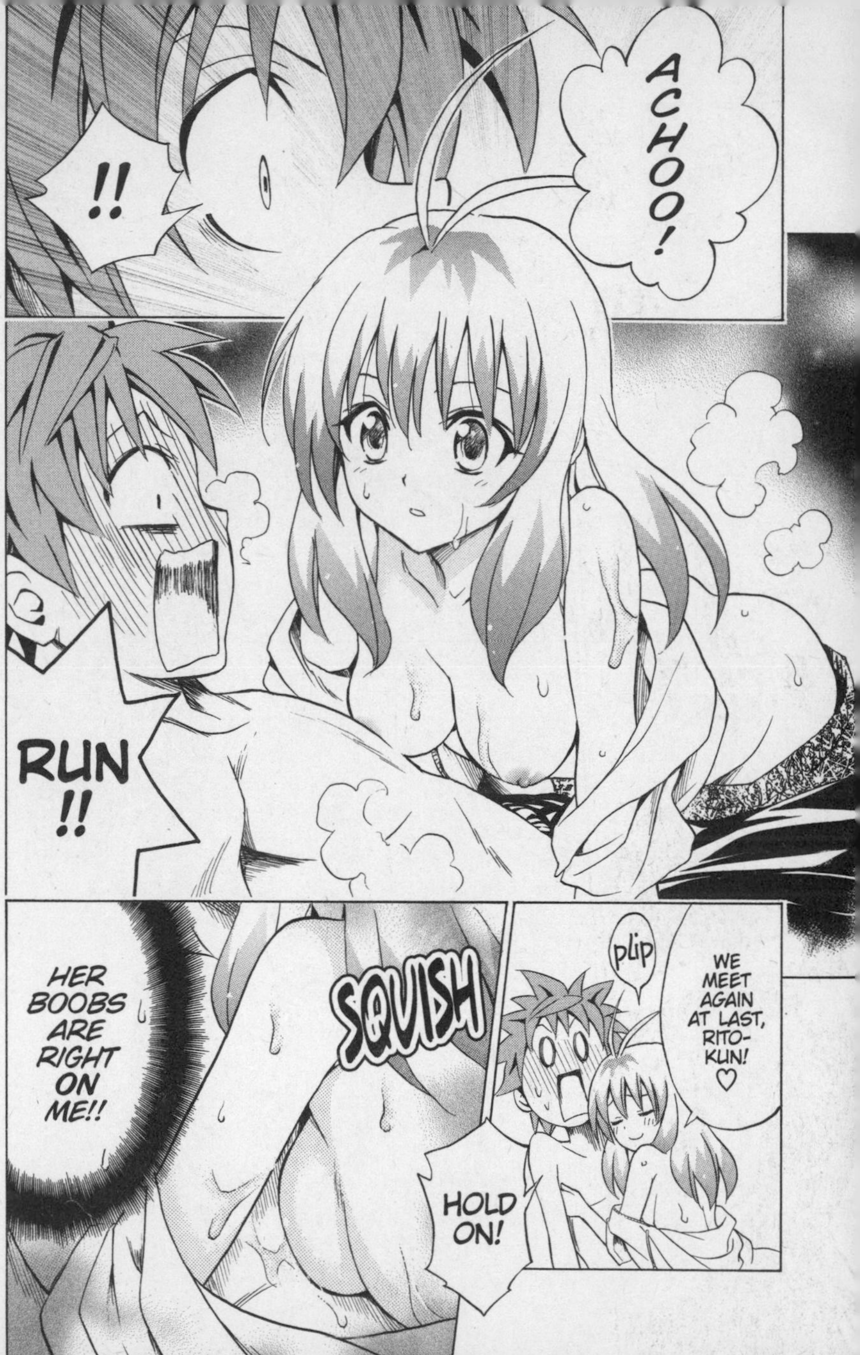
ACHOO!
!!
RUN!!
plip
WE MEET AGAIN AT LAST, RITO-KUN! ♡
HOLD ON!
SQUISH
HER BOOBS ARE RIGHT ON ME!!

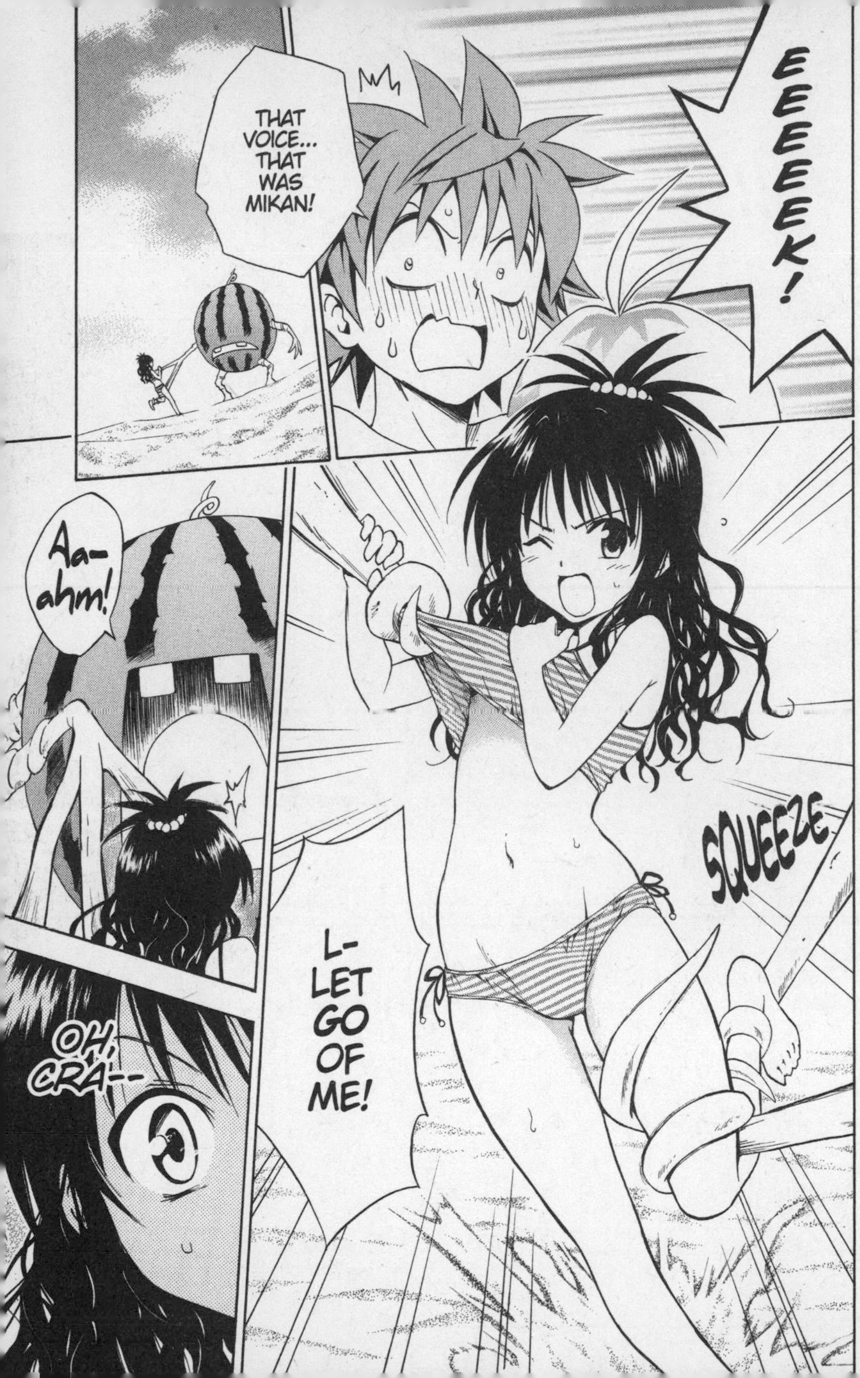
EEEEEK!
THAT VOICE... THAT WAS MIKAN!
SQUEEZE
L-LET GO OF ME!
Aa-ahm!
OH, CRA--

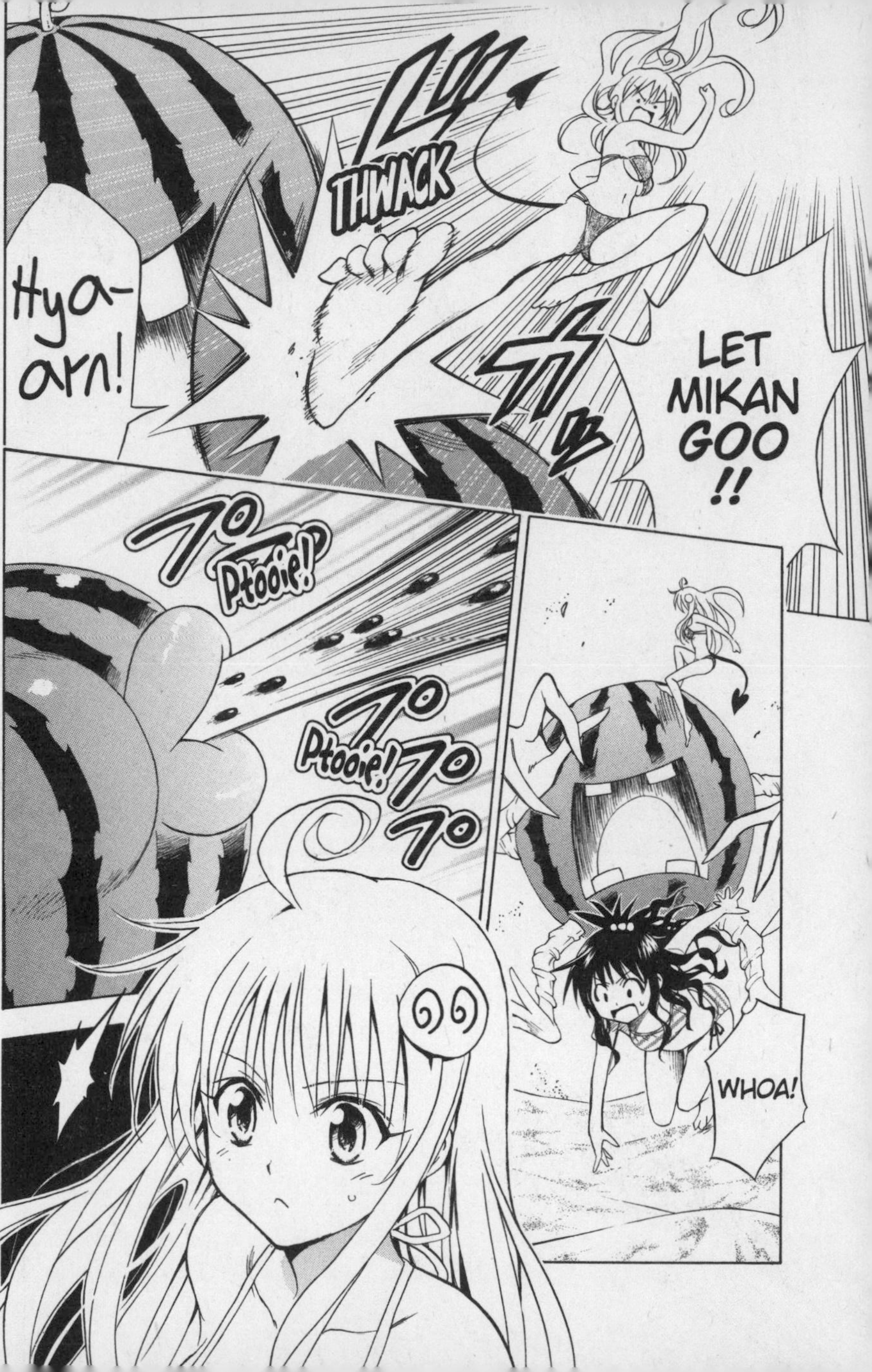
LET MIKAN GOO!!
THWACK
Hya-arn!
WHOA!
Ptooie!
Ptooie!

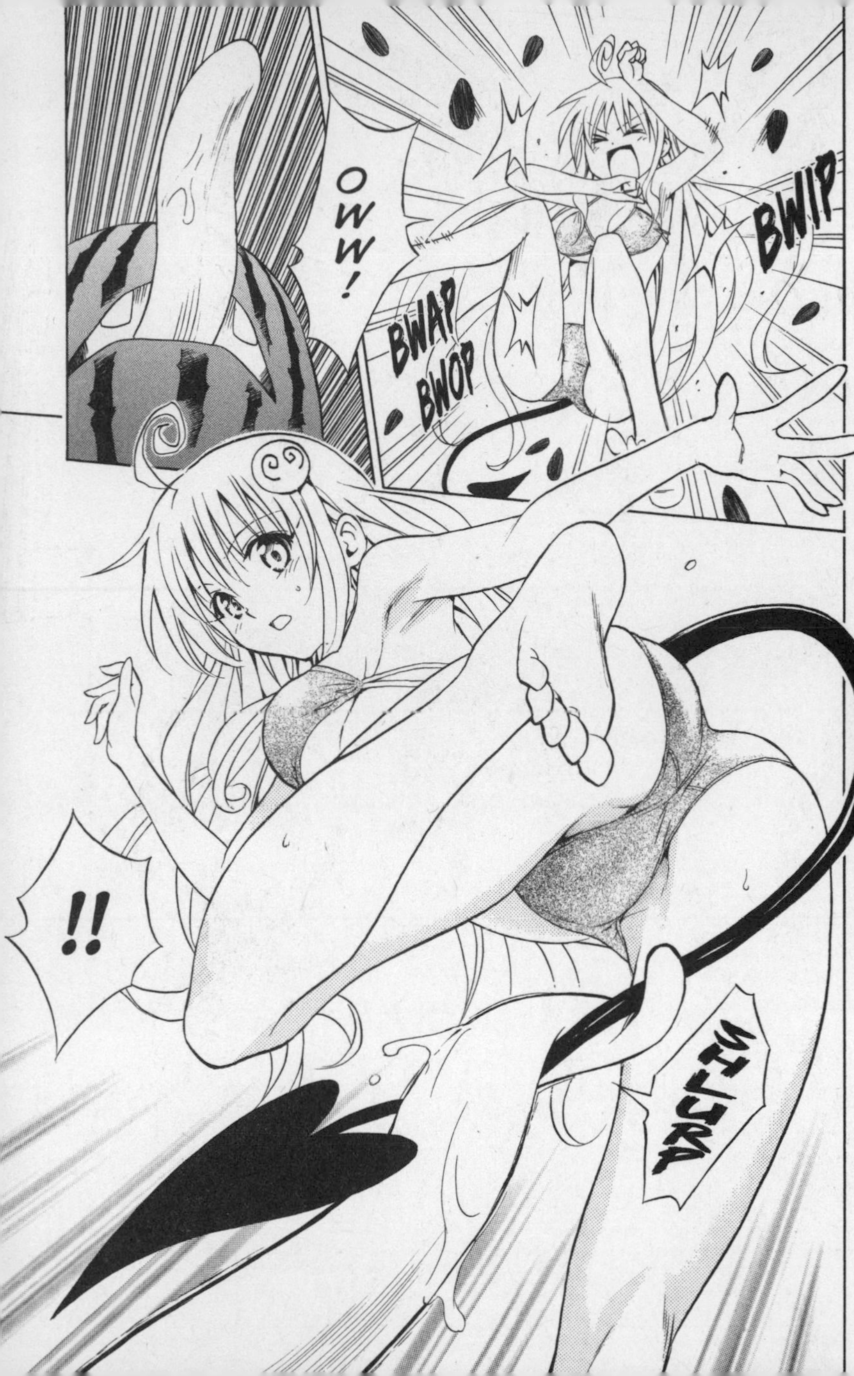
BWIP
OWW!
BWAP
BWOP
!!
SHURA

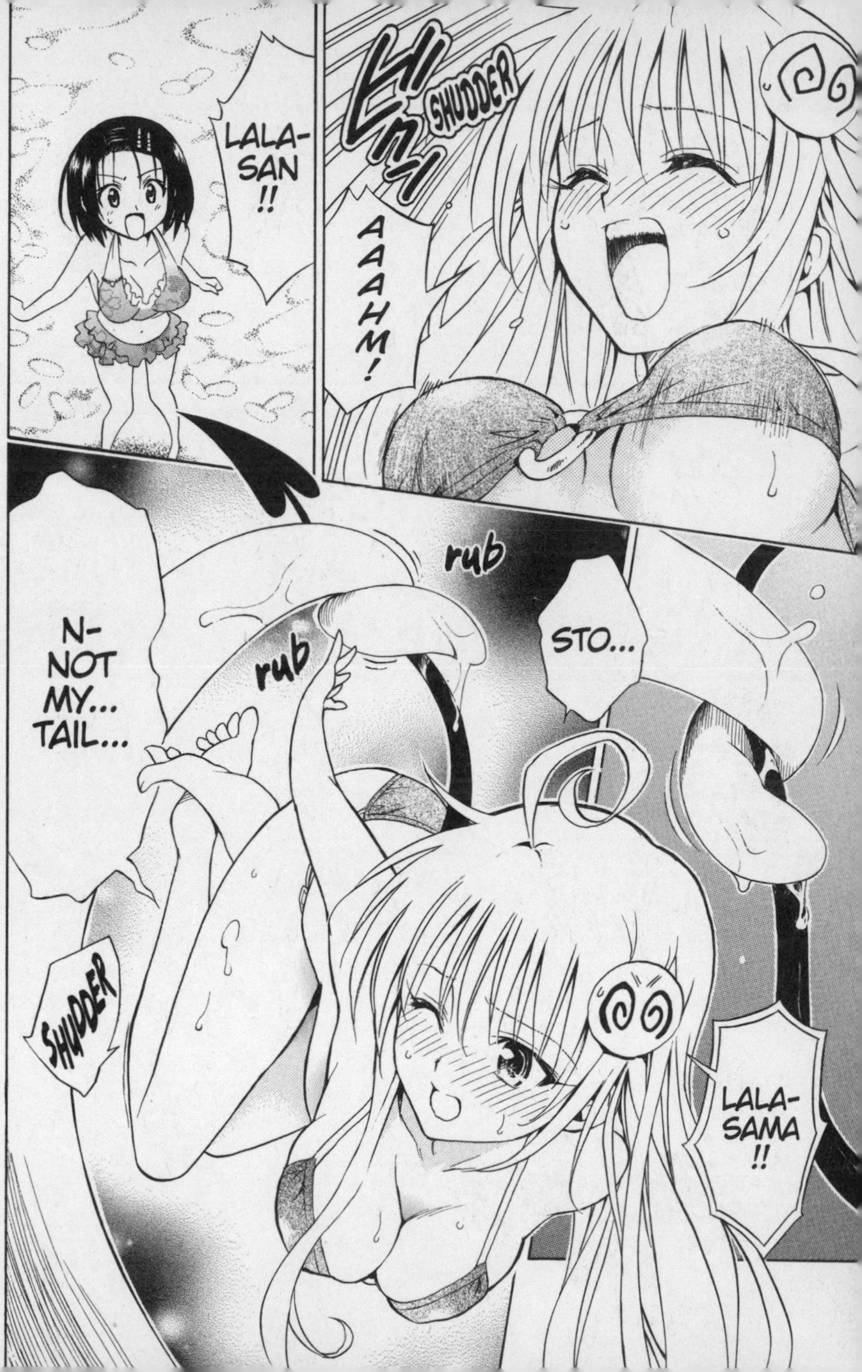
SHUDDER
AAAAHM!
LALA-SAN!!
STO...
rub
rub
N-NOT MY... TAIL...
LALA-SAMA!!
SHUDDER

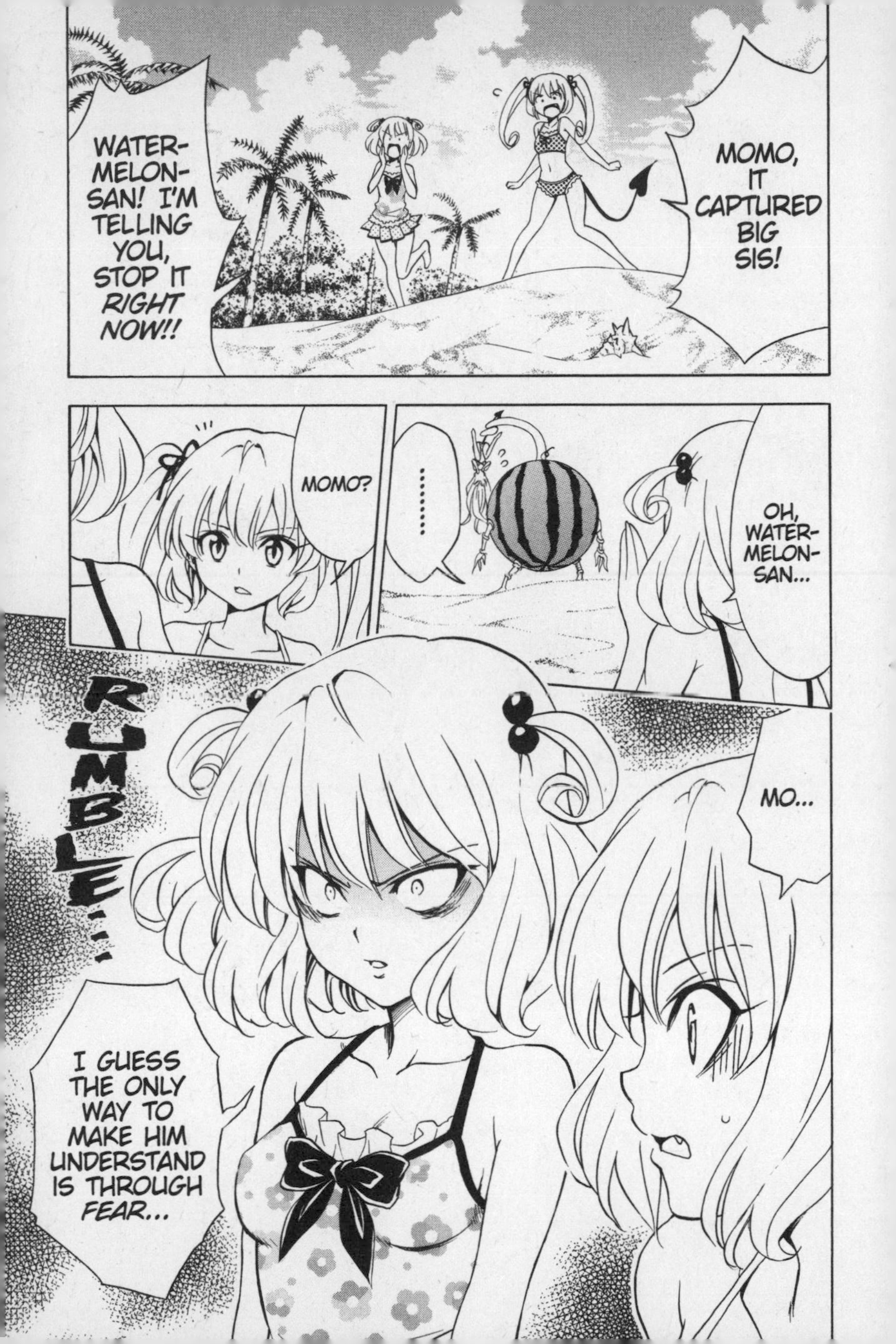
MOMO, IT CAPTURED BIG SIS!
WATER-MELON-SAN! I'M TELLING YOU, STOP IT RIGHT NOW!!
OH, WATER-MELON-SAN...
......
MOMO?
MO...
RUMBLE...
I GUESS THE ONLY WAY TO MAKE HIM UNDERSTAND IS THROUGH FEAR...

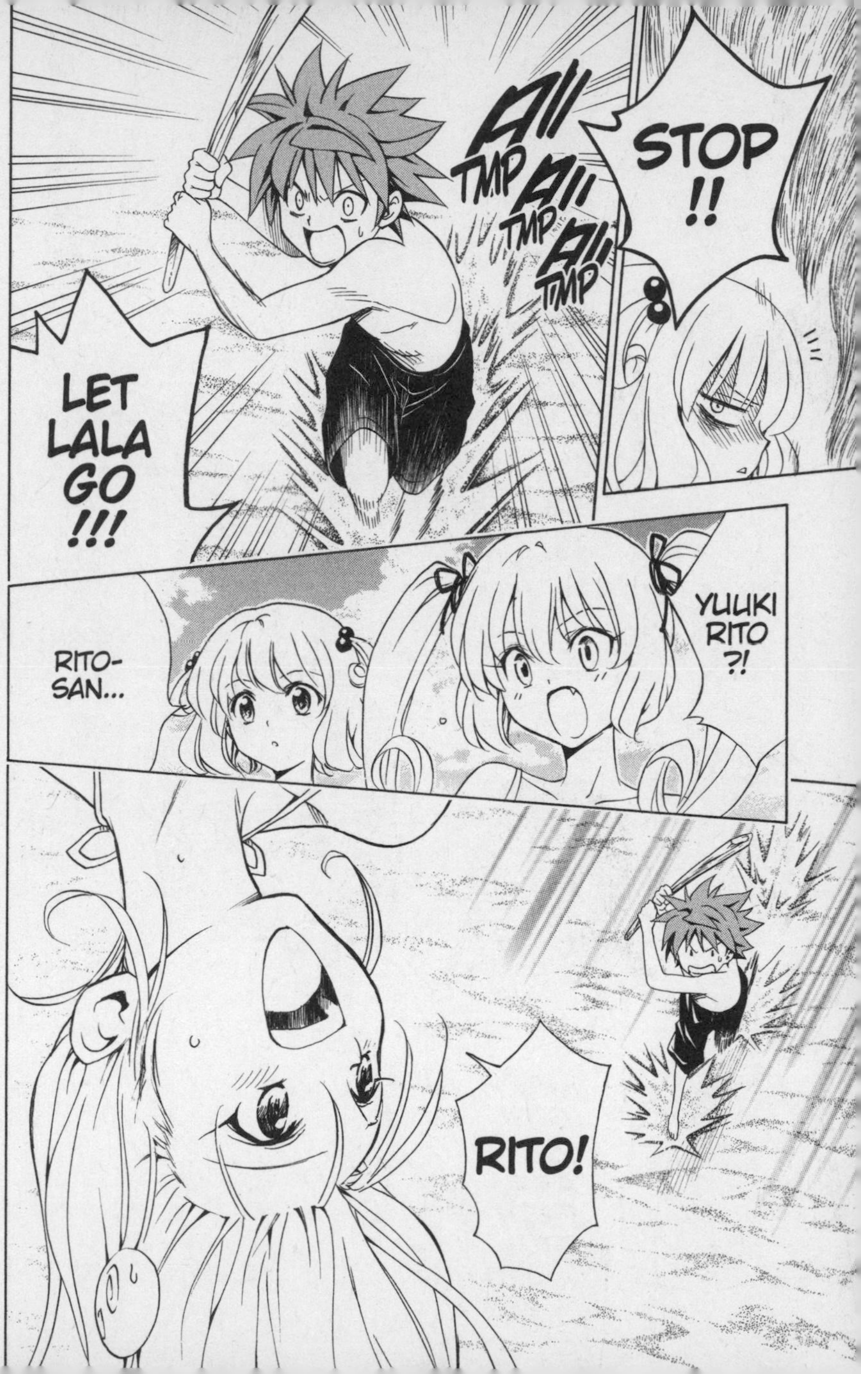
STOP !!
TMP
TMP
TMP
LET LALA GO !!!
YUUKI RITO ?!
RITO-SAN...
RITO!

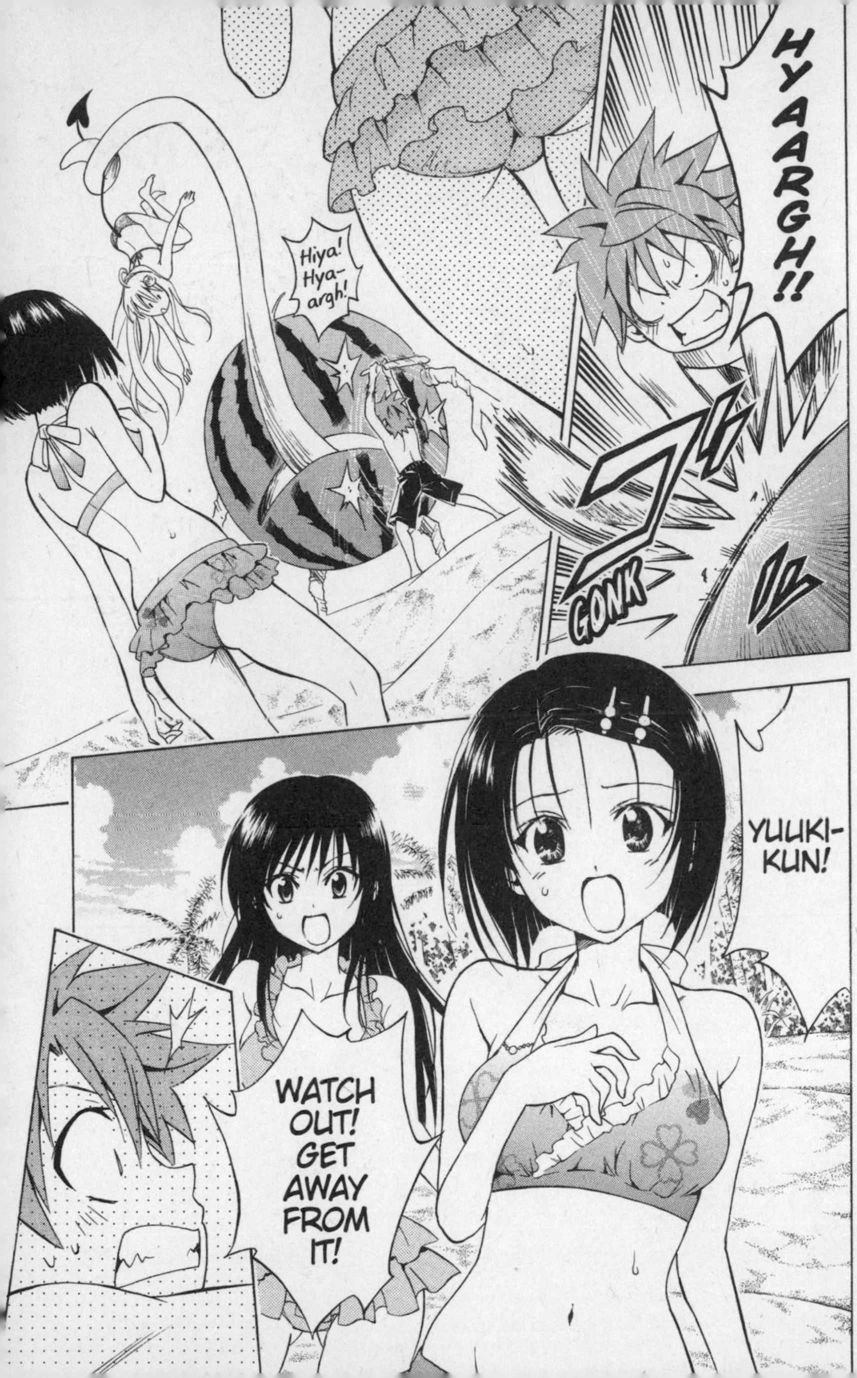

HYAARGH!!
Hiya! Hya-argh!
GONK
YUUKI-KUN!
WATCH OUT! GET AWAY FROM IT!

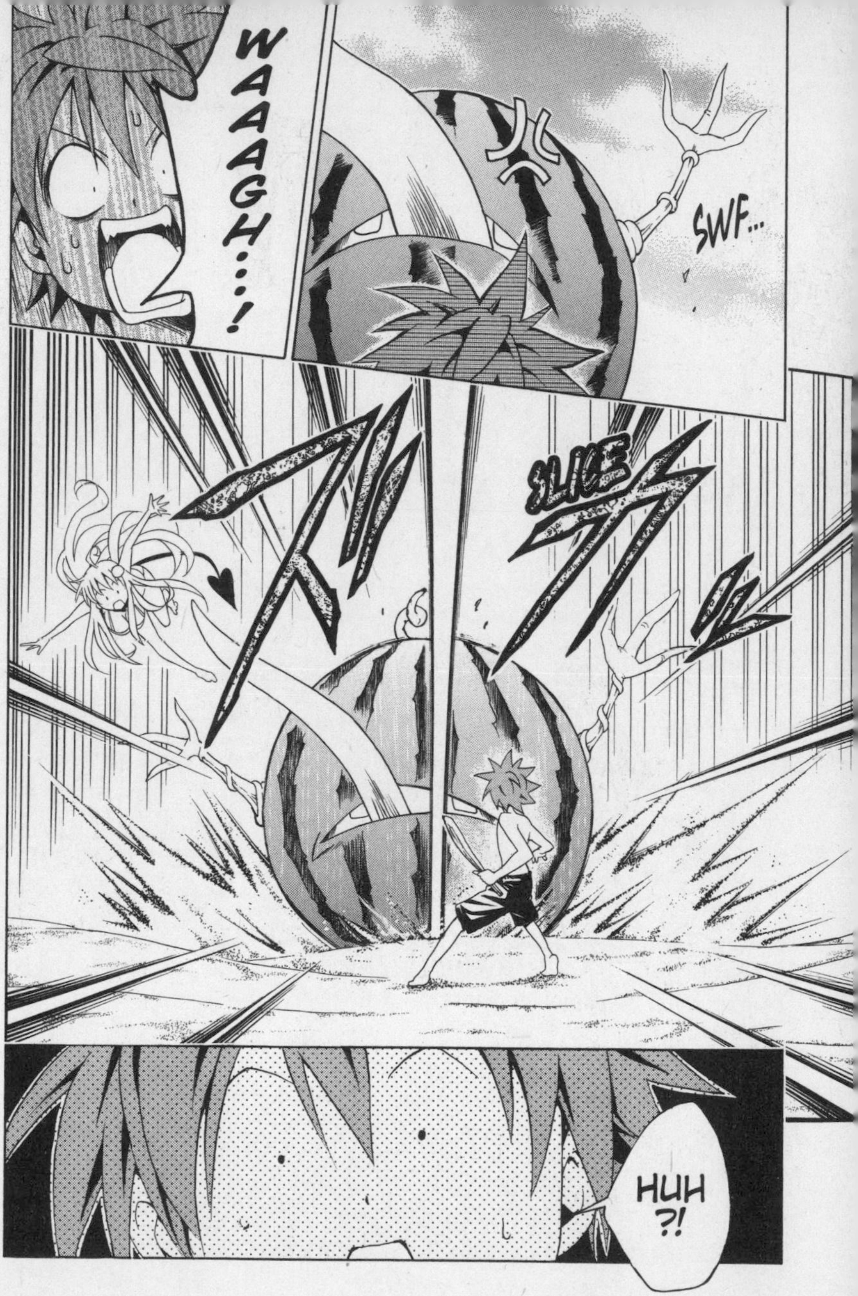
SWF...
WAAAAGH...!
SLICE
HUH ?!

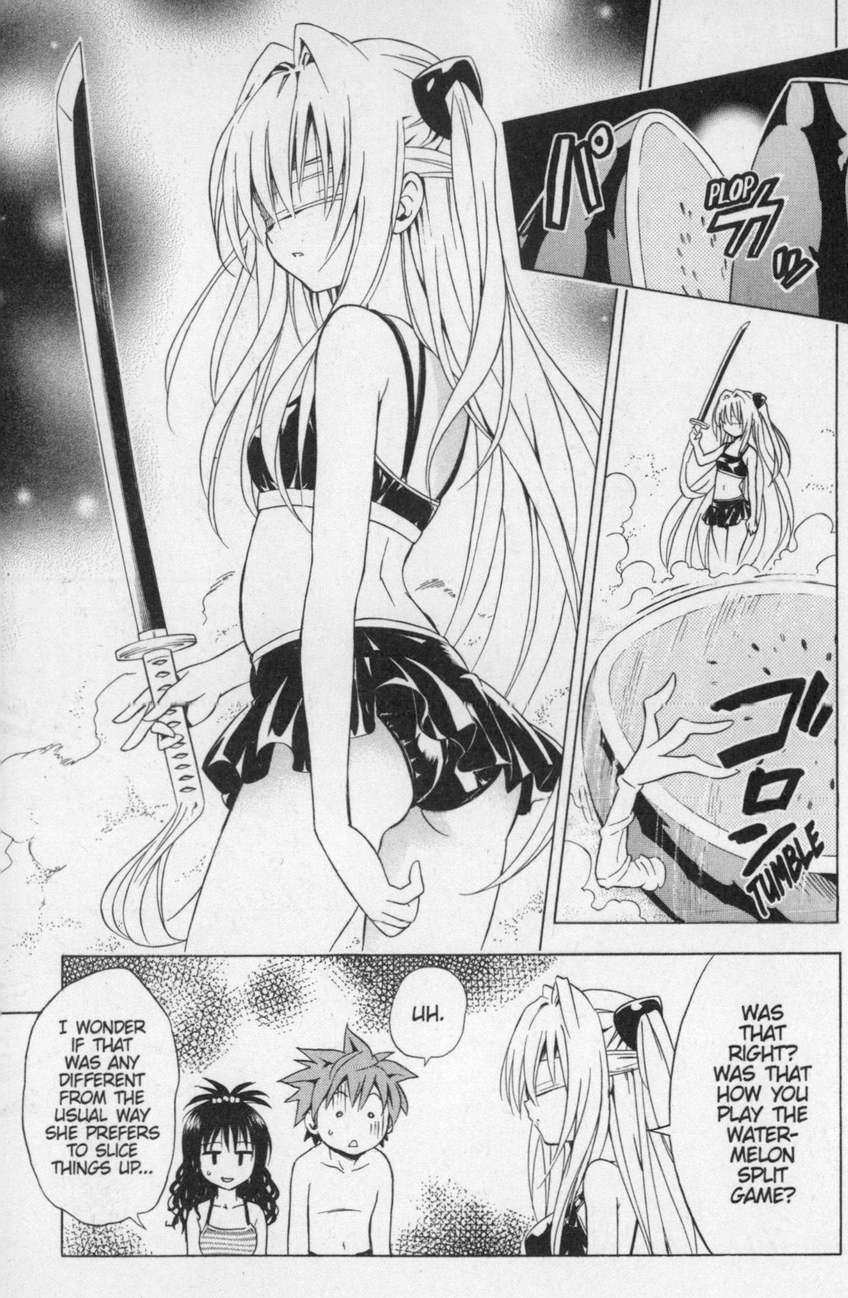
パ
PLOP
ゴロン
TUMBLE
WAS THAT RIGHT? WAS THAT HOW YOU PLAY THE WATER-MELON SPLIT GAME?
UH.
I WONDER IF THAT WAS ANY DIFFERENT FROM THE USUAL WAY SHE PREFERS TO SLICE THINGS UP...

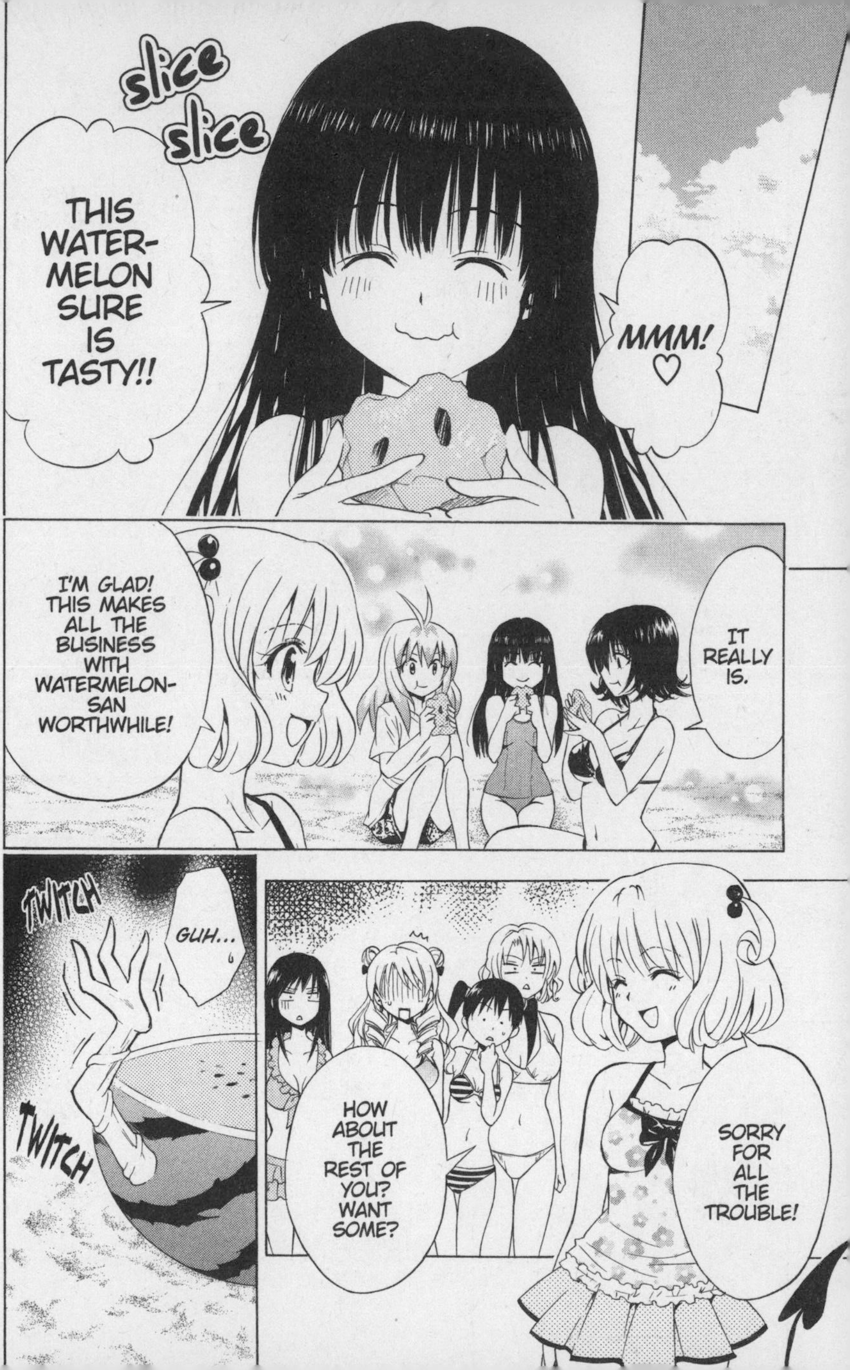
slice slice
MMM! ♡
THIS WATER-MELON SURE IS TASTY!!
IT REALLY IS.
I'M GLAD! THIS MAKES ALL THE BUSINESS WITH WATERMELON-SAN WORTHWHILE!
SORRY FOR ALL THE TROUBLE!
HOW ABOUT THE REST OF YOU? WANT SOME?
TWITCH
GUH...
TWITCH

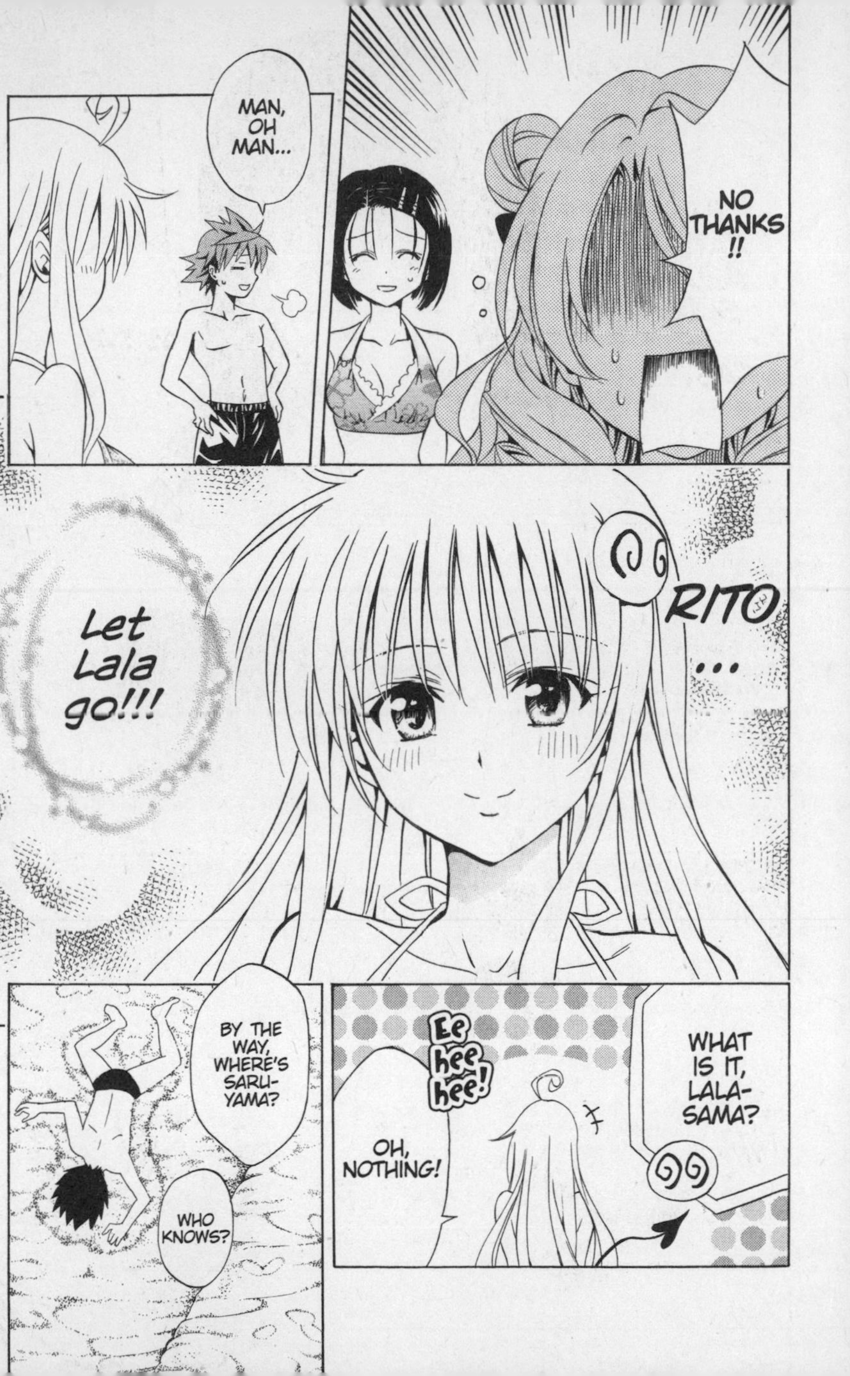
NO THANKS!!
MAN, OH MAN...
RITO...
Let Lala go!!!
WHAT IS IT, LALA-SAMA?
Ee hee hee!
OH, NOTHING!
BY THE WAY, WHERE'S SARU-YAMA?
WHO KNOWS?

Character File

Nana Asta Deviluke
Momo Belia Deviluke

☆Nana & Momo
Lala's twin sisters. Somehow, I think they manage to seem slightly older than Mikan.

●●●●●●●●●●●●●●●●●●●●●●

☆New Characters
From a relatively early stage, we had plans for Lala to have a younger sister, but we finally were able to find a place to debut both of them that corresponded nicely with our story needs for new characters.

●●●●●●●●●●●●●●●●●●●●●●

☆Twins
I wanted to make characters who are twins for quite some time, and in fact, inside my head, I tried to debut Yami as a character with a twin sister, one being rather dark and the other being comparatively nice. However, after a meeting, we decided to wait on that idea, and the concepts left over were inherited by Nana and Momo.

●●●●●●●●●●●●●●●●●●●●●●

☆Troubles
I struggled with their personalities and peculiarities. As readers know, we'd already debuted a lot of different personality types in the series, so we had to come up with something different from all the others (sweatdrop!). I had a lot of meetings with Yabuki-san about this, and what ended up coming from it was Nana's affinity for animals and Momo's for plants. This allowed us to link them with Celine and Maron nicely too.

●●●●●●●●●●●●●●●●●●●●●●

☆Their Personalities
Nana is straight-laced and cheerful, and more childlike than Momo. Momo (on the surface) is quieter and more ladylike, and tends to have a more mature way of thinking than Nana (and Lala). Beyond that, she's got a dark, sadistic side too... (Mwa ha ha!)

●●●●●●●●●●●●●●●●●●●●●●

☆Coming Next...
As for future developments, I think I'd like to first showcase more of Nana's innocence while also demonstrating how she matures into adulthood. In particular, I think there's a lot she still doesn't know about love. As for Momo, while she's got that devilish side, I think future stories ought to contrast that against her inner kindness.

In any case, there's a lot about both of them that we haven't been able to delve into yet, so I'm hoping we can find lots of ways forward to do so! Now, you tell me, readers: who do you prefer, Nana or Momo?

Hasemi

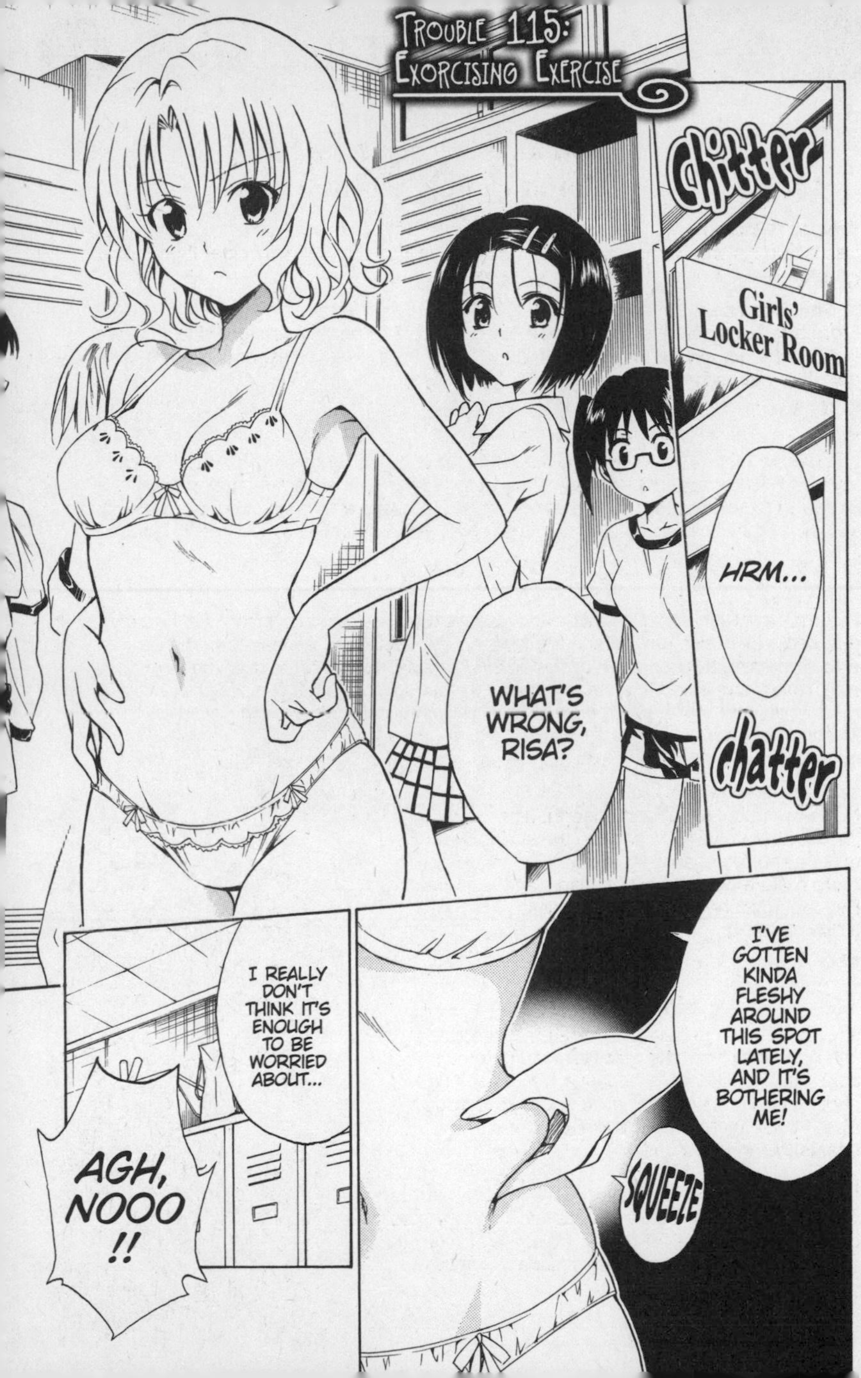
Trouble 115: Exorcising Exercise
Chitter
Girls' Locker Room
HRM...
chatter
WHAT'S WRONG, RISA?
I'VE GOTTEN KINDA FLESHY AROUND THIS SPOT LATELY, AND IT'S BOTHERING ME!
SQUEEZE
I REALLY DON'T THINK IT'S ENOUGH TO BE WORRIED ABOUT...
AGH, NOOO !!

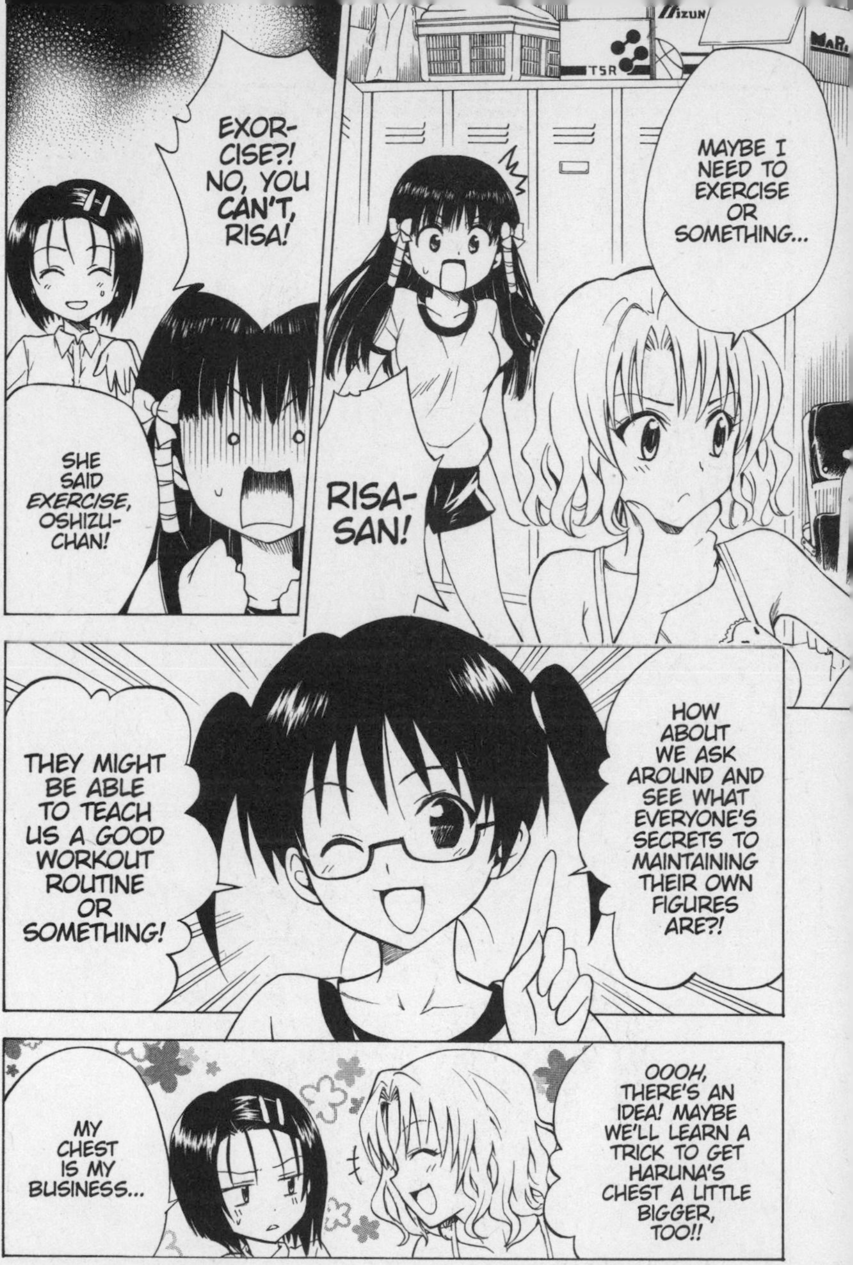
MAYBE I NEED TO EXERCISE OR SOMETHING...
RISA-SAN!
EXORCISE?! NO, YOU CAN'T, RISA!
SHE SAID *EXERCISE*, OSHIZU-CHAN!
HOW ABOUT WE ASK AROUND AND SEE WHAT EVERYONE'S SECRETS TO MAINTAINING THEIR OWN FIGURES ARE?!
THEY MIGHT BE ABLE TO TEACH US A GOOD WORKOUT ROUTINE OR SOMETHING!
OOOH, THERE'S AN IDEA! MAYBE WE'LL LEARN A TRICK TO GET HARUNA'S CHEST A LITTLE BIGGER, TOO!!
MY CHEST IS MY BUSINESS...

Trouble 115: Exorcising Exercise

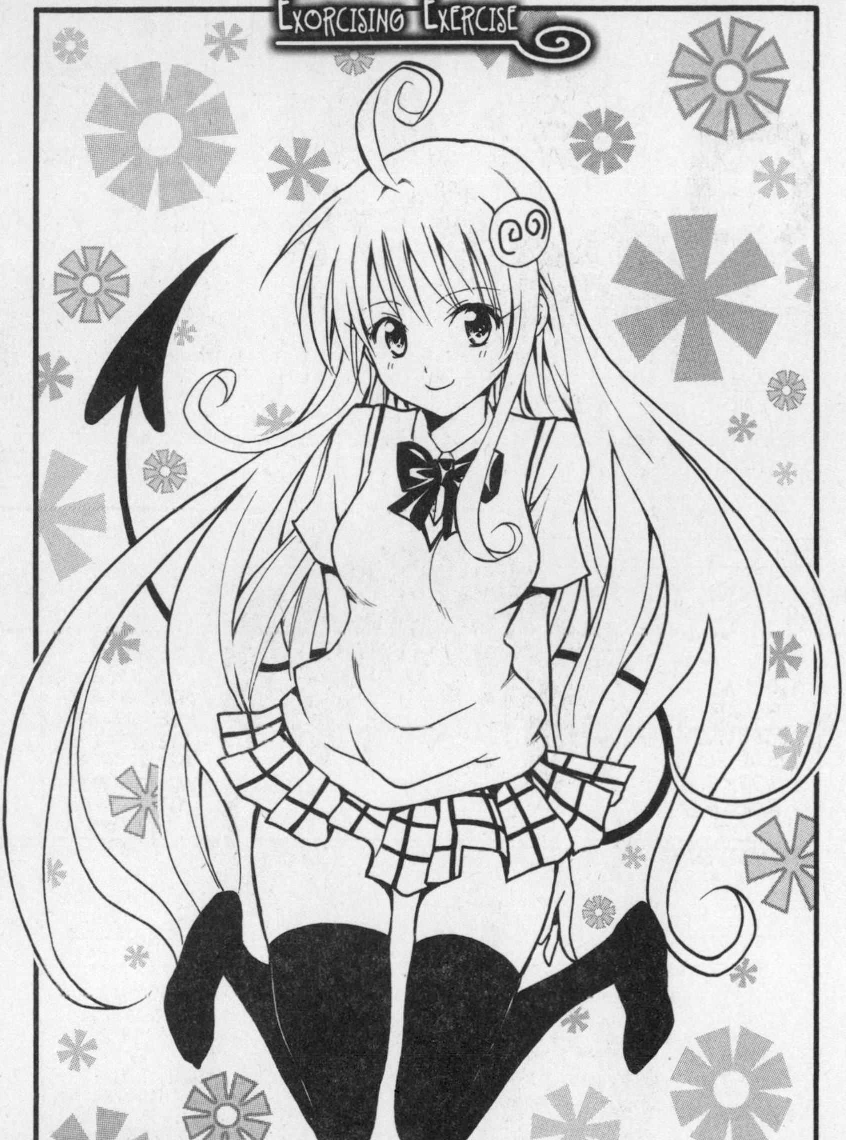

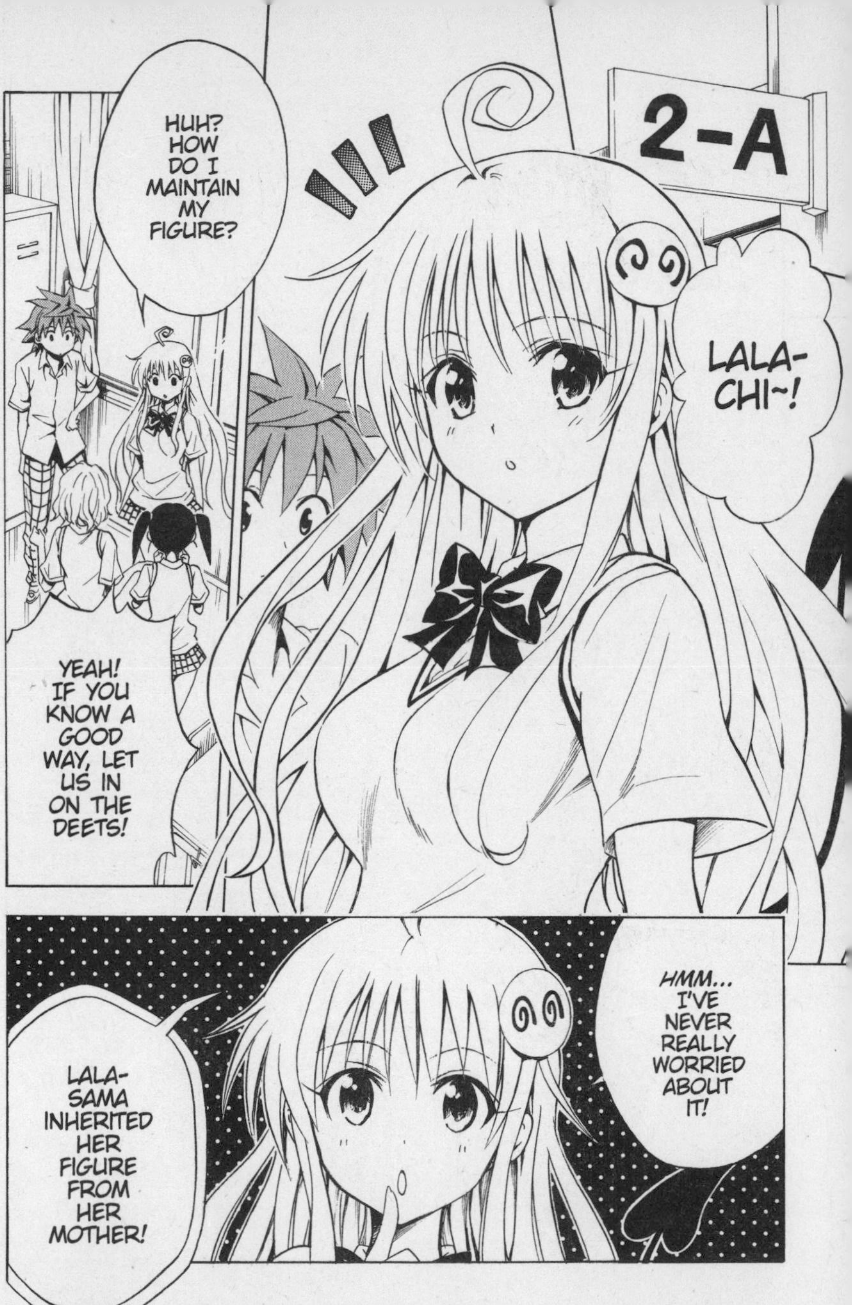
2-A
LALA-CHI~!
HUH? HOW DO I MAINTAIN MY FIGURE?
YEAH! IF YOU KNOW A GOOD WAY, LET US IN ON THE DEETS!
HMM... I'VE NEVER REALLY WORRIED ABOUT IT!
LALA-SAMA INHERITED HER FIGURE FROM HER MOTHER!

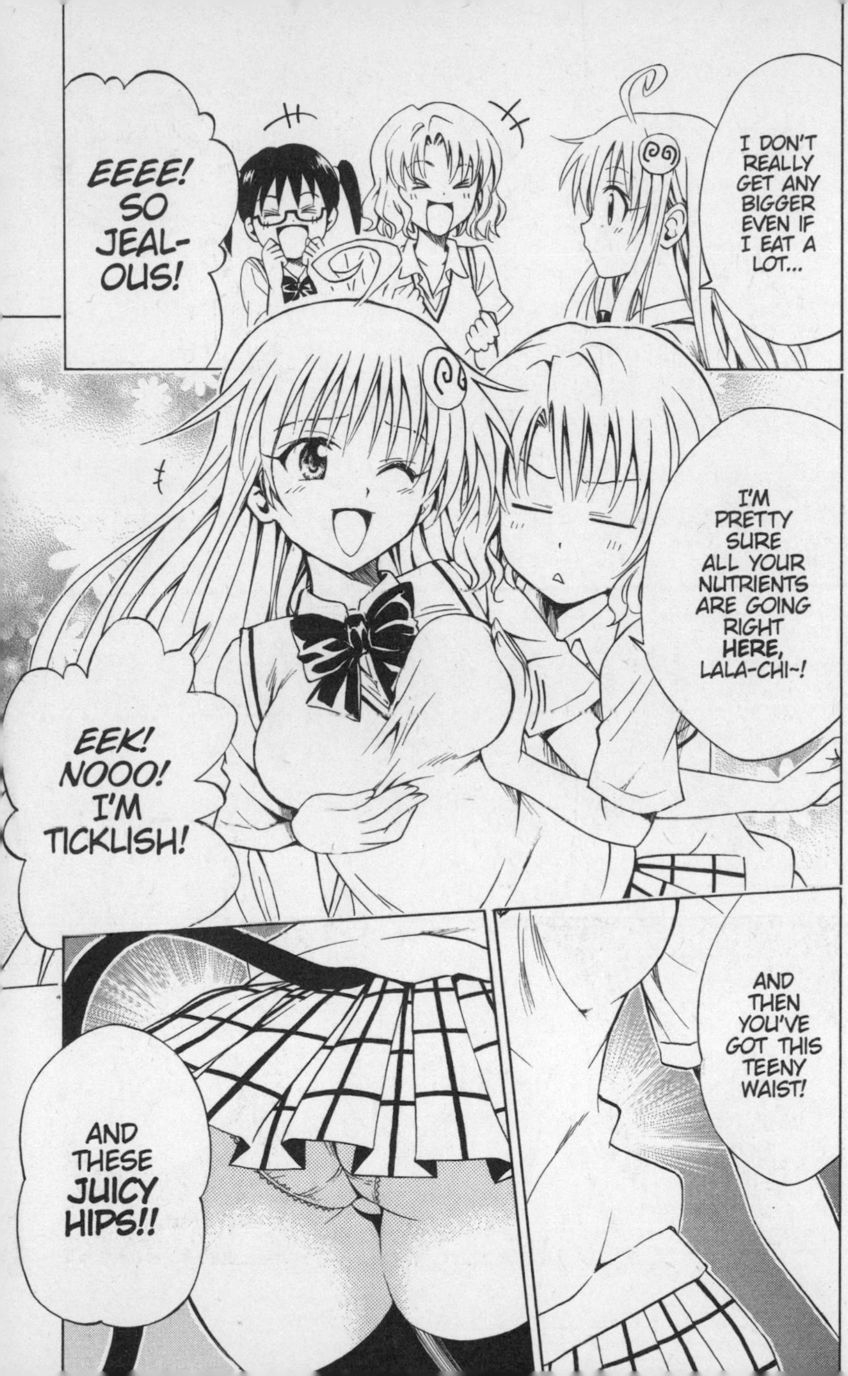
I DON'T REALLY GET ANY BIGGER EVEN IF I EAT A LOT...
EEEE! SO JEAL-OUS!
I'M PRETTY SURE ALL YOUR NUTRIENTS ARE GOING RIGHT HERE, LALA-CHI~!
EEK! NOOO! I'M TICKLISH!
AND THEN YOU'VE GOT THIS TEENY WAIST!
AND THESE JUICY HIPS!!

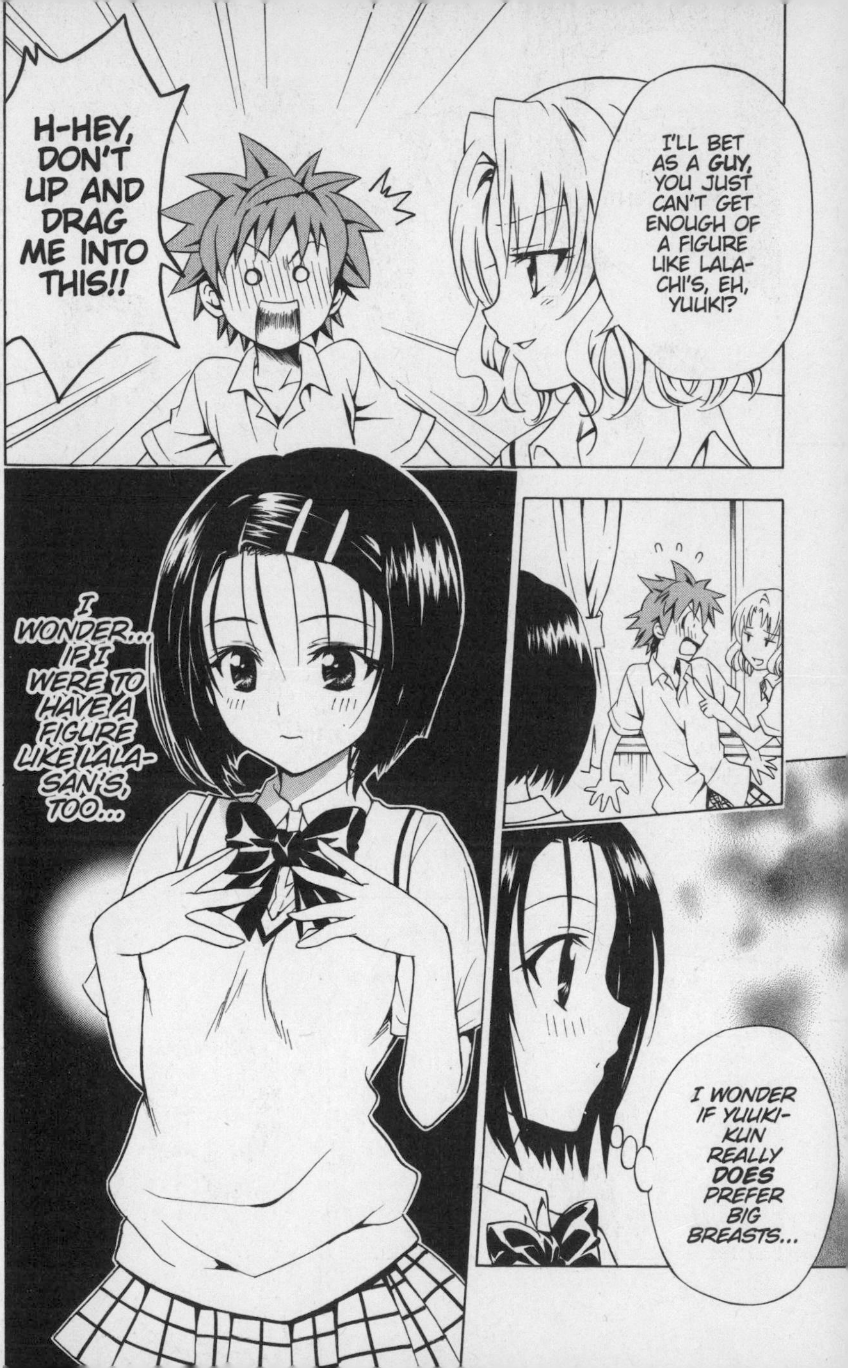
I'LL BET AS A GUY, YOU JUST CAN'T GET ENOUGH OF A FIGURE LIKE LALA-CHI'S, EH, YUUKI?
H-HEY, DON'T UP AND DRAG ME INTO THIS!!
I WONDER IF YUUKI-KUN REALLY DOES PREFER BIG BREASTS...
I WONDER... IF I WERE TO HAVE A FIGURE LIKE LALA-SAN'S, TOO...

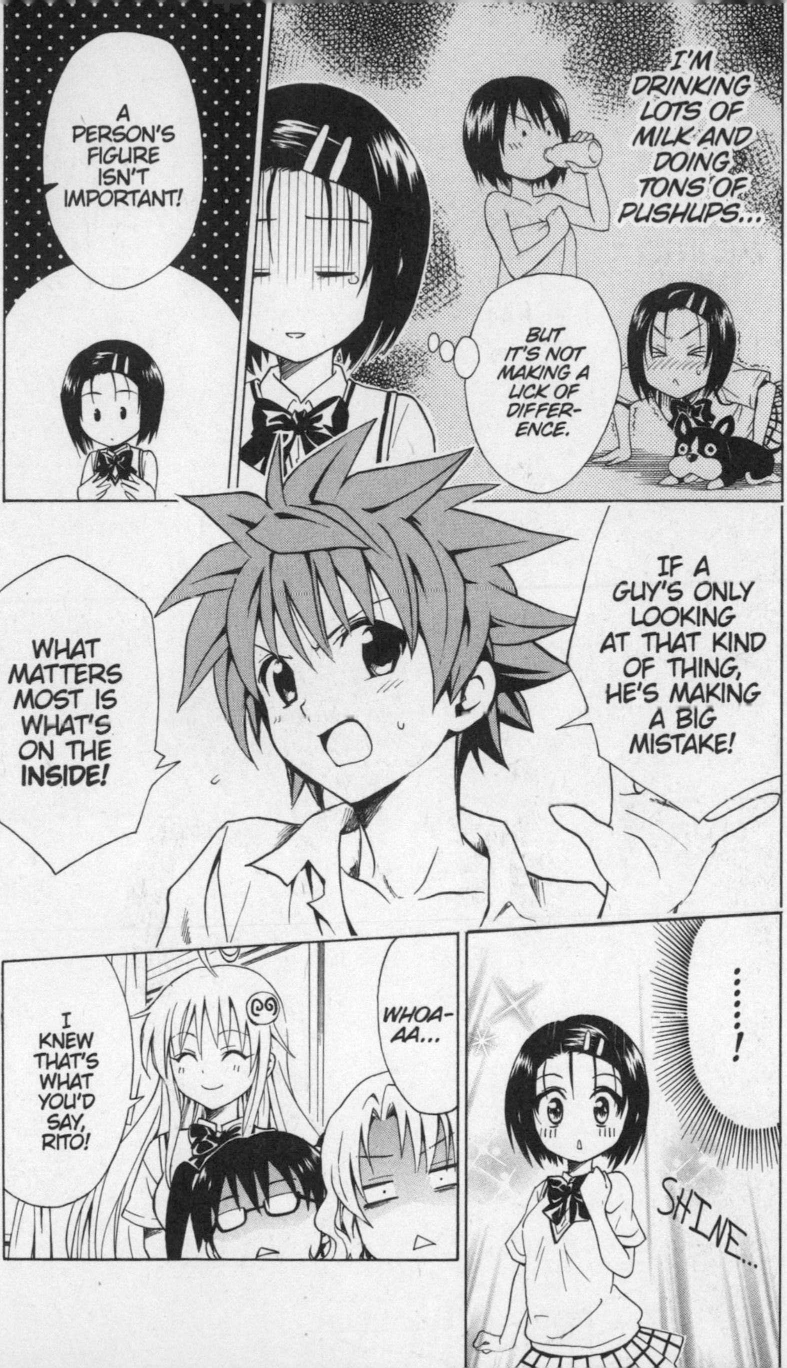
I'M DRINKING LOTS OF MILK AND DOING TONS OF PUSHUPS...
BUT IT'S NOT MAKING A LICK OF DIFFERENCE.
A PERSON'S FIGURE ISN'T IMPORTANT!
IF A GUY'S ONLY LOOKING AT THAT KIND OF THING, HE'S MAKING A BIG MISTAKE!
WHAT MATTERS MOST IS WHAT'S ON THE INSIDE!
......!
SHINE...
WHOA-AA...
I KNEW THAT'S WHAT YOU'D SAY, RITO!

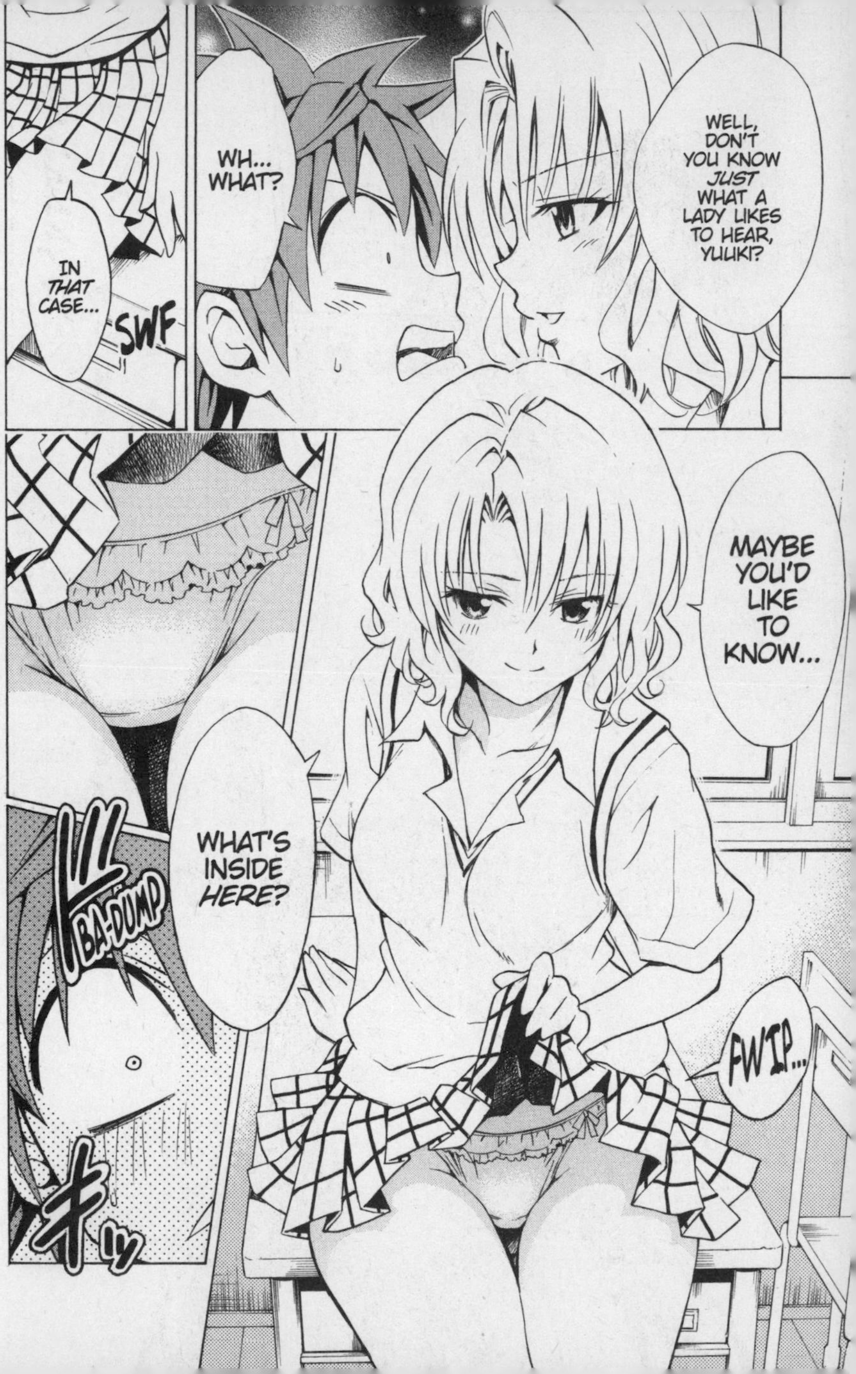
WELL, DON'T YOU KNOW *JUST* WHAT A LADY LIKES TO HEAR, YUUKI?
WH... WHAT?
IN *THAT* CASE...
SWF
MAYBE YOU'D LIKE TO KNOW...
WHAT'S INSIDE *HERE?*
FWIP...
BA-DUMP

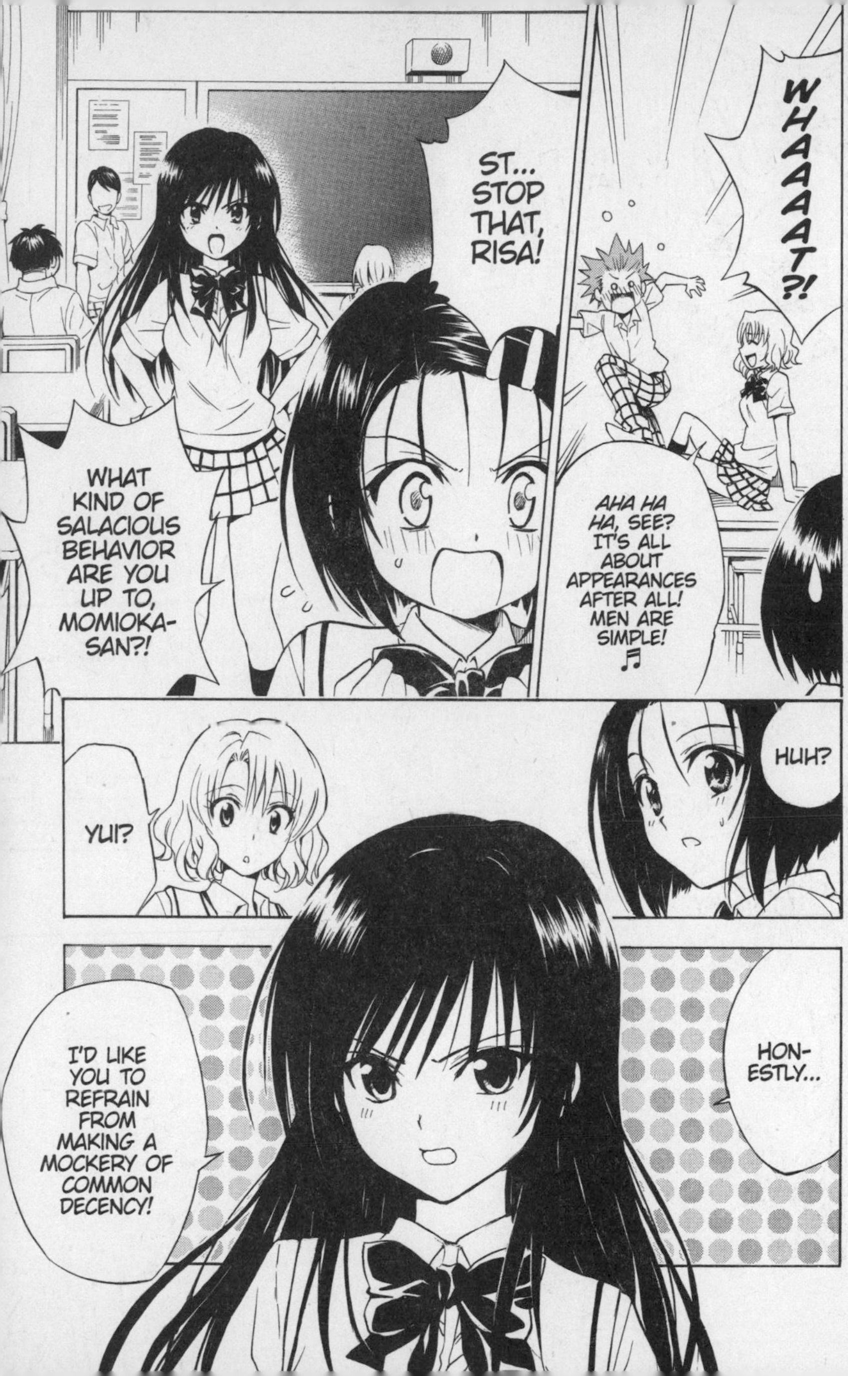
WHAAAAAT?!
AHA HA HA, SEE? IT'S ALL ABOUT APPEARANCES AFTER ALL! MEN ARE SIMPLE! ♬
ST... STOP THAT, RISA!
WHAT KIND OF SALACIOUS BEHAVIOR ARE YOU UP TO, MOMIOKA-SAN?!
HUH?
YUI?
HON-ESTLY...
I'D LIKE YOU TO REFRAIN FROM MAKING A MOCKERY OF COMMON DECENCY!

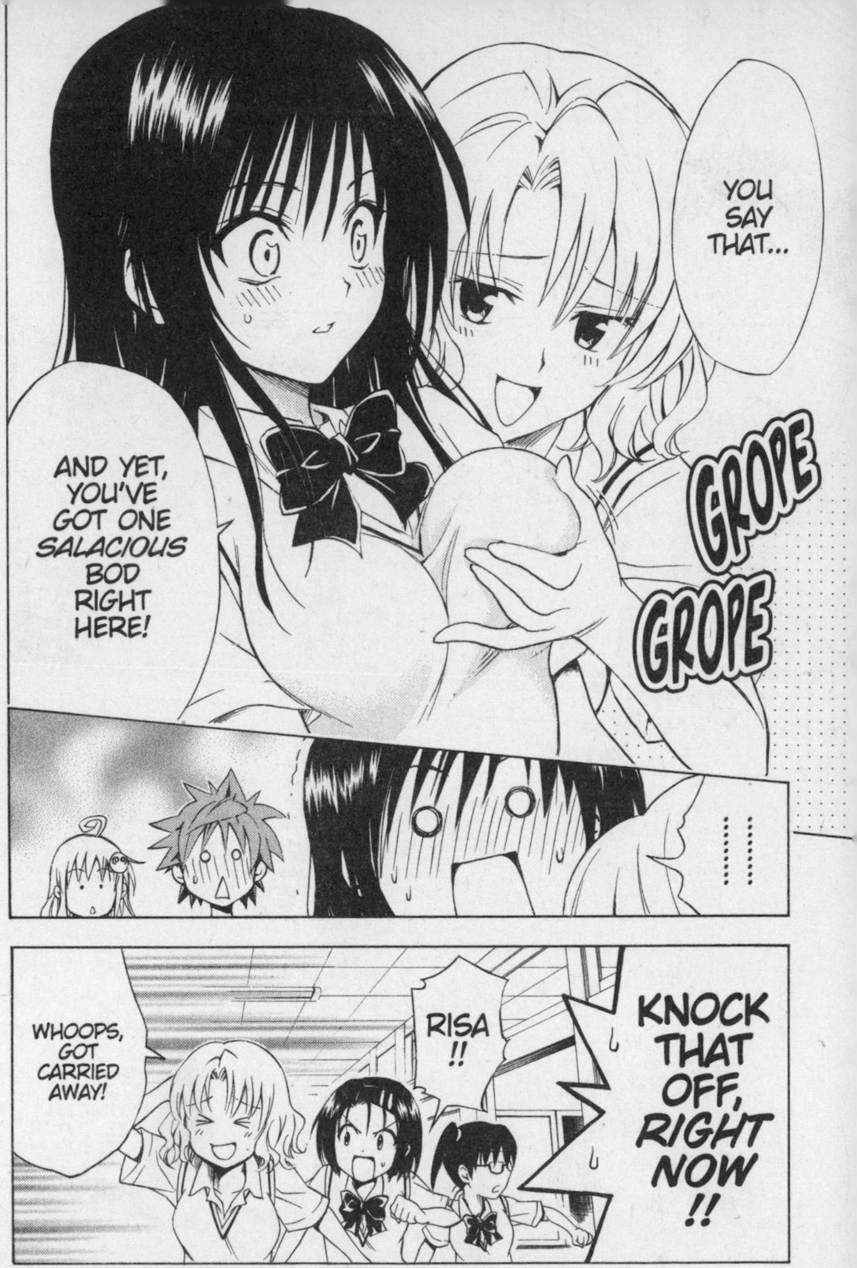
YOU SAY THAT...
AND YET, YOU'VE GOT ONE SALACIOUS BOD RIGHT HERE!
GROPE
GROPE
......
KNOCK THAT OFF, RIGHT NOW!!
RISA!!
WHOOPS, GOT CARRIED AWAY!

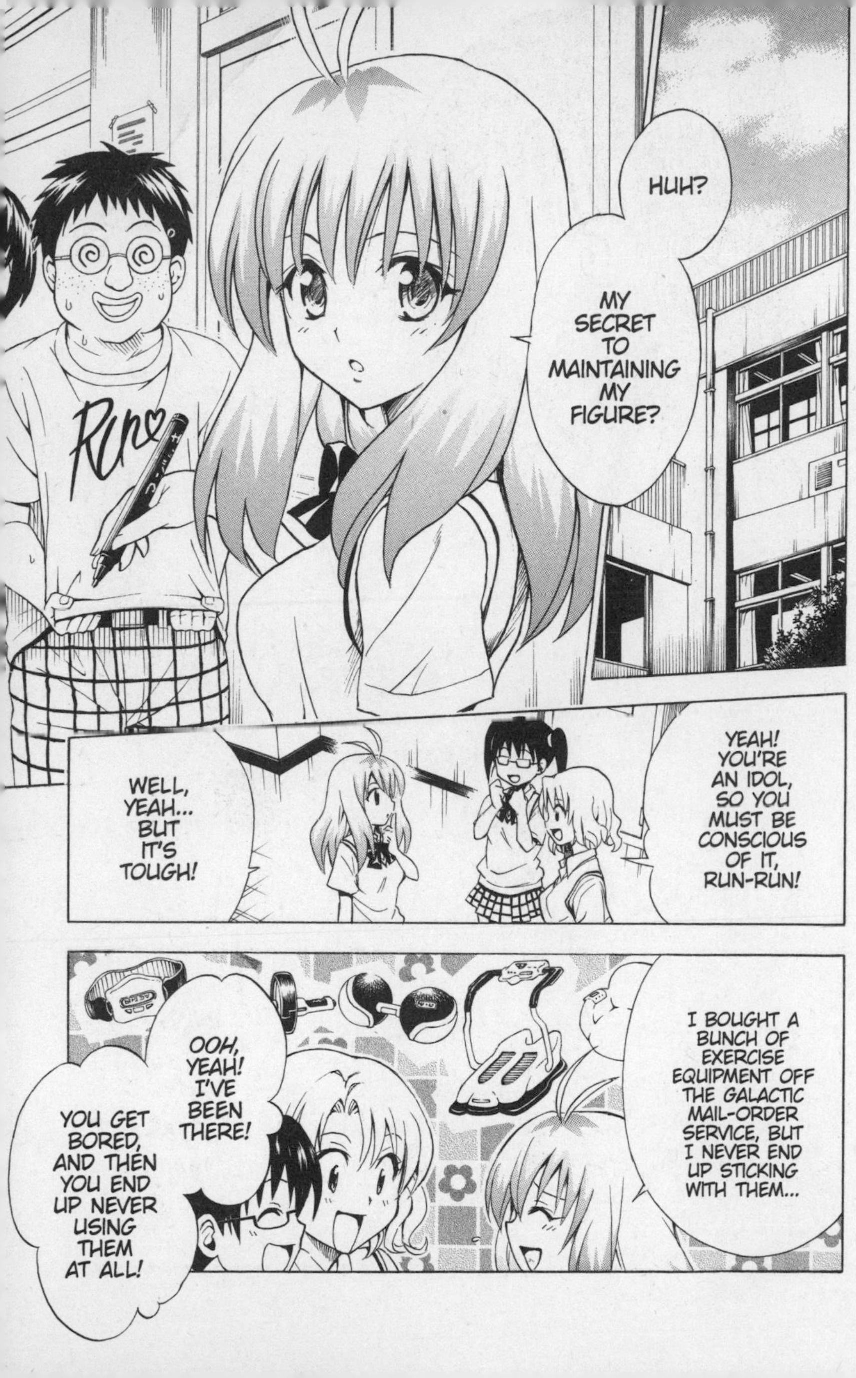
HUH?
MY SECRET TO MAINTAINING MY FIGURE?
Run
YEAH! YOU'RE AN IDOL, SO YOU MUST BE CONSCIOUS OF IT, RUN-RUN!
WELL, YEAH... BUT IT'S TOUGH!
I BOUGHT A BUNCH OF EXERCISE EQUIPMENT OFF THE GALACTIC MAIL-ORDER SERVICE, BUT I NEVER END UP STICKING WITH THEM...
OOH, YEAH! I'VE BEEN THERE!
YOU GET BORED, AND THEN YOU END UP NEVER USING THEM AT ALL!

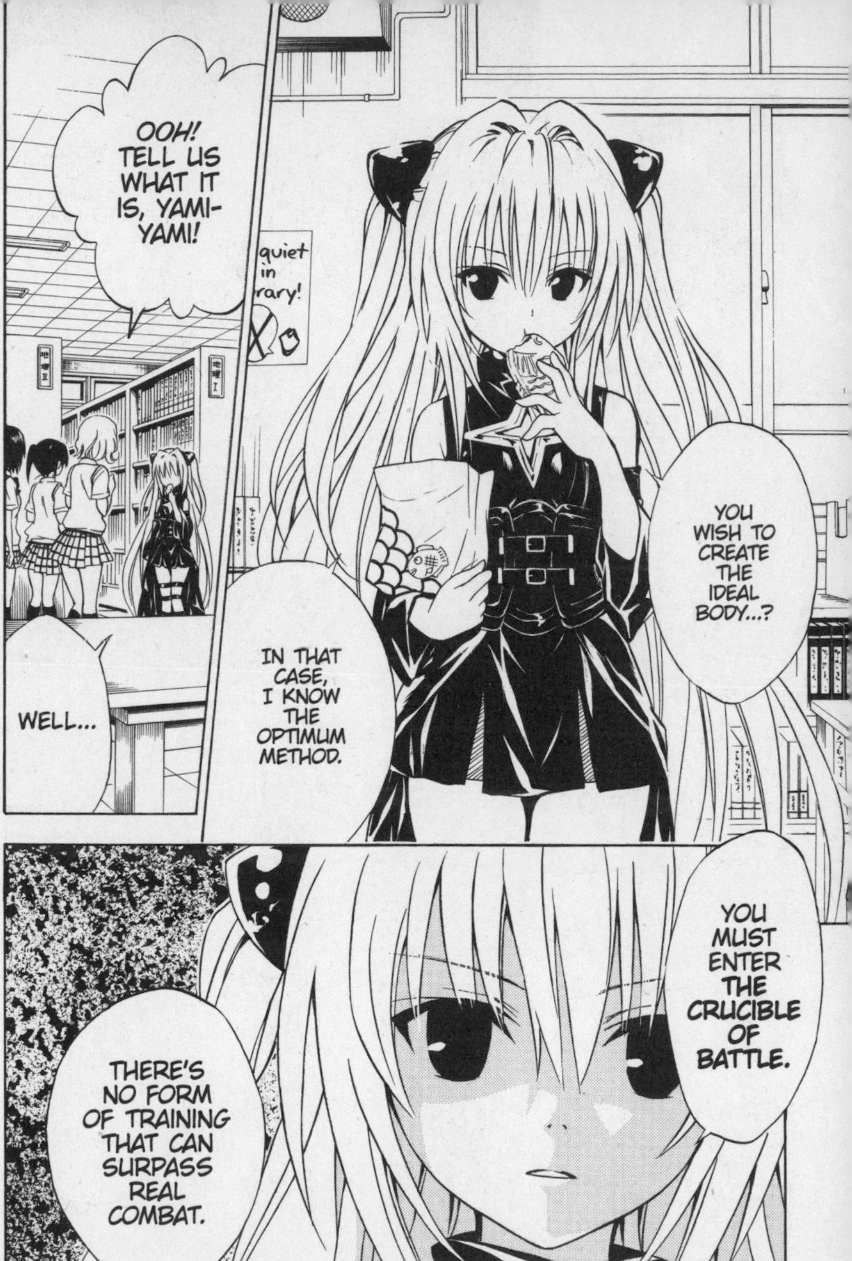
YOU WISH TO CREATE THE IDEAL BODY...?
IN THAT CASE, I KNOW THE OPTIMUM METHOD.
OOH! TELL US WHAT IT IS, YAMI-YAMI!
WELL...
YOU MUST ENTER THE CRUCIBLE OF BATTLE.
THERE'S NO FORM OF TRAINING THAT CAN SURPASS REAL COMBAT.

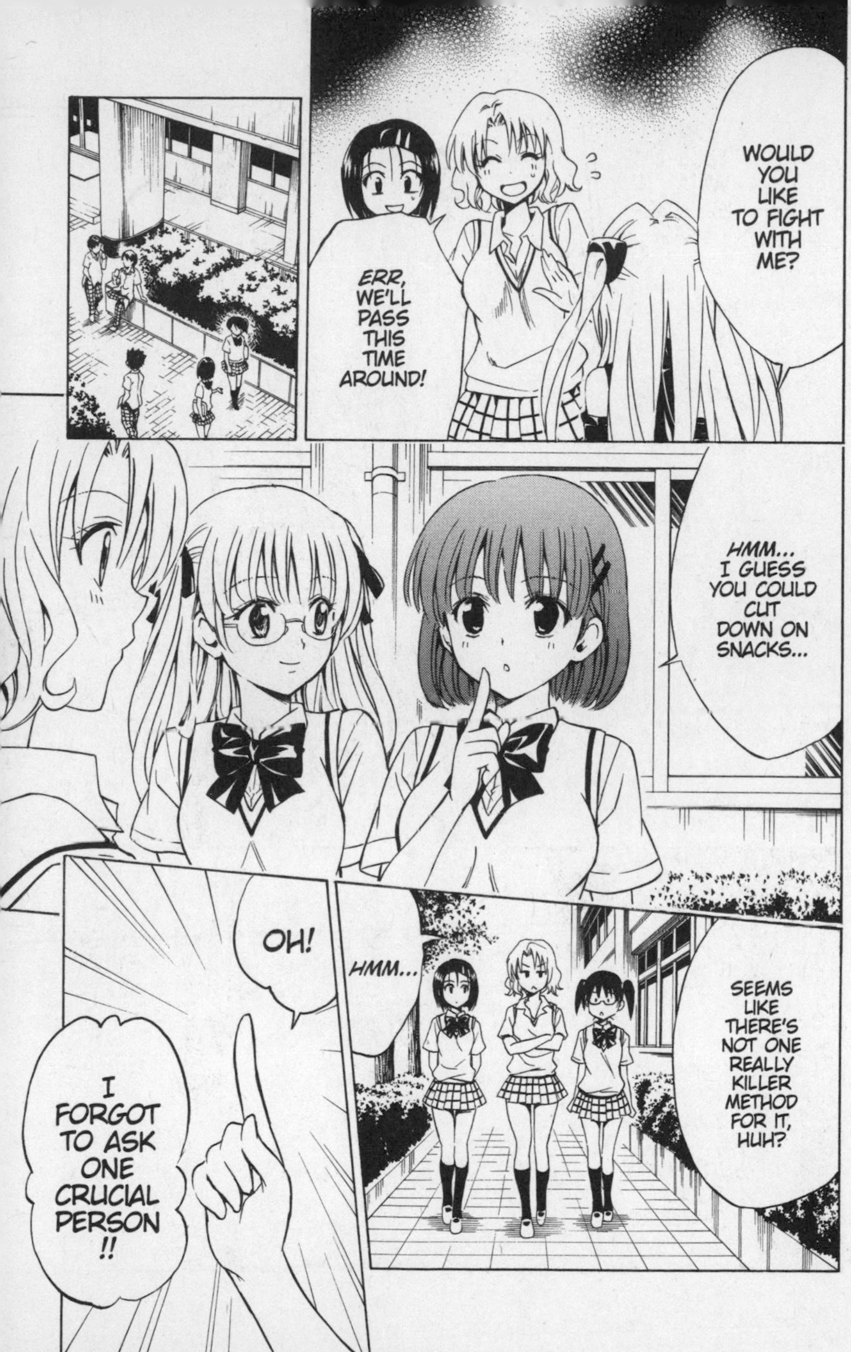
WOULD YOU LIKE TO FIGHT WITH ME?
ERR, WE'LL PASS THIS TIME AROUND!
HMM... I GUESS YOU COULD CUT DOWN ON SNACKS...
SEEMS LIKE THERE'S NOT ONE REALLY KILLER METHOD FOR IT, HUH?
HMM...
OH!
I FORGOT TO ASK ONE CRUCIAL PERSON !!

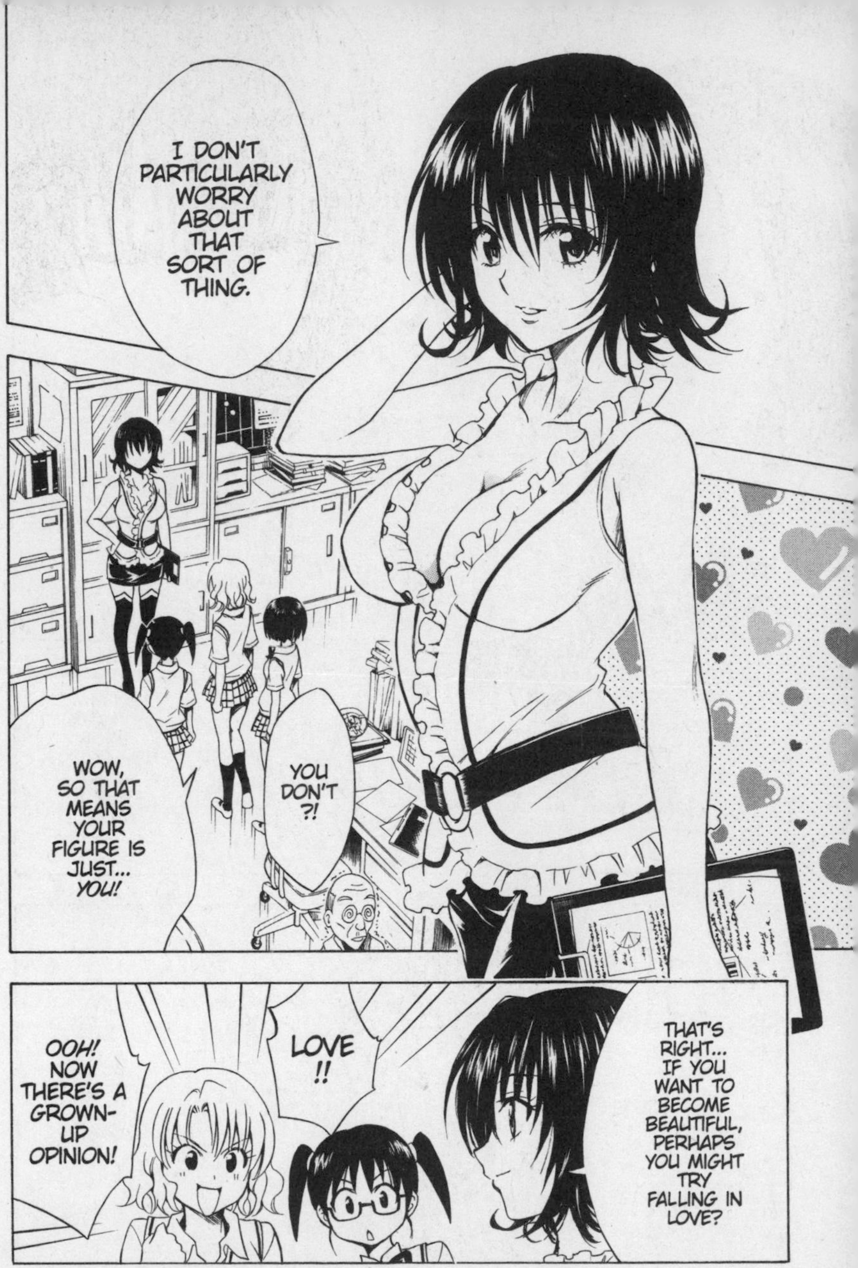
I DON'T PARTICULARLY WORRY ABOUT THAT SORT OF THING.
YOU DON'T ?!
WOW, SO THAT MEANS YOUR FIGURE IS JUST... *YOU!*
THAT'S RIGHT... IF YOU WANT TO BECOME BEAUTIFUL, PERHAPS YOU MIGHT TRY FALLING IN LOVE?
LOVE !!
OOH! NOW THERE'S A GROWN-UP OPINION!

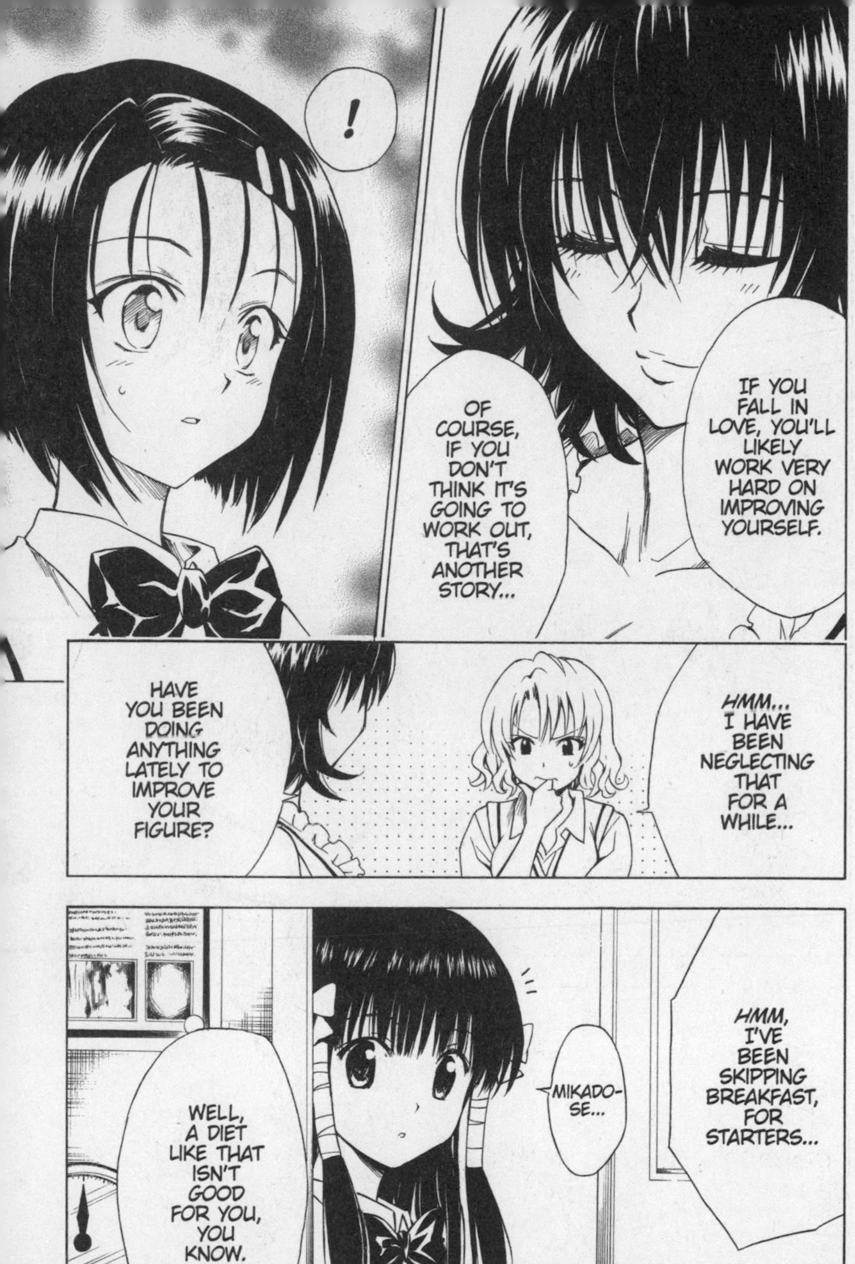
IF YOU FALL IN LOVE, YOU'LL LIKELY WORK VERY HARD ON IMPROVING YOURSELF.
OF COURSE, IF YOU DON'T THINK IT'S GOING TO WORK OUT, THAT'S ANOTHER STORY...
!
HMM... I HAVE BEEN NEGLECTING THAT FOR A WHILE...
HAVE YOU BEEN DOING ANYTHING LATELY TO IMPROVE YOUR FIGURE?
HMM, I'VE BEEN SKIPPING BREAKFAST, FOR STARTERS...
MIKADO-SE...
WELL, A DIET LIKE THAT ISN'T GOOD FOR YOU, YOU KNOW.

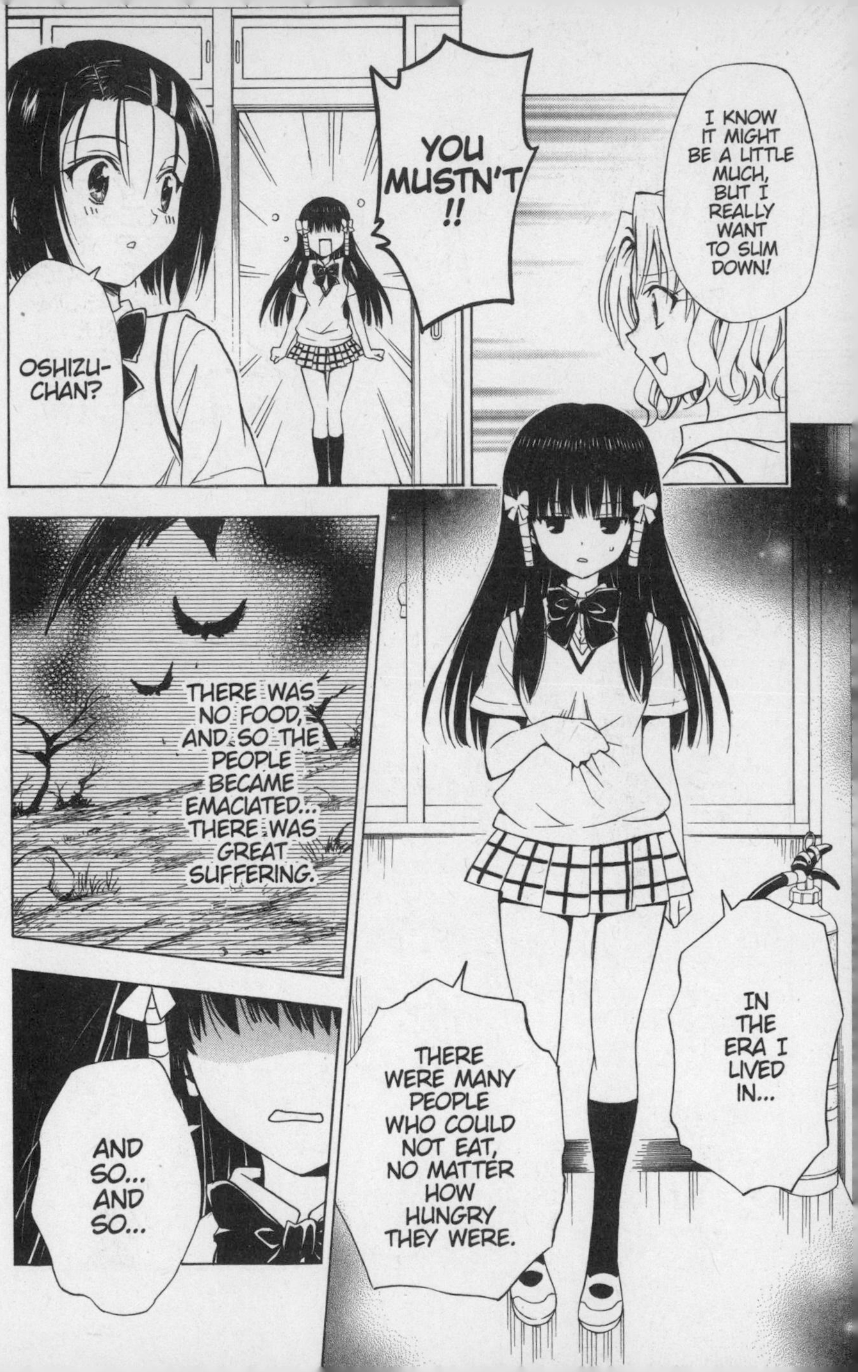
I KNOW IT MIGHT BE A LITTLE MUCH, BUT I REALLY WANT TO SLIM DOWN!
YOU MUSTN'T!!
OSHIZU-CHAN?
IN THE ERA I LIVED IN...
THERE WERE MANY PEOPLE WHO COULD NOT EAT, NO MATTER HOW HUNGRY THEY WERE.
THERE WAS NO FOOD, AND SO THE PEOPLE BECAME EMACIATED... THERE WAS GREAT SUFFERING.
AND SO... AND SO...

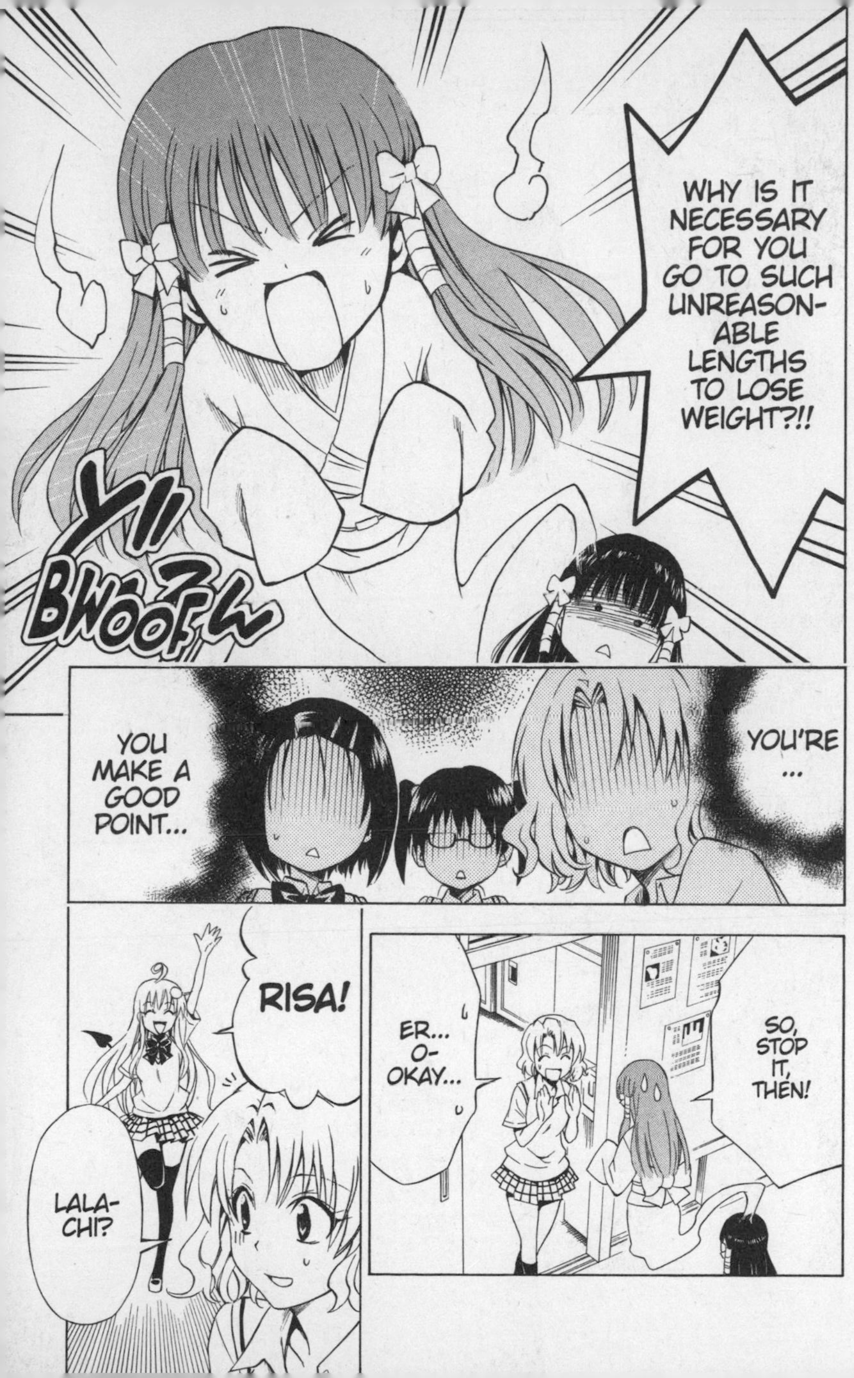
WHY IS IT NECESSARY FOR YOU GO TO SUCH UNREASON-ABLE LENGTHS TO LOSE WEIGHT?!!
BWOOF
YOU'RE ...
YOU MAKE A GOOD POINT...
SO, STOP IT, THEN!
ER... O-OKAY...
RISA!
LALA-CHI?

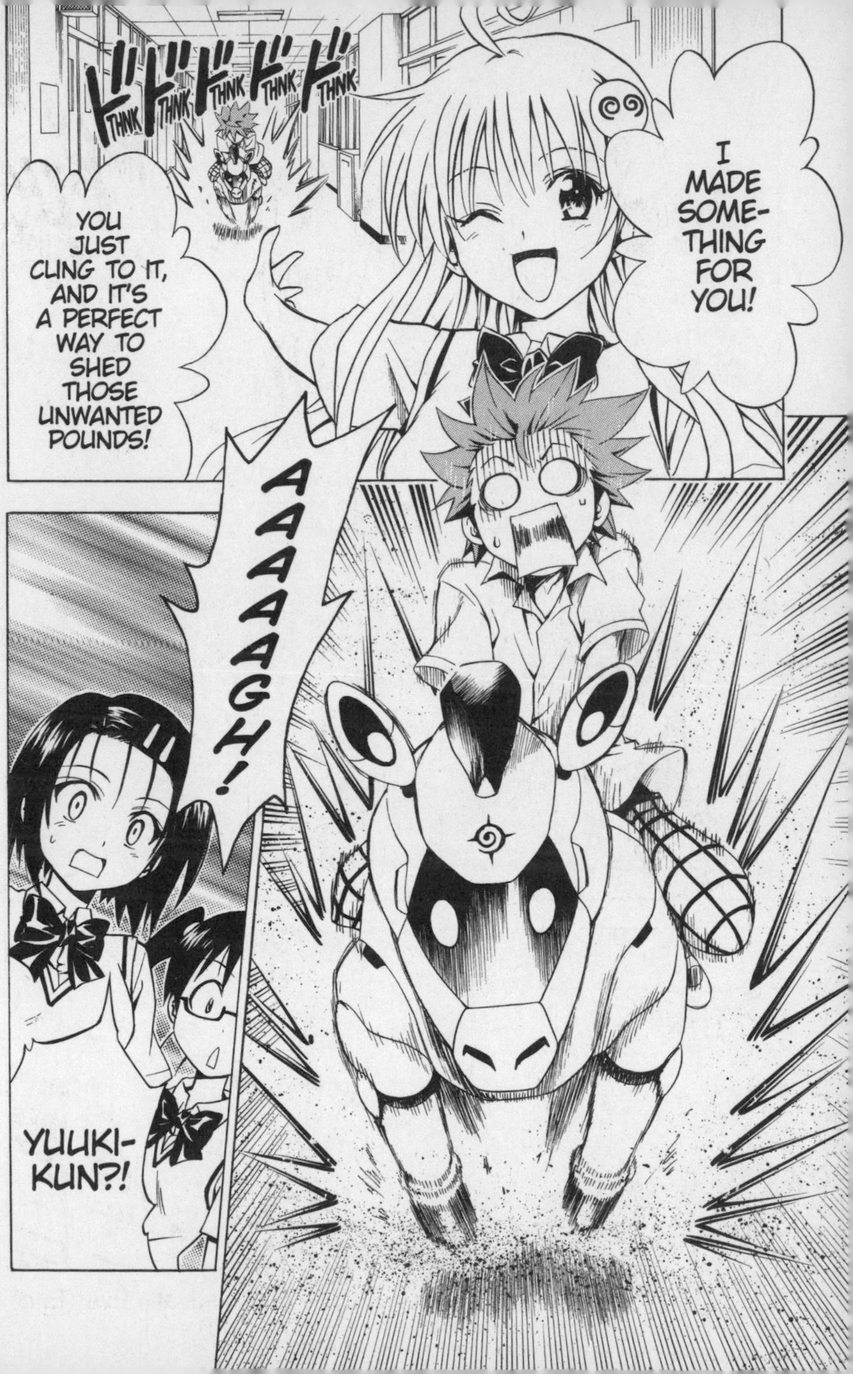
I MADE SOME-THING FOR YOU!
THNK THNK THNK THNK THNK
YOU JUST CLING TO IT, AND IT'S A PERFECT WAY TO SHED THOSE UNWANTED POUNDS!
AAAAAAAGH!
YUUKI-KUN?!

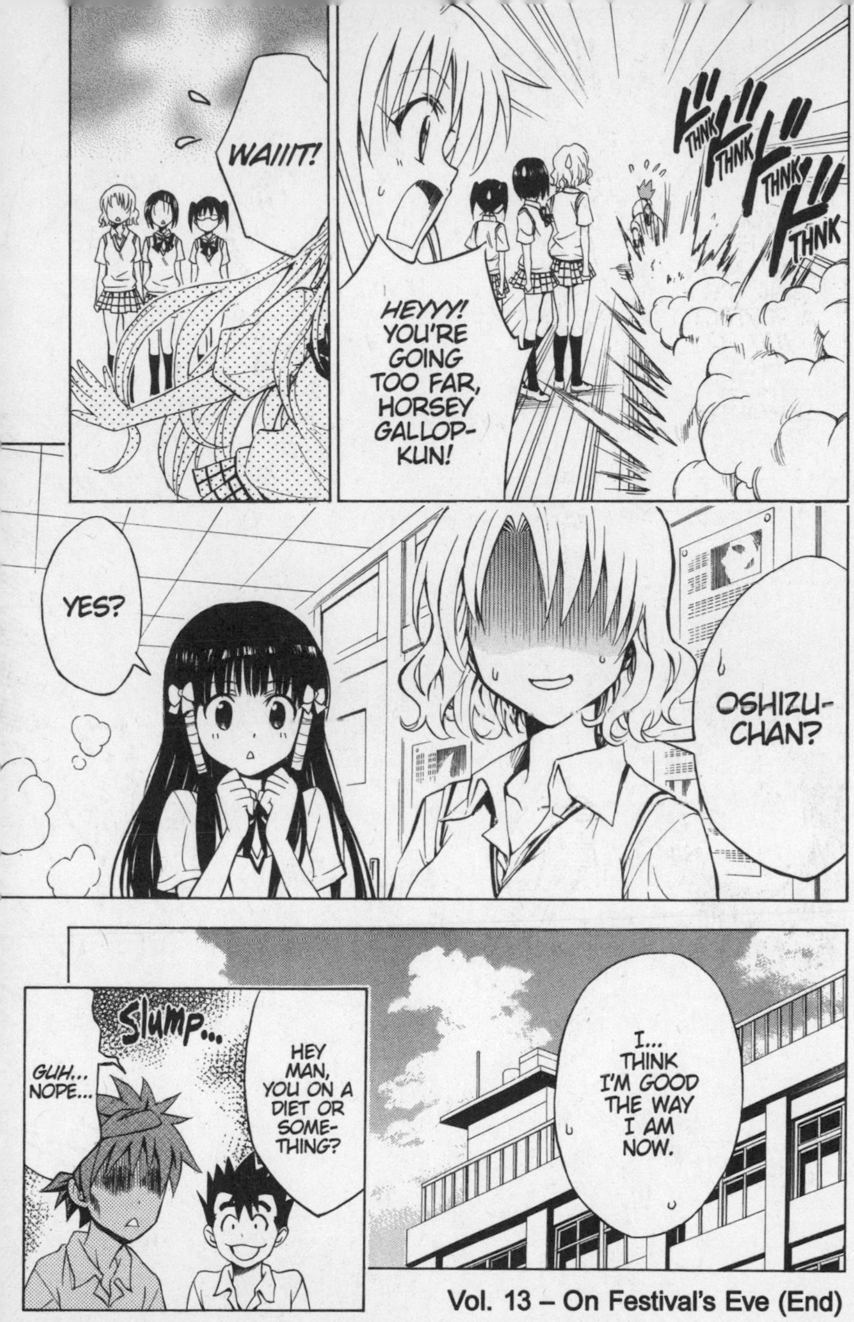
THNK
THNK
THNK
THNK
HEYYY! YOU'RE GOING TOO FAR, HORSEY GALLOP-KUN!
WAIIIT!
OSHIZU-CHAN?
YES?
I... THINK I'M GOOD THE WAY I AM NOW.
Slump...
HEY MAN, YOU ON A DIET OR SOME-THING?
GUH... NOPE...

Vol. 13 – On Festival's Eve (End)

To LOVE Ru

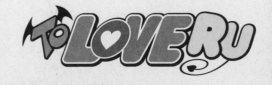

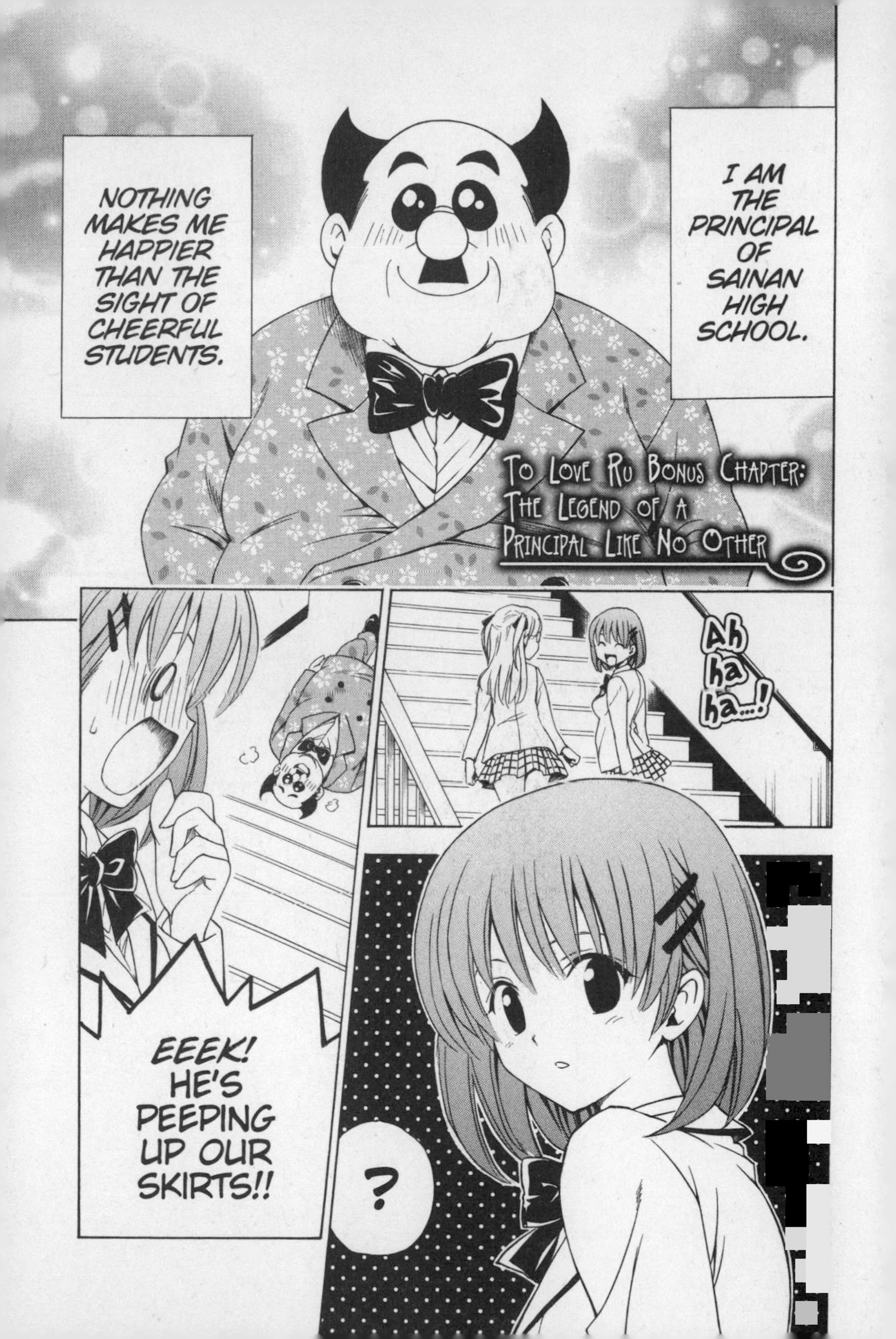
I AM THE PRINCIPAL OF SAINAN HIGH SCHOOL.
NOTHING MAKES ME HAPPIER THAN THE SIGHT OF CHEERFUL STUDENTS.
To Love Ru Bonus Chapter: The Legend of a Principal Like No Other
Ah ha ha...!
?
EEEK! HE'S PEEPING UP OUR SKIRTS!!

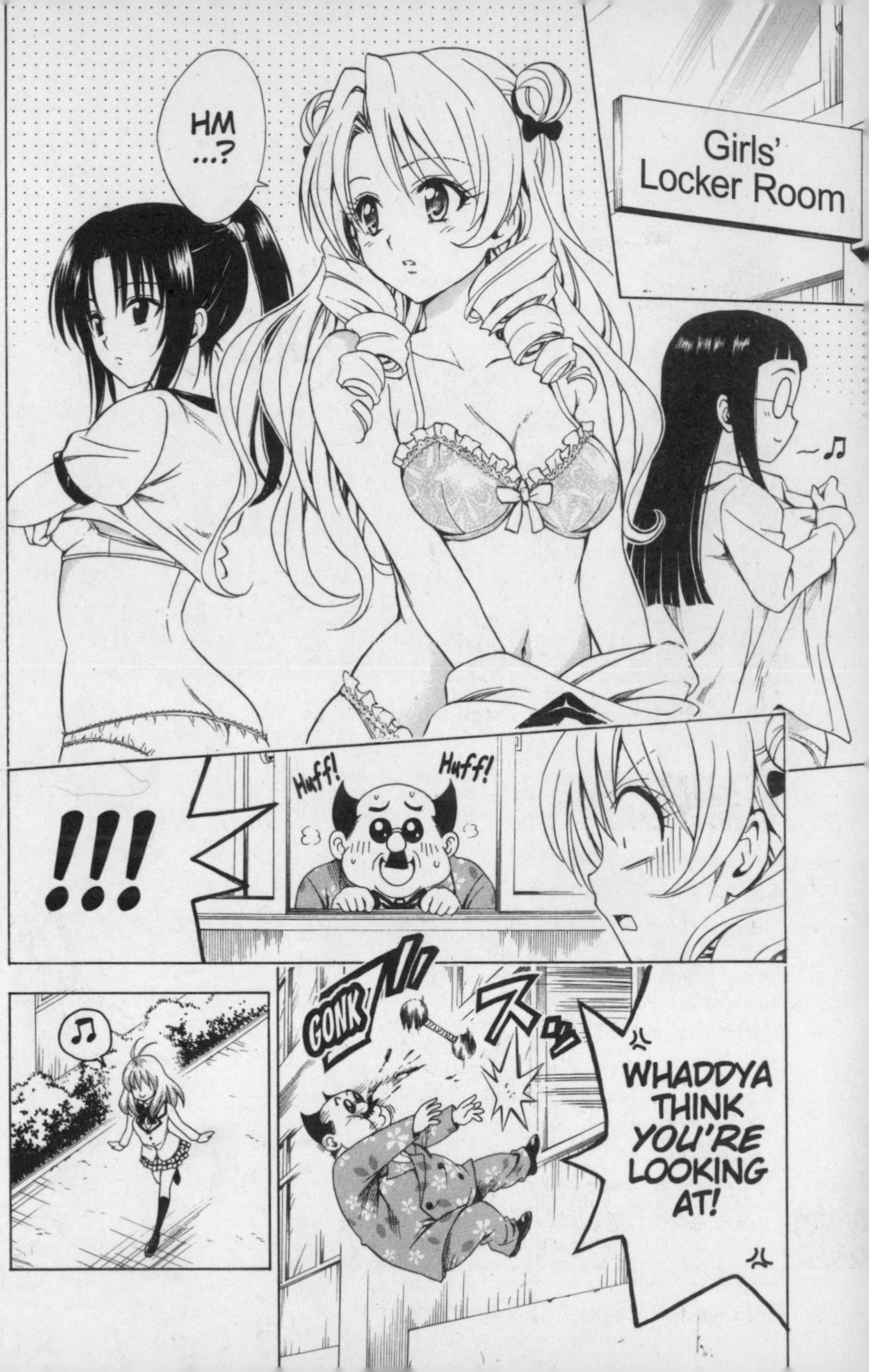
Girls' Locker Room
HM ...?
Huff!
Huff!
!!!
GONK
WHADDYA THINK YOU'RE LOOKING AT!

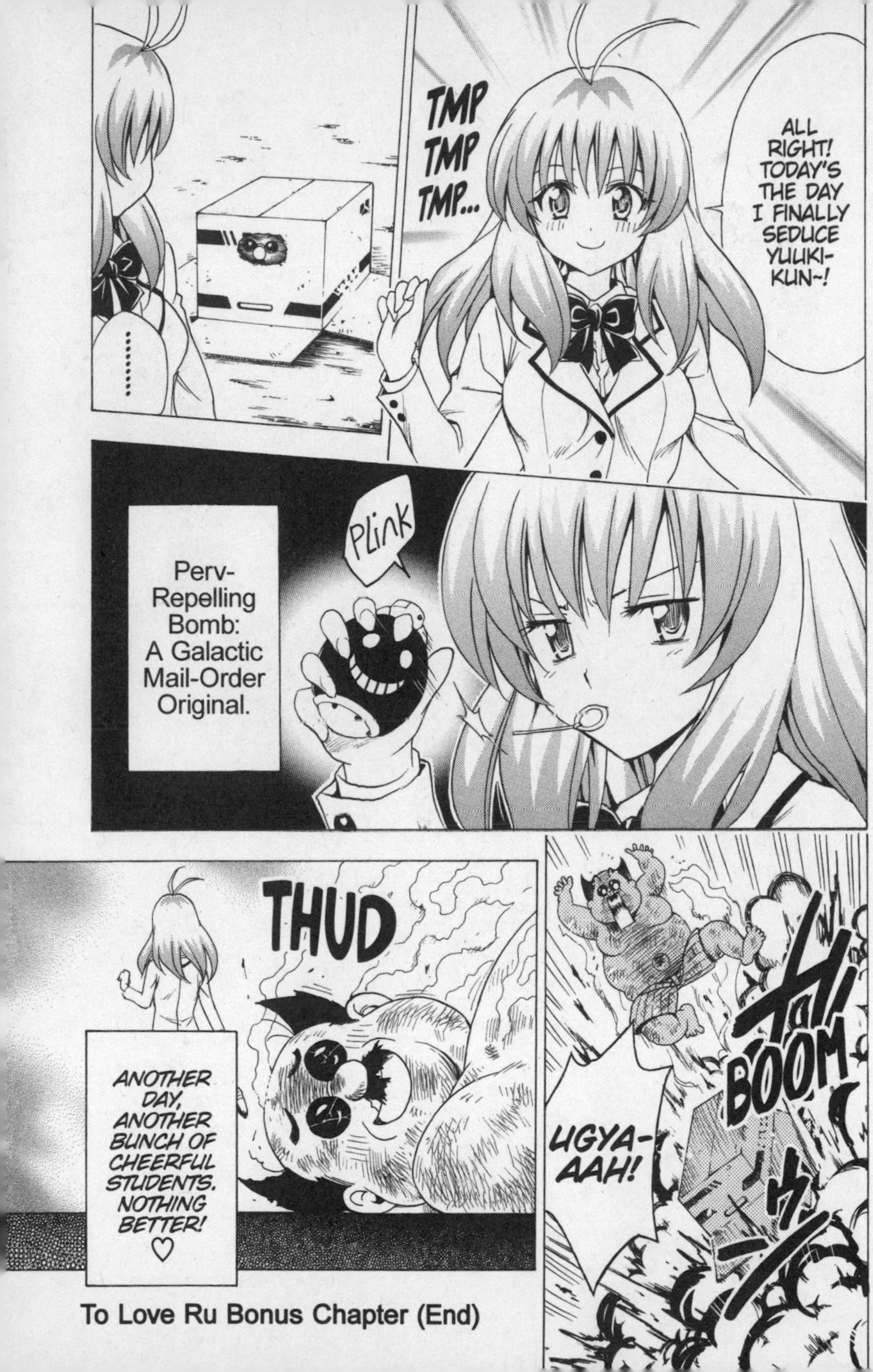
ALL RIGHT! TODAY'S THE DAY I FINALLY SEDUCE YUUKI-KUN~!
TMP TMP TMP...
......
PLINK
Perv-Repelling Bomb: A Galactic Mail-Order Original.
BOOM
UGYA-AAH!
THUD
ANOTHER DAY, ANOTHER BUNCH OF CHEERFUL STUDENTS. NOTHING BETTER! ♡

To Love Ru Bonus Chapter (End)

To LOVE Ru

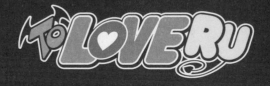

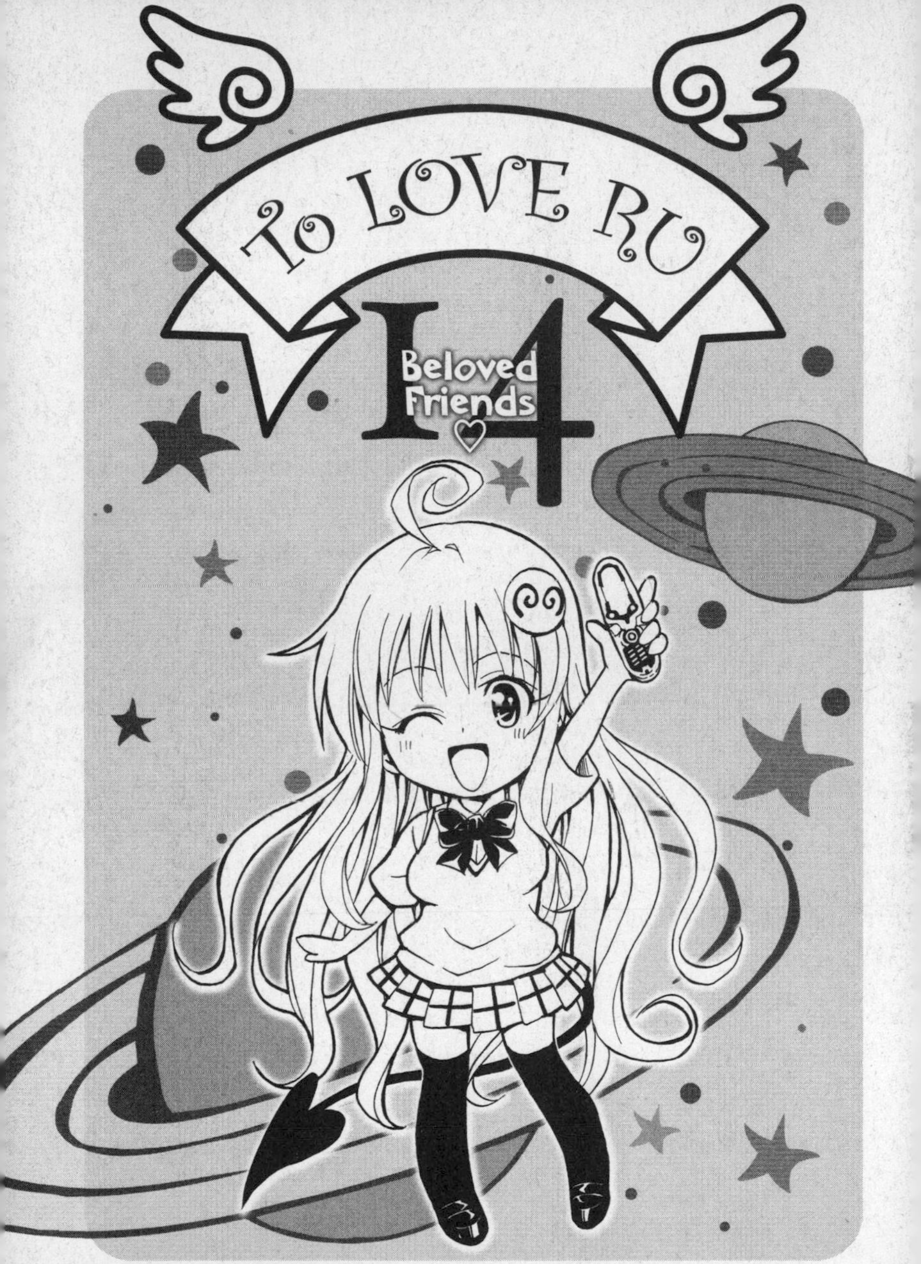
To LOVE RU
14
Beloved Friends

Story: Saki Hasemi Art: Kentaro Yabuki

To LOVE RU

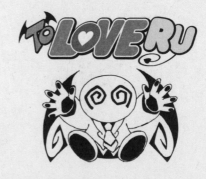

Trouble 116: Dandy Dogman

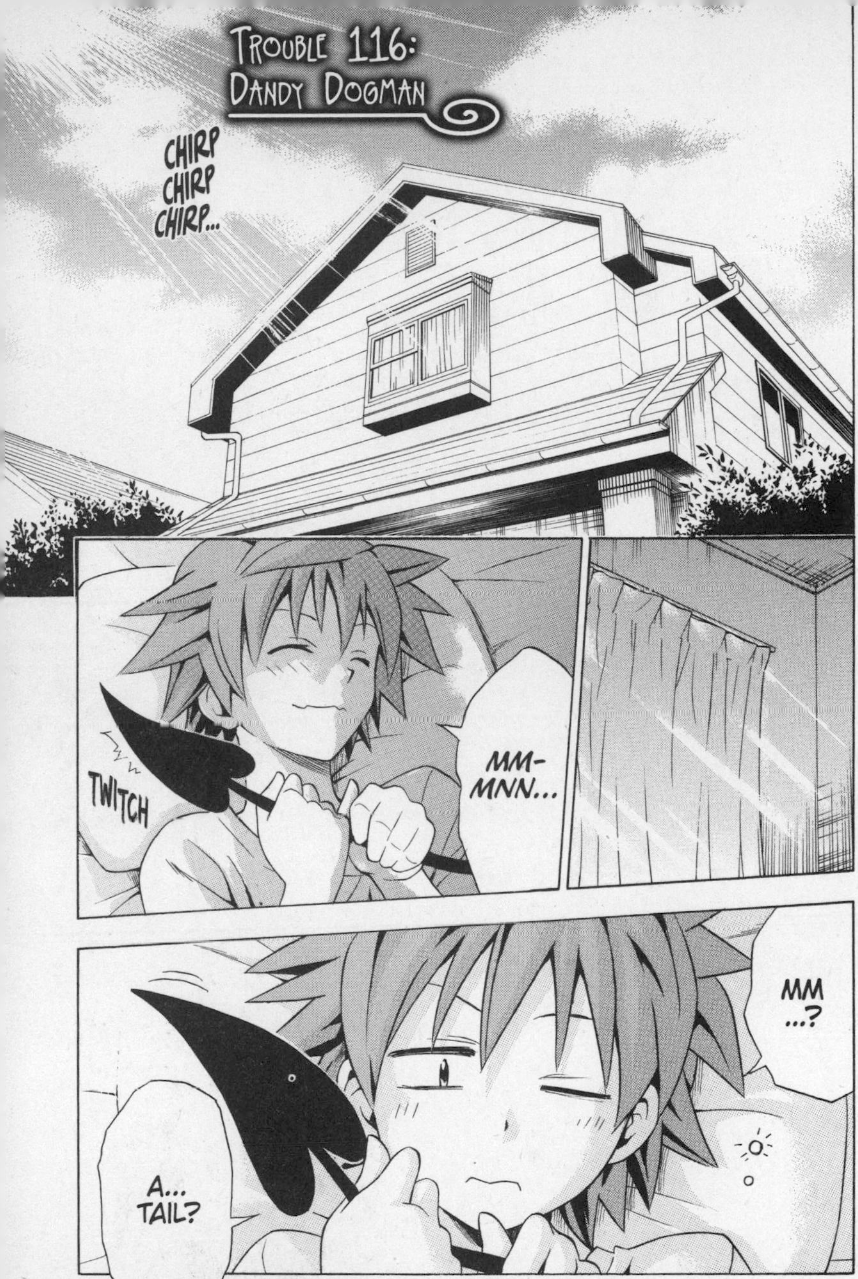
CHIRP CHIRP CHIRP...
MM-MNN...
TWITCH
MM ...?
A... TAIL?

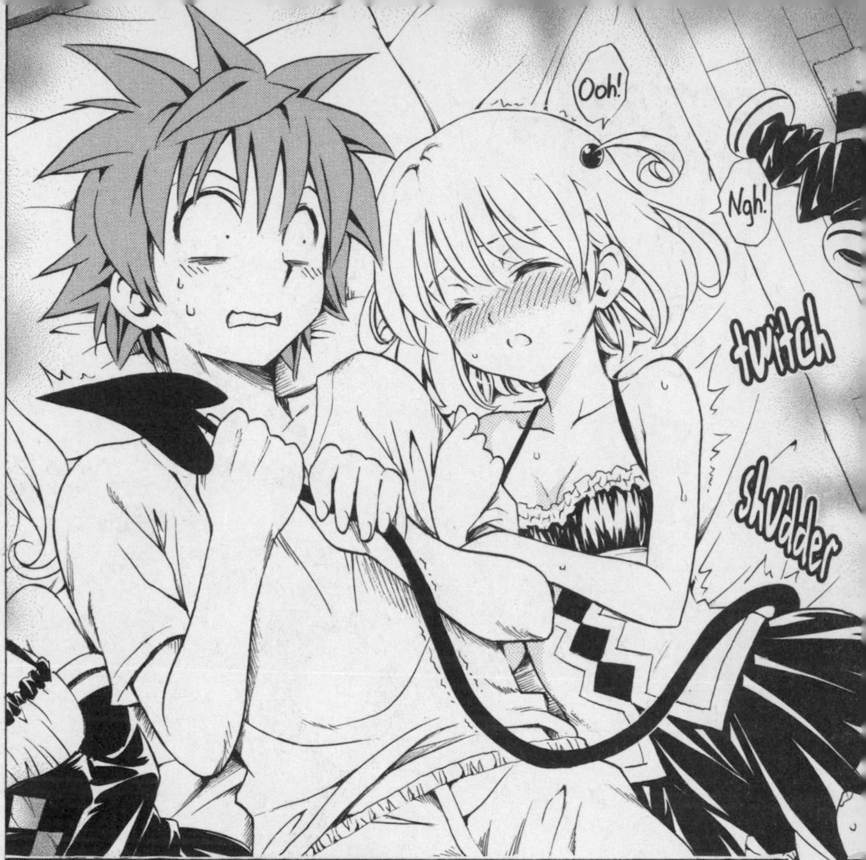
Ooh!
Ngh!
twitch
shudder
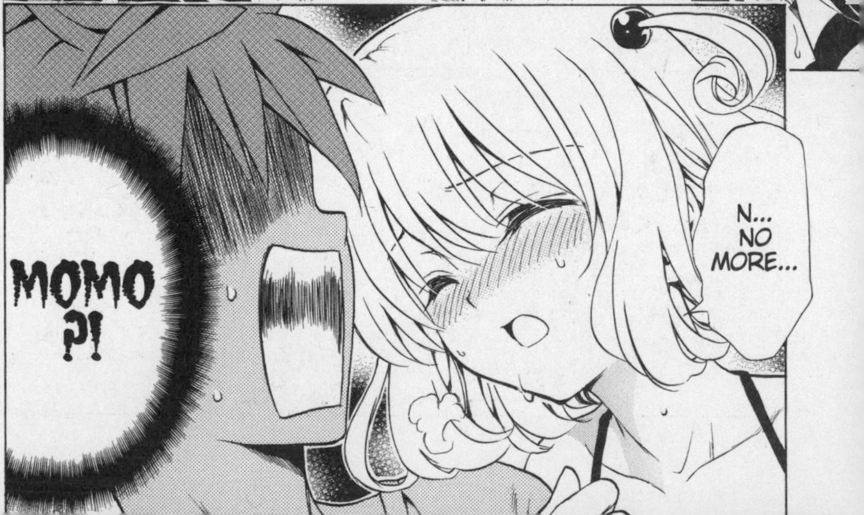
N... NO MORE...
MOMO ?!

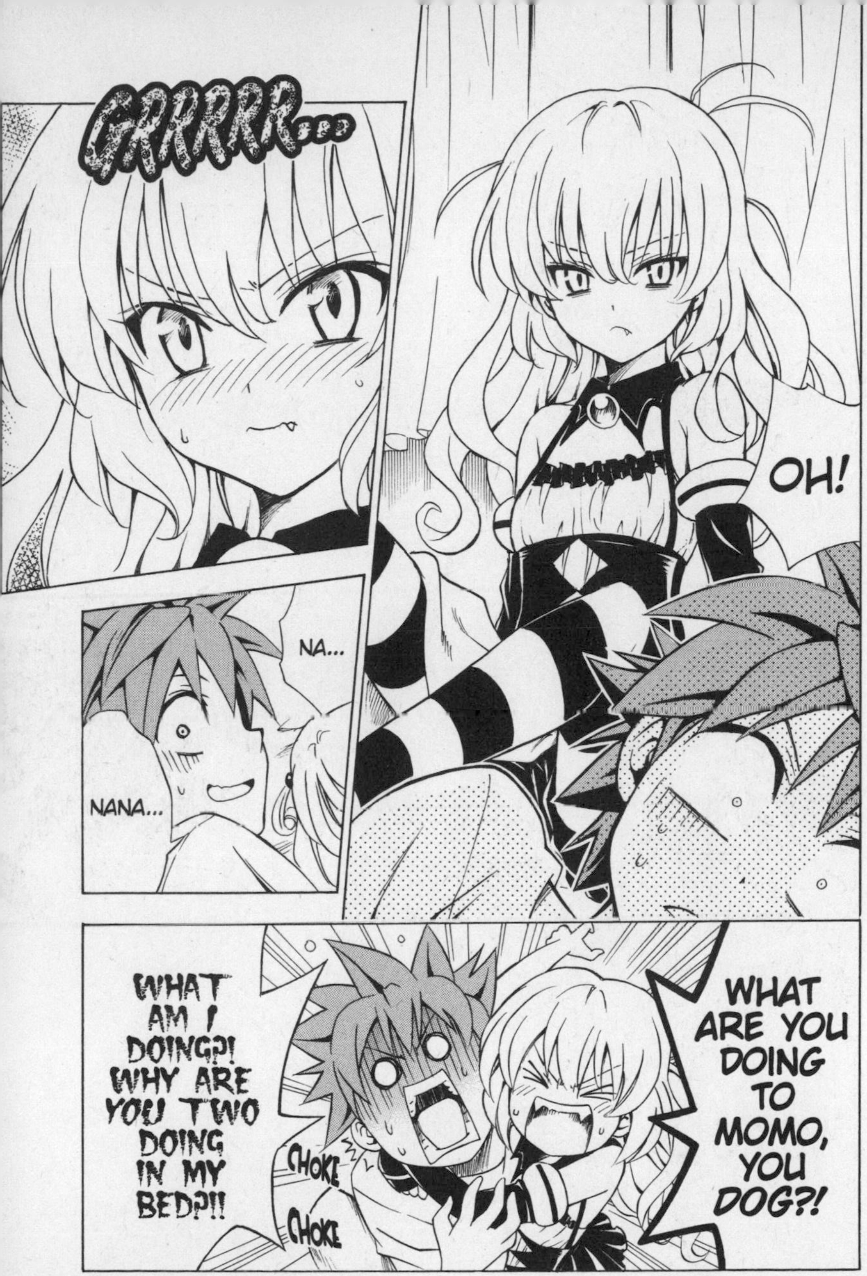
OH!
GRRRRR...
NA...
NANA...
WHAT ARE YOU DOING TO MOMO, YOU DOG?!
CHOKE
CHOKE
WHAT AM I DOING?! WHY ARE YOU TWO DOING IN MY BED?!!

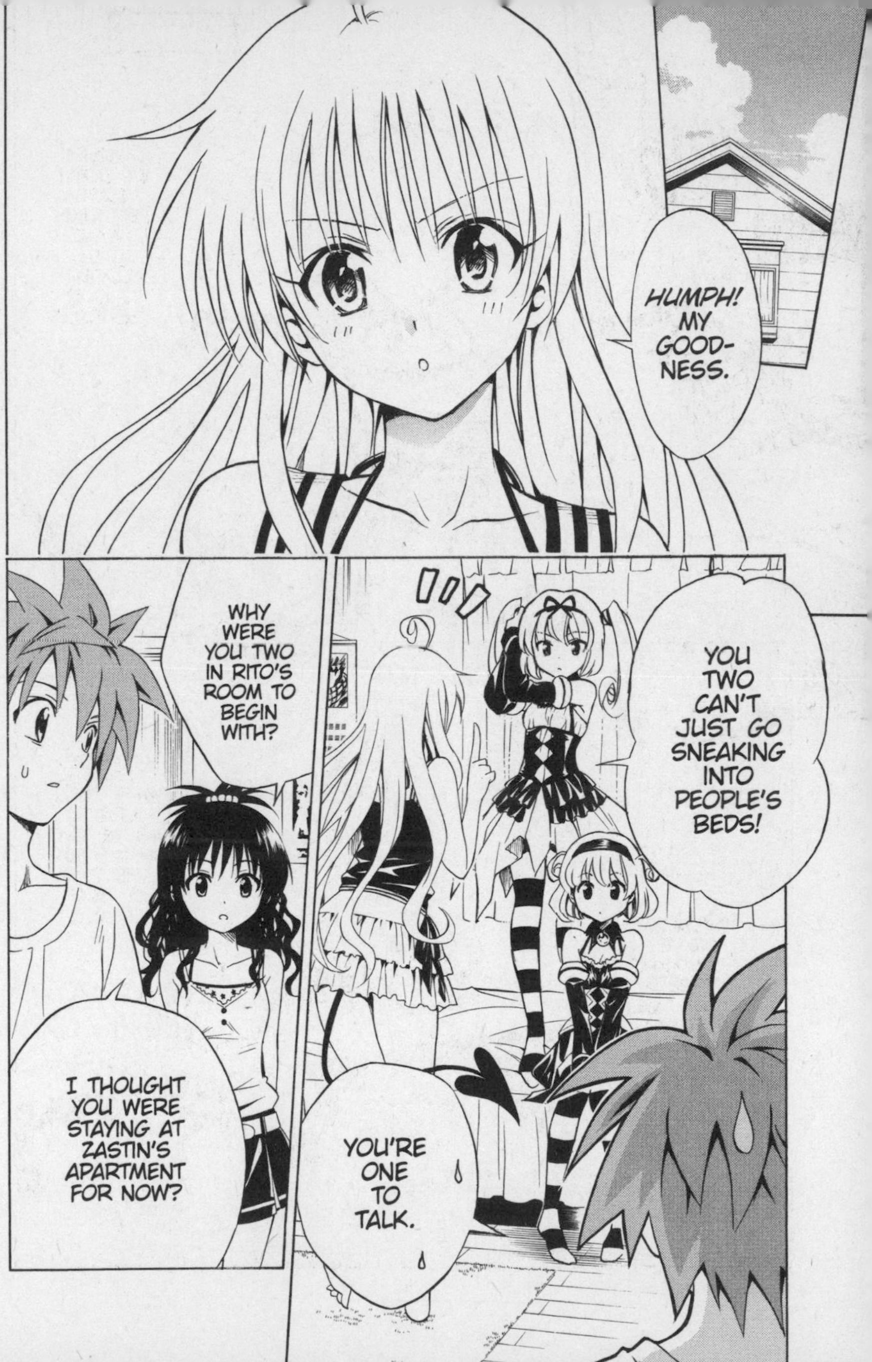
HUMPH! MY GOODNESS.
YOU TWO CAN'T JUST GO SNEAKING INTO PEOPLE'S BEDS!
YOU'RE ONE TO TALK.
WHY WERE YOU TWO IN RITO'S ROOM TO BEGIN WITH?
I THOUGHT YOU WERE STAYING AT ZASTIN'S APARTMENT FOR NOW?

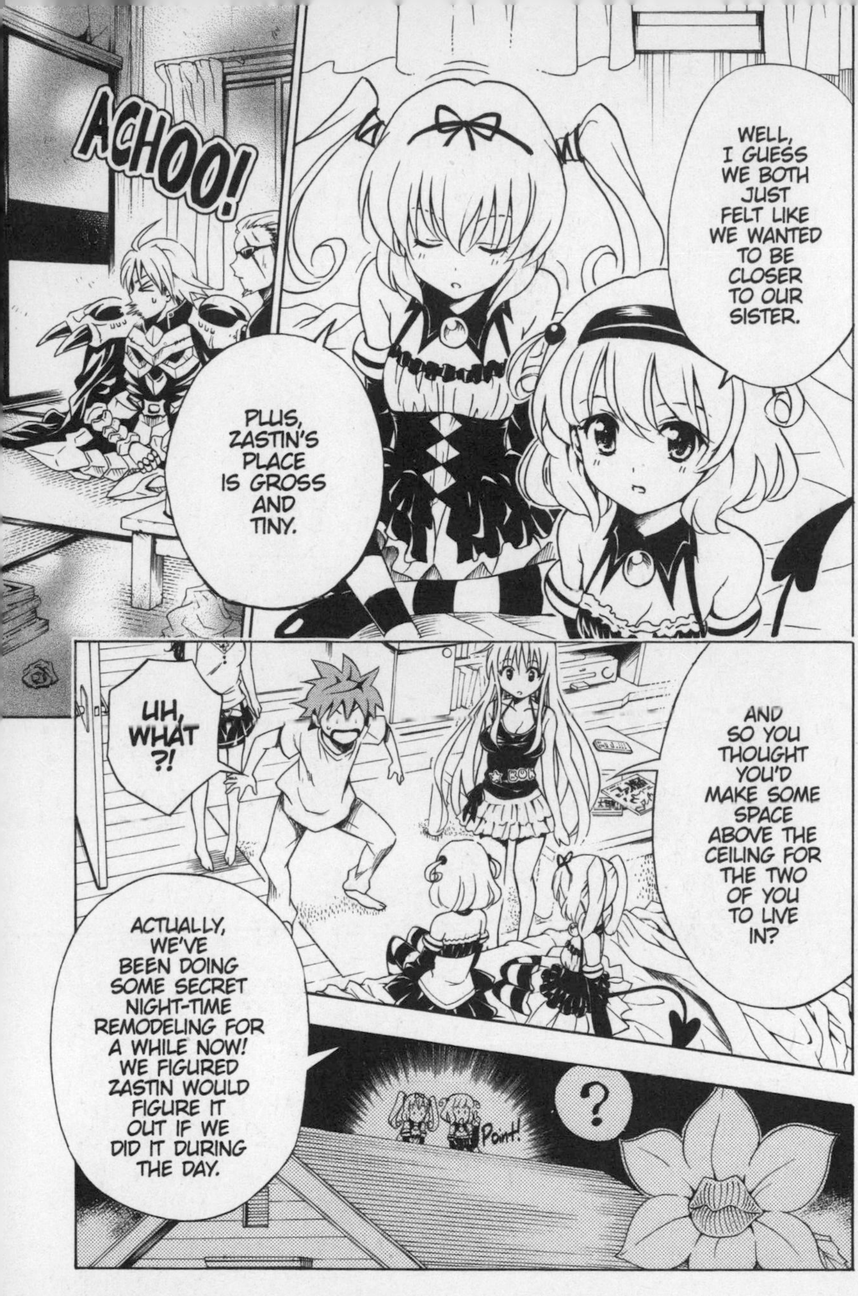
WELL, I GUESS WE BOTH JUST FELT LIKE WE WANTED TO BE CLOSER TO OUR SISTER.
PLUS, ZASTIN'S PLACE IS GROSS AND TINY.
ACHOO!
AND SO YOU THOUGHT YOU'D MAKE SOME SPACE ABOVE THE CEILING FOR THE TWO OF YOU TO LIVE IN?
UH, WHAT?!
?
Point!
ACTUALLY, WE'VE BEEN DOING SOME SECRET NIGHT-TIME REMODELING FOR A WHILE NOW! WE FIGURED ZASTIN WOULD FIGURE IT OUT IF WE DID IT DURING THE DAY.

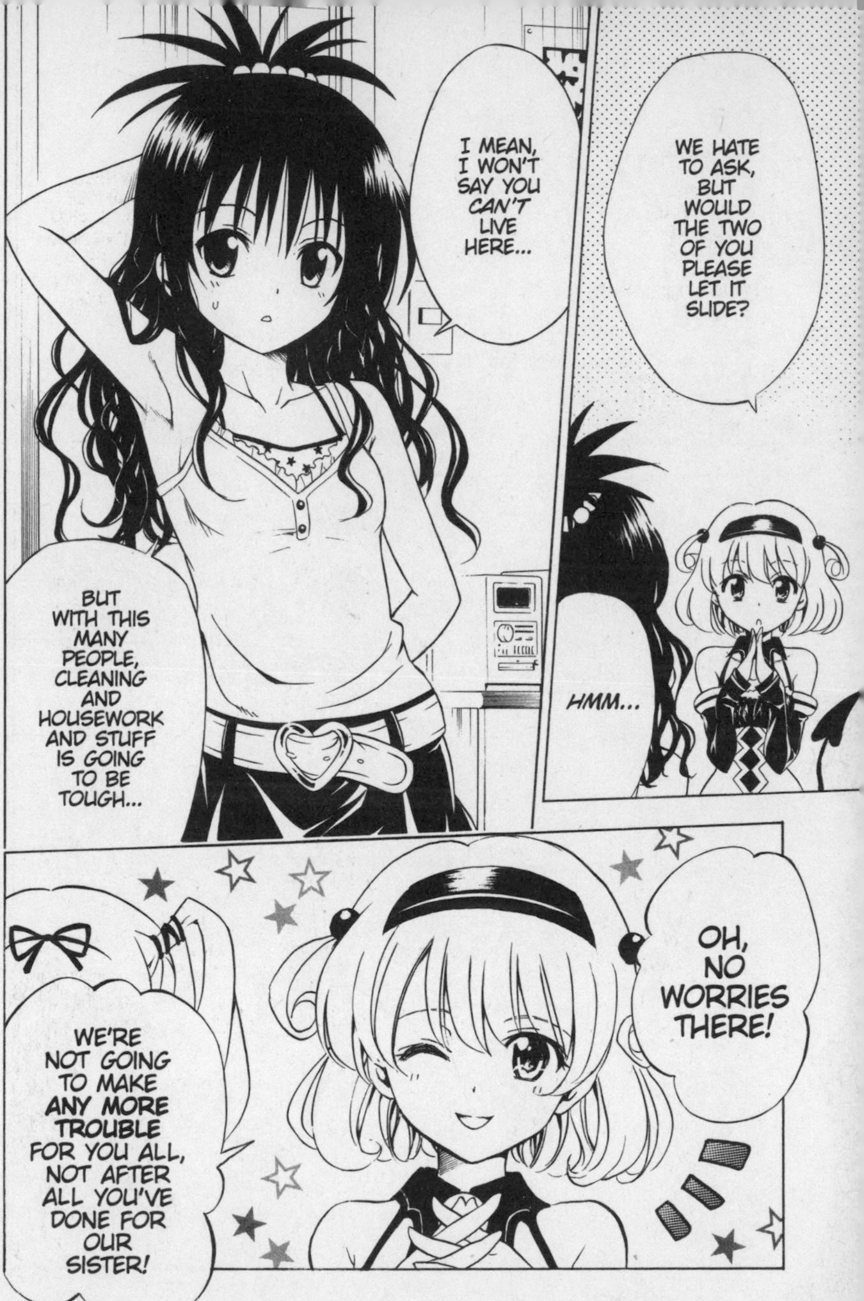
WE HATE TO ASK, BUT WOULD THE TWO OF YOU PLEASE LET IT SLIDE?
HMM...
I MEAN, I WON'T SAY YOU *CAN'T* LIVE HERE...
BUT WITH THIS MANY PEOPLE, CLEANING AND HOUSEWORK AND STUFF IS GOING TO BE TOUGH...
OH, NO WORRIES THERE!
WE'RE NOT GOING TO MAKE **ANY MORE TROUBLE** FOR YOU ALL, NOT AFTER ALL YOU'VE DONE FOR OUR SISTER!

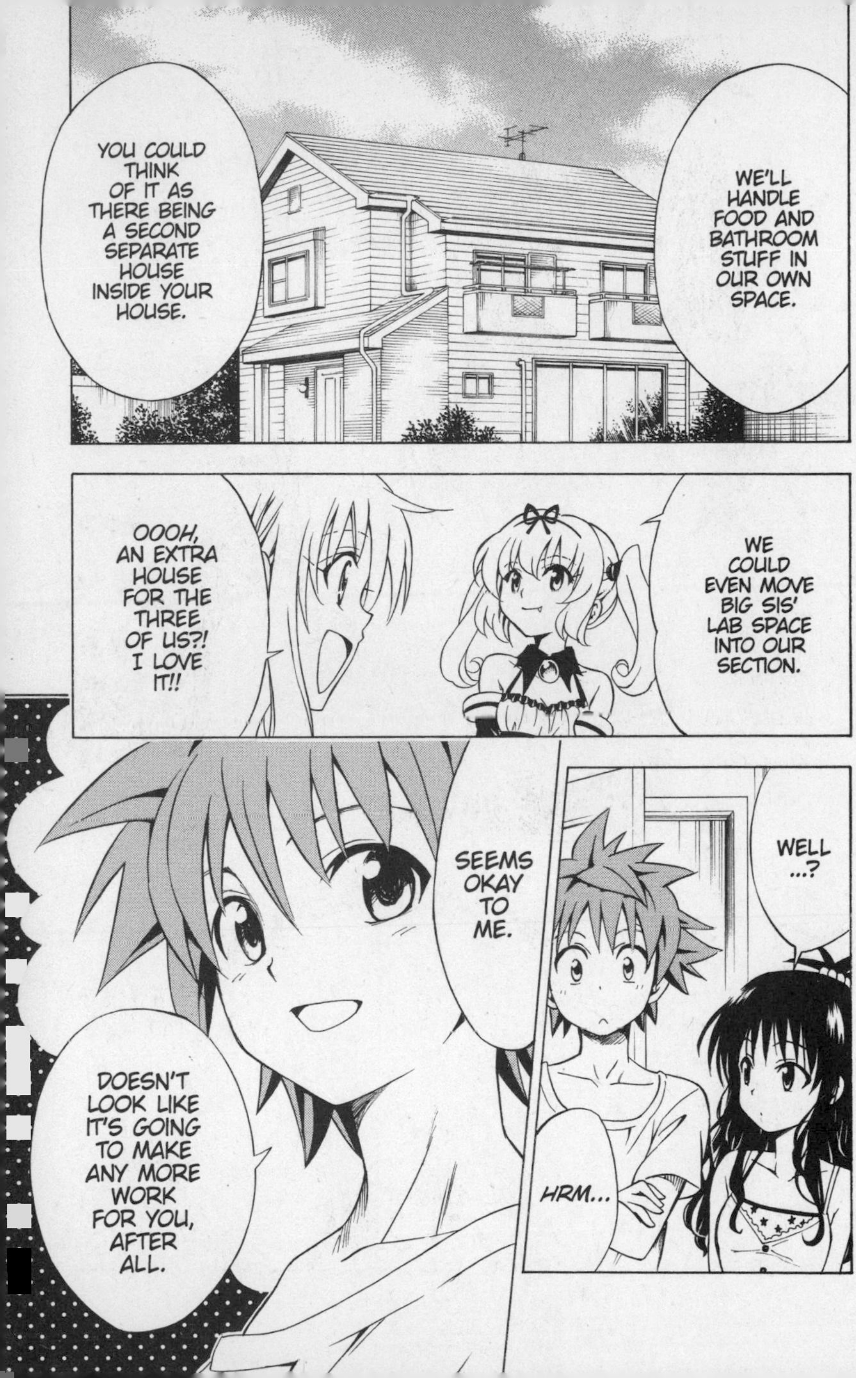
WE'LL HANDLE FOOD AND BATHROOM STUFF IN OUR OWN SPACE.
YOU COULD THINK OF IT AS THERE BEING A SECOND SEPARATE HOUSE INSIDE YOUR HOUSE.
WE COULD EVEN MOVE BIG SIS' LAB SPACE INTO OUR SECTION.
OOOH, AN EXTRA HOUSE FOR THE THREE OF US?! I LOVE IT!!
WELL ...?
HRM...
SEEMS OKAY TO ME.
DOESN'T LOOK LIKE IT'S GOING TO MAKE ANY MORE WORK FOR YOU, AFTER ALL.

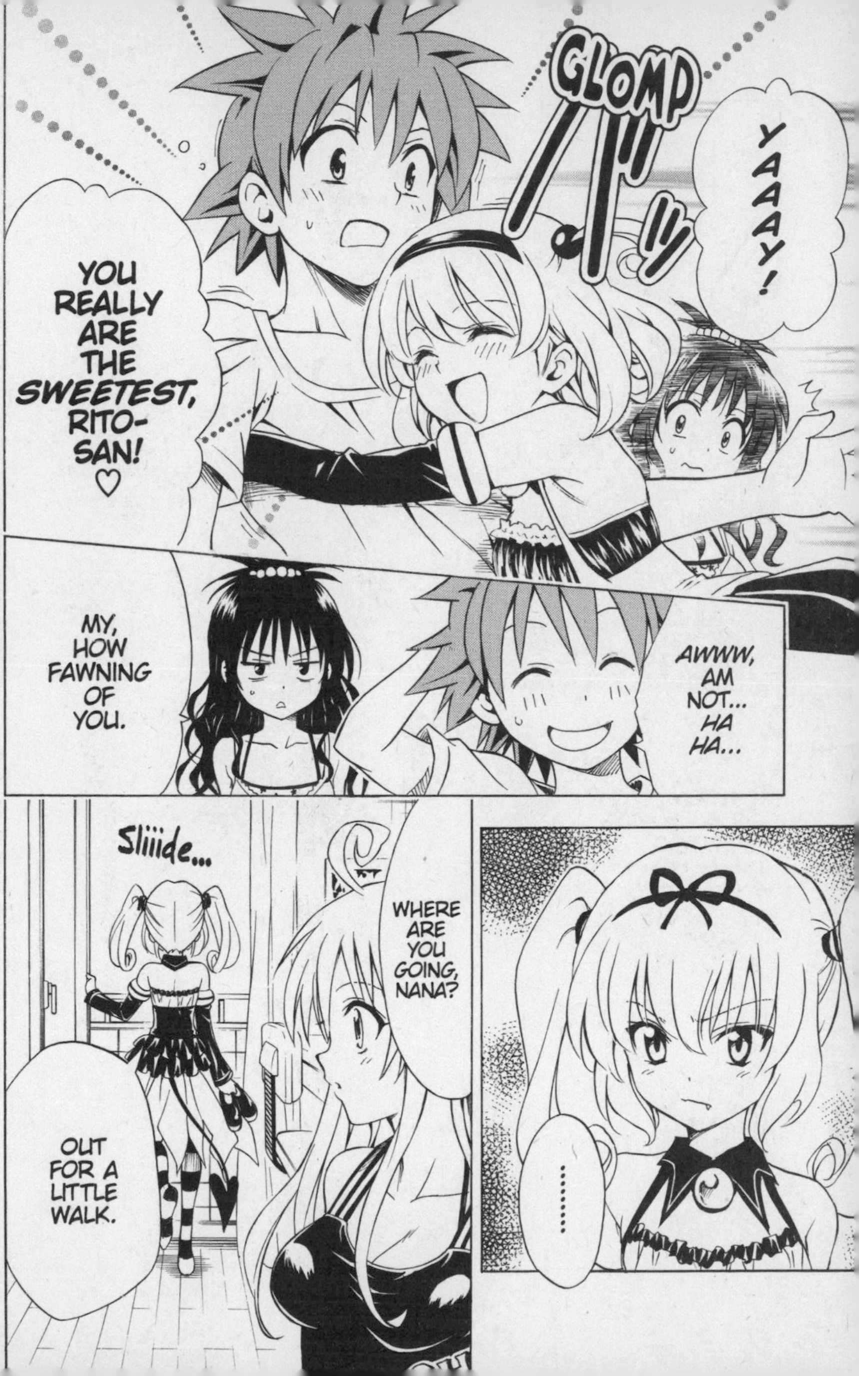
YAAAY!
GLOMP
YOU REALLY ARE THE SWEETEST, RITO-SAN! ♡
MY, HOW FAWNING OF YOU.
AWWW, AM NOT... HA HA...
......
Sliiide...
WHERE ARE YOU GOING, NANA?
OUT FOR A LITTLE WALK.

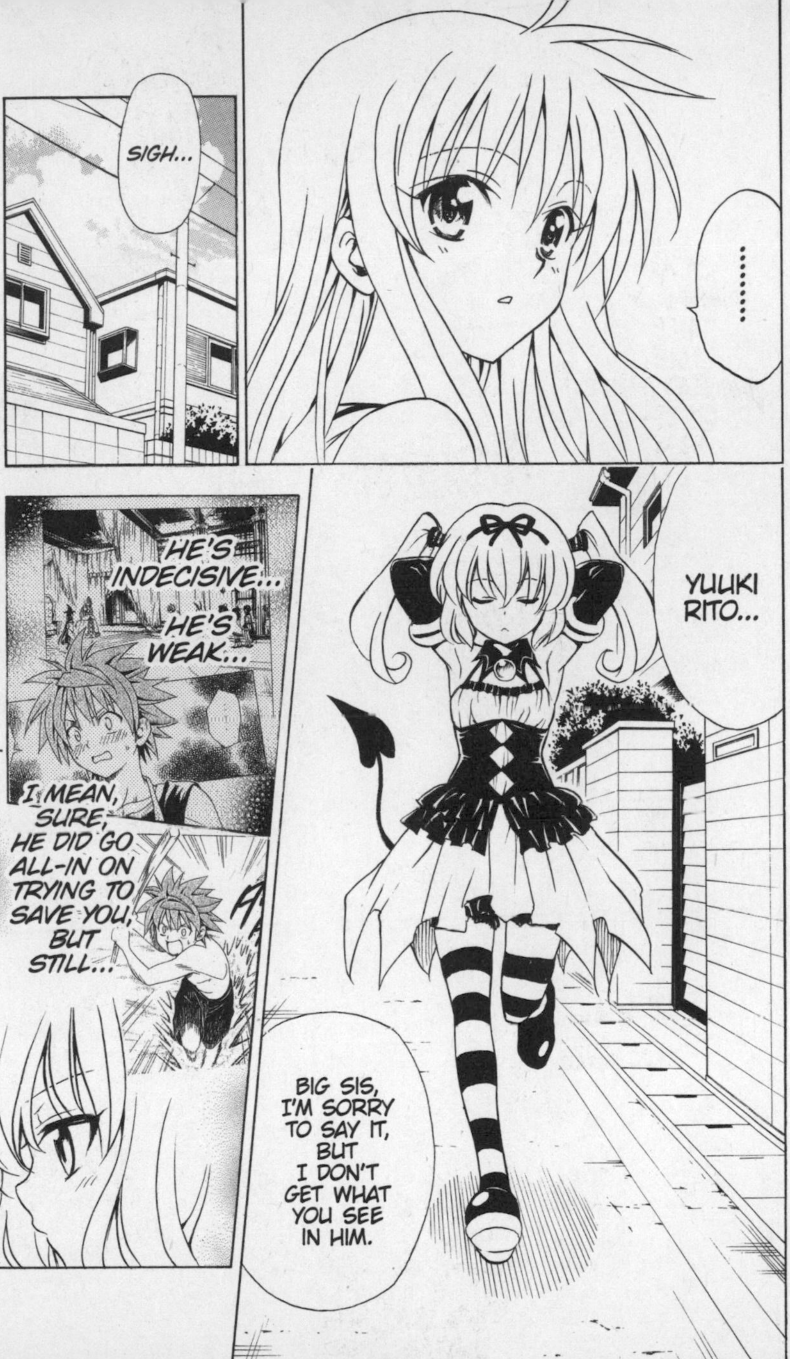
......
SIGH...
YUUKI RITO...
BIG SIS, I'M SORRY TO SAY IT, BUT I DON'T GET WHAT YOU SEE IN HIM.
HE'S INDECISIVE...
HE'S WEAK...
I MEAN, SURE, HE DID GO ALL-IN ON TRYING TO SAVE YOU, BUT STILL...

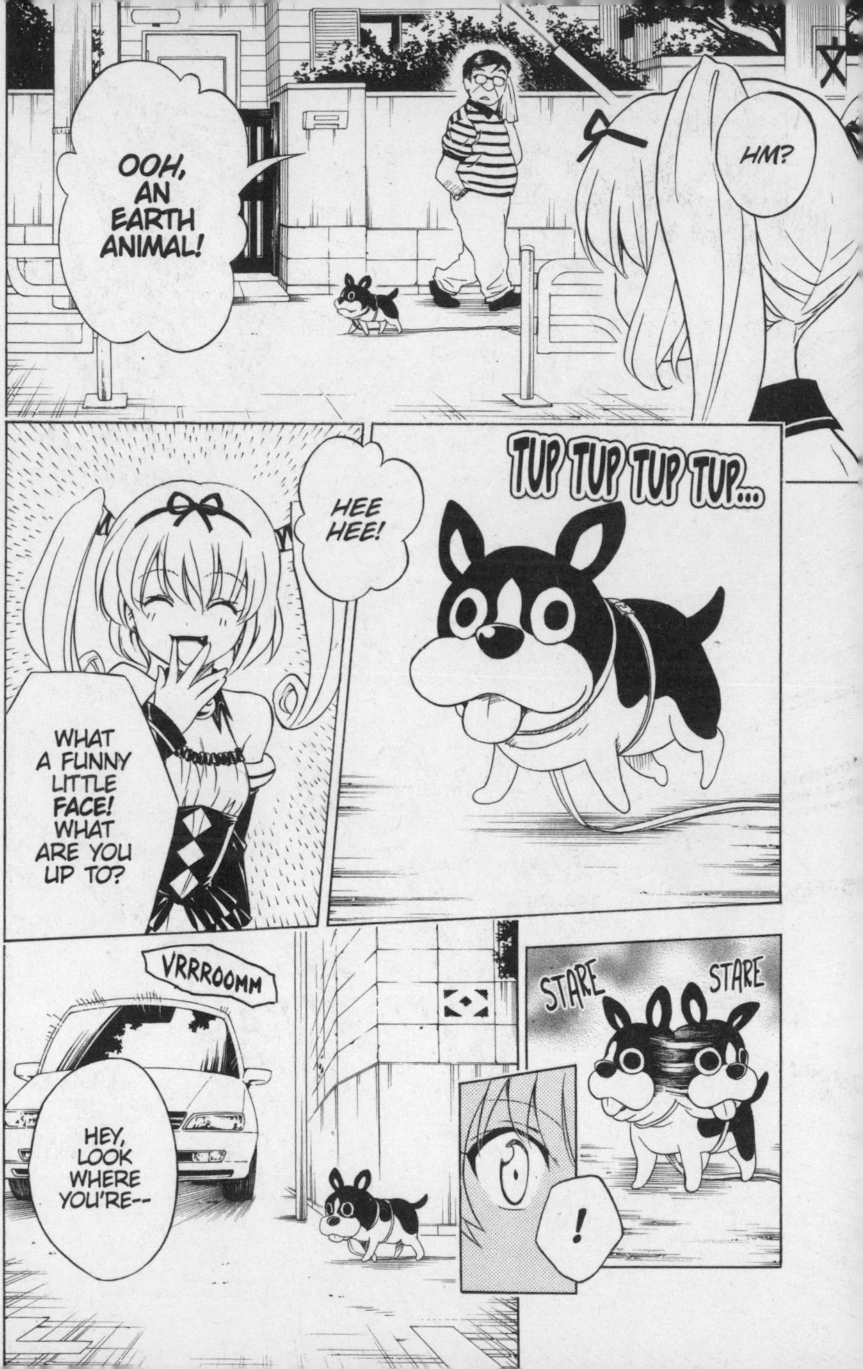
HM?
OOH, AN EARTH ANIMAL!
TUP TUP TUP TUP...
HEE HEE!
WHAT A FUNNY LITTLE FACE! WHAT ARE YOU UP TO?
STARE
STARE
!
VRRROOMM
HEY, LOOK WHERE YOU'RE--

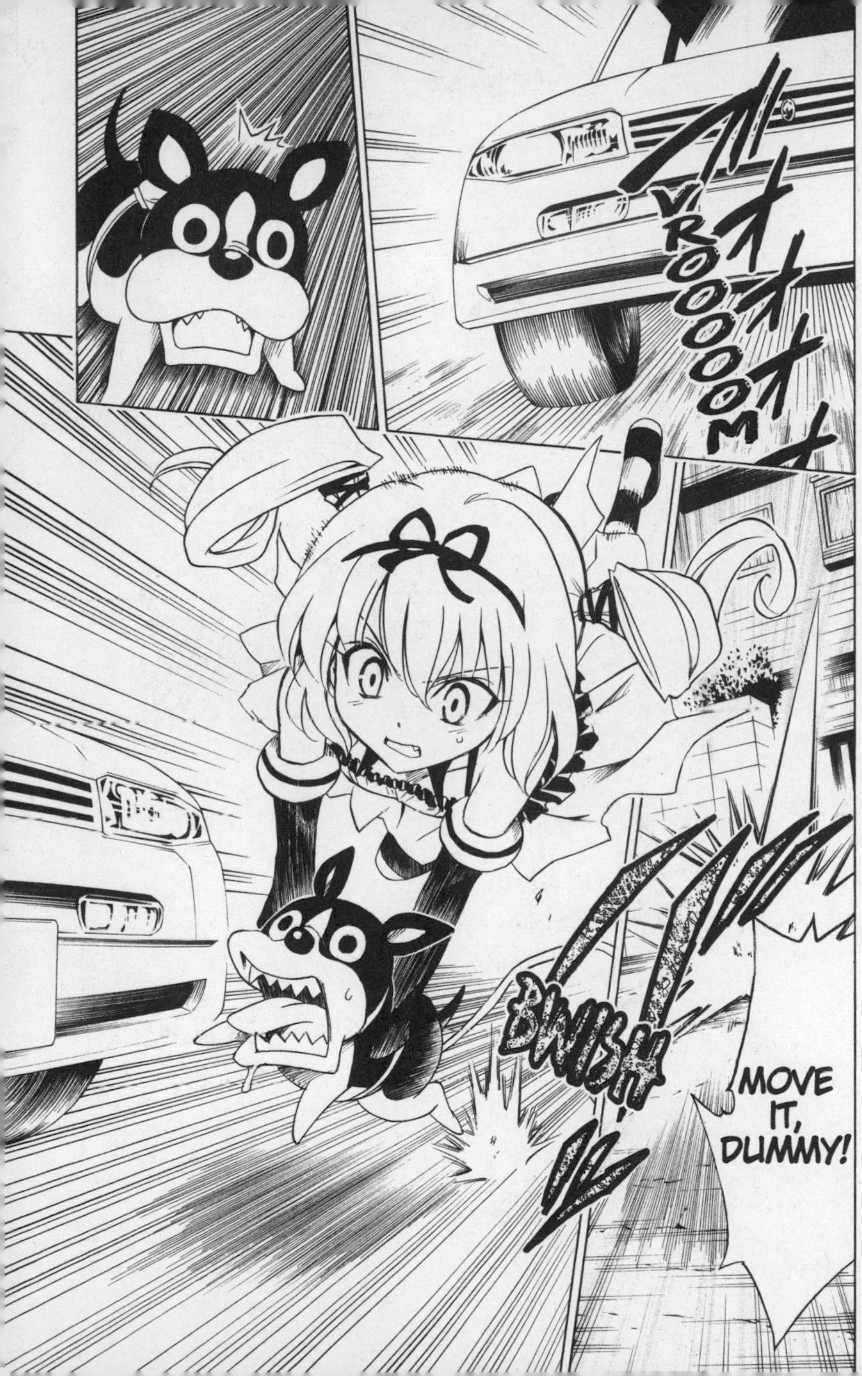
VROOOOOOM
BWISH
MOVE IT, DUMMY!

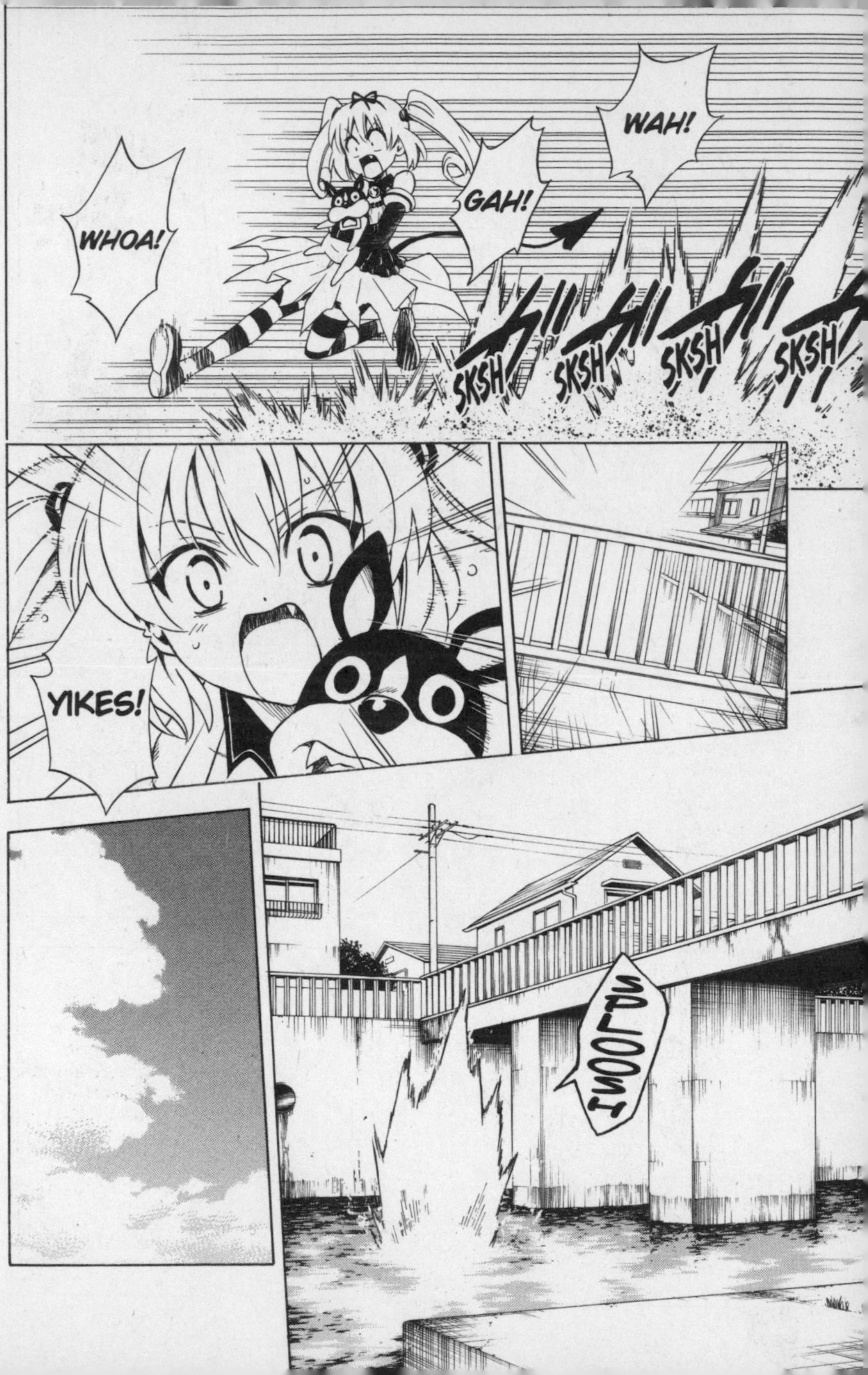
WAH!
GAH!
WHOA!
SKSH SKSH SKSH SKSH
YIKES!
SPLOOSH

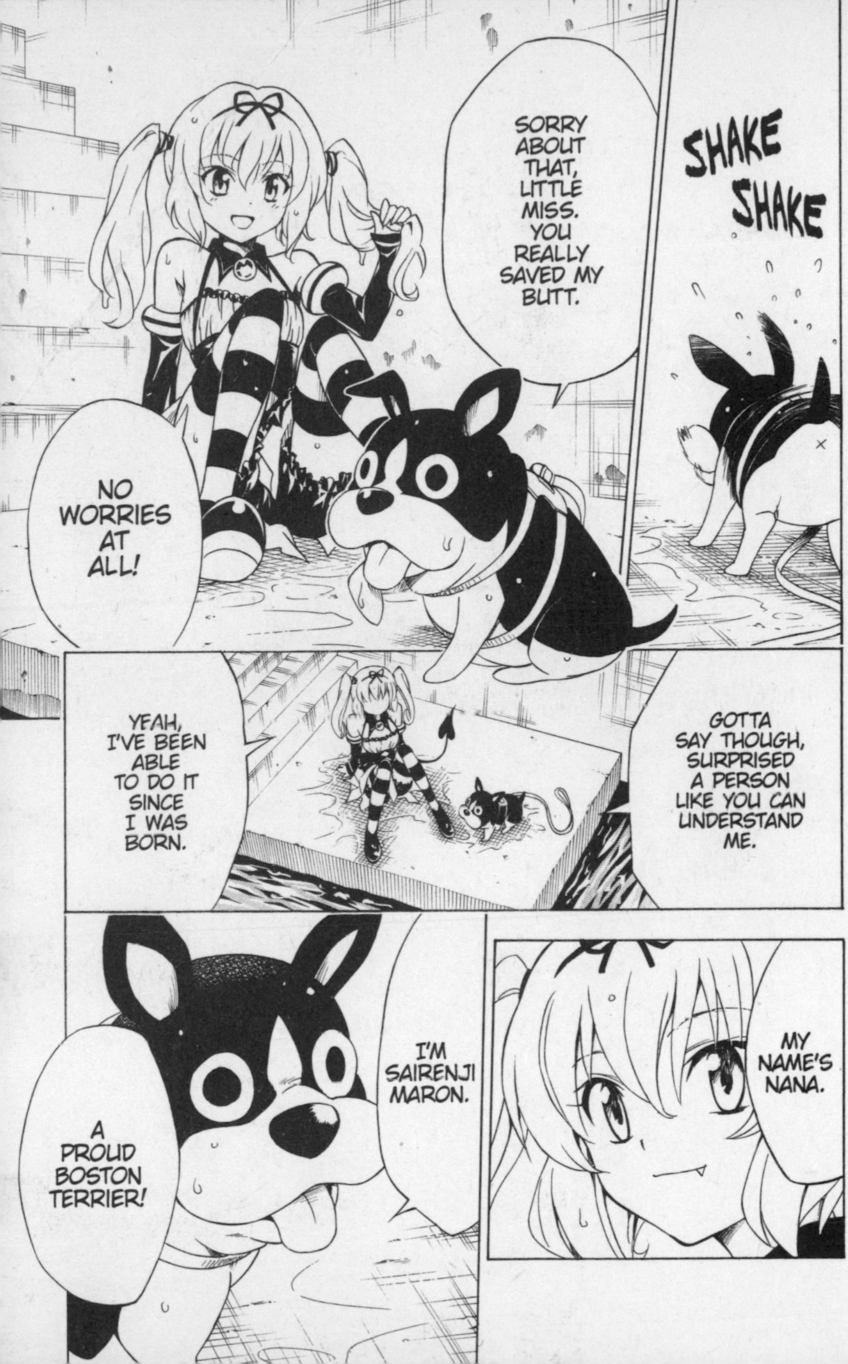
SHAKE SHAKE
SORRY ABOUT THAT, LITTLE MISS. YOU REALLY SAVED MY BUTT.
NO WORRIES AT ALL!
GOTTA SAY THOUGH, SURPRISED A PERSON LIKE YOU CAN UNDERSTAND ME.
YEAH, I'VE BEEN ABLE TO DO IT SINCE I WAS BORN.
MY NAME'S NANA.
I'M SAIRENJI MARON.
A PROUD BOSTON TERRIER!

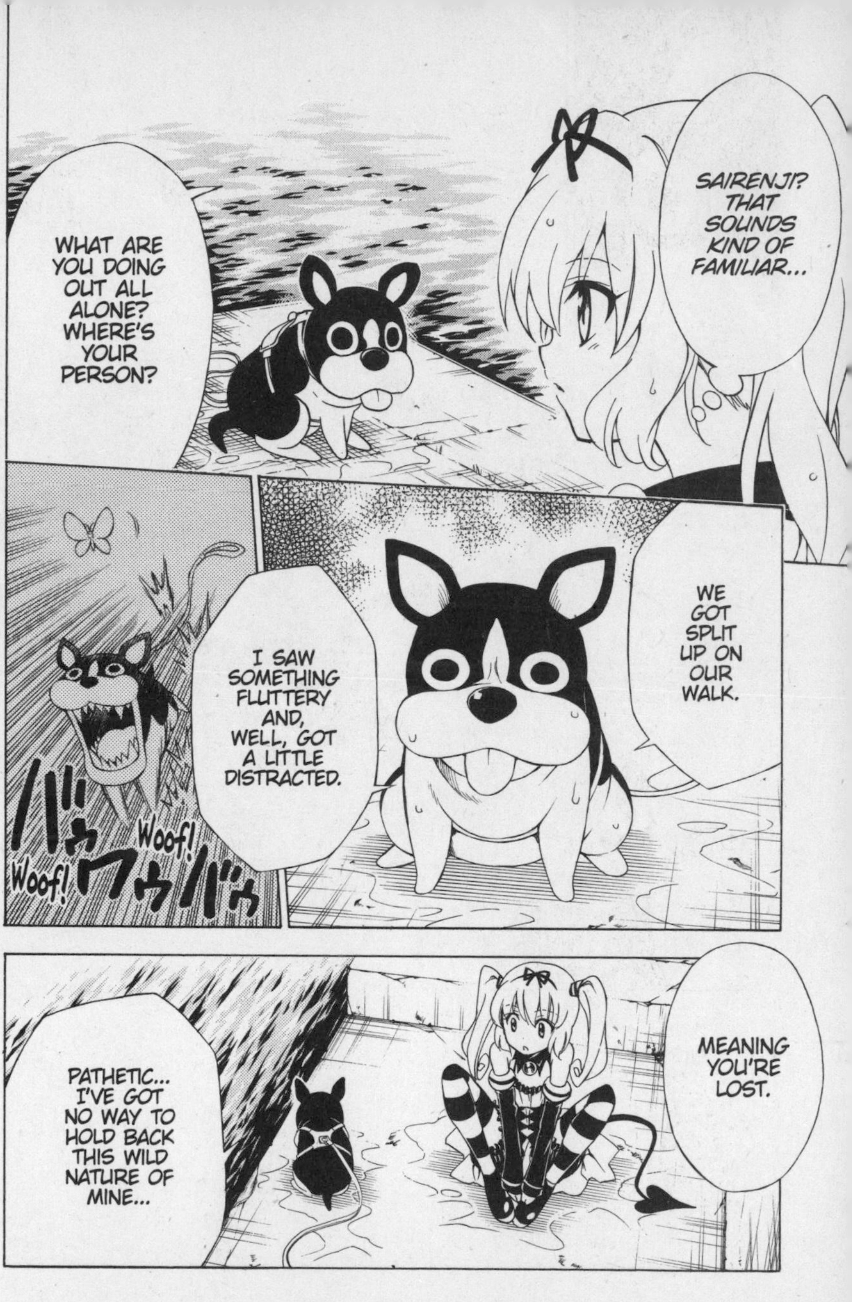
SAIRENJI? THAT SOUNDS KIND OF FAMILIAR...
WHAT ARE YOU DOING OUT ALL ALONE? WHERE'S YOUR PERSON?
WE GOT SPLIT UP ON OUR WALK.
I SAW SOMETHING FLUTTERY AND, WELL, GOT A LITTLE DISTRACTED.
バゥワゥバゥ
Woof! Woof!
MEANING YOU'RE LOST.
PATHETIC... I'VE GOT NO WAY TO HOLD BACK THIS WILD NATURE OF MINE...

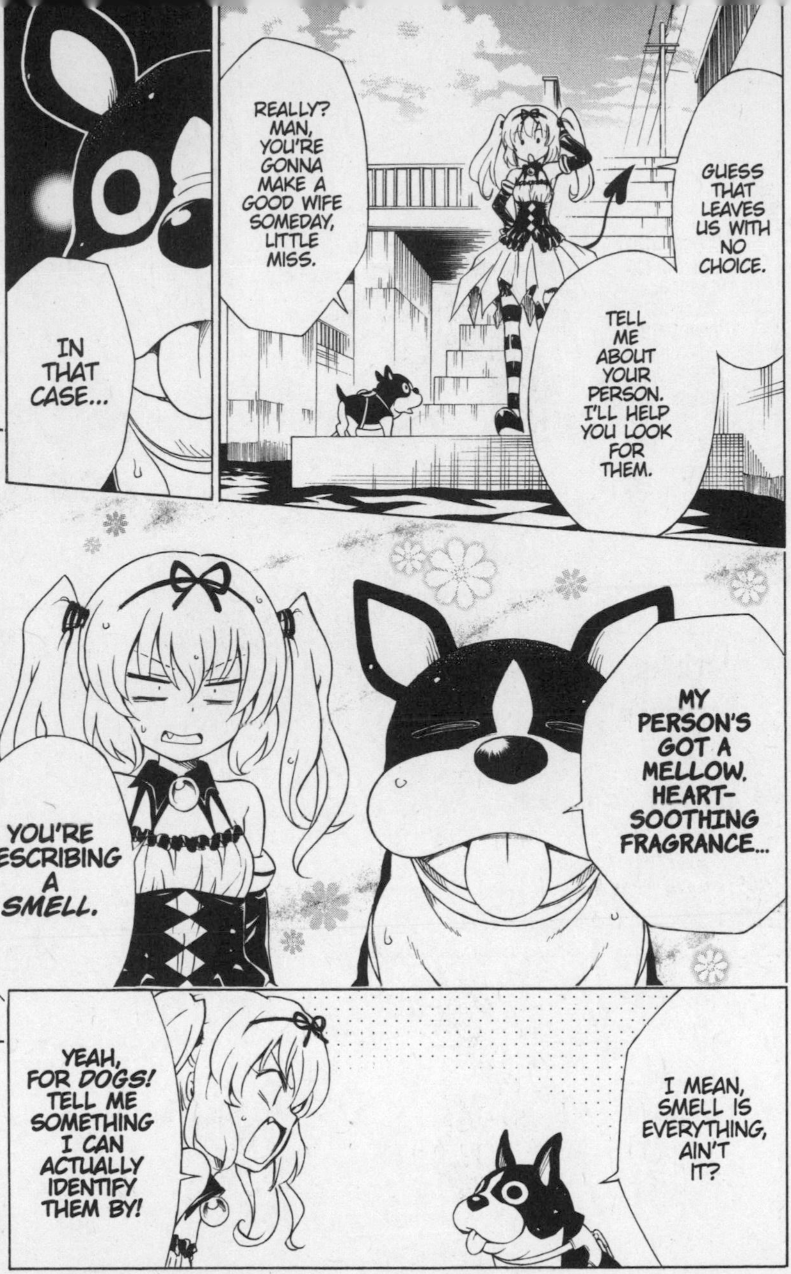
GUESS THAT LEAVES US WITH NO CHOICE.
TELL ME ABOUT YOUR PERSON. I'LL HELP YOU LOOK FOR THEM.
REALLY? MAN, YOU'RE GONNA MAKE A GOOD WIFE SOMEDAY, LITTLE MISS.
IN THAT CASE...
MY PERSON'S GOT A MELLOW, HEART-SOOTHING FRAGRANCE...
YOU'RE DESCRIBING A *SMELL*.
I MEAN, SMELL IS EVERYTHING, AIN'T IT?
YEAH, FOR *DOGS*! TELL ME SOMETHING I CAN ACTUALLY IDENTIFY THEM BY!

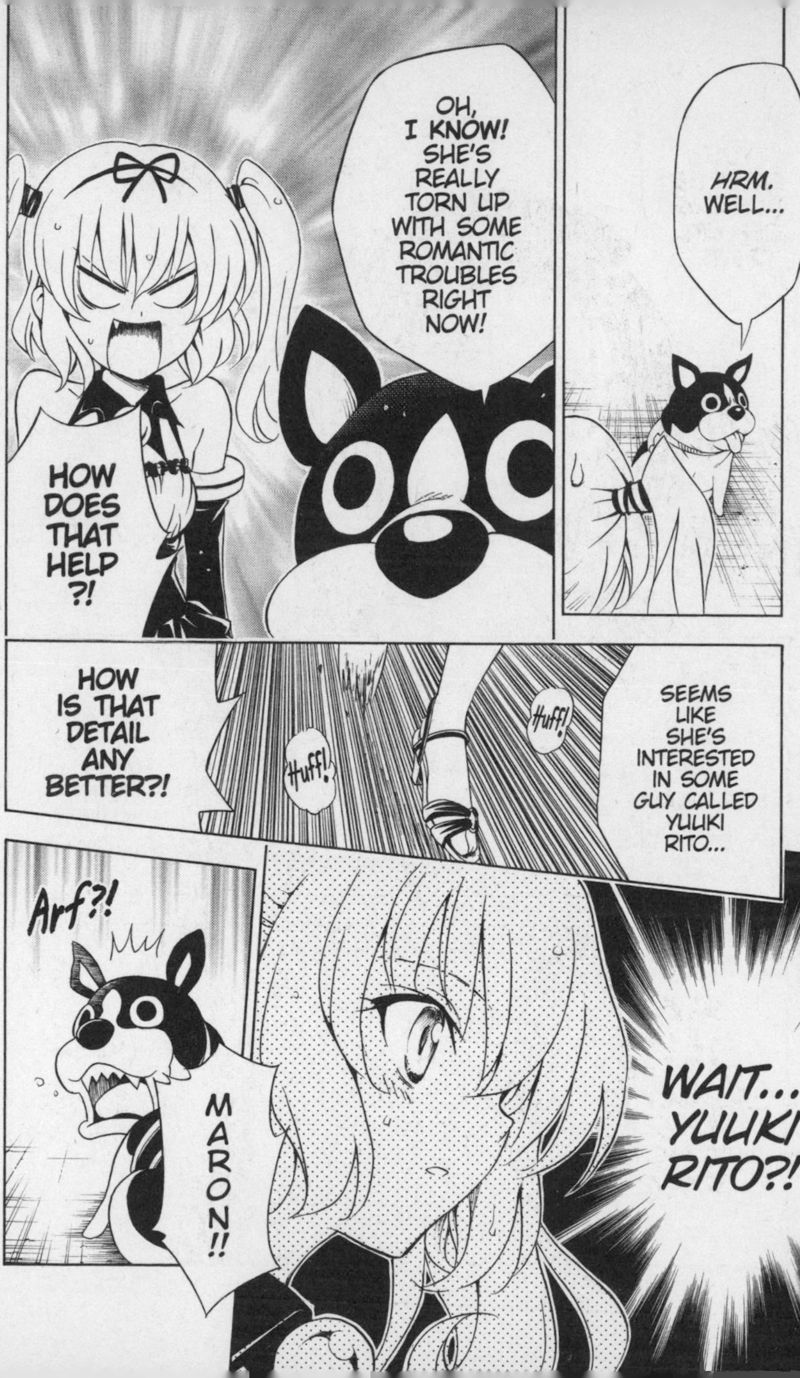
HRM. WELL...
OH, I KNOW! SHE'S REALLY TORN UP WITH SOME ROMANTIC TROUBLES RIGHT NOW!
HOW DOES THAT HELP?!
SEEMS LIKE SHE'S INTERESTED IN SOME GUY CALLED YUUKI RITO...
Huff!
Huff!
HOW IS THAT DETAIL ANY BETTER?!
WAIT... YUUKI RITO?!
Arf?!
MARON!!

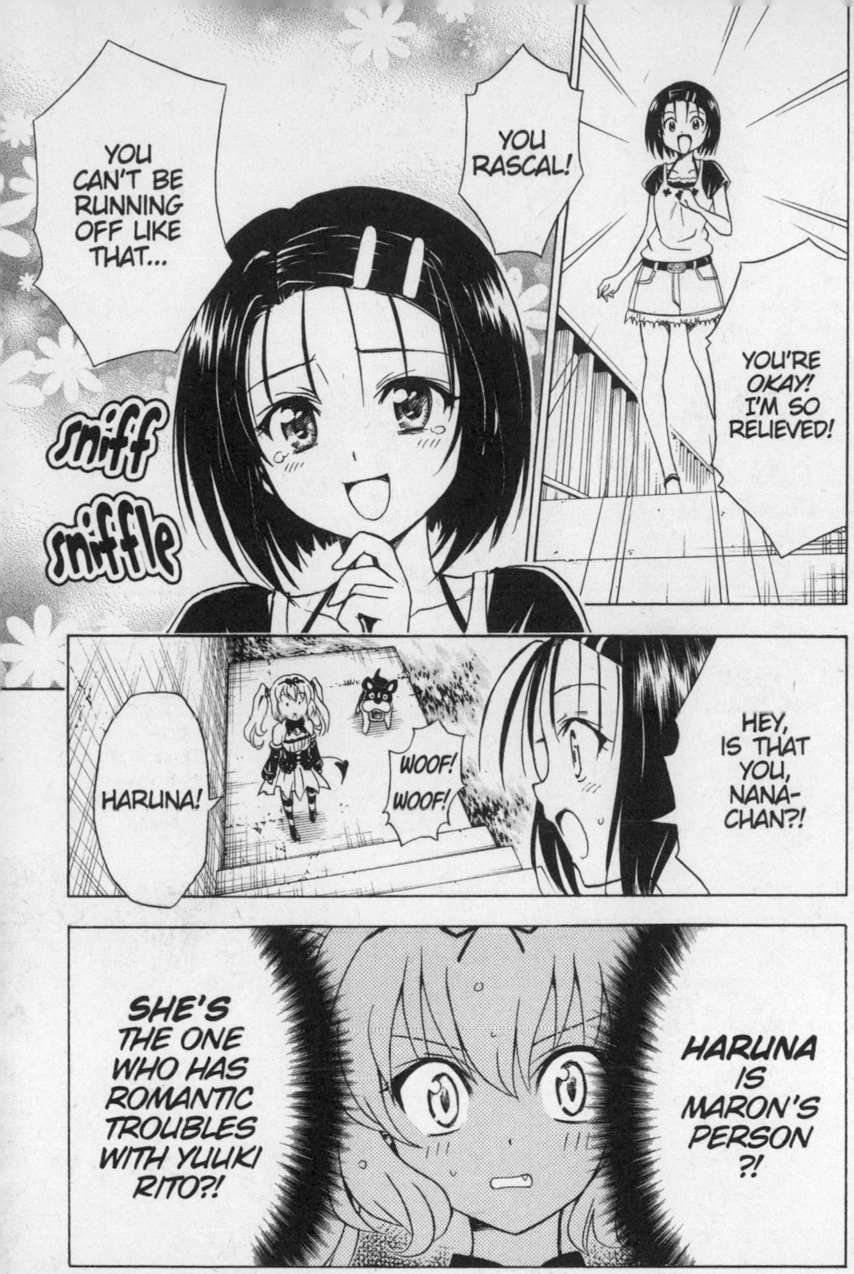
YOU RASCAL!
YOU'RE OKAY! I'M SO RELIEVED!
YOU CAN'T BE RUNNING OFF LIKE THAT...
sniff
sniffle
HEY, IS THAT YOU, NANA-CHAN?!
WOOF!
WOOF!
HARUNA!
HARUNA IS MARON'S PERSON ?!
SHE'S THE ONE WHO HAS ROMANTIC TROUBLES WITH YUUKI RITO?!

Character File
17
Sairenji Akiho

☆Akiho
Haruna's older sister. She works as an editor of a fashion magazine. She's also technically Maron's actual owner. She's currently on the lookout for a boyfriend of about 22 years of age? (lol!)

● ● ● ● ● ● ● ● ● ● ● ● ● ● ● ● ● ● ● ●

☆As an older sister
Her relationship with Haruna is messy, but good. She sometimes treats her sister like a child, but that's just the proof of how close they are!

● ● ● ● ● ● ● ● ● ● ● ● ● ● ● ● ● ● ● ●

☆Her relationships with men
Akiho seems to have a lot of male friends, and among them is Kotegawa Yuu (Yui's older brother). It's maybe a bit of untold backstory, but they actually met at a party among some mutual friends (haha!). Yuu is pretty serious, but Akiho kind of...isn't?

● ● ● ● ● ● ● ● ● ● ● ● ● ● ● ● ● ● ● ●

☆Hobbies
We haven't done much with this in the story yet, but Akiho loves pets like dogs and cats. However, with her work being really busy, Haruna often ends up responsible for Maron.

● ● ● ● ● ● ● ● ● ● ● ● ● ● ● ● ● ● ● ●

☆What's next...
Okay, I know everyone has been very interested in Akiho's relationship with Kotegawa Yuu! However, so far, Akiho has just been kind of a side character, so her future role will be based on how things in the story end up going. I'd like to use her in some kind of way that leaves an impression...but I don't know, maybe we'll start with something steamy? (Eheheh!)

Hasemi

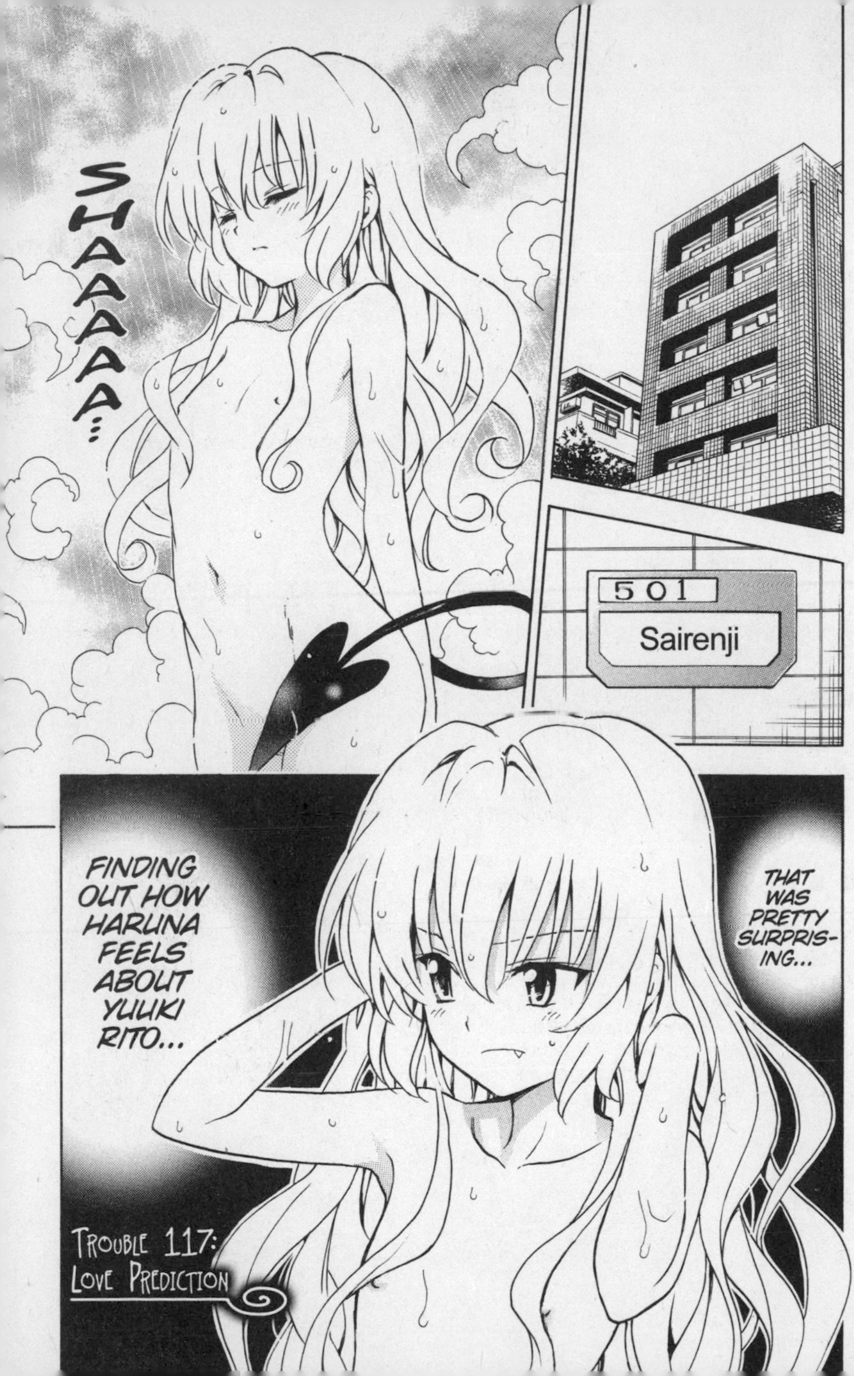
501
Sairenji
SHAAAAAA...
FINDING OUT HOW HARUNA FEELS ABOUT YUUKI RITO...
THAT WAS PRETTY SURPRIS-ING...
TROUBLE 117: LOVE PREDICTION

Trouble 117: Love Prediction

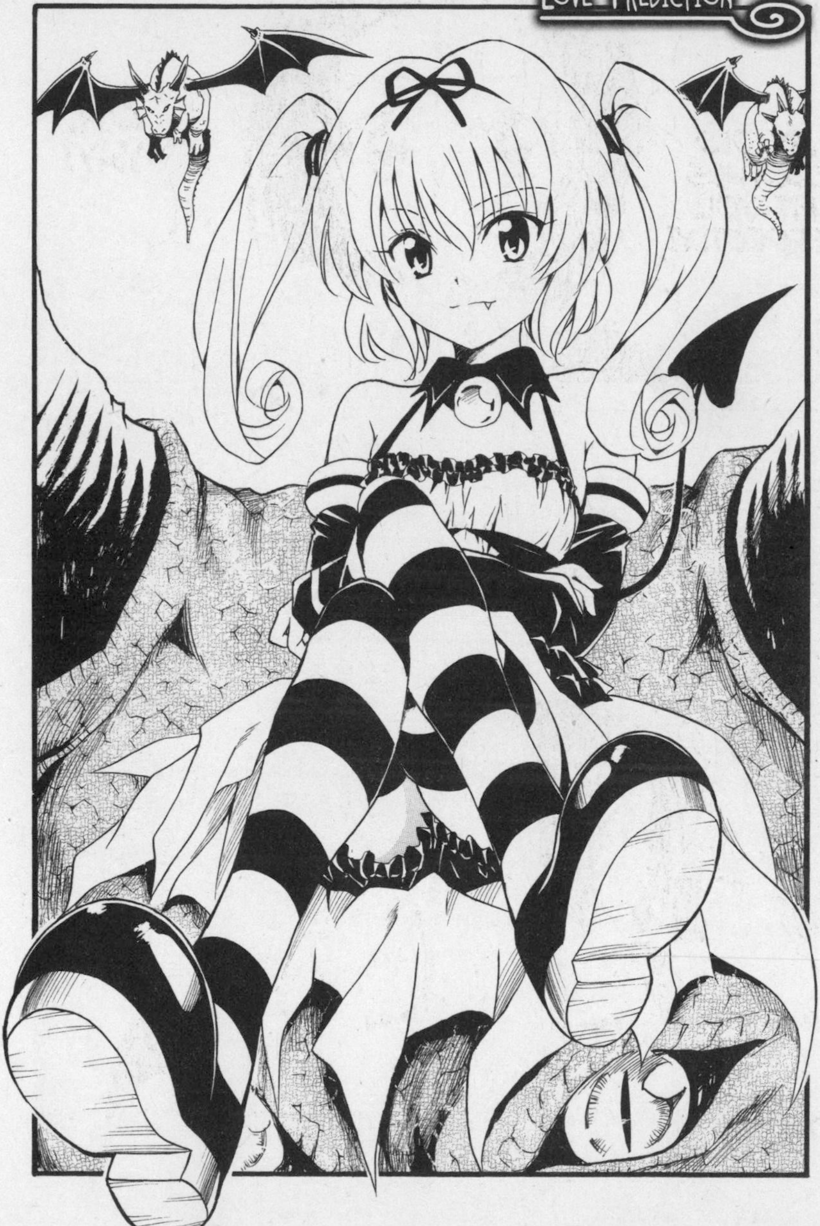

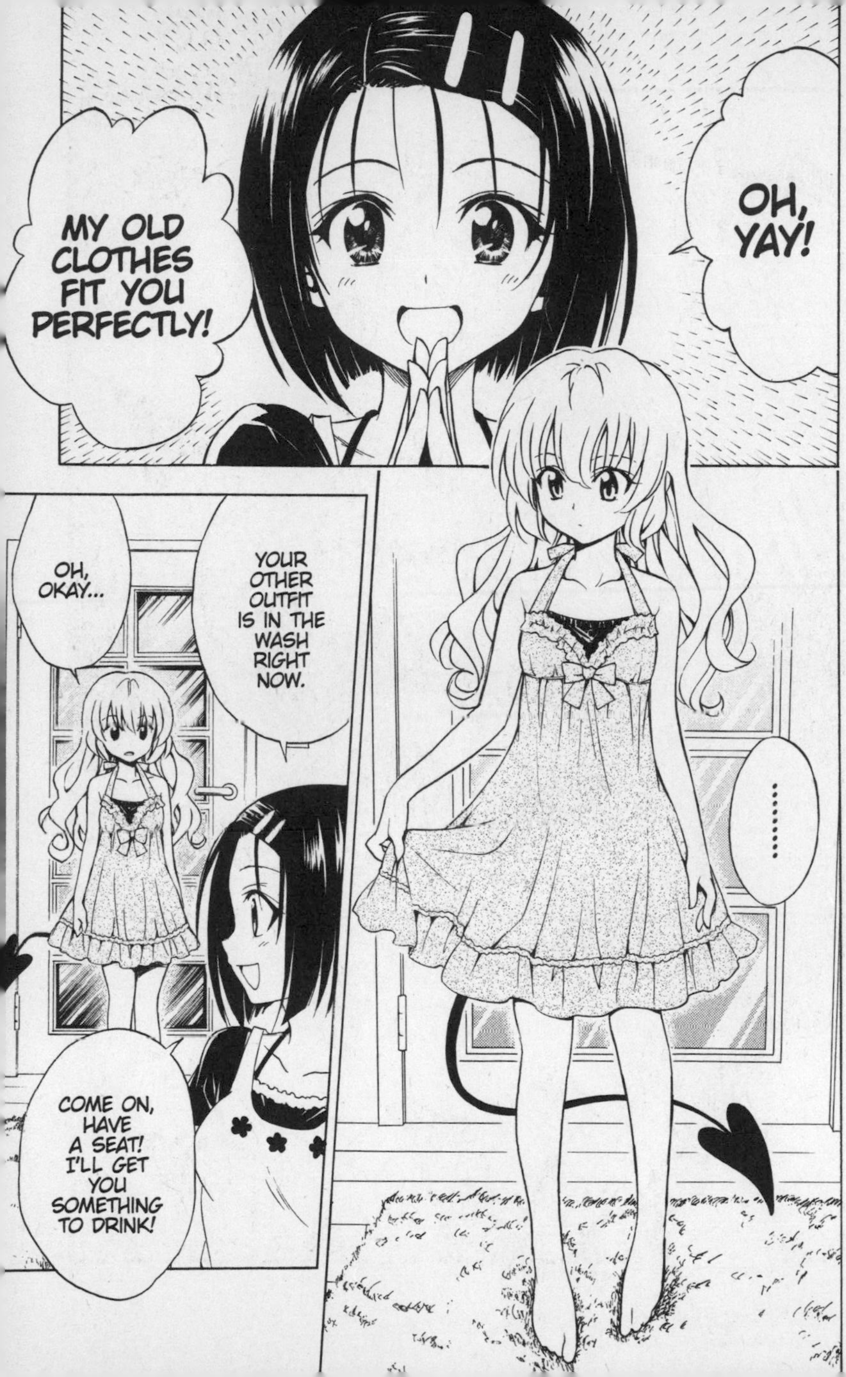
OH, YAY!
MY OLD CLOTHES FIT YOU PERFECTLY!
......
YOUR OTHER OUTFIT IS IN THE WASH RIGHT NOW.
OH, OKAY...
COME ON, HAVE A SEAT! I'LL GET YOU SOMETHING TO DRINK!

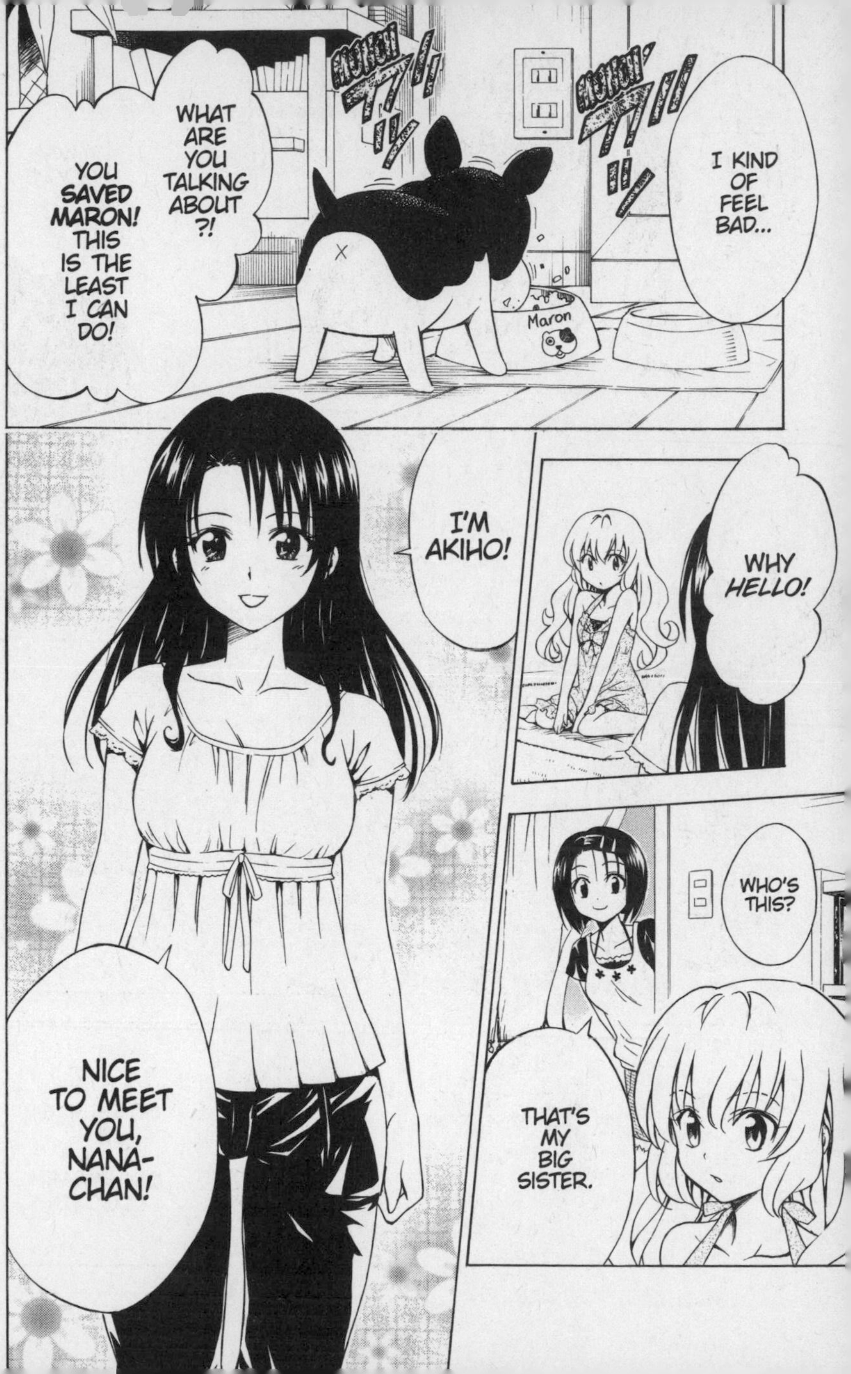
I KIND OF FEEL BAD...
WHAT ARE YOU TALKING ABOUT?!
YOU SAVED MARON! THIS IS THE LEAST I CAN DO!
Maron
WHY HELLO!
WHO'S THIS?
THAT'S MY BIG SISTER.
I'M AKIHO!
NICE TO MEET YOU, NANA-CHAN!

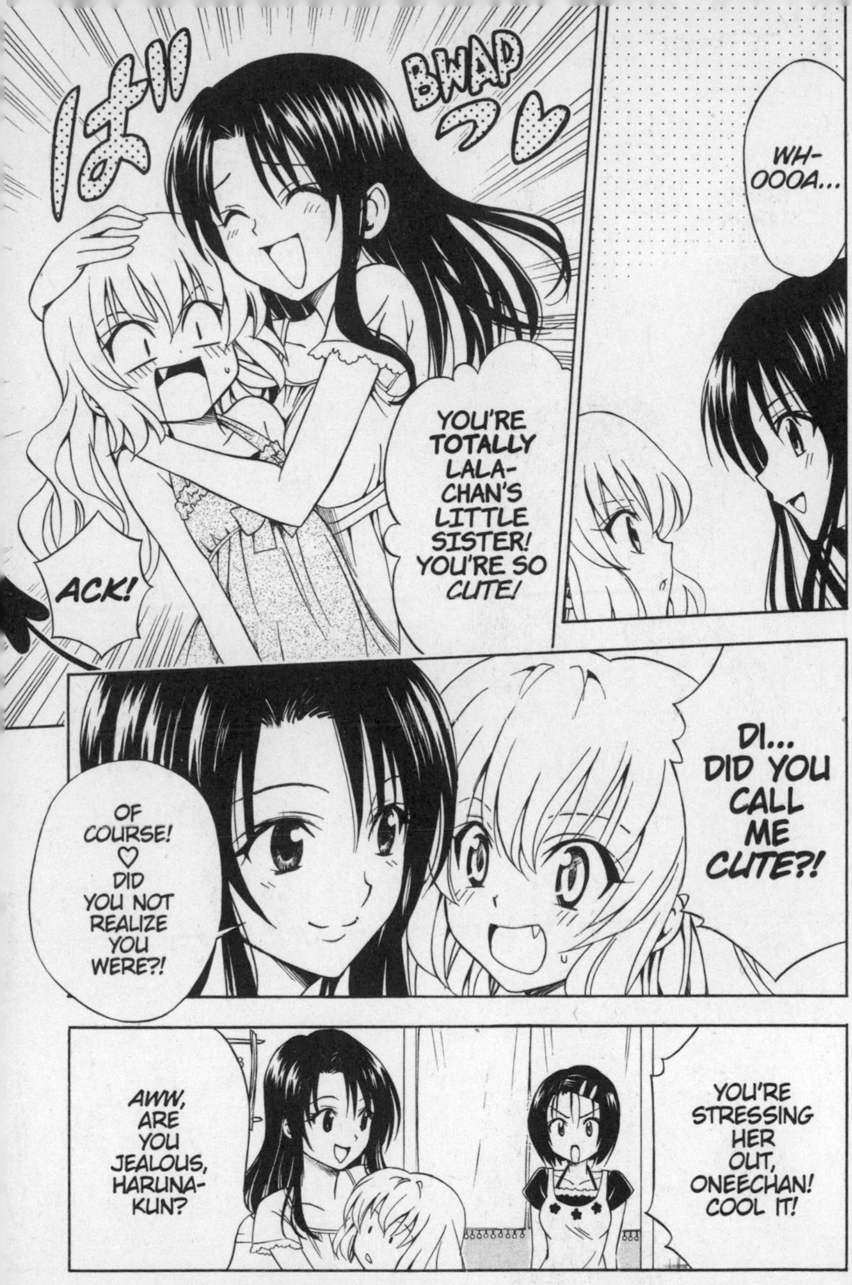
WH-OOOA...
ば
BWAP
っ♡
YOU'RE TOTALLY LALA-CHAN'S LITTLE SISTER! YOU'RE SO CUTE!
ACK!
DI... DID YOU CALL ME CUTE?!
OF COURSE! ♡ DID YOU NOT REALIZE YOU WERE?!
YOU'RE STRESSING HER OUT, ONEECHAN! COOL IT!
AWW, ARE YOU JEALOUS, HARUNA-KUN?

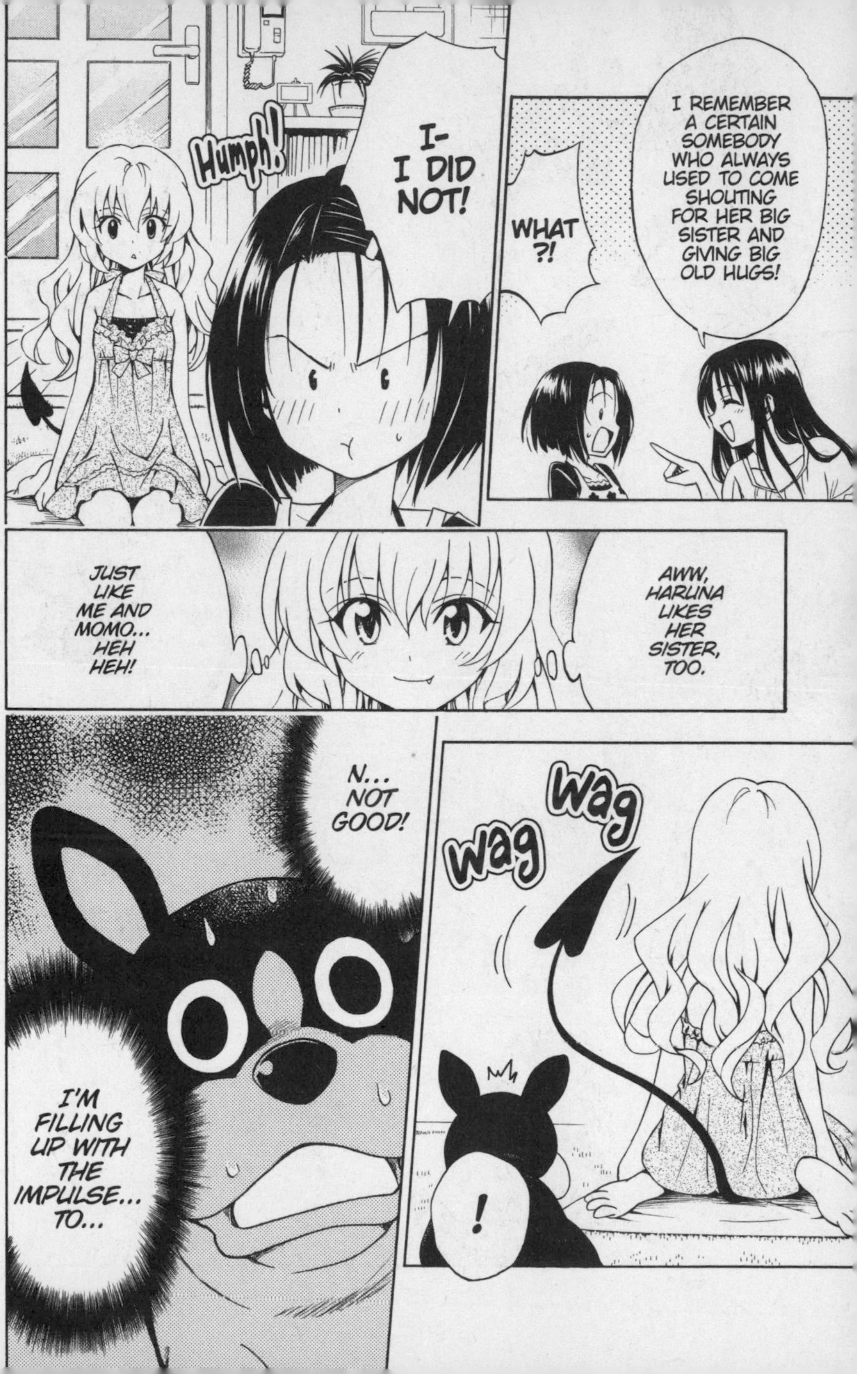
I REMEMBER A CERTAIN SOMEBODY WHO ALWAYS USED TO COME SHOUTING FOR HER BIG SISTER AND GIVING BIG OLD HUGS!
WHAT ?!
I- I DID NOT!
Humph!
AWW, HARUNA LIKES HER SISTER, TOO.
JUST LIKE ME AND MOMO... HEH HEH!
wag
wag
!
N... NOT GOOD!
I'M FILLING UP WITH THE IMPULSE... TO...

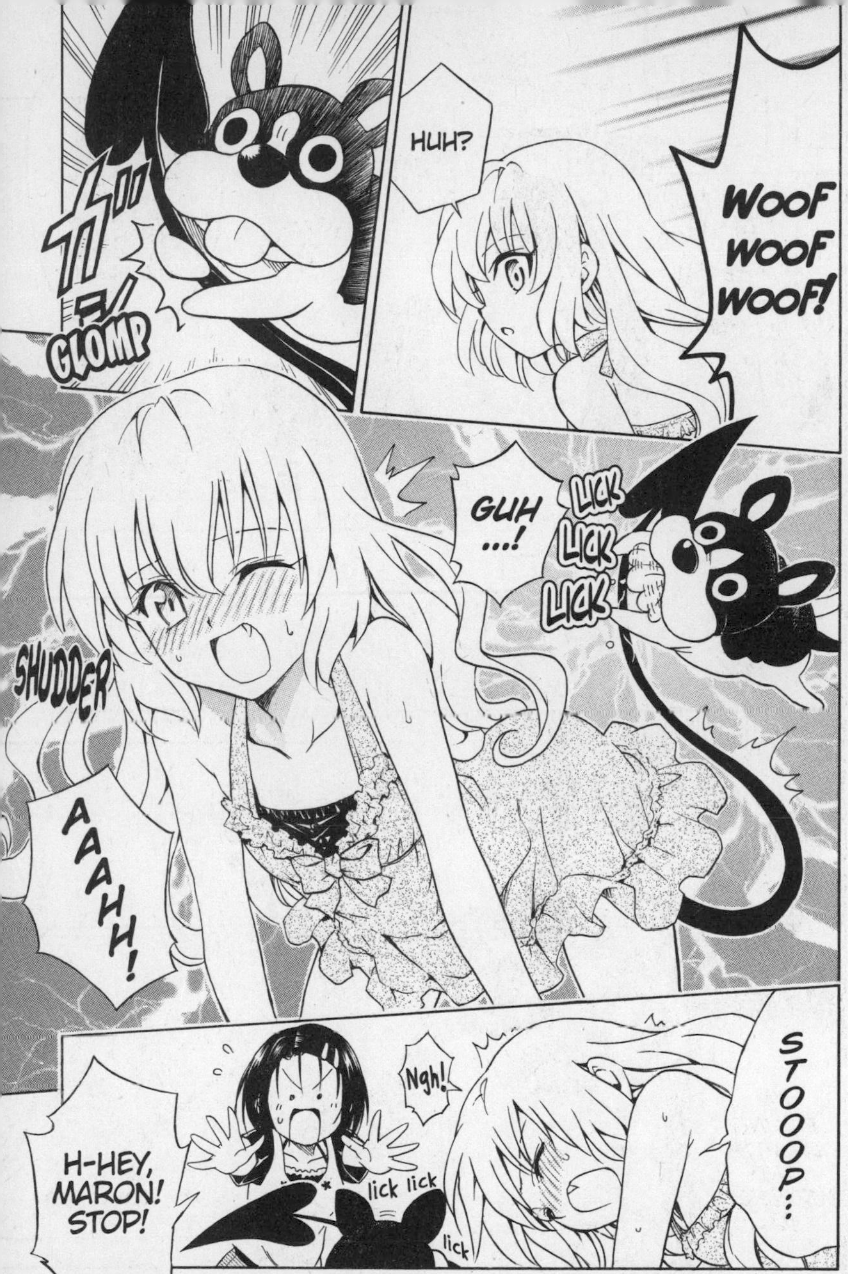
WOOF WOOF WOOF!
HUH?
GLOMP
LICK LICK LICK
GUH ...!
SHUDDER
AAAHH!
STOOOOP...
Ngh!
lick lick
lick
H-HEY, MARON! STOP!

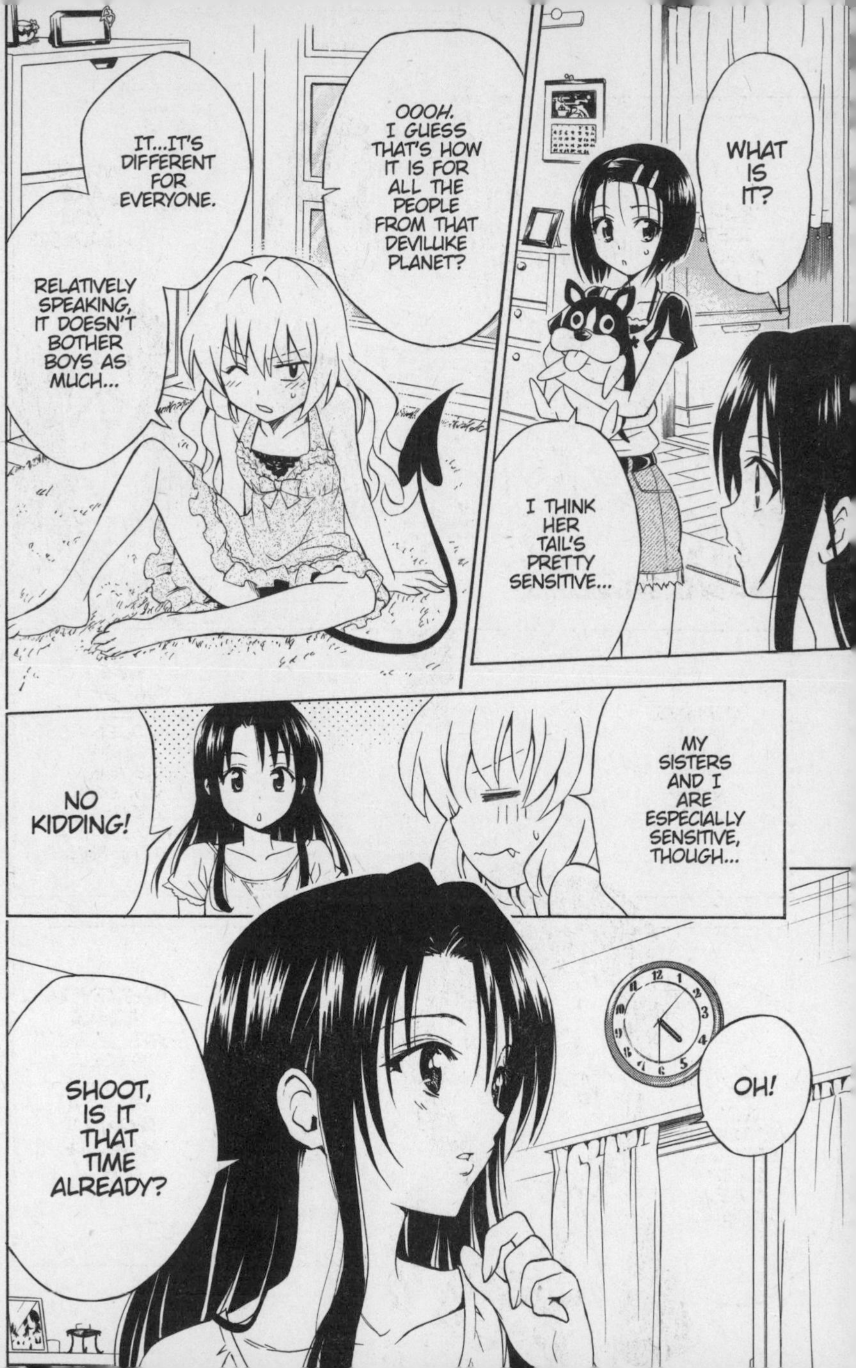
WHAT IS IT?
I THINK HER TAIL'S PRETTY SENSITIVE...
OOOH. I GUESS THAT'S HOW IT IS FOR ALL THE PEOPLE FROM THAT DEVILLIKE PLANET?
IT...IT'S DIFFERENT FOR EVERYONE.
RELATIVELY SPEAKING, IT DOESN'T BOTHER BOYS AS MUCH...
MY SISTERS AND I ARE ESPECIALLY SENSITIVE, THOUGH...
NO KIDDING!
OH!
SHOOT, IS IT THAT TIME ALREADY?

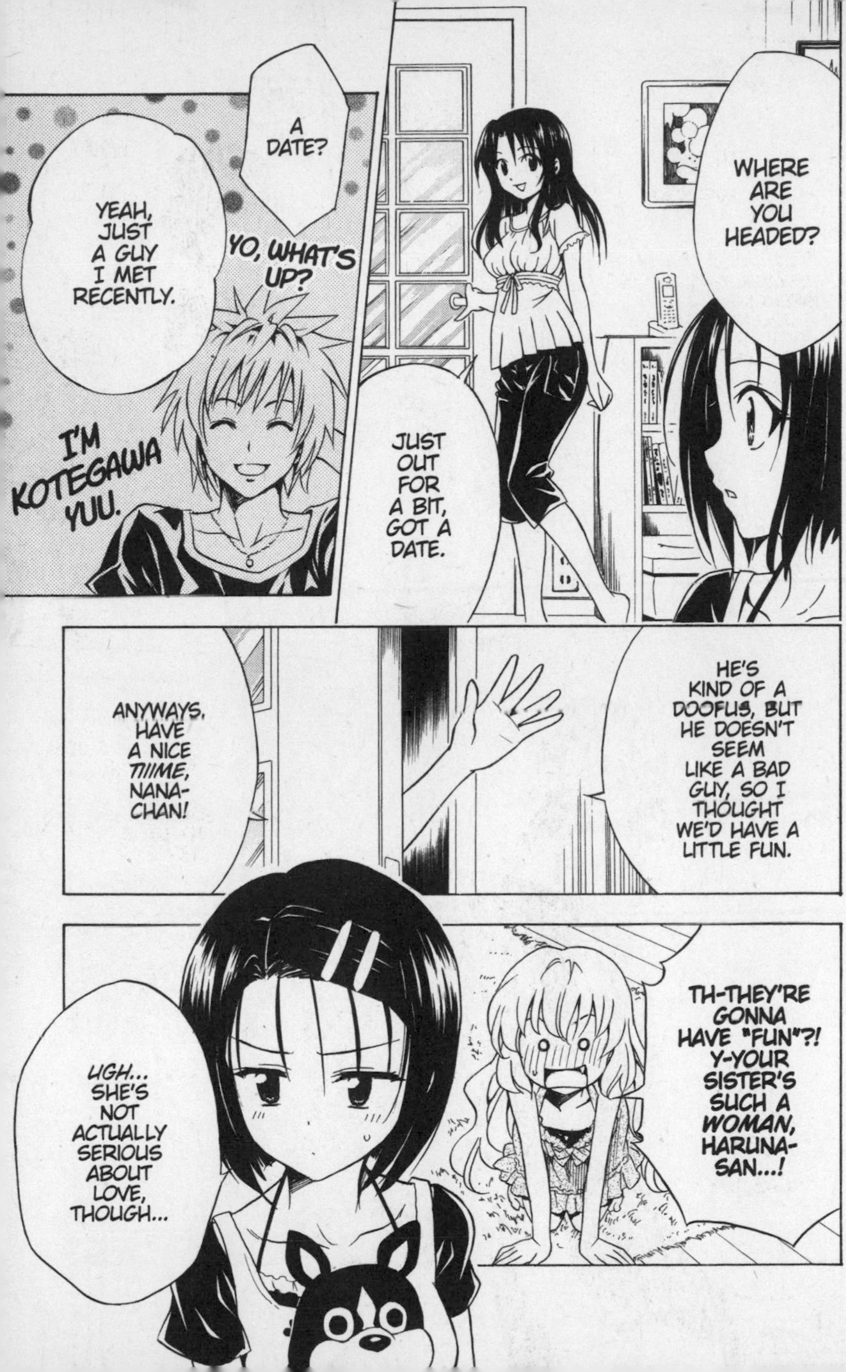
WHERE ARE YOU HEADED?
JUST OUT FOR A BIT, GOT A DATE.
A DATE?
YEAH, JUST A GUY I MET RECENTLY.
YO, WHAT'S UP?
I'M KOTEGAWA YUU.
HE'S KIND OF A DOOFUS, BUT HE DOESN'T SEEM LIKE A BAD GUY, SO I THOUGHT WE'D HAVE A LITTLE FUN.
ANYWAYS, HAVE A NICE TIIIME, NANA-CHAN!
TH-THEY'RE GONNA HAVE "FUN"?! Y-YOUR SISTER'S SUCH A WOMAN, HARUNA-SAN...!
UGH... SHE'S NOT ACTUALLY SERIOUS ABOUT LOVE, THOUGH...

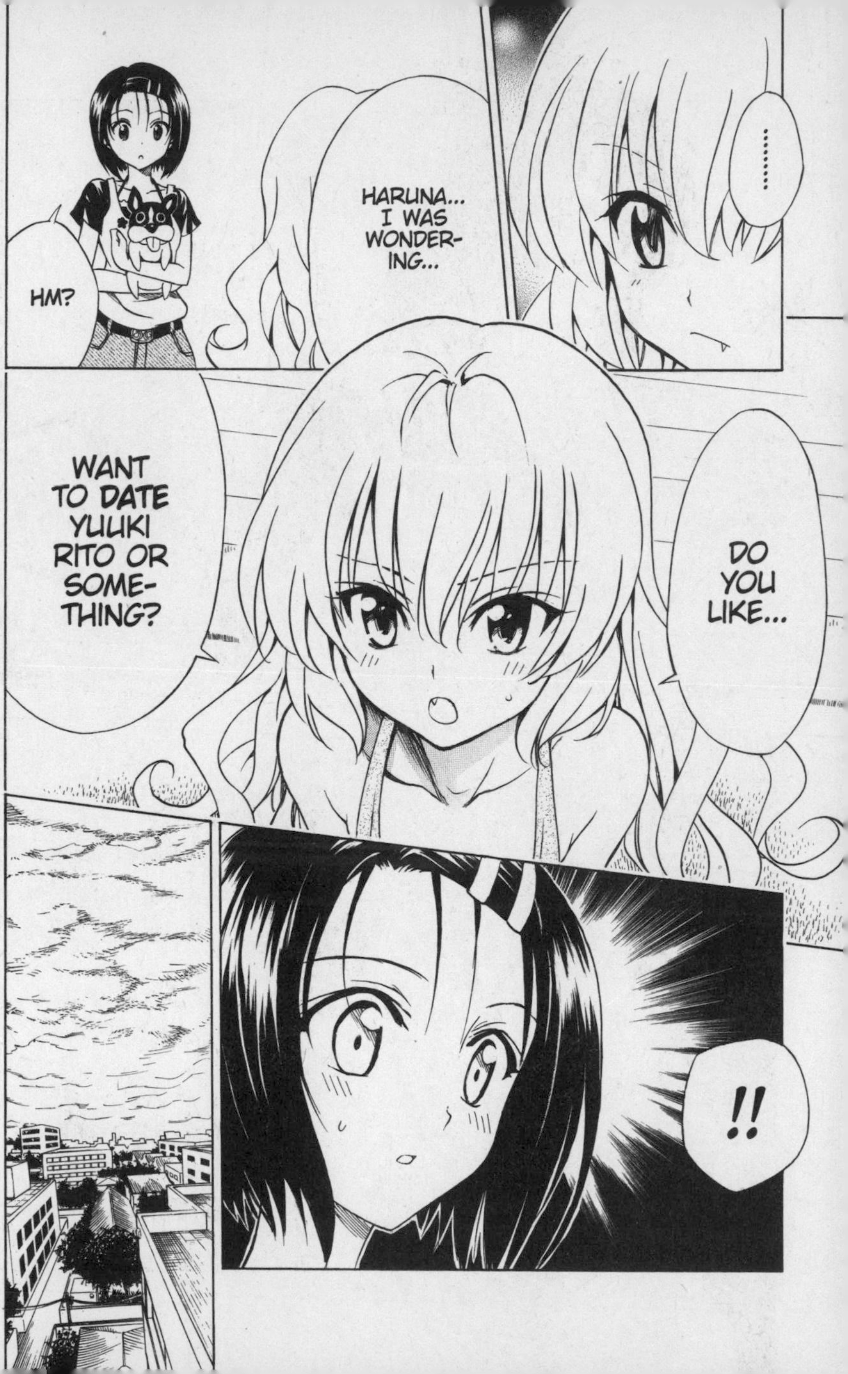
......
HARUNA... I WAS WONDERING...
HM?
DO YOU LIKE...
WANT TO DATE YUUKI RITO OR SOMETHING?
!!

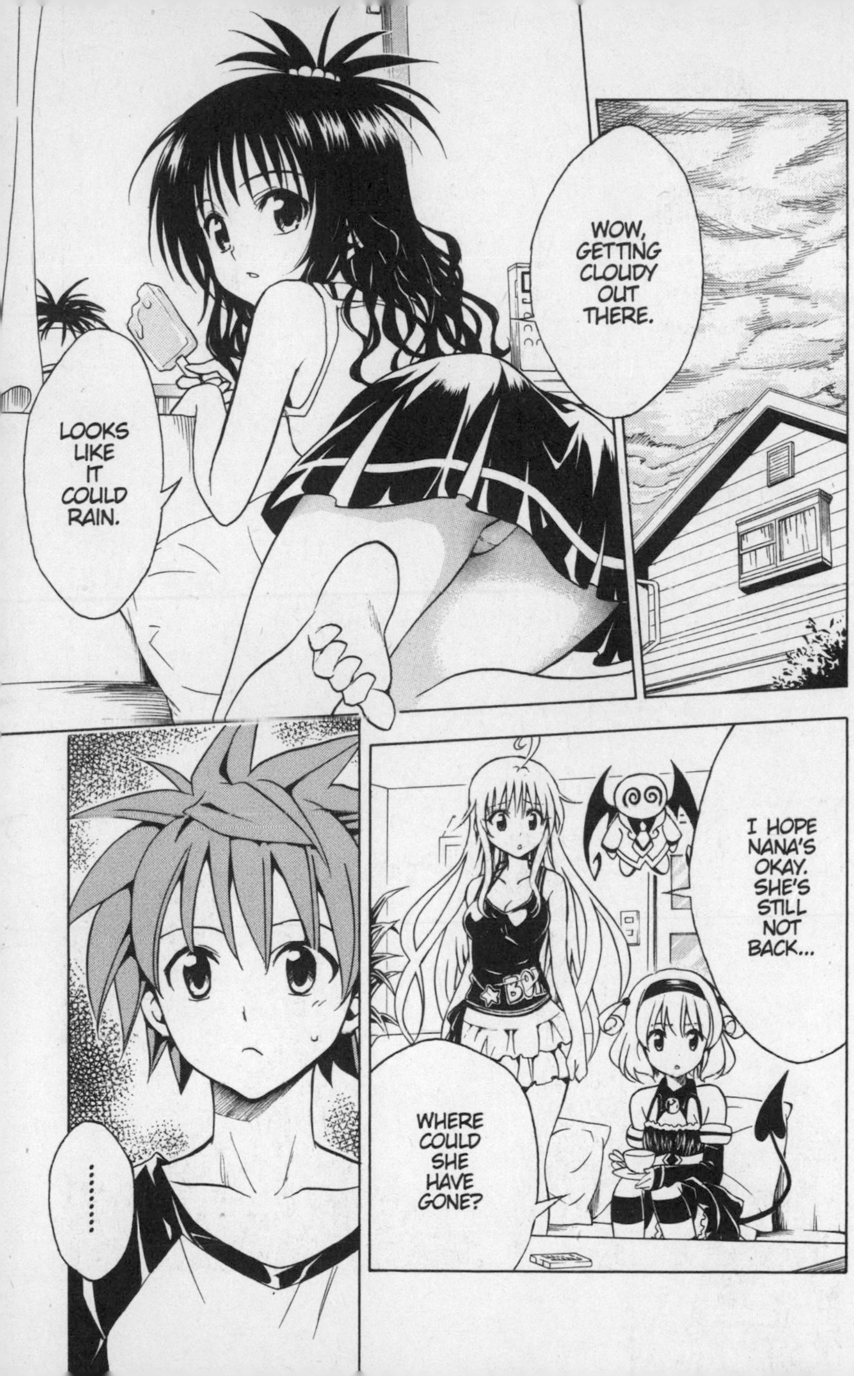
WOW, GETTING CLOUDY OUT THERE.
LOOKS LIKE IT COULD RAIN.
I HOPE NANA'S OKAY. SHE'S STILL NOT BACK...
WHERE COULD SHE HAVE GONE?
......

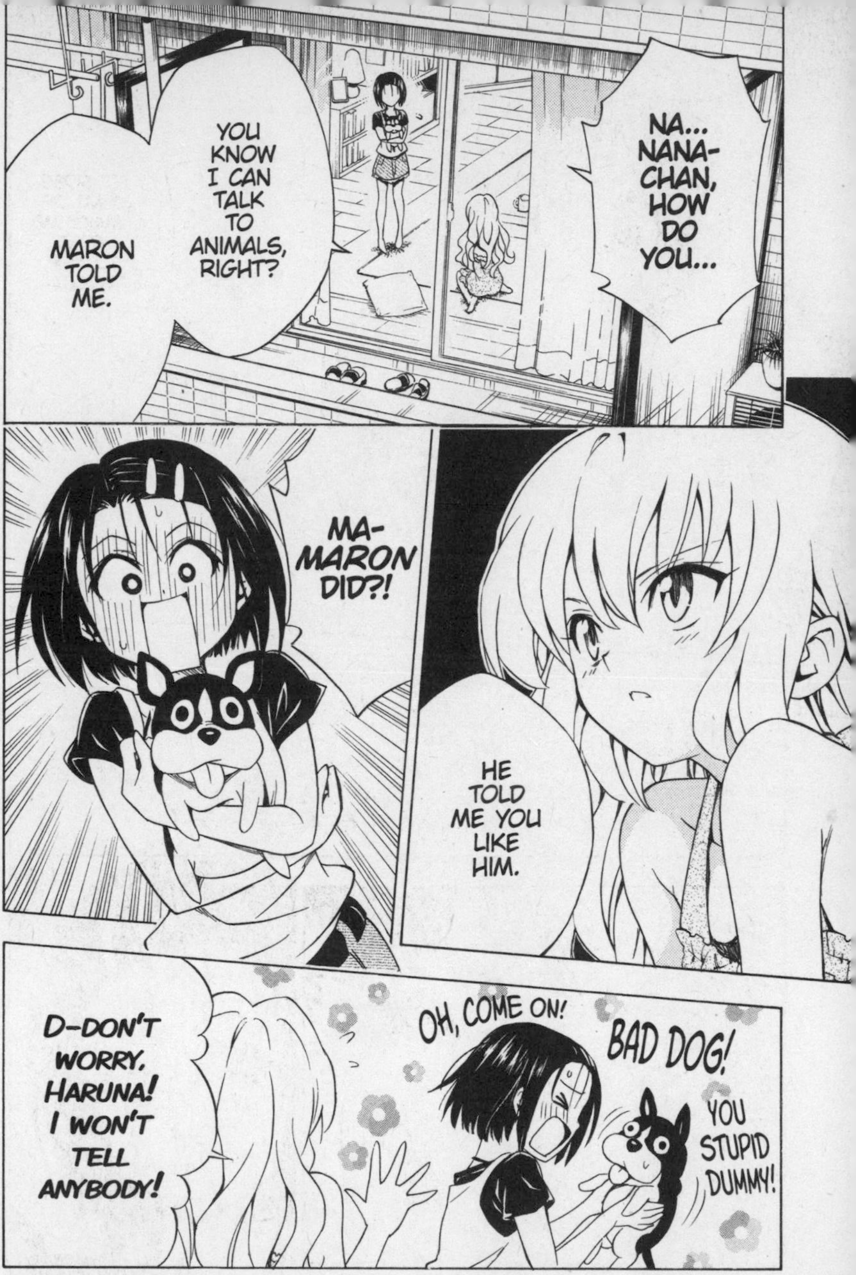
NA... NANA-CHAN, HOW DO YOU...
YOU KNOW I CAN TALK TO ANIMALS, RIGHT?
MARON TOLD ME.
HE TOLD ME YOU LIKE HIM.
MA-MARON DID?!
BAD DOG!
YOU STUPID DUMMY!
OH, COME ON!
D-DON'T WORRY, HARUNA! I WON'T TELL ANYBODY!

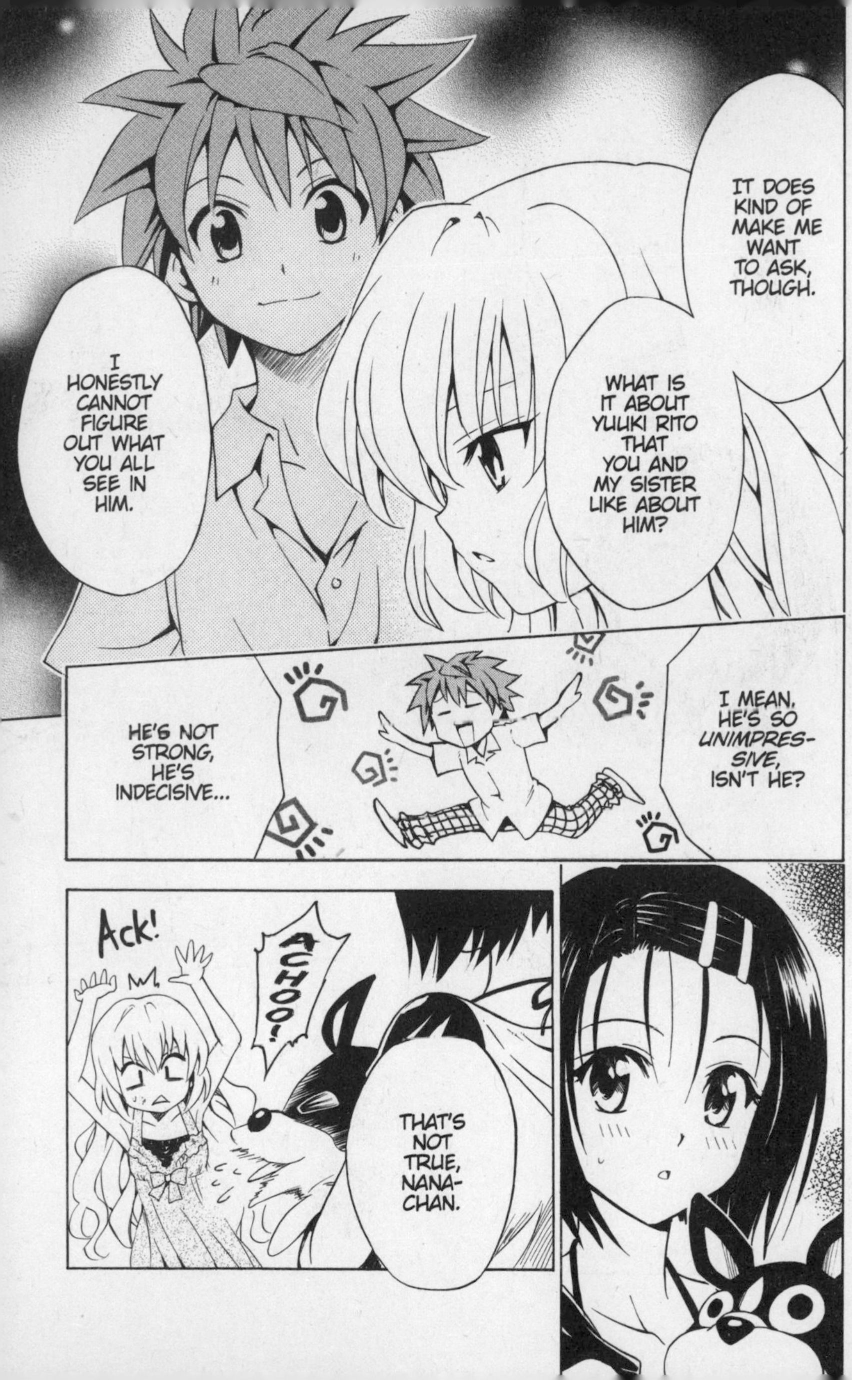
IT DOES KIND OF MAKE ME WANT TO ASK, THOUGH.
WHAT IS IT ABOUT YUUKI RITO THAT YOU AND MY SISTER LIKE ABOUT HIM?
I HONESTLY CANNOT FIGURE OUT WHAT YOU ALL SEE IN HIM.
I MEAN, HE'S SO *UNIMPRESSIVE*, ISN'T HE?
HE'S NOT STRONG, HE'S INDECISIVE...
THAT'S NOT TRUE, NANA-CHAN.
ACHOO!
Ack!

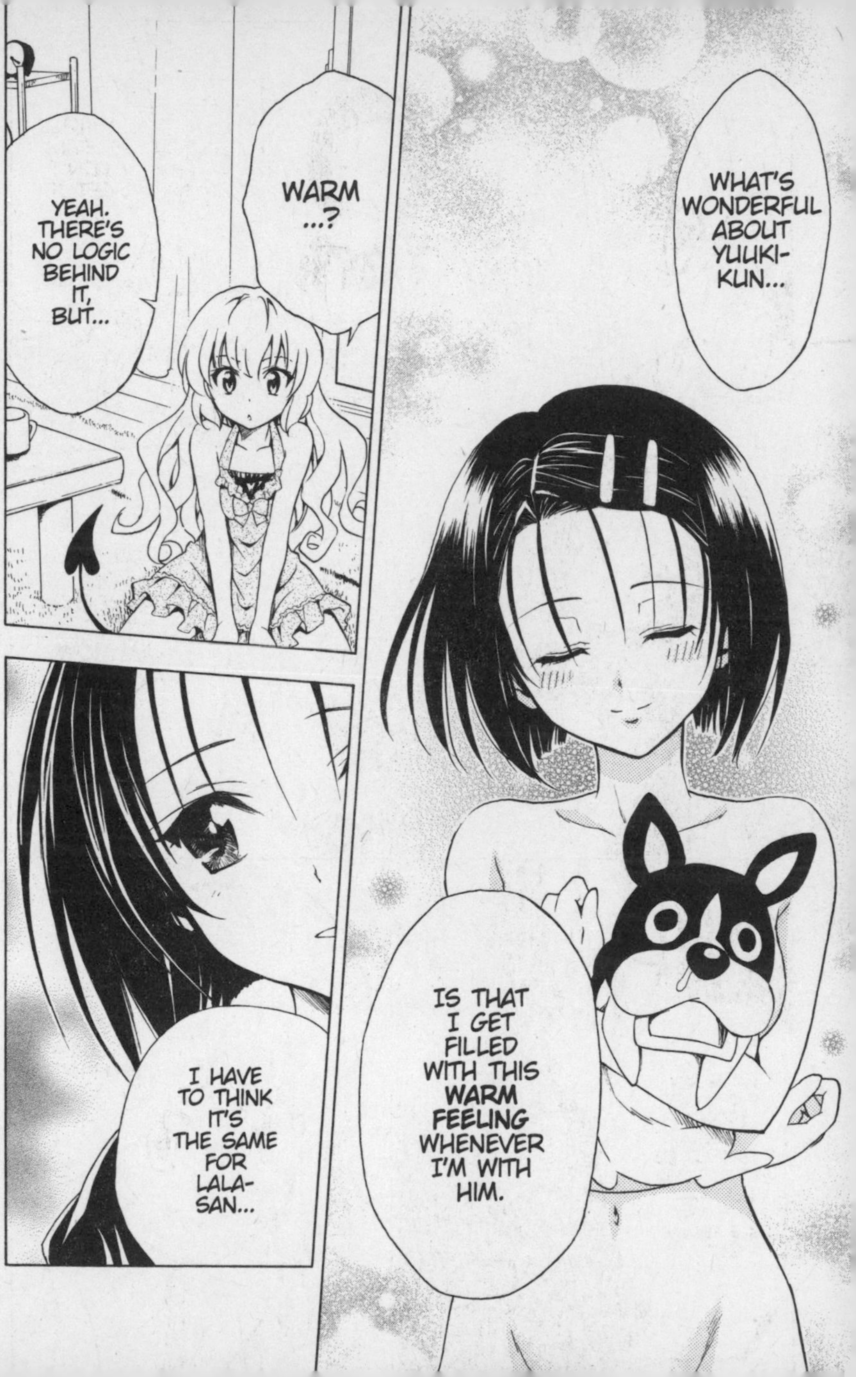
WHAT'S WONDERFUL ABOUT YUUKI-KUN...
IS THAT I GET FILLED WITH THIS **WARM FEELING** WHENEVER I'M WITH HIM.
WARM ...?
YEAH. THERE'S NO LOGIC BEHIND IT, BUT...
I HAVE TO THINK IT'S THE SAME FOR LALA-SAN...

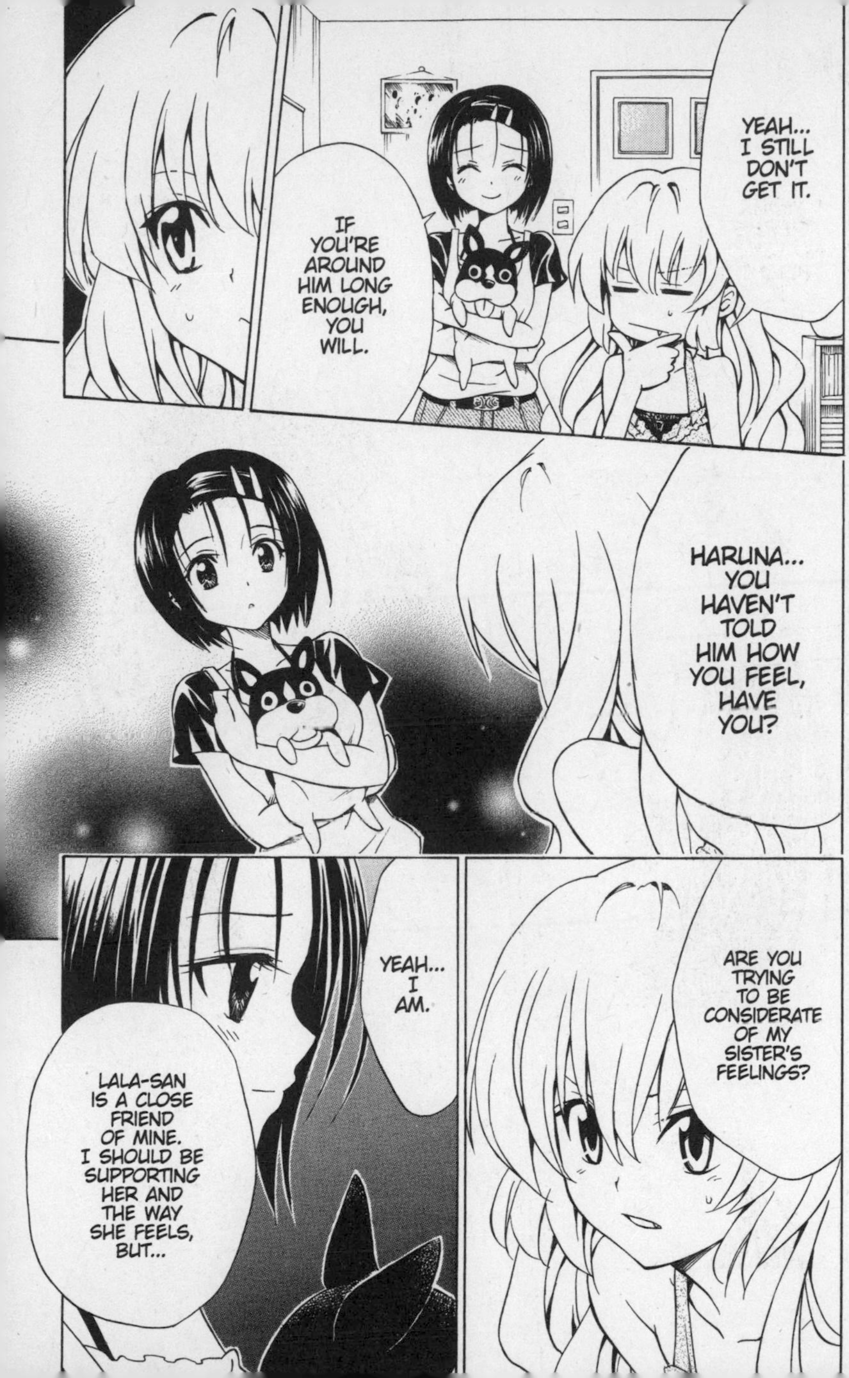
YEAH... I STILL DON'T GET IT.
IF YOU'RE AROUND HIM LONG ENOUGH, YOU WILL.
HARUNA... YOU HAVEN'T TOLD HIM HOW YOU FEEL, HAVE YOU?
ARE YOU TRYING TO BE CONSIDERATE OF MY SISTER'S FEELINGS?
YEAH... I AM.
LALA-SAN IS A CLOSE FRIEND OF MINE. I SHOULD BE SUPPORTING HER AND THE WAY SHE FEELS, BUT...

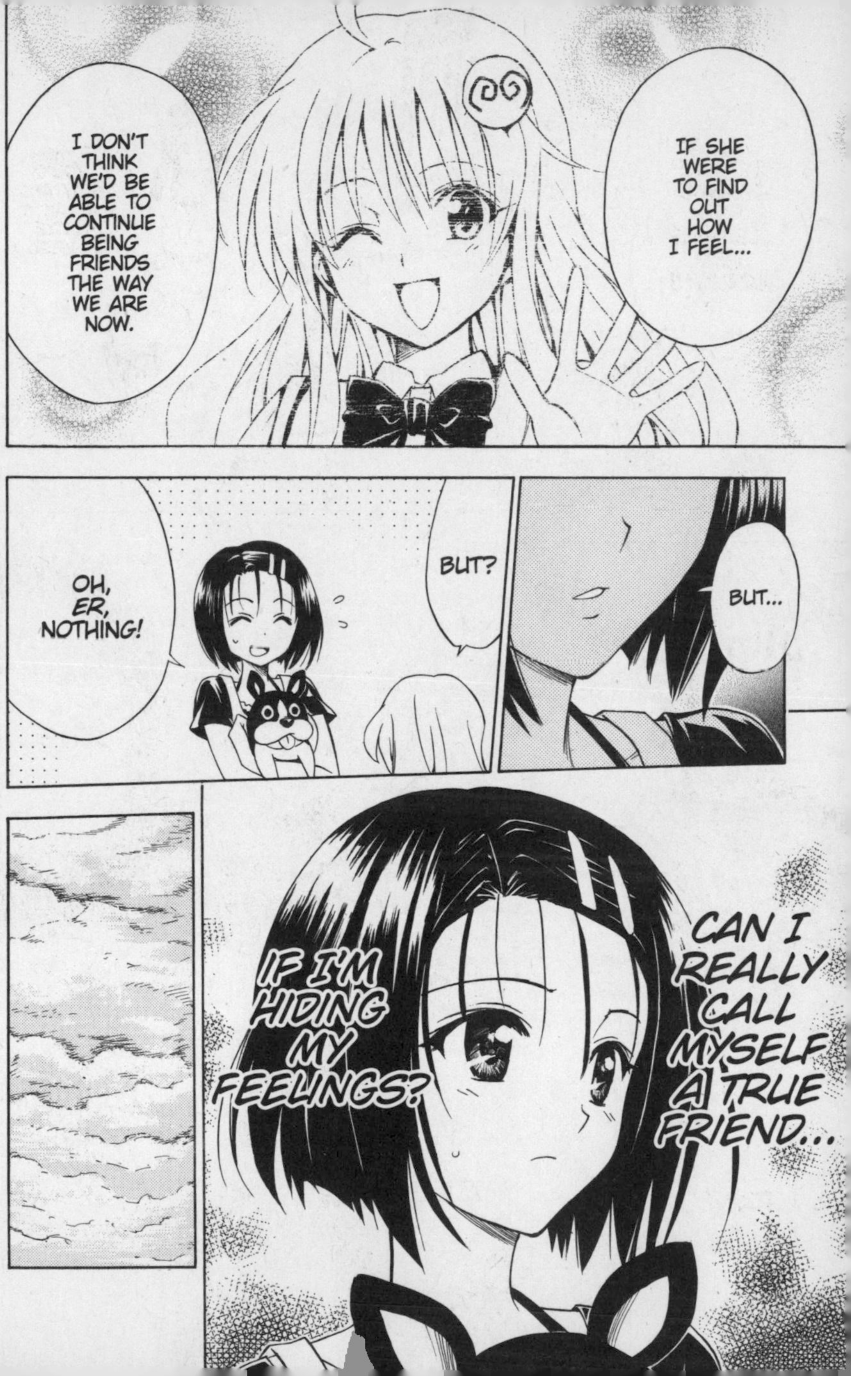
IF SHE WERE TO FIND OUT HOW I FEEL...
I DON'T THINK WE'D BE ABLE TO CONTINUE BEING FRIENDS THE WAY WE ARE NOW.
BUT...
BUT?
OH, ER, NOTHING!
CAN I REALLY CALL MYSELF A TRUE FRIEND...
IF I'M HIDING MY FEELINGS?

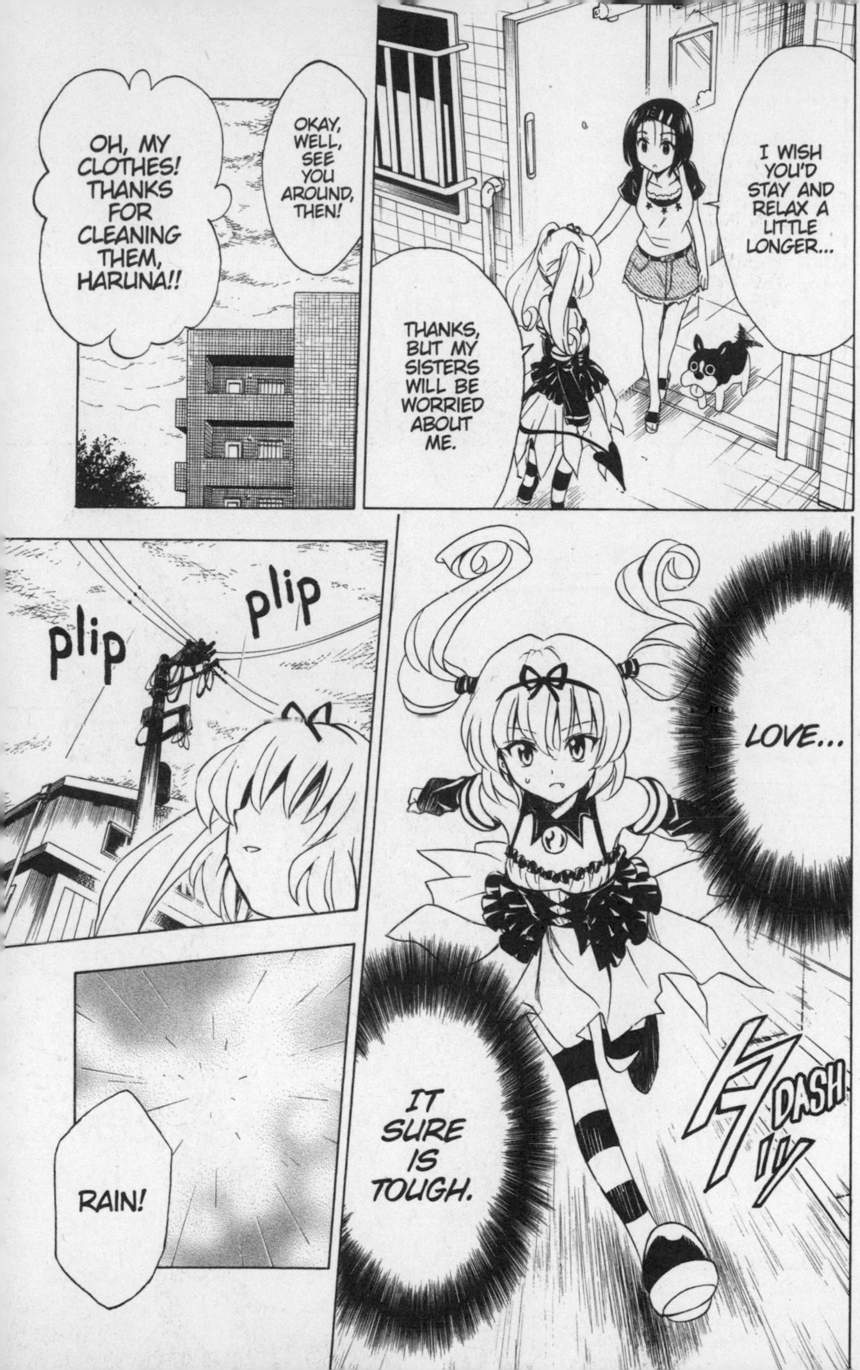
I WISH YOU'D STAY AND RELAX A LITTLE LONGER...
THANKS, BUT MY SISTERS WILL BE WORRIED ABOUT ME.
OKAY, WELL, SEE YOU AROUND, THEN!
OH, MY CLOTHES! THANKS FOR CLEANING THEM, HARUNA!!
LOVE...
IT SURE IS TOUGH.
DASH
plip
plip
RAIN!

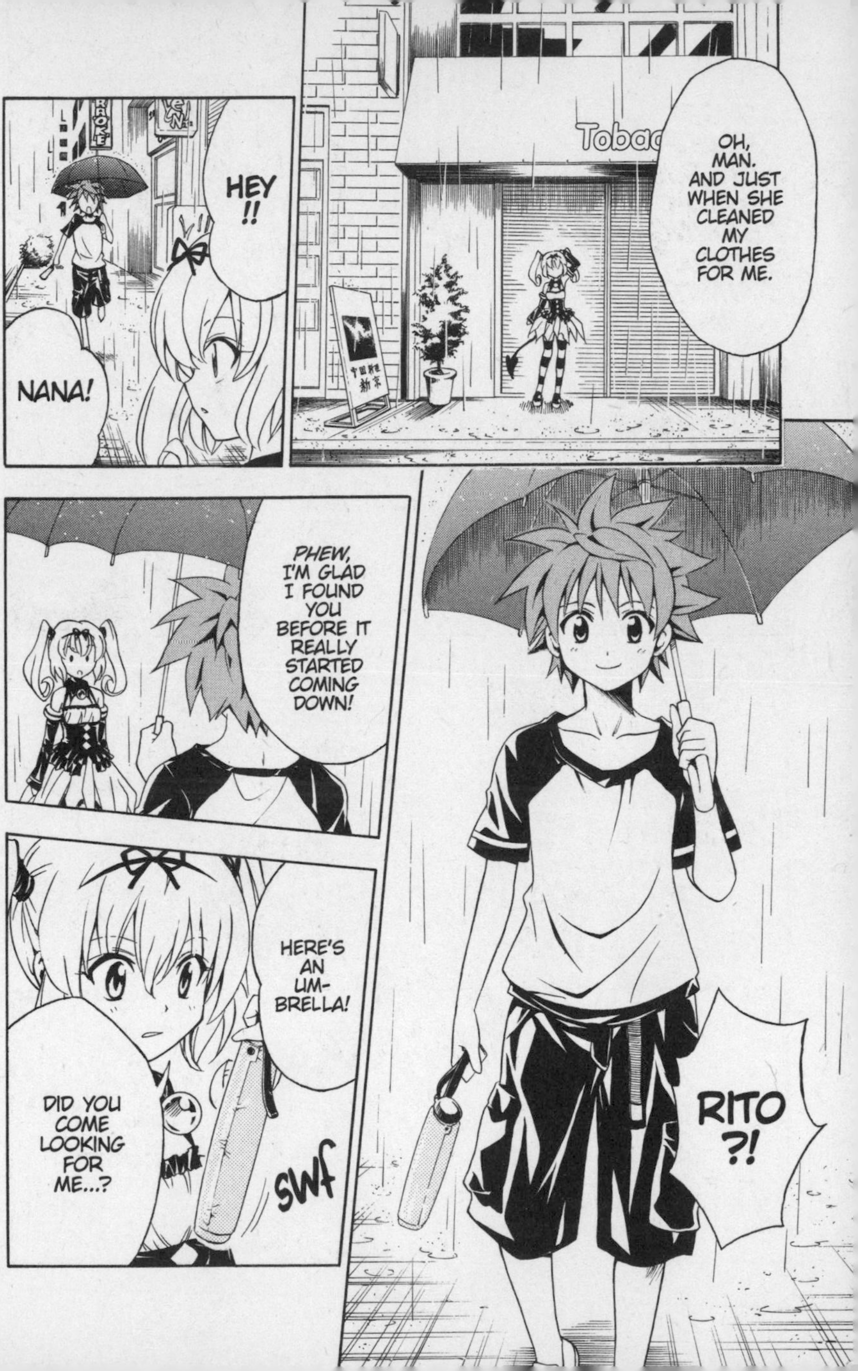
Tobac
OH, MAN. AND JUST WHEN SHE CLEANED MY CLOTHES FOR ME.
HEY !!
NANA!
RITO ?!
PHEW, I'M GLAD I FOUND YOU BEFORE IT REALLY STARTED COMING DOWN!
HERE'S AN UM-BRELLA!
SWF
DID YOU COME LOOKING FOR ME...?

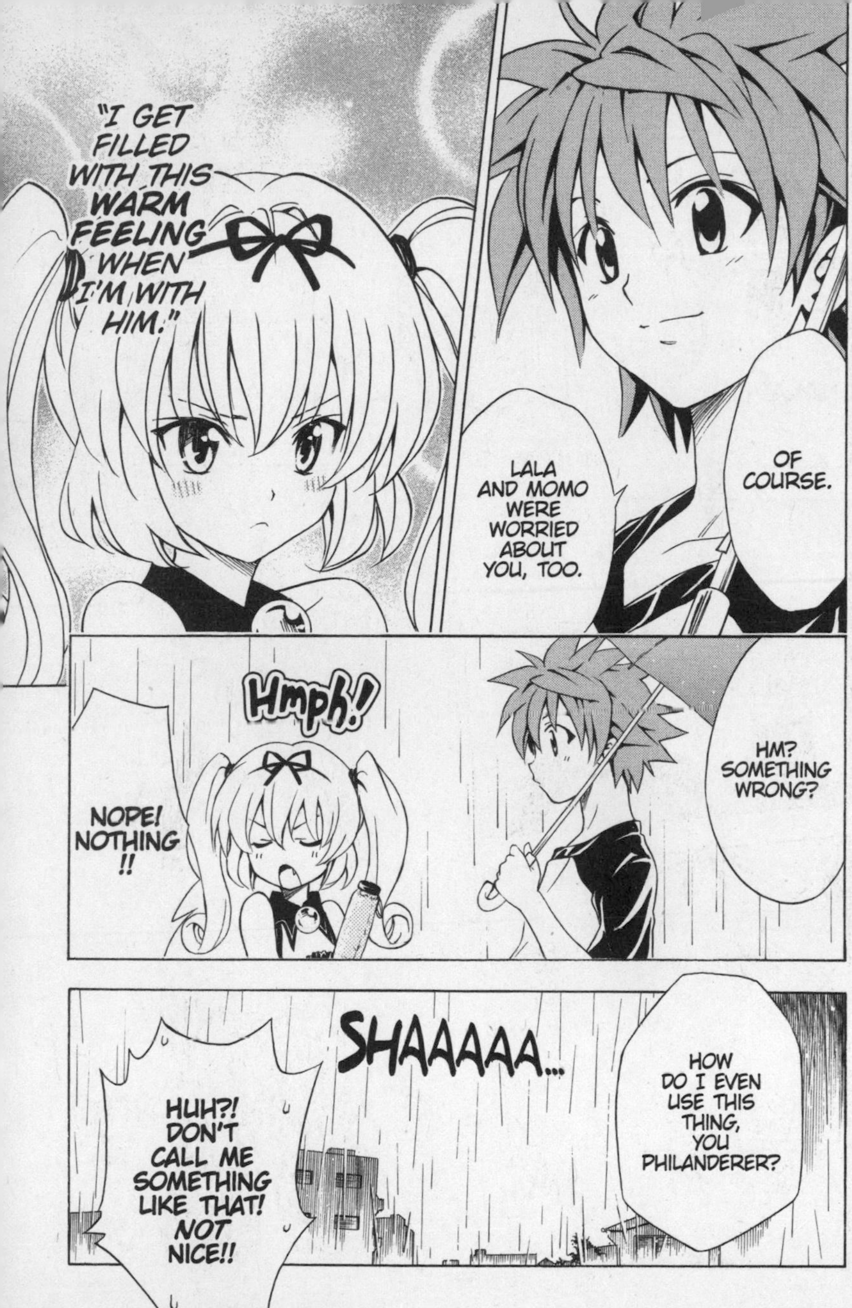
OF COURSE.
LALA AND MOMO WERE WORRIED ABOUT YOU, TOO.
"I GET FILLED WITH THIS WARM FEELING WHEN I'M WITH HIM."
HM? SOMETHING WRONG?
Hmph!
NOPE! NOTHING!!
HOW DO I EVEN USE THIS THING, YOU PHILANDERER?
SHAAAAA...
HUH?! DON'T CALL ME SOMETHING LIKE THAT! NOT NICE!!

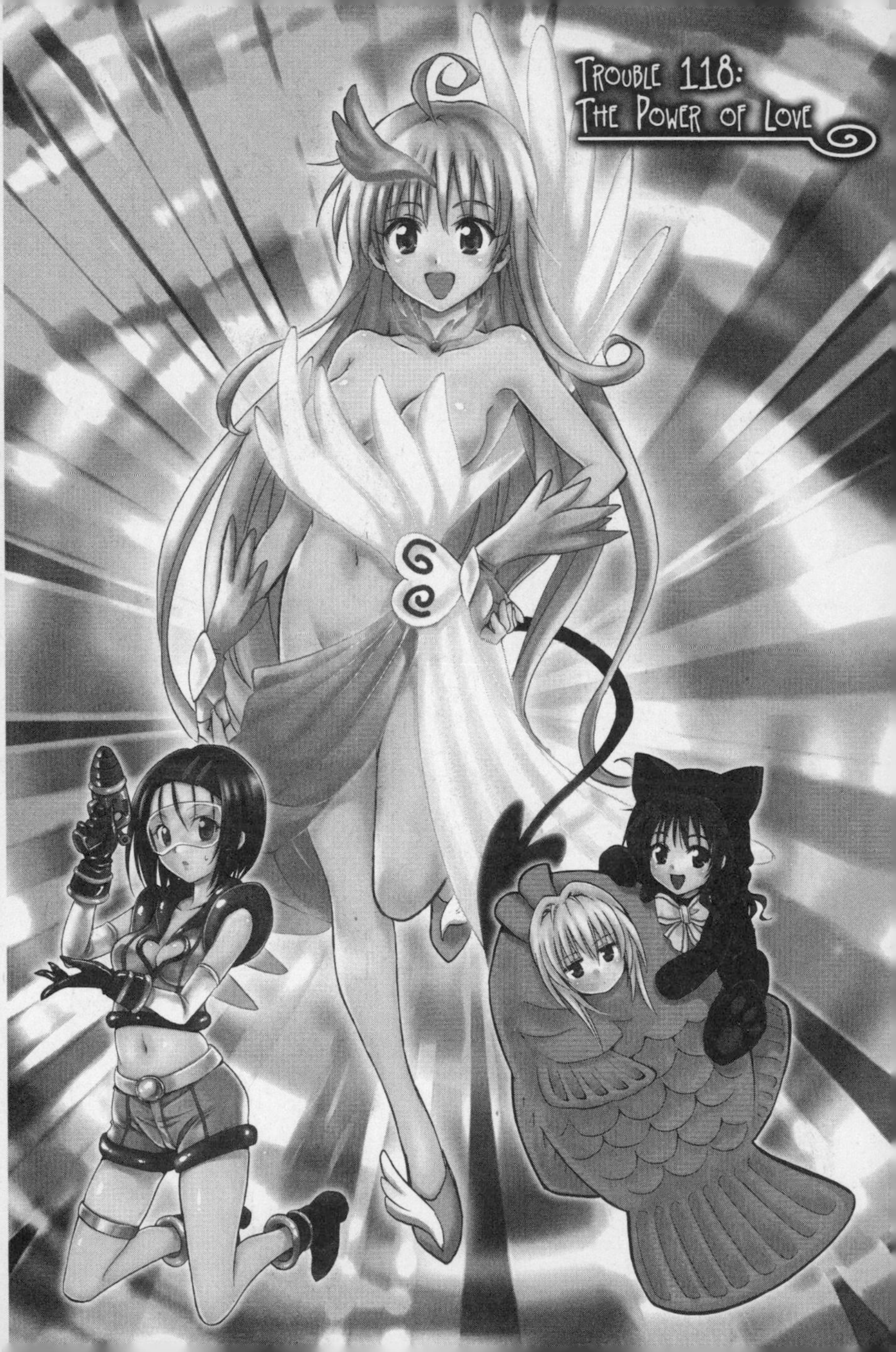
Trouble 118:
The Power of Love

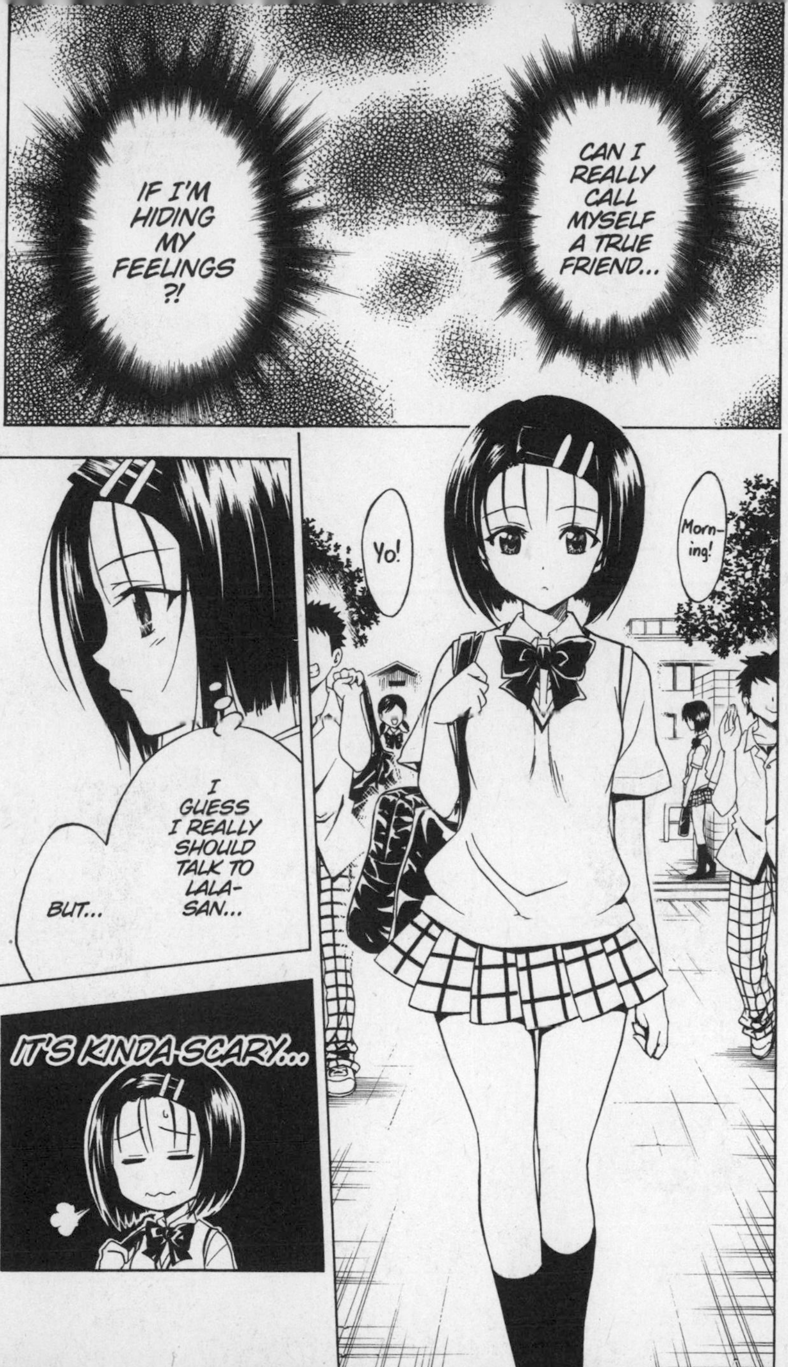
CAN I REALLY CALL MYSELF A TRUE FRIEND...
IF I'M HIDING MY FEELINGS ?!
Morn-ing!
Yo!
I GUESS I REALLY SHOULD TALK TO LALA-SAN...
BUT...
IT'S KINDA SCARY...

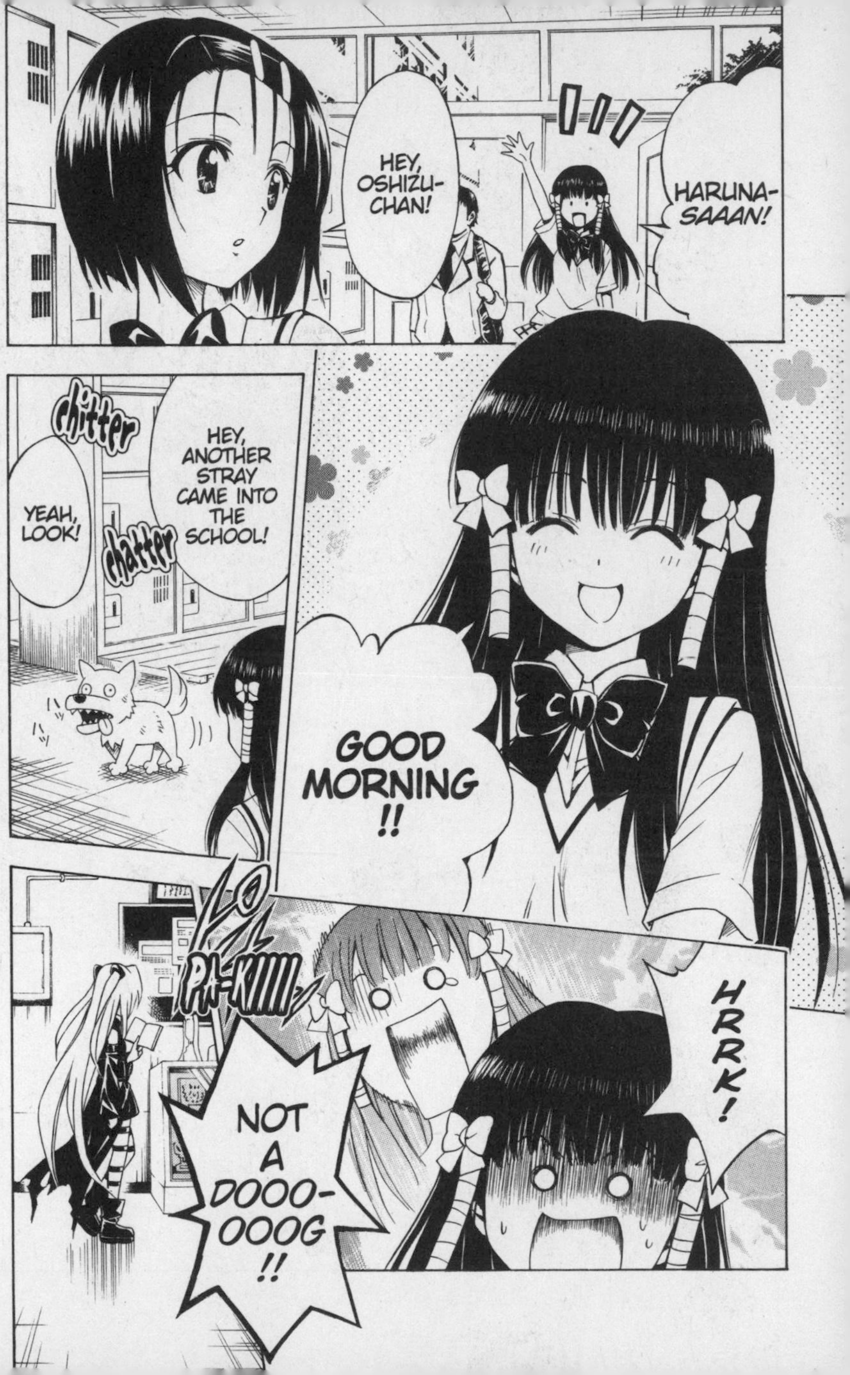
HARUNA-SAAAN!
HEY, OSHIZU-CHAN!
GOOD MORNING !!
HEY, ANOTHER STRAY CAME INTO THE SCHOOL!
chitter
chatter
YEAH, LOOK!
HRRK!
PA-KIIII
NOT A DOOOO-OOOG !!

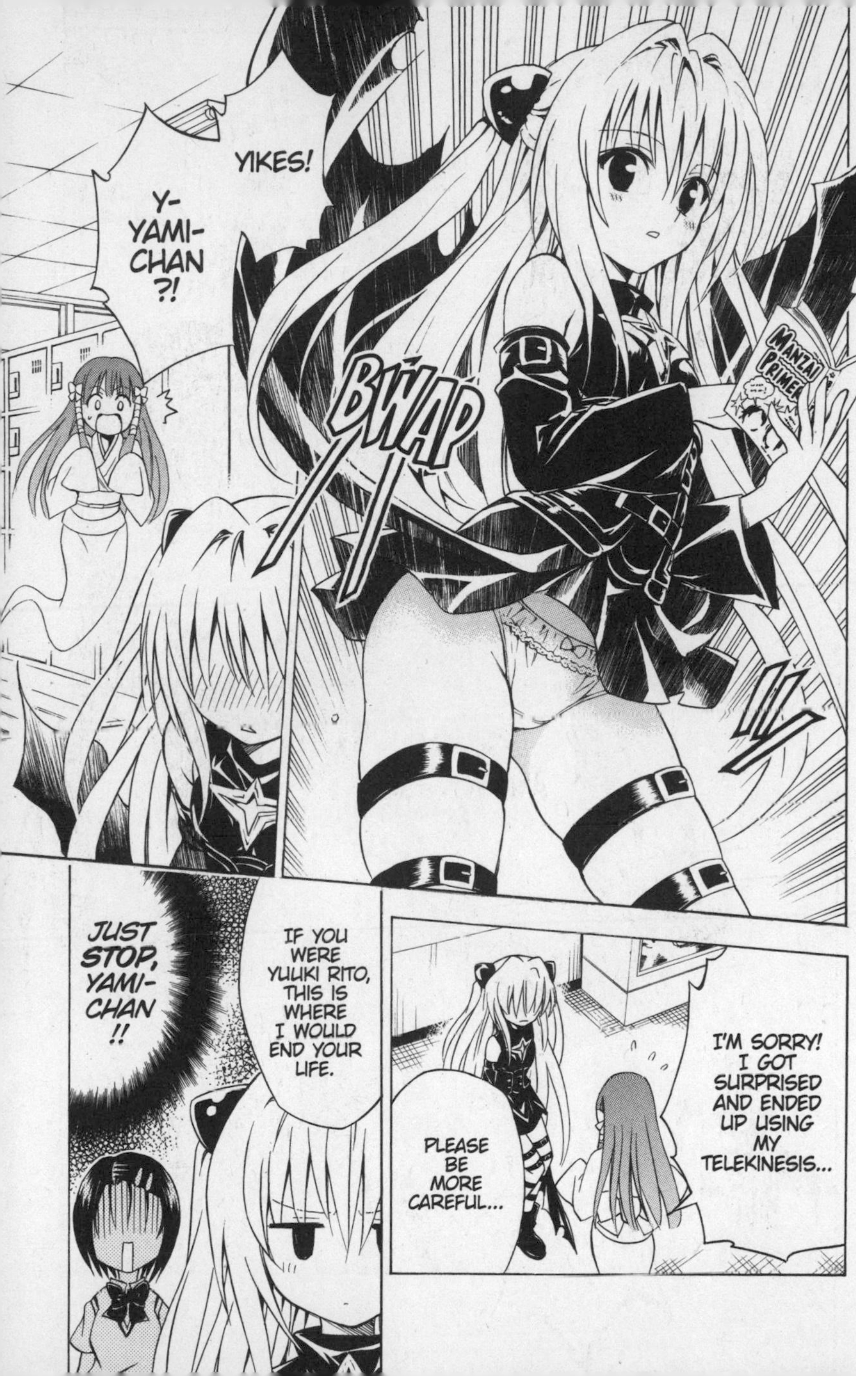
MANZAI PRIMER
YIKES!
Y-YAMI-CHAN?!
BWAP
I'M SORRY! I GOT SURPRISED AND ENDED UP USING MY TELEKINESIS...
PLEASE BE MORE CAREFUL...
IF YOU WERE YUUKI RITO, THIS IS WHERE I WOULD END YOUR LIFE.
JUST STOP, YAMI-CHAN!!

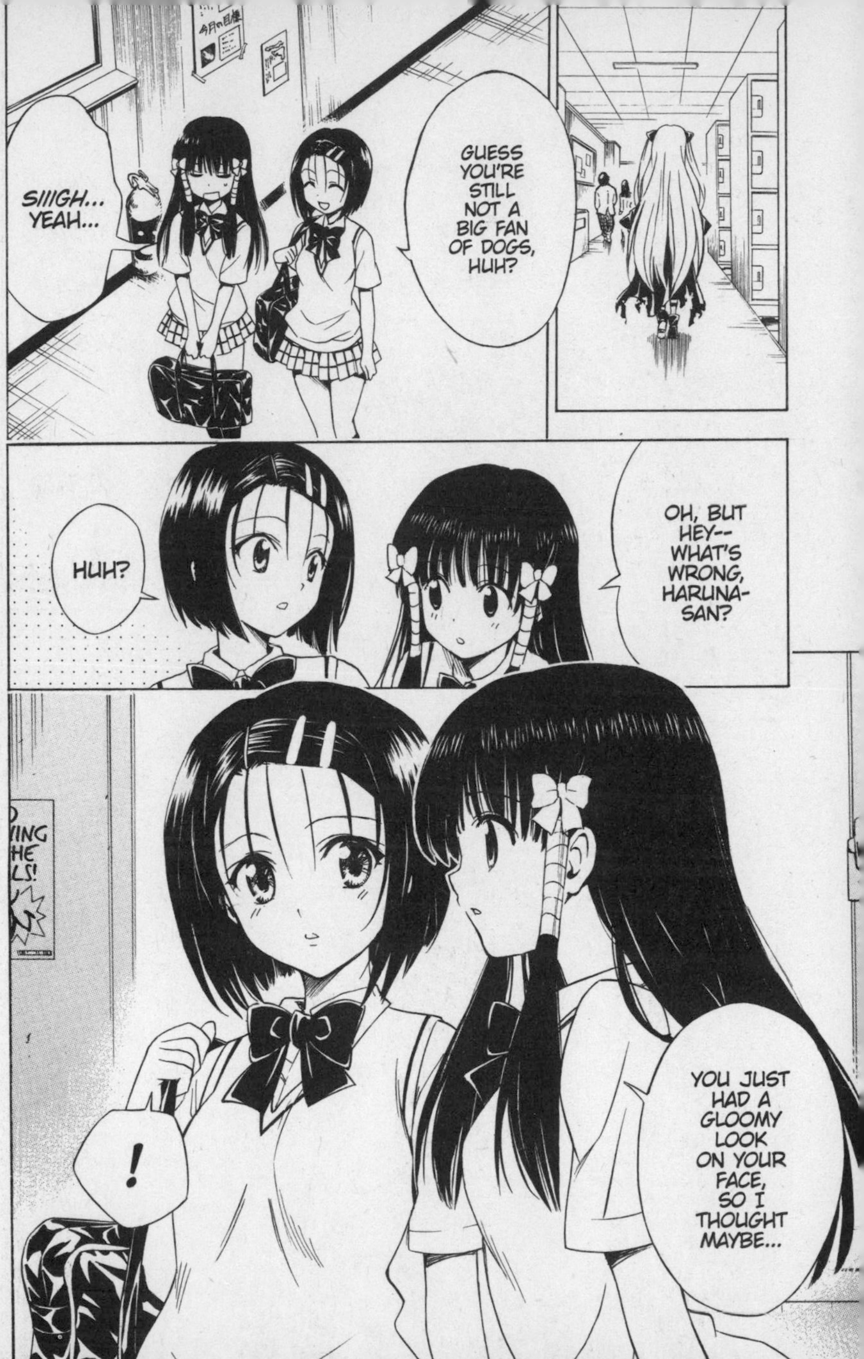
GUESS YOU'RE STILL NOT A BIG FAN OF DOGS, HUH?
SIIIGH... YEAH...
OH, BUT HEY-- WHAT'S WRONG, HARUNA-SAN?
HUH?
YOU JUST HAD A GLOOMY LOOK ON YOUR FACE, SO I THOUGHT MAYBE...
!

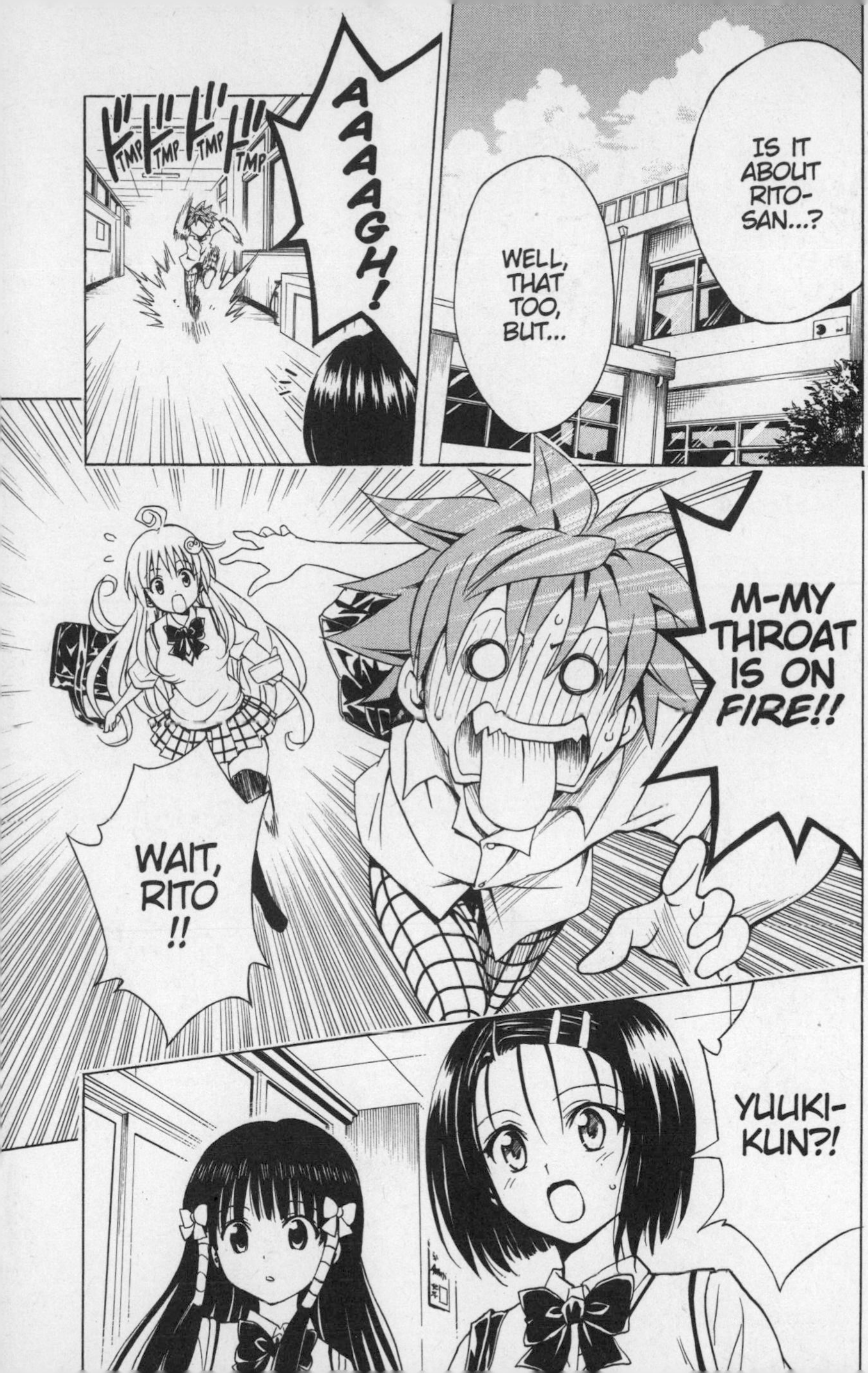
IS IT ABOUT RITO-SAN...?
WELL, THAT TOO, BUT...
ドドドド
TMP TMP TMP TMP
AAAAAGH!
M-MY THROAT IS ON FIRE!!
WAIT, RITO!!
YUUKI-KUN?!

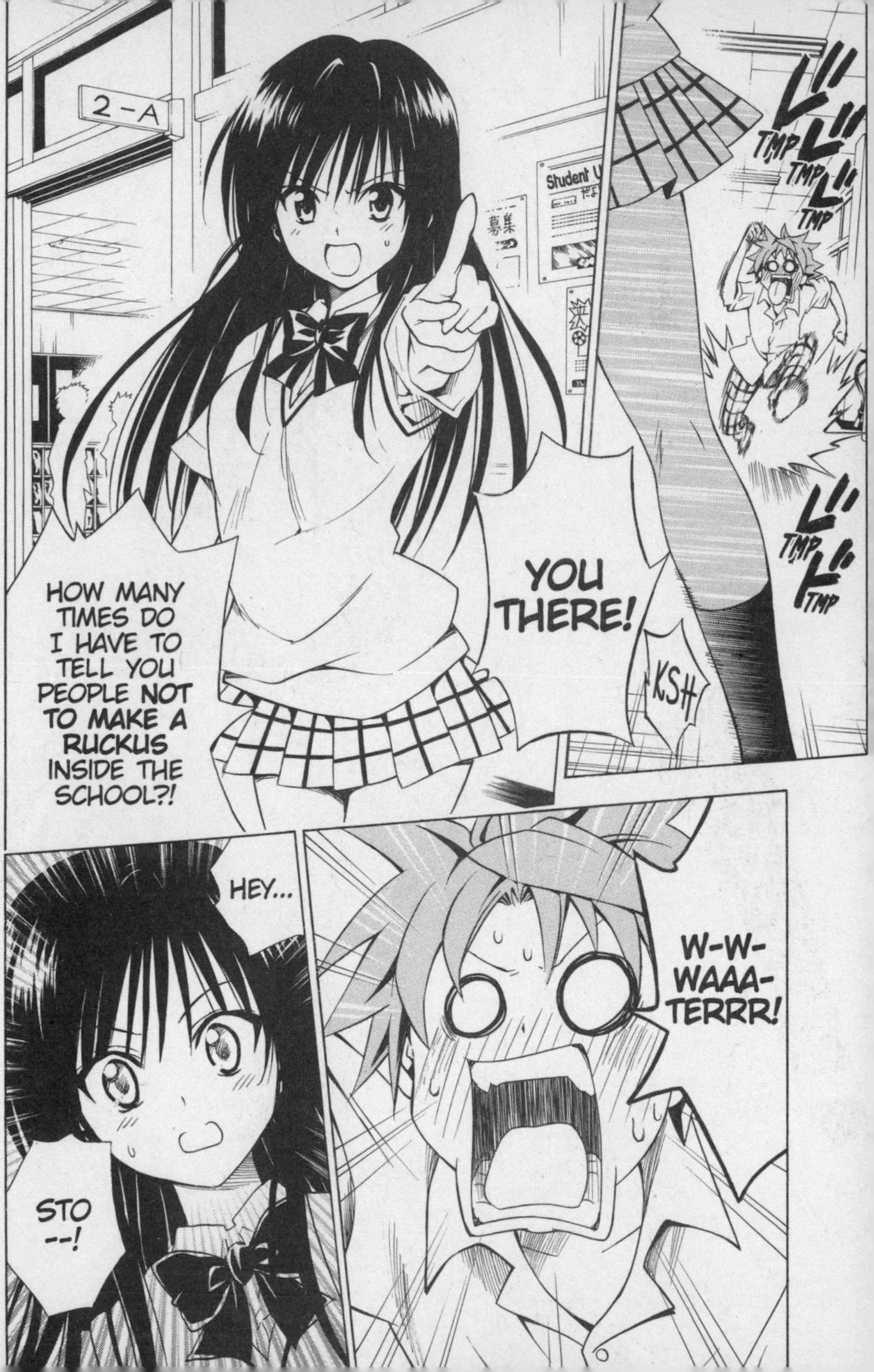
TMP
TMP
TMP
TMP
TMP
2-A
募集
YOU THERE!
KSH
HOW MANY TIMES DO I HAVE TO TELL YOU PEOPLE NOT TO MAKE A RUCKUS INSIDE THE SCHOOL?!
W-W-WAAA-TERRR!
HEY...
STO--!

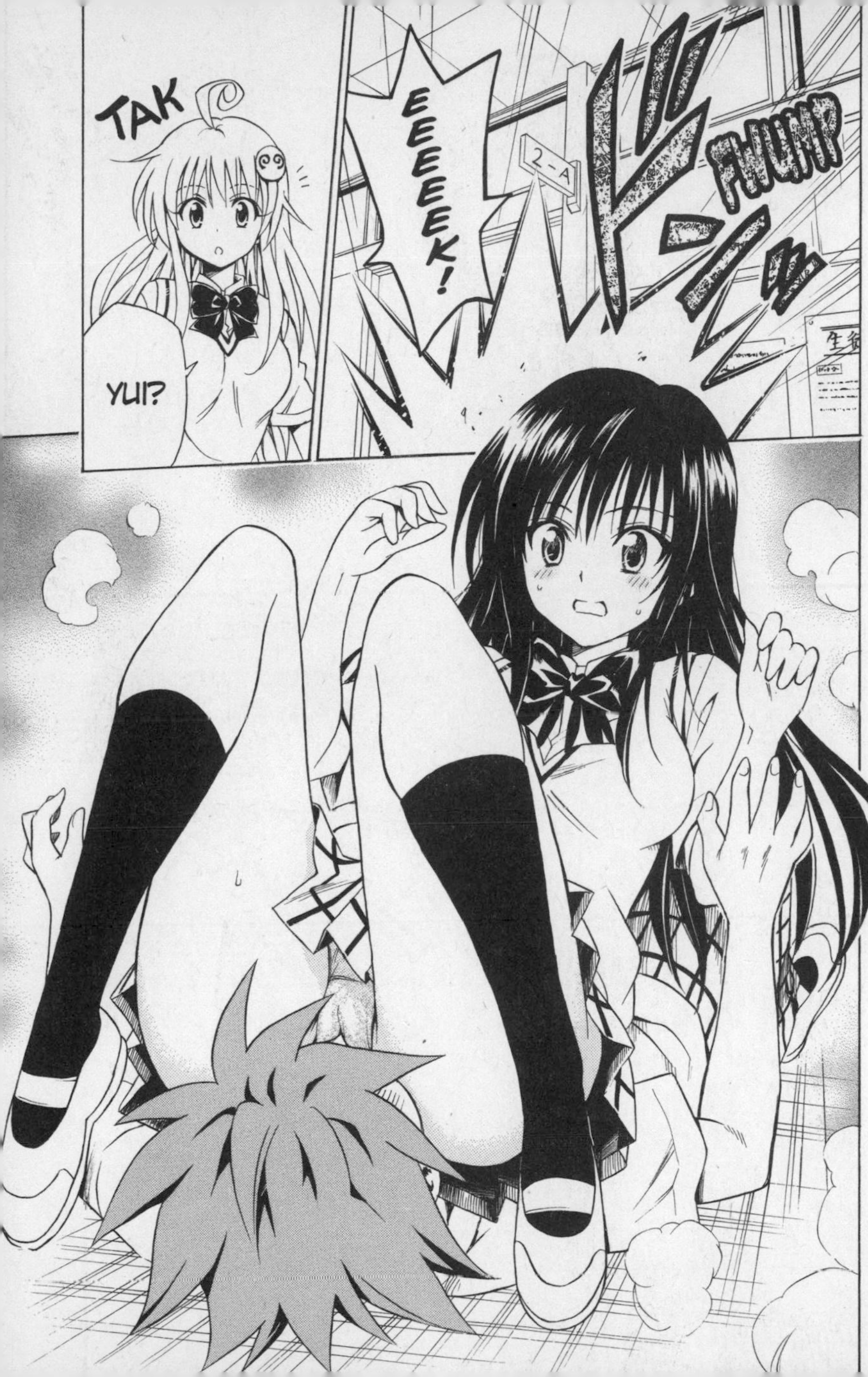
EEEEEK!
2-A
FWUMP
TAK
YUI?

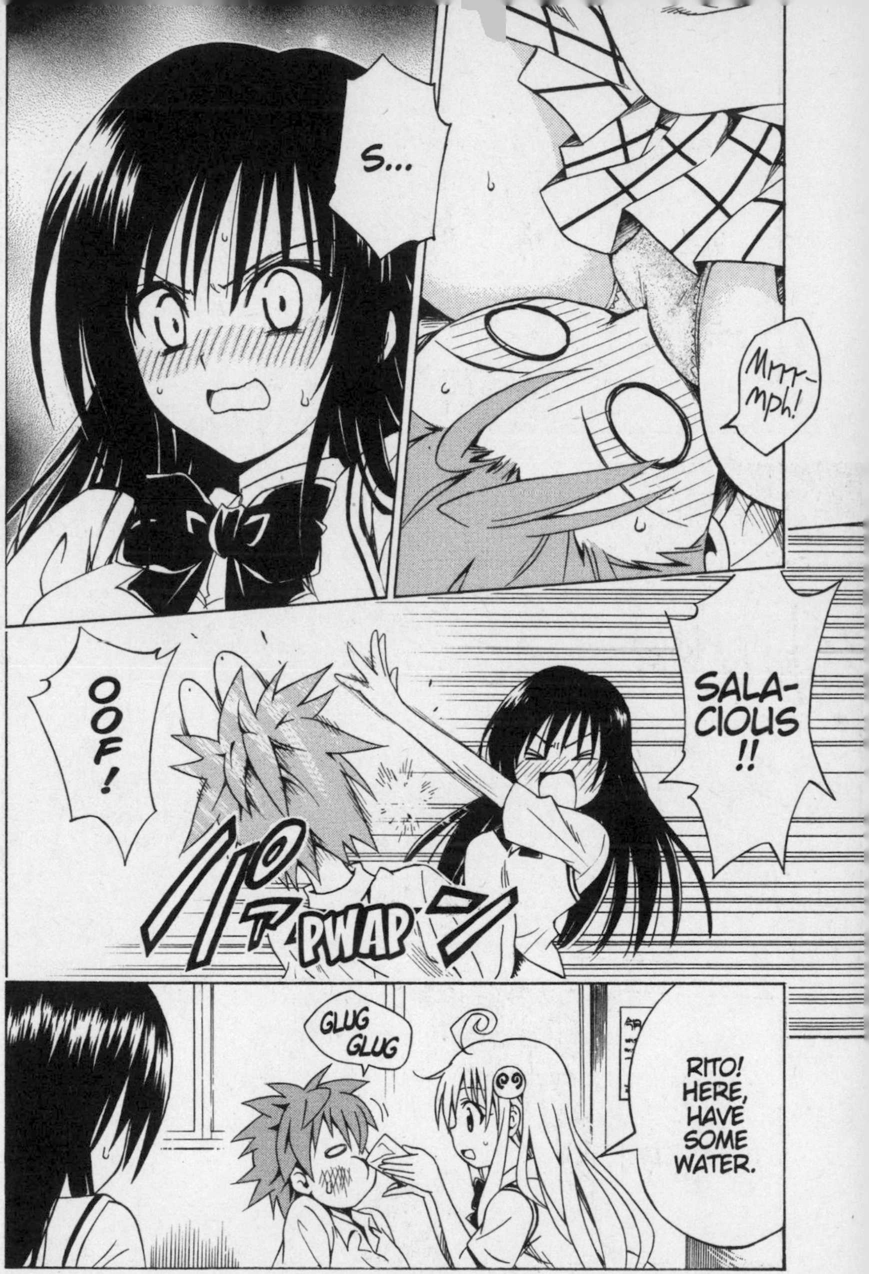
Mrrr-mph!
S...
SALACIOUS!!
OOF!
PWAP
RITO! HERE, HAVE SOME WATER.
GLUG GLUG

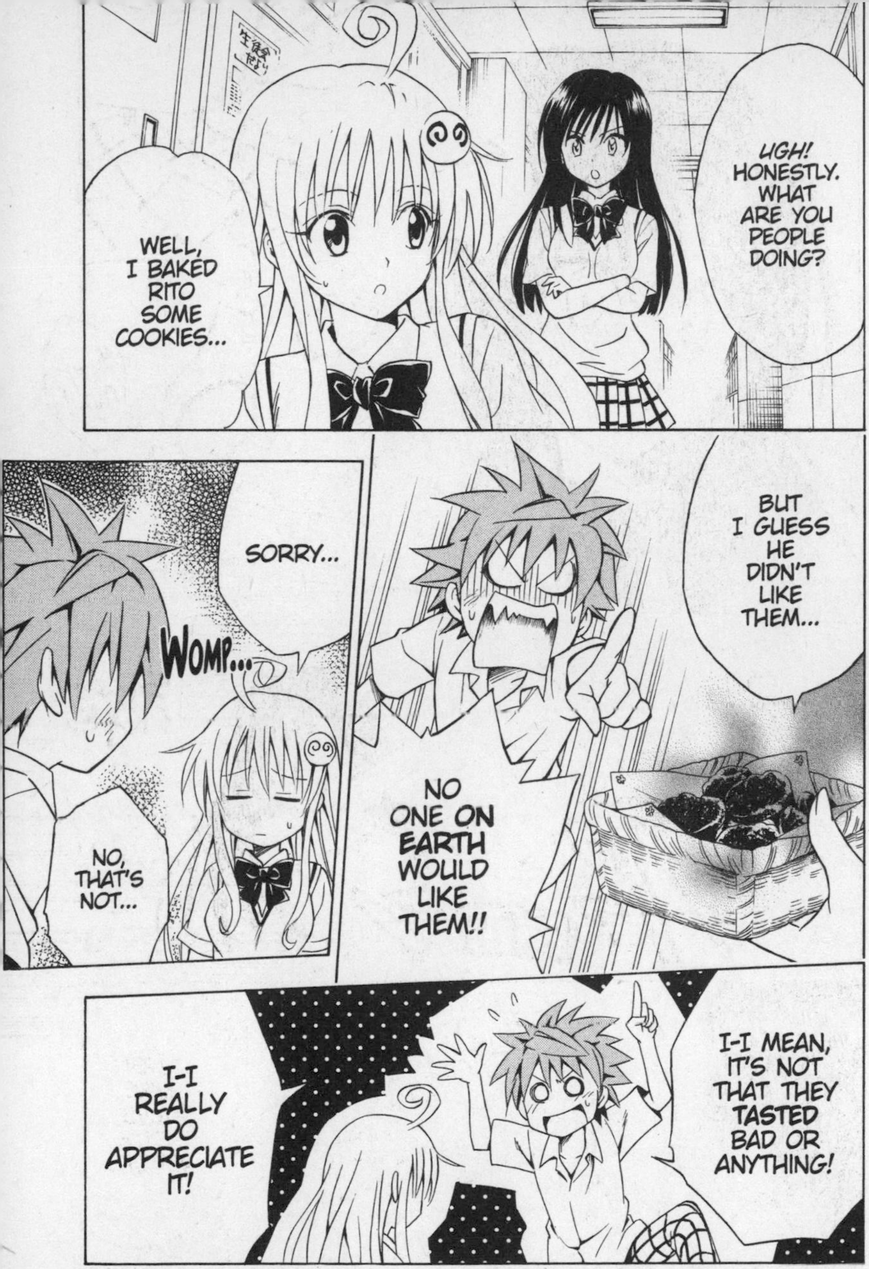
UGH! HONESTLY. WHAT ARE YOU PEOPLE DOING?
WELL, I BAKED RITO SOME COOKIES...
BUT I GUESS HE DIDN'T LIKE THEM...
NO ONE ON EARTH WOULD LIKE THEM!!
SORRY...
WOMP...
NO, THAT'S NOT...
I-I MEAN, IT'S NOT THAT THEY TASTED BAD OR ANYTHING!
I-I REALLY DO APPRECIATE IT!

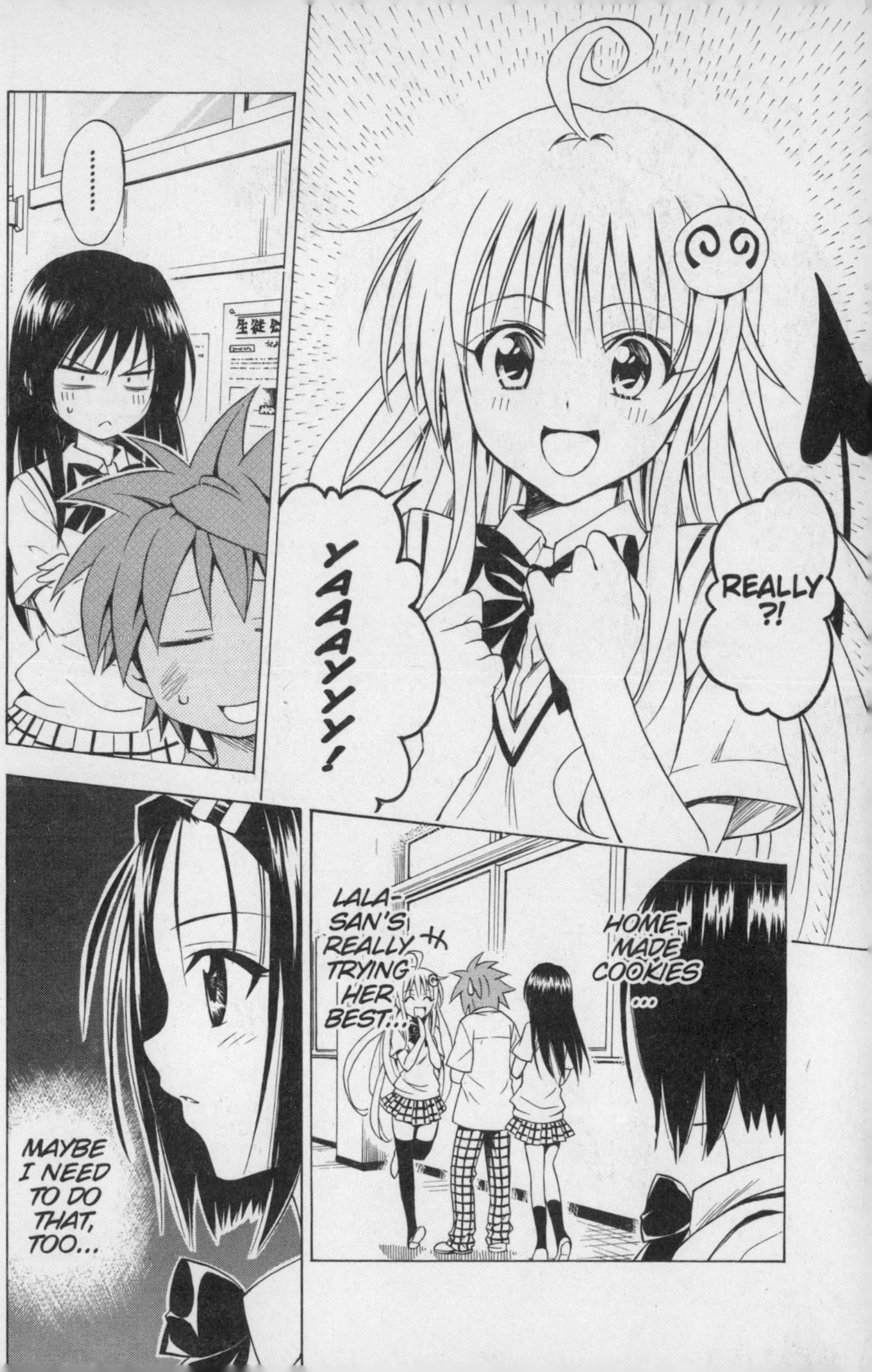
REALLY ?!
YAAAAYYY!
......
HOME-MADE COOKIES ...
LALA-SAN'S REALLY TRYING HER BEST...
MAYBE I NEED TO DO THAT, TOO...

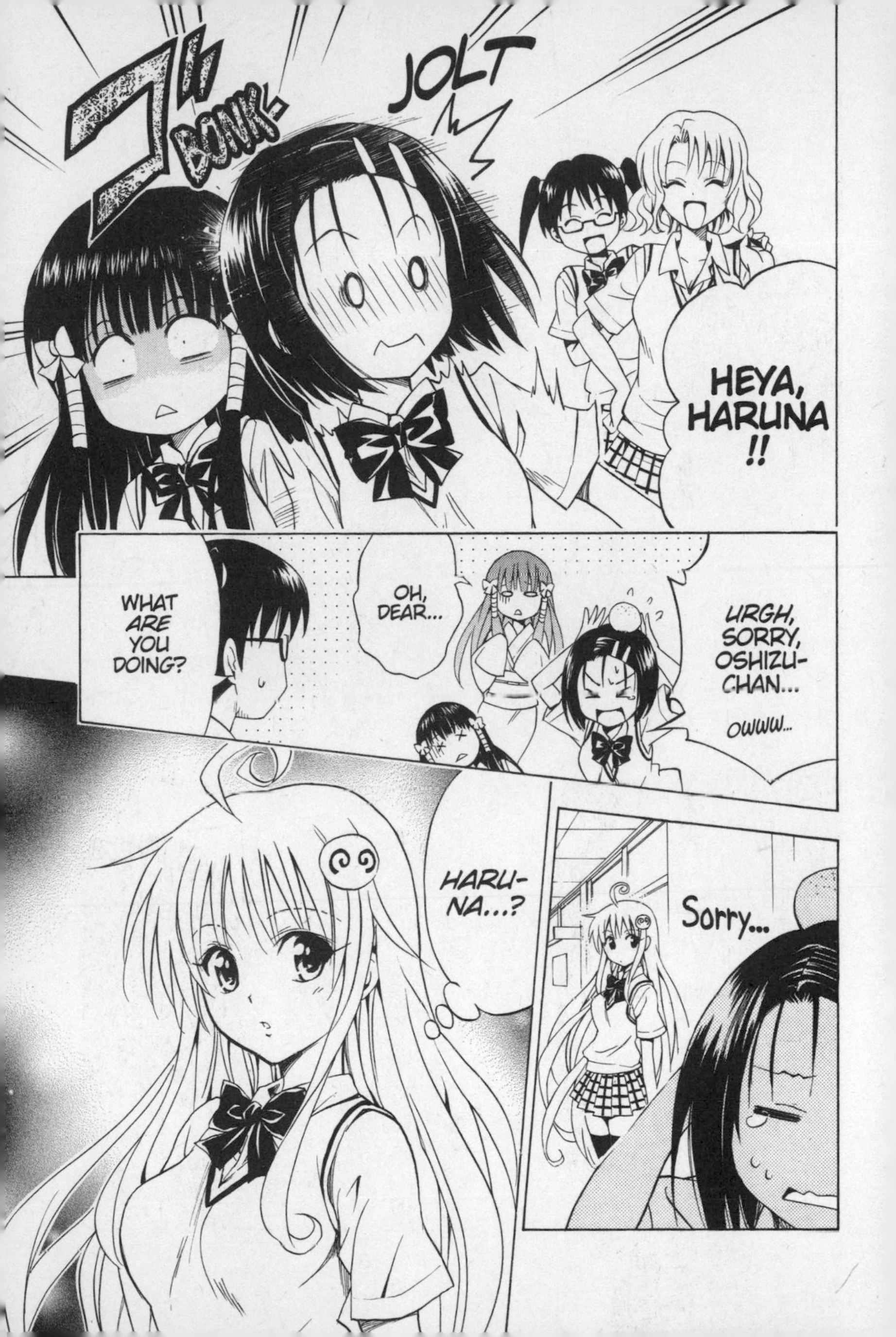
HEYA, HARUNA !!
JOLT
BONK!
URGH, SORRY, OSHIZU-CHAN...
OWWW...
OH, DEAR...
WHAT ARE YOU DOING?
Sorry...
HARU-NA...?

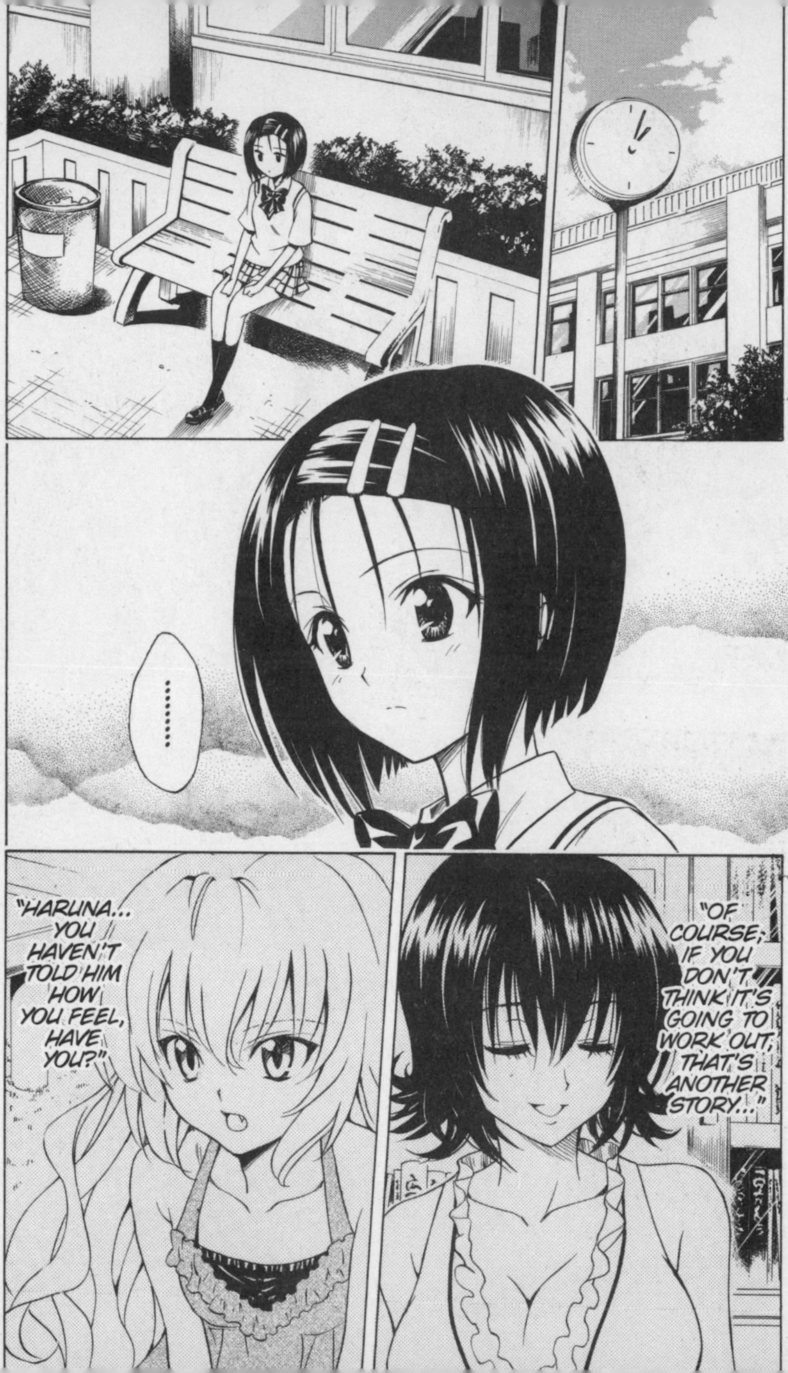
......
"OF COURSE; IF YOU DON'T THINK IT'S GOING TO WORK OUT, THAT'S ANOTHER STORY..."
"HARUNA... YOU HAVEN'T TOLD HIM HOW YOU FEEL, HAVE YOU?"

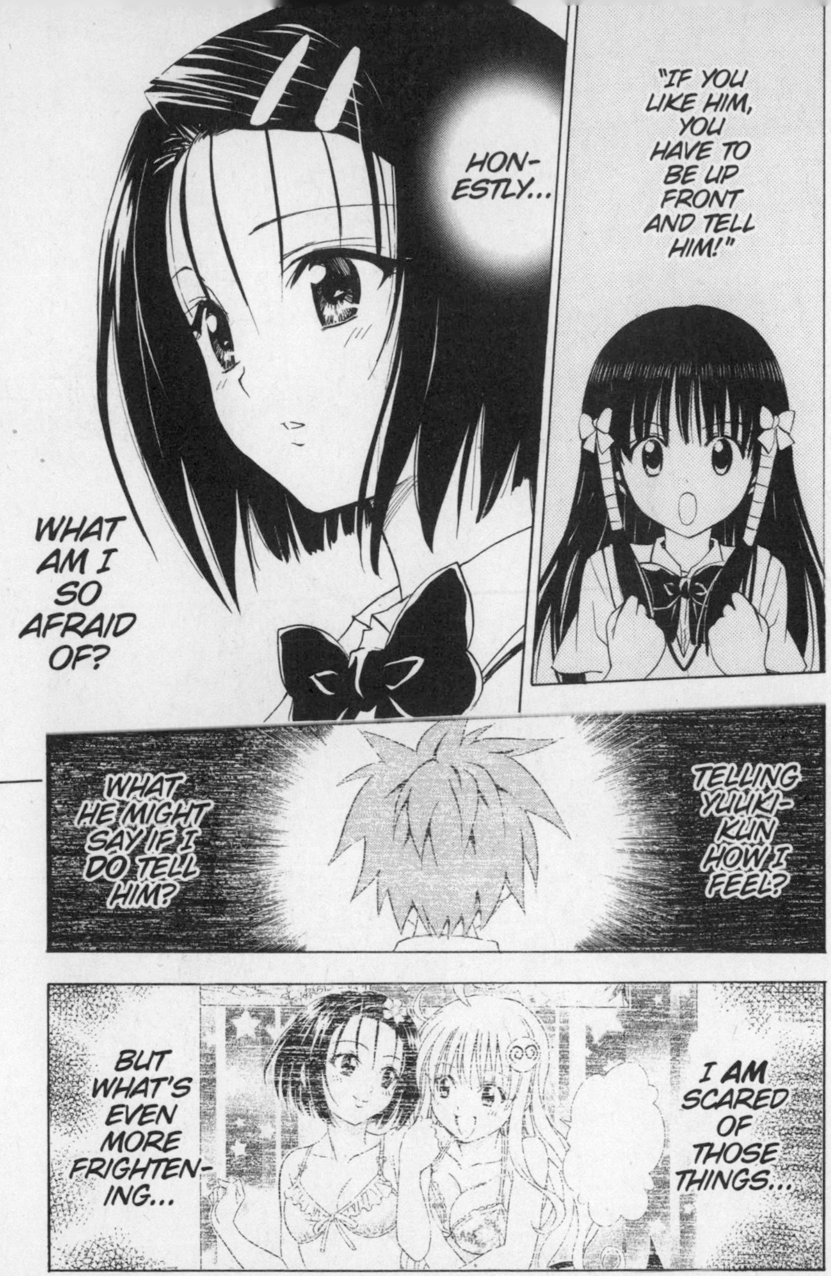
"IF YOU LIKE HIM, YOU HAVE TO BE UP FRONT AND TELL HIM!"
HON-ESTLY...
WHAT AM I SO AFRAID OF?
TELLING YUUKI-KUN HOW I FEEL?
WHAT HE MIGHT SAY IF I DO TELL HIM?
I AM SCARED OF THOSE THINGS...
BUT WHAT'S EVEN MORE FRIGHTEN-ING...

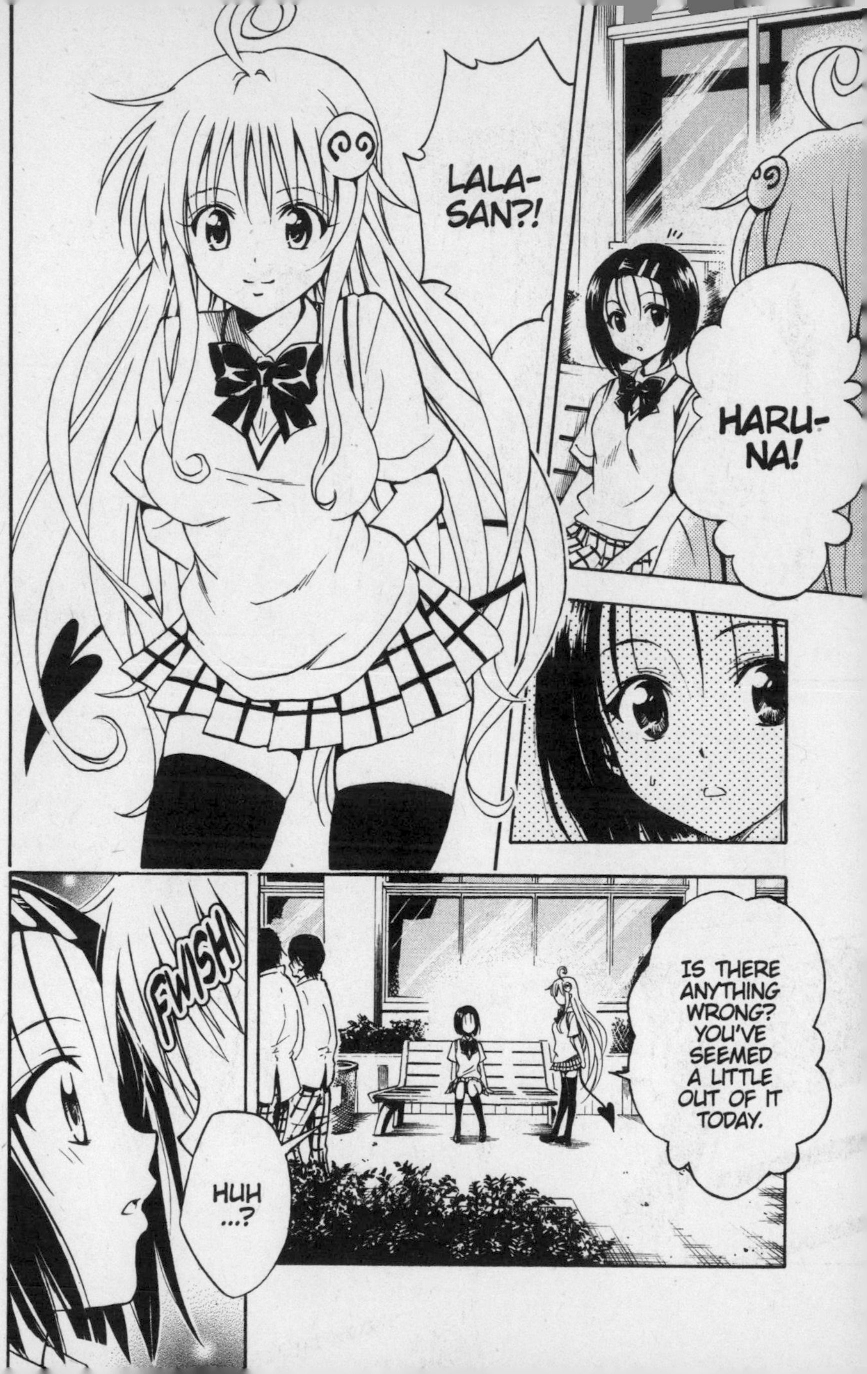
HARU-NA!
LALA-SAN?!
IS THERE ANYTHING WRONG? YOU'VE SEEMED A LITTLE OUT OF IT TODAY.
FWISH
HUH ...?

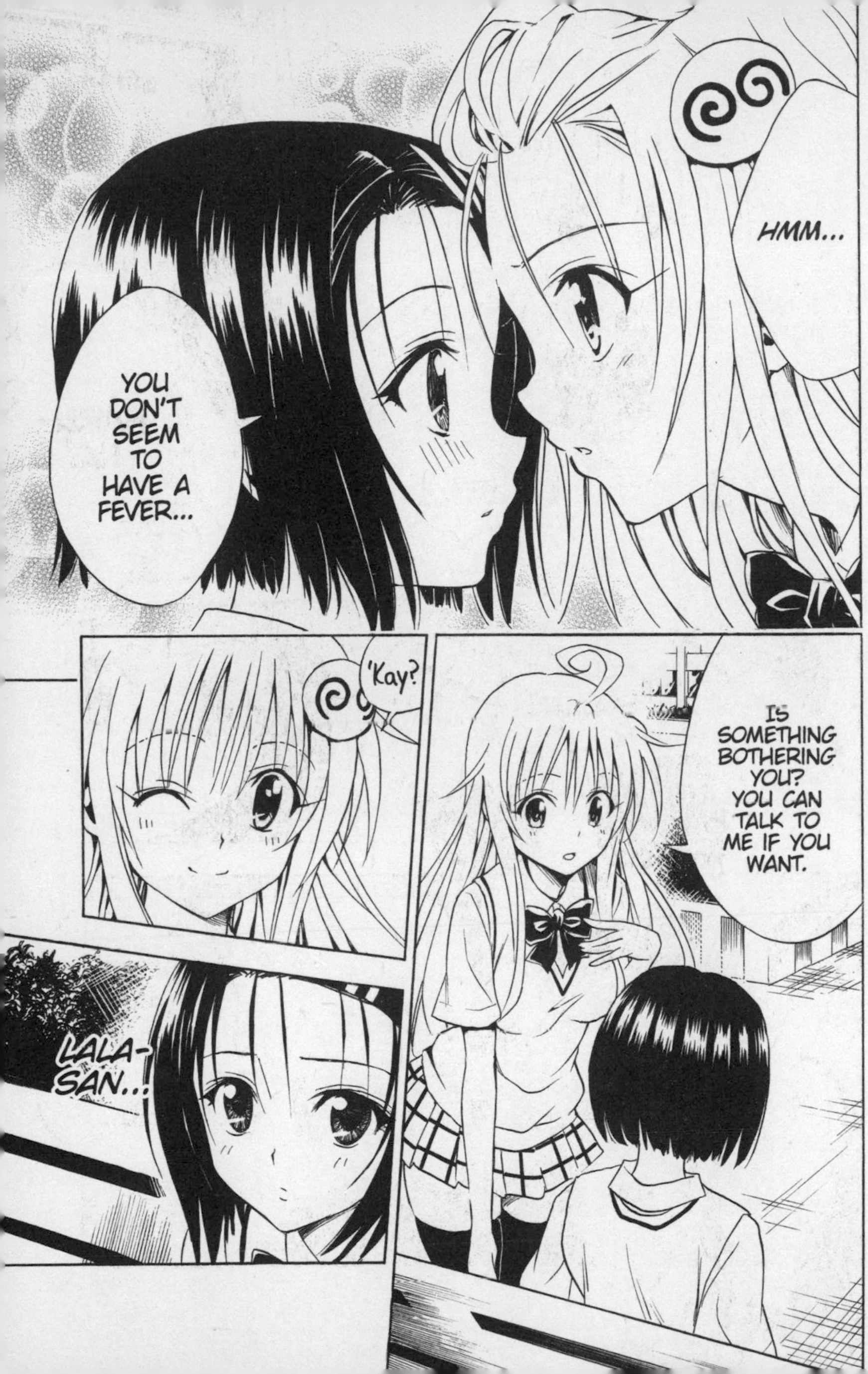

HMM...
YOU DON'T SEEM TO HAVE A FEVER...
IS SOMETHING BOTHERING YOU? YOU CAN TALK TO ME IF YOU WANT.
'Kay?
LALA-SAN...

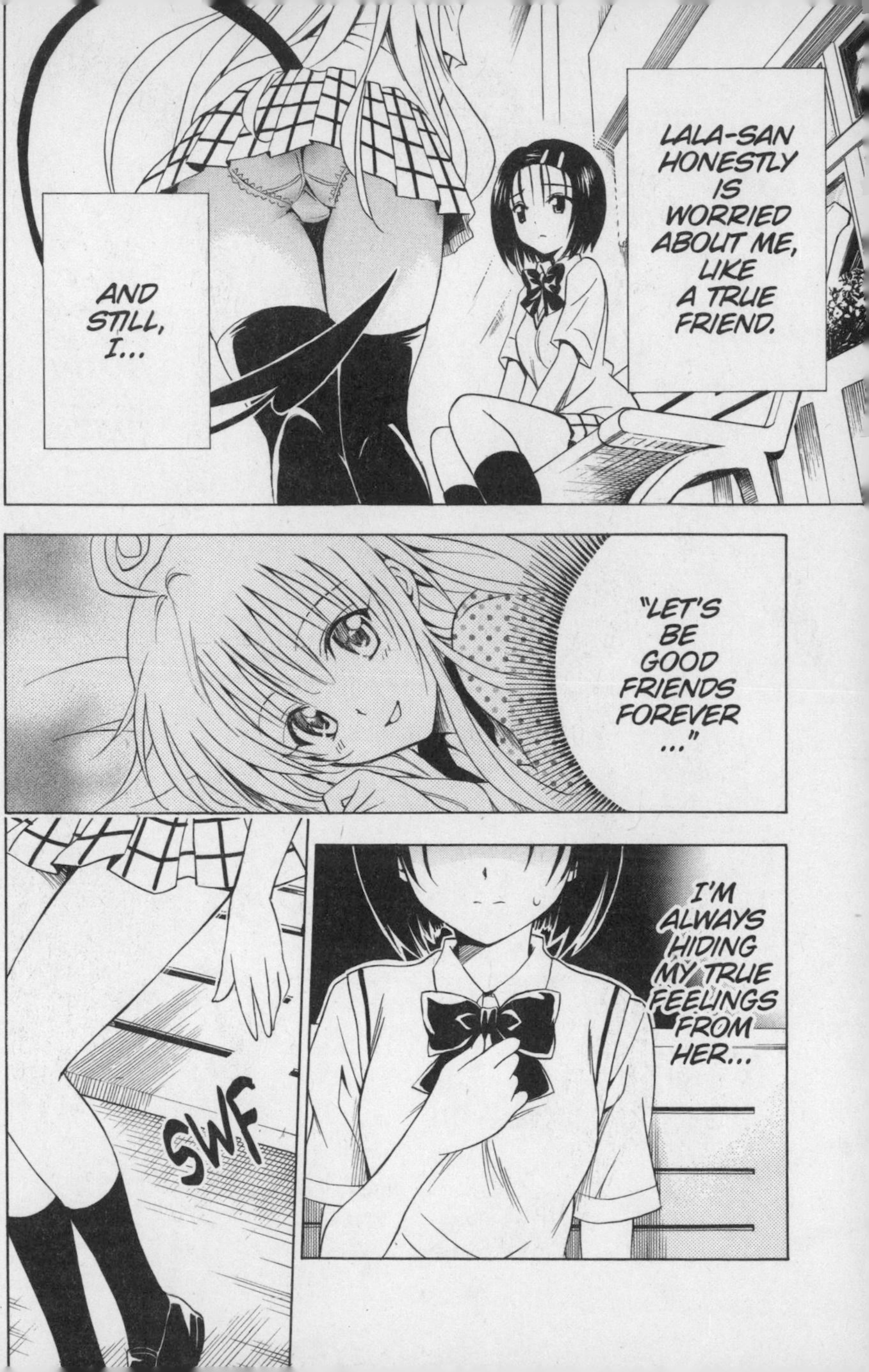
LALA-SAN HONESTLY IS WORRIED ABOUT ME, LIKE A TRUE FRIEND.
AND STILL, I...
"LET'S BE GOOD FRIENDS FOREVER..."
I'M ALWAYS HIDING MY TRUE FEELINGS FROM HER...
SWF

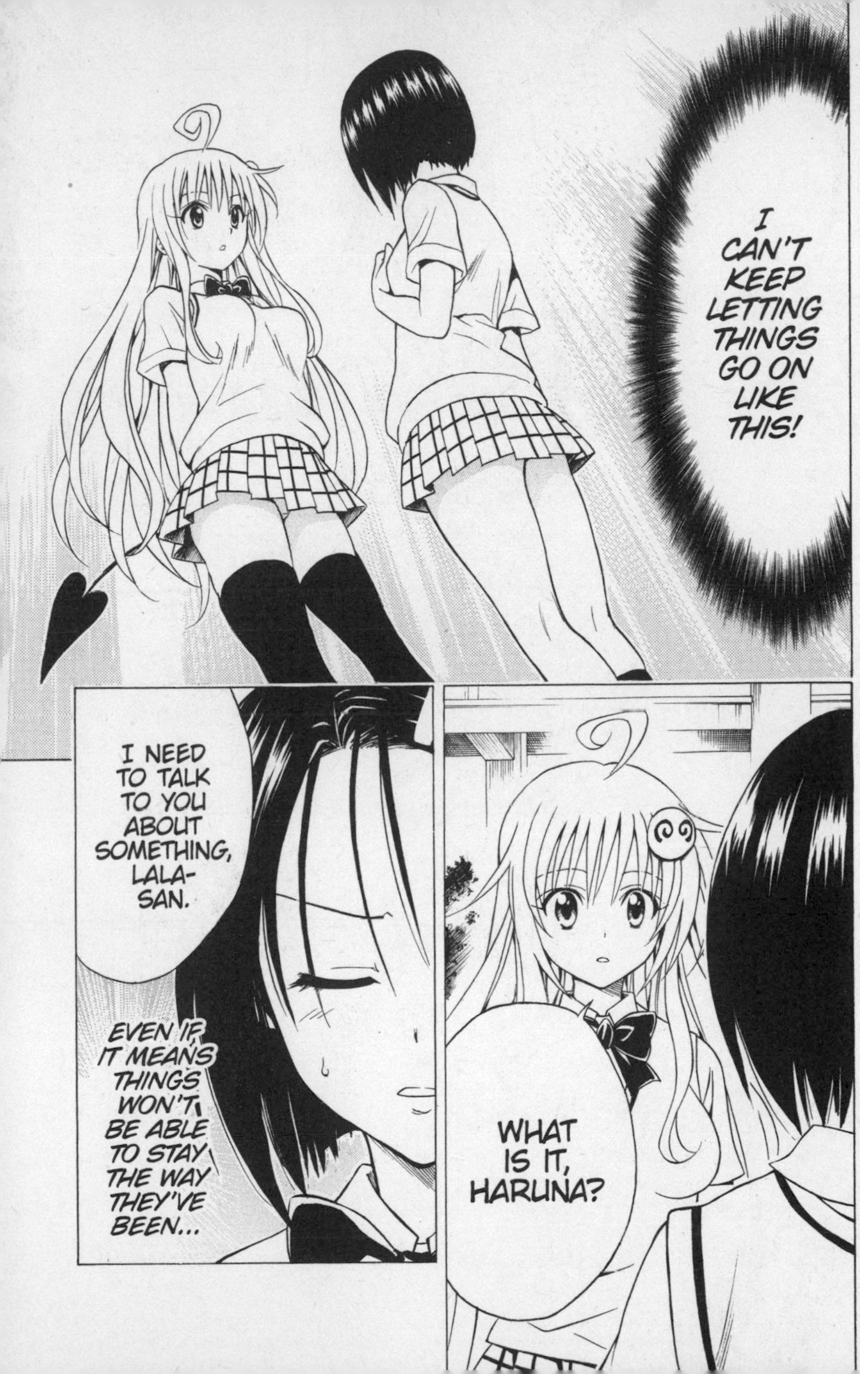
I CAN'T KEEP LETTING THINGS GO ON LIKE THIS!
WHAT IS IT, HARUNA?
I NEED TO TALK TO YOU ABOUT SOMETHING, LALA-SAN.
EVEN IF IT MEANS THINGS WON'T BE ABLE TO STAY THE WAY THEY'VE BEEN...

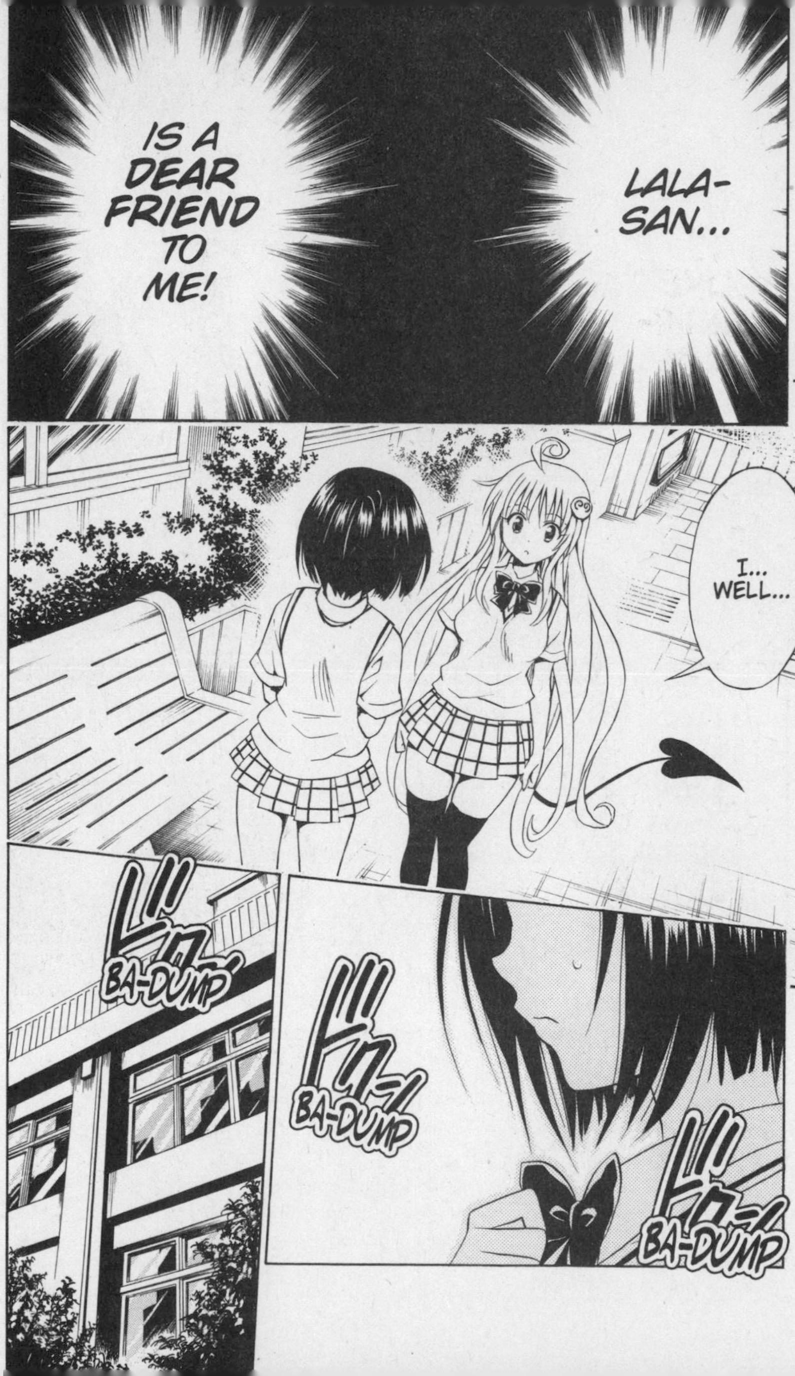
LALA-SAN...
IS A DEAR FRIEND TO ME!
I... WELL...
BA-DUMP
BA-DUMP
BA-DUMP

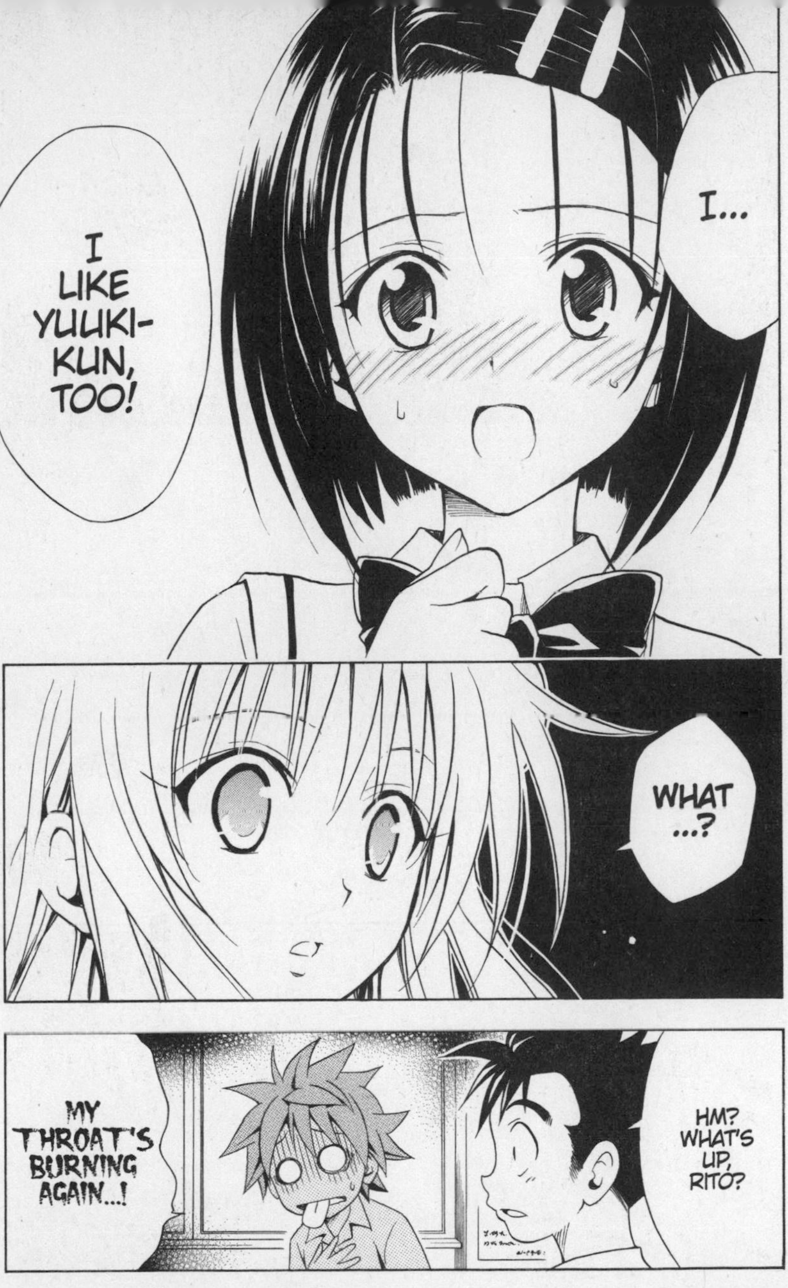
I...
I LIKE YUUKI-KUN, TOO!
WHAT ...?
HM? WHAT'S UP, RITO?
MY THROAT'S BURNING AGAIN...!

To LOVE Ru

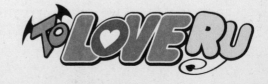

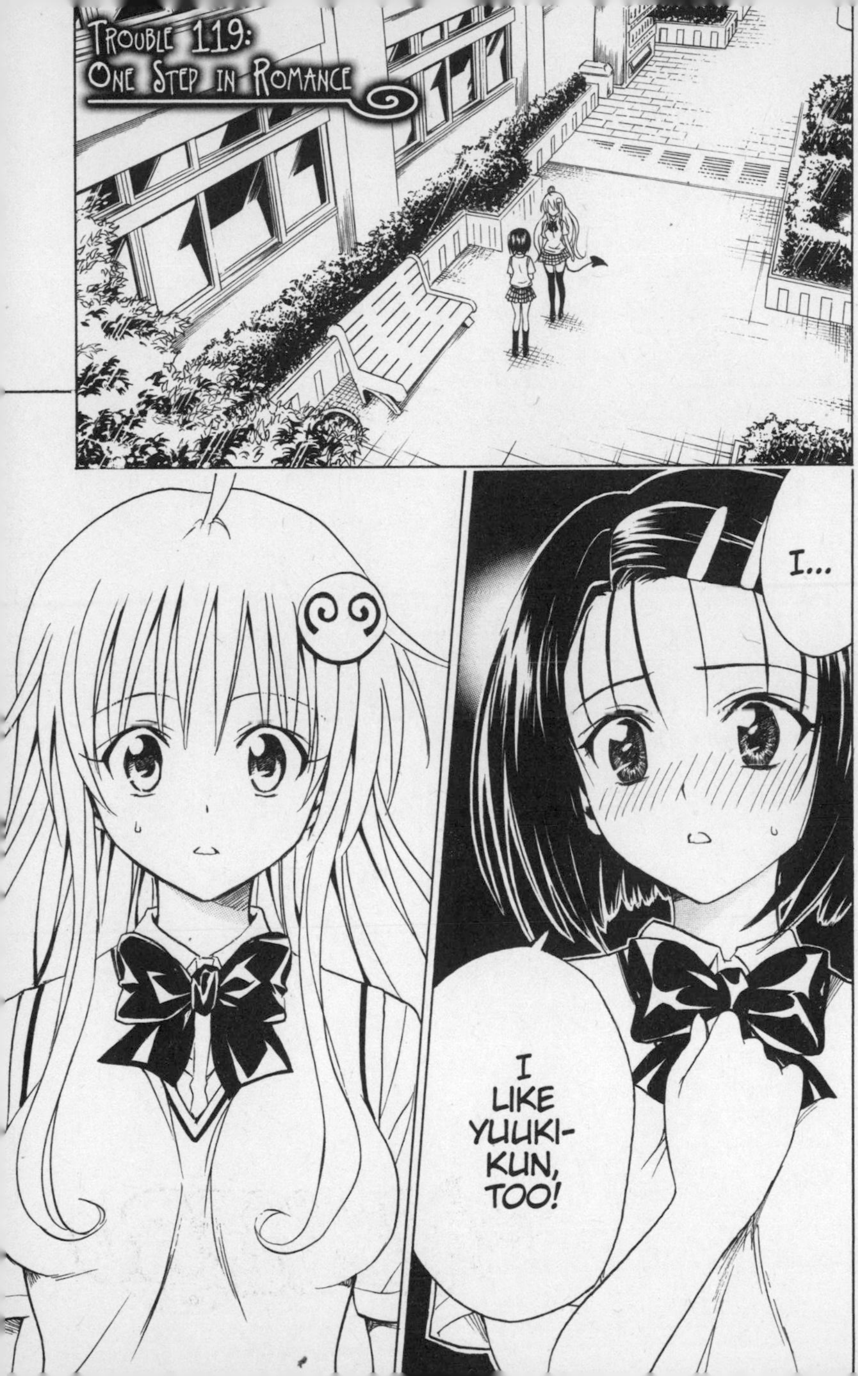
Trouble 119:
One Step in Romance
I...
I like Yuuki-kun, too!

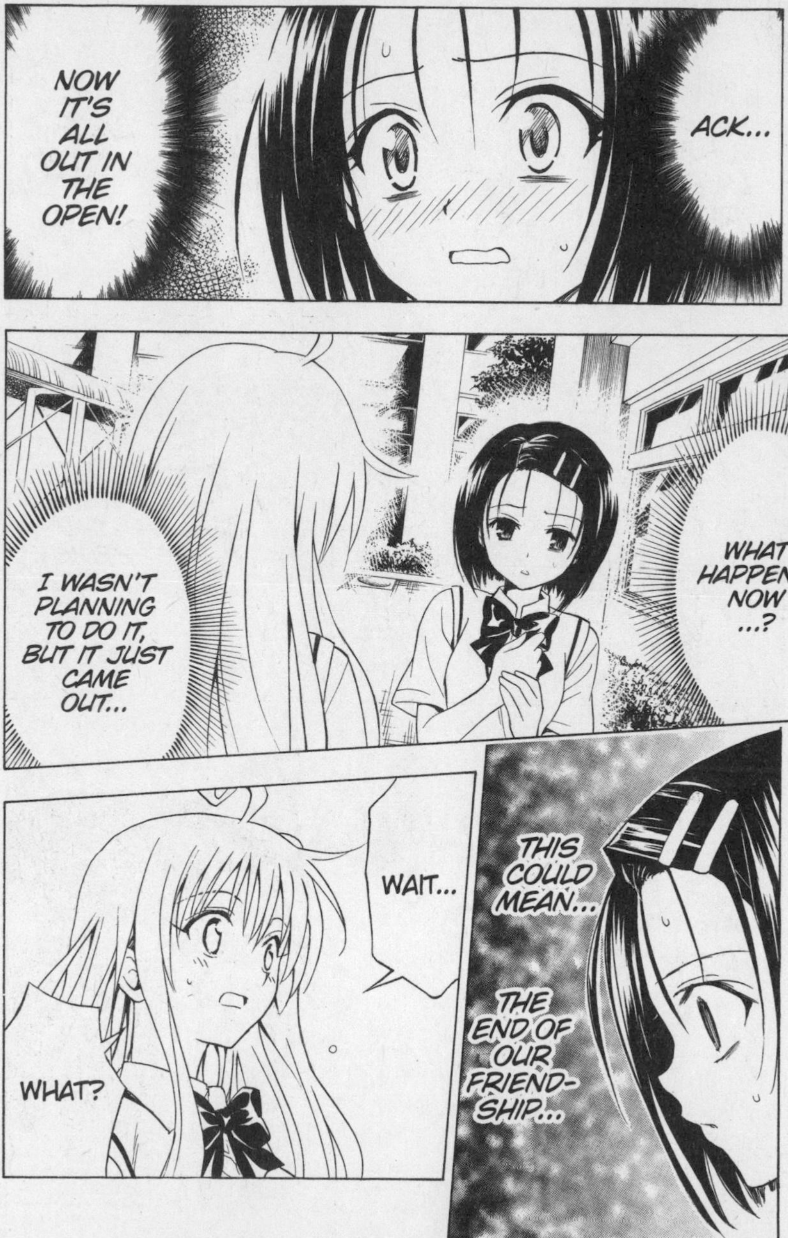
ACK...
NOW IT'S ALL OUT IN THE OPEN!
WHAT HAPPENS NOW ...?
I WASN'T PLANNING TO DO IT, BUT IT JUST CAME OUT...
THIS COULD MEAN...
THE END OF OUR FRIEND-SHIP...
WAIT...
WHAT?

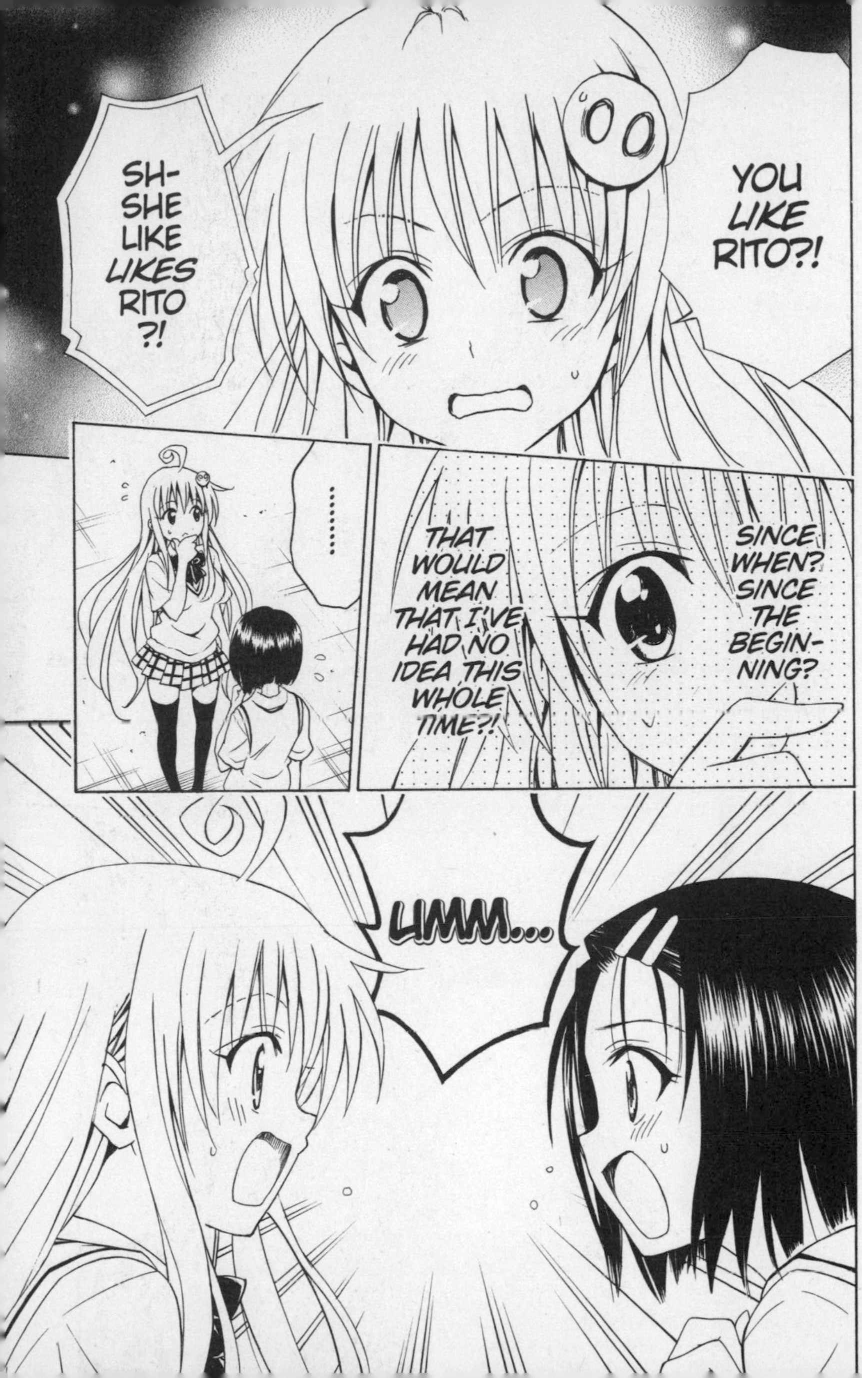
YOU LIKE RITO?!
SH-SHE LIKE LIKES RITO?!
SINCE WHEN? SINCE THE BEGIN-NING?
THAT WOULD MEAN THAT I'VE HAD NO IDEA THIS WHOLE TIME?!
......
UMM...

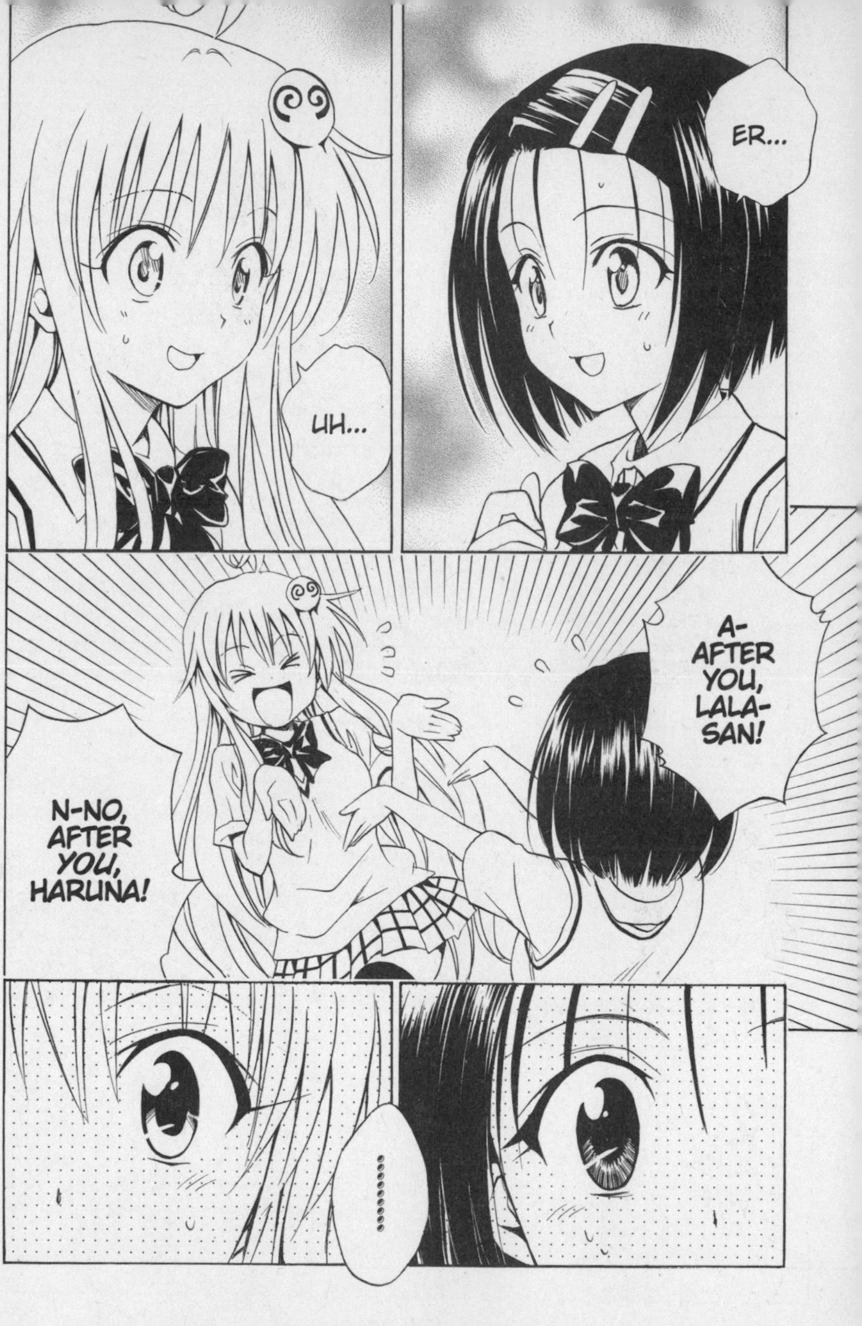

ER...
UH...
A-AFTER YOU, LALA-SAN!
N-NO, AFTER YOU, HARUNA!
....

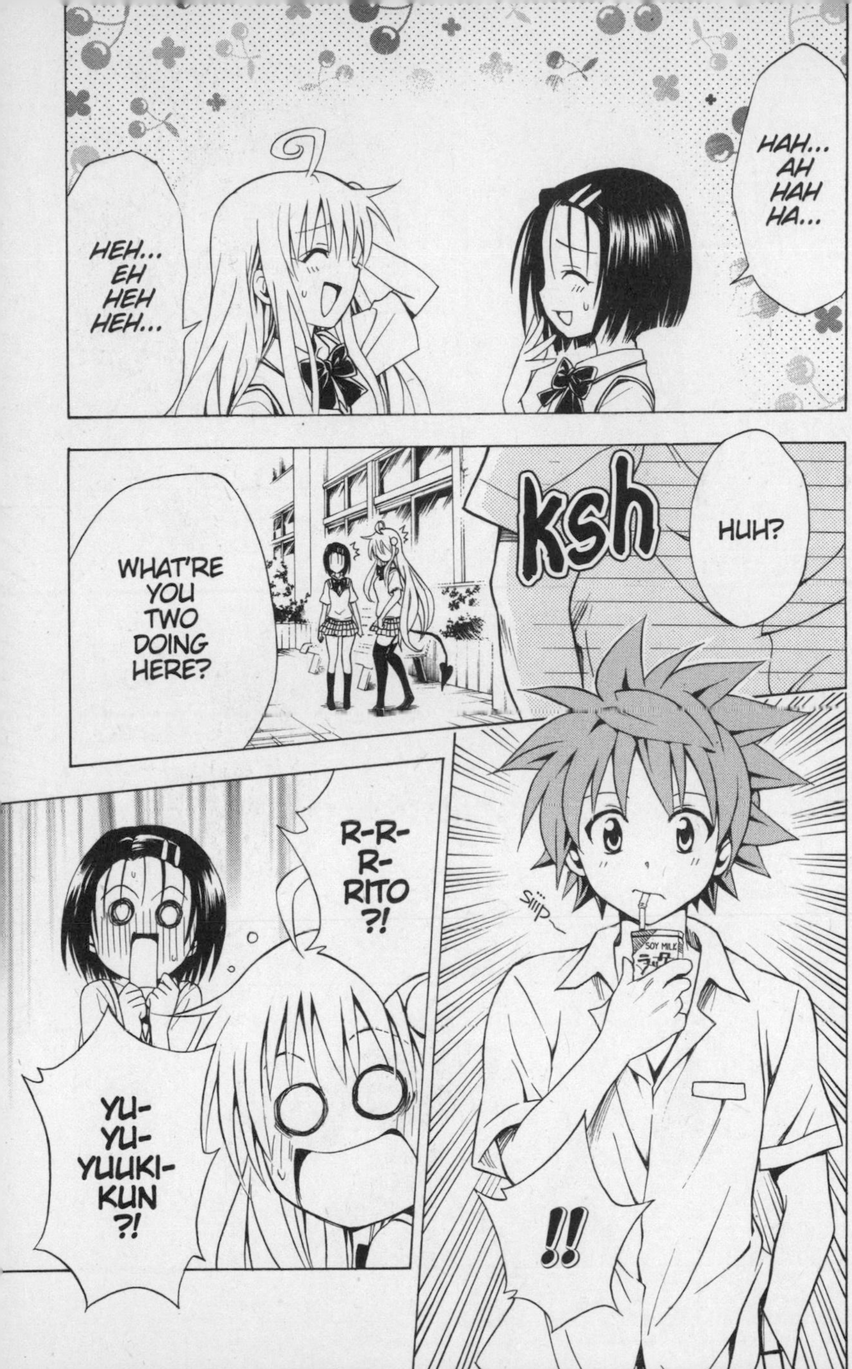
HAH... AH HAH HA...
HEH... EH HEH HEH...
ksh
HUH?
SIIIP
SOY MILK
!!
WHAT'RE YOU TWO DOING HERE?
R-R-R-RITO?!
YU-YU-YUUKI-KUN?!

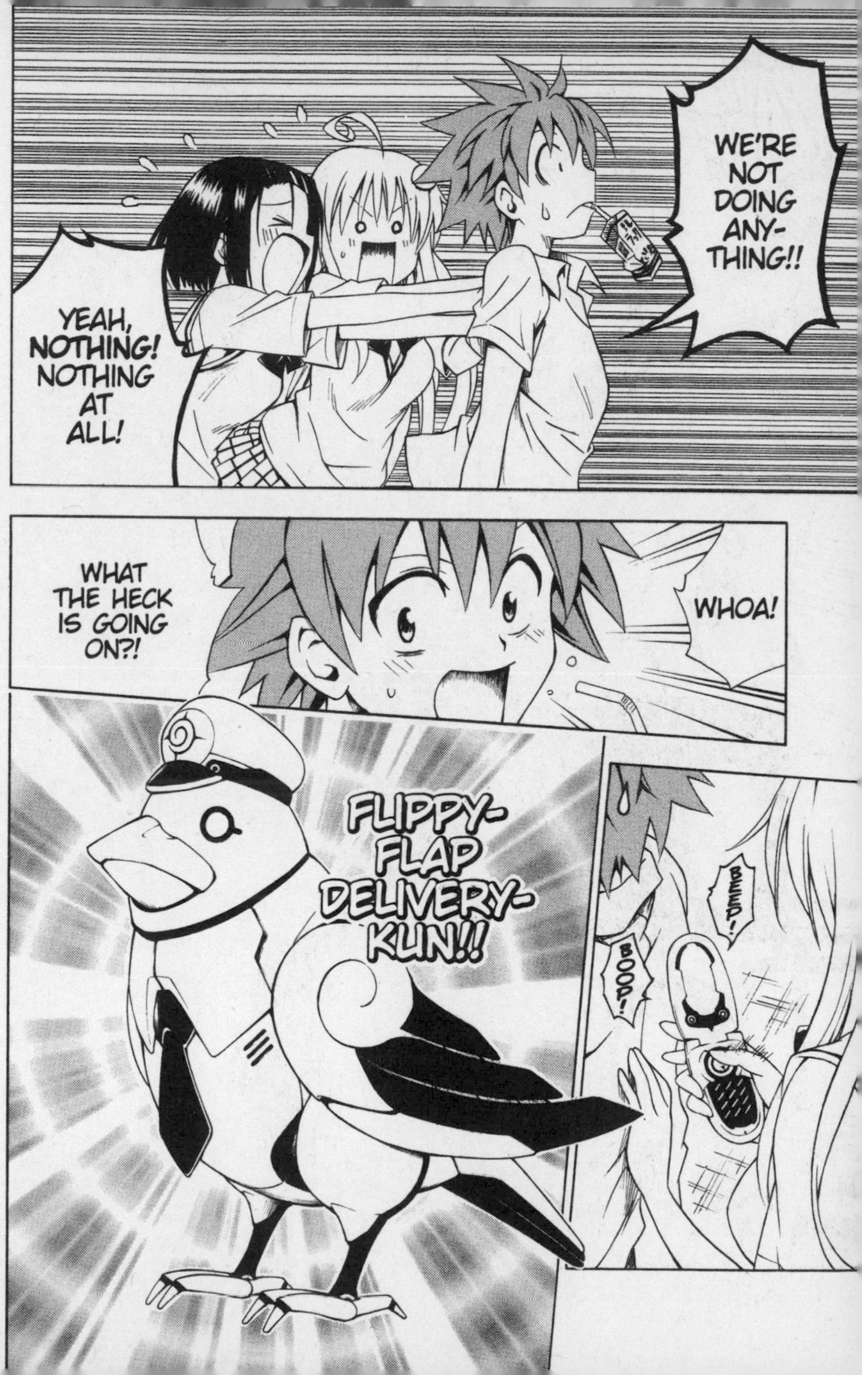
WE'RE NOT DOING ANY-THING!!
YEAH, NOTHING! NOTHING AT ALL!
WHOA!
WHAT THE HECK IS GOING ON?!
BEEP!
BOOP!
FLIPPY-FLAP DELIVERY-KUN!!

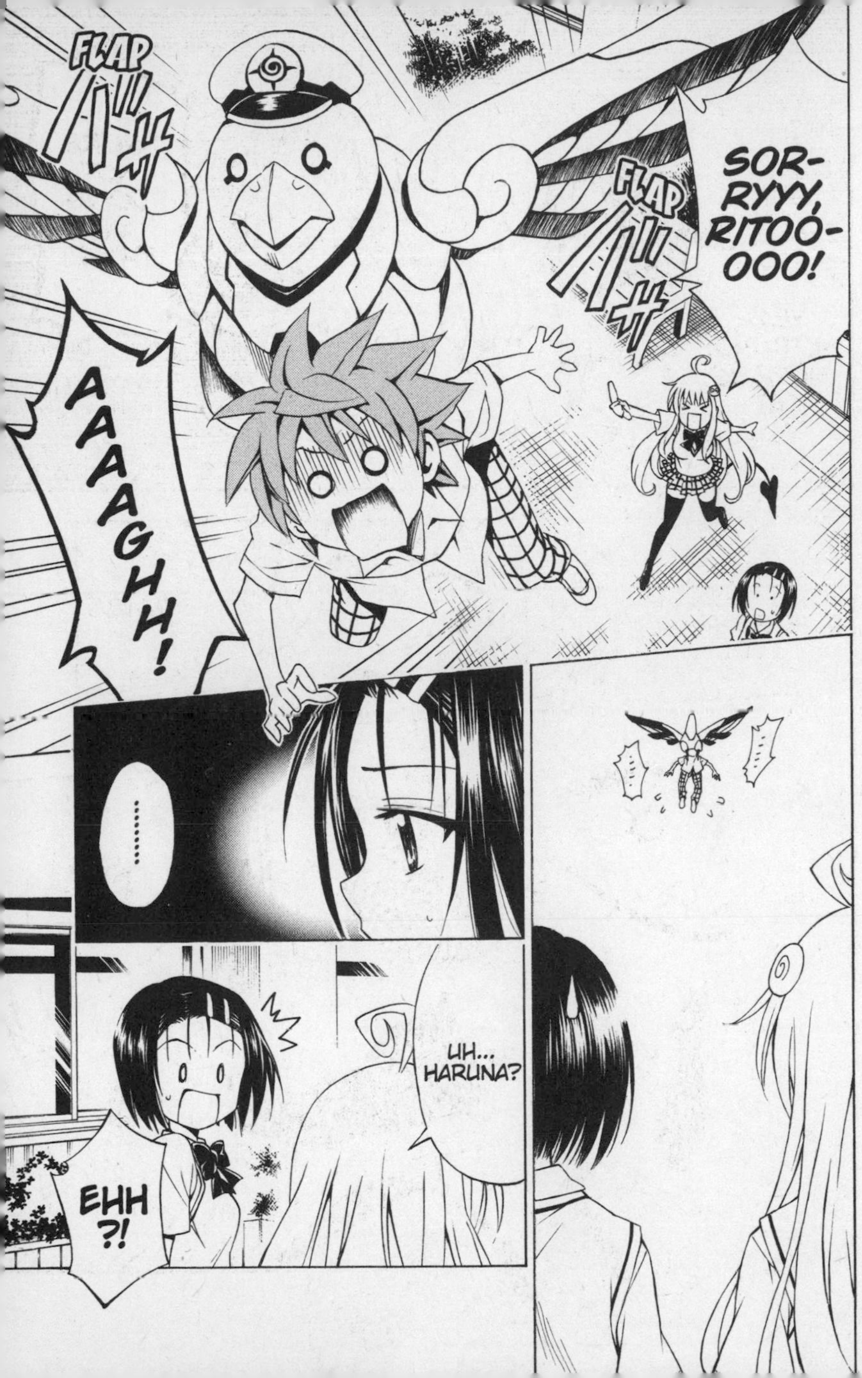
SOR-
RYYY,
RITOO-
OOO!
FLAP
FLAP
AAAAGHH!
......
UH...
HARUNA?
EHH
?!

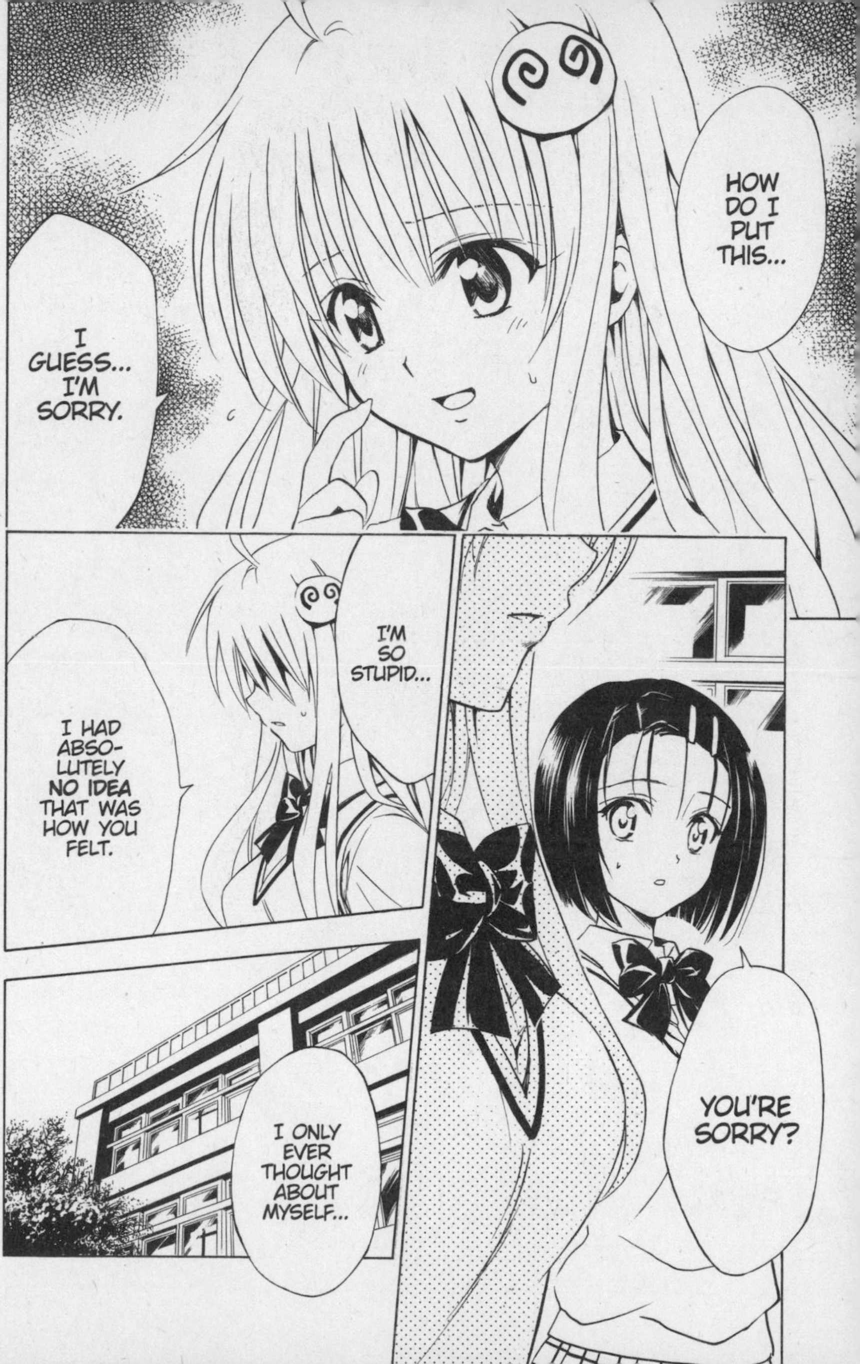
HOW DO I PUT THIS...
I GUESS... I'M SORRY.
YOU'RE SORRY?
I'M SO STUPID...
I HAD ABSO-LUTELY NO IDEA THAT WAS HOW YOU FELT.
I ONLY EVER THOUGHT ABOUT MYSELF...

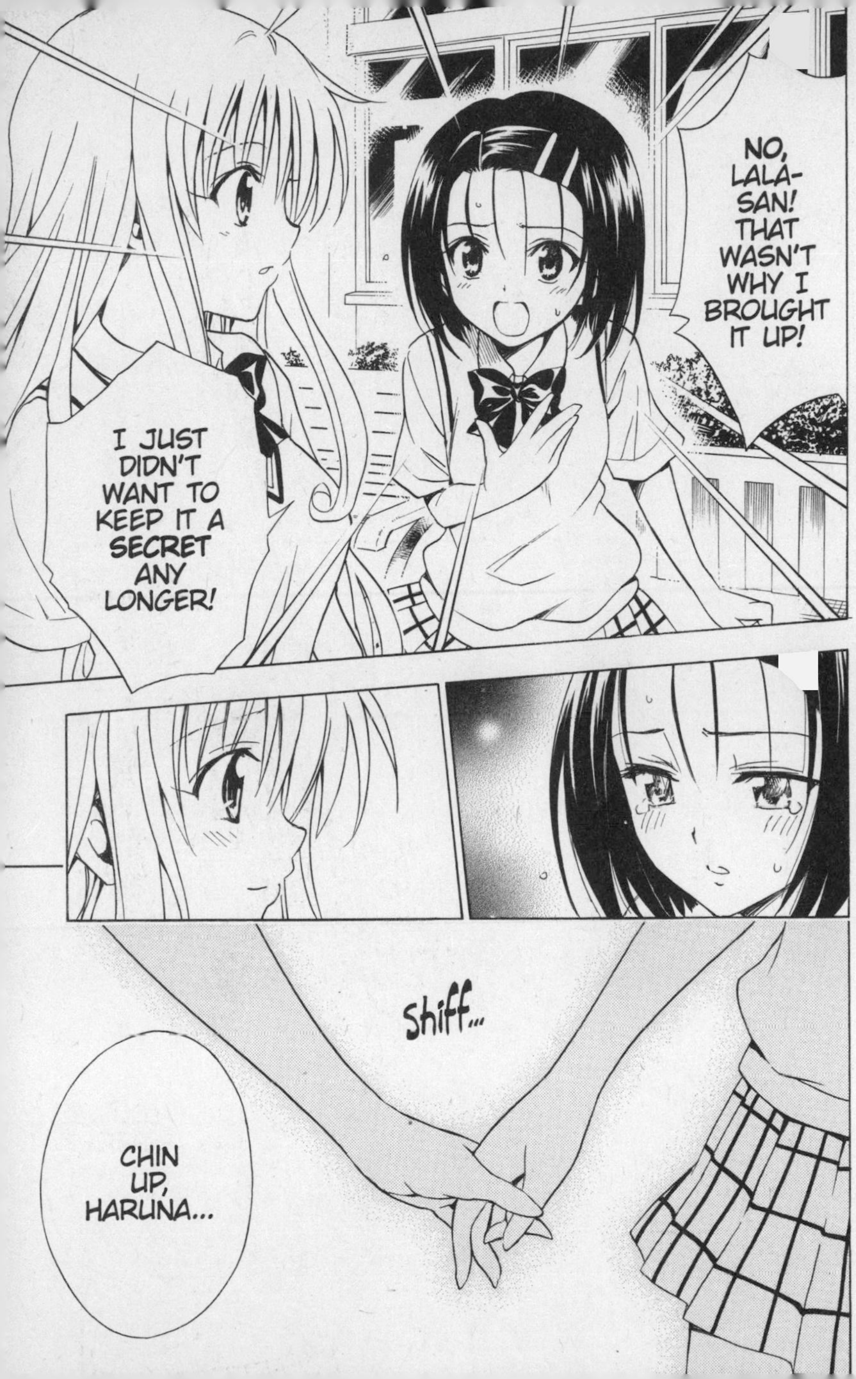
NO, LALA-SAN! THAT WASN'T WHY I BROUGHT IT UP!
I JUST DIDN'T WANT TO KEEP IT A SECRET ANY LONGER!
Shiff...
CHIN UP, HARUNA...

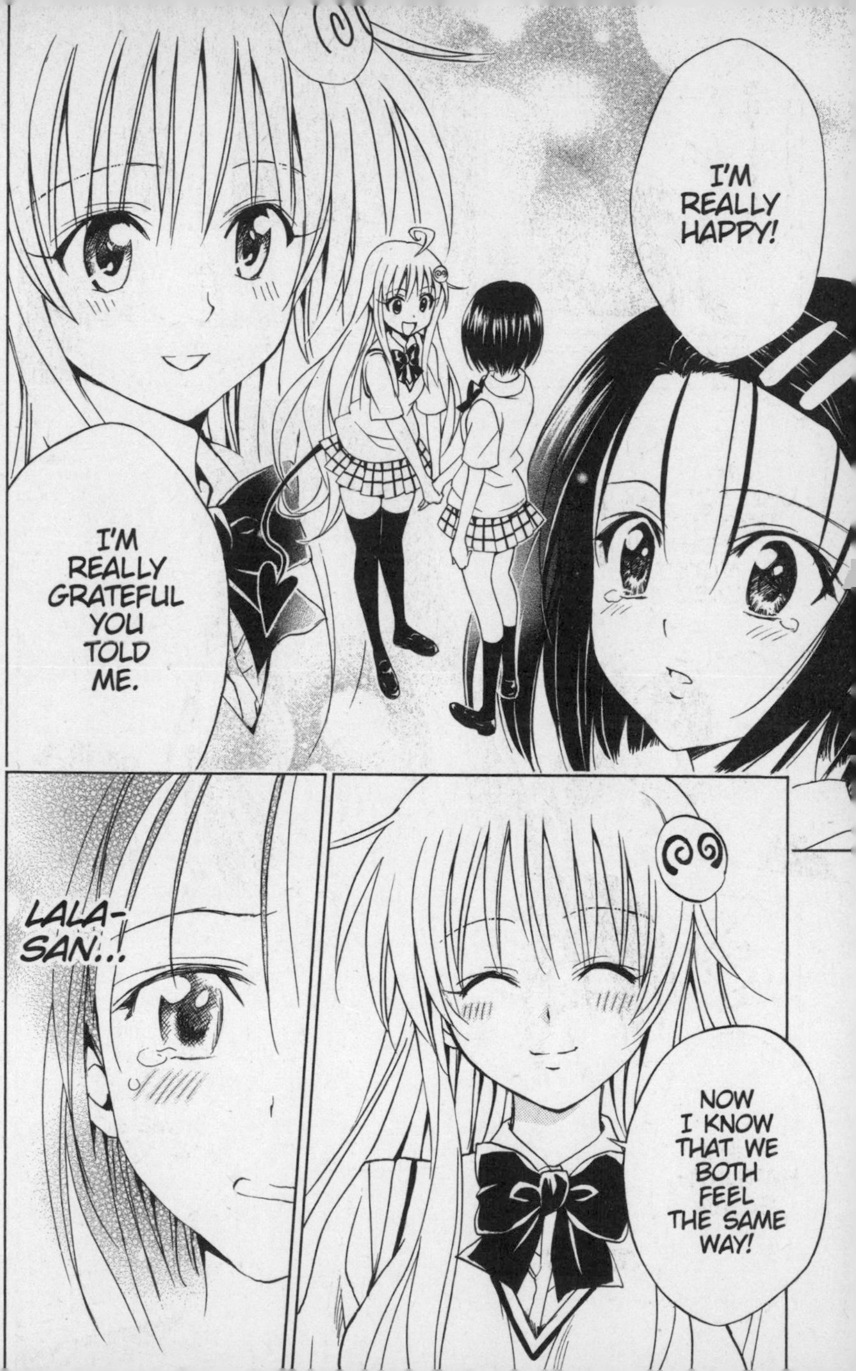
I'M REALLY HAPPY!
I'M REALLY GRATEFUL YOU TOLD ME.
NOW I KNOW THAT WE BOTH FEEL THE SAME WAY!
LALA-SAN..!

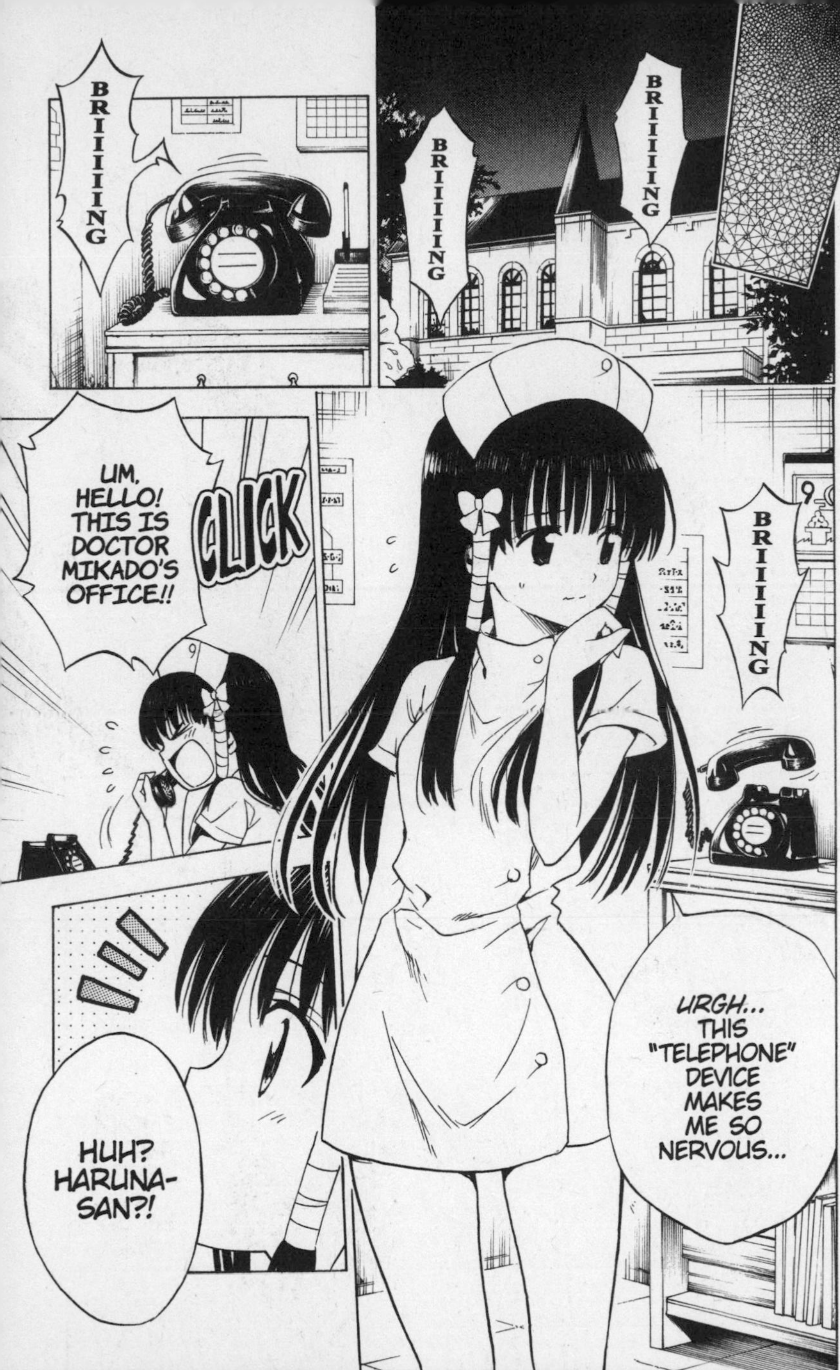
BRIIIIING
BRIIIIING
BRIIIIING
BRIIIIING
URGH... THIS "TELEPHONE" DEVICE MAKES ME SO NERVOUS...
UM. HELLO! THIS IS DOCTOR MIKADO'S OFFICE!!
CLICK
HUH? HARUNA-SAN?!

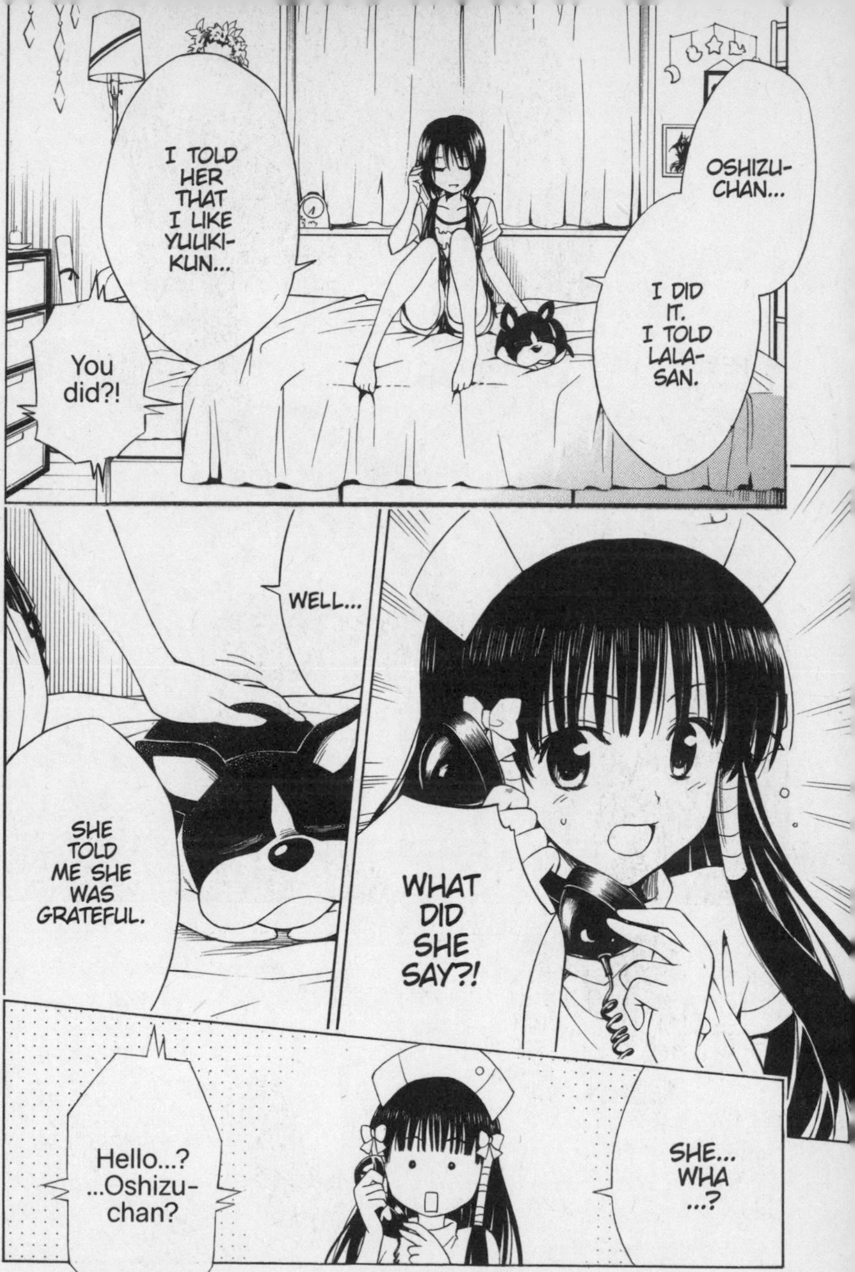

OSHIZU-CHAN...
I DID IT. I TOLD LALA-SAN.
I TOLD HER THAT I LIKE YUUKI-KUN...
You did?!
WHAT DID SHE SAY?!
WELL...
SHE TOLD ME SHE WAS GRATEFUL.
SHE... WHA ...?
Hello...? ...Oshizu-chan?

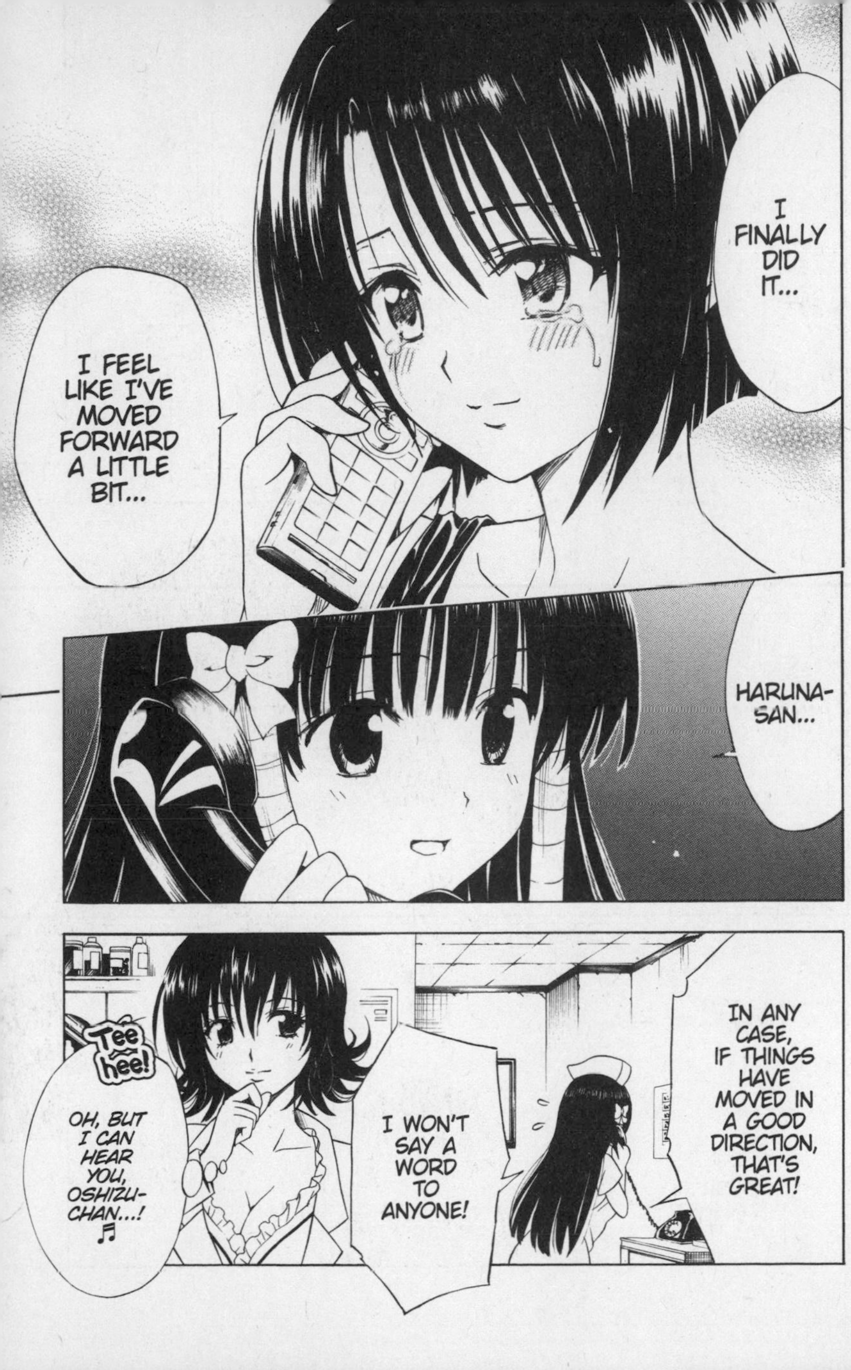
I FINALLY DID IT...
I FEEL LIKE I'VE MOVED FORWARD A LITTLE BIT...
HARUNA-SAN...
IN ANY CASE, IF THINGS HAVE MOVED IN A GOOD DIRECTION, THAT'S GREAT!
I WON'T SAY A WORD TO ANYONE!
Tee hee!
OH, BUT I CAN HEAR YOU, OSHIZU-CHAN...! ♫

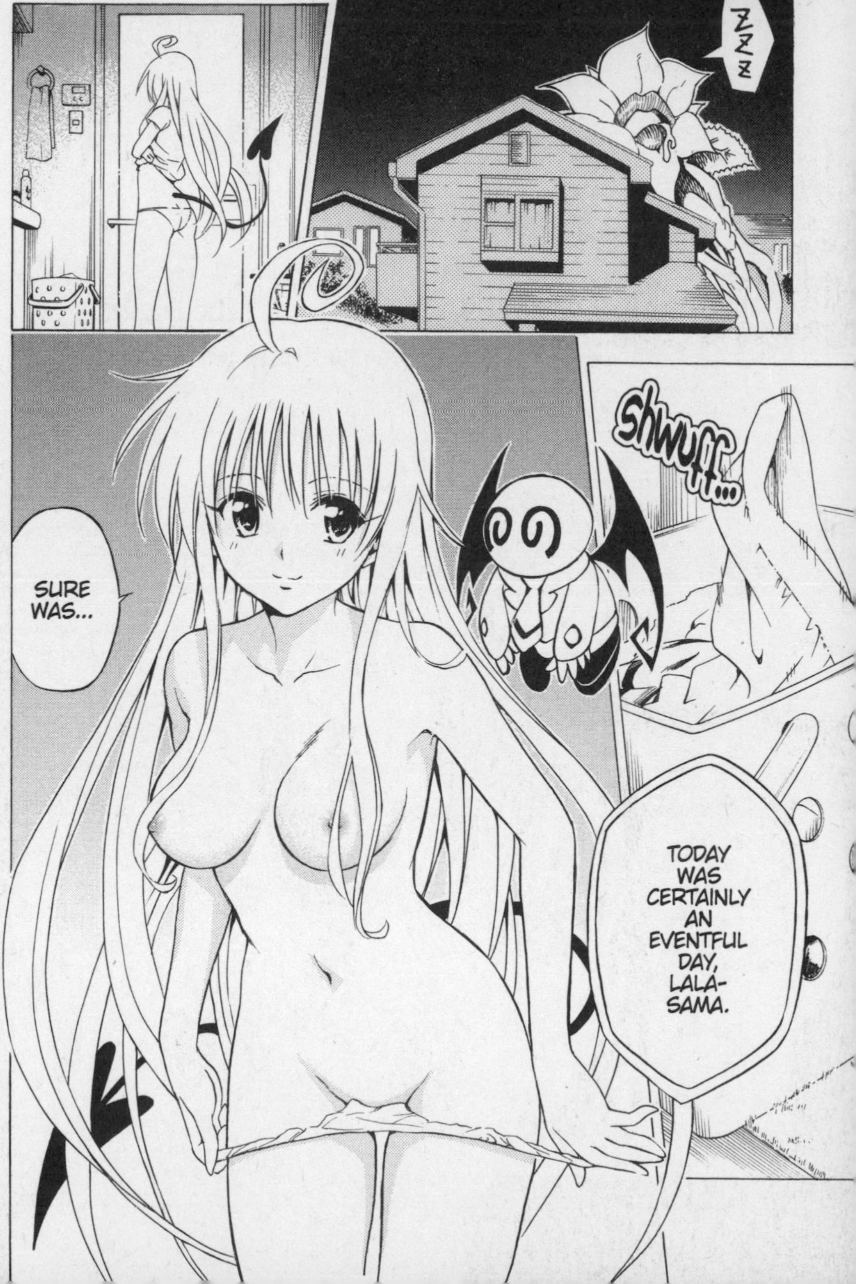
ZZZ
shwuff...
TODAY WAS CERTAINLY AN EVENTFUL DAY, LALA-SAMA.
SURE WAS...

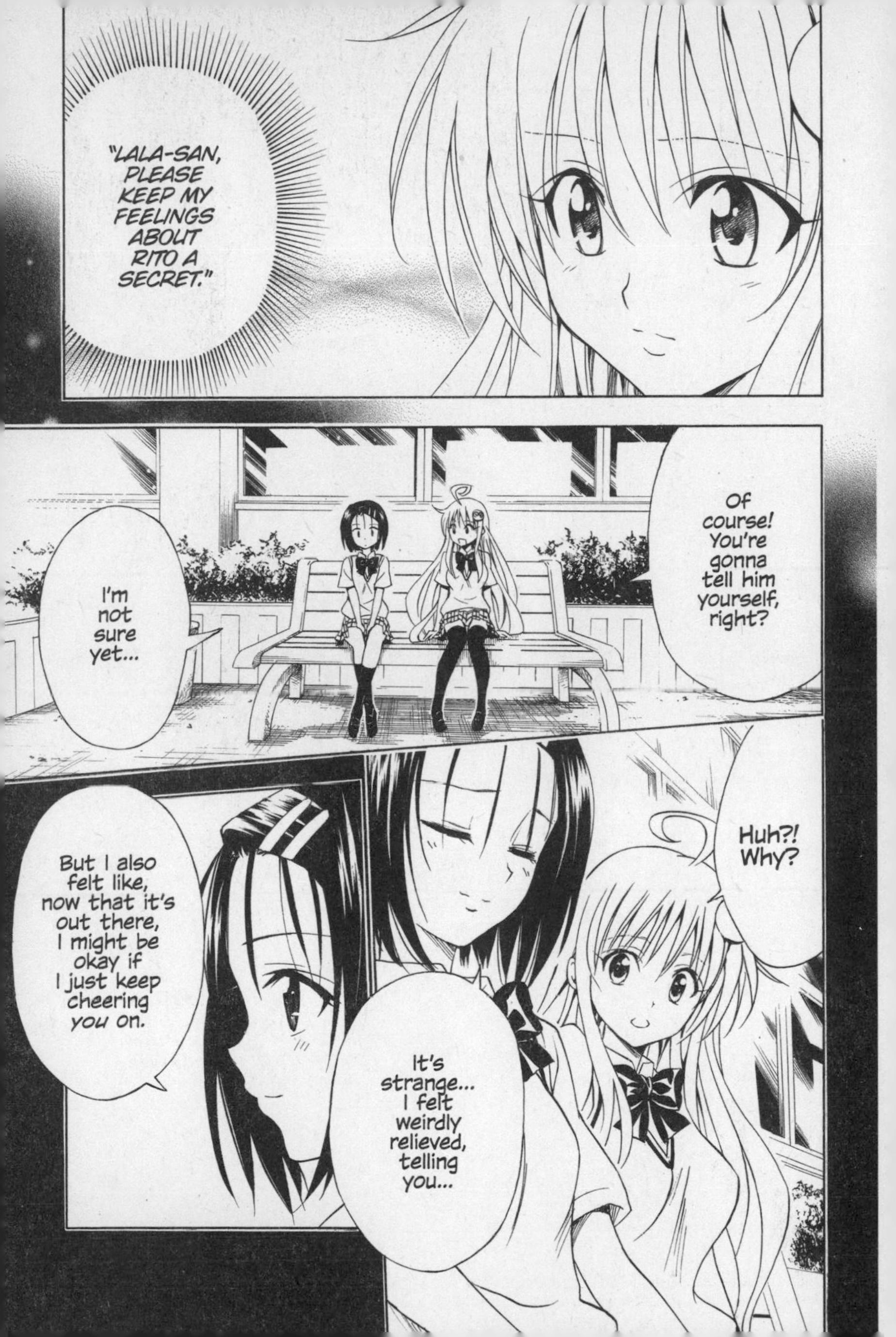
"LALA-SAN, PLEASE KEEP MY FEELINGS ABOUT RITO A SECRET."
Of course! You're gonna tell him yourself, right?
I'm not sure yet...
Huh?! Why?
It's strange... I felt weirdly relieved, telling you...
But I also felt like, now that it's out there, I might be okay if I just keep cheering you on.

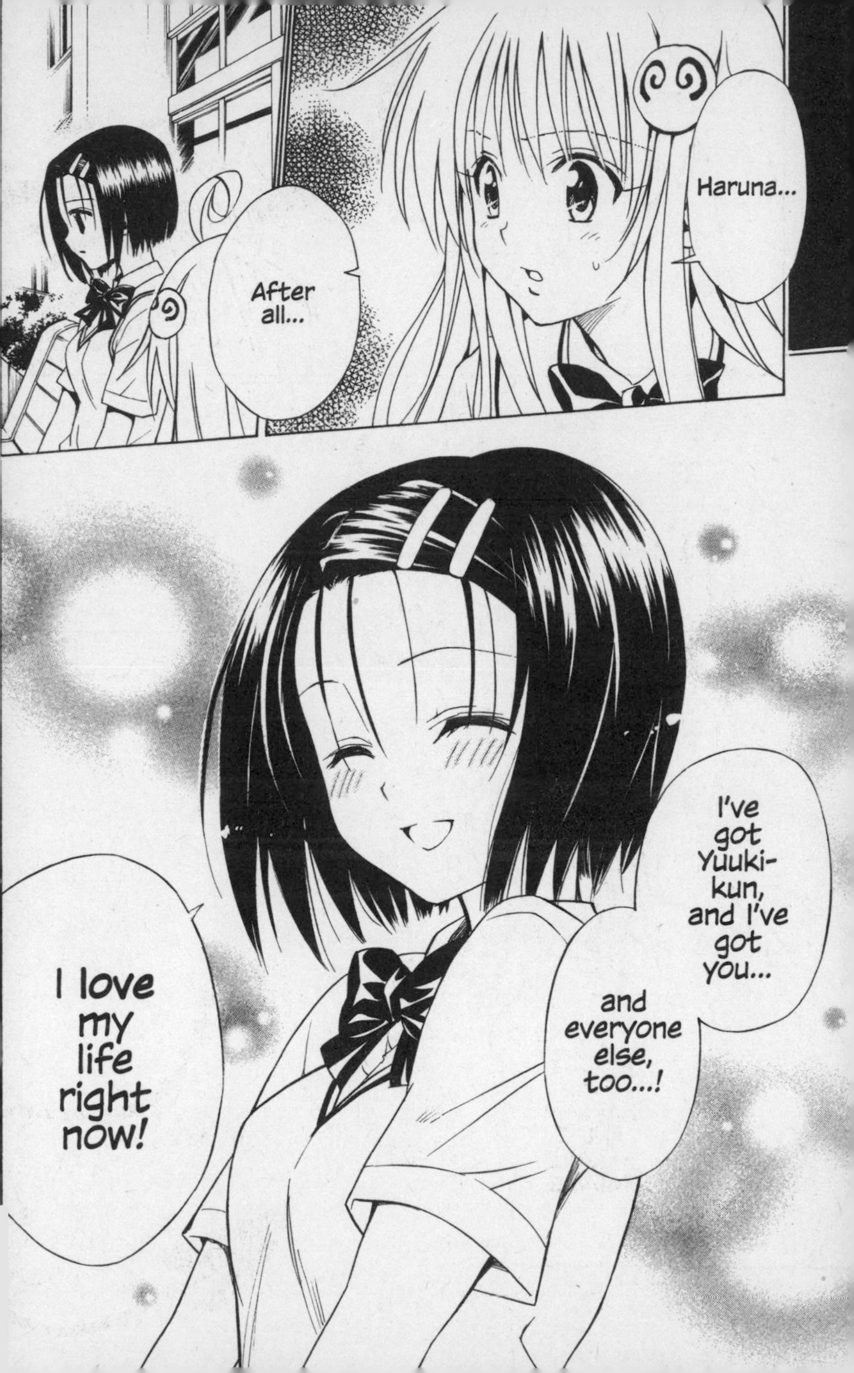
Haruna...
After all...
I've got Yuuki-kun, and I've got you...
and everyone else, too...!
I love my life right now!

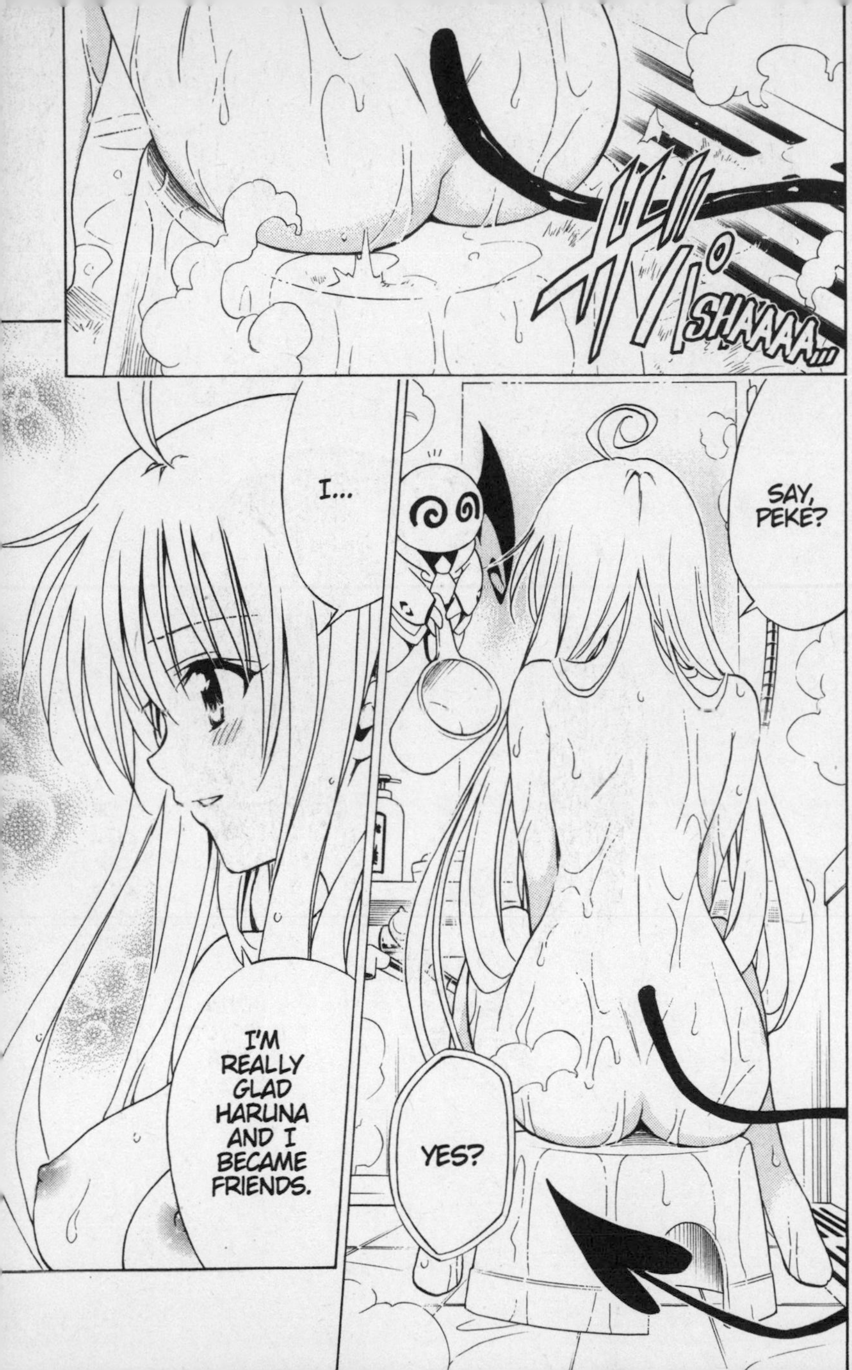
SHAAAA...
SAY, PEKE?
YES?
I...
I'M REALLY GLAD HARUNA AND I BECAME FRIENDS.

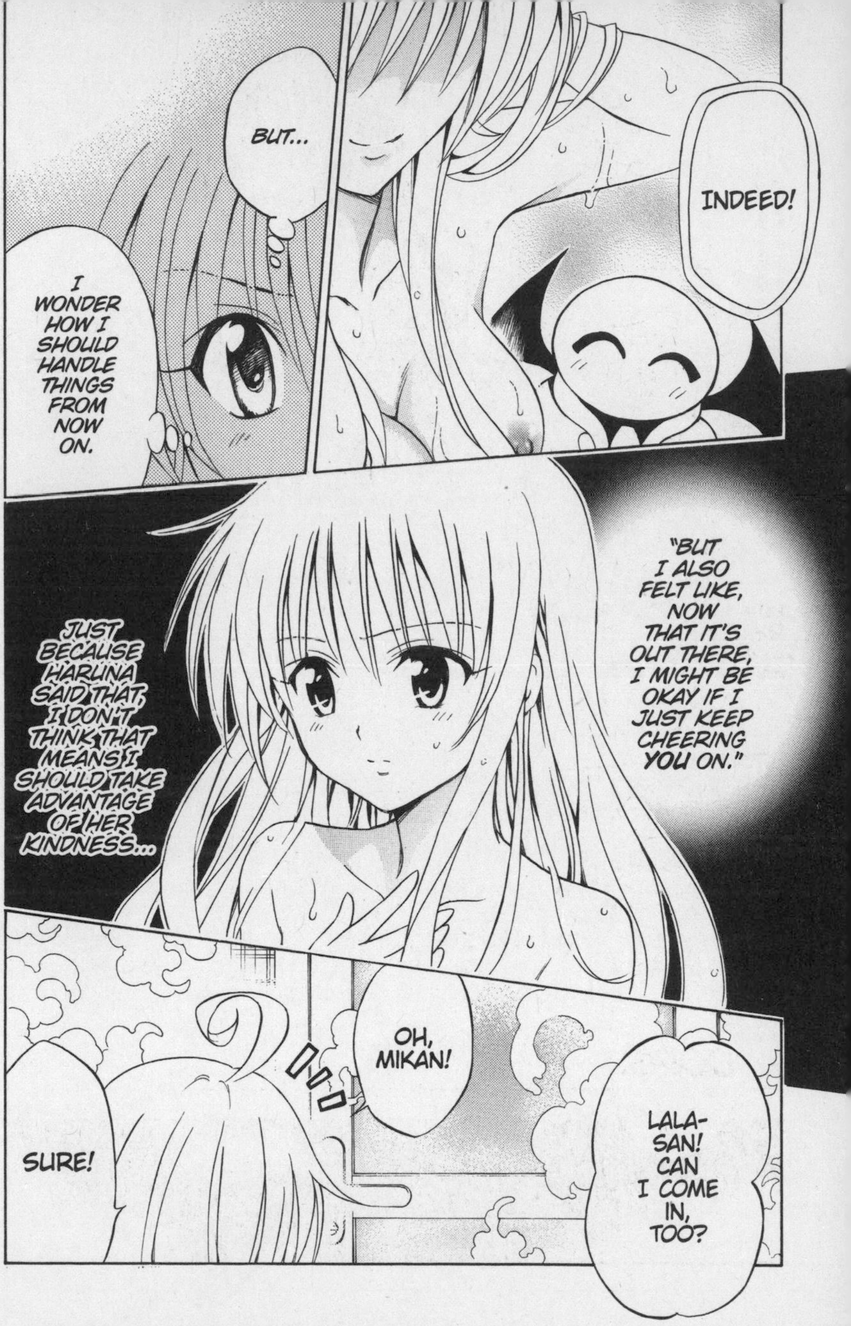
INDEED!
BUT...
I WONDER HOW I SHOULD HANDLE THINGS FROM NOW ON.
"BUT I ALSO FELT LIKE, NOW THAT IT'S OUT THERE, I MIGHT BE OKAY IF I JUST KEEP CHEERING YOU ON."
JUST BECAUSE HARUNA SAID THAT, I DON'T THINK THAT MEANS I SHOULD TAKE ADVANTAGE OF HER KINDNESS...
LALA-SAN! CAN I COME IN, TOO?
OH, MIKAN!
SURE!

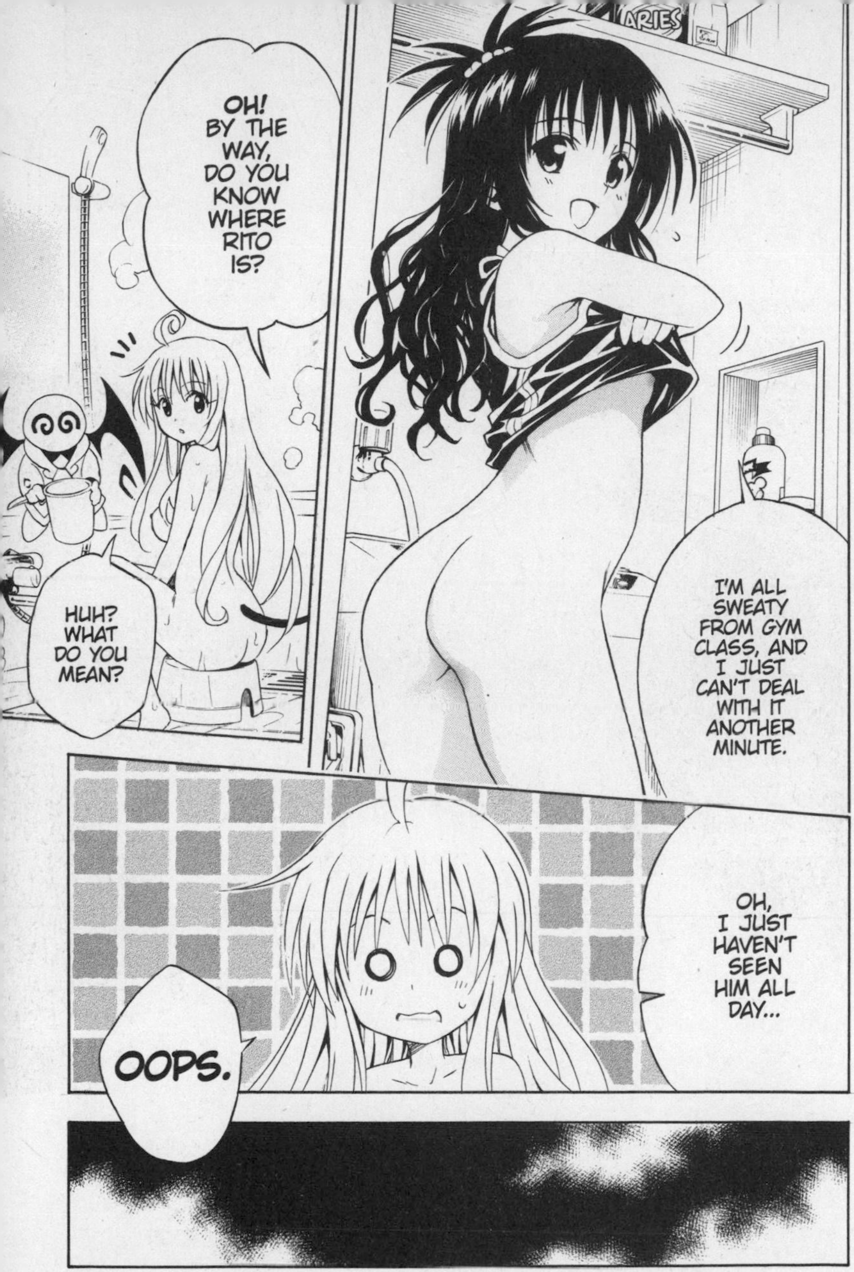
I'M ALL SWEATY FROM GYM CLASS, AND I JUST CAN'T DEAL WITH IT ANOTHER MINUTE.
OH! BY THE WAY, DO YOU KNOW WHERE RITO IS?
HUH? WHAT DO YOU MEAN?
OH, I JUST HAVEN'T SEEN HIM ALL DAY...
OOPS.

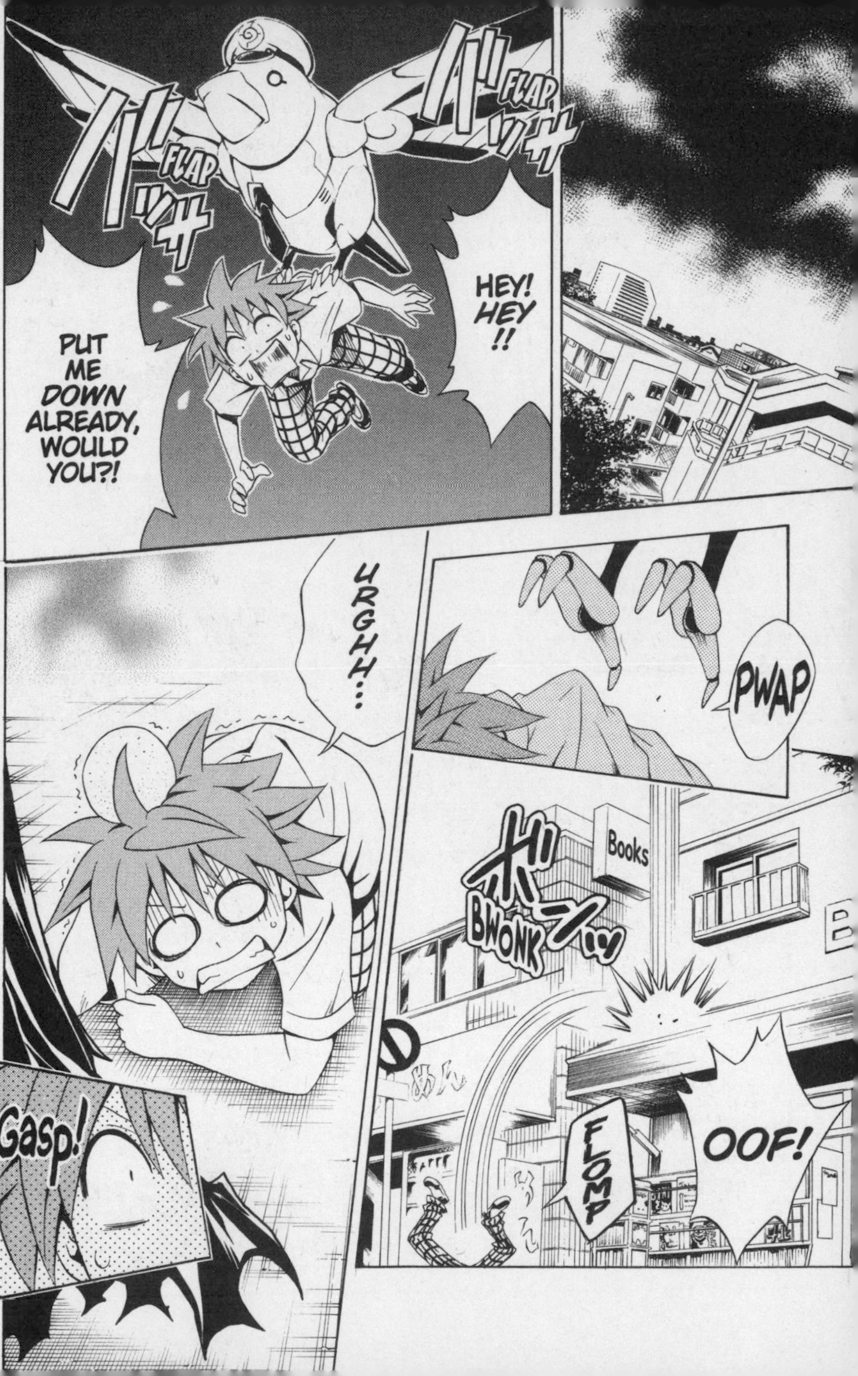
FLAP
FLAP
HEY! HEY!!
PUT ME DOWN ALREADY, WOULD YOU?!
PWAP
Books
BWONK
OOF!
FLOMP
URGHH...
Gasp!

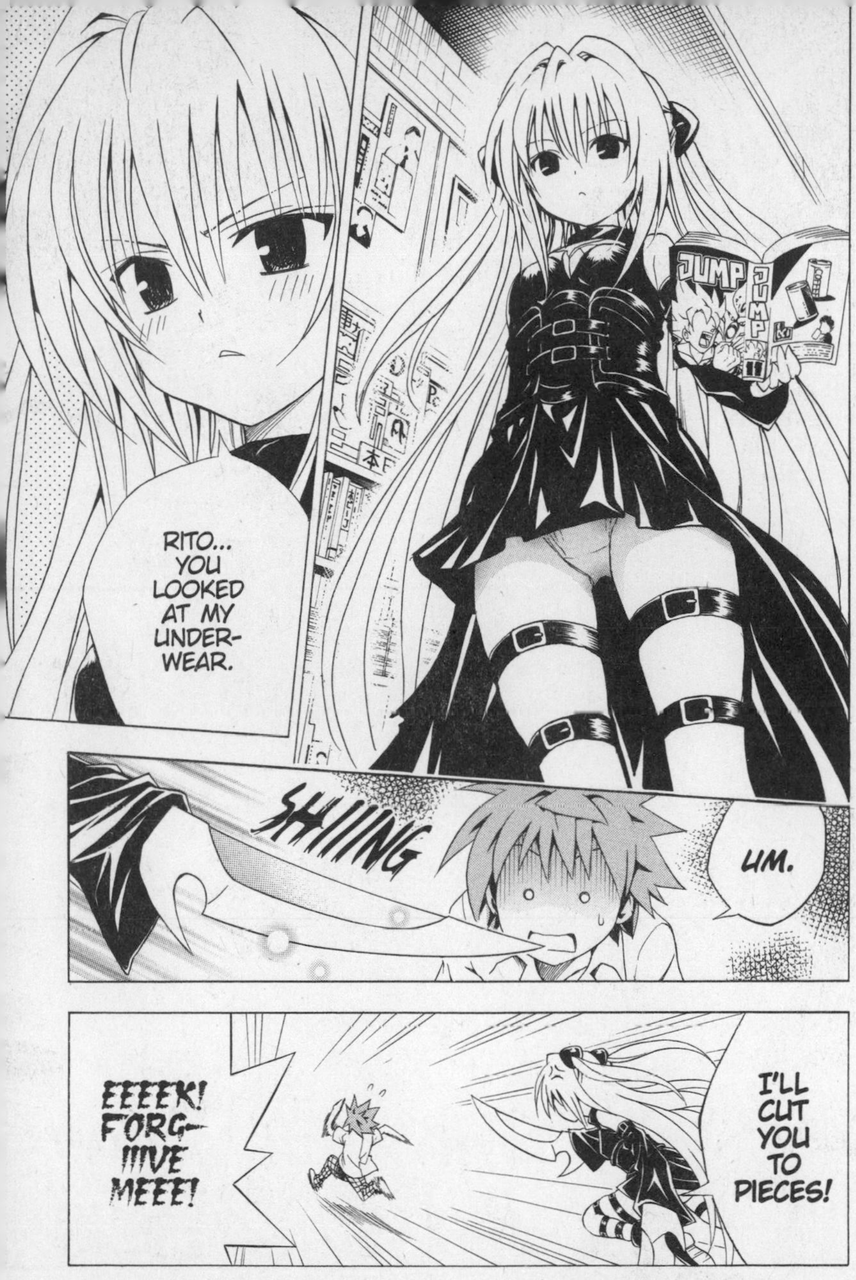
JUMP
JUMP
RITO... YOU LOOKED AT MY UNDER-WEAR.
UM.
SHIIING
I'LL CUT YOU TO PIECES!
EEEEK! FORG-IIIVE MEEE!

To LOVE Ru

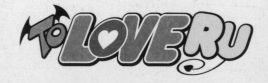

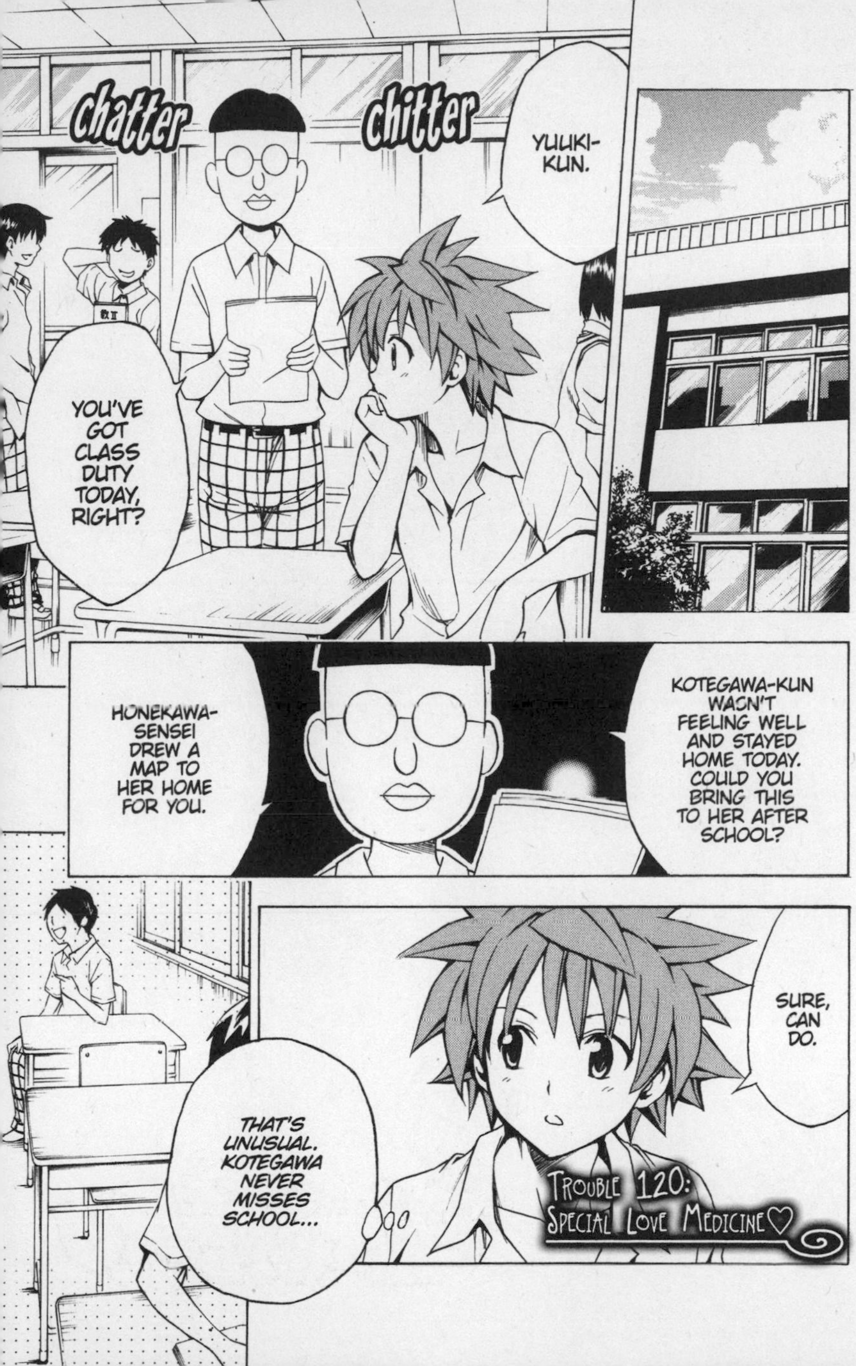
YUUKI-KUN.
chitter
chatter
YOU'VE GOT CLASS DUTY TODAY, RIGHT?
KOTEGAWA-KUN WASN'T FEELING WELL AND STAYED HOME TODAY. COULD YOU BRING THIS TO HER AFTER SCHOOL?
HONEKAWA-SENSEI DREW A MAP TO HER HOME FOR YOU.
SURE, CAN DO.
TROUBLE 120: SPECIAL LOVE MEDICINE♡
THAT'S UNUSUAL. KOTEGAWA NEVER MISSES SCHOOL...

Trouble 120: Special Love Medicine♡

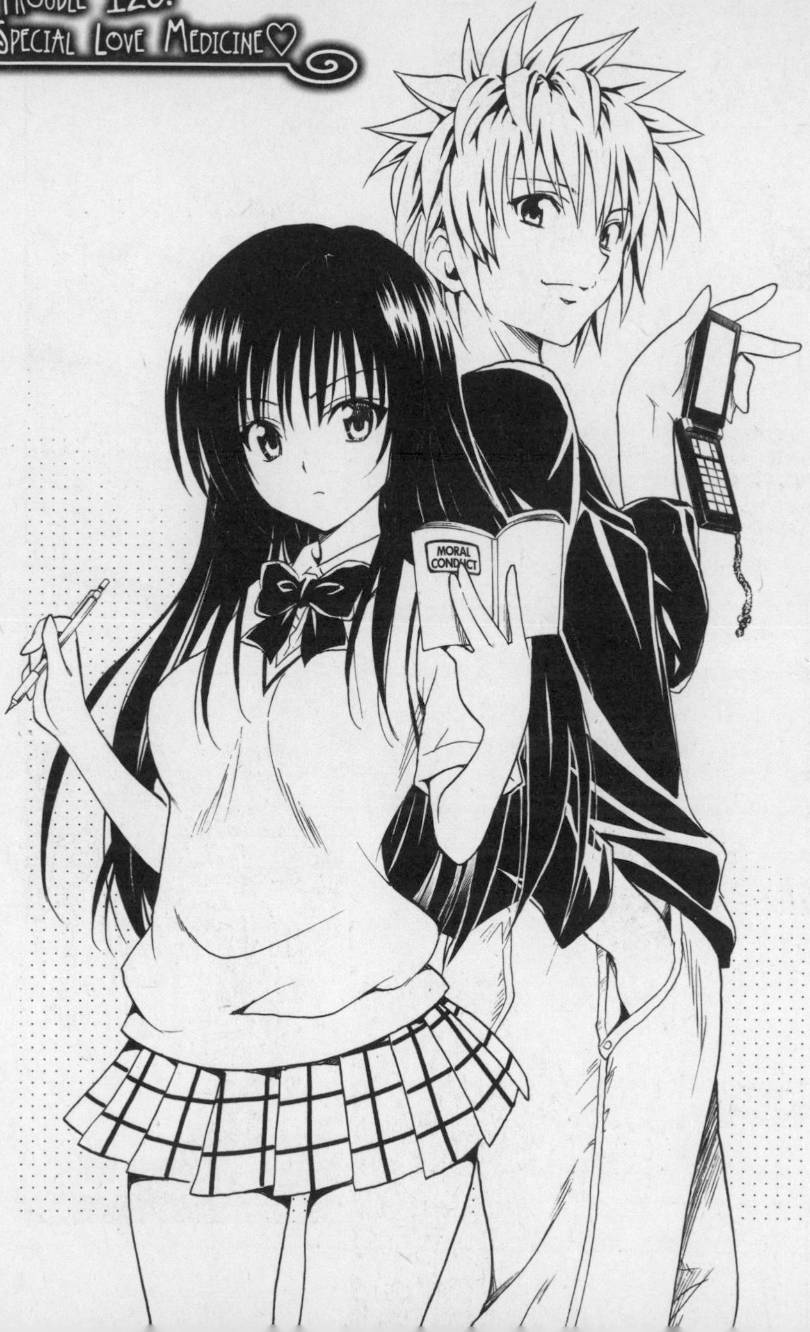
MORAL CONDUCT

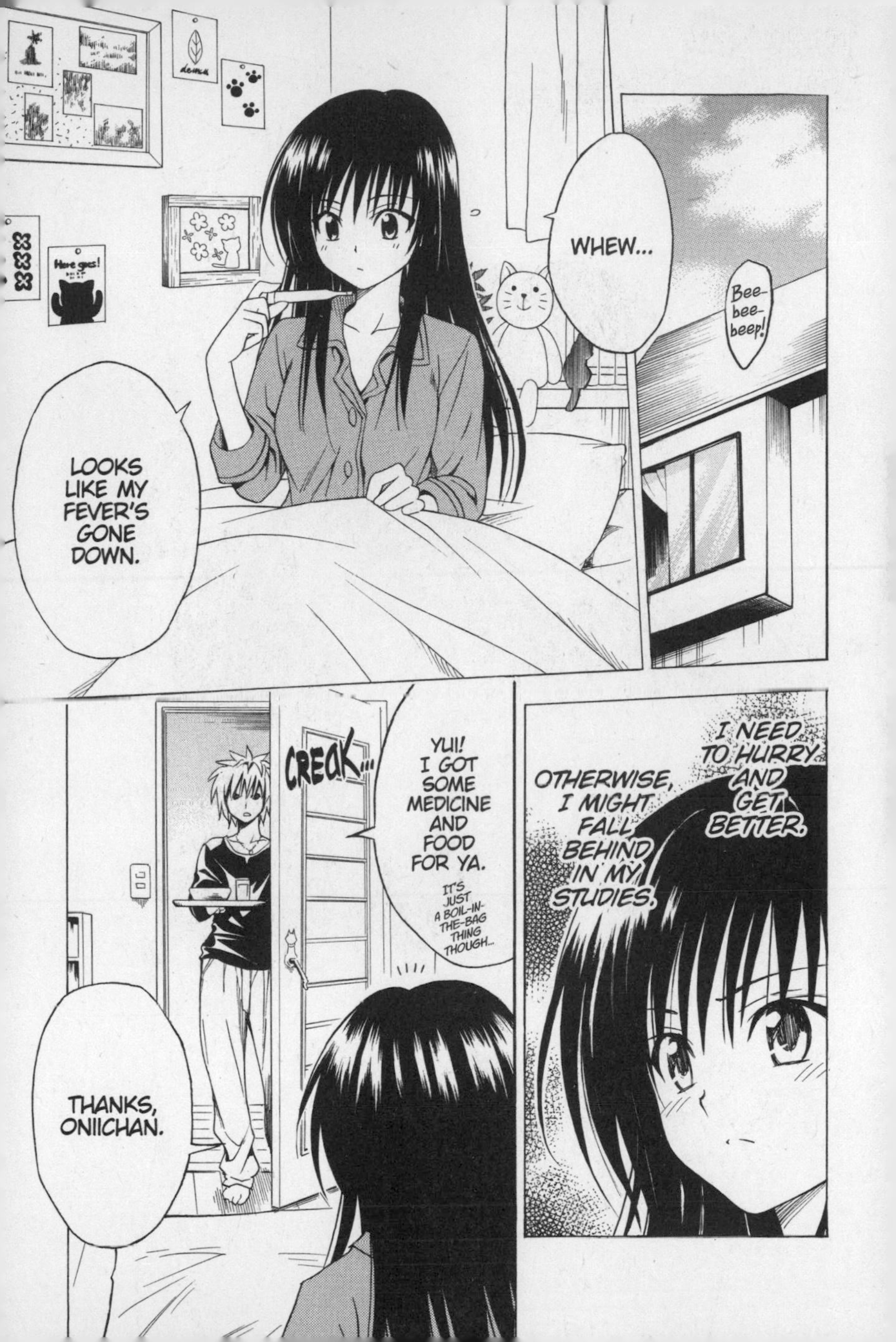
Bee-bee-beep!
WHEW...
Here goes!
LOOKS LIKE MY FEVER'S GONE DOWN.
I NEED TO HURRY AND GET BETTER.
OTHERWISE, I MIGHT FALL BEHIND IN MY STUDIES.
CREAK...
YUI! I GOT SOME MEDICINE AND FOOD FOR YA.
IT'S JUST A BOIL-IN-THE-BAG THING THOUGH...
THANKS, ONIICHAN.

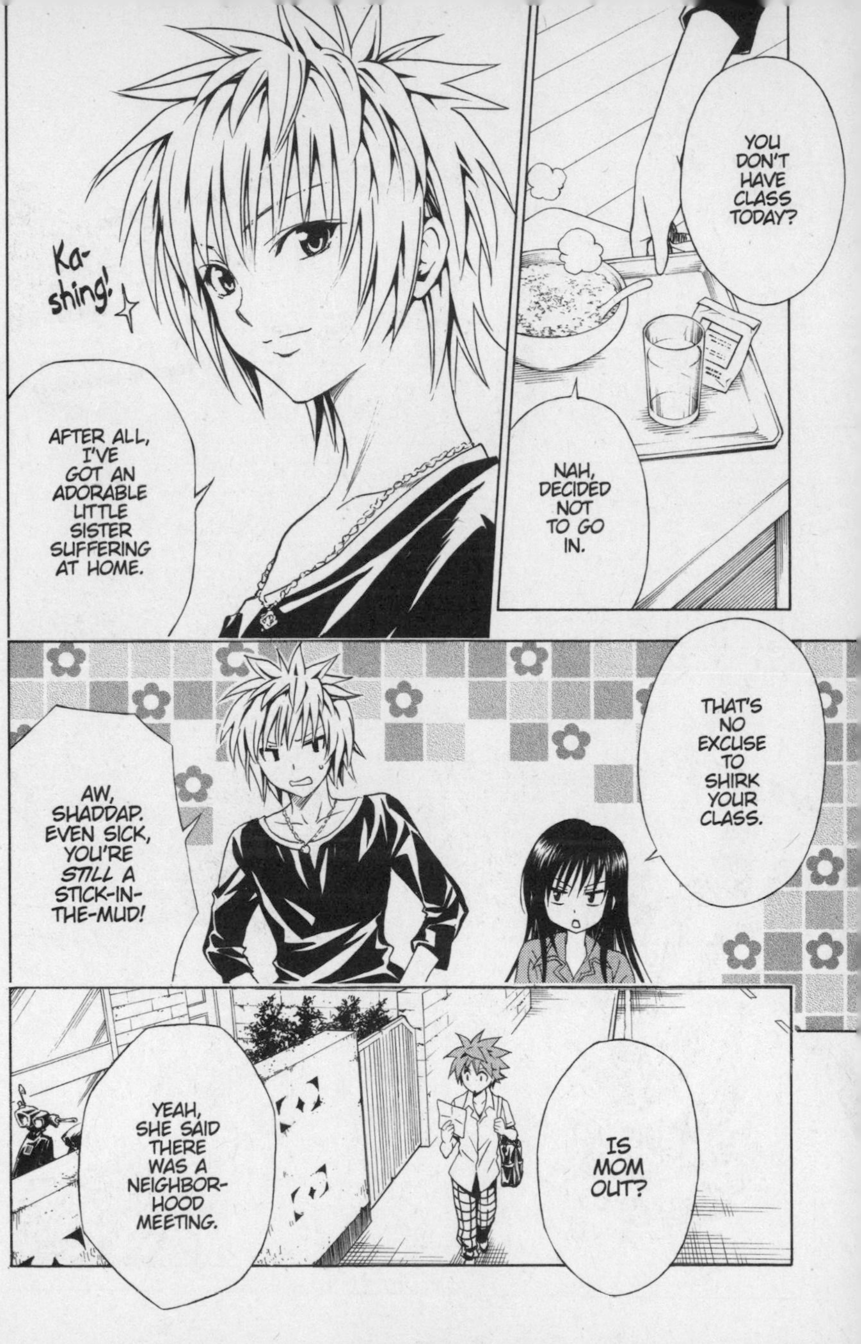

YOU DON'T HAVE CLASS TODAY?
NAH, DECIDED NOT TO GO IN.
Ka-shing!
AFTER ALL, I'VE GOT AN ADORABLE LITTLE SISTER SUFFERING AT HOME.
THAT'S NO EXCUSE TO SHIRK YOUR CLASS.
AW, SHADDAP. EVEN SICK, YOU'RE STILL A STICK-IN-THE-MUD!
IS MOM OUT?
YEAH, SHE SAID THERE WAS A NEIGHBOR-HOOD MEETING.

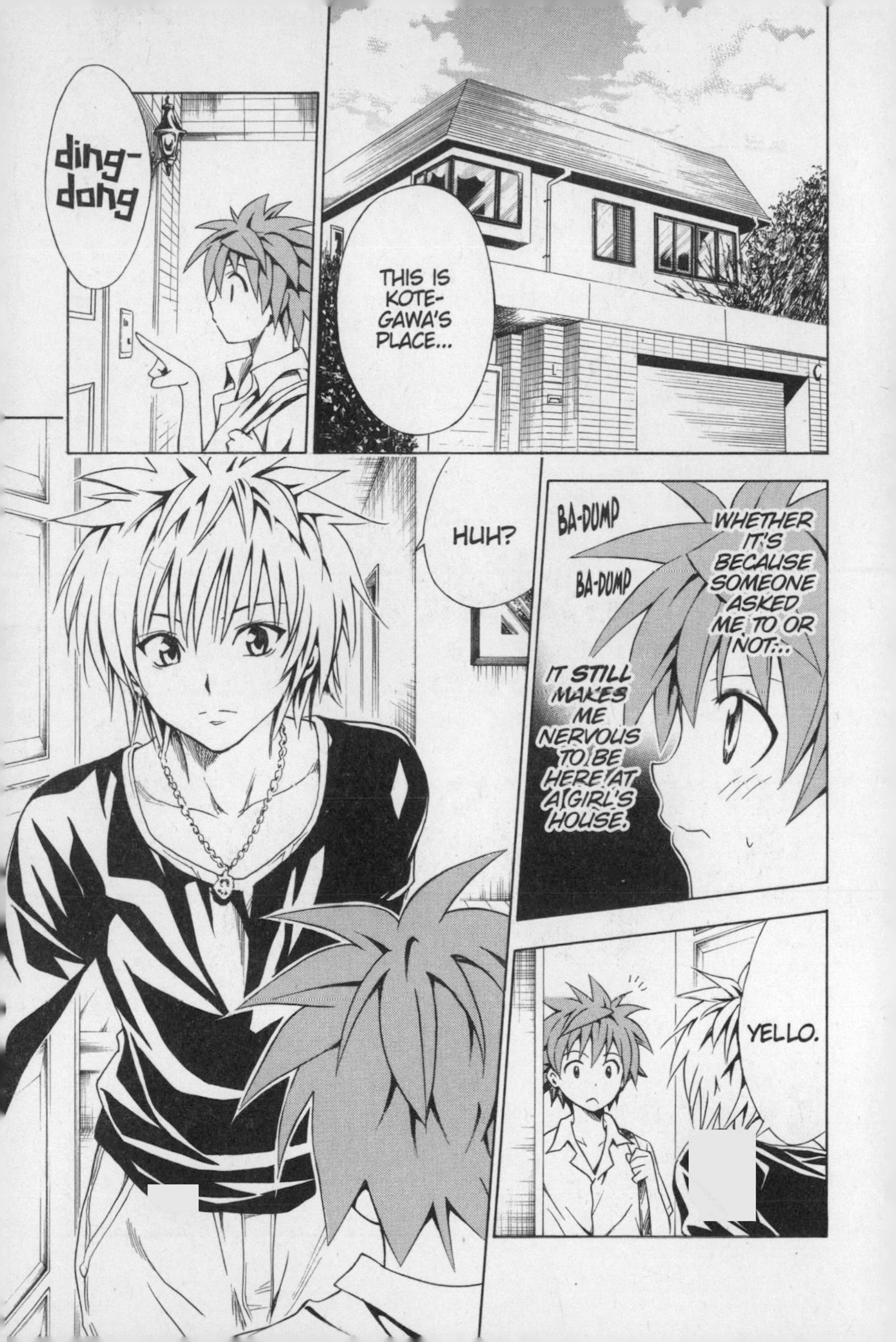
THIS IS KOTE-GAWA'S PLACE...
ding-dong
BA-DUMP
BA-DUMP
WHETHER IT'S BECAUSE SOMEONE ASKED ME TO OR NOT...
IT STILL MAKES ME NERVOUS TO BE HERE AT A GIRL'S HOUSE.
YELLO.
HUH?

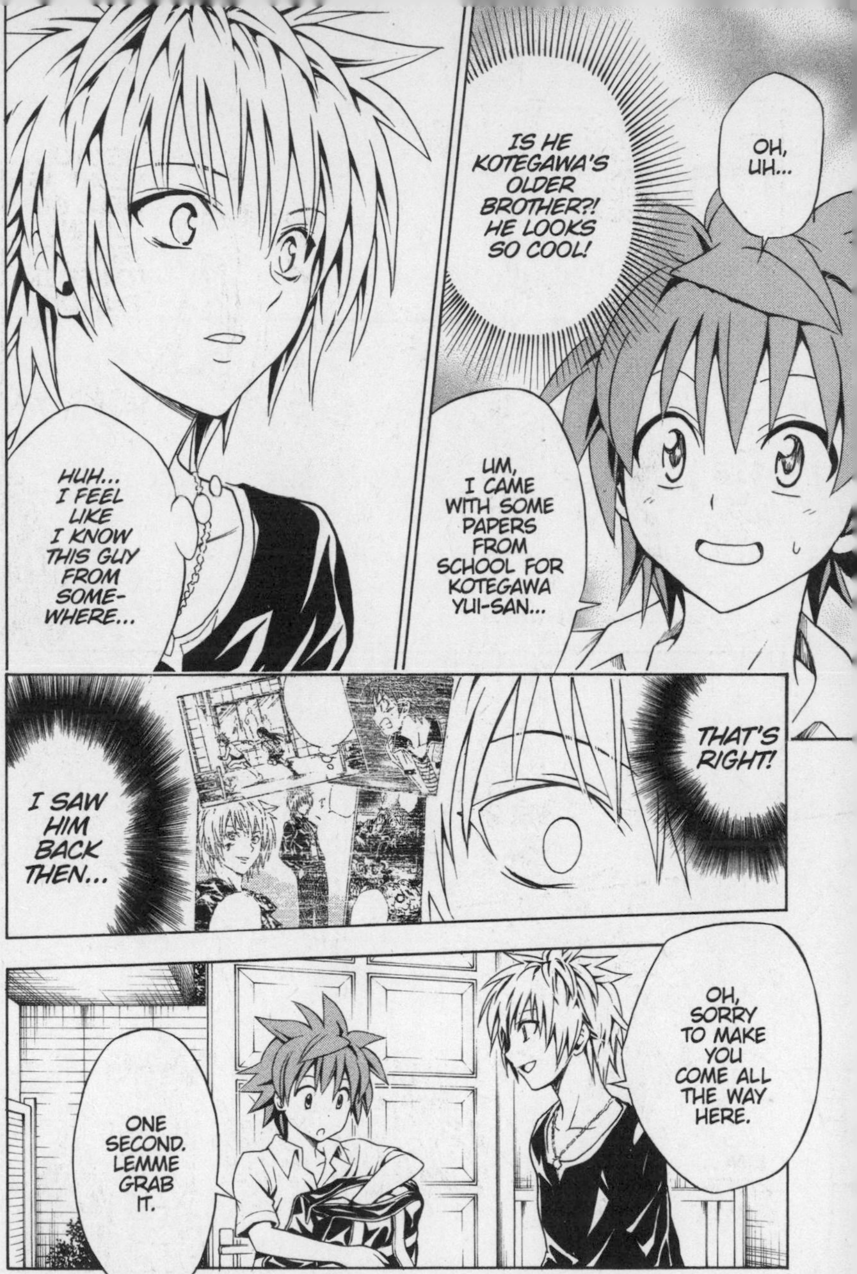
OH, UH...
IS HE KOTEGAWA'S OLDER BROTHER?! HE LOOKS SO COOL!
UM, I CAME WITH SOME PAPERS FROM SCHOOL FOR KOTEGAWA YUI-SAN...
HUH... I FEEL LIKE I KNOW THIS GUY FROM SOME-WHERE...
THAT'S RIGHT!
I SAW HIM BACK THEN...
OH, SORRY TO MAKE YOU COME ALL THE WAY HERE.
ONE SECOND. LEMME GRAB IT.

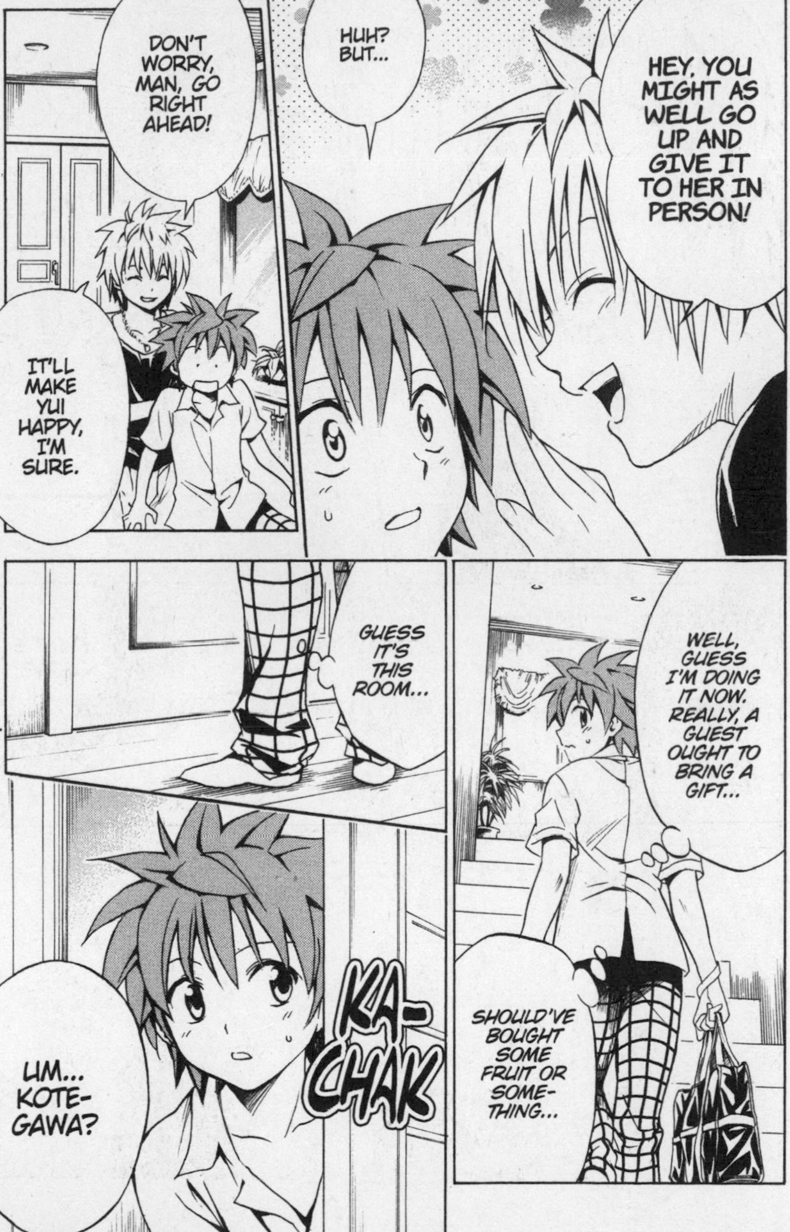
HEY, YOU MIGHT AS WELL GO UP AND GIVE IT TO HER IN PERSON!
HUH? BUT...
DON'T WORRY, MAN, GO RIGHT AHEAD!
IT'LL MAKE YUI HAPPY, I'M SURE.
WELL, GUESS I'M DOING IT NOW. REALLY, A GUEST OUGHT TO BRING A GIFT...
SHOULD'VE BOUGHT SOME FRUIT OR SOME-THING...
GUESS IT'S THIS ROOM...
KA-CHAK
UM... KOTE-GAWA?

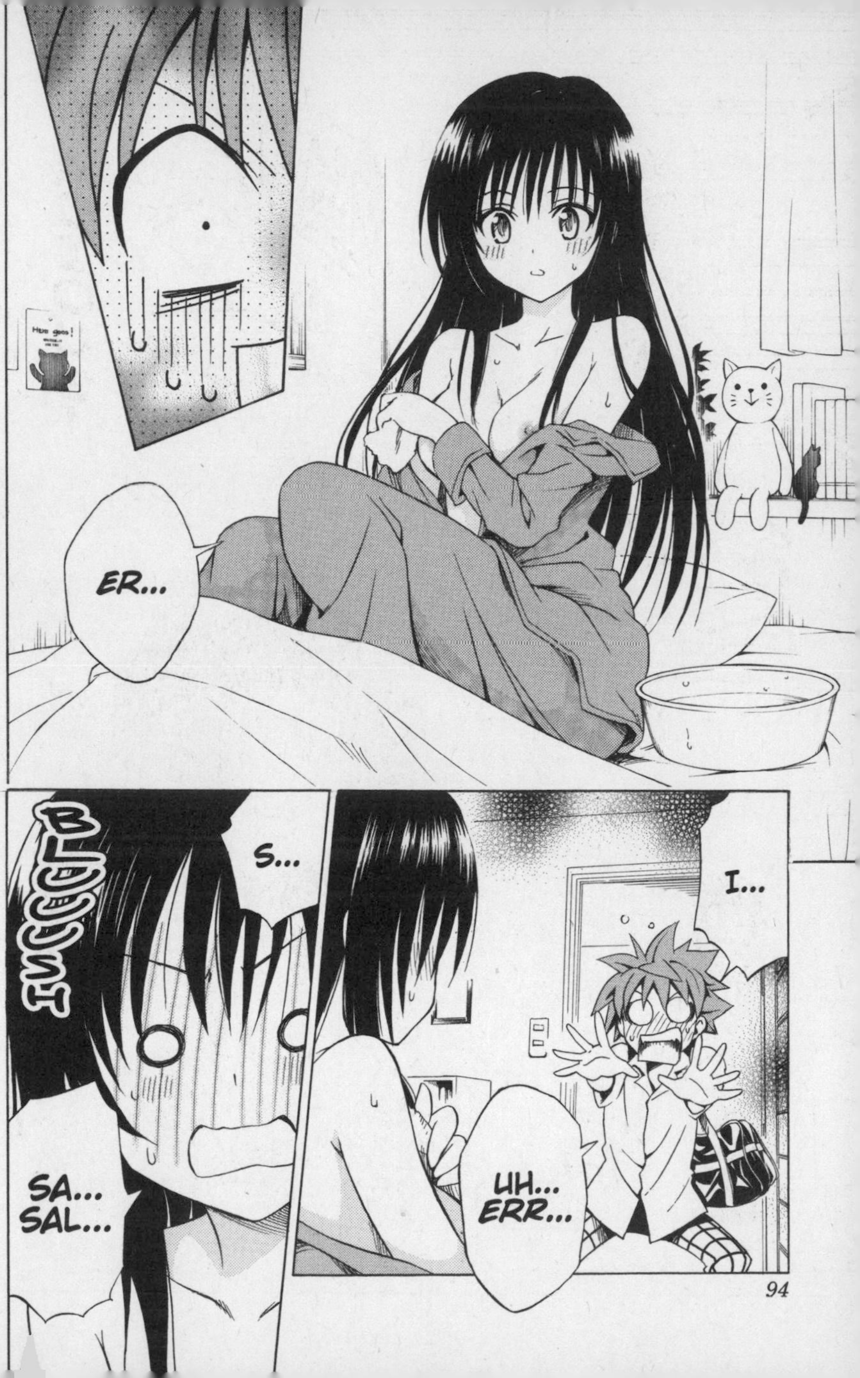
ER...
I...
UH... ERR...
S...
BLUUUSH
SA... SAL...

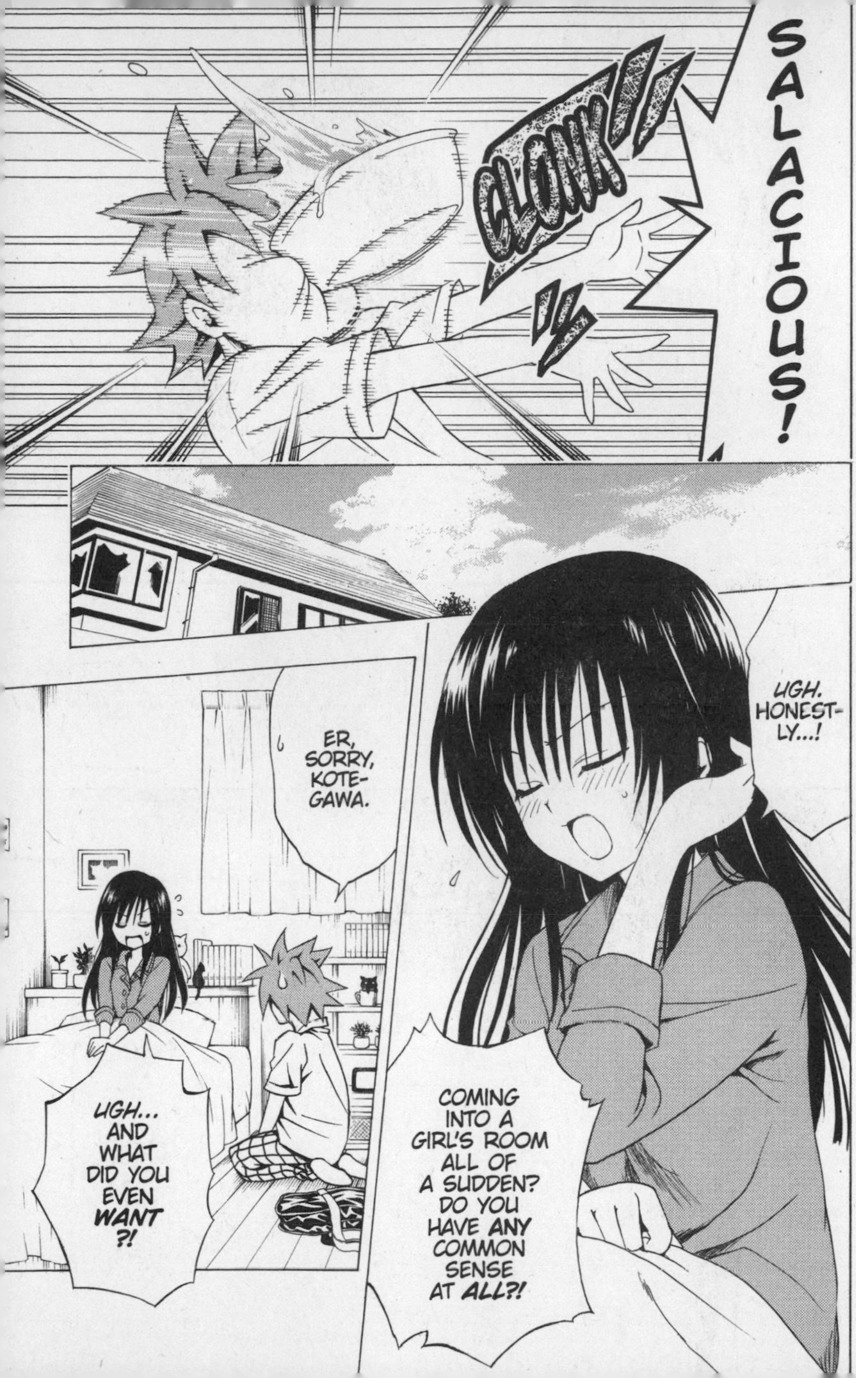
SALACIOUS!
CLONK!!
UGH. HONESTLY...!
COMING INTO A GIRL'S ROOM ALL OF A SUDDEN? DO YOU HAVE ANY COMMON SENSE AT ALL?!
ER, SORRY, KOTEGAWA.
UGH... AND WHAT DID YOU EVEN WANT?!

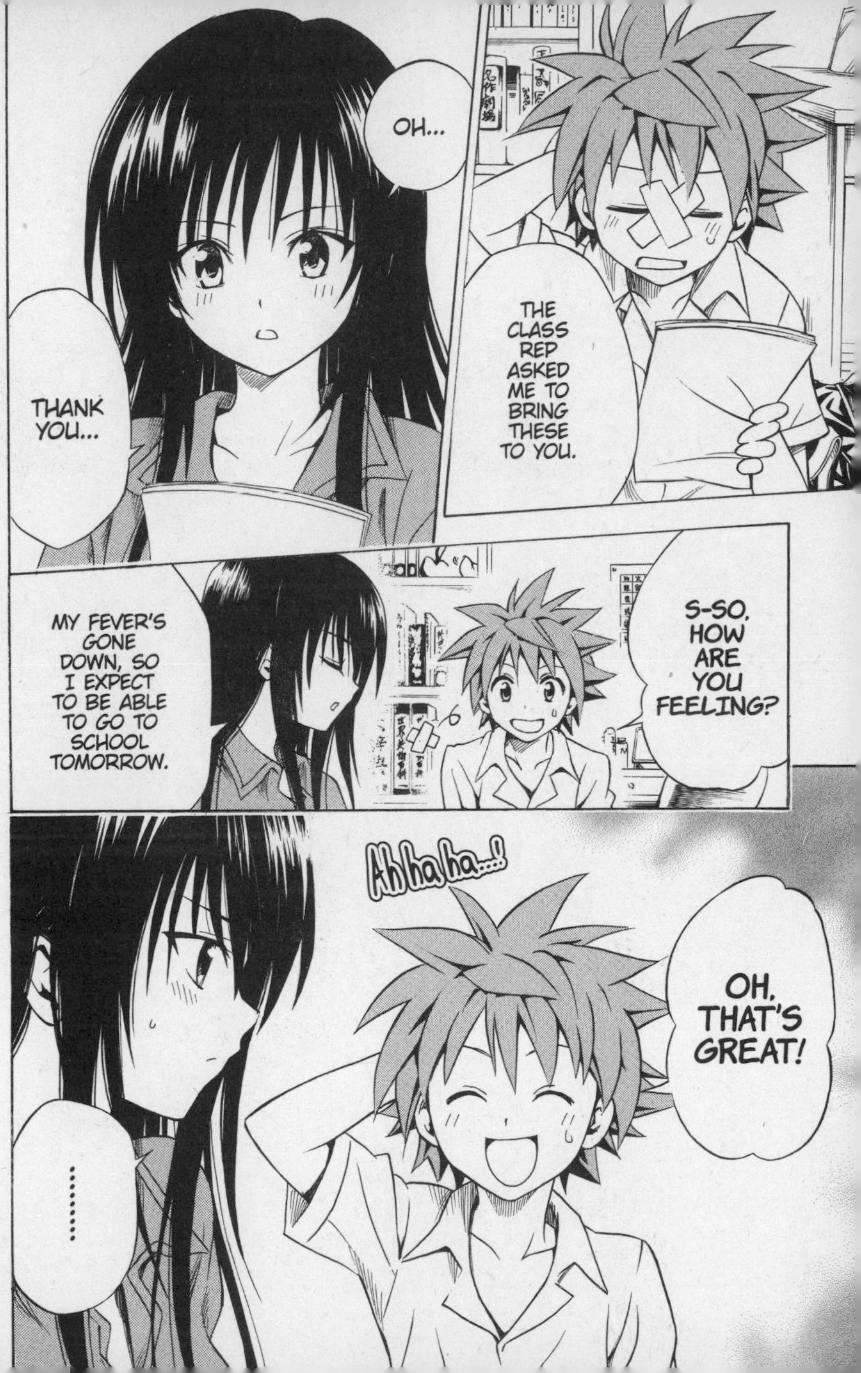
THE CLASS REP ASKED ME TO BRING THESE TO YOU.
OH...
THANK YOU...
S-SO, HOW ARE YOU FEELING?
MY FEVER'S GONE DOWN, SO I EXPECT TO BE ABLE TO GO TO SCHOOL TOMORROW.
Ah ha ha...!
OH, THAT'S GREAT!
....

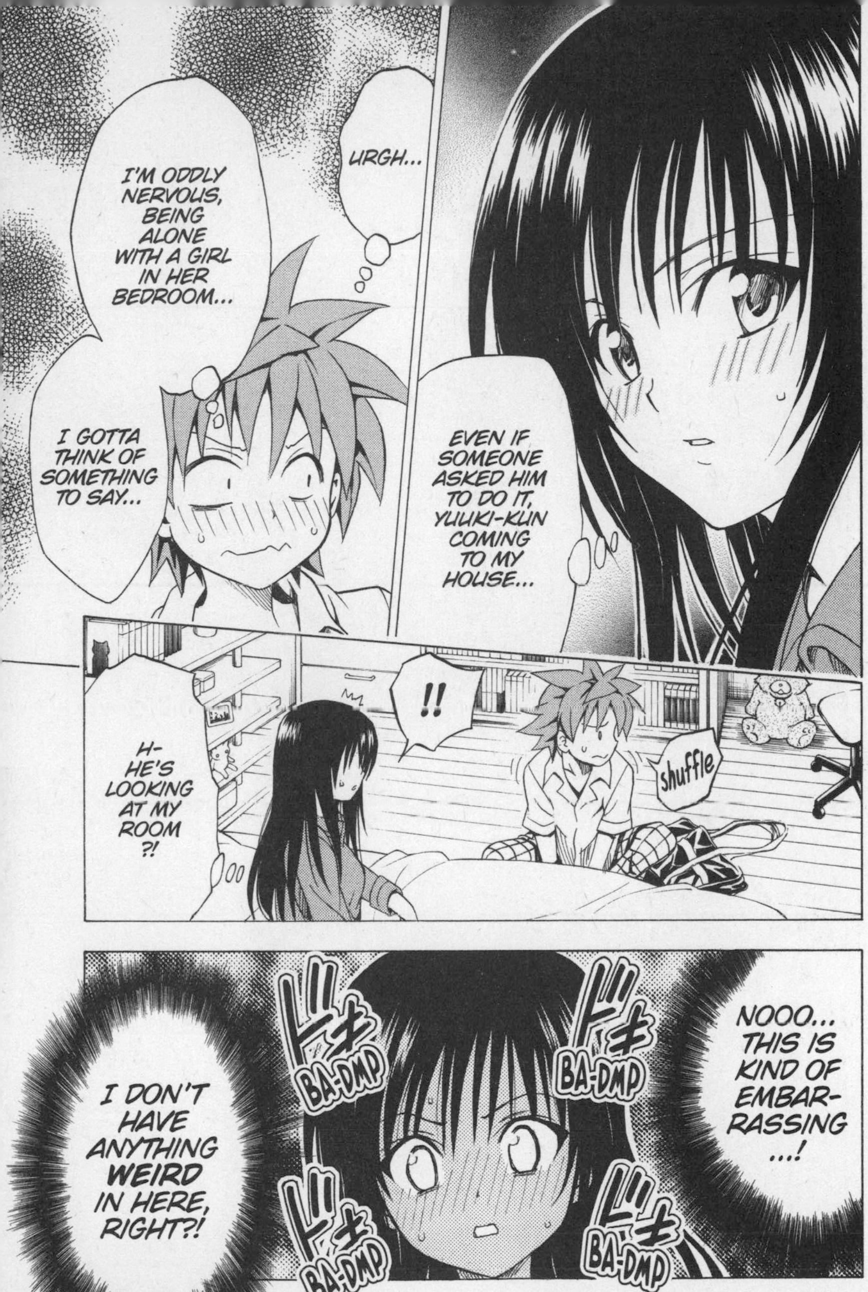
EVEN IF SOMEONE ASKED HIM TO DO IT, YUUKI-KUN COMING TO MY HOUSE...
URGH...
I'M ODDLY NERVOUS, BEING ALONE WITH A GIRL IN HER BEDROOM...
I GOTTA THINK OF SOMETHING TO SAY...
shuffle
!!
H-HE'S LOOKING AT MY ROOM?!
NOOO... THIS IS KIND OF EMBARRASSING...!
ドキ BA-DMP
ドキ BA-DMP
ドキ BA-DMP
ドキ BA-DMP
I DON'T HAVE ANYTHING WEIRD IN HERE, RIGHT?!

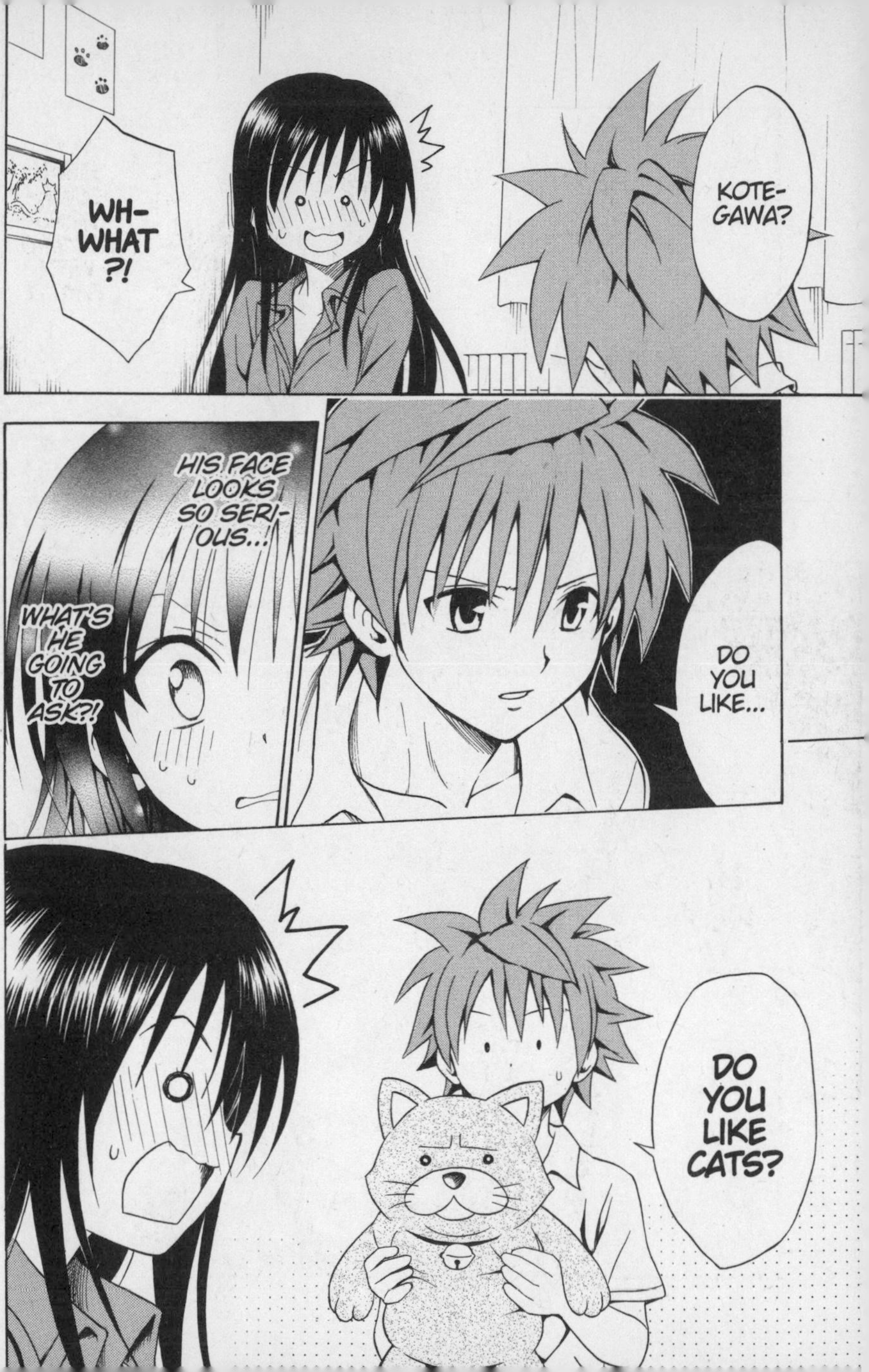
KOTE-GAWA?
WH-WHAT?!
DO YOU LIKE...
HIS FACE LOOKS SO SERI-OUS...!
WHAT'S HE GOING TO ASK?!
DO YOU LIKE CATS?

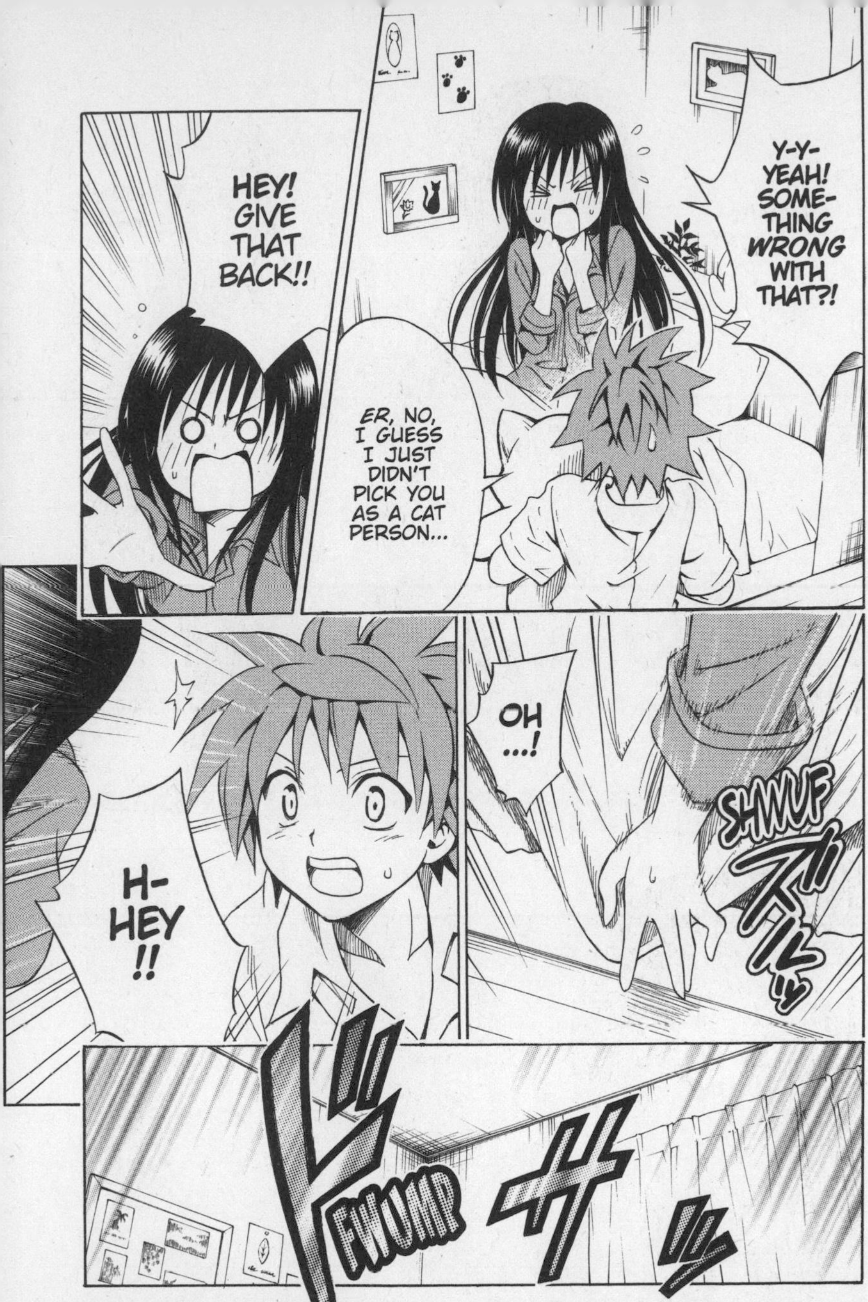
Y-Y-YEAH! SOMETHING WRONG WITH THAT?!
ER, NO, I GUESS I JUST DIDN'T PICK YOU AS A CAT PERSON...
HEY! GIVE THAT BACK!!
OH ...!
SHWUF
H-HEY !!
FWUMP

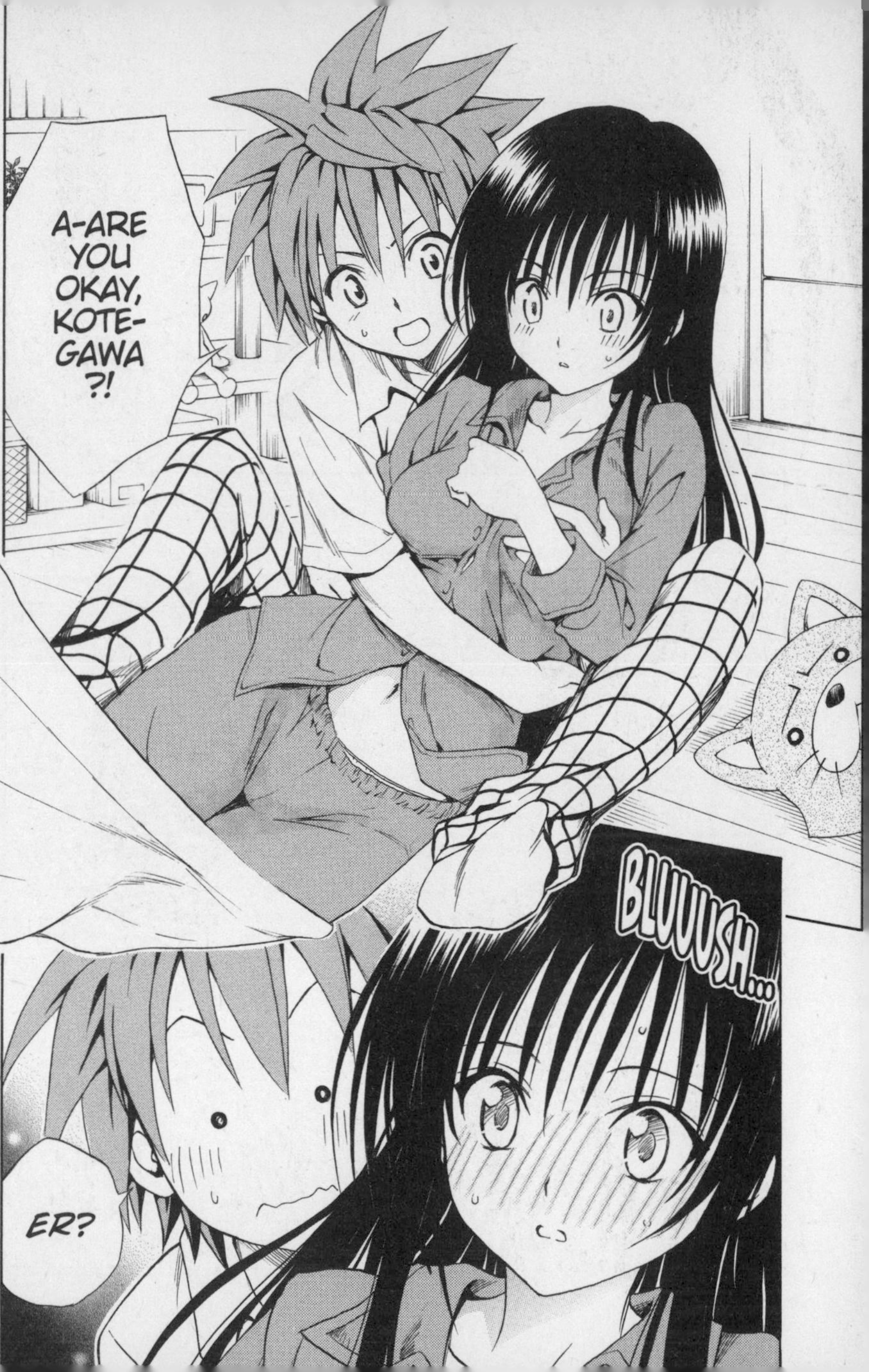
A-ARE YOU OKAY, KOTE-GAWA ?!
BLUUUSH...
ER?

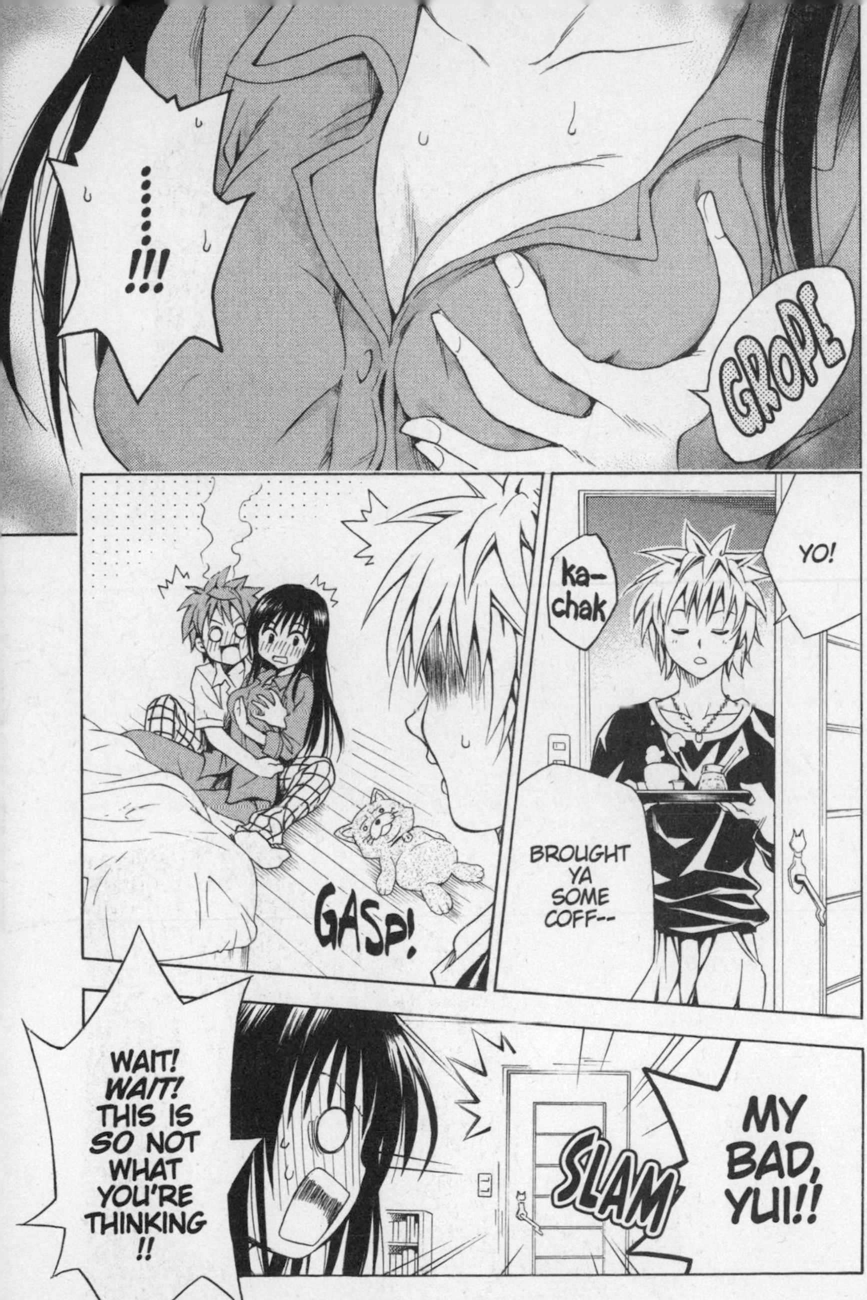

GROPE
......!!!
YO!
ka-chak
BROUGHT YA SOME COFF--
GASP!
MY BAD, YUI!!
SLAM
WAIT! WAIT! THIS IS SO NOT WHAT YOU'RE THINKING!!

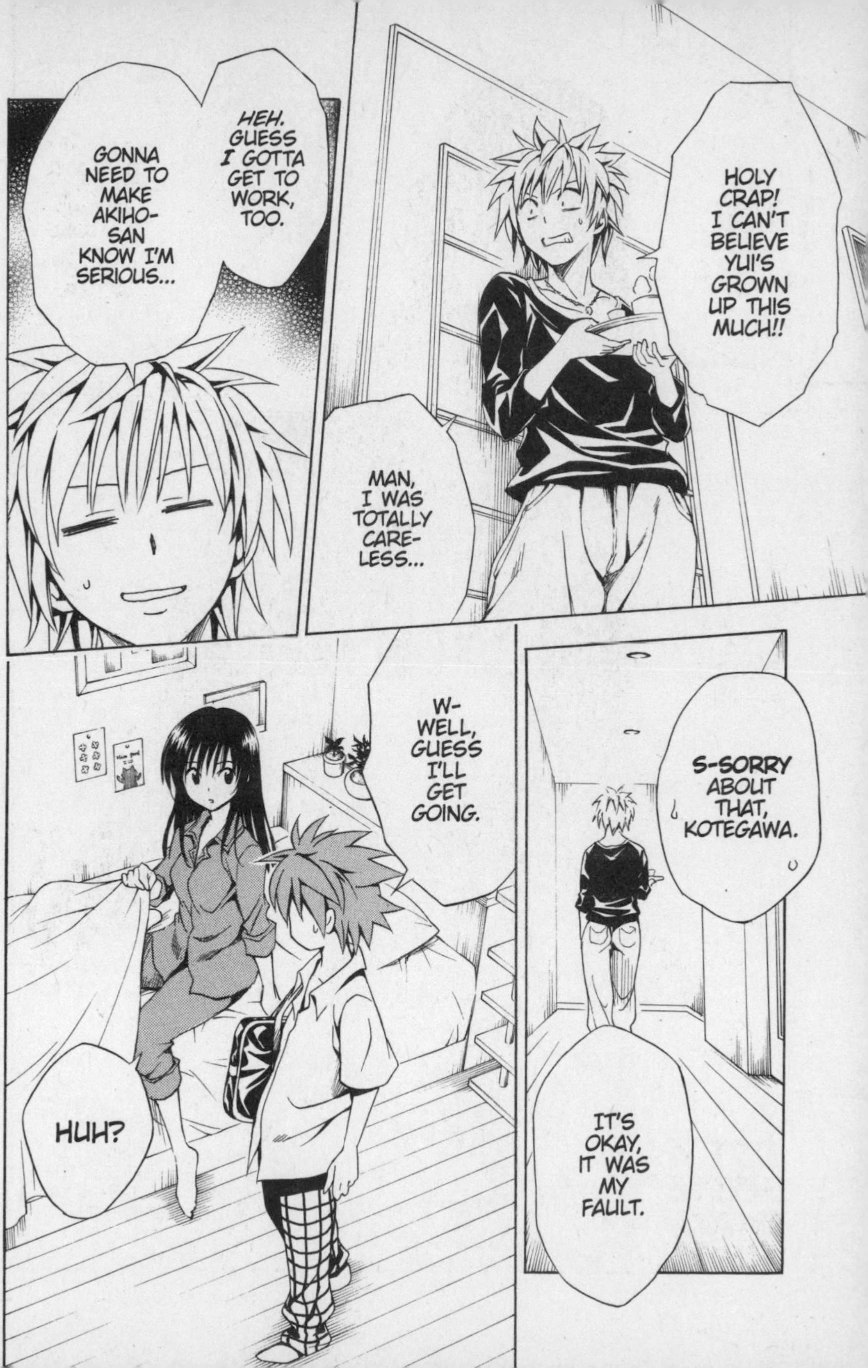
HOLY CRAP! I CAN'T BELIEVE YUI'S GROWN UP THIS MUCH!!
MAN, I WAS TOTALLY CARE-LESS...
HEH. GUESS I GOTTA GET TO WORK, TOO.
GONNA NEED TO MAKE AKIHO-SAN KNOW I'M SERIOUS...
S-SORRY ABOUT THAT, KOTEGAWA.
IT'S OKAY, IT WAS MY FAULT.
W-WELL, GUESS I'LL GET GOING.
HUH?

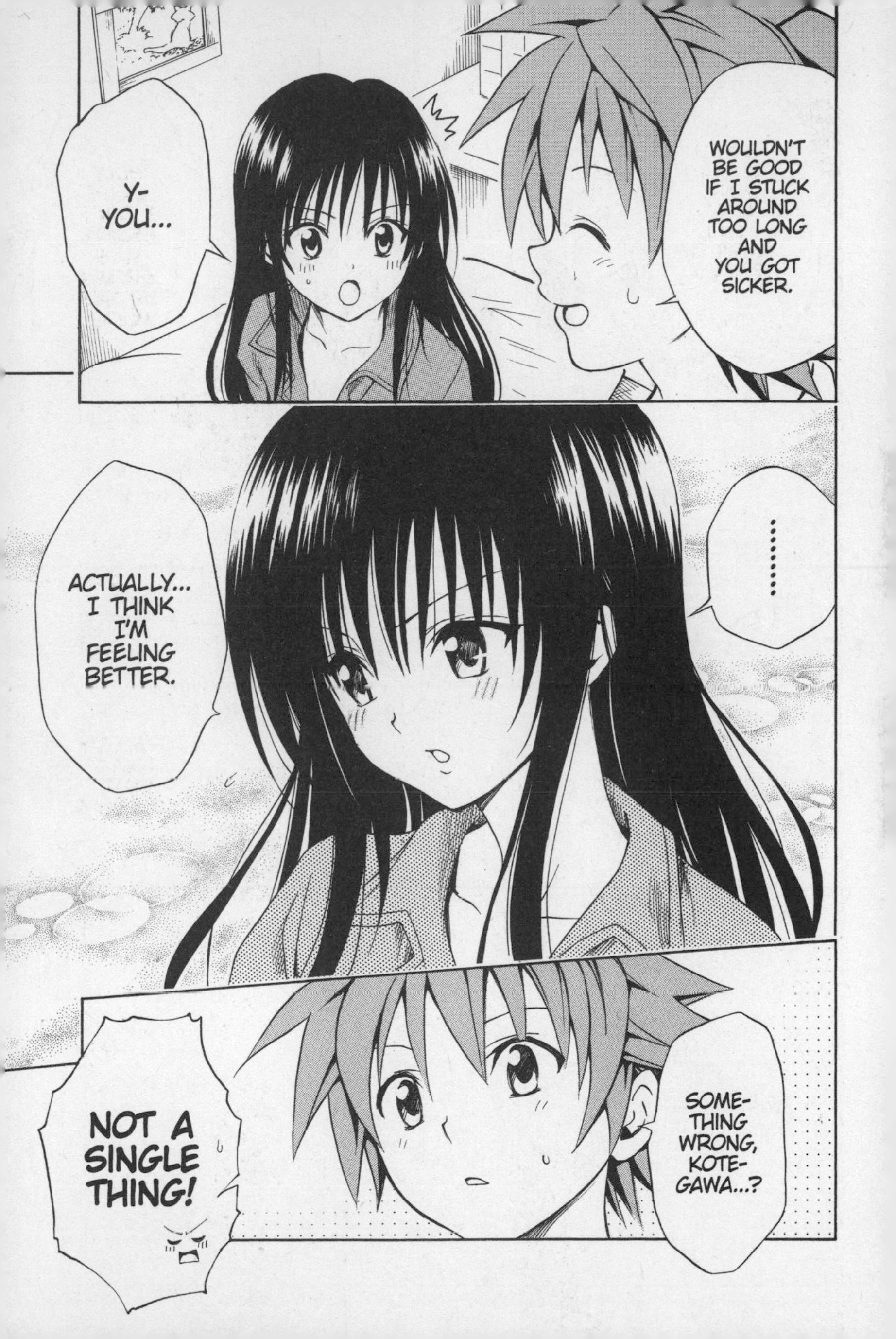
WOULDN'T BE GOOD IF I STUCK AROUND TOO LONG AND YOU GOT SICKER.
Y- YOU...
......
ACTUALLY... I THINK I'M FEELING BETTER.
SOME- THING WRONG, KOTE- GAWA...?
NOT A SINGLE THING!

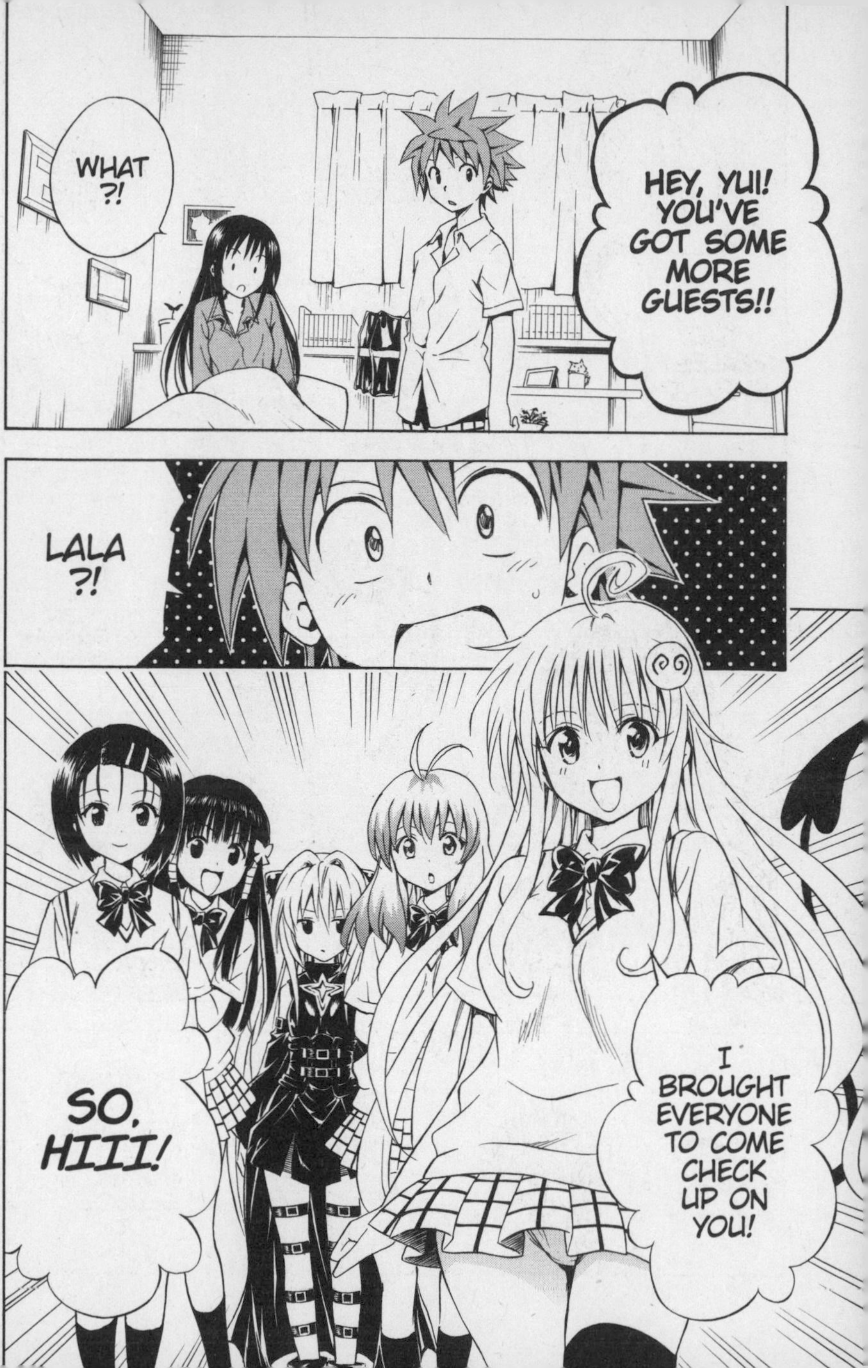
HEY, YUI! YOU'VE GOT SOME MORE GUESTS!!
WHAT ?!
LALA ?!
I BROUGHT EVERYONE TO COME CHECK UP ON YOU!
SO, HIII!

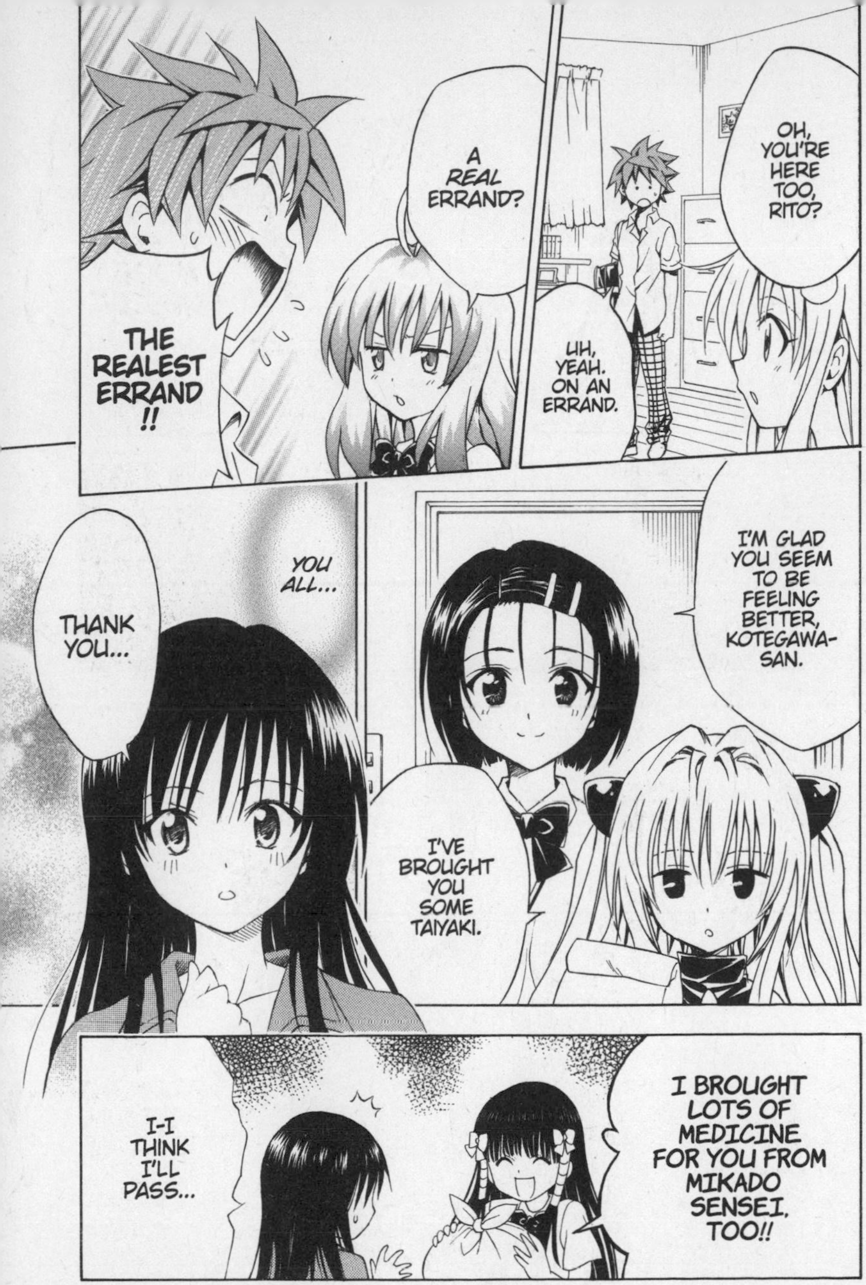
OH, YOU'RE HERE TOO, RITO?
UH, YEAH. ON AN ERRAND.
A REAL ERRAND?
THE REALEST ERRAND !!
I'M GLAD YOU SEEM TO BE FEELING BETTER, KOTEGAWA-SAN.
I'VE BROUGHT YOU SOME TAIYAKI.
YOU ALL...
THANK YOU...
I BROUGHT LOTS OF MEDICINE FOR YOU FROM MIKADO SENSEI, TOO!!
I-I THINK I'LL PASS...

To LOVE Ru

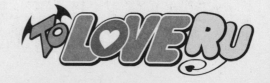

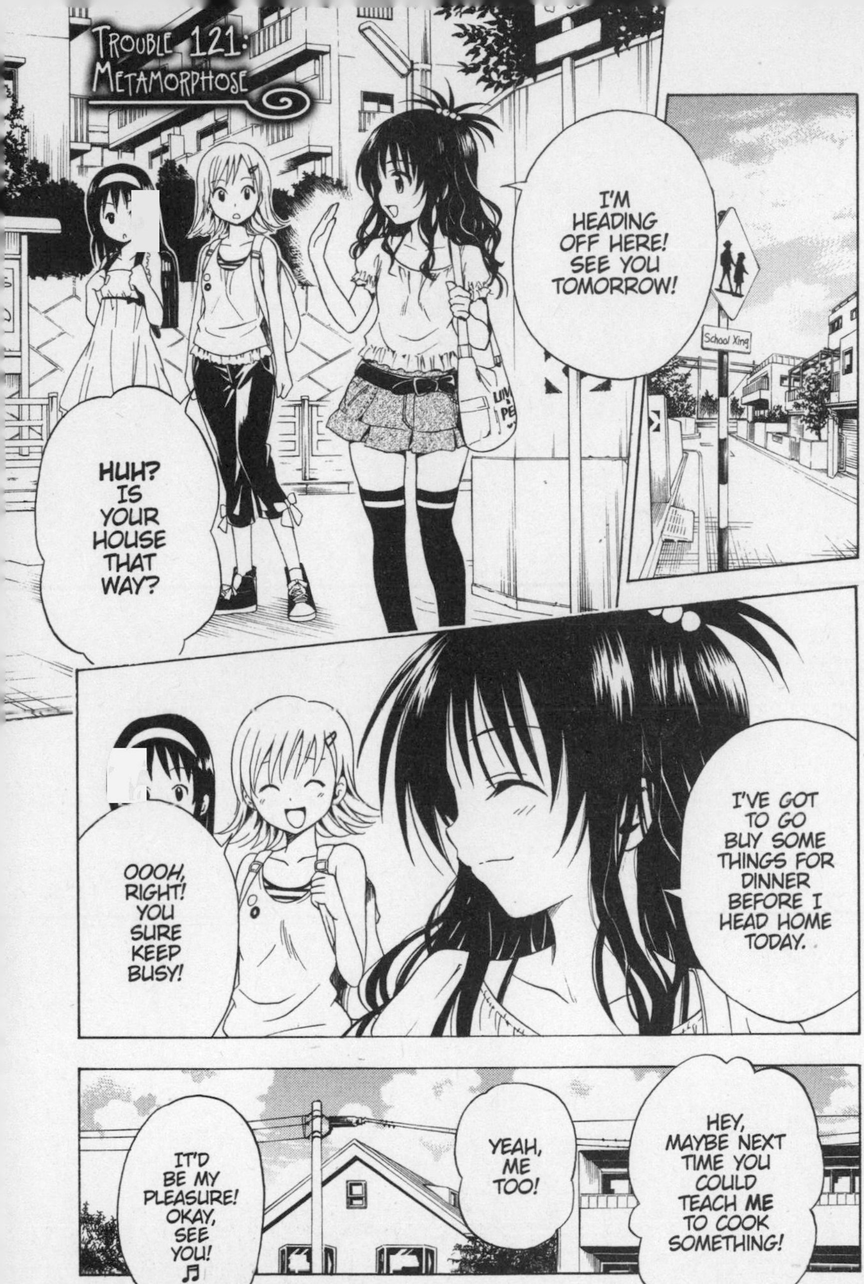
Trouble 121: Metamorphose
I'M HEADING OFF HERE! SEE YOU TOMORROW!
School Xing
HUH? IS YOUR HOUSE THAT WAY?
I'VE GOT TO GO BUY SOME THINGS FOR DINNER BEFORE I HEAD HOME TODAY.
OOOH, RIGHT! YOU SURE KEEP BUSY!
HEY, MAYBE NEXT TIME YOU COULD TEACH ME TO COOK SOMETHING!
YEAH, ME TOO!
IT'D BE MY PLEASURE! OKAY, SEE YOU! ♫

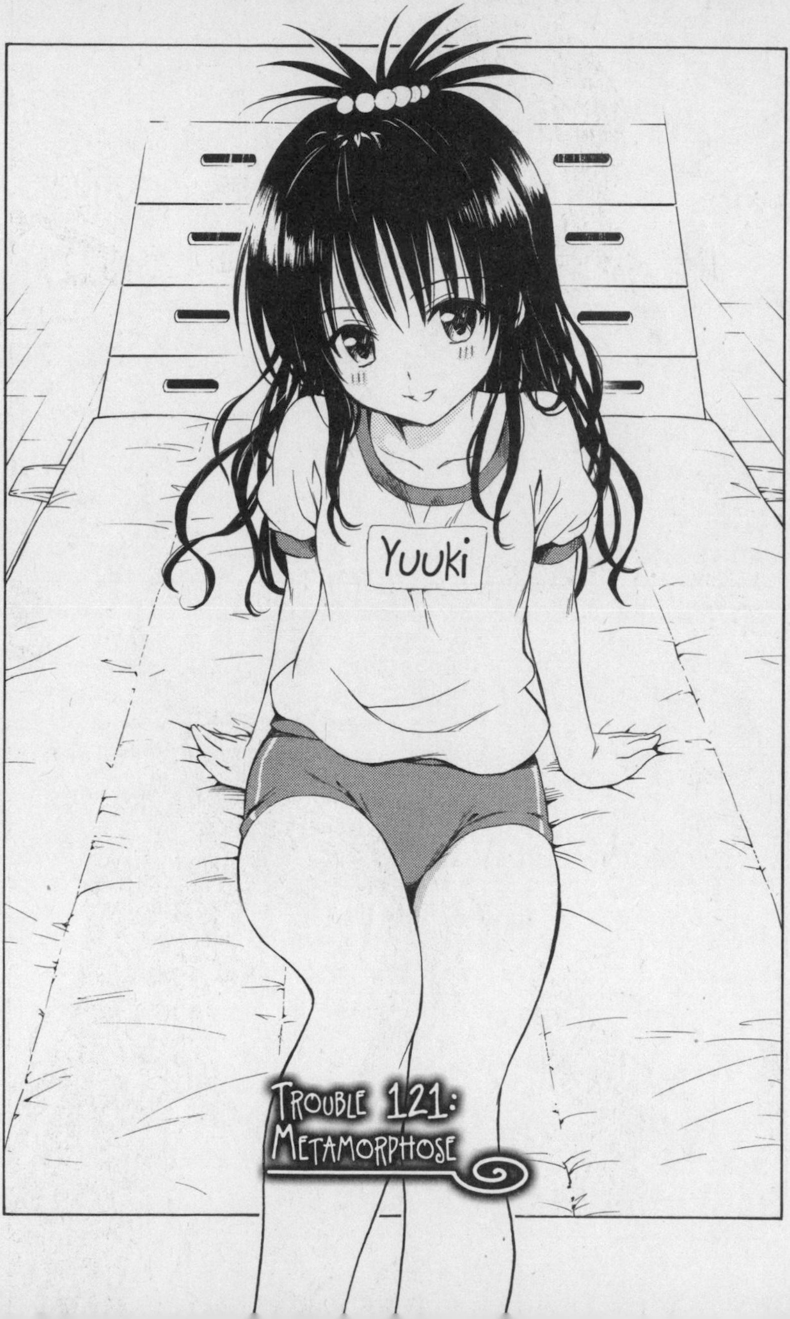
Yuuki
Trouble 121:
Metamorphose

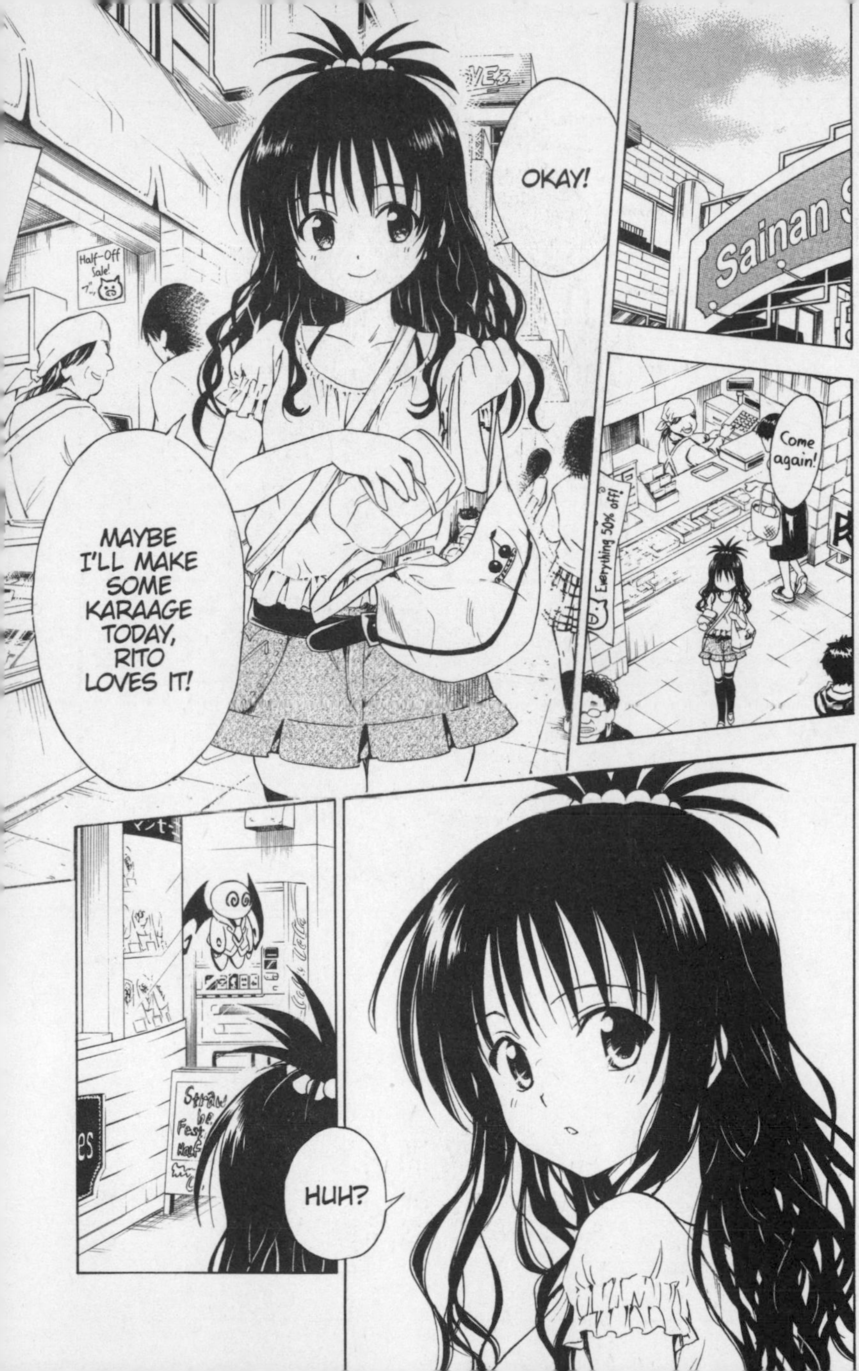

Sainan
Come again!
Everything 50% off!
OKAY!
MAYBE I'LL MAKE SOME KARAAGE TODAY, RITO LOVES IT!
Half-Off Sale!
HUH?

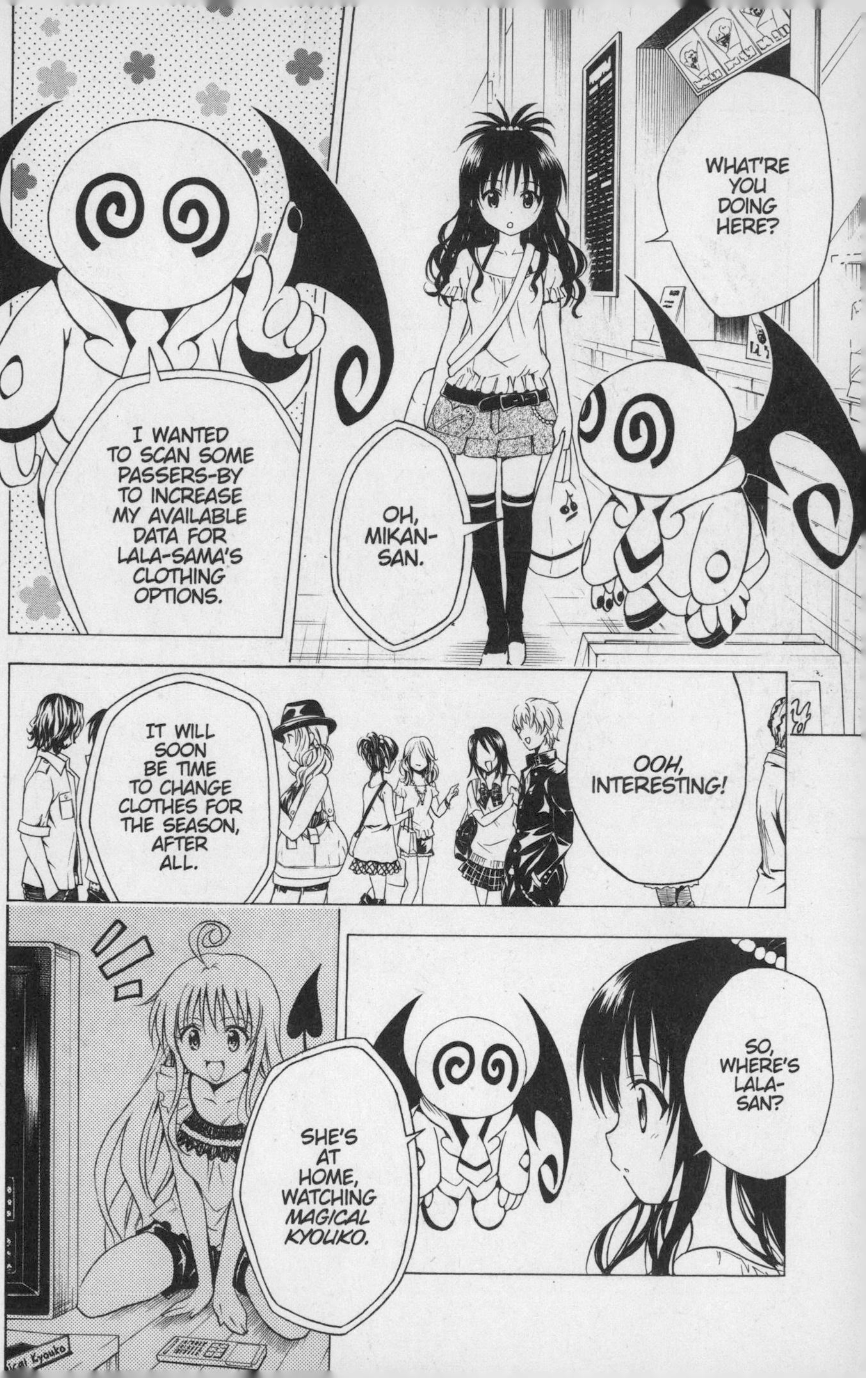
WHAT'RE YOU DOING HERE?
OH, MIKAN-SAN.
I WANTED TO SCAN SOME PASSERS-BY TO INCREASE MY AVAILABLE DATA FOR LALA-SAMA'S CLOTHING OPTIONS.
OOH, INTERESTING!
IT WILL SOON BE TIME TO CHANGE CLOTHES FOR THE SEASON, AFTER ALL.
SO, WHERE'S LALA-SAN?
SHE'S AT HOME, WATCHING MAGICAL KYOUKO.

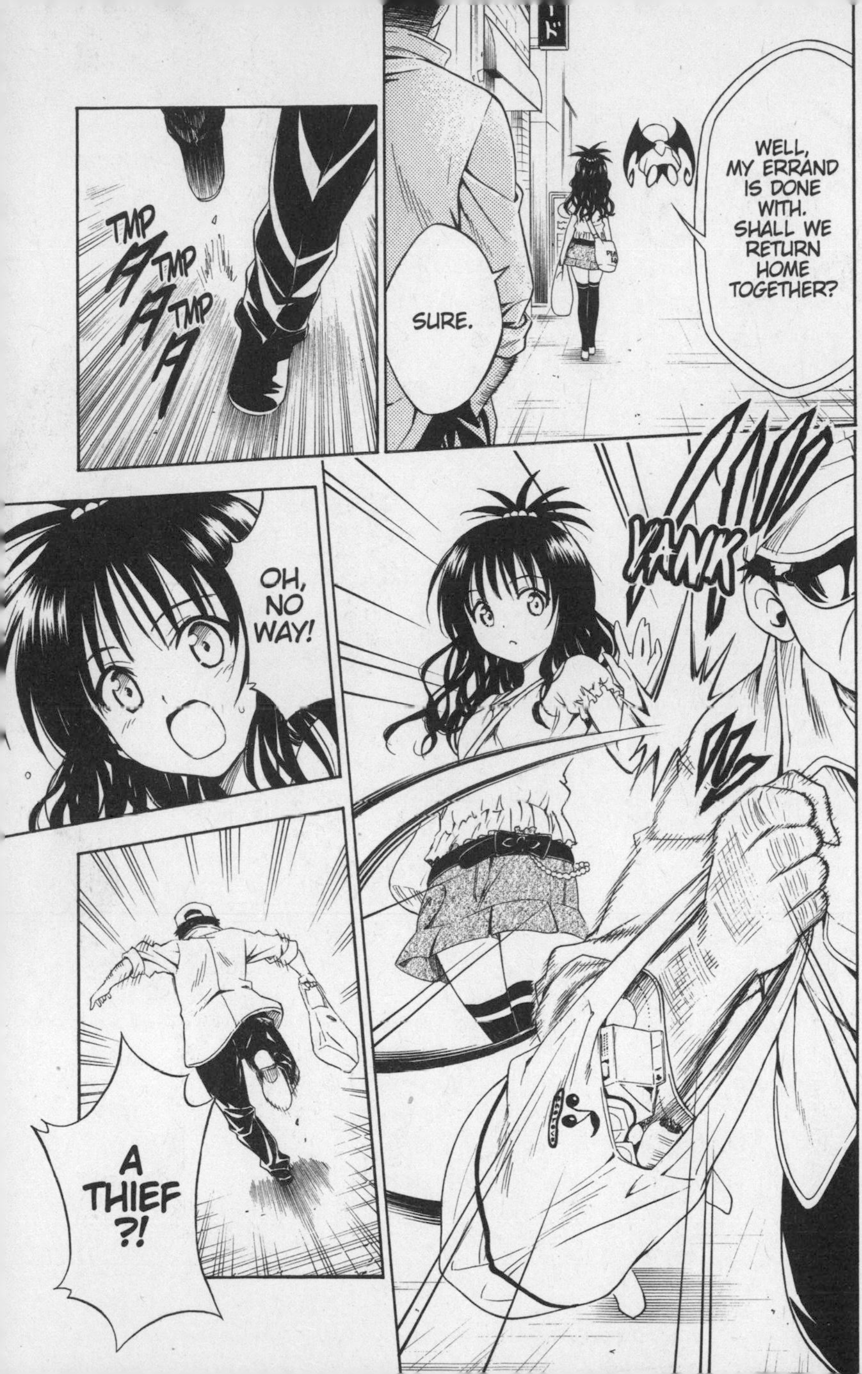
WELL, MY ERRAND IS DONE WITH. SHALL WE RETURN HOME TOGETHER?
SURE.
TMP
TMP
TMP
YANK
OH, NO WAY!
A THIEF?!

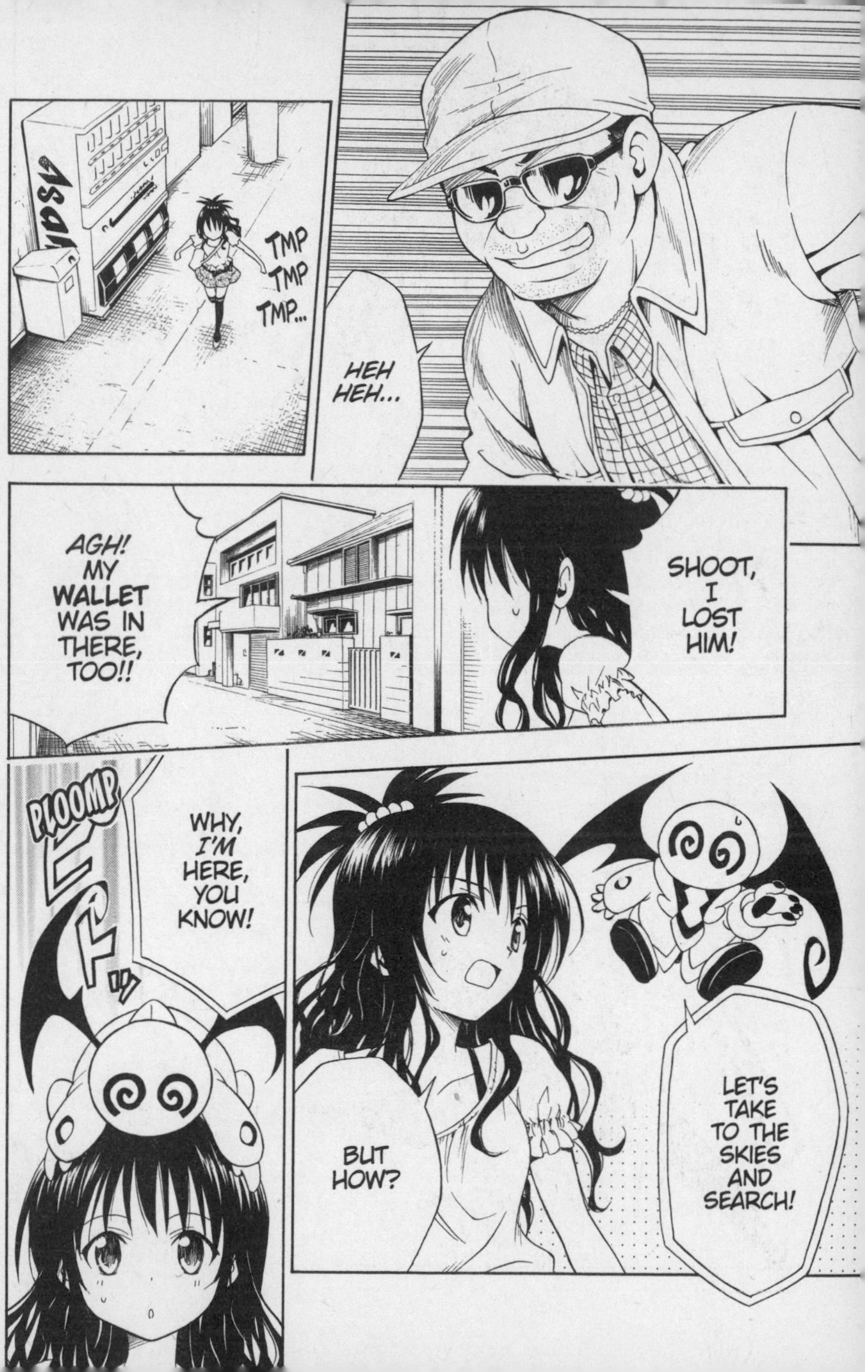
HEH HEH...
TMP TMP TMP...
SHOOT, I LOST HIM!
AGH! MY WALLET WAS IN THERE, TOO!!
LET'S TAKE TO THE SKIES AND SEARCH!
BUT HOW?
PLOOMP
WHY, I'M HERE, YOU KNOW!

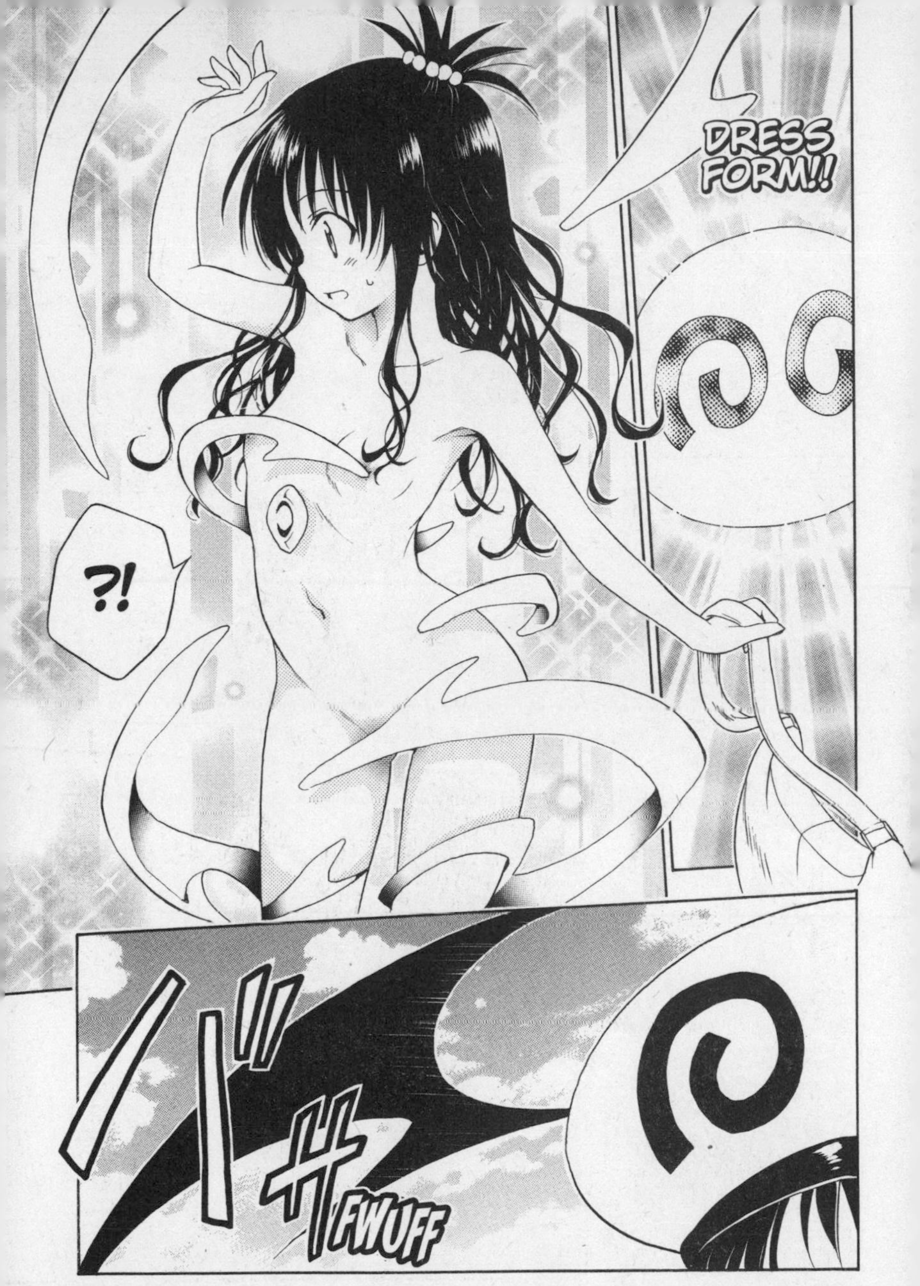
DRESS FORM!!
?!
FWUFF

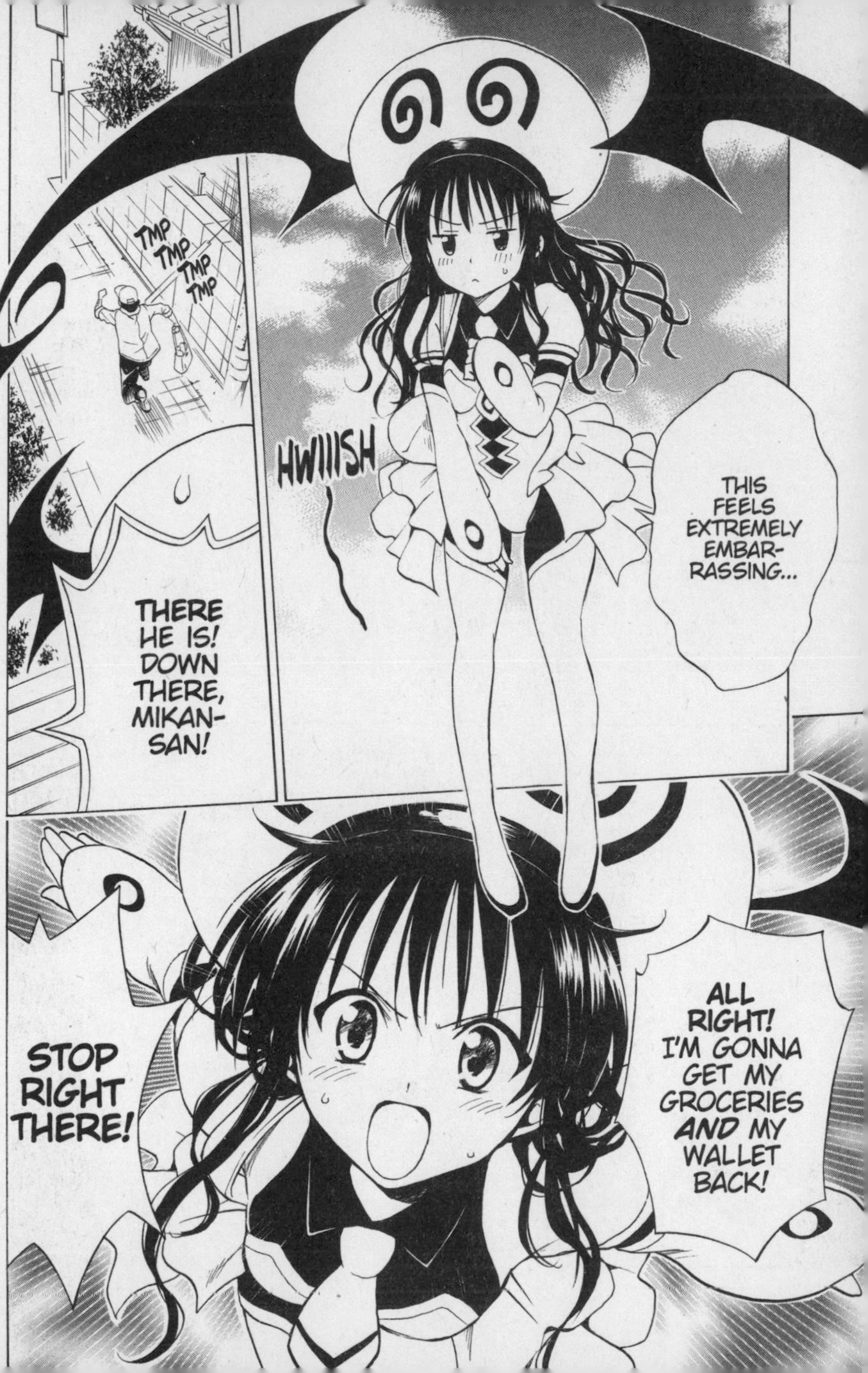
THIS FEELS EXTREMELY EMBAR-RASSING...
HWIIISH
TMP TMP TMP TMP
THERE HE IS! DOWN THERE, MIKAN-SAN!
ALL RIGHT! I'M GONNA GET MY GROCERIES AND MY WALLET BACK!
STOP RIGHT THERE!

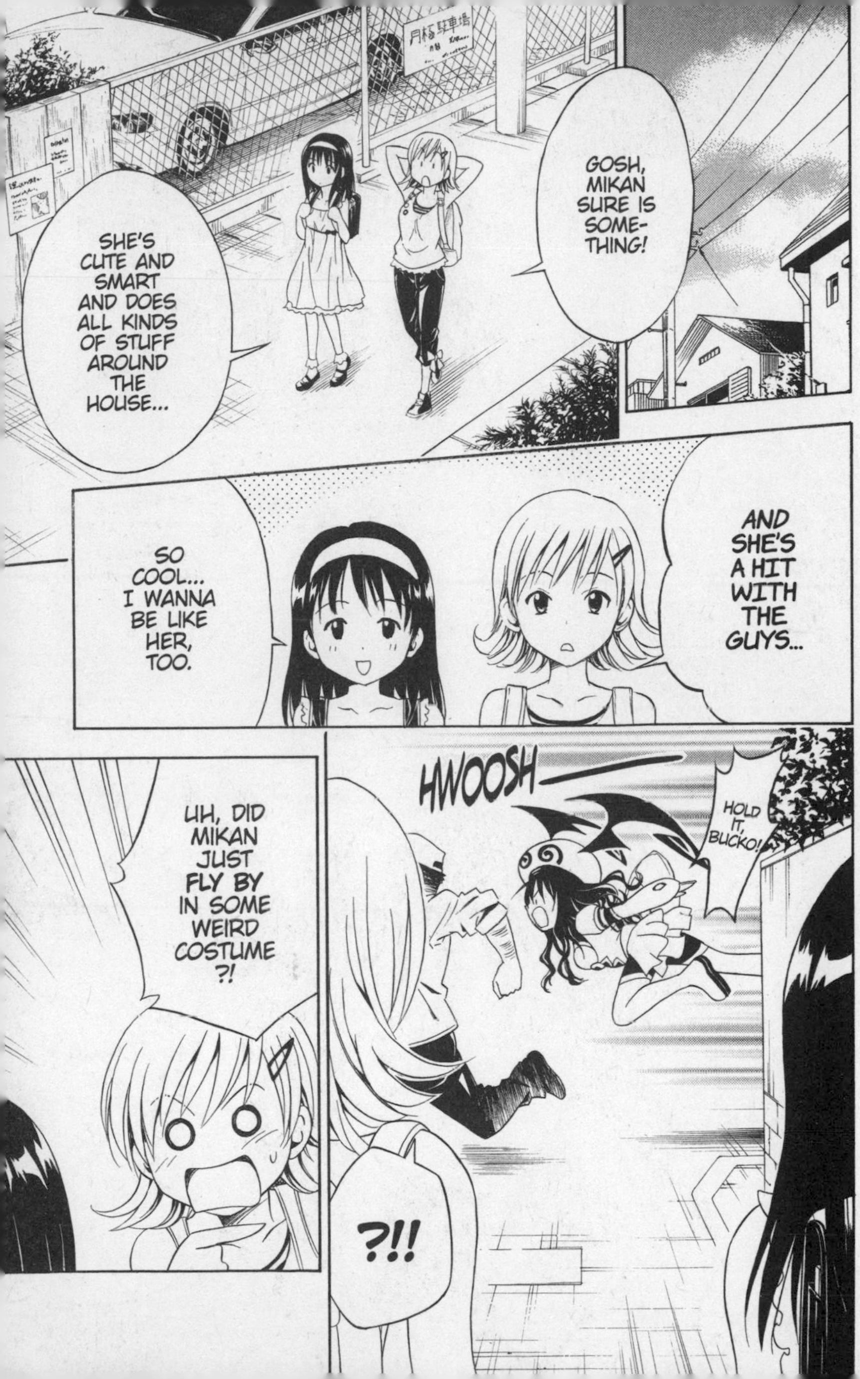
月極駐車場
GOSH, MIKAN SURE IS SOME-THING!
SHE'S CUTE AND SMART AND DOES ALL KINDS OF STUFF AROUND THE HOUSE...
AND SHE'S A HIT WITH THE GUYS...
SO COOL... I WANNA BE LIKE HER, TOO.
HWOOSH—
HOLD IT, BUCKO!
?!!
UH, DID MIKAN JUST FLY BY IN SOME WEIRD COSTUME?!

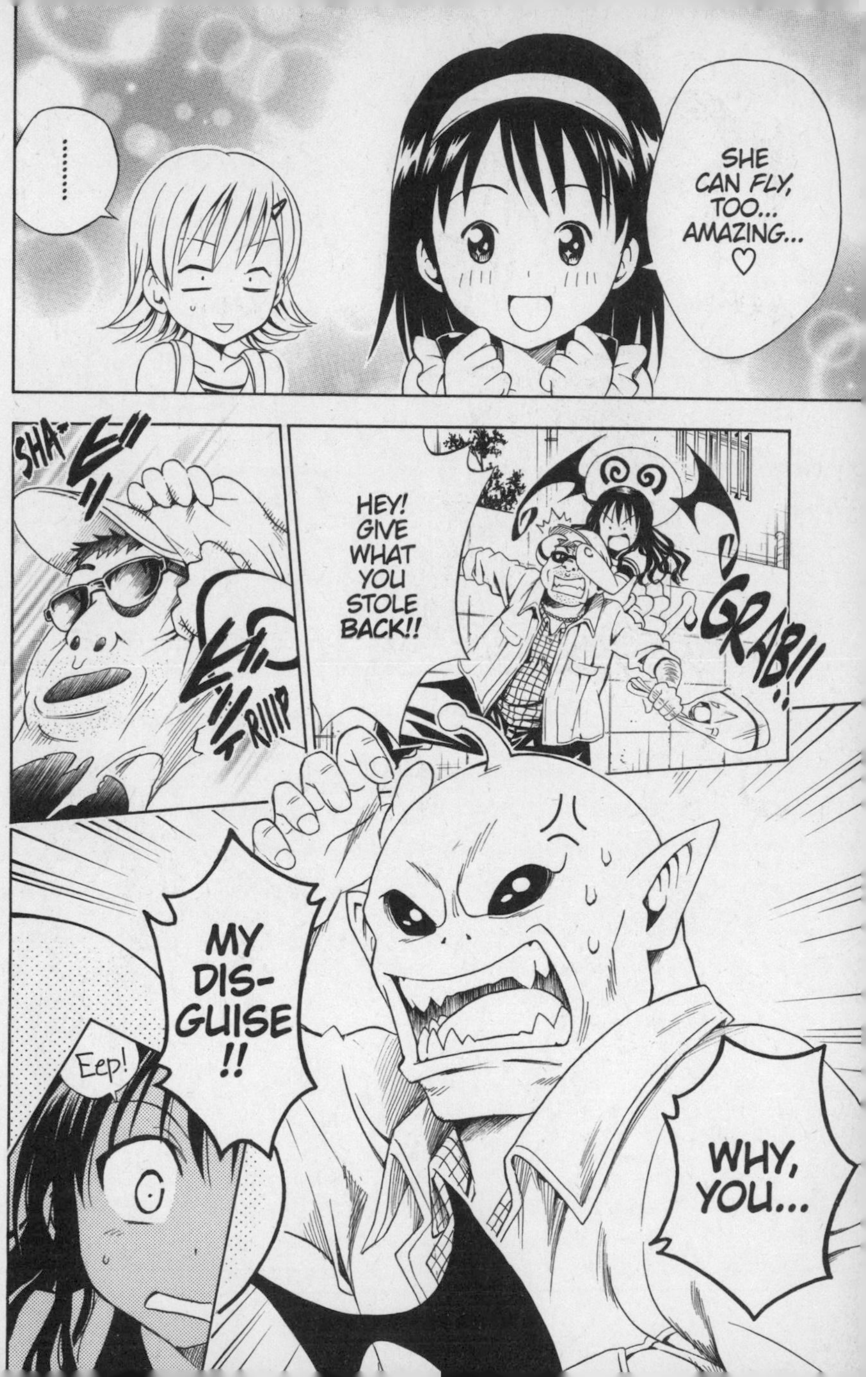
SHE CAN FLY, TOO... AMAZING... ♡
......
HEY! GIVE WHAT YOU STOLE BACK!!
GRAB!!
SHA-
RIIIP
MY DIS-GUISE!!
WHY, YOU...
Eep!

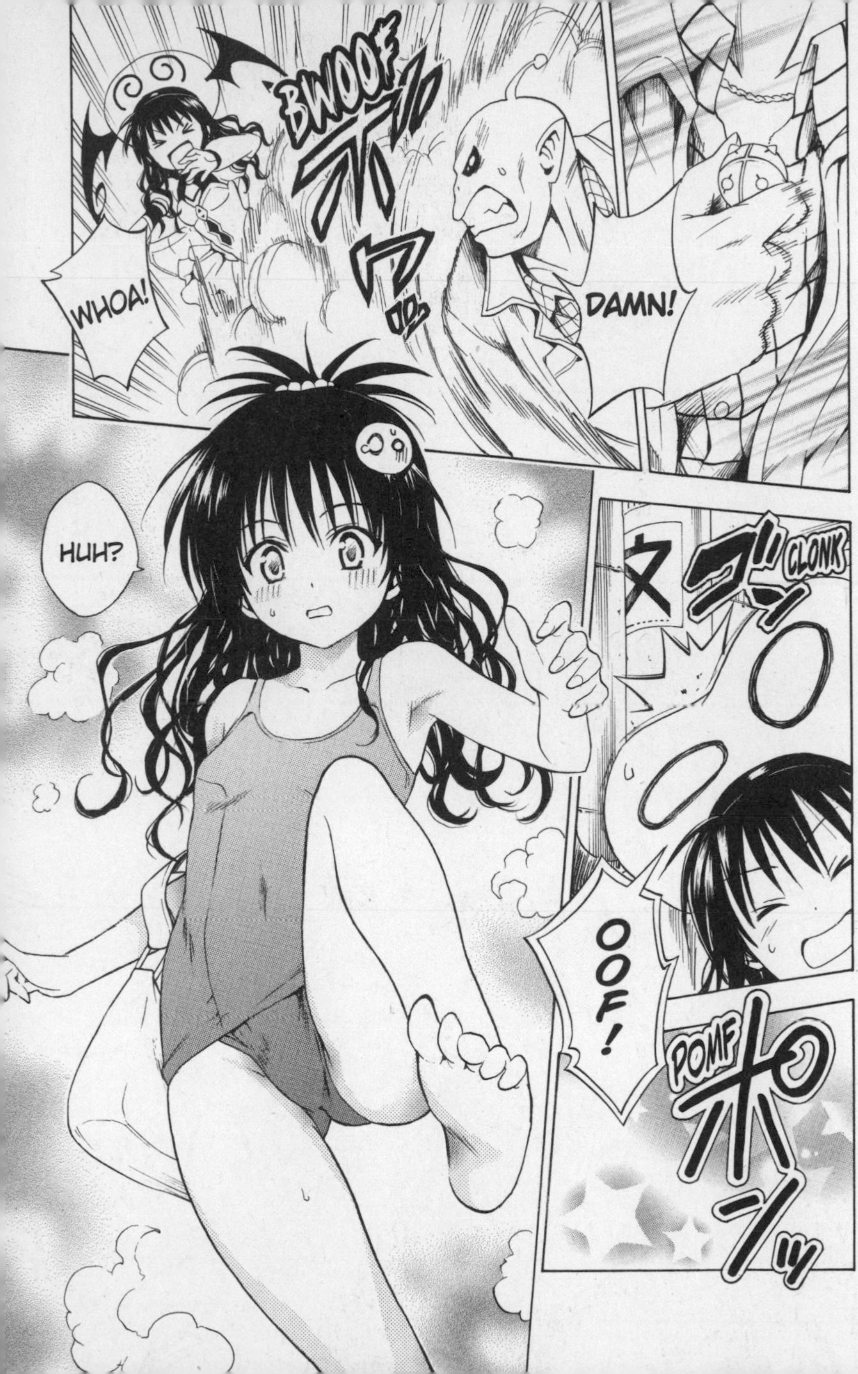
DAMN!
BWOOF
WHOA!
CLONK
OOF!
POMF
HUH?

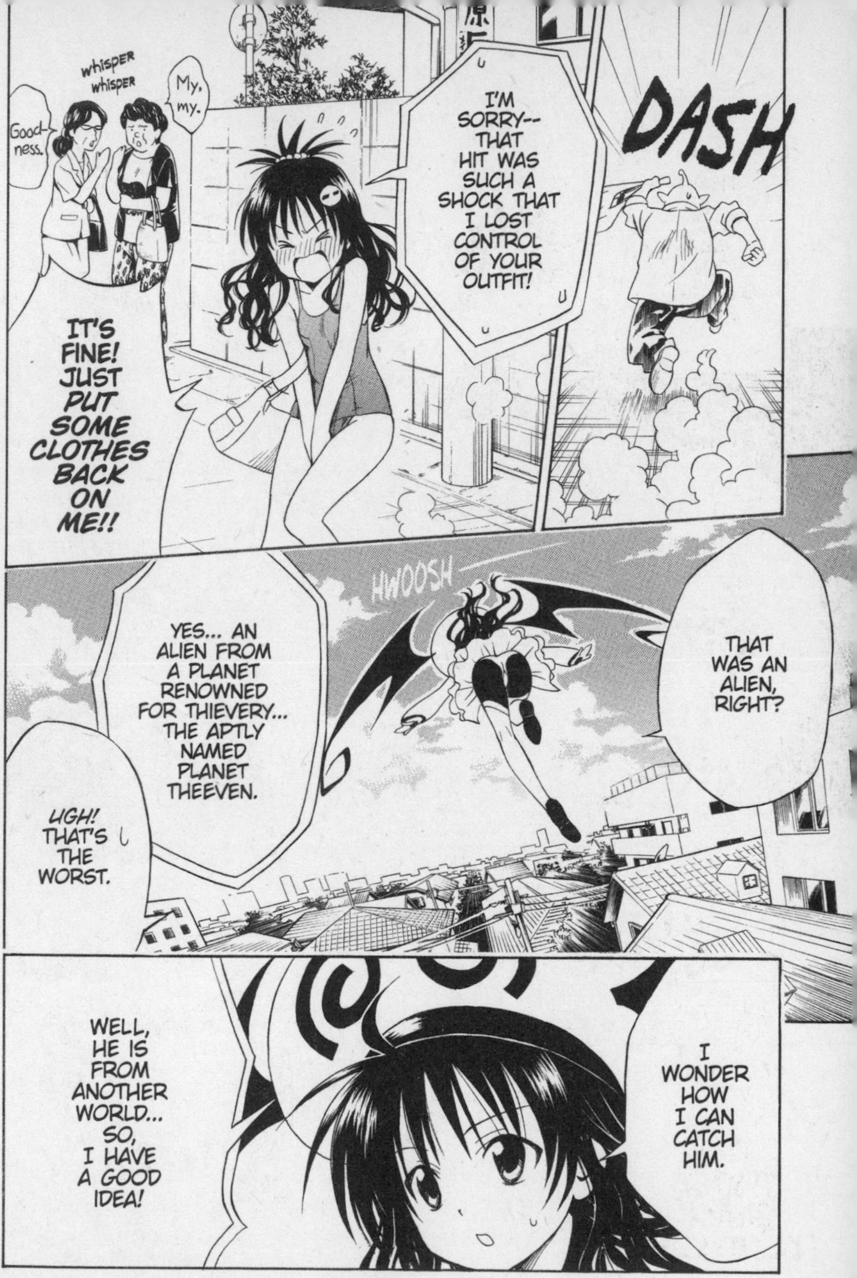
DASH
I'M SORRY-- THAT HIT WAS SUCH A SHOCK THAT I LOST CONTROL OF YOUR OUTFIT!
My, my.
whisper whisper
Goodness.
IT'S FINE! JUST PUT SOME CLOTHES BACK ON ME!!
THAT WAS AN ALIEN, RIGHT?
HWOOSH
YES... AN ALIEN FROM A PLANET RENOWNED FOR THIEVERY... THE APTLY NAMED PLANET THEEVEN.
UGH! THAT'S THE WORST.
I WONDER HOW I CAN CATCH HIM.
WELL, HE IS FROM ANOTHER WORLD... SO, I HAVE A GOOD IDEA!

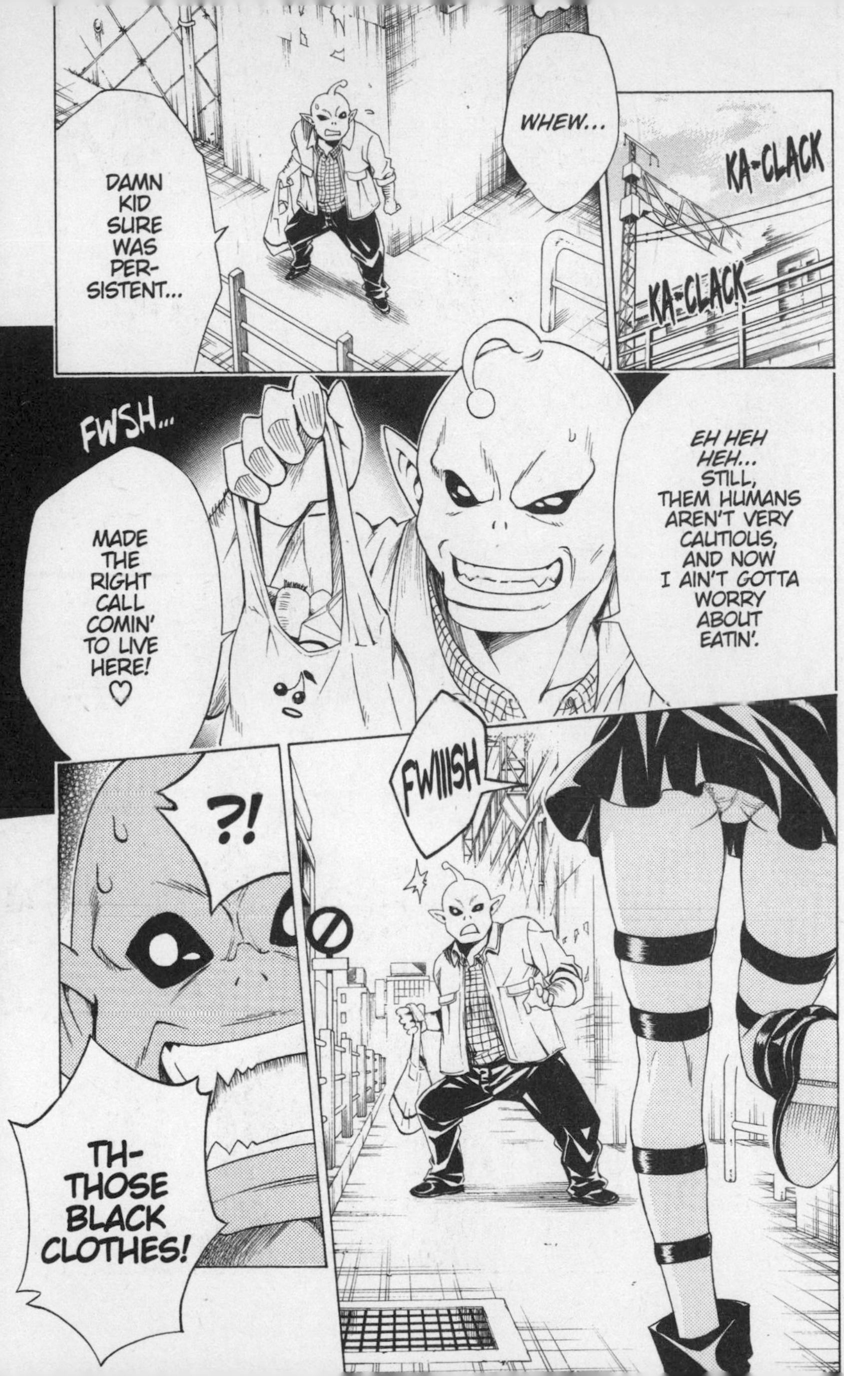
KA-CLACK
KA-CLACK
WHEW...
DAMN KID SURE WAS PER- SISTENT...
EH HEH HEH... STILL, THEM HUMANS AREN'T VERY CAUTIOUS, AND NOW I AIN'T GOTTA WORRY ABOUT EATIN'.
FWSH...
MADE THE RIGHT CALL COMIN' TO LIVE HERE! ♡
FWIIISH
?!
TH- THOSE BLACK CLOTHES!

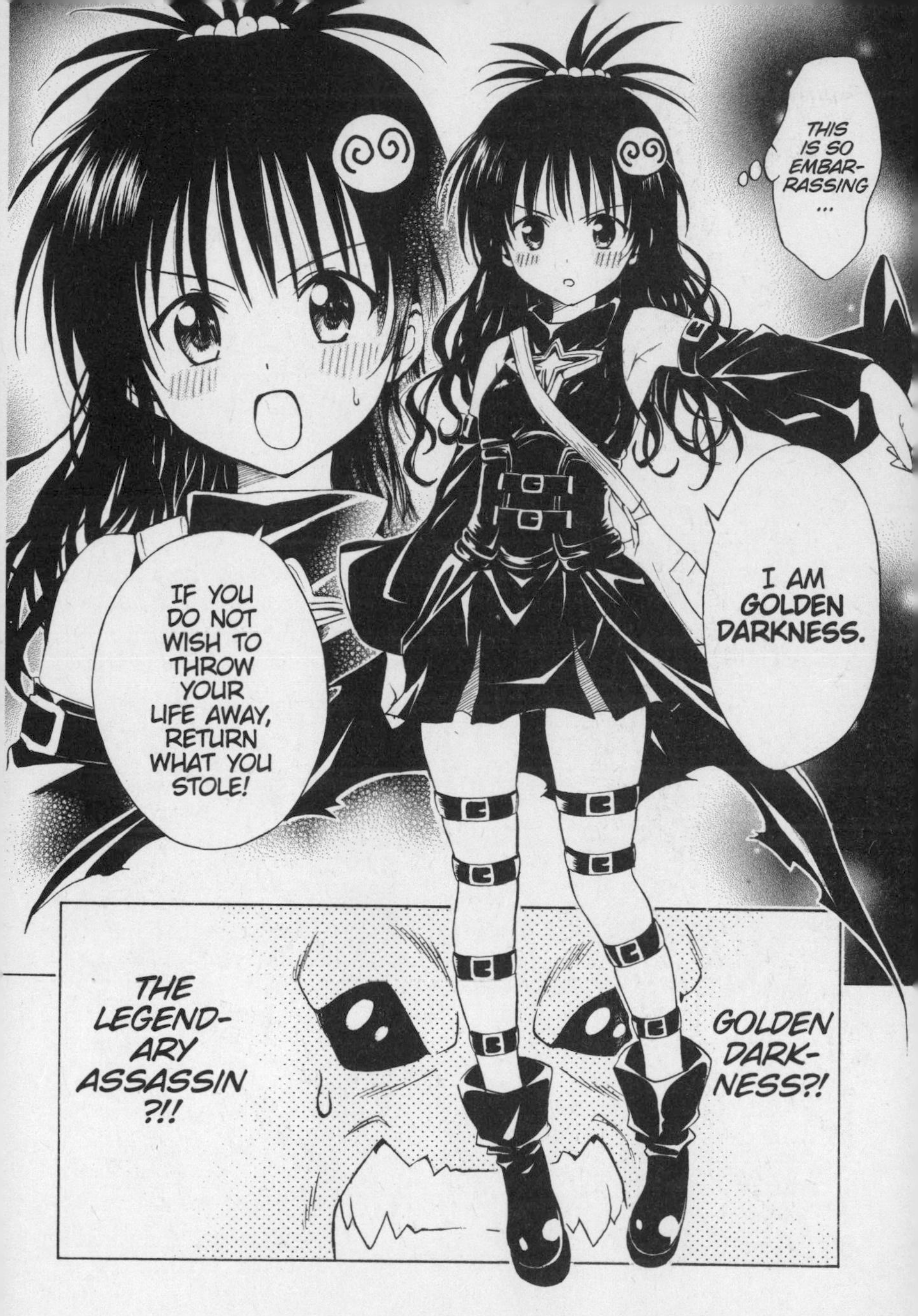
THIS IS SO EMBAR-RASSING...
I AM GOLDEN DARKNESS.
IF YOU DO NOT WISH TO THROW YOUR LIFE AWAY, RETURN WHAT YOU STOLE!
GOLDEN DARK-NESS?!
THE LEGEND-ARY ASSASSIN?!!

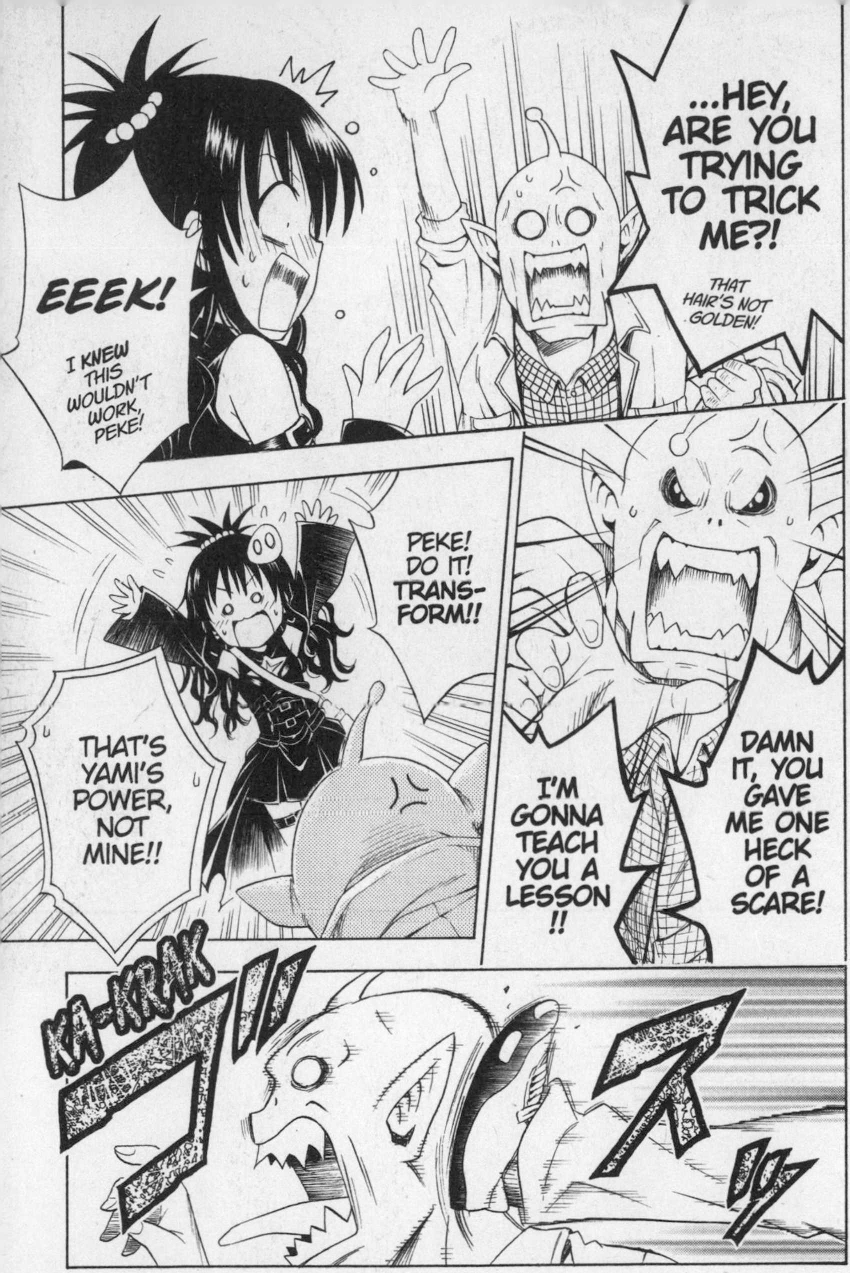
...HEY, ARE YOU TRYING TO TRICK ME?!
THAT HAIR'S NOT GOLDEN!
EEEK!
I KNEW THIS WOULDN'T WORK, PEKE!
DAMN IT, YOU GAVE ME ONE HECK OF A SCARE!
I'M GONNA TEACH YOU A LESSON!!
PEKE! DO IT! TRANSFORM!!
THAT'S YAMI'S POWER, NOT MINE!!
KA-KRAK

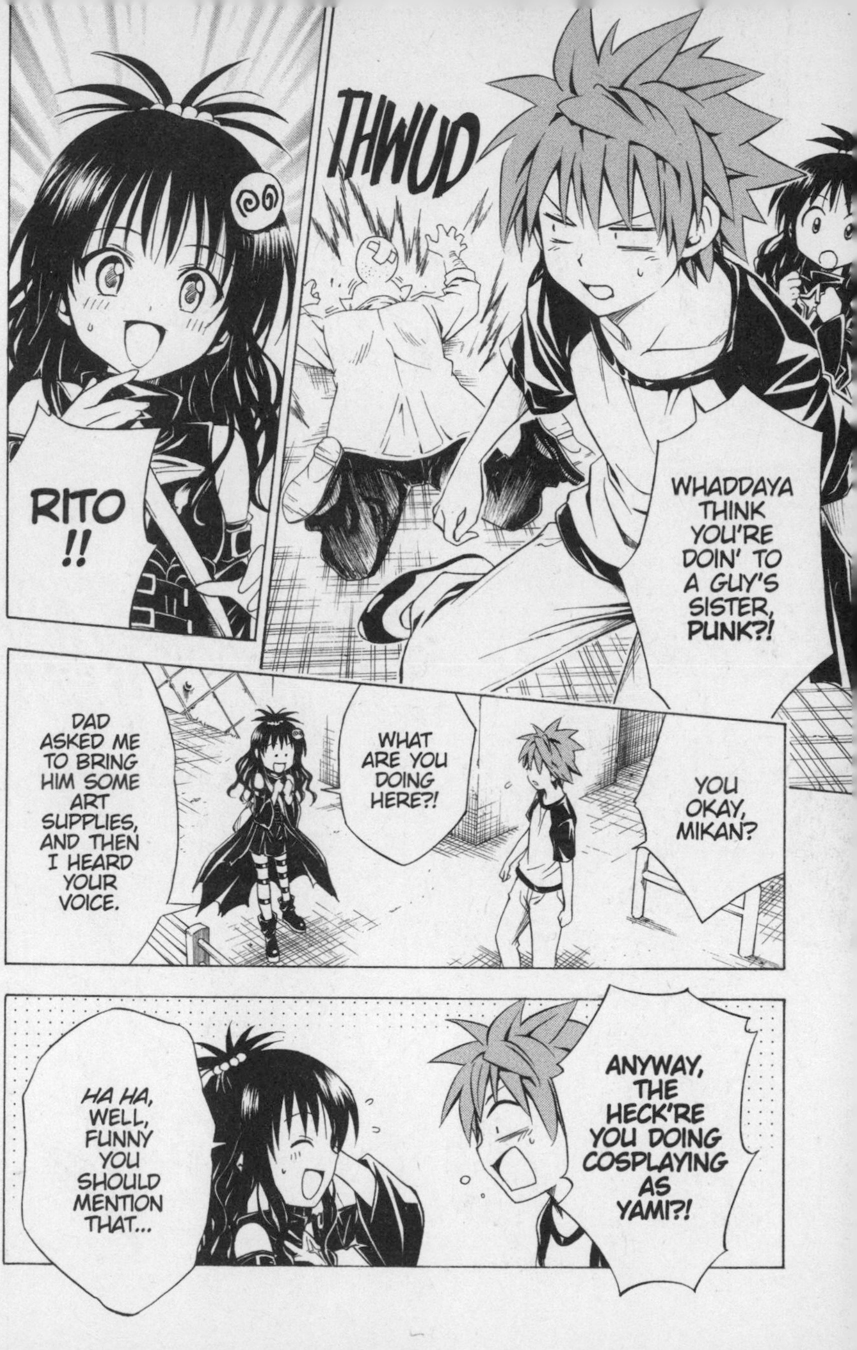
THWUD
WHADDAYA THINK YOU'RE DOIN' TO A GUY'S SISTER, PUNK?!
RITO !!
YOU OKAY, MIKAN?
WHAT ARE YOU DOING HERE?!
DAD ASKED ME TO BRING HIM SOME ART SUPPLIES, AND THEN I HEARD YOUR VOICE.
ANYWAY, THE HECK'RE YOU DOING COSPLAYING AS YAMI?!
HA HA, WELL, FUNNY YOU SHOULD MENTION THAT...

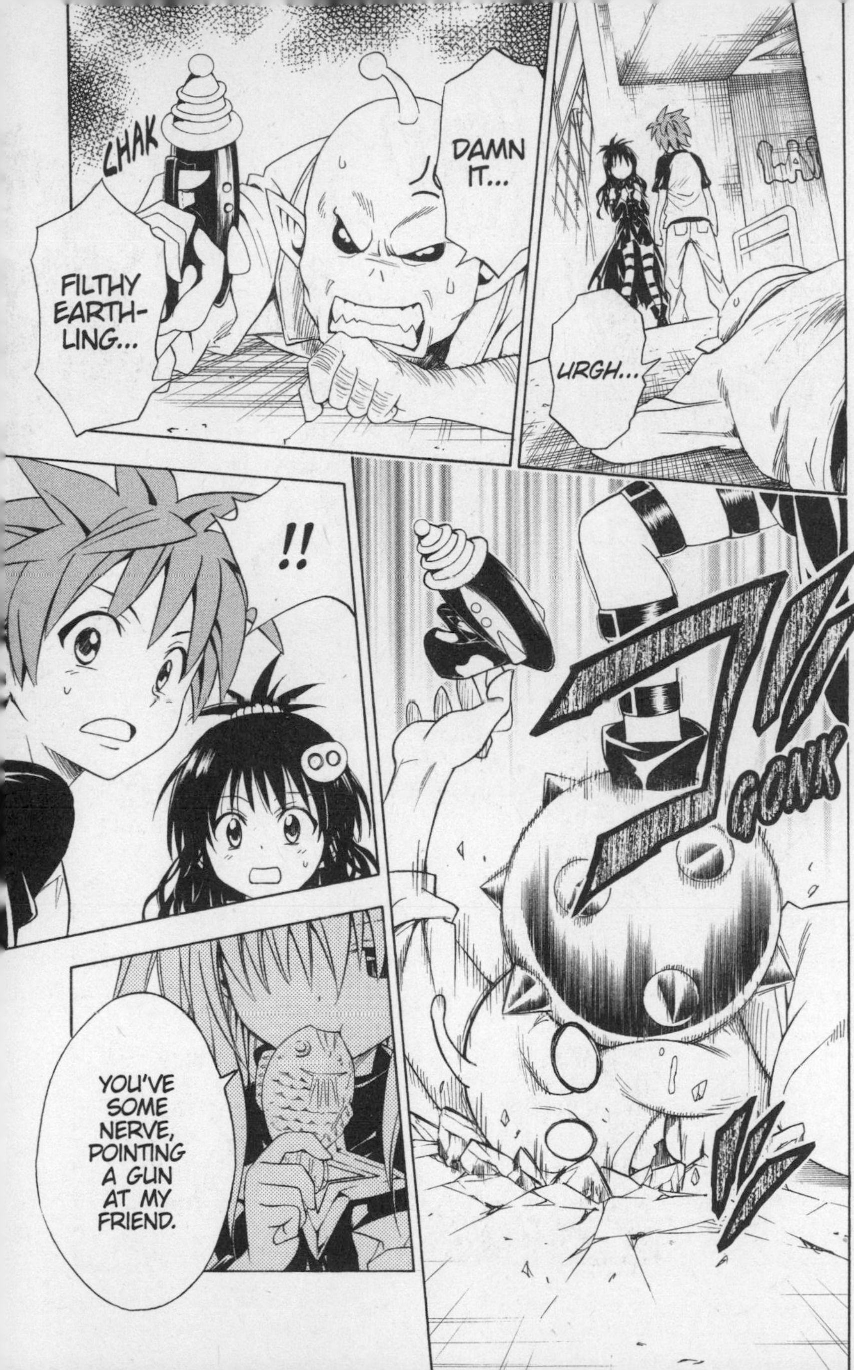
URGH...
DAMN IT...
CHAK
FILTHY EARTHLING...
GONK
!!
YOU'VE SOME NERVE, POINTING A GUN AT MY FRIEND.

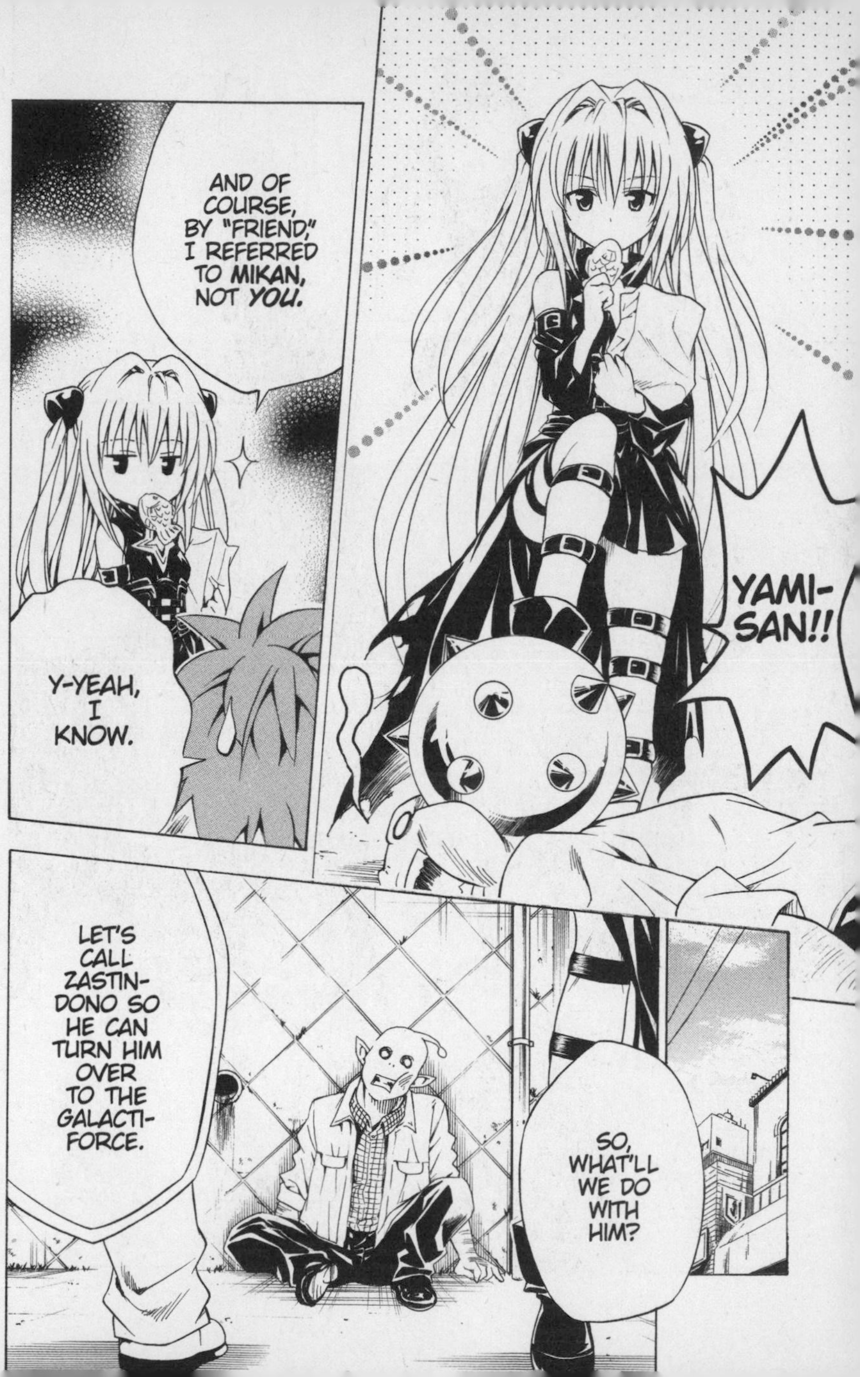
YAMI-SAN!!
AND OF COURSE, BY "FRIEND," I REFERRED TO MIKAN, NOT *YOU*.
Y-YEAH, I KNOW.
SO, WHAT'LL WE DO WITH HIM?
LET'S CALL ZASTIN-DONO SO HE CAN TURN HIM OVER TO THE GALACTI-FORCE.

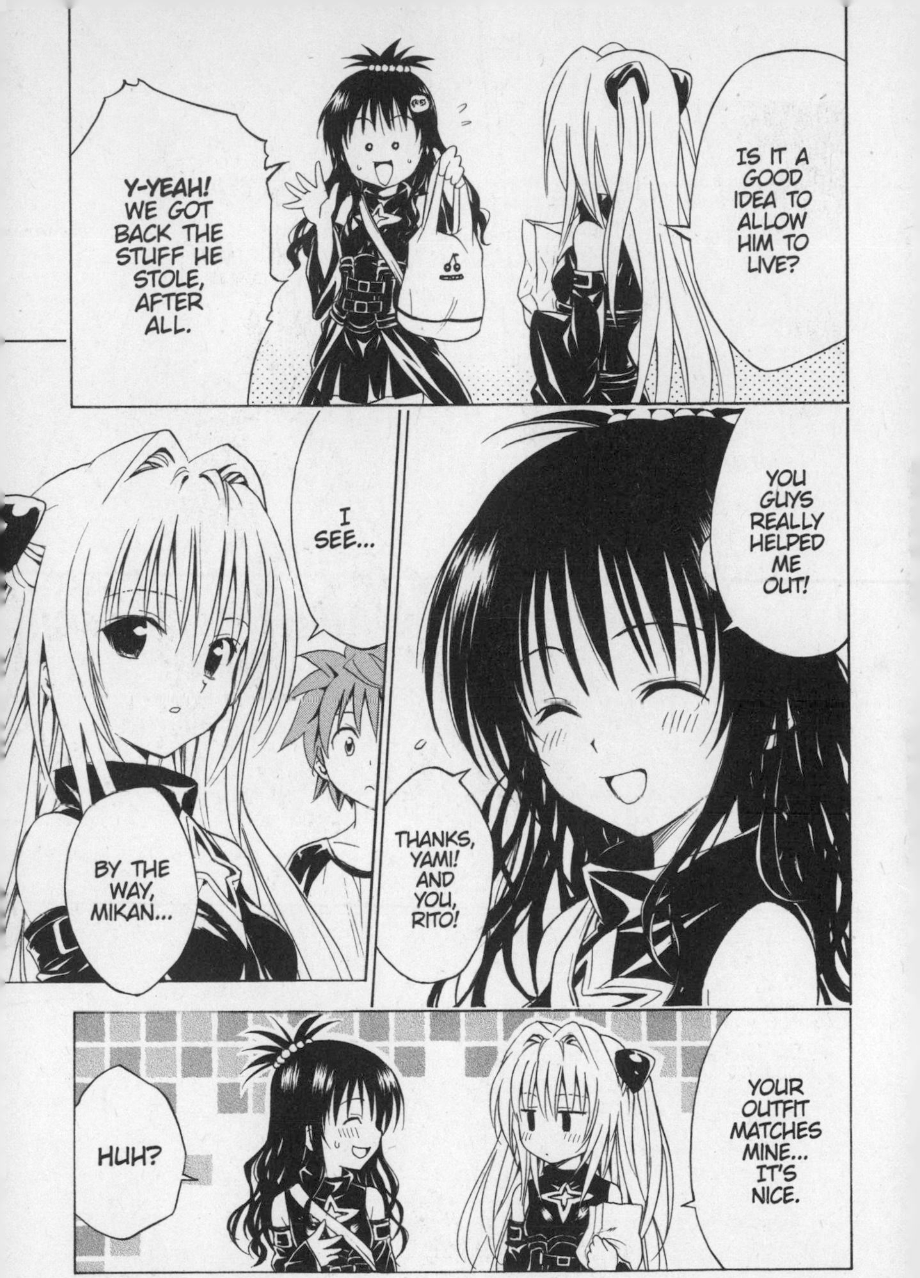
IS IT A GOOD IDEA TO ALLOW HIM TO LIVE?
Y-YEAH! WE GOT BACK THE STUFF HE STOLE, AFTER ALL.
YOU GUYS REALLY HELPED ME OUT!
THANKS, YAMI! AND YOU, RITO!
I SEE...
BY THE WAY, MIKAN...
YOUR OUTFIT MATCHES MINE... IT'S NICE.
HUH?

Mikan's Observation Log 5

Thok! Thok! The sound of the knife repeated over and over.

The pot next to her bubbled away, the sound of gurgling water and chopping knife mingling into a kind of duet.

×　　　×　　　×

"All right, dinner's almost done!"

Standing on her tiptoes, Mikan reached into the top cabinet and took out some dishes. Her twin bunny slippers also stretched out together...

"Today sure was a calamity, though... A weird alien from planet Feever...or was it...? Oh, whatever. Important thing is, he stole the groceries..."

×　　　×　　　×

Thok! Thok! In a steady rhythm, the chopping of the vegetables continued.

"It was pretty fun dressing like Yami-san, though..."

"..."

The rhythm of the knife stopped...

"Maybe I should ask Peke to help me transform like that again! Hee hee! ♪"

THIS IS SO EMBAR-RASSING...

Her cheeks grew slightly red, and she let out a slightly strained laugh to herself.

Thok! Thok! The rhythm of the knife resumed, blade to vegetables once again.

×　　　×　　　×

"A whole lot of wacky stuff happened today, but I'm really happy Rito and Yami-san saved me, too! ♪"

"Okay!"

×　　　×　　　×

Mikan placed the chopped vegetables on some plates, and with that, the salad was done.

She hollered towards the living room: "Rito! Lala-saan! Nana-san! Momo-san! Dinner's just about ready!"

I AM GOLDEN DARKNESS.

With her large eyes and cute, smiling face, Mikan seemed to be enjoying herself. The dinner table at the Yuuki residence would probably be quite lively again today...

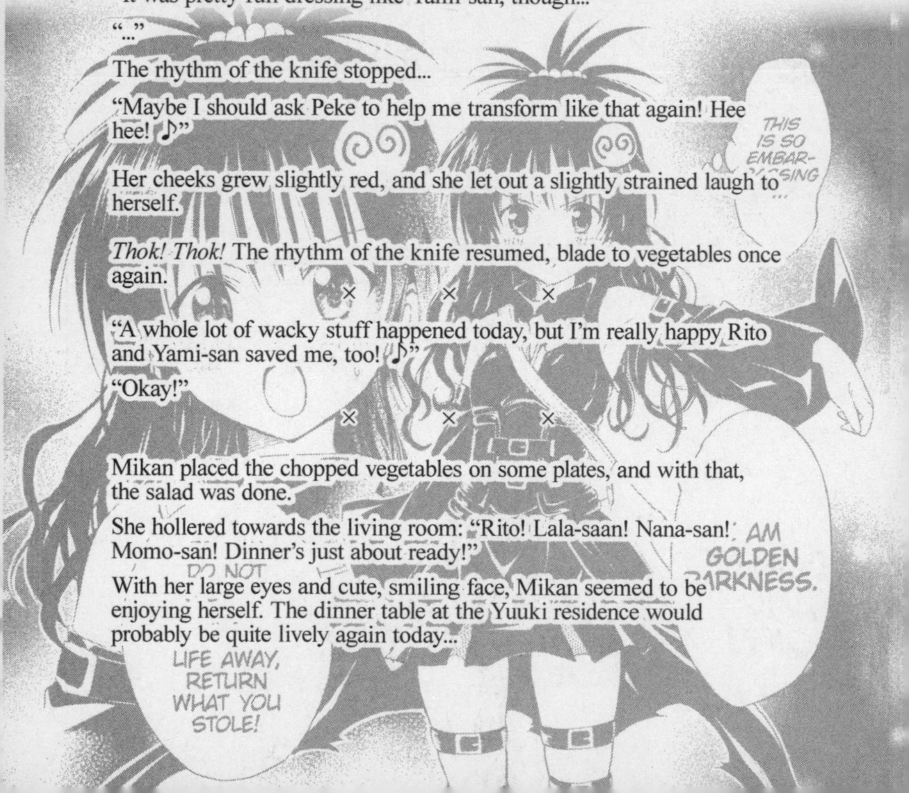

DO NOT

LIFE AWAY, RETURN WHAT YOU STOLE!

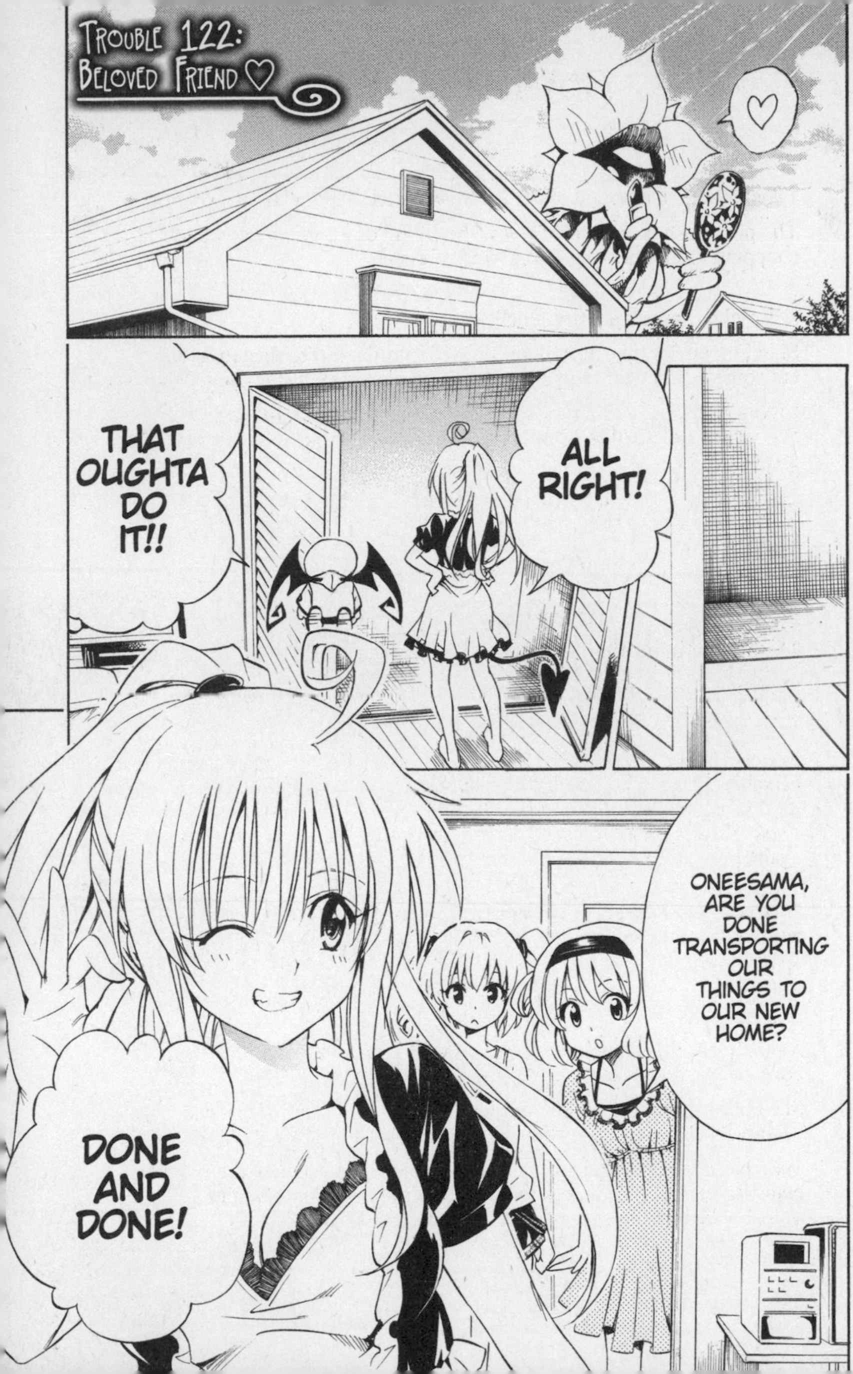
Trouble 122: Beloved Friend ♡
♡
ALL RIGHT!
THAT OUGHTA DO IT!!
ONEESAMA, ARE YOU DONE TRANSPORTING OUR THINGS TO OUR NEW HOME?
DONE AND DONE!

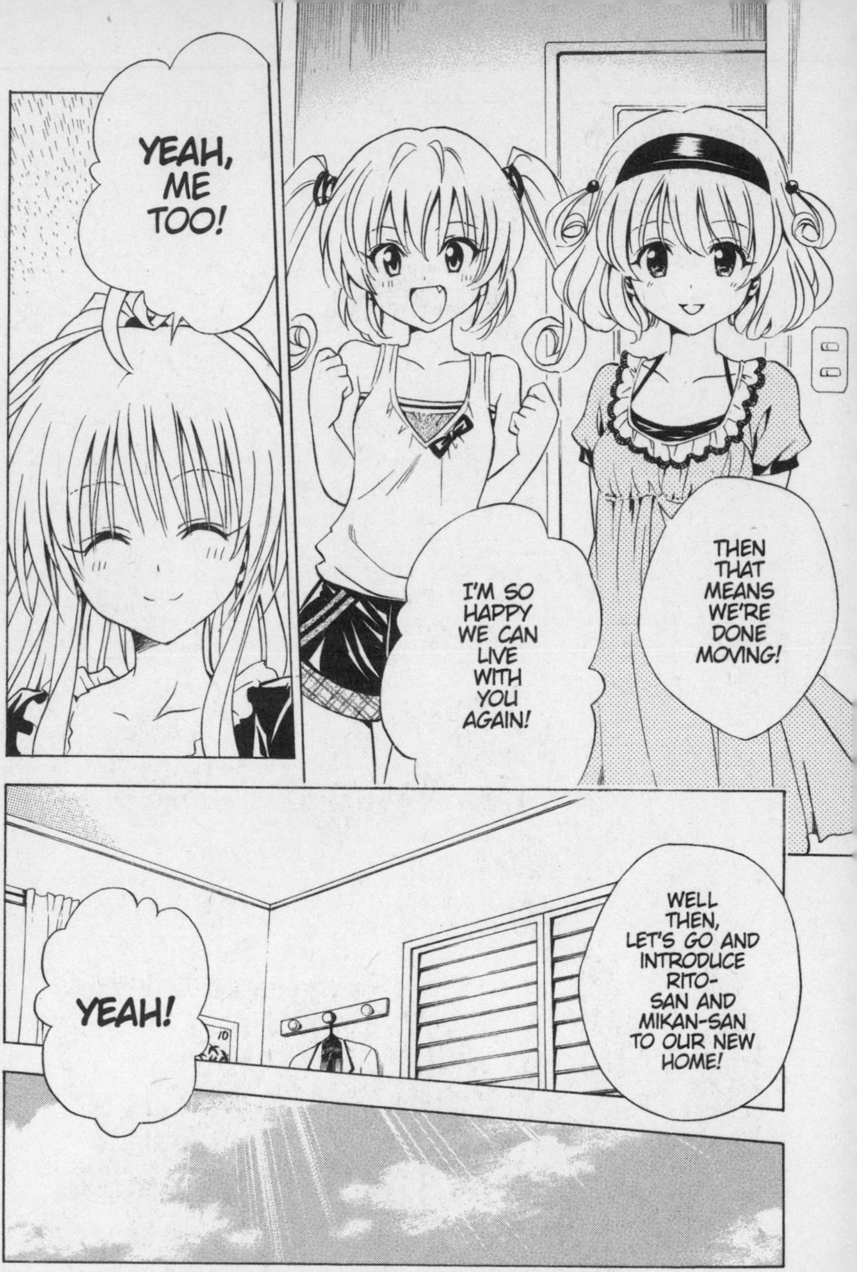
THEN THAT MEANS WE'RE DONE MOVING!
I'M SO HAPPY WE CAN LIVE WITH YOU AGAIN!
YEAH, ME TOO!
WELL THEN, LET'S GO AND INTRODUCE RITO-SAN AND MIKAN-SAN TO OUR NEW HOME!
YEAH!

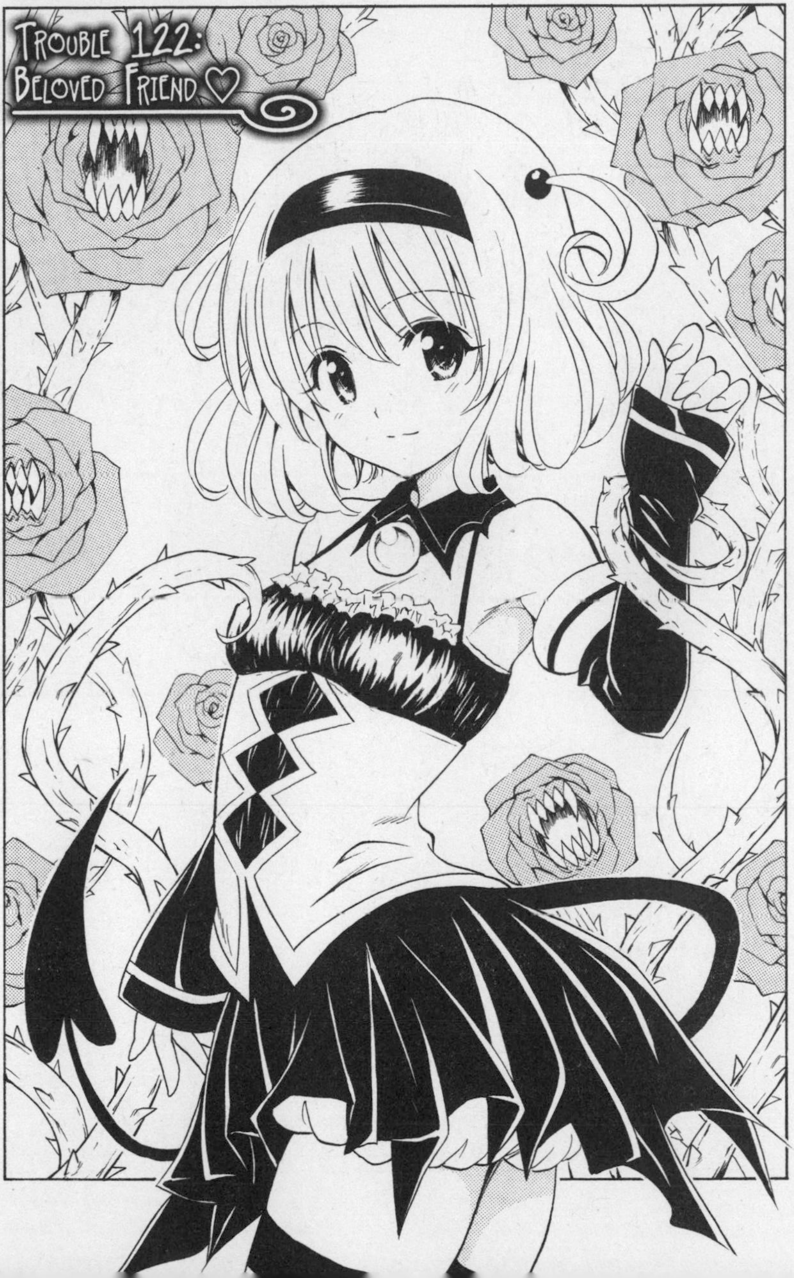
TROUBLE 122:
BELOVED FRIEND ♡

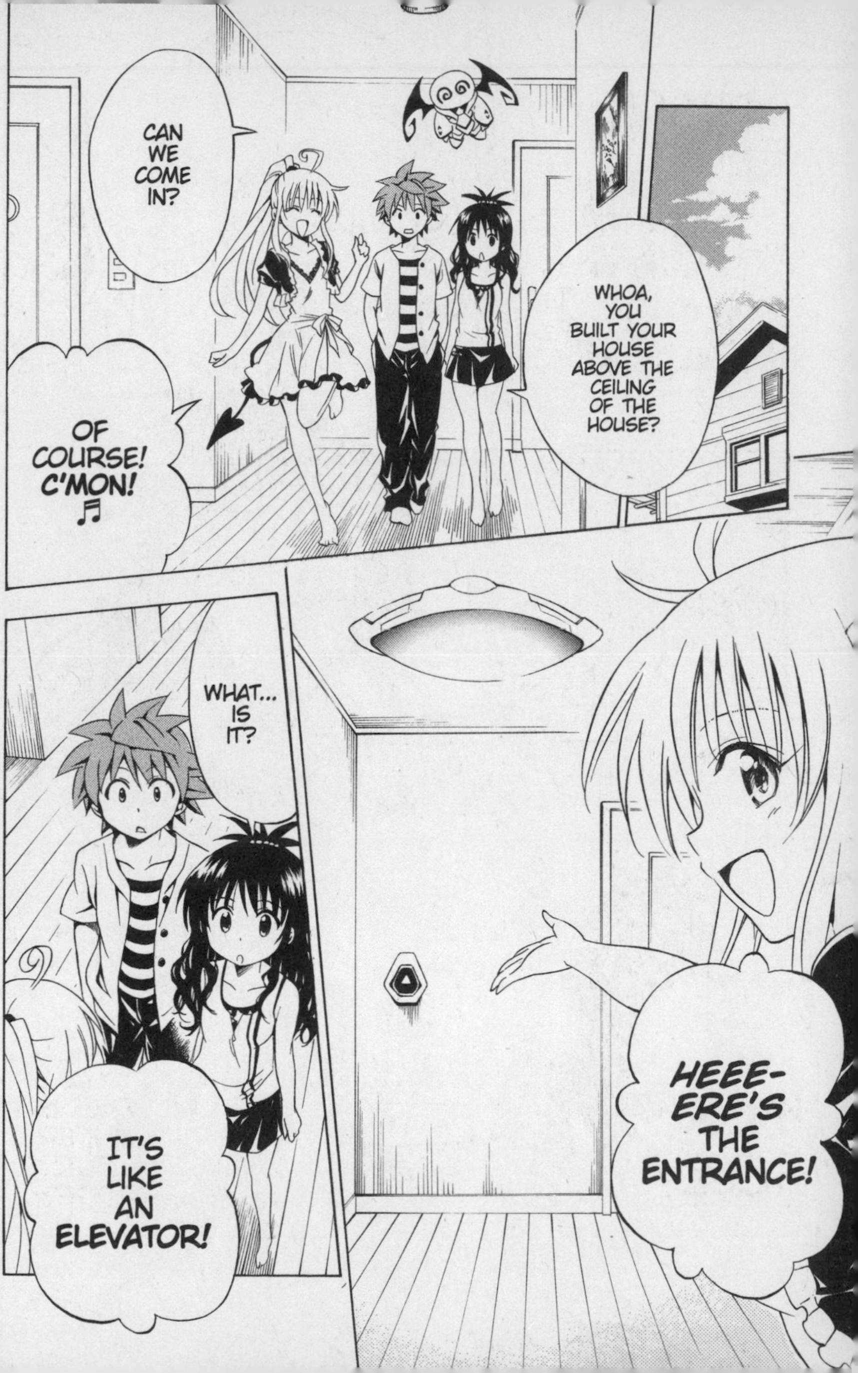

WHOA, YOU BUILT YOUR HOUSE ABOVE THE CEILING OF THE HOUSE?
CAN WE COME IN?
OF COURSE! C'MON! ♬
HEEEE-ERE'S THE ENTRANCE!
WHAT... IS IT?
IT'S LIKE AN ELEVATOR!

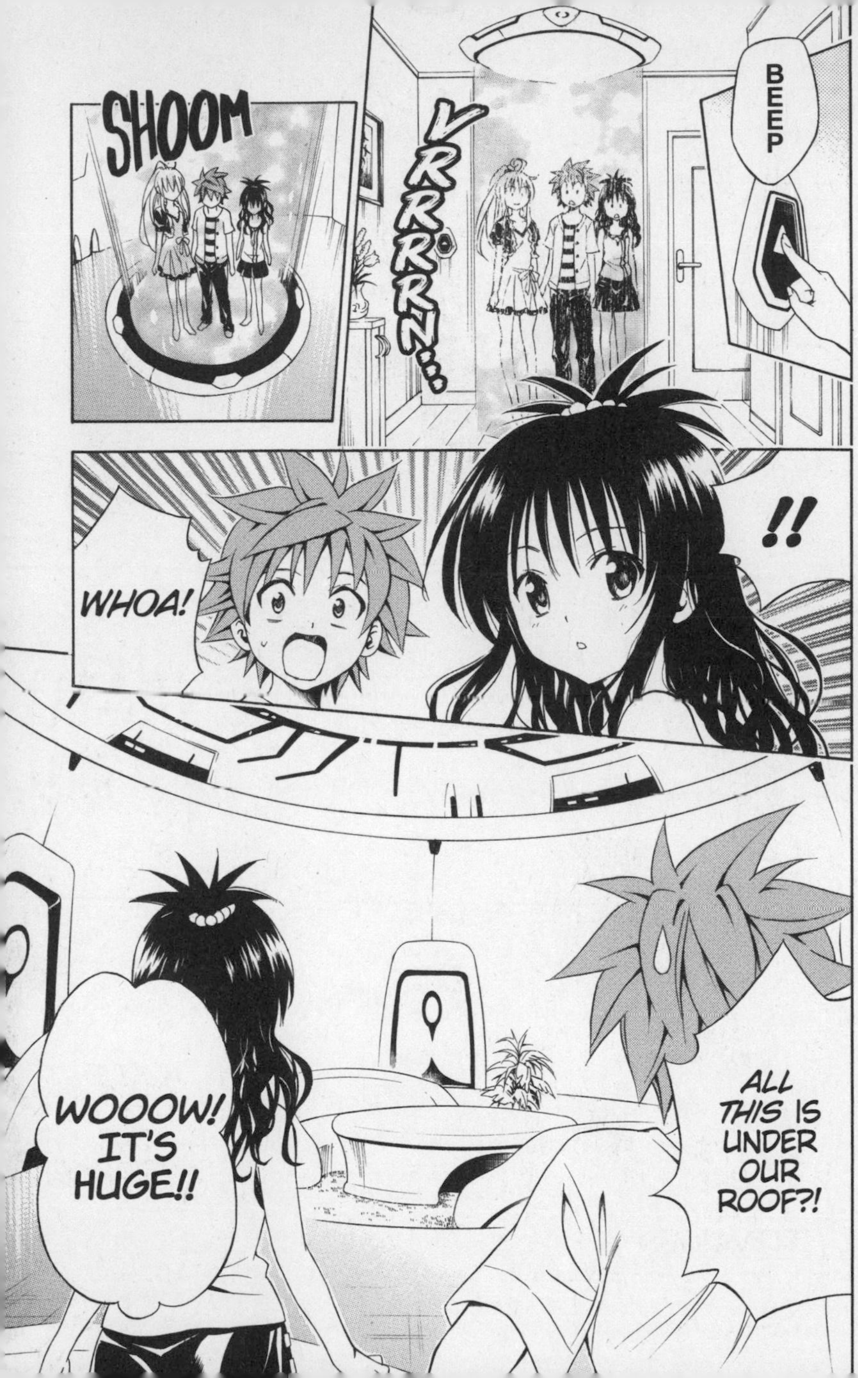

BEEP
VRRRRN...
SHOOM
!!
WHOA!
ALL THIS IS UNDER OUR ROOF?!
WOOOW! IT'S HUGE!!

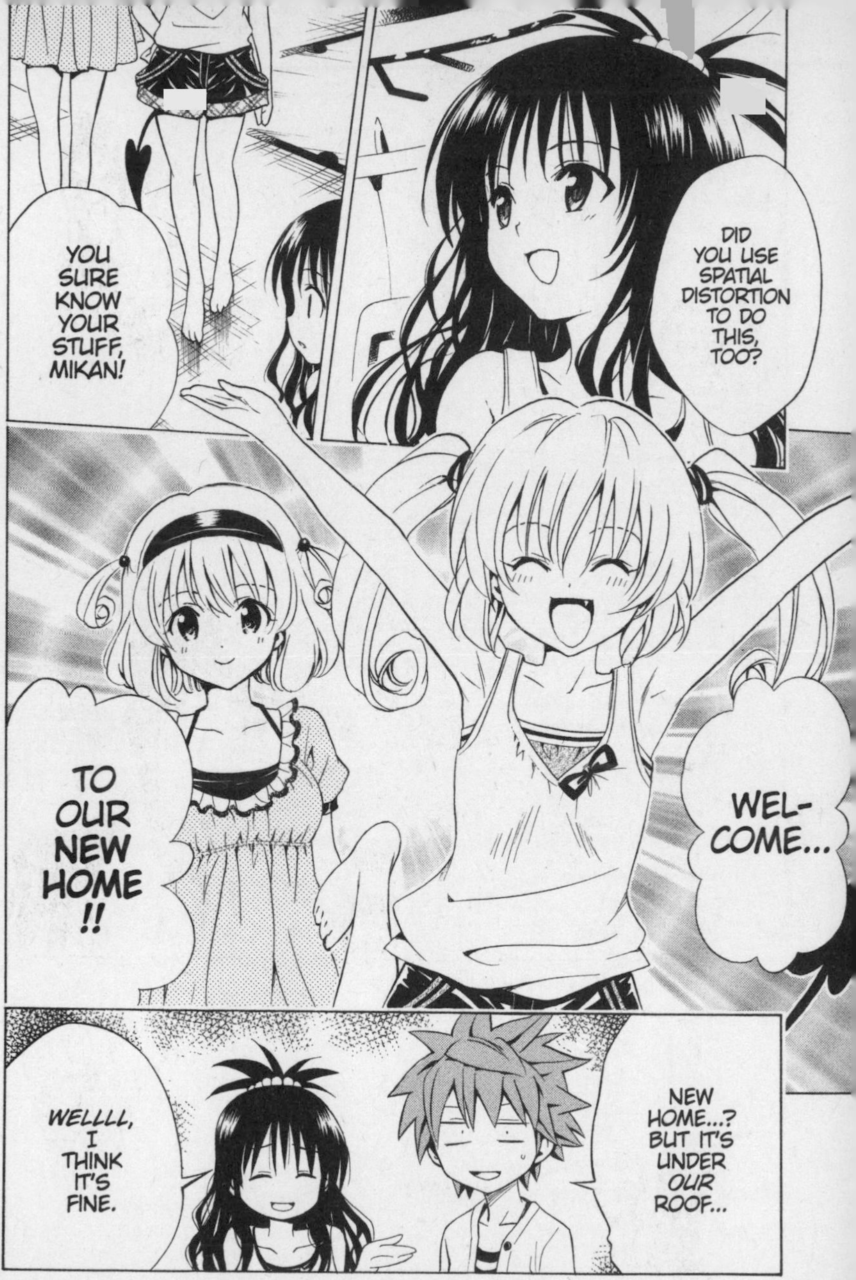
DID YOU USE SPATIAL DISTORTION TO DO THIS, TOO?
YOU SURE KNOW YOUR STUFF, MIKAN!
WEL- COME...
TO OUR NEW HOME !!
NEW HOME...? BUT IT'S UNDER OUR ROOF...
WELLLL, I THINK IT'S FINE.

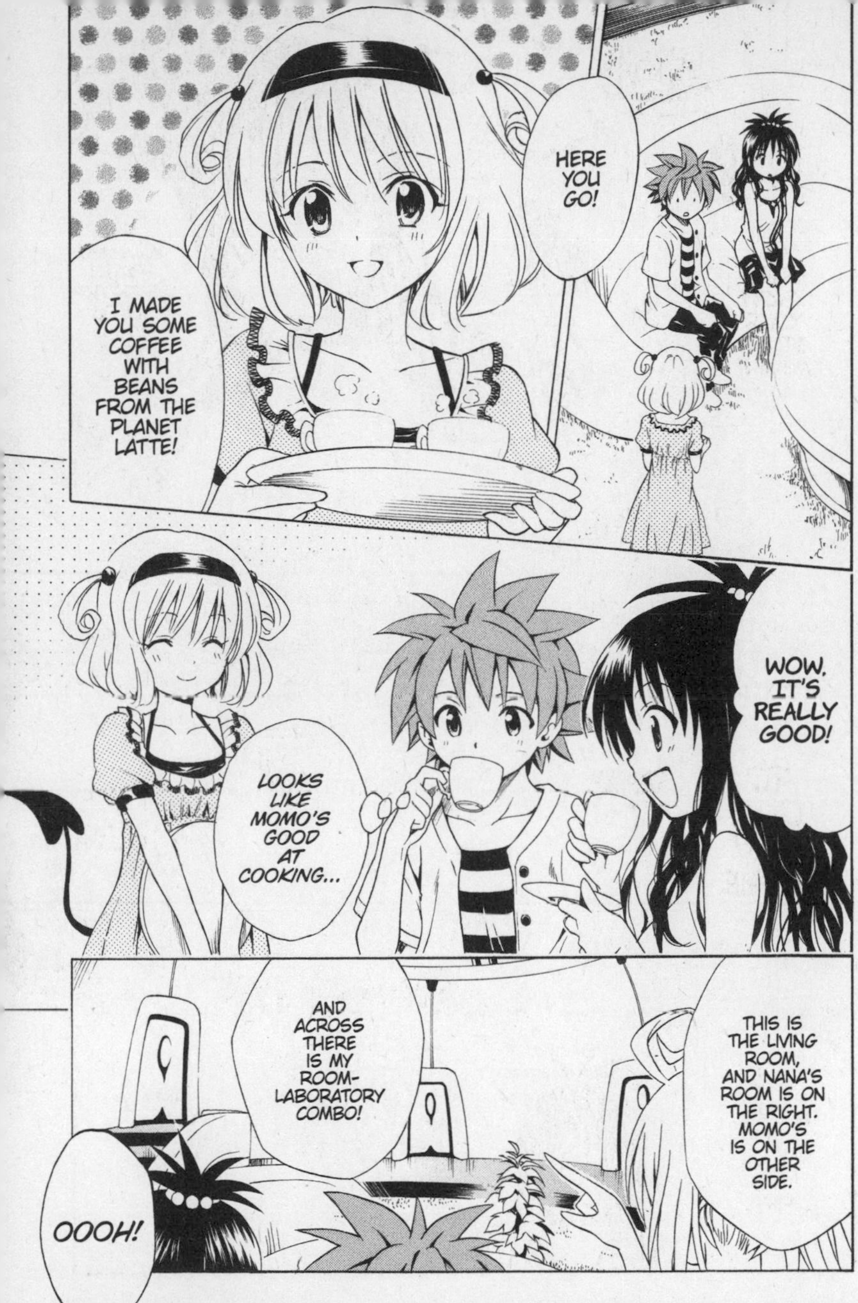
HERE YOU GO!
I MADE YOU SOME COFFEE WITH BEANS FROM THE PLANET LATTE!
WOW. IT'S REALLY GOOD!
LOOKS LIKE MOMO'S GOOD AT COOKING...
THIS IS THE LIVING ROOM, AND NANA'S ROOM IS ON THE RIGHT. MOMO'S IS ON THE OTHER SIDE.
AND ACROSS THERE IS MY ROOM-LABORATORY COMBO!
OOOH!

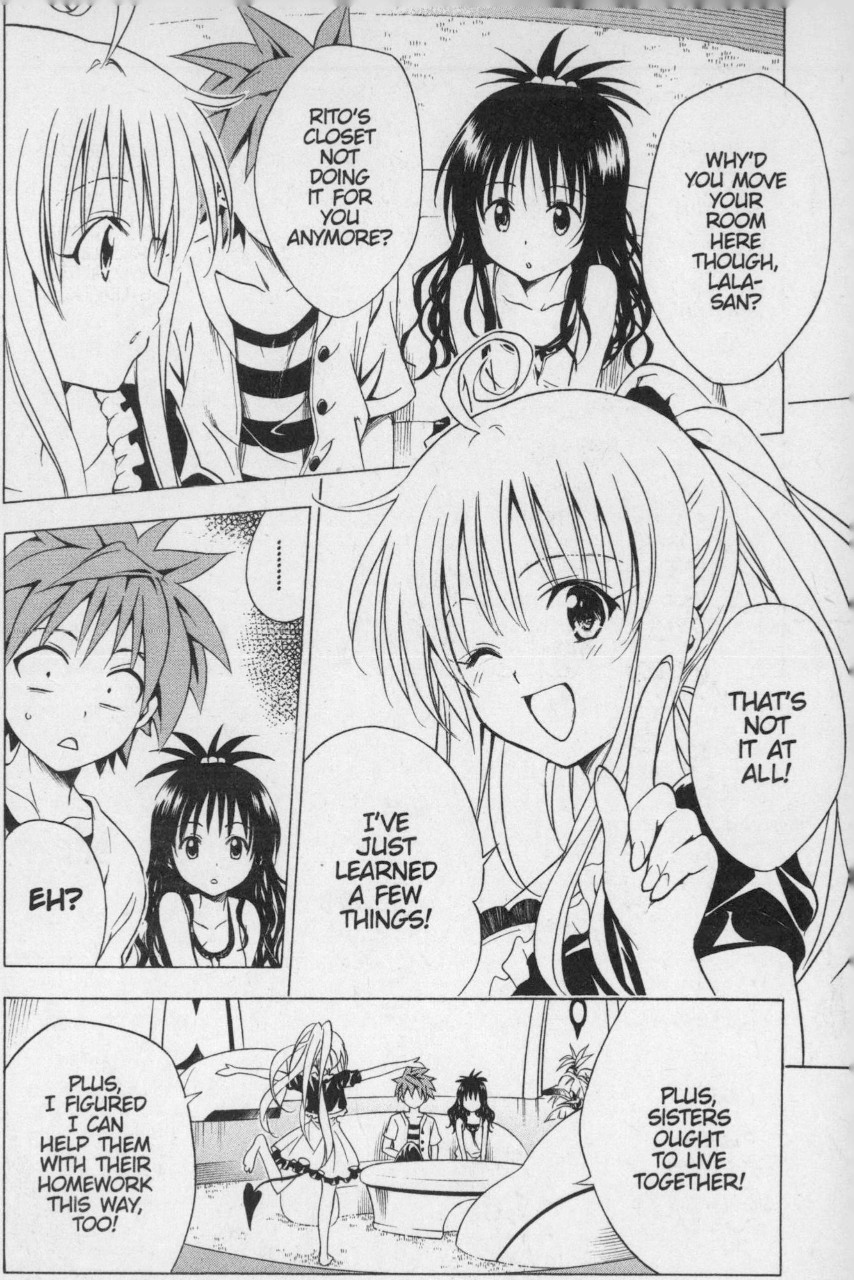
WHY'D YOU MOVE YOUR ROOM HERE THOUGH, LALA-SAN?
RITO'S CLOSET NOT DOING IT FOR YOU ANYMORE?
THAT'S NOT IT AT ALL!
I'VE JUST LEARNED A FEW THINGS!
......
EH?
PLUS, SISTERS OUGHT TO LIVE TOGETHER!
PLUS, I FIGURED I CAN HELP THEM WITH THEIR HOMEWORK THIS WAY, TOO!

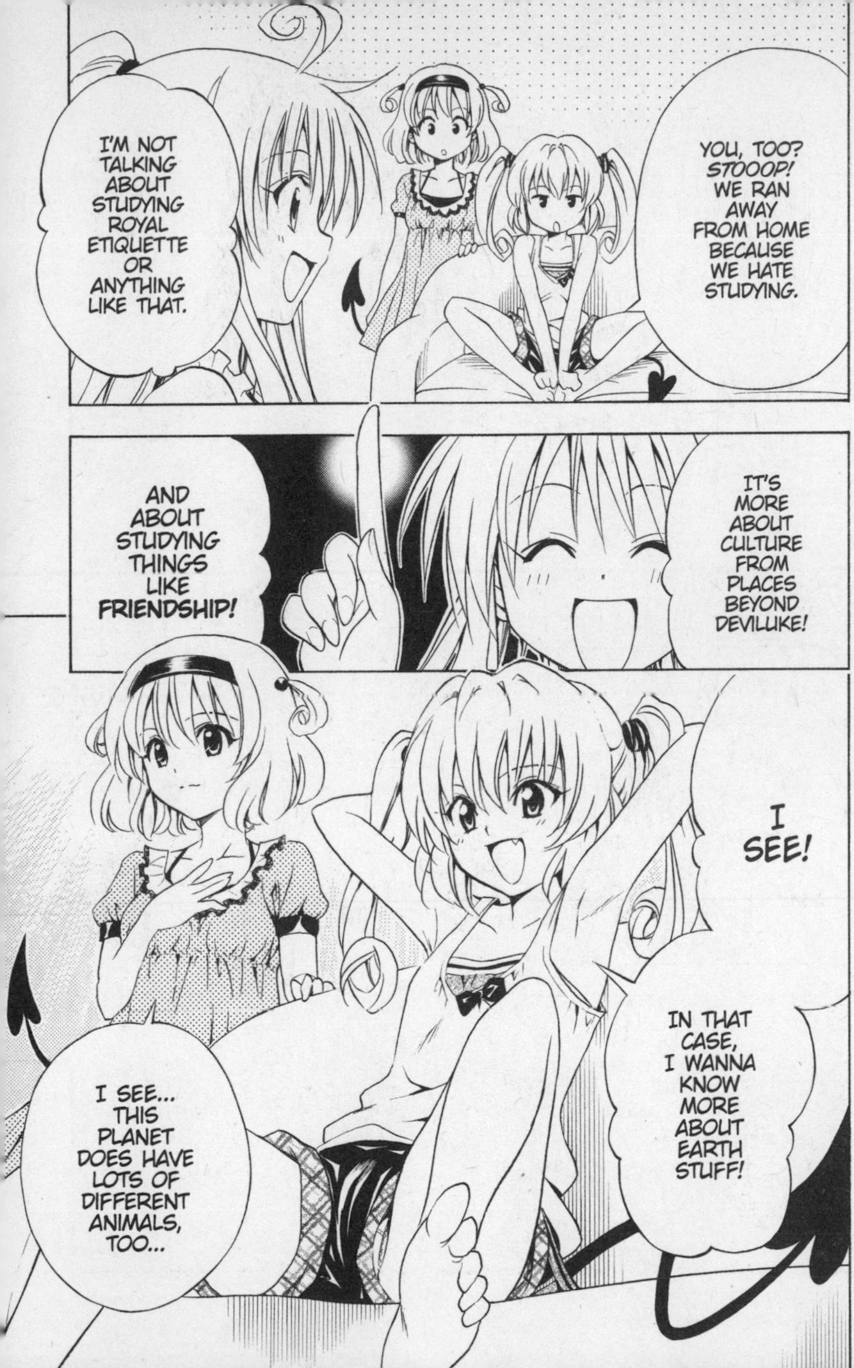
YOU, TOO? STOOOP! WE RAN AWAY FROM HOME BECAUSE WE HATE STUDYING.
I'M NOT TALKING ABOUT STUDYING ROYAL ETIQUETTE OR ANYTHING LIKE THAT.
IT'S MORE ABOUT CULTURE FROM PLACES BEYOND DEVILUKE!
AND ABOUT STUDYING THINGS LIKE FRIENDSHIP!
I SEE!
IN THAT CASE, I WANNA KNOW MORE ABOUT EARTH STUFF!
I SEE... THIS PLANET DOES HAVE LOTS OF DIFFERENT ANIMALS, TOO...

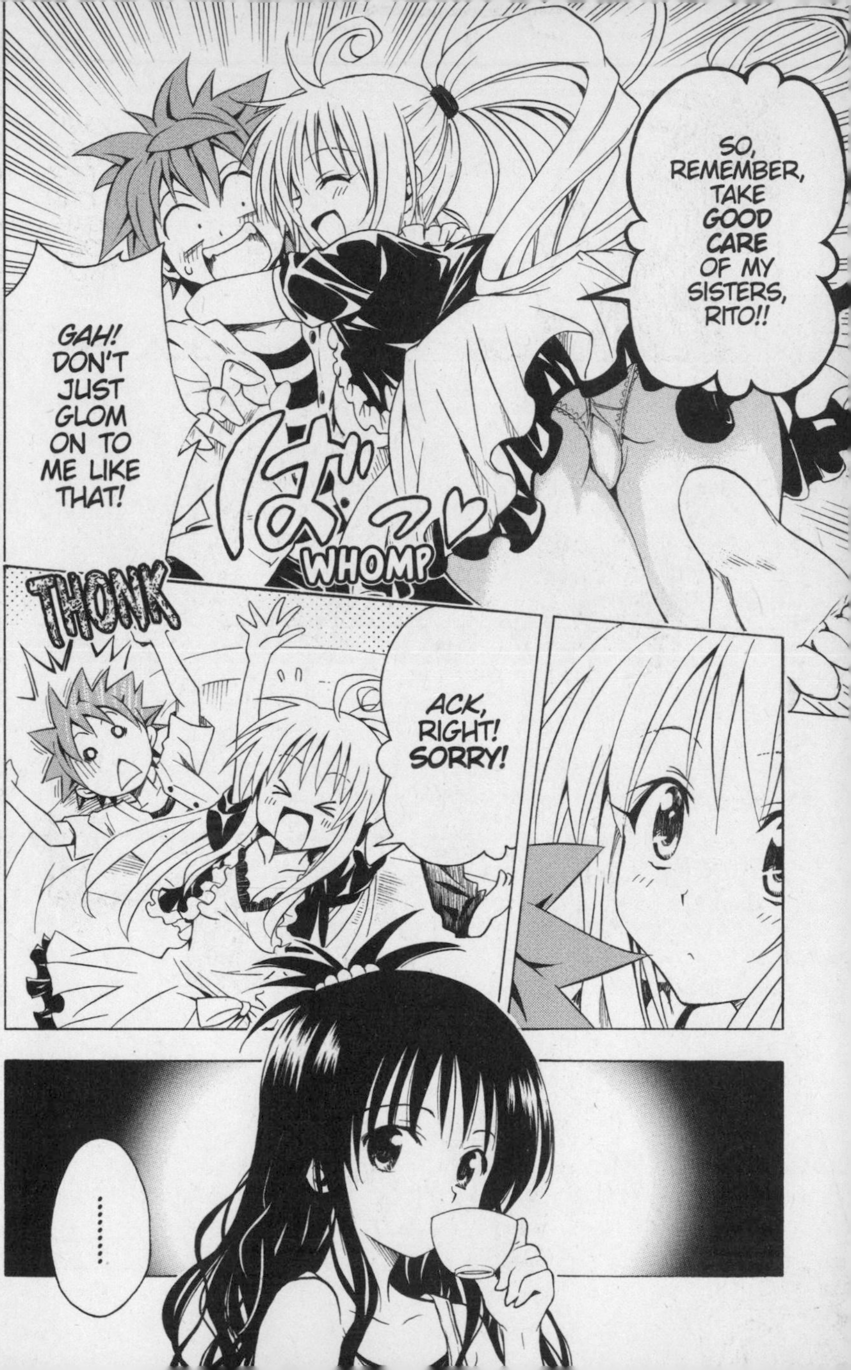
SO, REMEMBER, TAKE GOOD CARE OF MY SISTERS, RITO!!
GAH! DON'T JUST GLOM ON TO ME LIKE THAT!
ばっ
WHOMP
ACK, RIGHT! SORRY!
THONK
......

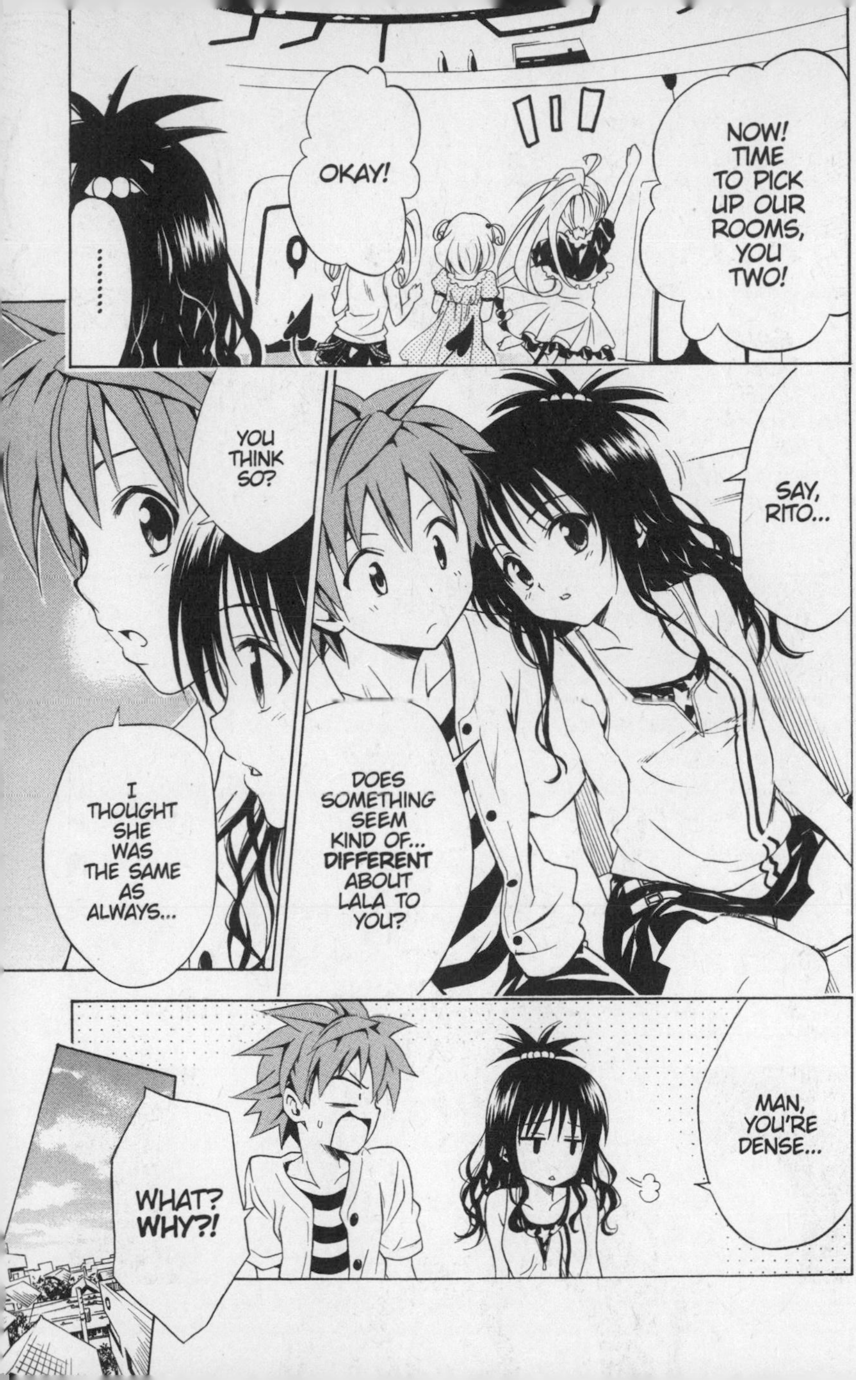
NOW! TIME TO PICK UP OUR ROOMS, YOU TWO!
OKAY!
......
SAY, RITO...
DOES SOMETHING SEEM KIND OF... DIFFERENT ABOUT LALA TO YOU?
YOU THINK SO?
I THOUGHT SHE WAS THE SAME AS ALWAYS...
MAN, YOU'RE DENSE...
WHAT? WHY?!

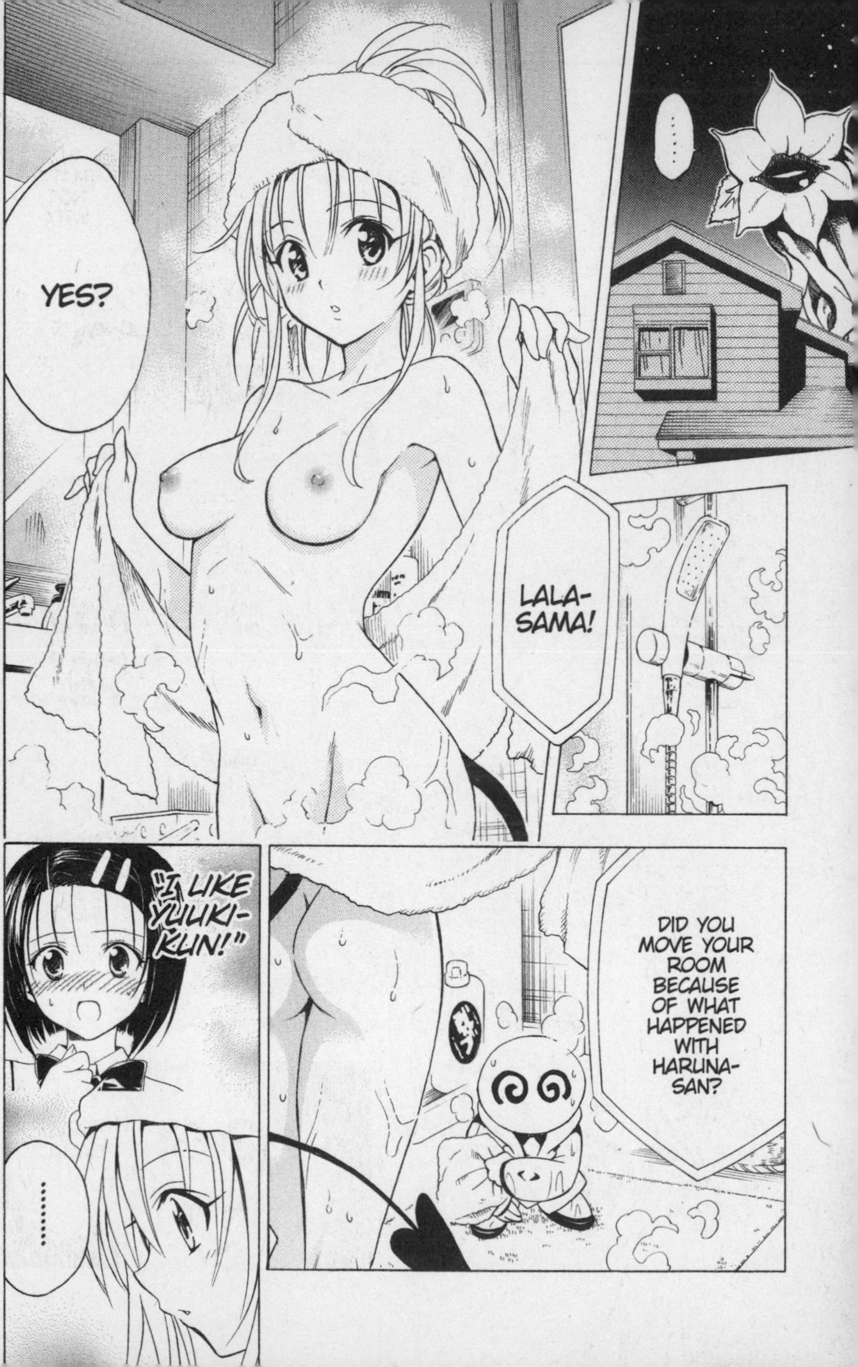
……
LALA-SAMA!
YES?
DID YOU MOVE YOUR ROOM BECAUSE OF WHAT HAPPENED WITH HARUNA-SAN?
"I LIKE YUUKI-KUN!"
……

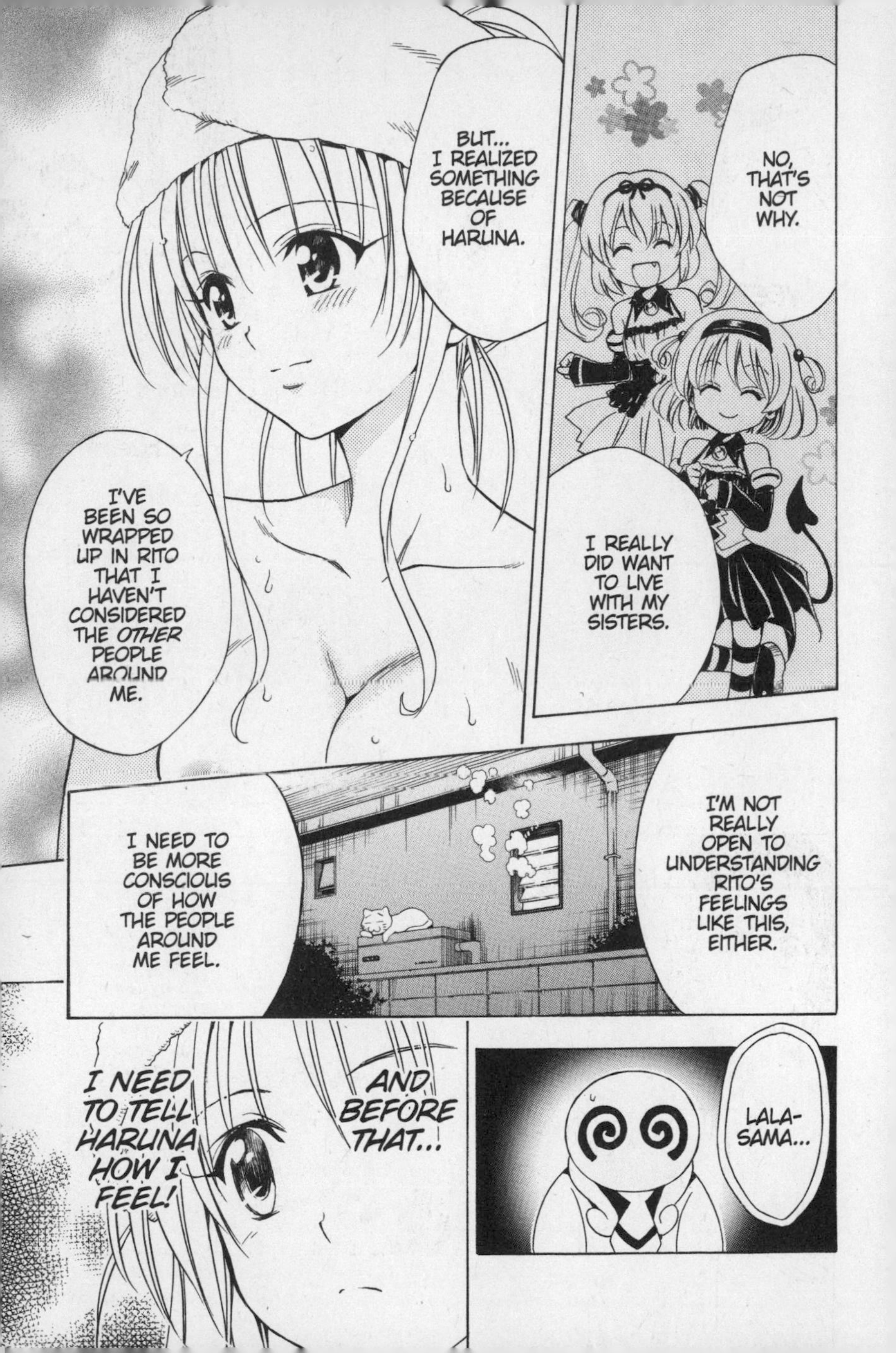
NO, THAT'S NOT WHY.
I REALLY DID WANT TO LIVE WITH MY SISTERS.
BUT... I REALIZED SOMETHING BECAUSE OF HARUNA.
I'VE BEEN SO WRAPPED UP IN RITO THAT I HAVEN'T CONSIDERED THE *OTHER* PEOPLE AROUND ME.
I'M NOT REALLY OPEN TO UNDERSTANDING RITO'S FEELINGS LIKE THIS, EITHER.
I NEED TO BE MORE CONSCIOUS OF HOW THE PEOPLE AROUND ME FEEL.
LALA-SAMA...
AND BEFORE THAT...
I NEED TO TELL HARUNA HOW I FEEL!

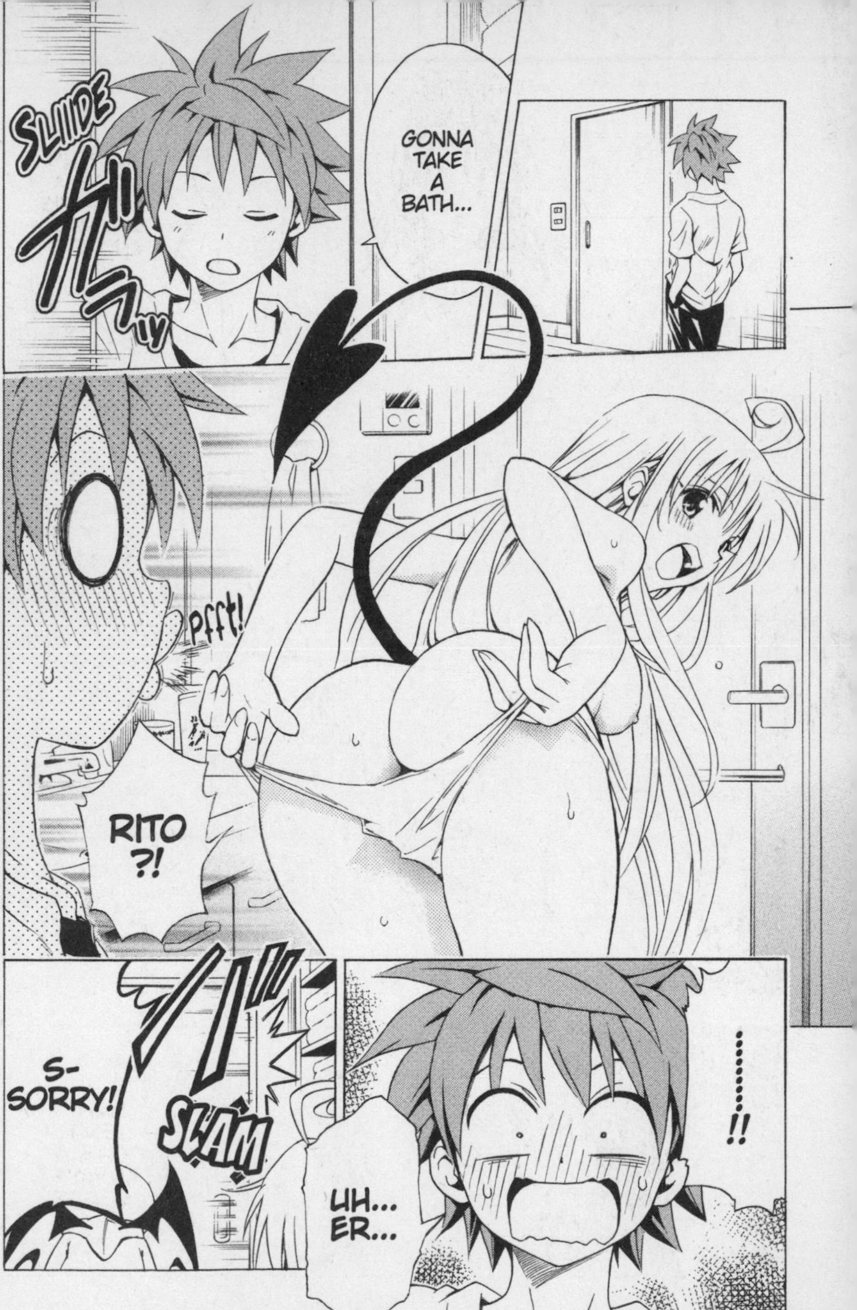
GONNA TAKE A BATH...
SLIIDE
Pfft!
RITO ?!
......!!
UH... ER...
S-SORRY!
SLAM

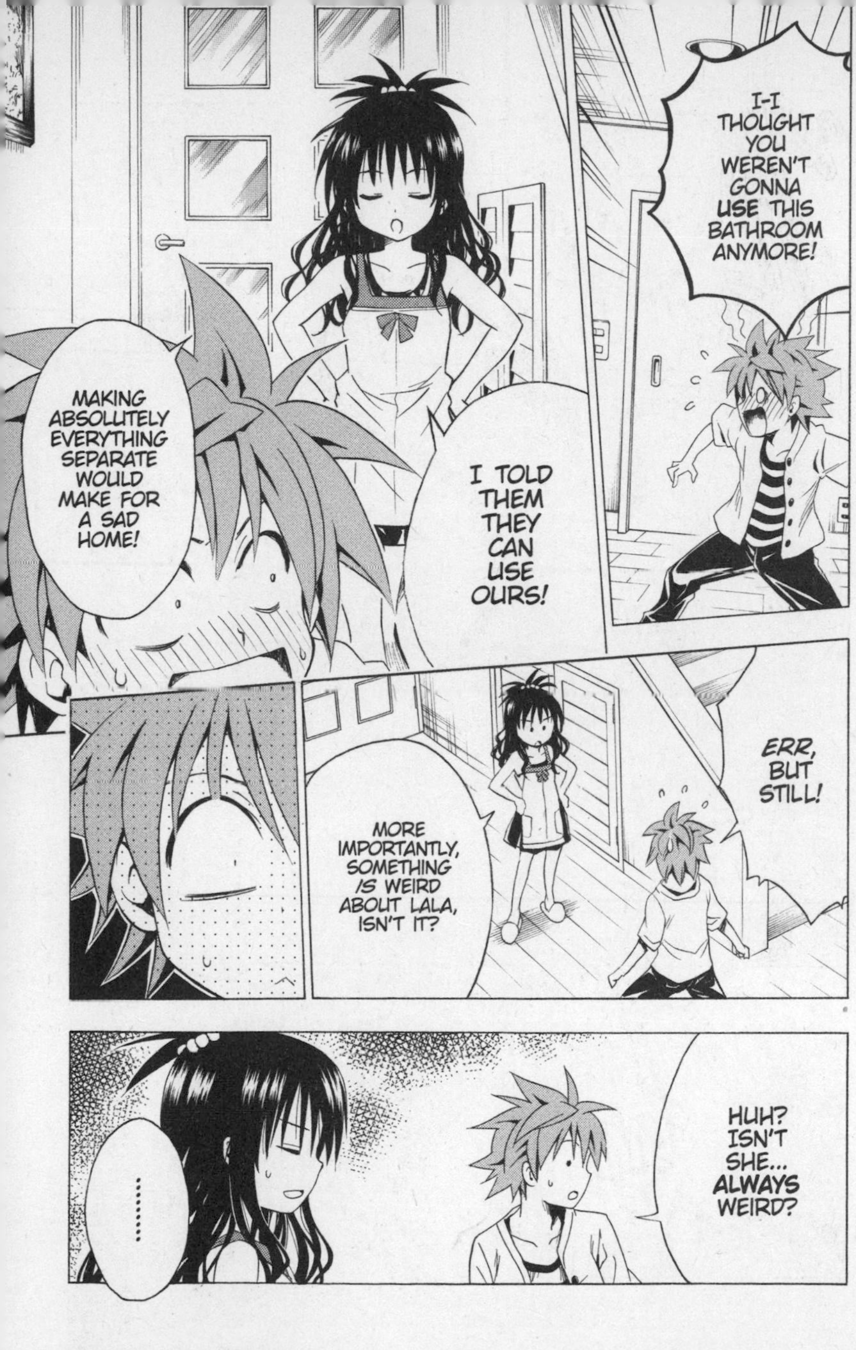
I-I THOUGHT YOU WEREN'T GONNA USE THIS BATHROOM ANYMORE!
I TOLD THEM THEY CAN USE OURS!
MAKING ABSOLUTELY EVERYTHING SEPARATE WOULD MAKE FOR A SAD HOME!
ERR, BUT STILL!
MORE IMPORTANTLY, SOMETHING IS WEIRD ABOUT LALA, ISN'T IT?
HUH? ISN'T SHE... ALWAYS WEIRD?
......

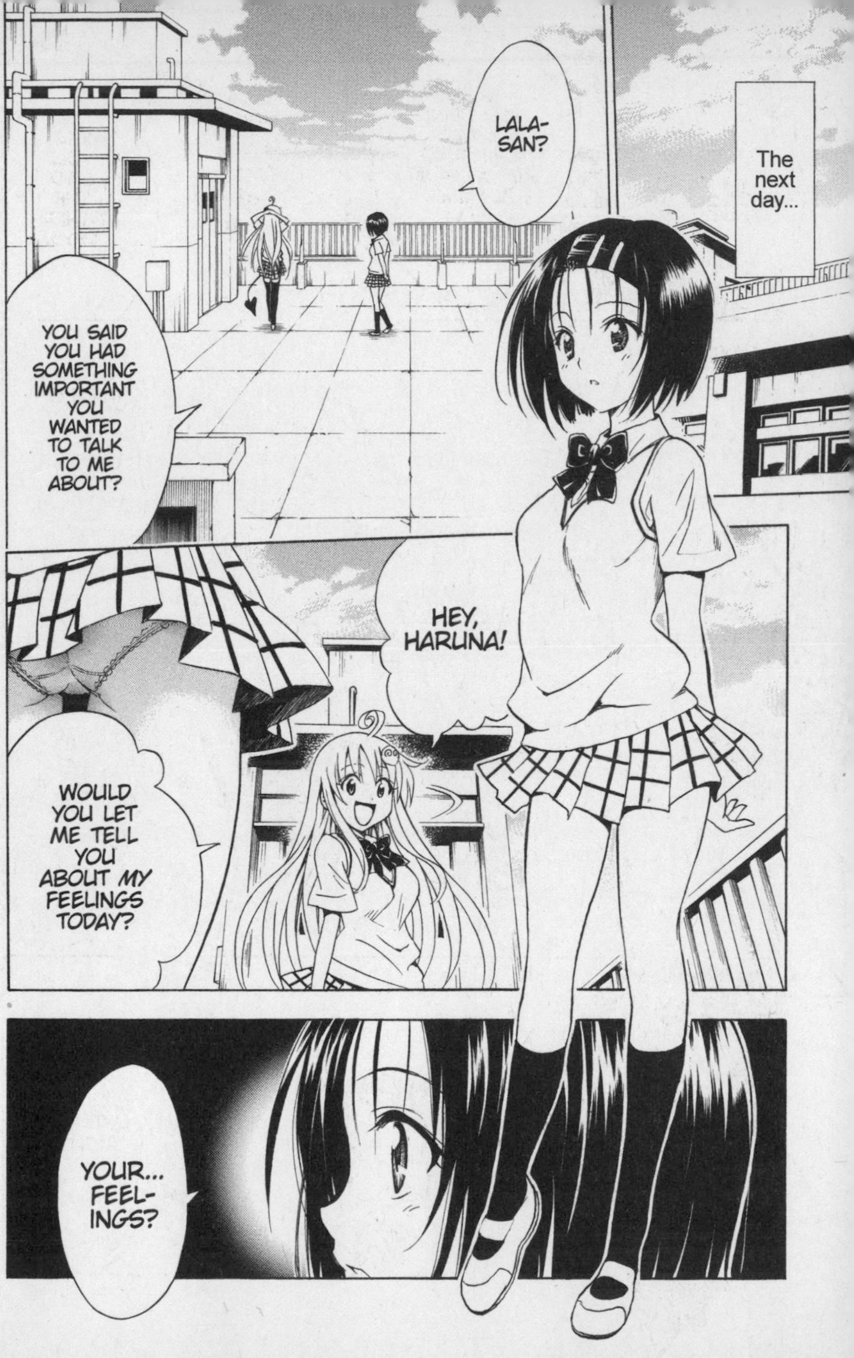
The next day...
LALA-SAN?
YOU SAID YOU HAD SOMETHING IMPORTANT YOU WANTED TO TALK TO ME ABOUT?
HEY, HARUNA!
WOULD YOU LET ME TELL YOU ABOUT MY FEELINGS TODAY?
YOUR... FEEL-INGS?

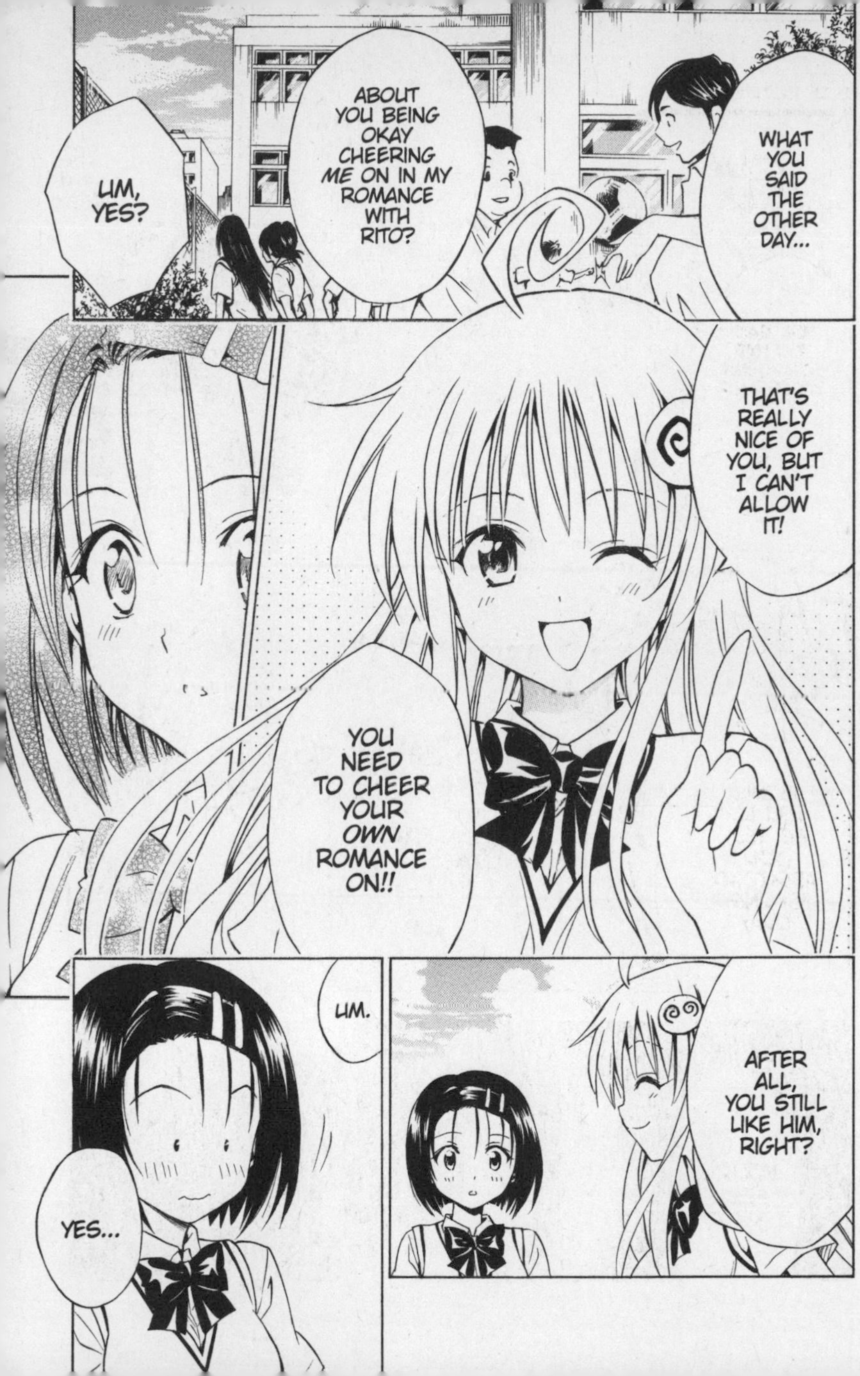
WHAT YOU SAID THE OTHER DAY...
ABOUT YOU BEING OKAY CHEERING *ME* ON IN MY ROMANCE WITH RITO?
UM, YES?
THAT'S REALLY NICE OF YOU, BUT I CAN'T ALLOW IT!
YOU NEED TO CHEER YOUR *OWN* ROMANCE ON!!
AFTER ALL, YOU STILL LIKE HIM, RIGHT?
UM.
YES...

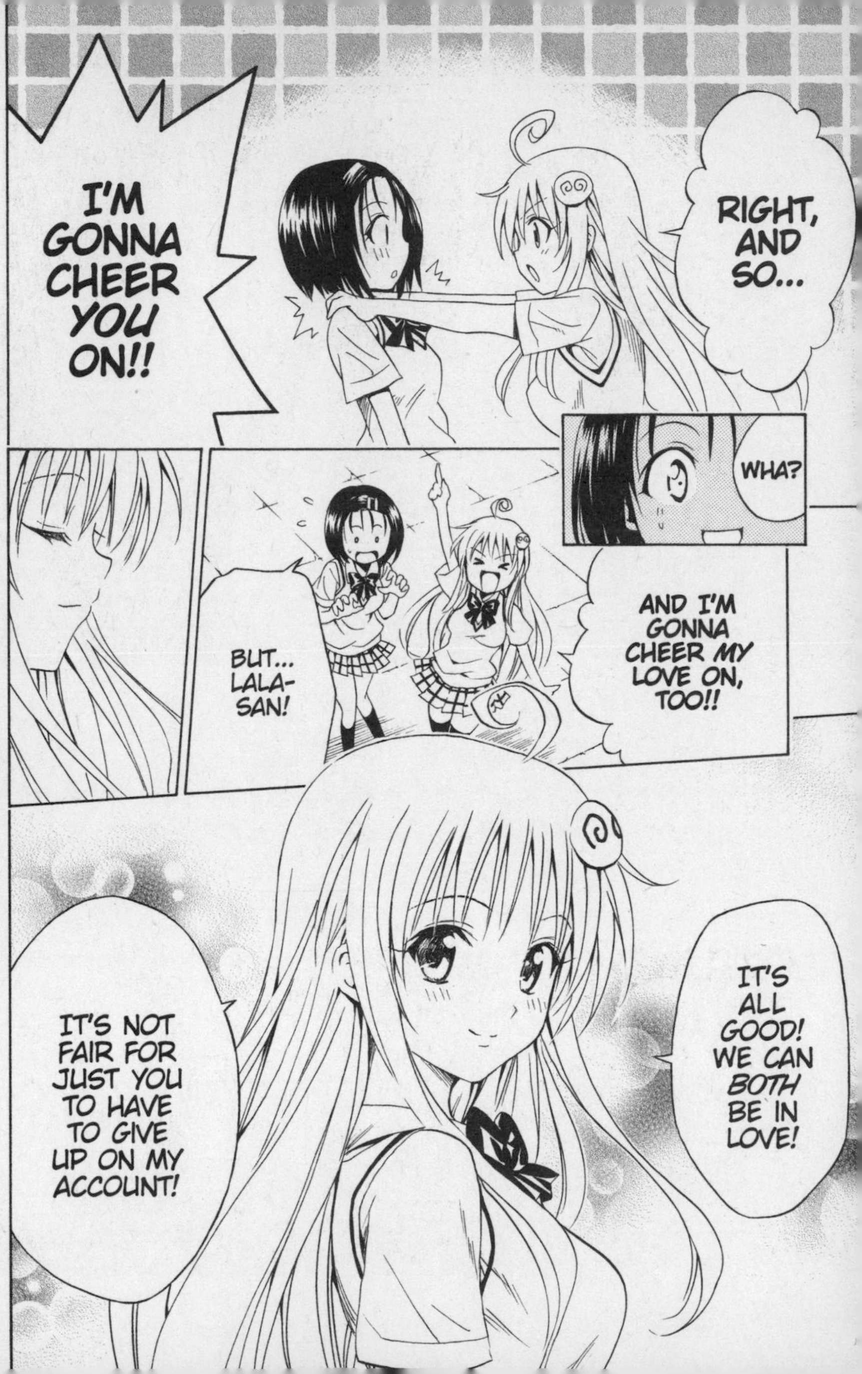
RIGHT, AND SO...
I'M GONNA CHEER YOU ON!!
WHA?
AND I'M GONNA CHEER MY LOVE ON, TOO!!
BUT... LALA-SAN!
IT'S ALL GOOD! WE CAN BOTH BE IN LOVE!
IT'S NOT FAIR FOR JUST YOU TO HAVE TO GIVE UP ON MY ACCOUNT!

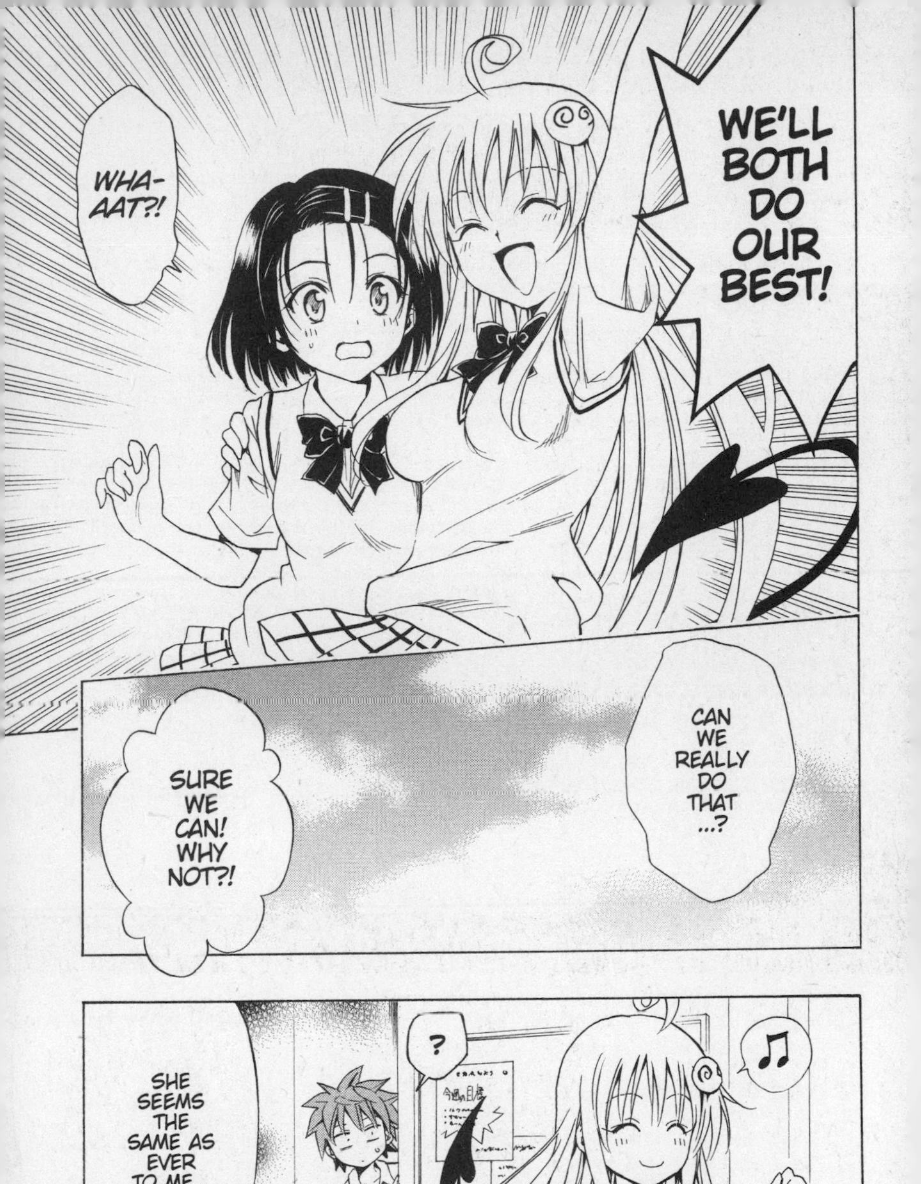
WE'LL BOTH DO OUR BEST!
WHA-AAT?!
CAN WE REALLY DO THAT ...?
SURE WE CAN! WHY NOT?!
♫
?
SHE SEEMS THE SAME AS EVER TO ME... RIGHT?

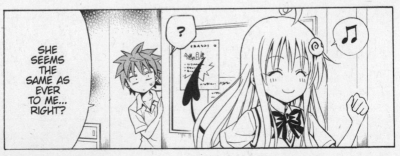

To Love Ru Bonus Info:
Magical Kyouko, the Dynamite Girl: Part 1

All Info Taken From: Free Encyclopedia (ukiuki ♪ pedian)

Magical Kyouko, the Dynamite Girl:
An original animated television show aimed at young girls.
51 episodes in total.

Plot Summary:
Uzarth is a mysterious organization that sows the seeds of stress around the world. But there is one brave girl who stands against them, Magical Kyouko—her adventures make up this slightly naughty romantic comedy aimed at young girls!

Characters:

• Kirisaki Kyouko
A magical girl from another world who is a sophomore in high school. She's quite busy worrying about love and style, but supposedly, she's only interested in looks. She can transform into Magical Kyouko, the Dynamite Girl. Her tendency to solve all her problems by lighting them on fire can be something of an issue at times.

• Shirone
Kyouko's support character. A stylish white cat wearing a ribbon. It can talk!

• Ikemen Yuuto
A.K.A. "Dreamboat-Senpai." A bass player in a band and Kyouko's senior in school. He's a handsome guy, buuut a bit of a perv. He's madly in love with Kyouko, but she really only seems interested in his face. He knows Kyouko's real identity, and helps her in the fight against Uzarth.

• Dark Lord Uzarth
The leader of the mysterious organization Uzarth. His true identity remains a mystery.

• General Mojack
One of Uzarth's commanders. Accompanied by a squadron of Stress-Makers, he burns with a passion to defeat Kyouko. Has an afro, but no one really knows why. You have to respect that hair.

• The Stress-Makers
The so-called villains of the week, they appear in antagonistic roles each episode. Count Gemuu, Baron Mobile, Prince Night, Secretary Stockings, Colonel Toothbrush, and more round out this dastardly group.

Publication
Shuueisha has published six volumes, one light novel, and two magazine books (or *mook*). A short story collection is in the final stages of production, with original characters from designer Mr. Kentaro, which will differ from the serialization that appeared in monthly magazines.

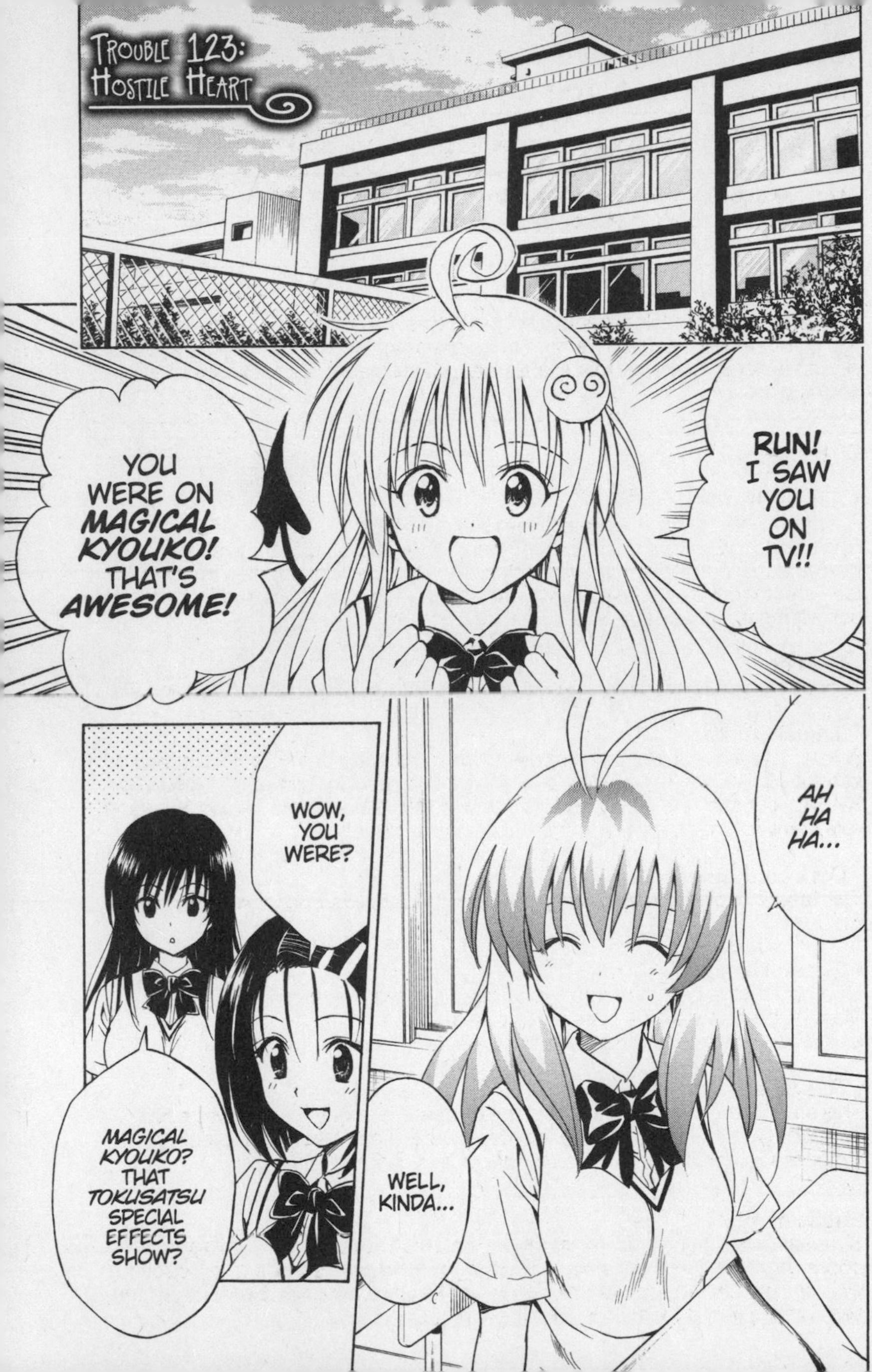
Trouble 123: Hostile Heart
RUN! I SAW YOU ON TV!!
YOU WERE ON MAGICAL KYOUKO! THAT'S AWESOME!
AH HA HA...
WELL, KINDA...
WOW, YOU WERE?
MAGICAL KYOUKO? THAT TOKUSATSU SPECIAL EFFECTS SHOW?

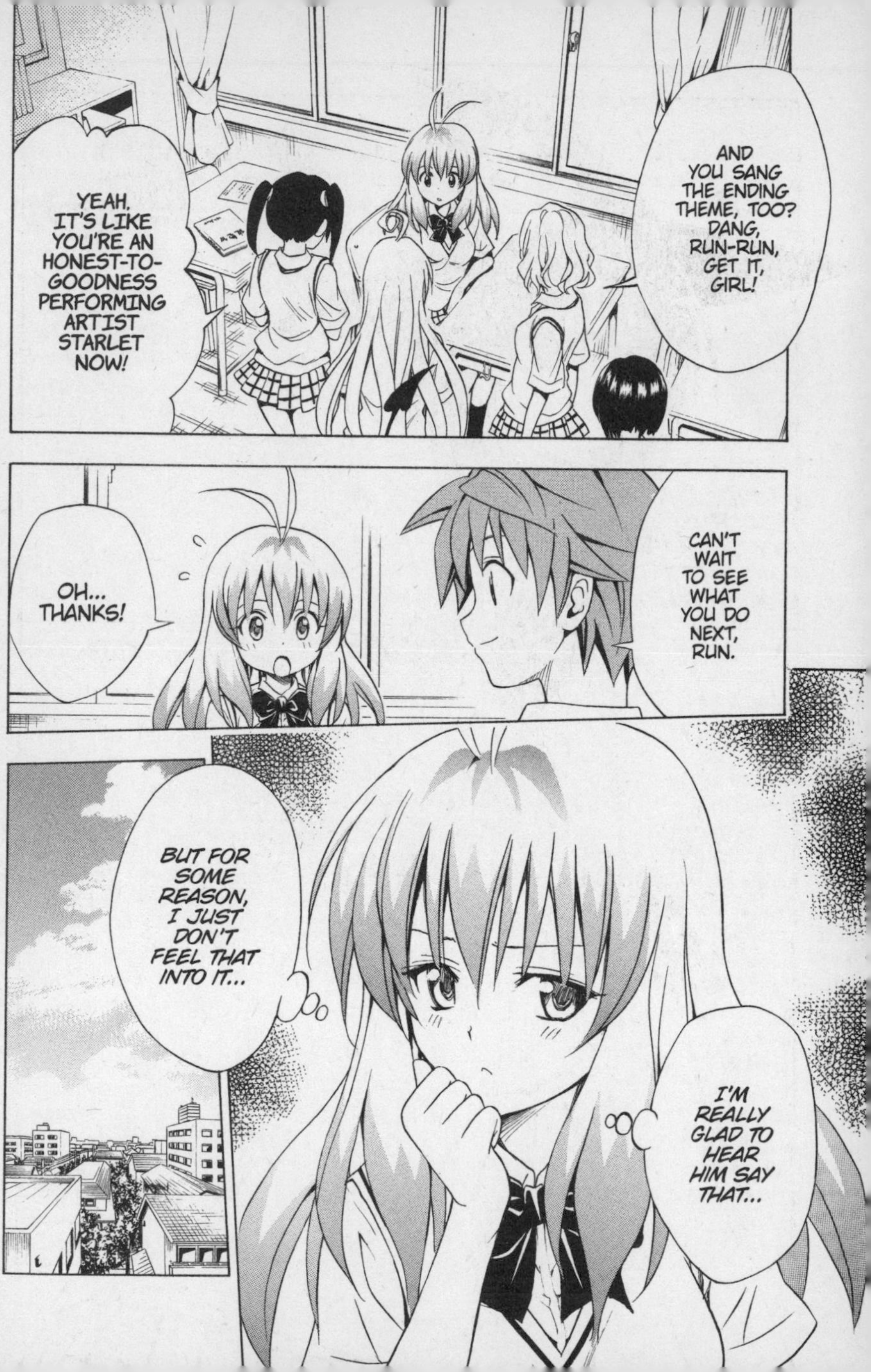
AND YOU SANG THE ENDING THEME, TOO? DANG, RUN-RUN, GET IT, GIRL!
YEAH. IT'S LIKE YOU'RE AN HONEST-TO-GOODNESS PERFORMING ARTIST STARLET NOW!
CAN'T WAIT TO SEE WHAT YOU DO NEXT, RUN.
OH... THANKS!
I'M REALLY GLAD TO HEAR HIM SAY THAT...
BUT FOR SOME REASON, I JUST DON'T FEEL THAT INTO IT...

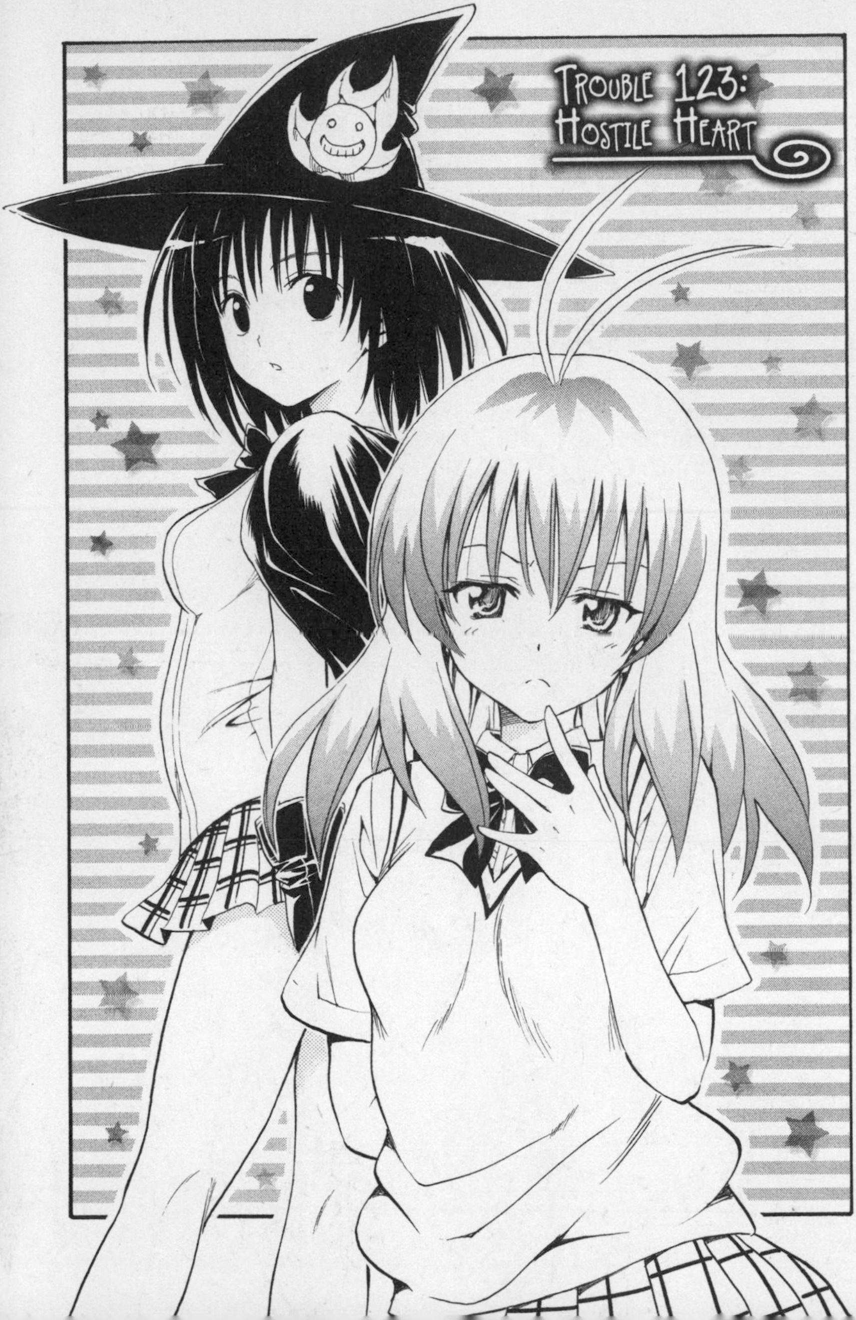
Trouble 123:
Hostile Heart

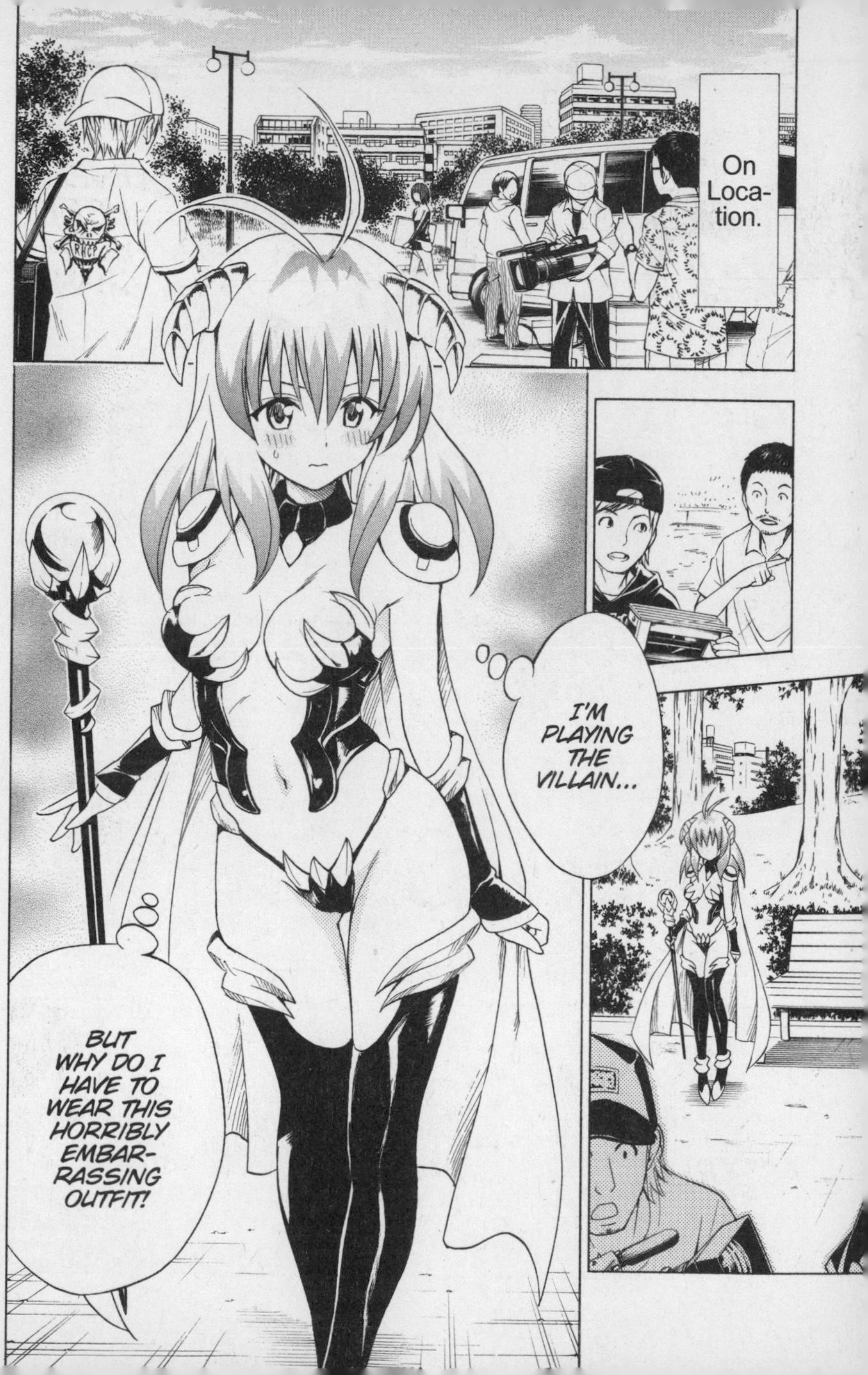
On Location.
I'M PLAYING THE VILLAIN...
BUT WHY DO I HAVE TO WEAR THIS HORRIBLY EMBARRASSING OUTFIT!

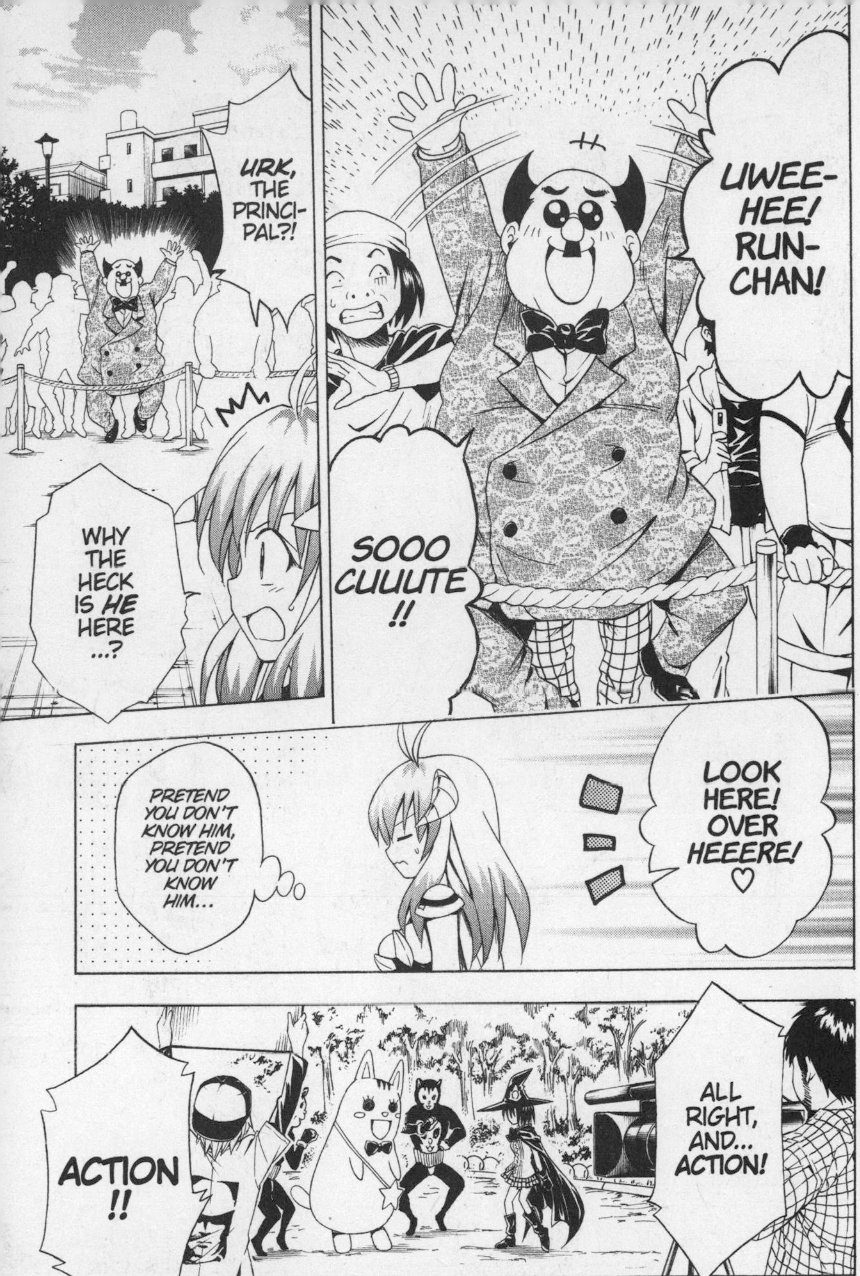
UWEE-HEE! RUN-CHAN!
SOOO CUUUTE !!
URK, THE PRINCIPAL?!
WHY THE HECK IS *HE* HERE ...?
LOOK HERE! OVER HEEERE! ♡
PRETEND YOU DON'T KNOW HIM, PRETEND YOU DON'T KNOW HIM...
ALL RIGHT, AND... ACTION!
ACTION !!

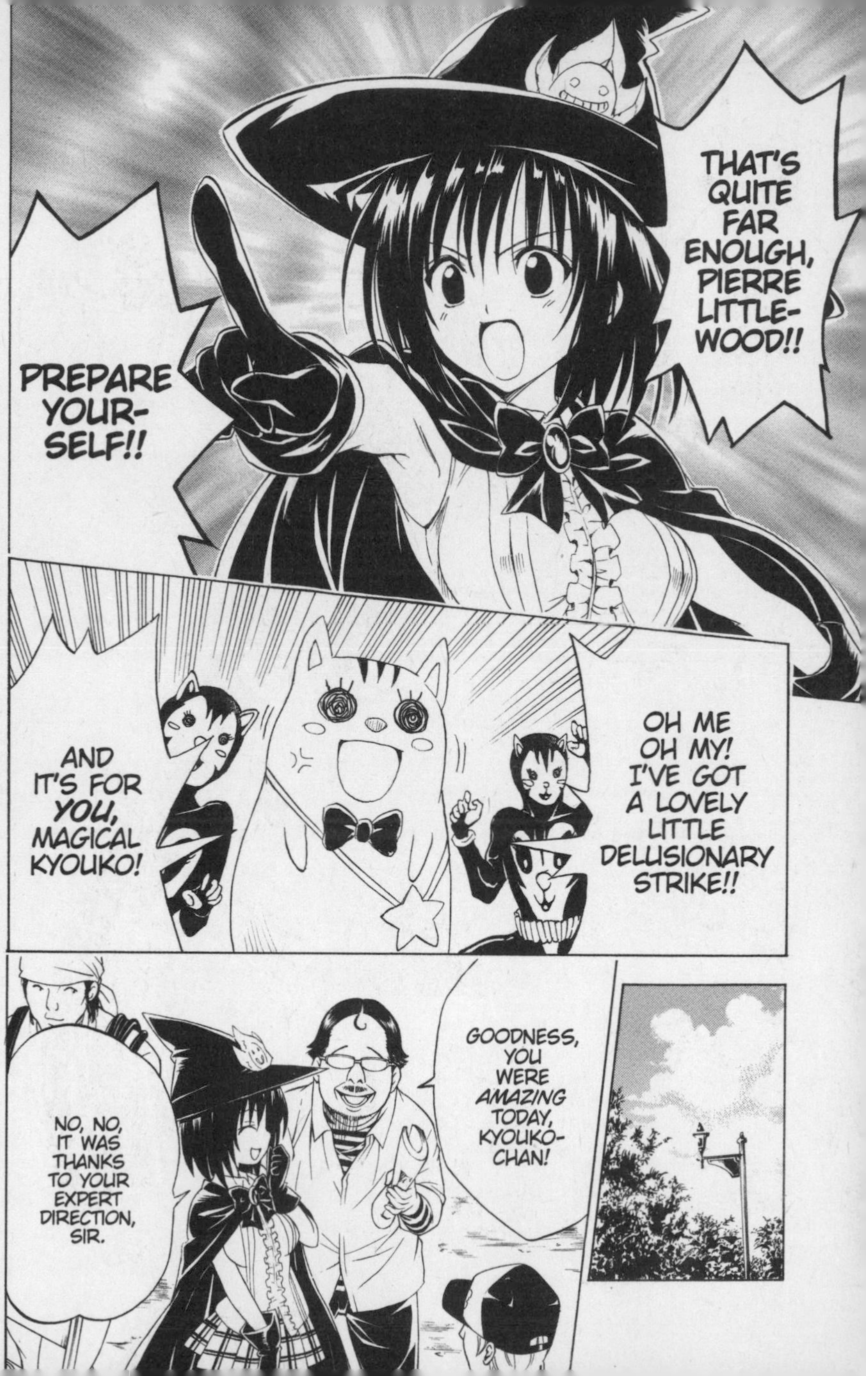
THAT'S QUITE FAR ENOUGH, PIERRE LITTLEWOOD!!
PREPARE YOURSELF!!
OH ME OH MY! I'VE GOT A LOVELY LITTLE DELUSIONARY STRIKE!!
AND IT'S FOR *YOU*, MAGICAL KYOUKO!
GOODNESS, YOU WERE *AMAZING* TODAY, KYOUKO-CHAN!
NO, NO, IT WAS THANKS TO YOUR EXPERT DIRECTION, SIR.

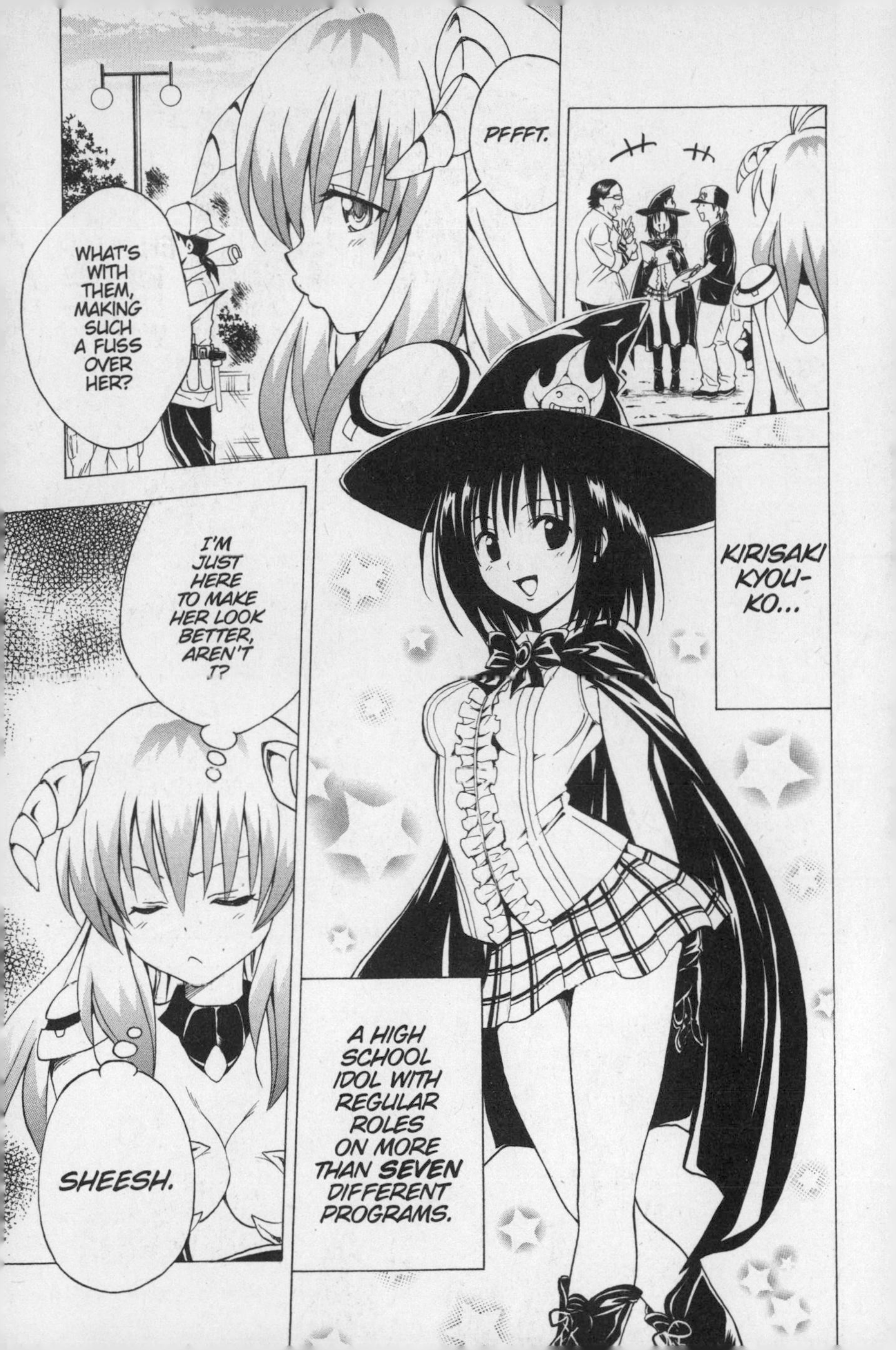
PFFFT.
WHAT'S WITH THEM, MAKING SUCH A FUSS OVER HER?
KIRISAKI KYOU-KO...
A HIGH SCHOOL IDOL WITH REGULAR ROLES ON MORE THAN SEVEN DIFFERENT PROGRAMS.
I'M JUST HERE TO MAKE HER LOOK BETTER, AREN'T I?
SHEESH.

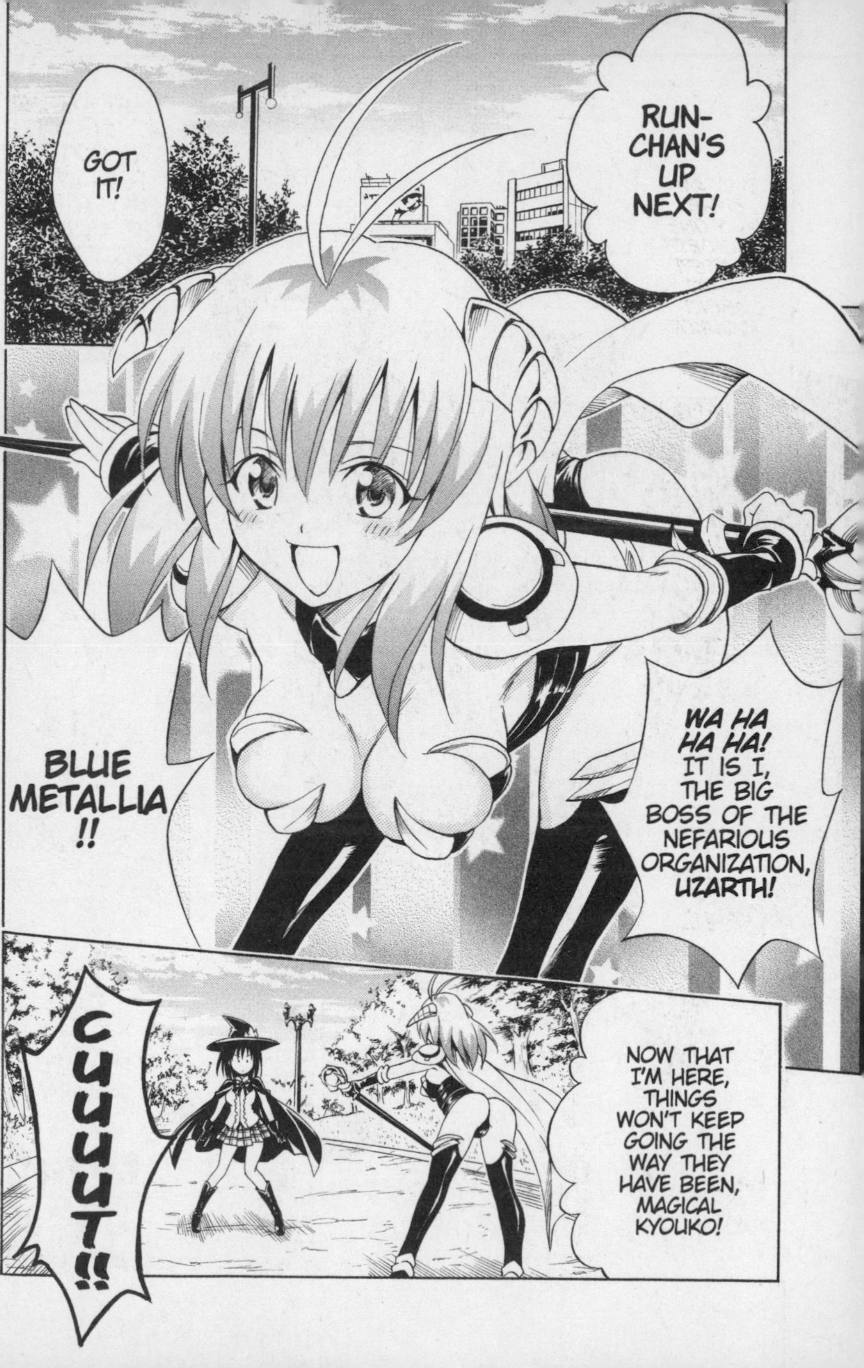
RUN-CHAN'S UP NEXT!
GOT IT!
WA HA HA HA! IT IS I, THE BIG BOSS OF THE NEFARIOUS ORGANIZATION, UZARTH!
BLUE METALLIA !!
NOW THAT I'M HERE, THINGS WON'T KEEP GOING THE WAY THEY HAVE BEEN, MAGICAL KYOUKO!
CUUUUT!!

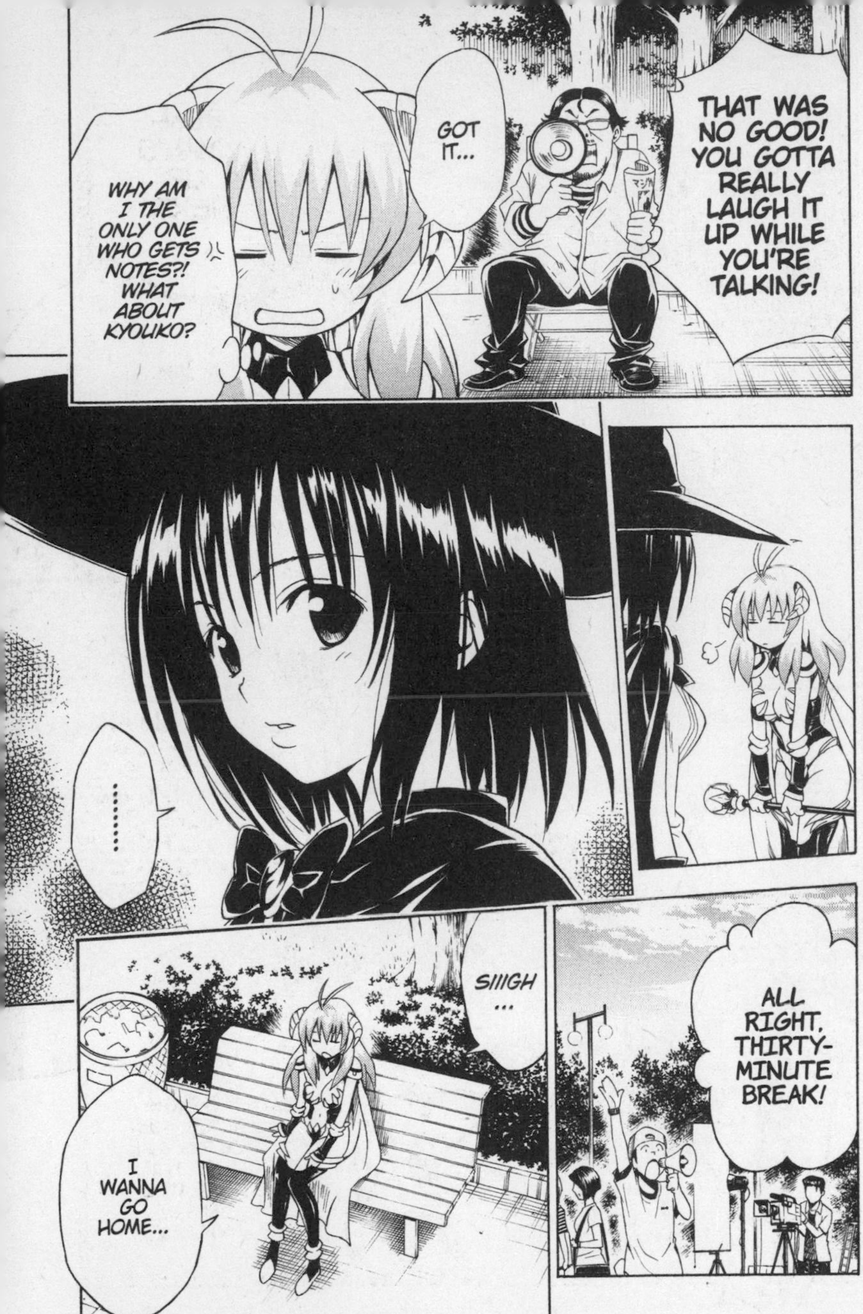
THAT WAS NO GOOD! YOU GOTTA REALLY LAUGH IT UP WHILE YOU'RE TALKING!
GOT IT...
WHY AM I THE ONLY ONE WHO GETS NOTES?! WHAT ABOUT KYOUKO?
......
ALL RIGHT, THIRTY-MINUTE BREAK!
SIIIGH ...
I WANNA GO HOME...

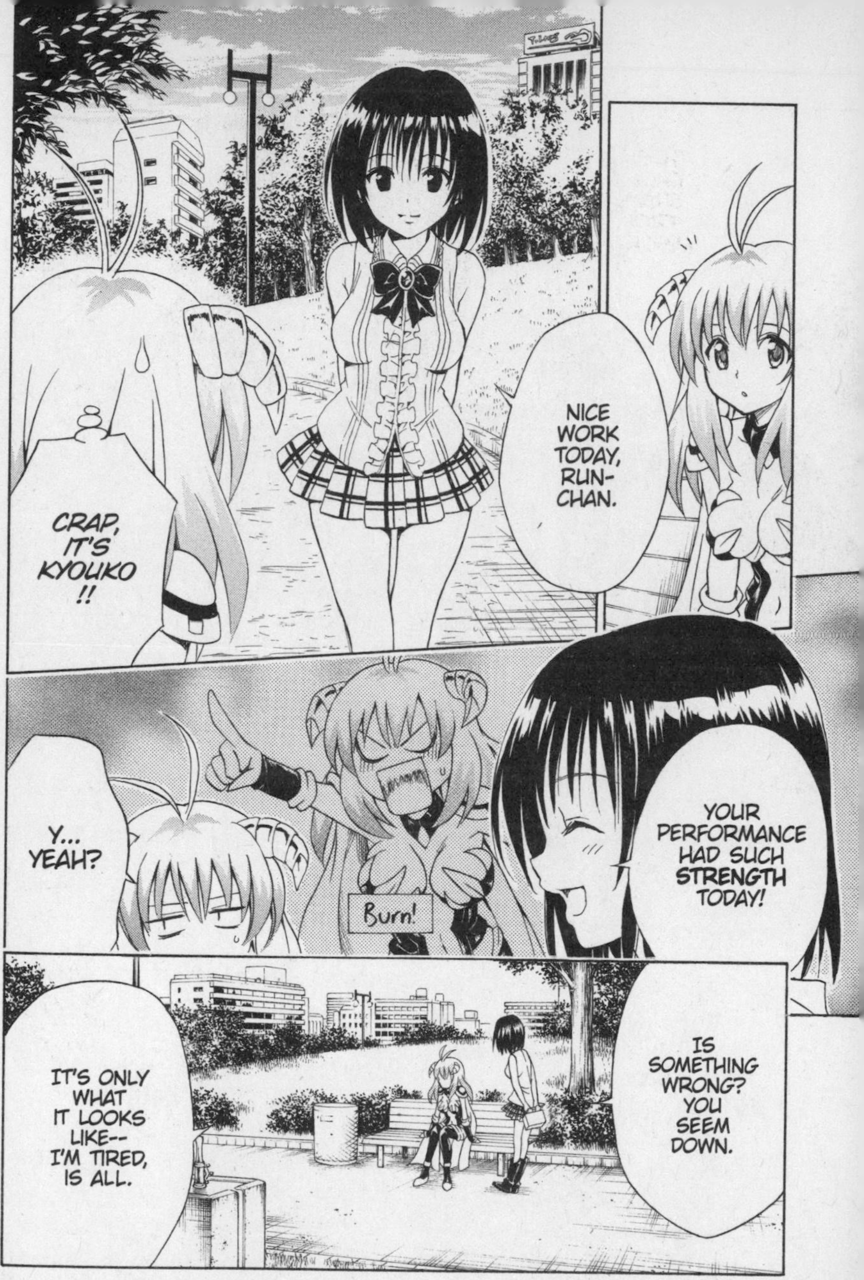
NICE WORK TODAY, RUN-CHAN.
CRAP, IT'S KYOUKO!!
YOUR PERFORMANCE HAD SUCH STRENGTH TODAY!
Burn!
Y... YEAH?
IS SOMETHING WRONG? YOU SEEM DOWN.
IT'S ONLY WHAT IT LOOKS LIKE-- I'M TIRED, IS ALL.

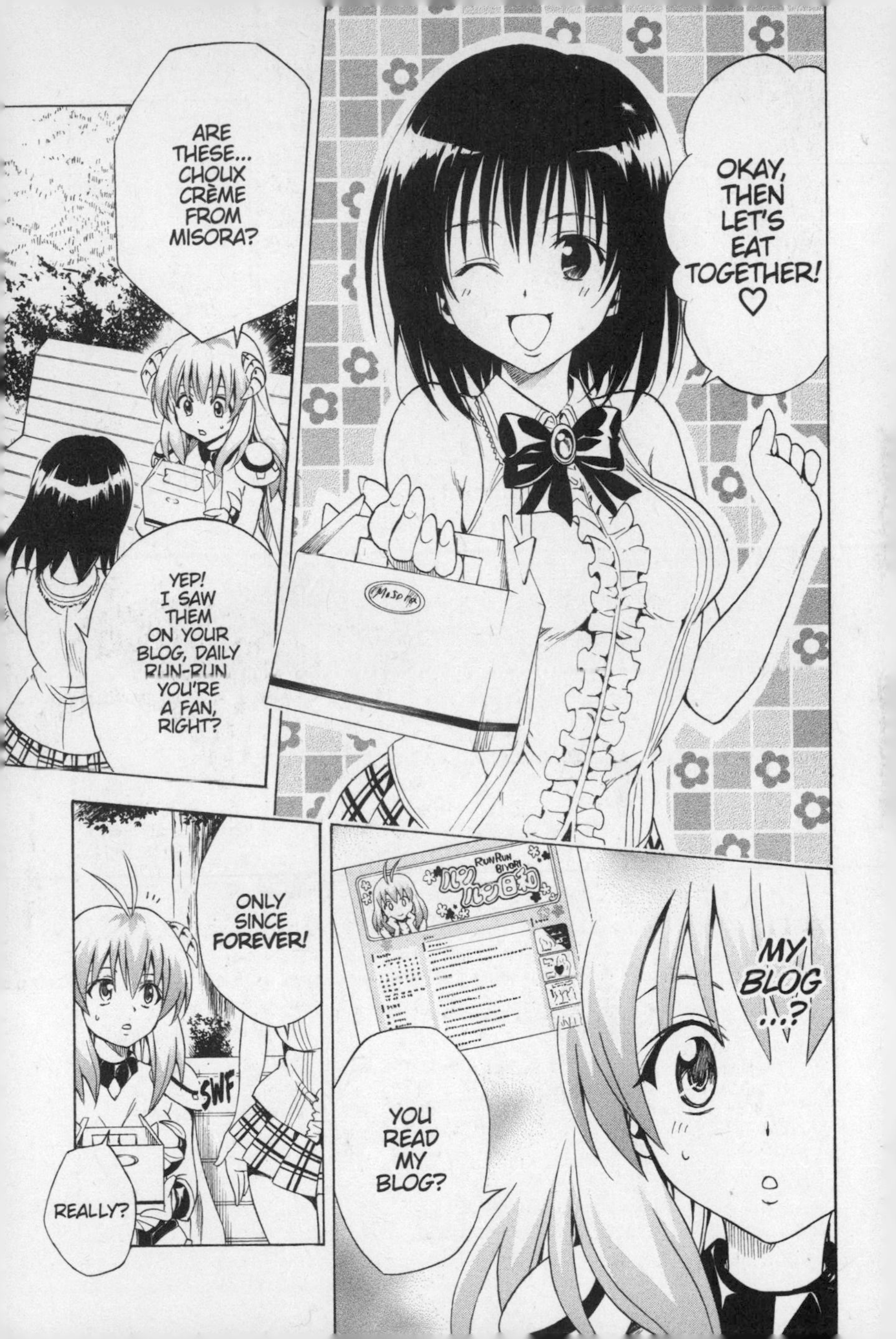
OKAY, THEN LET'S EAT TOGETHER! ♡
ARE THESE... CHOUX CRÈME FROM MISORA?
YEP! I SAW THEM ON YOUR BLOG, DAILY RUN-RUN YOU'RE A FAN, RIGHT?
RUN RUN BIYORI
ルンルン日和
MY BLOG ...?
YOU READ MY BLOG?
ONLY SINCE FOREVER!
SWF
REALLY?

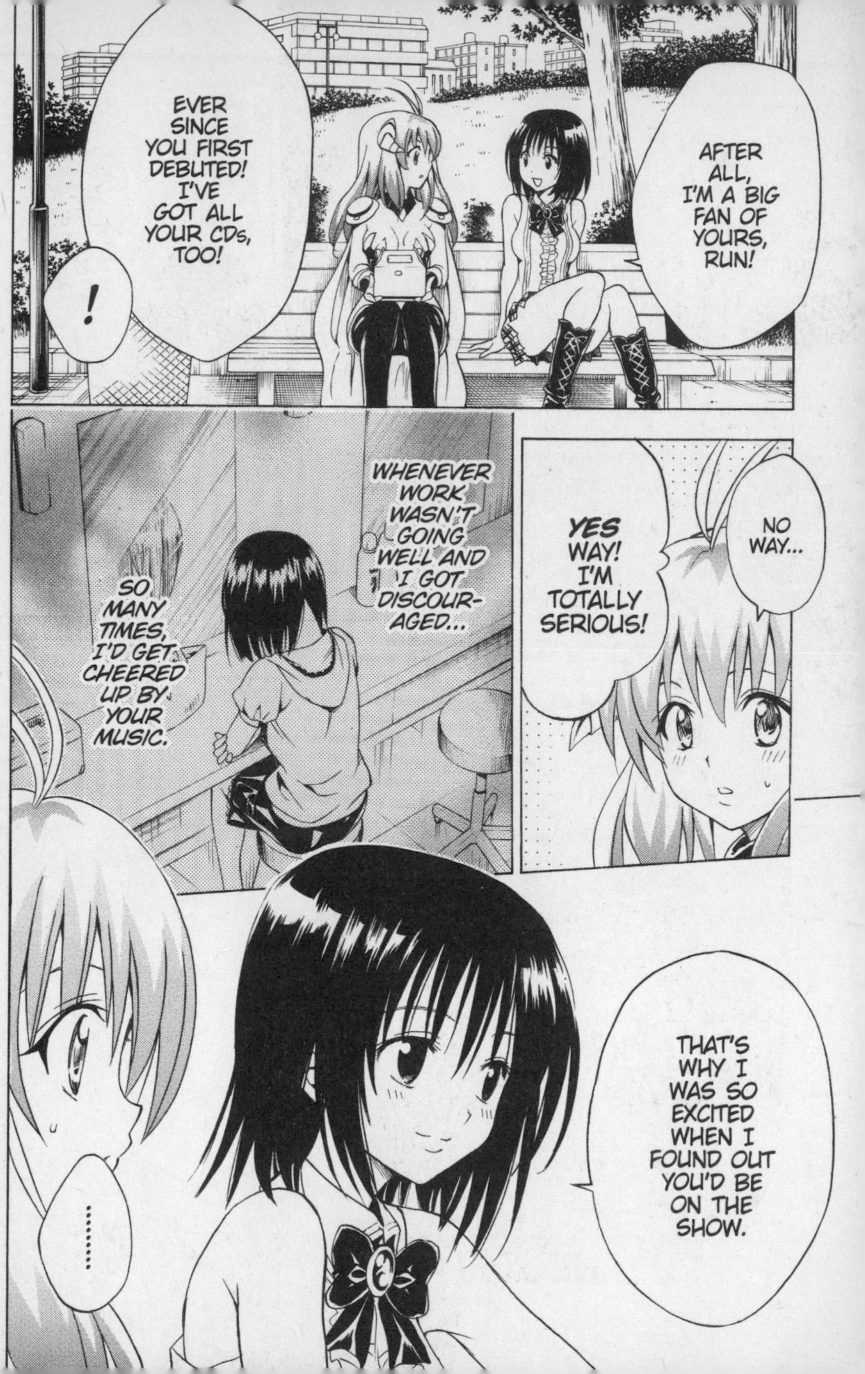
AFTER ALL, I'M A BIG FAN OF YOURS, RUN!
EVER SINCE YOU FIRST DEBUTED! I'VE GOT ALL YOUR CDs, TOO!
!
NO WAY...
YES WAY! I'M TOTALLY SERIOUS!
WHENEVER WORK WASN'T GOING WELL AND I GOT DISCOURAGED...
SO MANY TIMES, I'D GET CHEERED UP BY YOUR MUSIC.
THAT'S WHY I WAS SO EXCITED WHEN I FOUND OUT YOU'D BE ON THE SHOW.
......

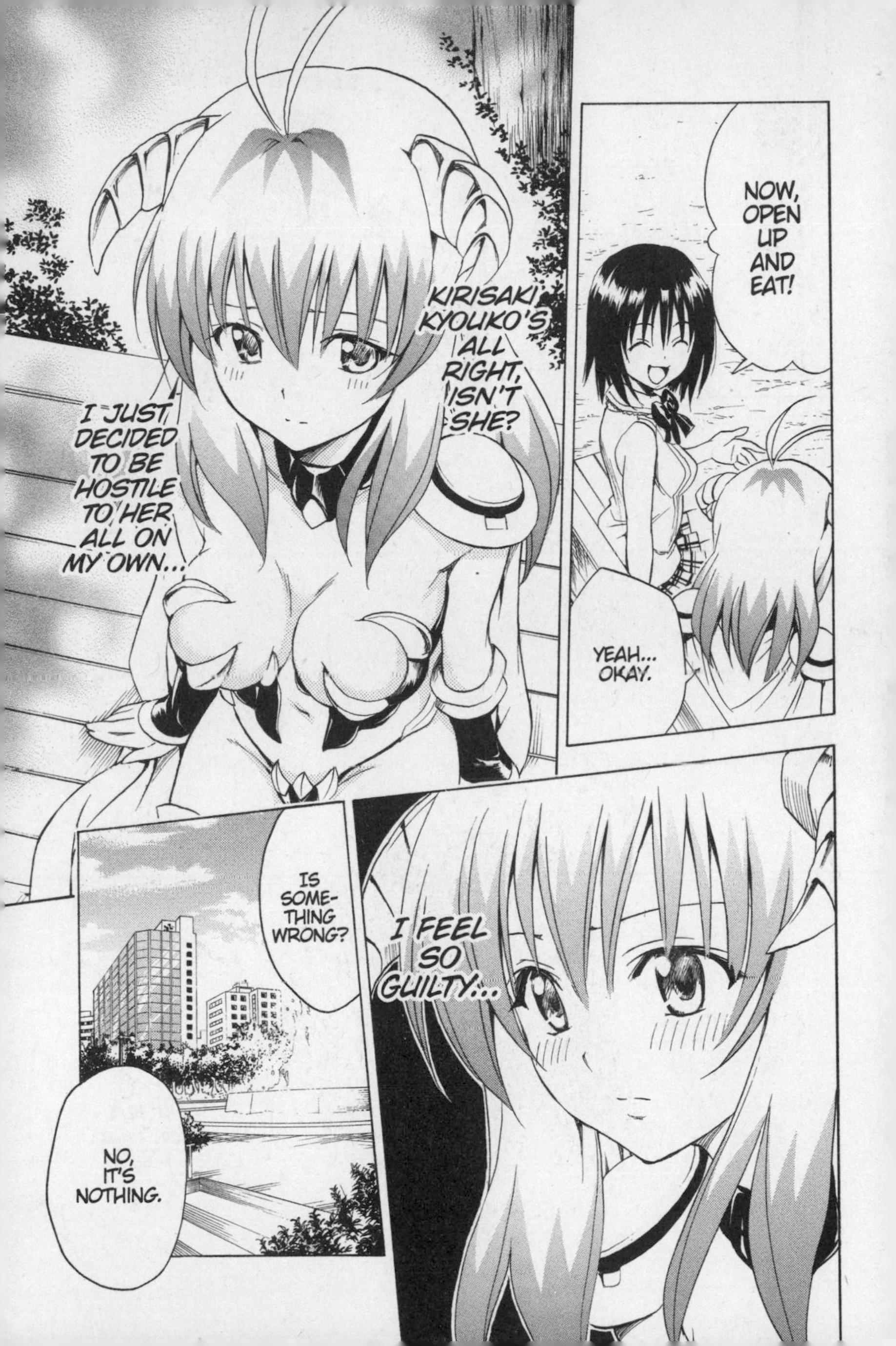
NOW, OPEN UP AND EAT!
YEAH... OKAY.
KIRISAKI KYOUKO'S ALL RIGHT, ISN'T SHE?
I JUST DECIDED TO BE HOSTILE TO HER ALL ON MY OWN...
I FEEL SO GUILTY...
IS SOME-THING WRONG?
NO, IT'S NOTHING.

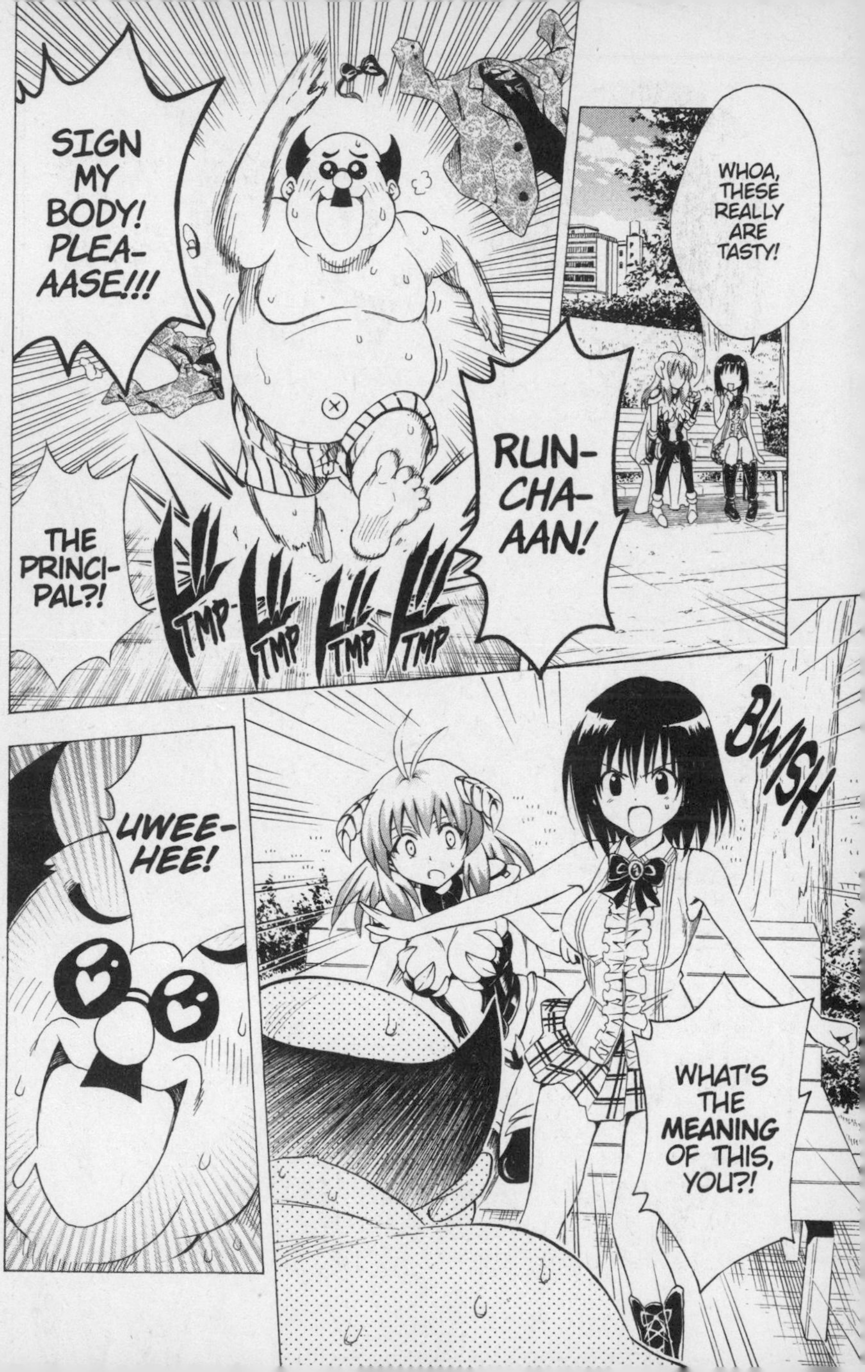
WHOA, THESE REALLY ARE TASTY!
RUN-CHA-AAN!
SIGN MY BODY! PLEA-AASE!!!
THE PRINCI-PAL?!
TMP-TMP TMP TMP
BWISH
WHAT'S THE MEANING OF THIS, YOU?!
UWEE-HEE!

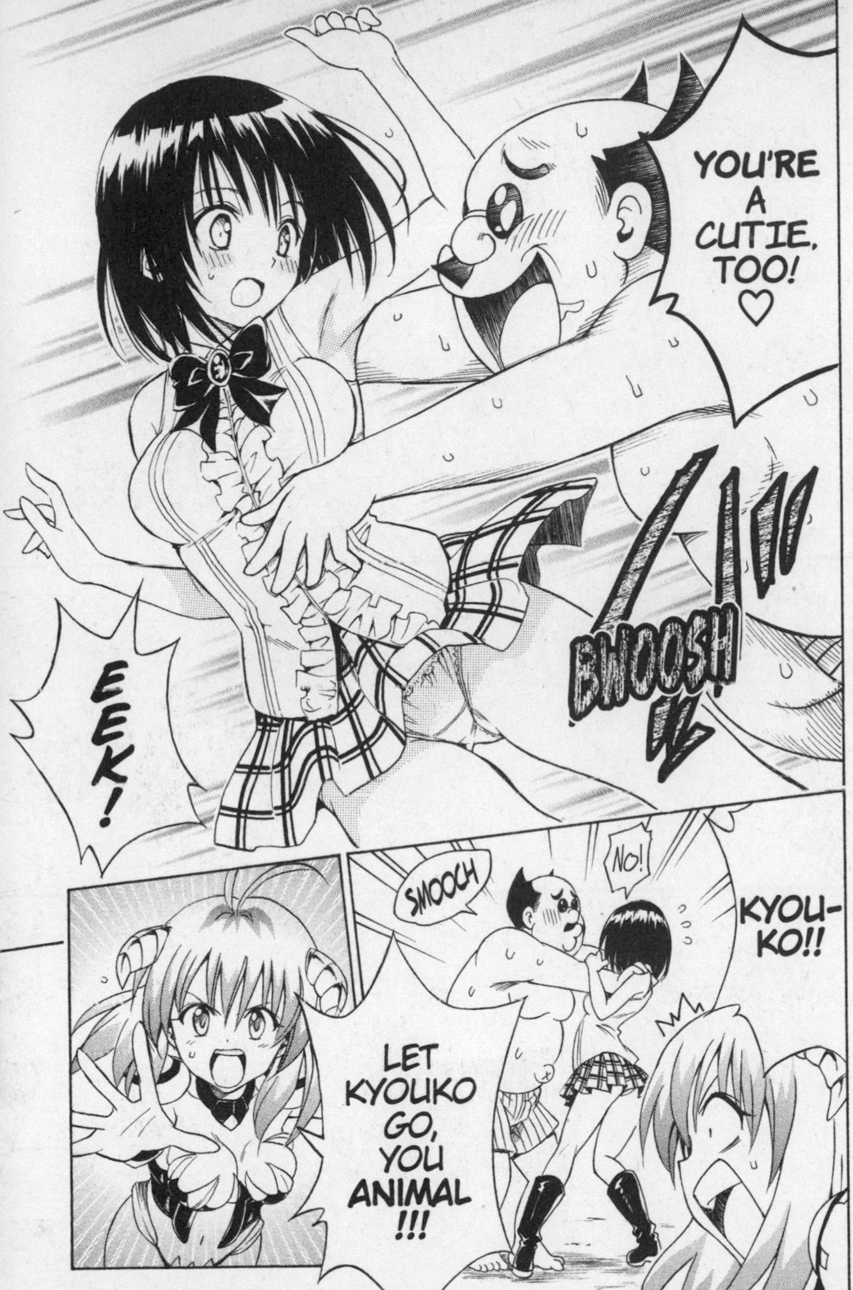
YOU'RE A CUTIE, TOO! ♡
BWOOSH
EEK!
KYOU-KO!!
NO!
SMOOCH
LET KYOUKO GO, YOU ANIMAL!!!

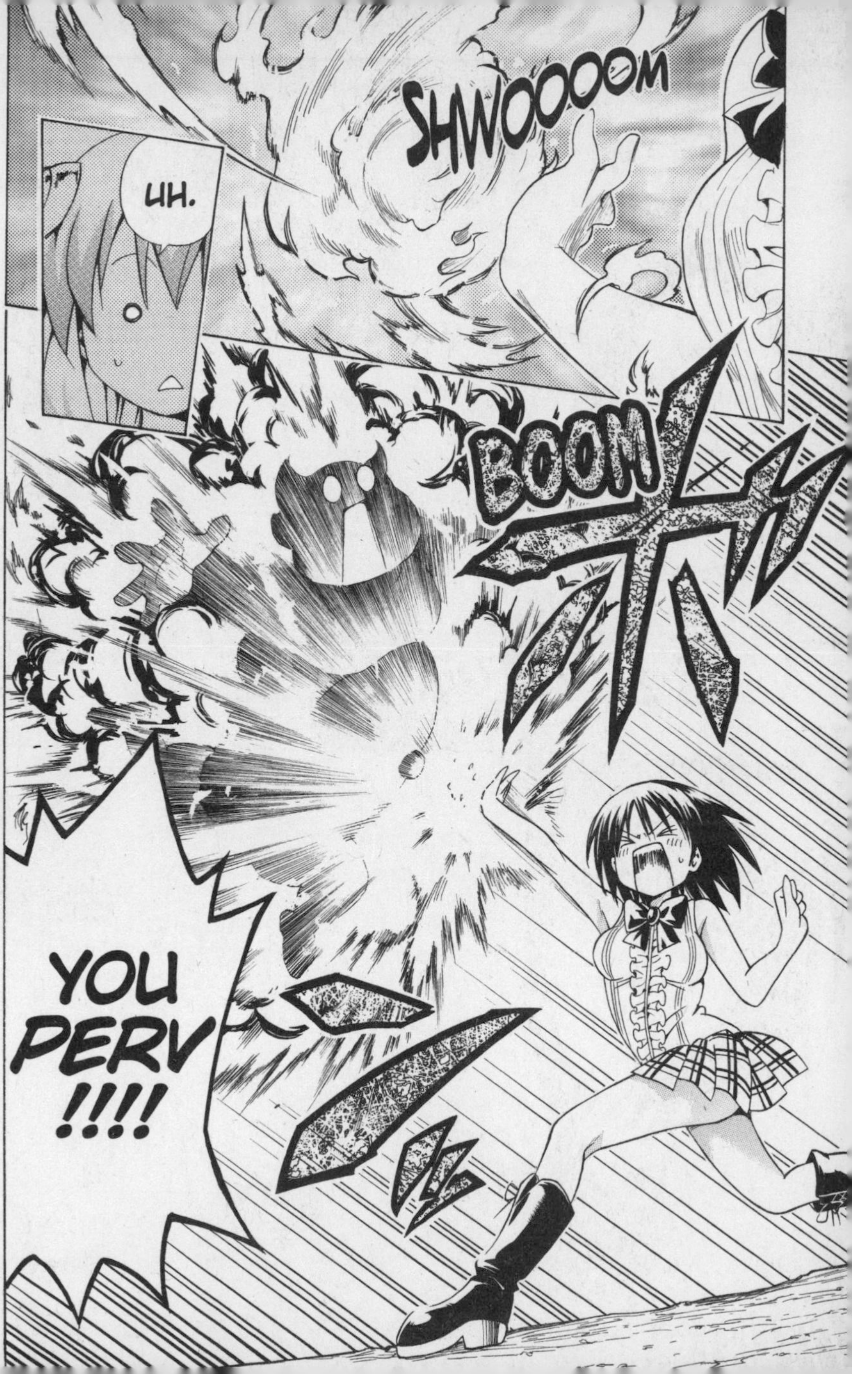
SHWOOOOM
UH.
BOOM
YOU PERV!!!!

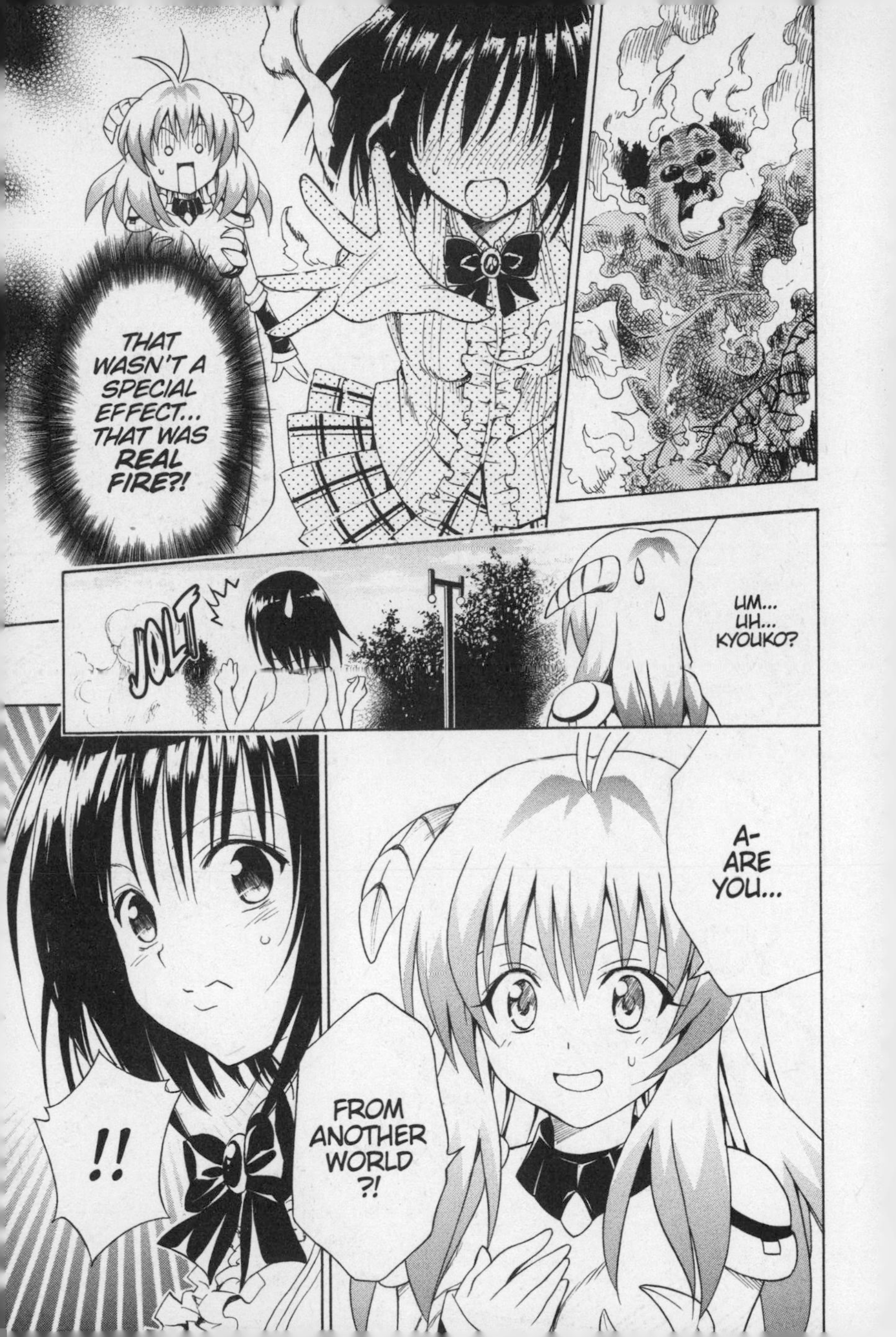
THAT WASN'T A SPECIAL EFFECT... THAT WAS REAL FIRE?!
UM... UH... KYOUKO?
JOLT
A- ARE YOU...
FROM ANOTHER WORLD ?!
!!

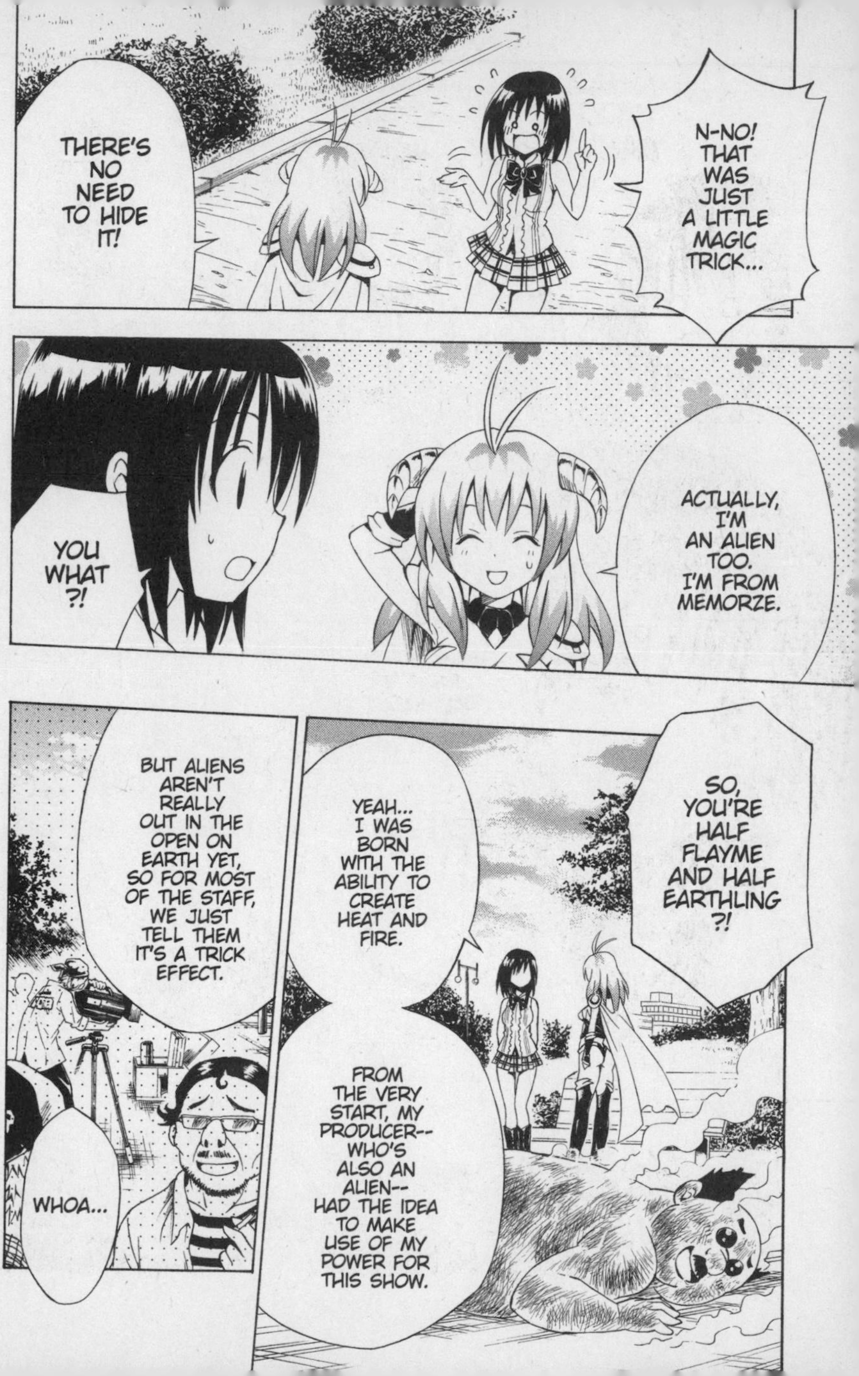
N-NO! THAT WAS JUST A LITTLE MAGIC TRICK...
THERE'S NO NEED TO HIDE IT!
ACTUALLY, I'M AN ALIEN TOO. I'M FROM MEMORZE.
YOU WHAT?!
SO, YOU'RE HALF FLAYME AND HALF EARTHLING?!
YEAH... I WAS BORN WITH THE ABILITY TO CREATE HEAT AND FIRE.
FROM THE VERY START, MY PRODUCER--WHO'S ALSO AN ALIEN--HAD THE IDEA TO MAKE USE OF MY POWER FOR THIS SHOW.
BUT ALIENS AREN'T REALLY OUT IN THE OPEN ON EARTH YET, SO FOR MOST OF THE STAFF, WE JUST TELL THEM IT'S A TRICK EFFECT.
WHOA...

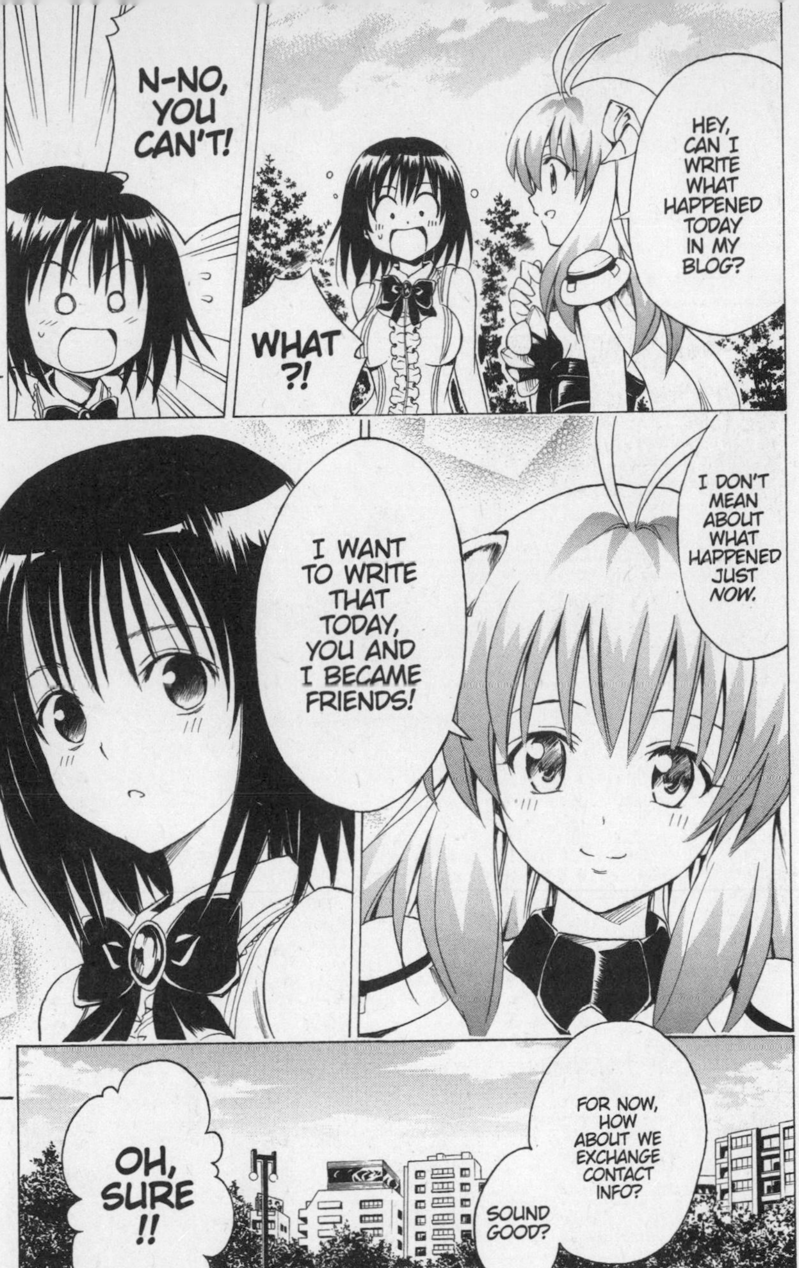
HEY, CAN I WRITE WHAT HAPPENED TODAY IN MY BLOG?
WHAT ?!
N-NO, YOU CAN'T!
I DON'T MEAN ABOUT WHAT HAPPENED JUST NOW.
I WANT TO WRITE THAT TODAY, YOU AND I BECAME FRIENDS!
FOR NOW, HOW ABOUT WE EXCHANGE CONTACT INFO?
SOUND GOOD?
OH, SURE !!

To Love Ru Bonus Info:

Magical Kyouko, the Dynamite Girl: Part 2

All Info Taken From: Free Encyclopedia (ukiuki ♪ pedian)

Drama CD:
Features an original story composed by the series planner, Saki Hasemi. A drama CD ostensibly aimed at young girls, sales were halted due to the contents being adult-oriented in more ways than one. With only a few sold, they fetch a high price now on internet auction sites.

Series OP and ED Themes:
Opening Theme – Burn! Magical Kyouko (Episodes 1-26)
Lyrics: Kentaro Music/Arrangement: Ucchii Vocals: Kirisaki Kyouko & the Firegals

Opening Theme – The Dynamite Girl's Fury! (Episodes 27-51)
Lyrics: Kentaro Music/Arrangement: Ucchii Vocals: Kirisaki Kyouko & the Firegals

Ending Theme – Maiden's Blaze (Episodes 1-26)
Lyrics: Kentaro Music/Arrangement: Ucchii Vocals: Kirisaki Kyouko

Ending Theme – March of Dynamite: Hot Hot Hot! (Episodes 27-33)
Lyrics: Kentaro Music/Arrangement: Ucchii Vocals: Kirisaki Kyouko + That Cat Over There

Ending Theme – March of Dynamite: Hot Hot Hot! (Episodes 34-51)
Lyrics: Kentaro Music/Arrangement: Ucchii Vocals: Kirisaki Kyouko + General Mojack & The Stress-Makers

OVA:
On sale separate from the main series are two OVAs (Original Video Animation). Episodes in this run carried the title *Magical Kyouko, the Dynamite Girl – Burning!* The tagline for the OVA version is "dear friends." First-run copies came with a postcard with a hidden secret. Also features audio commentary tracks (Old Man Who Unexpectedly Walked, Part-Timer on the Sound Crew, the Director's Son, a Cat).

Feature Film:
A theatrical release targeted for Golden Week. "One day, mysterious panties fall from the sky. Thrills and Suspense! Kyouko and her friends explode onto the screen! Feel the pulse of sorrow..." Showing with: *Shirone's Bon Holiday.*

Note:
Magical Kyouko relies on strong word-of-mouth to achieve box office and financial success; the franchise has no children's toys aimed at the younger market. Kyouko will return next year with the debut of a new series: *Magical Kyouko, the Dynamite Girl – Flame.*

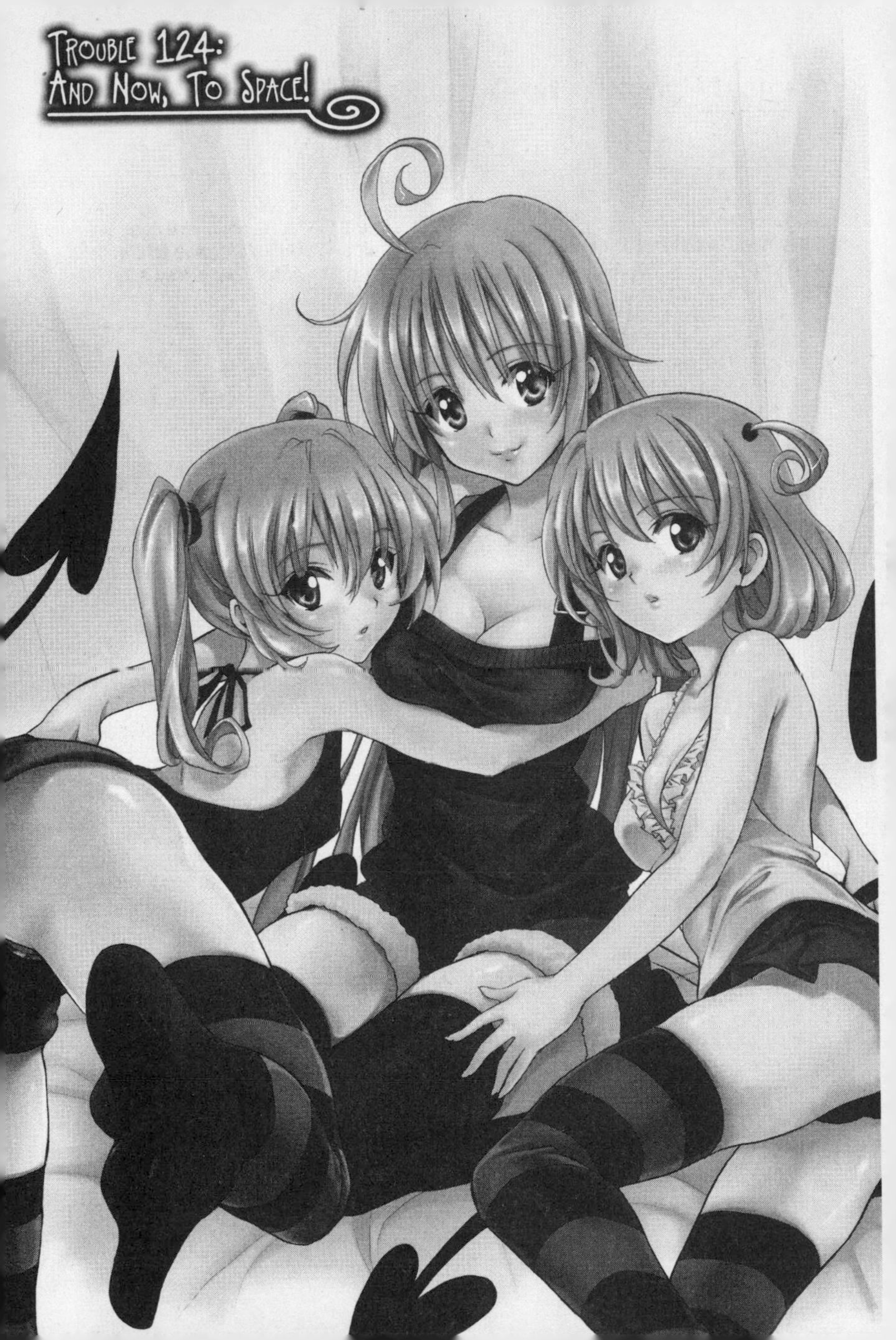
Trouble 124:
And Now, To Space!

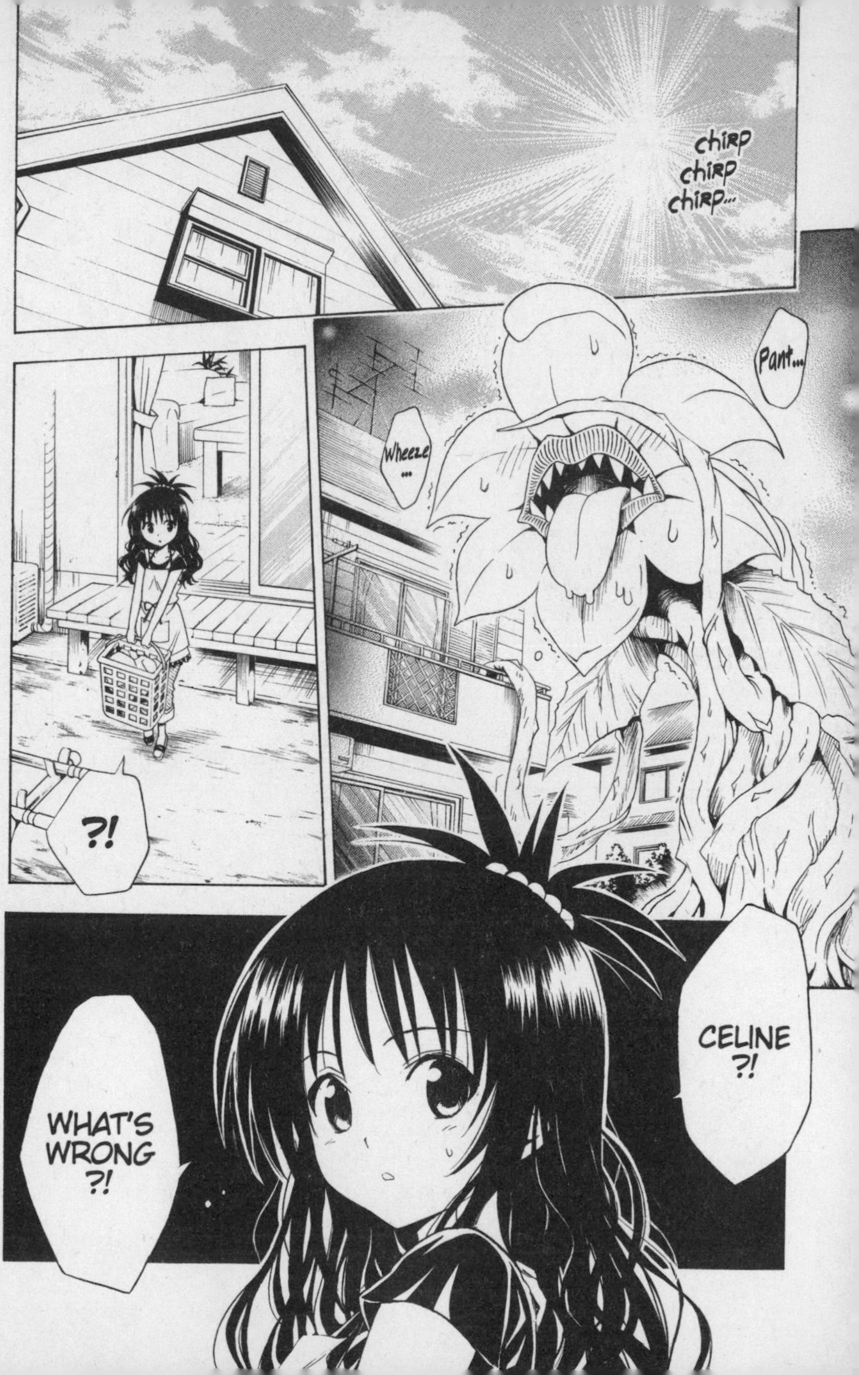
chirp
chirp
chirp...
Pant...
Wheeze ...
?!
CELINE ?!
WHAT'S WRONG ?!

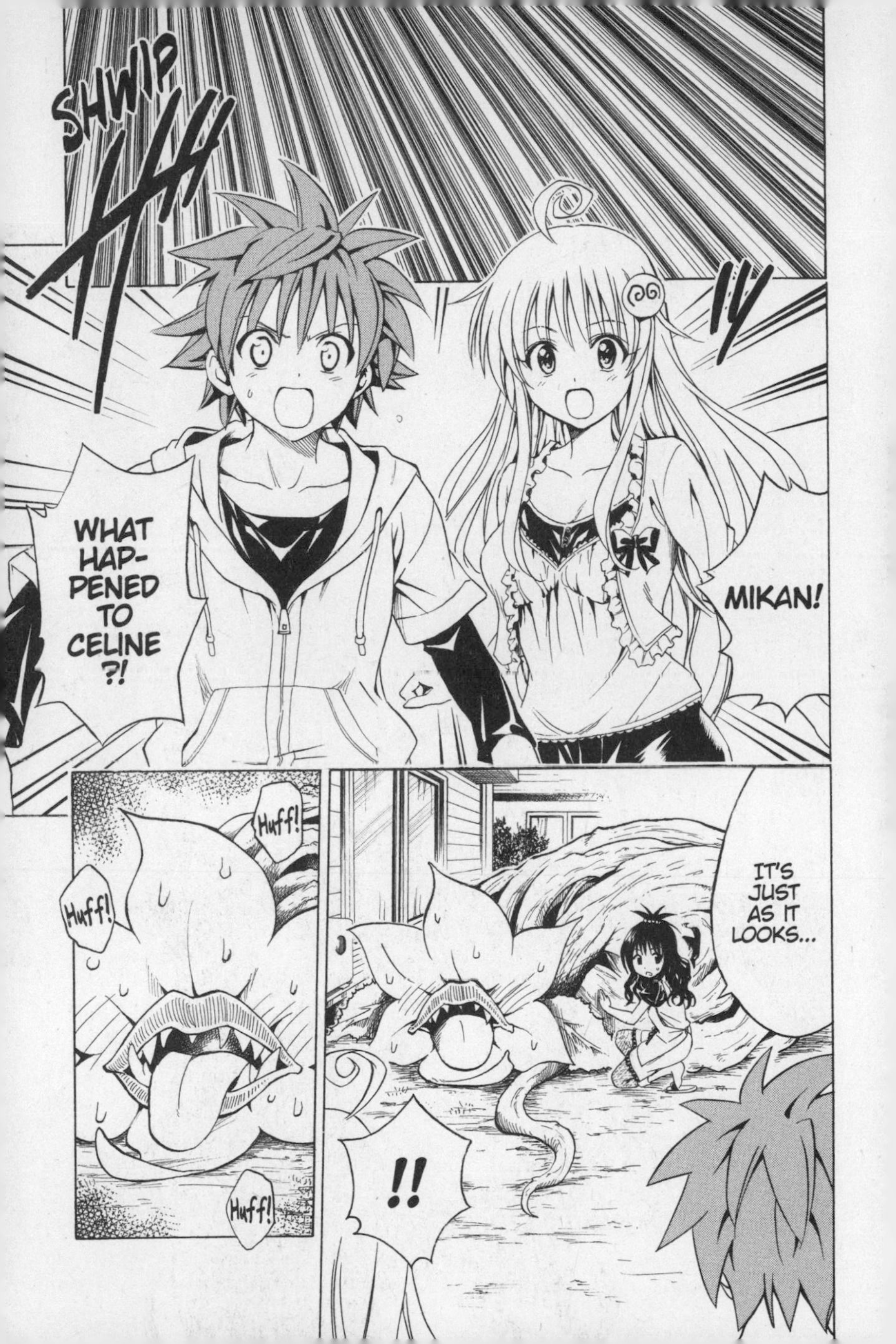
MIKAN!
SHWIP
WHAT HAP-PENED TO CELINE?!
IT'S JUST AS IT LOOKS...
!!
Huff!
Huff!
Huff!

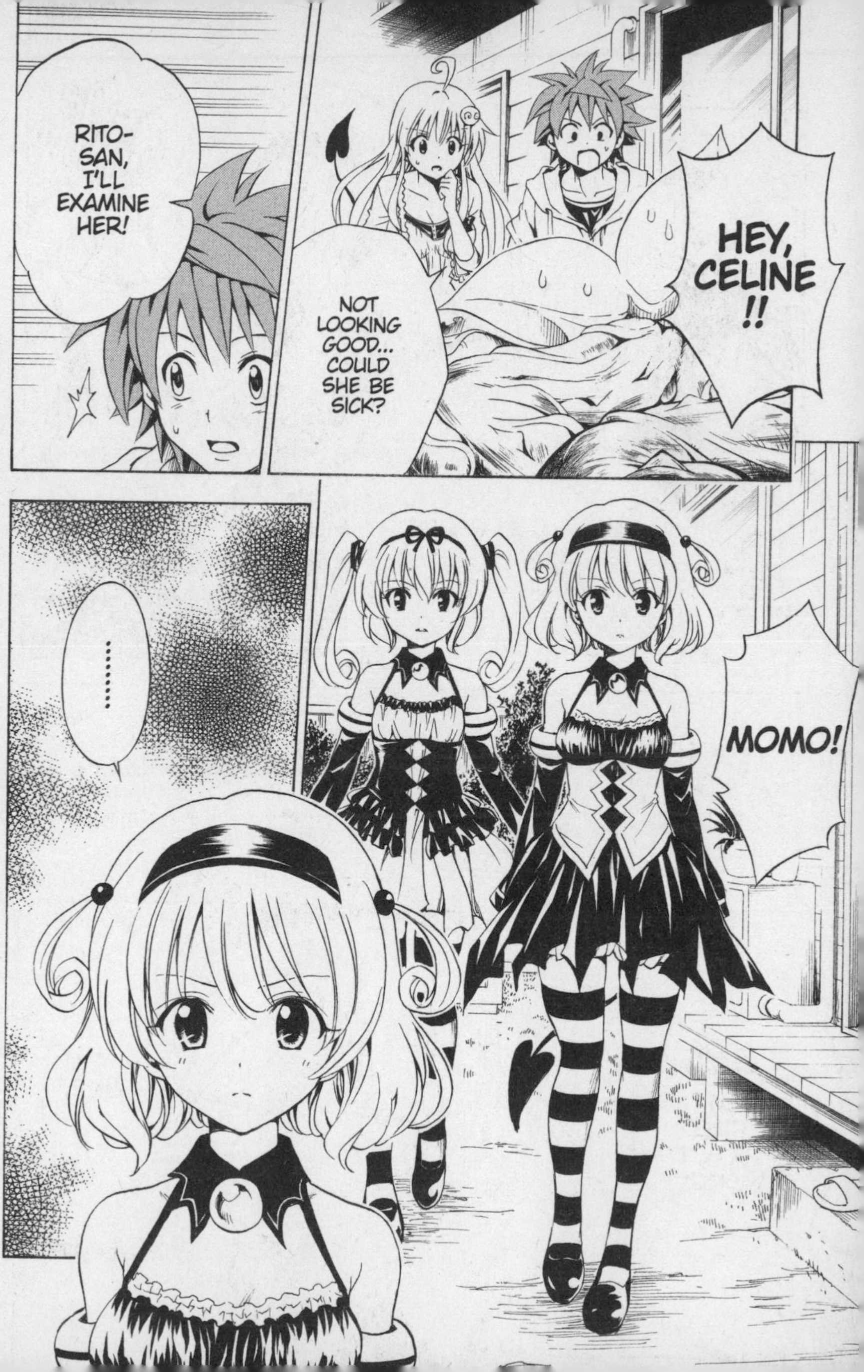
HEY, CELINE!!
NOT LOOKING GOOD... COULD SHE BE SICK?
RITO-SAN, I'LL EXAMINE HER!
MOMO!
......

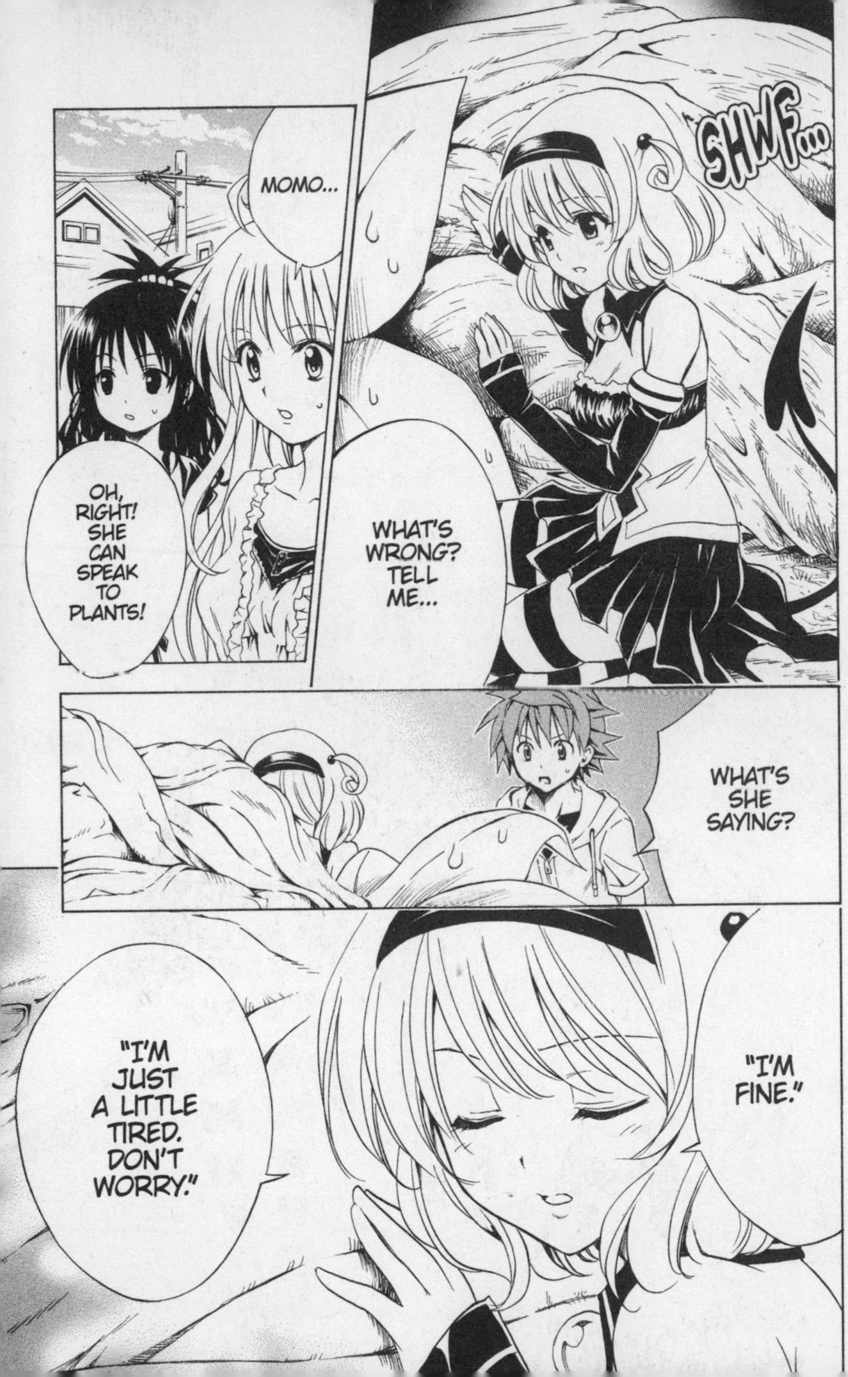
SHWF...
WHAT'S WRONG? TELL ME...
MOMO...
OH, RIGHT! SHE CAN SPEAK TO PLANTS!
WHAT'S SHE SAYING?
"I'M FINE."
"I'M JUST A LITTLE TIRED. DON'T WORRY."

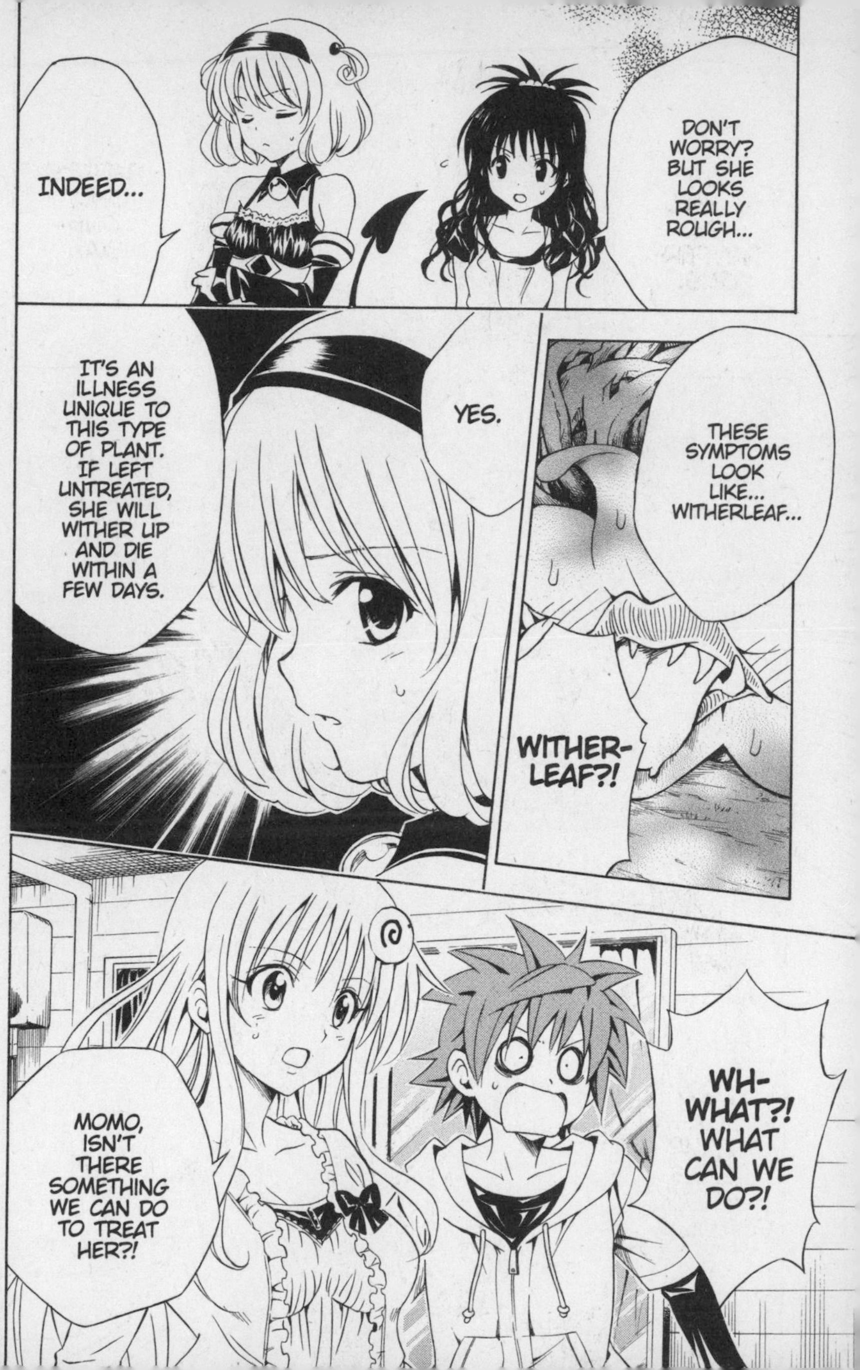
DON'T WORRY? BUT SHE LOOKS REALLY ROUGH...
INDEED...
THESE SYMPTOMS LOOK LIKE... WITHERLEAF...
WITHER-LEAF?!
YES.
IT'S AN ILLNESS UNIQUE TO THIS TYPE OF PLANT. IF LEFT UNTREATED, SHE WILL WITHER UP AND DIE WITHIN A FEW DAYS.
WH-WHAT?! WHAT CAN WE DO?!
MOMO, ISN'T THERE SOMETHING WE CAN DO TO TREAT HER?!

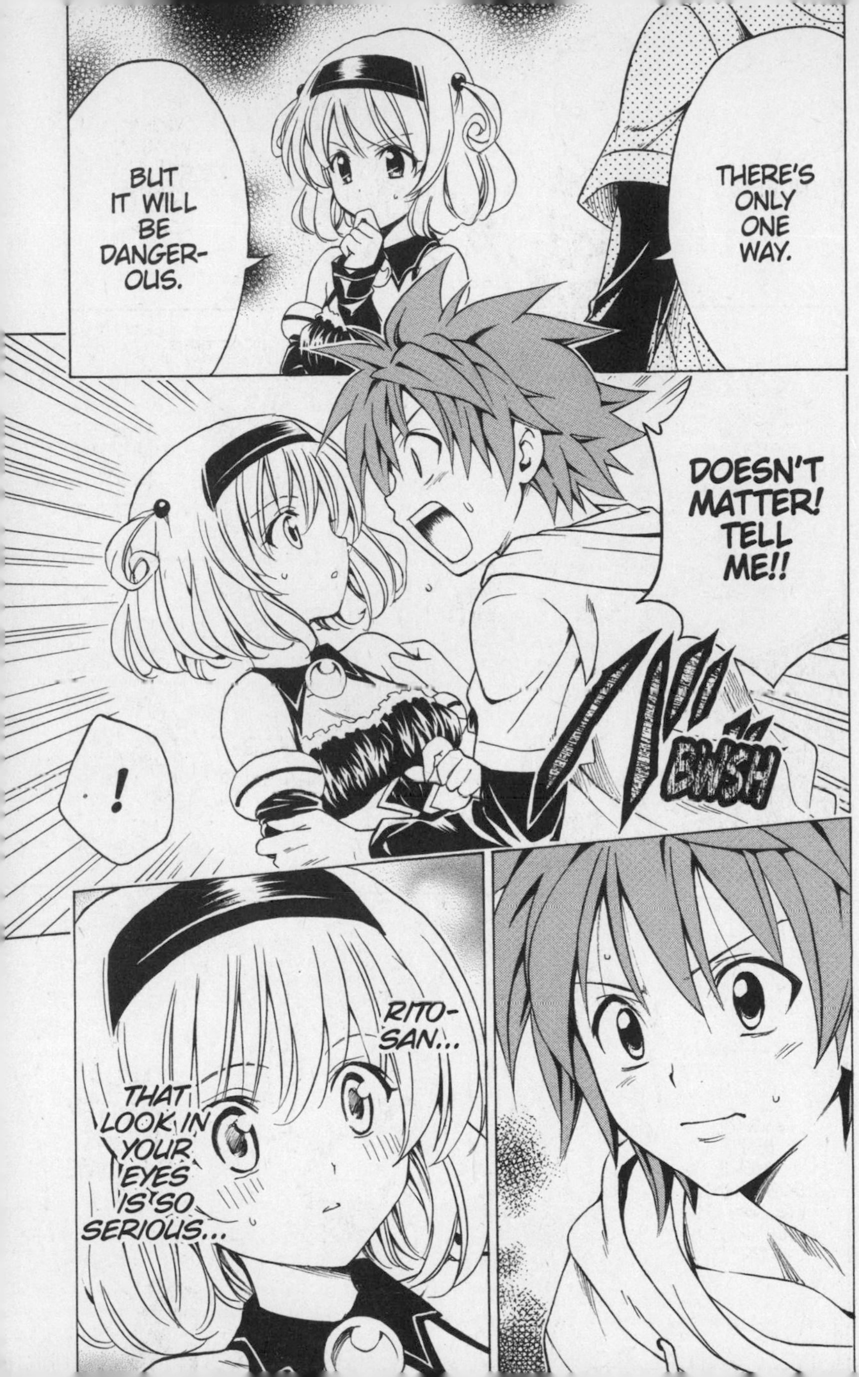
THERE'S ONLY ONE WAY.
BUT IT WILL BE DANGER-OUS.
DOESN'T MATTER! TELL ME!!
BWSH
!
RITO-SAN...
THAT LOOK IN YOUR EYES IS SO SERIOUS...

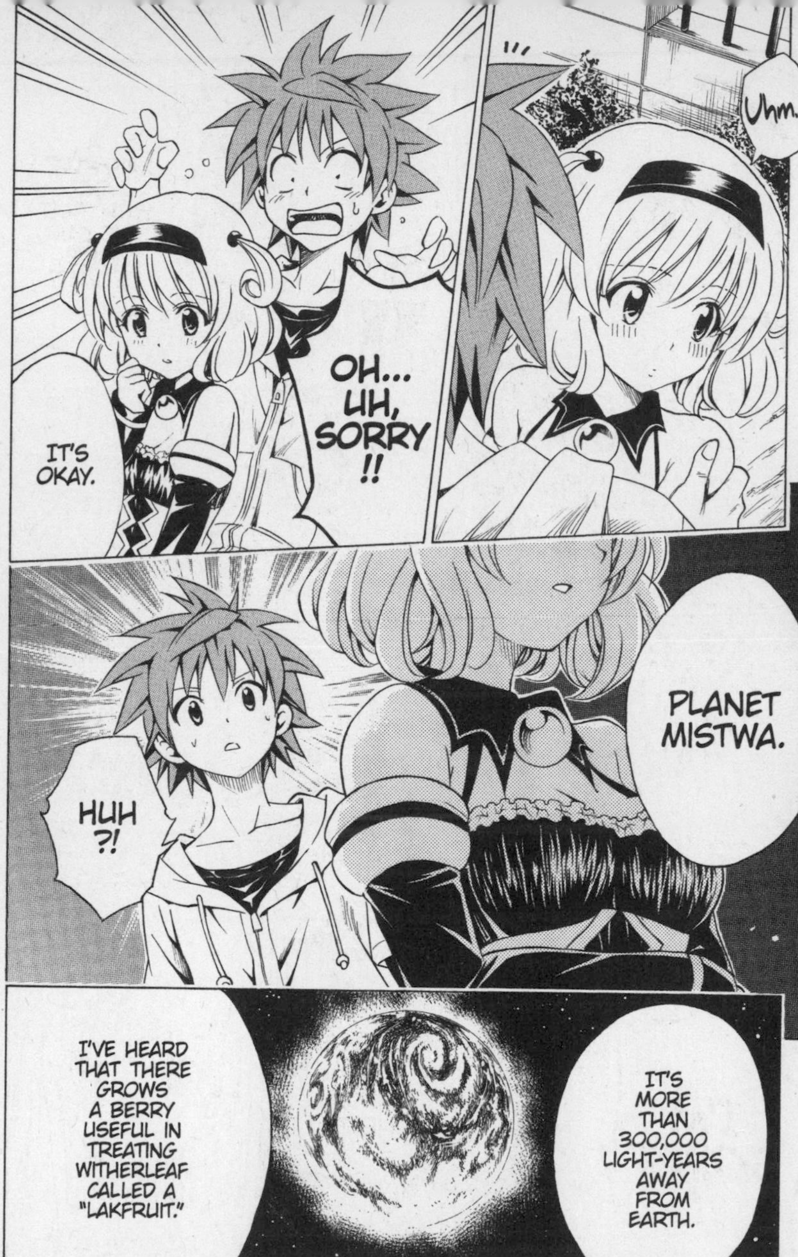
Uhm...
OH... UH, SORRY!!
IT'S OKAY.
PLANET MISTWA.
HUH?!
IT'S MORE THAN 300,000 LIGHT-YEARS AWAY FROM EARTH.
I'VE HEARD THAT THERE GROWS A BERRY USEFUL IN TREATING WITHERLEAF CALLED A "LAKFRUIT."

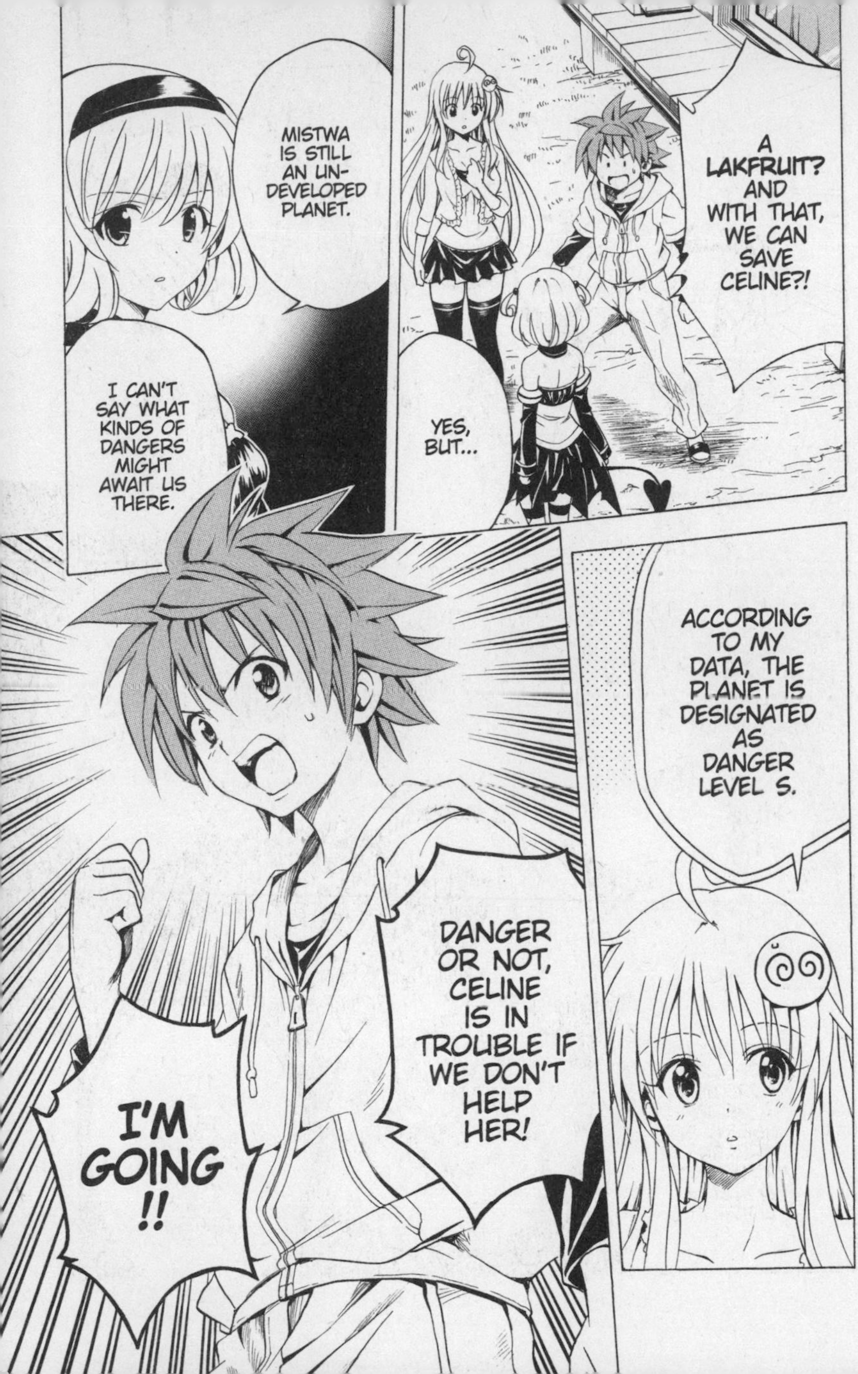
A LAKFRUIT? AND WITH THAT, WE CAN SAVE CELINE?!
YES, BUT...
MISTWA IS STILL AN UN-DEVELOPED PLANET.
I CAN'T SAY WHAT KINDS OF DANGERS MIGHT AWAIT US THERE.
ACCORDING TO MY DATA, THE PLANET IS DESIGNATED AS DANGER LEVEL S.
DANGER OR NOT, CELINE IS IN TROUBLE IF WE DON'T HELP HER!
I'M GOING!!

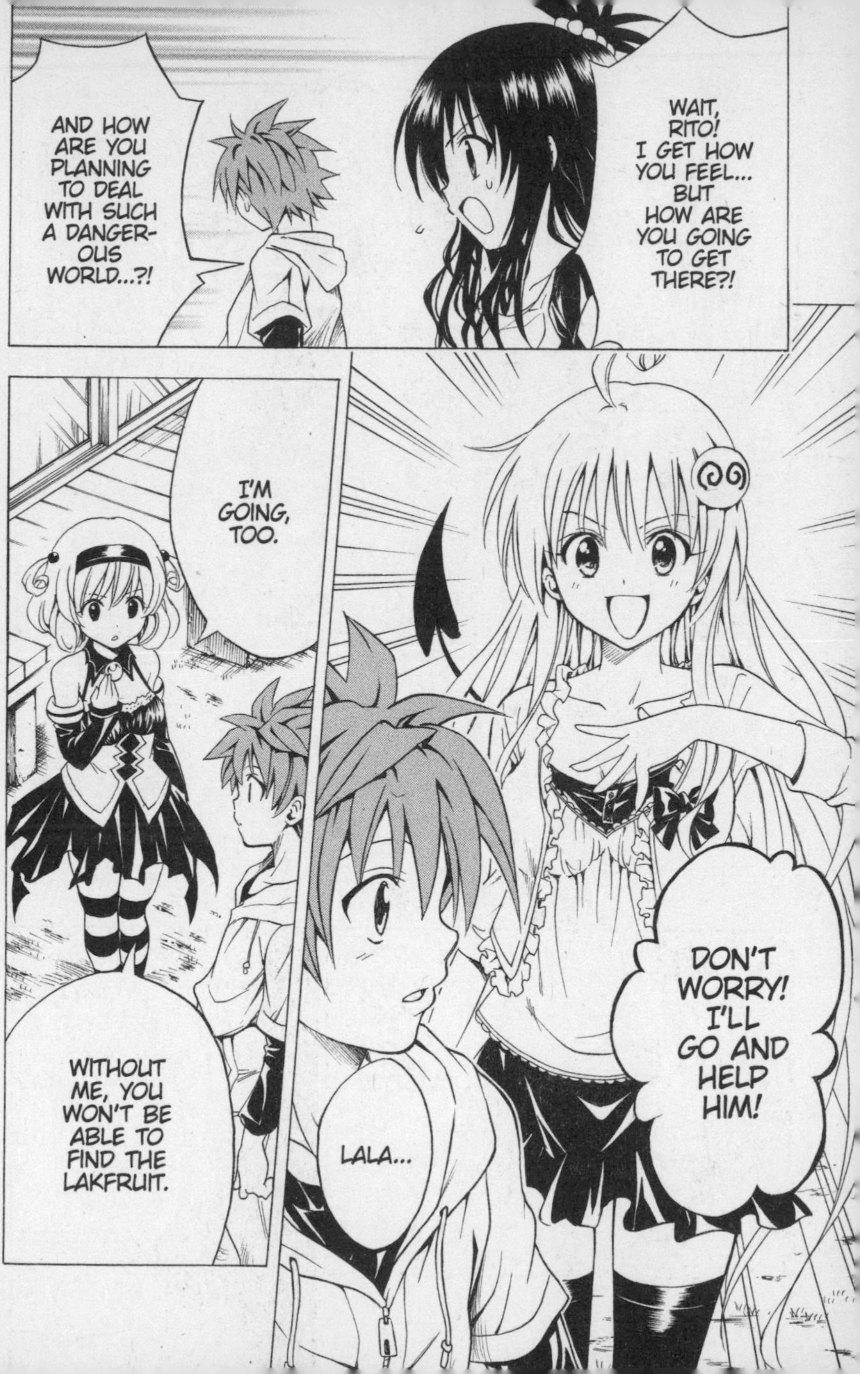
WAIT, RITO! I GET HOW YOU FEEL... BUT HOW ARE YOU GOING TO GET THERE?!
AND HOW ARE YOU PLANNING TO DEAL WITH SUCH A DANGER-OUS WORLD...?!
DON'T WORRY! I'LL GO AND HELP HIM!
LALA...
I'M GOING, TOO.
WITHOUT ME, YOU WON'T BE ABLE TO FIND THE LAKFRUIT.

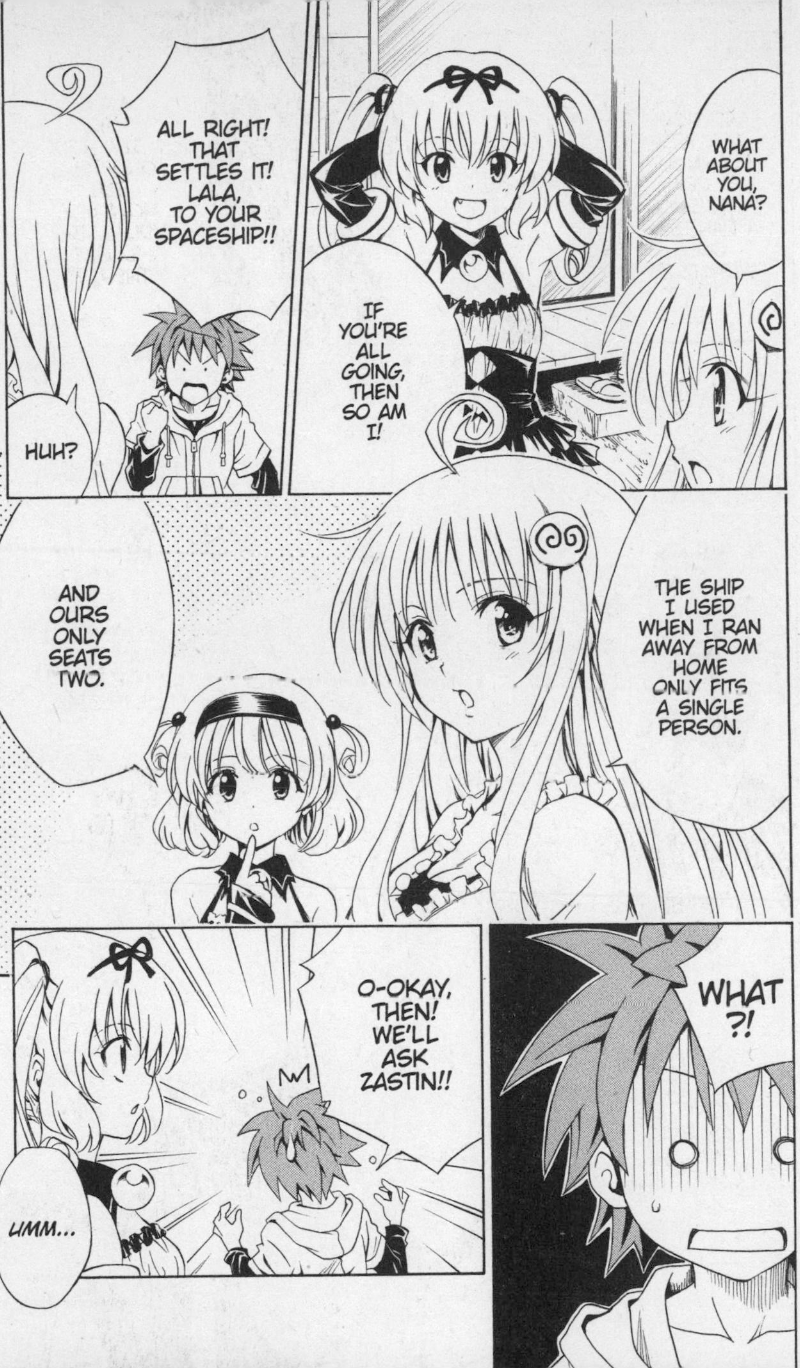
WHAT ABOUT YOU, NANA?
IF YOU'RE ALL GOING, THEN SO AM I!
ALL RIGHT! THAT SETTLES IT! LALA, TO YOUR SPACESHIP!!
HUH?
THE SHIP I USED WHEN I RAN AWAY FROM HOME ONLY FITS A SINGLE PERSON.
AND OURS ONLY SEATS TWO.
WHAT ?!
O-OKAY, THEN! WE'LL ASK ZASTIN!!
UMM...

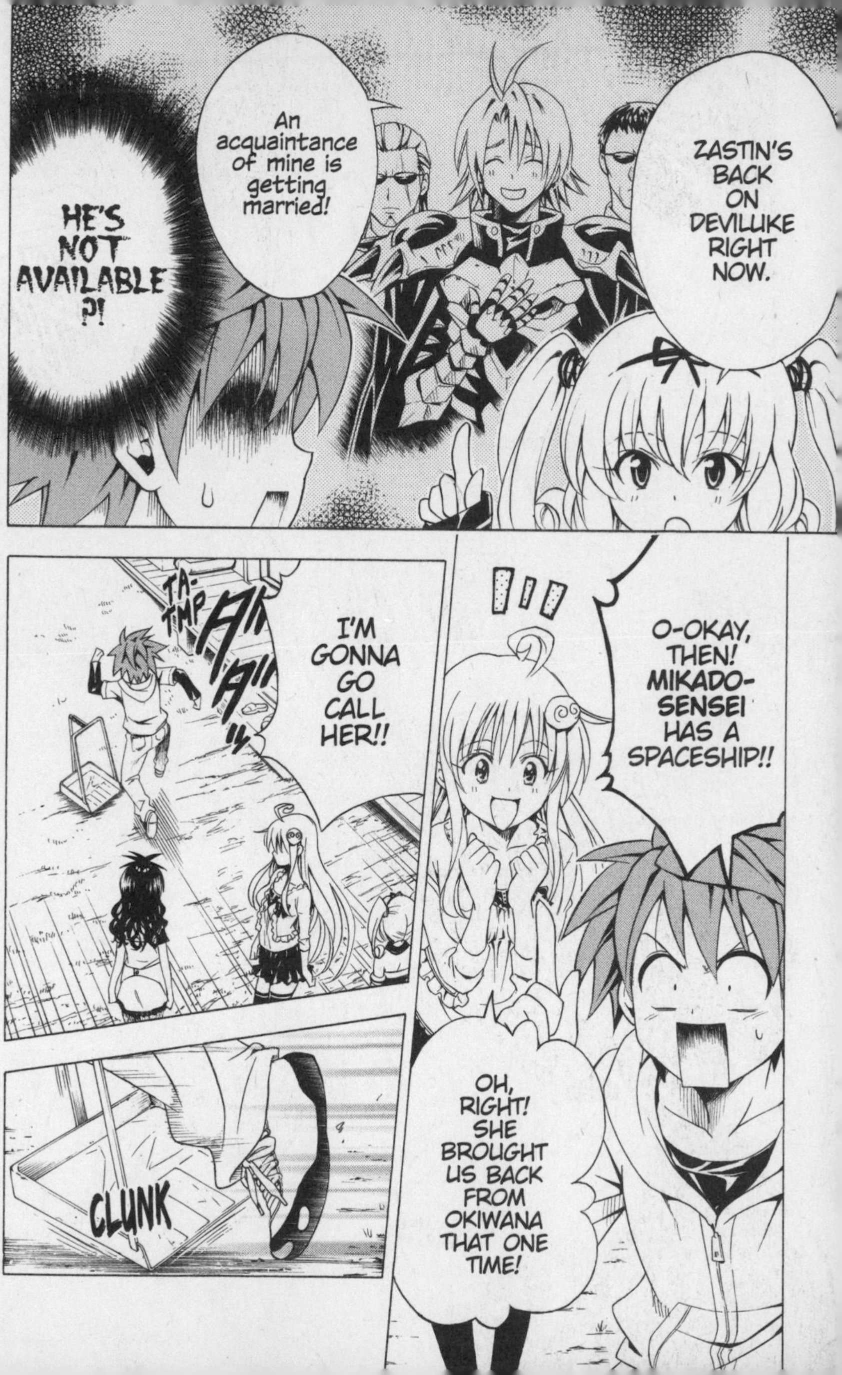
ZASTIN'S BACK ON DEVILUKE RIGHT NOW.
An acquaintance of mine is getting married!
HE'S NOT AVAILABLE ?!
!!!
O-OKAY, THEN! MIKADO-SENSEI HAS A SPACESHIP!!
OH, RIGHT! SHE BROUGHT US BACK FROM OKIWANA THAT ONE TIME!
I'M GONNA GO CALL HER!!
TA-TMP
CLUNK

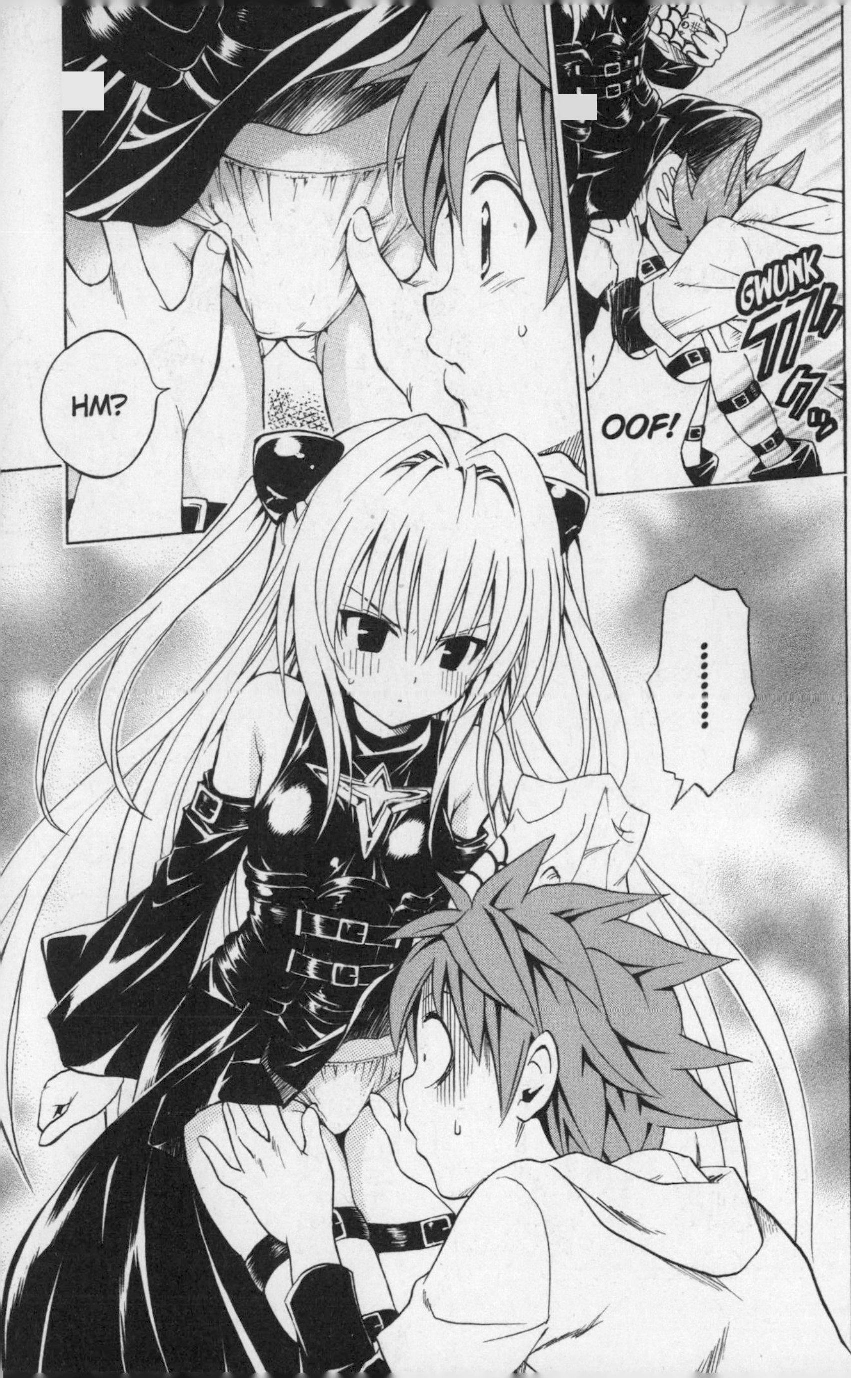
GWUNK
OOF!
HM?
......

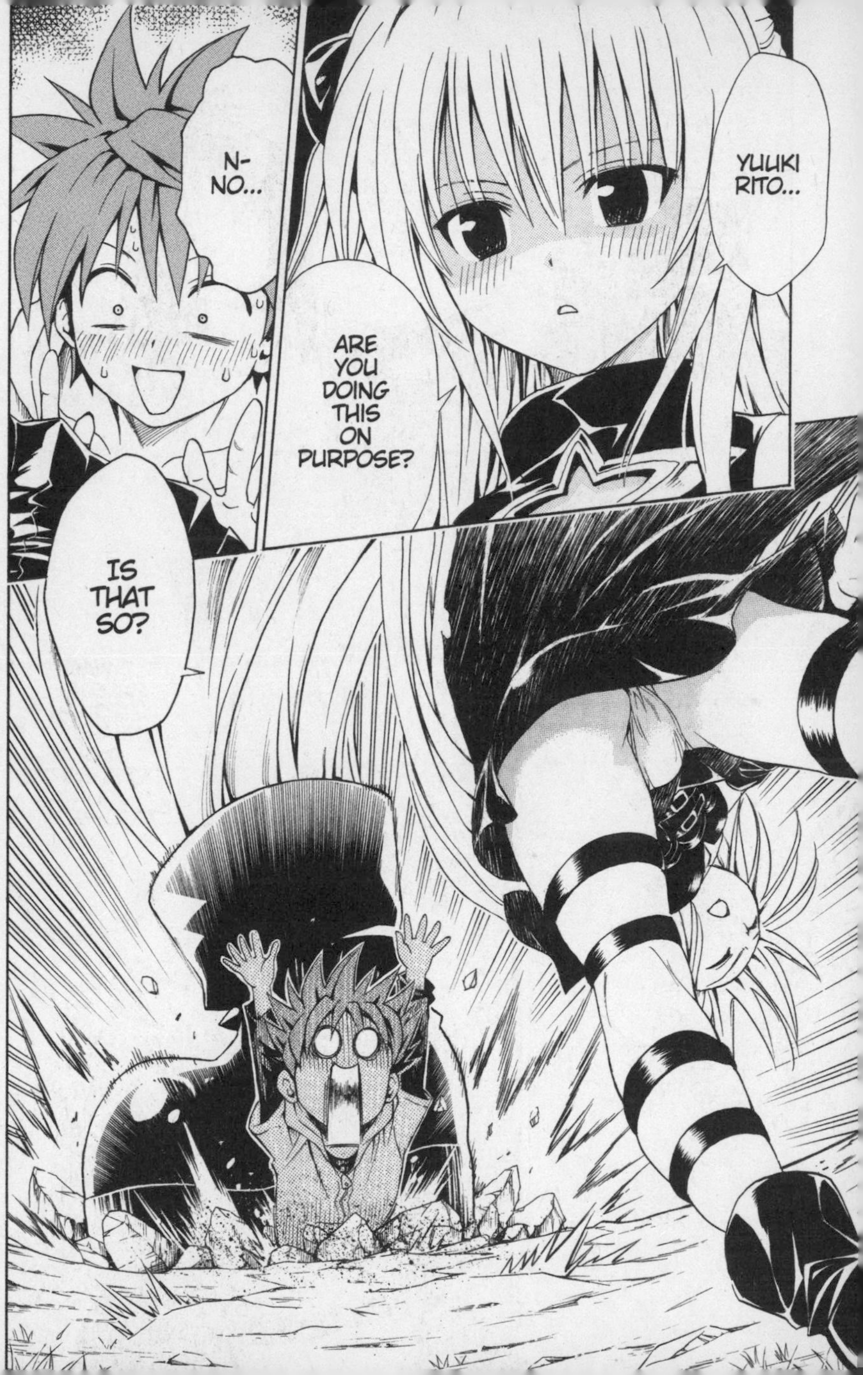
YUUKI RITO...
ARE YOU DOING THIS ON PURPOSE?
N-NO...
IS THAT SO?

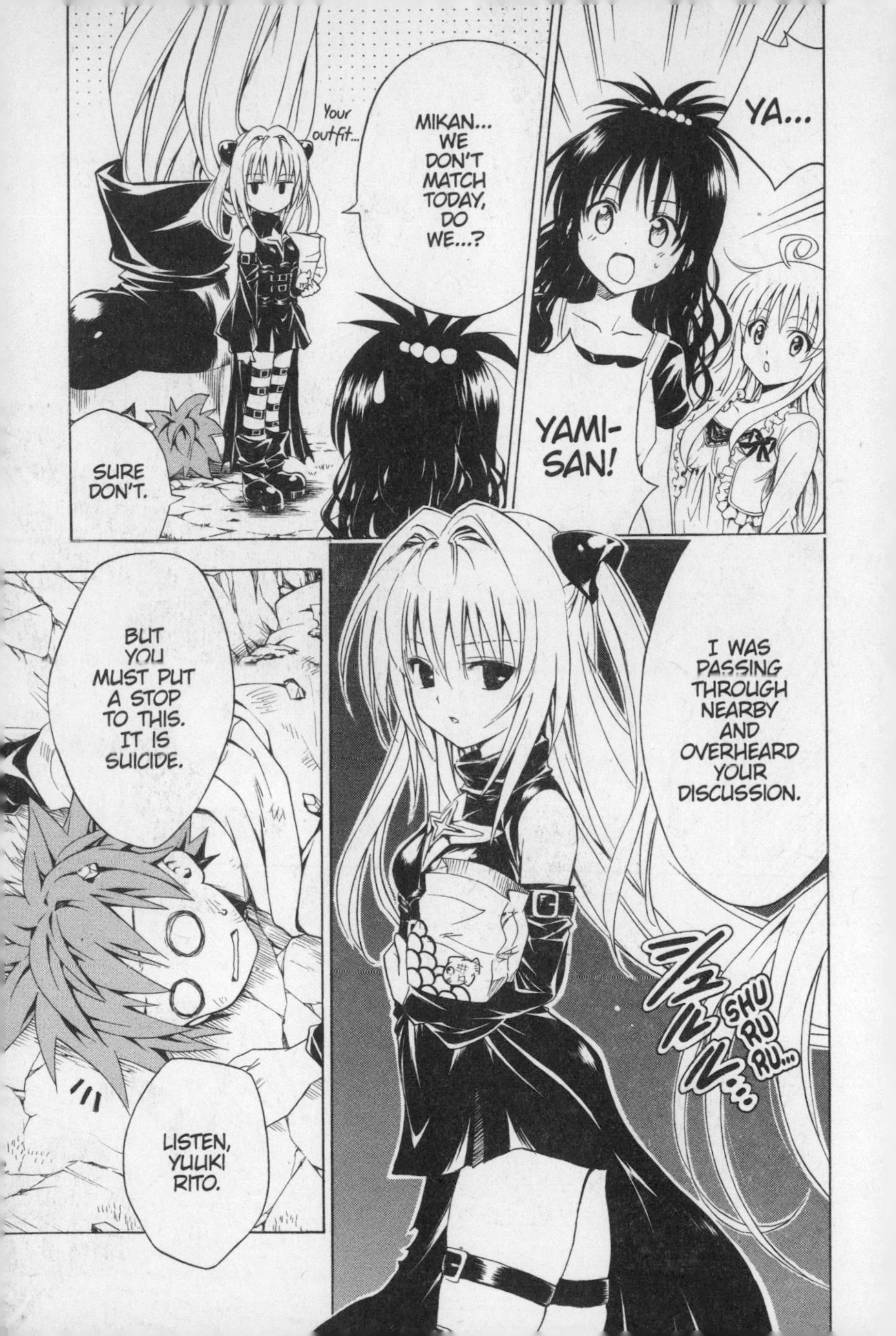
YA...
YAMI-SAN!
MIKAN... WE DON'T MATCH TODAY, DO WE...?
Your outfit...
SURE DON'T.
I WAS PASSING THROUGH NEARBY AND OVERHEARD YOUR DISCUSSION.
SHURURU...
BUT YOU MUST PUT A STOP TO THIS. IT IS SUICIDE.
LISTEN, YUUKI RITO.

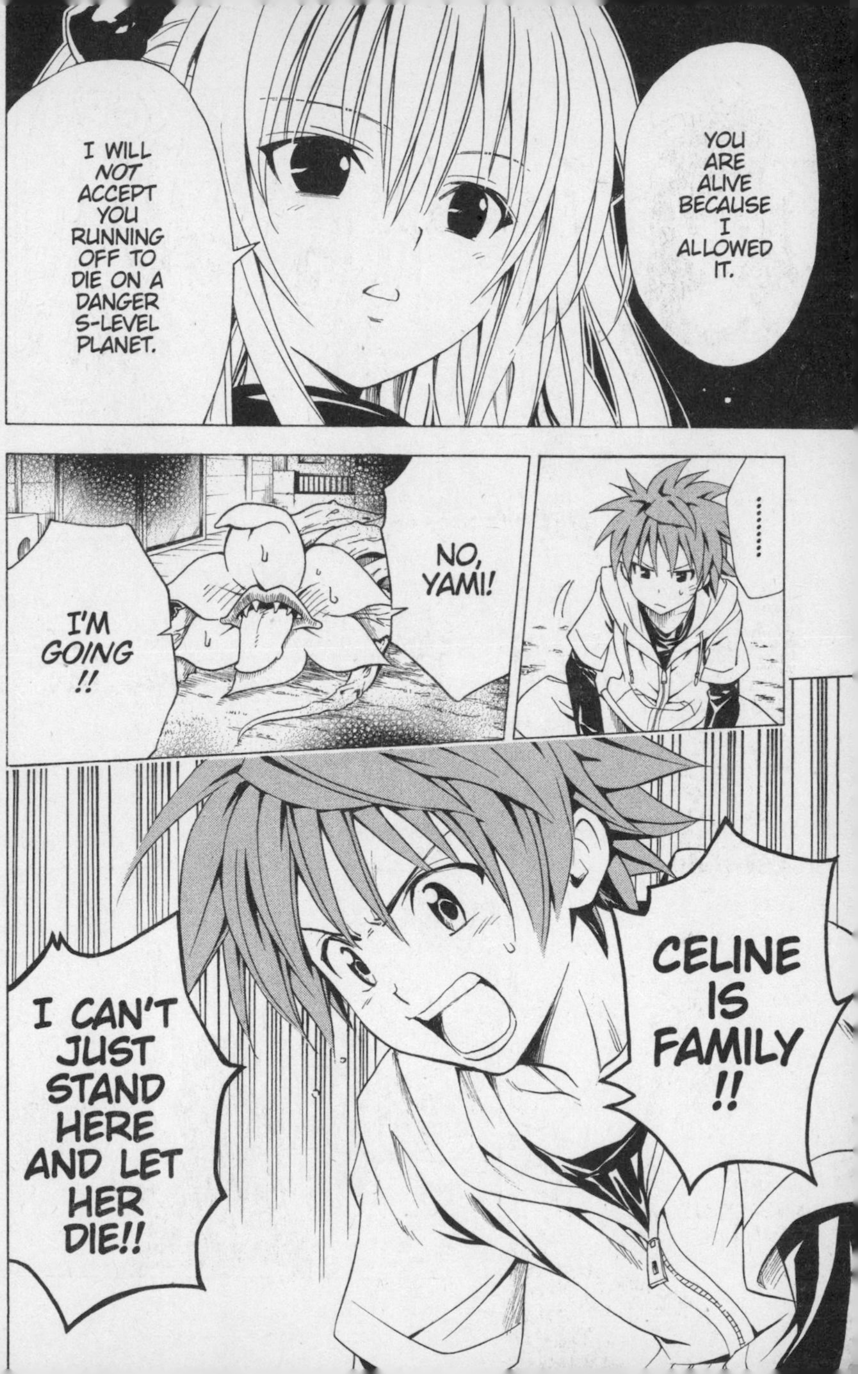

YOU ARE ALIVE BECAUSE I ALLOWED IT.
I WILL *NOT* ACCEPT YOU RUNNING OFF TO DIE ON A DANGER S-LEVEL PLANET.
......
NO, YAMI!
I'M GOING!!
CELINE IS FAMILY!!
I CAN'T JUST STAND HERE AND LET HER DIE!!

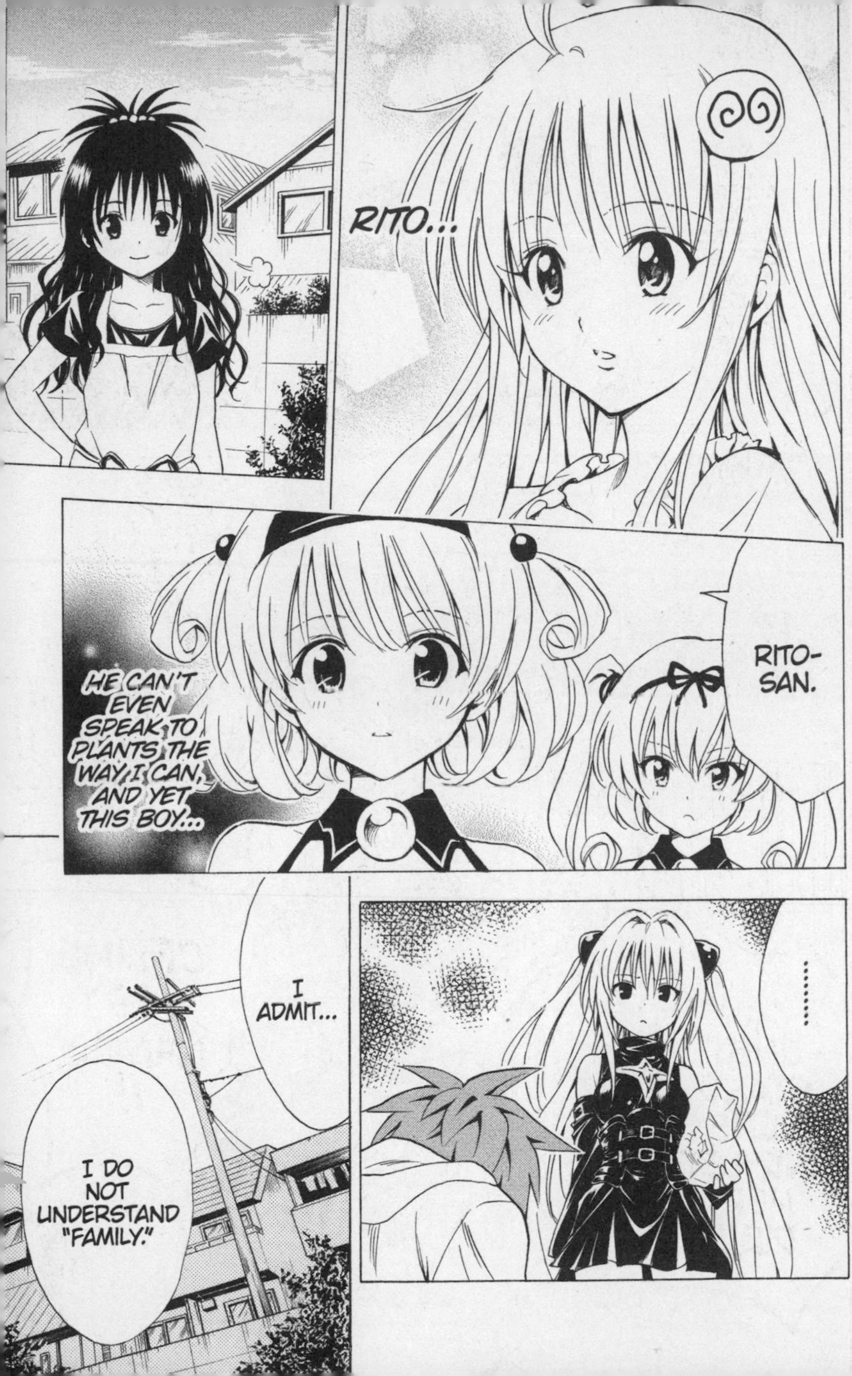
RITO...
RITO-SAN.
HE CAN'T EVEN SPEAK TO PLANTS THE WAY I CAN, AND YET THIS BOY...
......
I ADMIT...
I DO NOT UNDERSTAND "FAMILY."

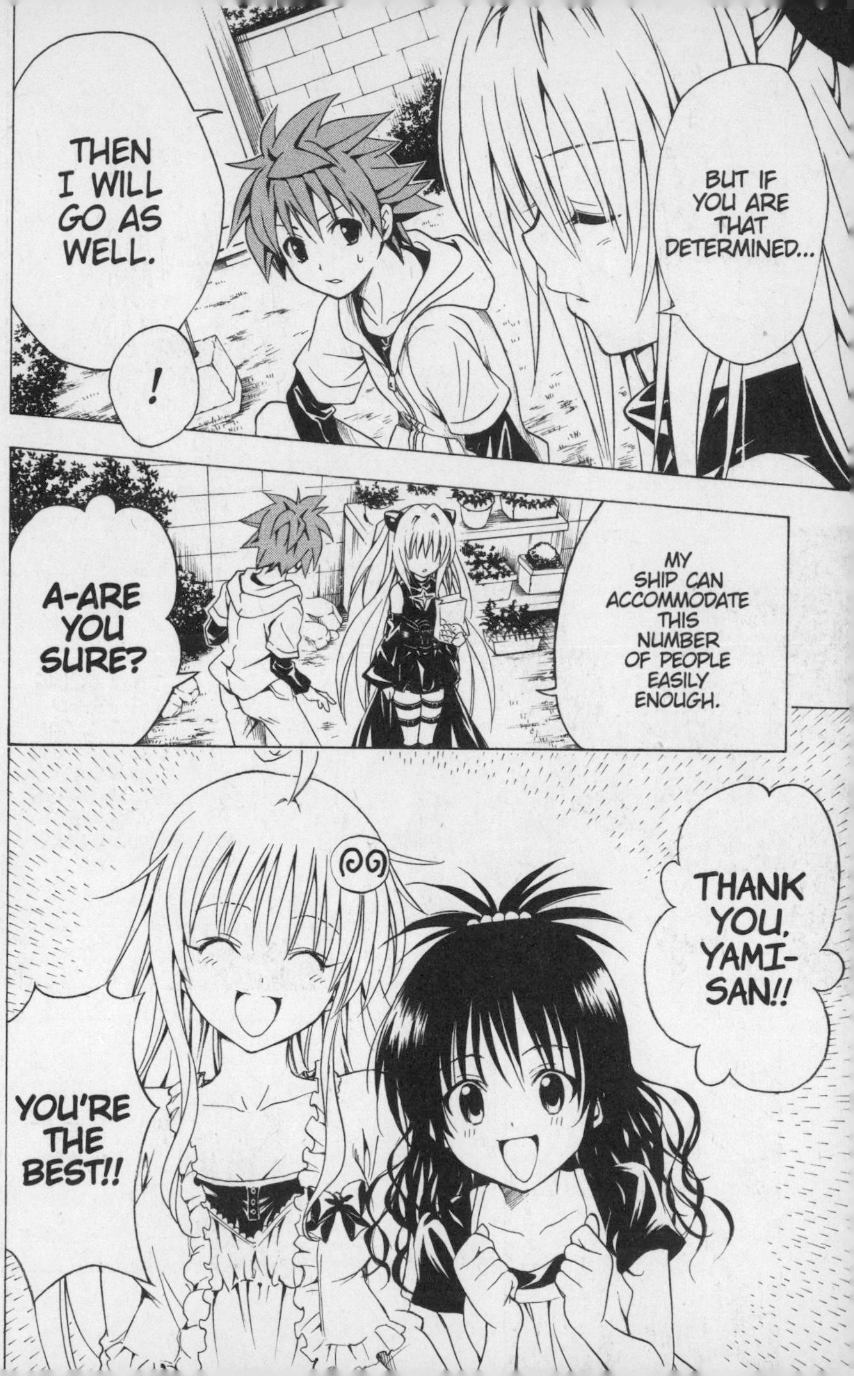
BUT IF YOU ARE THAT DETERMINED...
THEN I WILL GO AS WELL.
!
MY SHIP CAN ACCOMMODATE THIS NUMBER OF PEOPLE EASILY ENOUGH.
A-ARE YOU SURE?
THANK YOU, YAMI-SAN!!
YOU'RE THE BEST!!

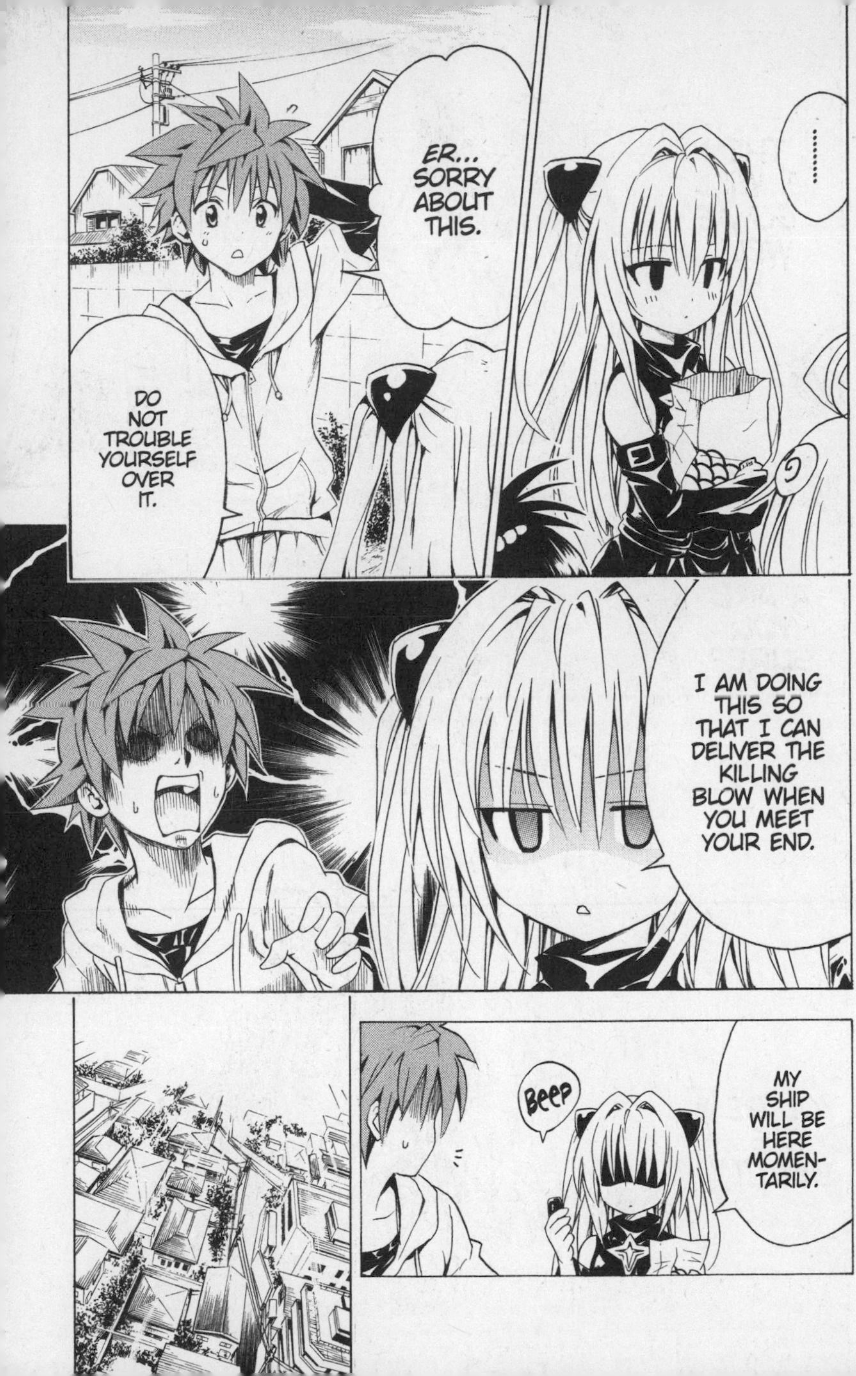

......
ER... SORRY ABOUT THIS.
DO NOT TROUBLE YOURSELF OVER IT.
I AM DOING THIS SO THAT I CAN DELIVER THE KILLING BLOW WHEN YOU MEET YOUR END.
MY SHIP WILL BE HERE MOMENTARILY.
Beep

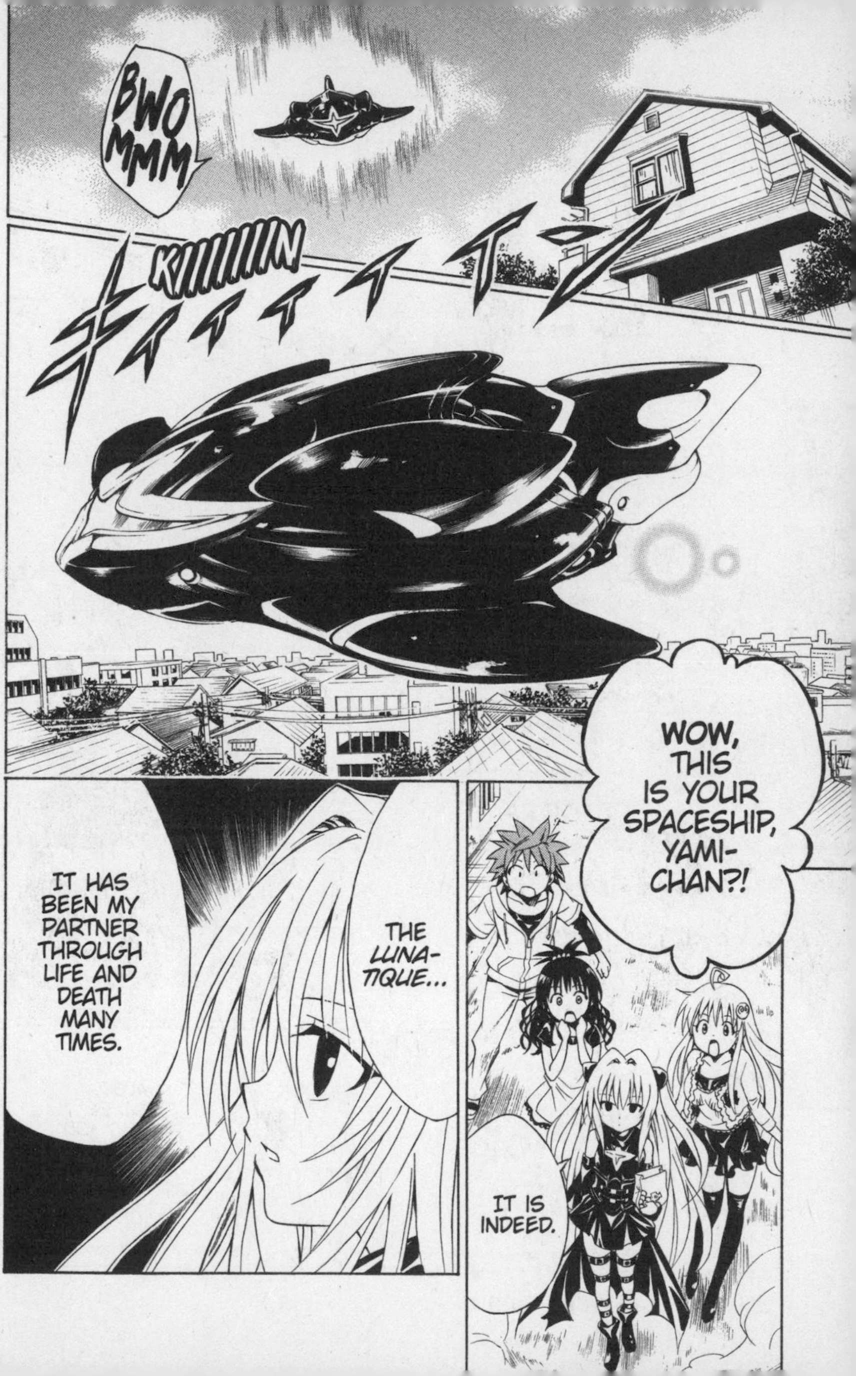
BWOMMM
KIIIIIIN
WOW, THIS IS YOUR SPACESHIP, YAMI-CHAN?!
IT IS INDEED.
THE LUNATIQUE...
IT HAS BEEN MY PARTNER THROUGH LIFE AND DEATH MANY TIMES.

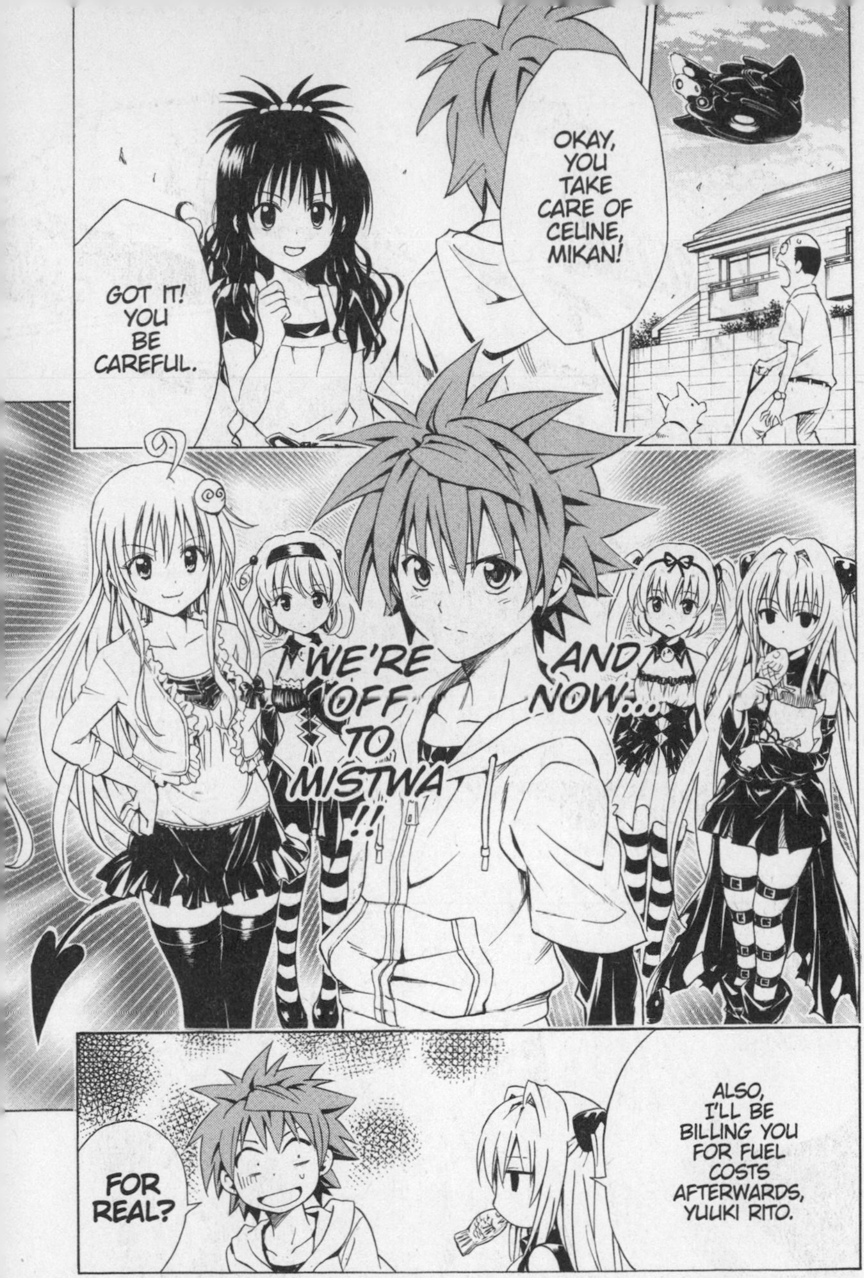
OKAY, YOU TAKE CARE OF CELINE, MIKAN!
GOT IT! YOU BE CAREFUL.
AND NOW...
WE'RE OFF TO MISTWA!!
ALSO, I'LL BE BILLING YOU FOR FUEL COSTS AFTERWARDS, YUUKI RITO.
FOR REAL?

Vol. 14 – Beloved Friends♡

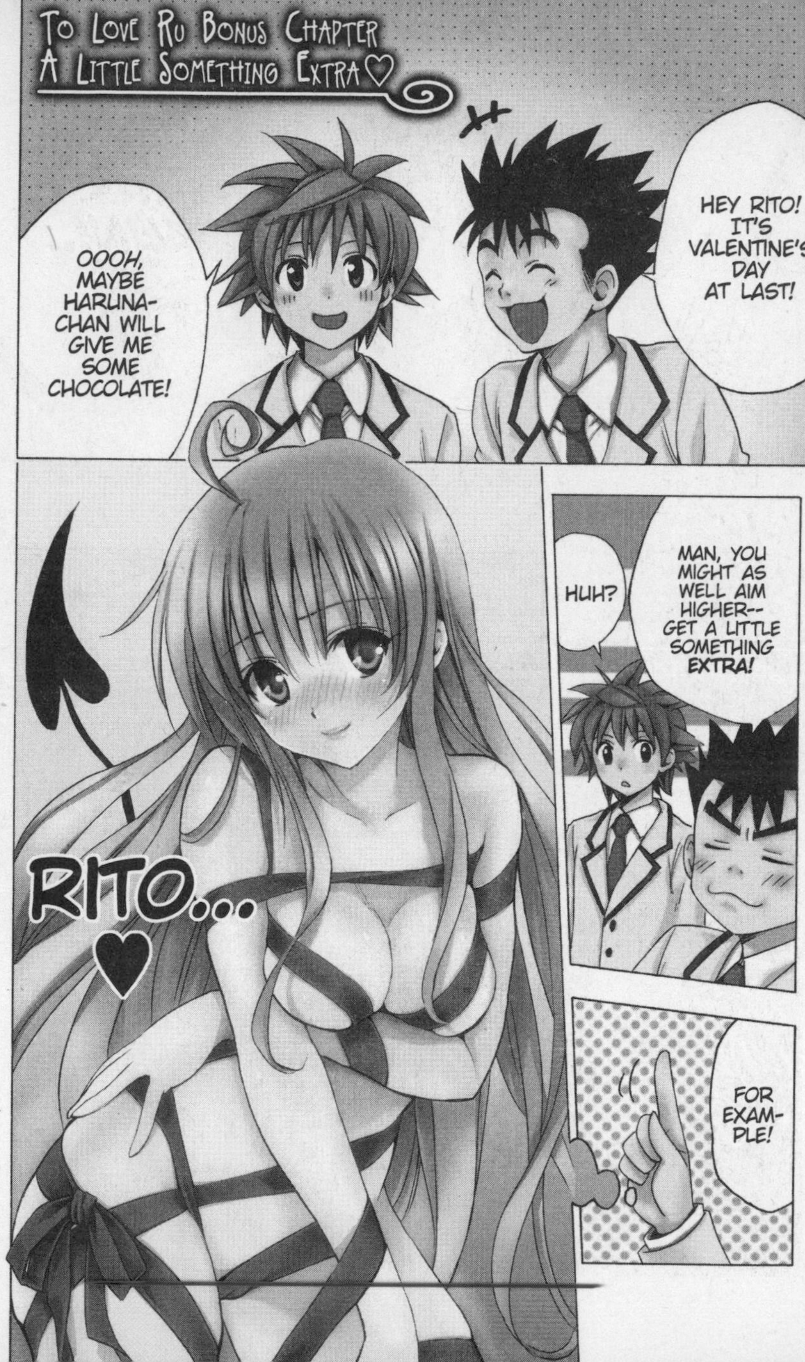
TO LOVE RU BONUS CHAPTER
A LITTLE SOMETHING EXTRA♡
HEY RITO! IT'S VALENTINE'S DAY AT LAST!
OOOH, MAYBE HARUNA-CHAN WILL GIVE ME SOME CHOCOLATE!
MAN, YOU MIGHT AS WELL AIM HIGHER-- GET A LITTLE SOMETHING EXTRA!
HUH?
FOR EXAMPLE!
RITO... ♥

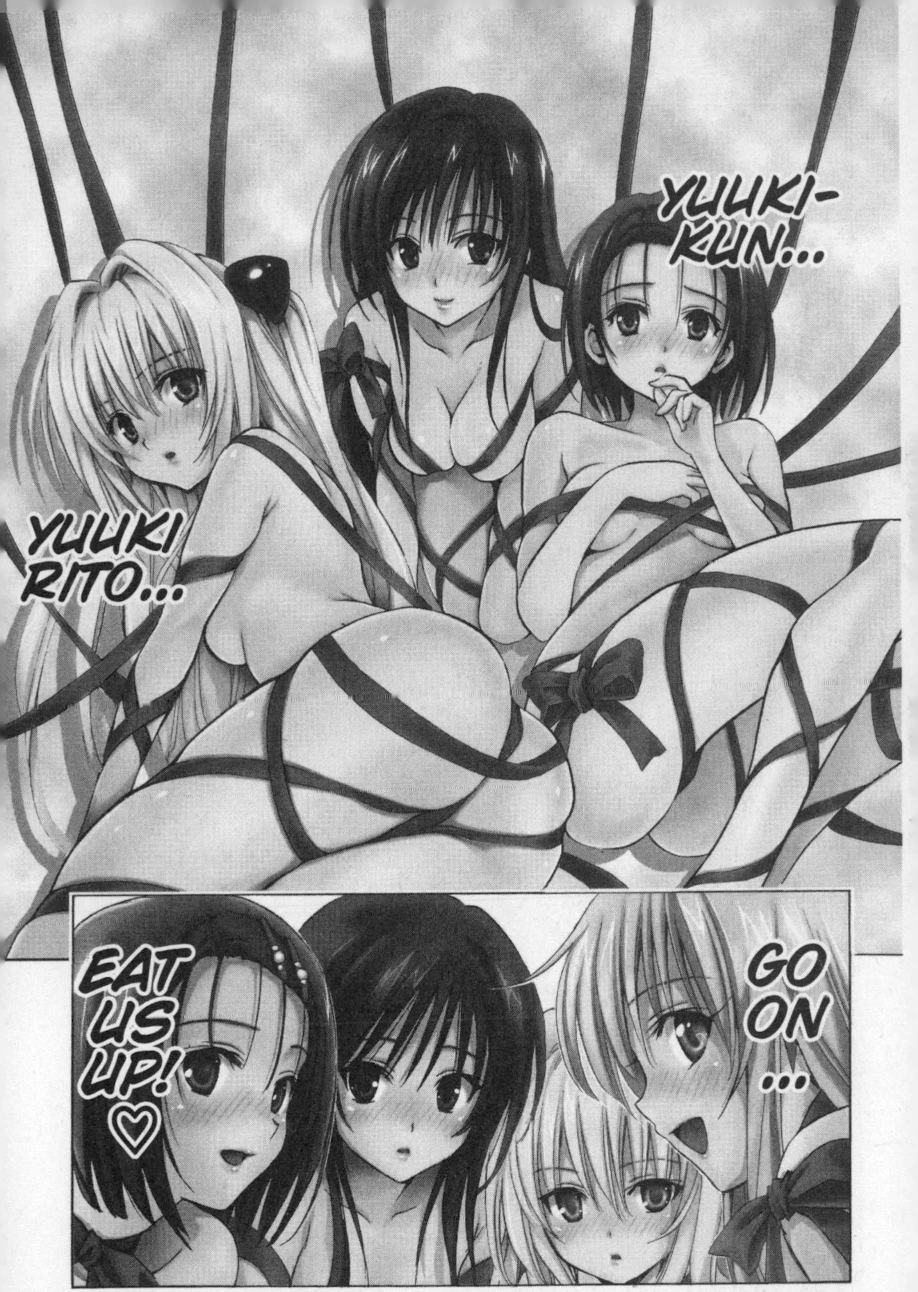
YUUKI-KUN...
YUUKI RITO...
GO ON ...
EAT US UP! ♡

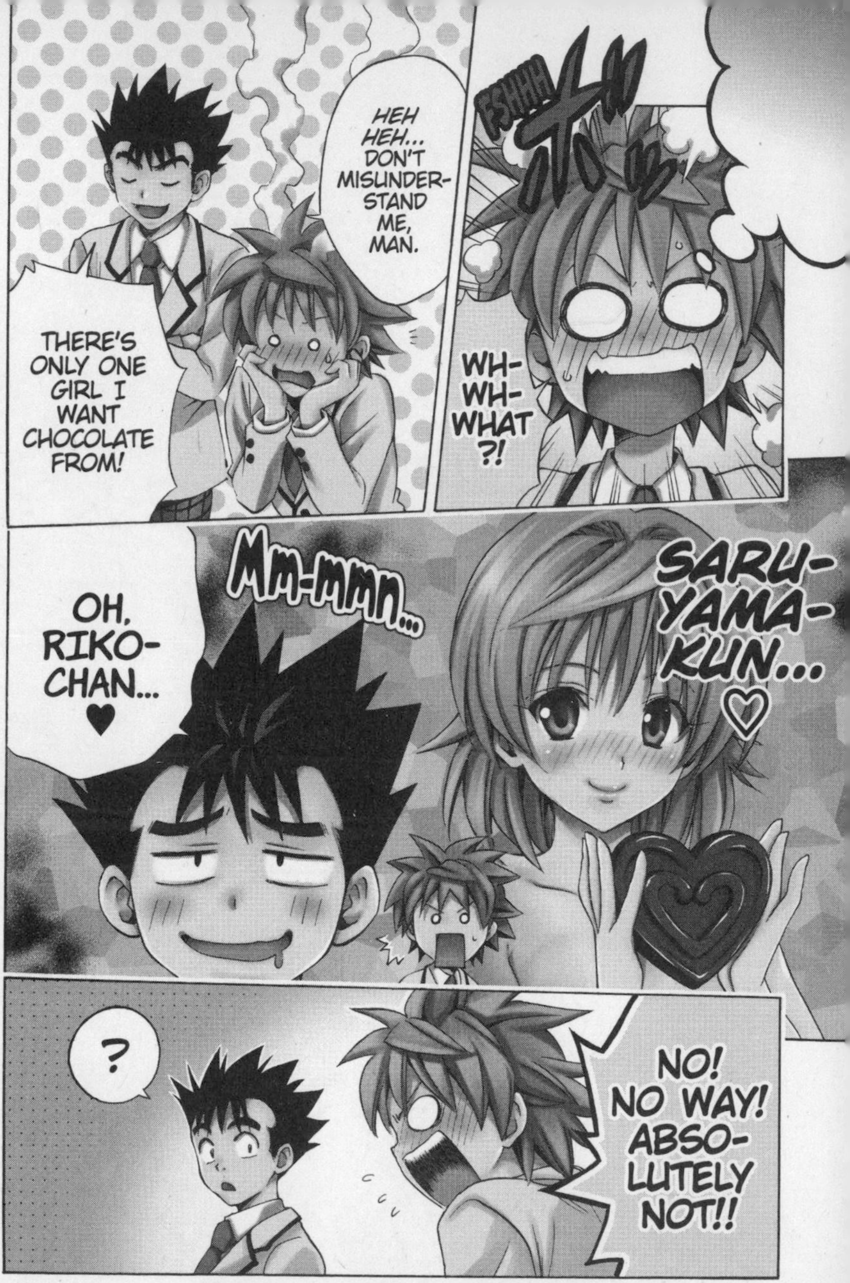
FSHHH
WH-WH-WHAT?!
HEH HEH... DON'T MISUNDER-STAND ME, MAN.
THERE'S ONLY ONE GIRL I WANT CHOCOLATE FROM!
SARU-YAMA-KUN... ♡
Mm-mmn...
OH, RIKO-CHAN... ♥
NO! NO WAY! ABSO-LUTELY NOT!!
?

To Love Ru Bonus Chapter (End)

To LOVE Ru

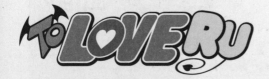

SEVEN SEAS' GHOST SHIP PRESENTS

TO LOVE RU

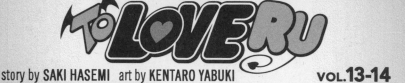

story by **SAKI HASEMI** art by **KENTARO YABUKI**

VOL. 13-14

TRANSLATION
Alex Gaspard

LETTERING AND LAYOUT
Paweł Szczęszek

LOGO DESIGN
Larry Kotef

COVER DESIGN
Nicky Lim

PROOFREADER
Janet Houck
Tom Speelman

EDITOR
J.P. Sullivan

PRODUCTION MANAGER
Lissa Pattillo

MANAGING EDITOR
Julie Davis

EDITOR-IN-CHIEF
Adam Arnold

PUBLISHER
Jason DeAngelis

First published in Japan in 2006 by SHUEISHA Inc., Tokyo.
English translation rights arranged by SHUEISHA Inc.
through TOHAN CORPORATION, Tokyo.

Seven Seas press and purchase enquiries can be sent to Marketing Manager Lianne Sentar at press@gomanga.com. Information regarding the distribution and purchase of digital editions is available from Digital Manager CK Russell at digital@gomanga.com.

ISBN: 978-1-947804-31-9

Printed in Canada

First Printing: June 2019

10 9 8 7 6 5 4 3 2 1

FOLLOW US ONLINE: ***www.ghostshipmanga.com***

READING DIRECTIONS

This book reads from ***right to left***, Japanese style. If this is your first time reading manga, you start reading from the top right panel on each page and take it from there. If you get lost, just follow the numbered diagram here. It may seem backwards at first, but you'll get the hang of it! Have fun!!

1
2
3
4
5
6
7
8
9

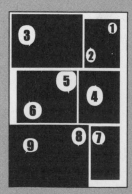